The Great Melody

The Great Melody

*A Thematic Biography and Commented
Anthology of Edmund Burke*

Conor Cruise O'Brien

THE UNIVERSITY OF CHICAGO PRESS

For
Deirdre Levinson Bergson
who brought the Message from the Master.

The University of Chicago Press, Chicago 60637
Sinclair-Stevenson Ltd, London

© 1992 by Conor Cruise O'Brien
All rights reserved. Published 1992
Paperback edition 1993

Printed in Great Britain
01 00 99 98 97 96 95 94 93   2 3 4 5 6

ISBN: 0-226-61650-9 (cloth); 0226-61651-7 (paper)

This book is printed on acid-free paper

Library of Congress Cataloging-in-Publication Data

O'Brien, Conor Cruise, 1917–
    The great melody: a thematic biography and
commented anthology of Edmund Burke /
Conor Cruise O'Brien.
       p.   cm.
    Includes bibliographical references and index.
    ISBN 0-226-61650-9 (cloth)
    1. Burke. Edmund, 1729–1797. 2. Statesmen – Great Britain –
Biography. 3. Political scientists – Great Britain – Biography.
4. Great Britain – Politics and government – 1760–1820.   I. Title.
DA506.B9029   1992
941.07'3'092–dc20   92-7302
    [B]   CIP

Contents

Lord Rockingham and Edmund Burke, unfinished portrait by
Sir Joshua Reynolds. 'Not Lord Rockingham's right hand, but both
his hands.' (p. 99)

List of Illustrations

Acknowledgements

THIS BOOK could not have been written without the encouragement, advice, criticism and other forms of assistance from a number of friends, several of whom are also members of my family. Some of those concerned are no longer with us.

Let me speak first of my late father, Francis Cruise O'Brien, and my late father-in-law, Sean MacEntee.

My father was an admirer of Edmund Burke, although he himself belonged in a category which Burke held in low esteem: that of agnostics, whom Burke always referred to as 'Atheists', not a term of endearment. Yet my father was an agnostic with a difference, and the difference is one that Burke would have appreciated, somewhat wryly. Francis Cruise O'Brien was an agnostic who was intensely proud of his Catholic ancestors – O'Briens of Ennistymon Co. Clare – who clung to their faith under the Penal Laws, when it would have been greatly to their advantage to renounce it, and pretend to be Protestants. In early twentieth century Ireland, on the other hand, it would have been greatly to my father's advantage to pretend to believe in the teachings of the Catholic Church. In refusing to do so, he believed that he was treading – in a somewhat paradoxical manner – in the footsteps of his penalised Catholic ancestors. Like them, he refused to pretend to believe things which he did not in fact believe, and like them he paid a price for that refusal. There is of course an element of 'cussedness' in this position, and this is a characteristic which I have observed in a number of members of my family.

Burke's predicament under the Penal Laws (explored in Chapter 1 and elsewhere) was different from that of our family's Catholic ancestors: his being more fraught and complex. I know that my father would have been fascinated by the exploration of that predicament in the present study, and that knowledge helped to sustain me in carrying out that exploration and – above all – in returning to it, after a period of discouragement (see Preface).

My father died long before I could develop any serious interest in Edmund Burke. My father-in-law, Sean MacEntee – also an admirer of Burke's – had read and liked my introduction to the Penguin Classics edition of *Reflections on the Revolution in France*. He encouraged me to persevere with writing a biography of Burke and when I gave up on that (see Preface) he made known his disappointment, and his hope that I would ultimately come back to Burke. Especially after his death (in January 1984) I felt sorry about having disappointed him, and this *eventually* inclined me to what he had hoped I would do. My only regret, now, is that I was not able to complete the book during his lifetime.

Among the living, those of whom my thanks are due fall into three groups. The first group consists of those concerned with publication. Elaine Greene has been my friend as well as my literary agent since 1961, known in my life as 'the year of the Congo' (or, as my children put it, following James Thurber, 'the Year the Bed fell on Father'). For the past twenty years, she has been involved with my Burke project, or rather projects (again, see Preface). The early years were years of frustration in this project, of slow and unsatisfactory progress, culminating in the abandonment of the whole thing. Elaine can be testy enough, on occasion, with an author who is doing well, but when her author is in real trouble, as I was over Burke Mark I, she is capable of endless patience and kindness, as she demonstrated in my case.

Then about five years after giving up on Mark I, I came back with Burke Mark II. Elaine promptly found me a publisher, and the publisher was the same person who had endured the frustrations associated with Burke Mark One. Christopher Sinclair-Stevenson has been involved with my Burke projects for almost as long as Elaine has. It was he who conveyed to me – he being then with Hamish Hamilton – that Burke Mark I would not do. I am grateful to him in retrospect for that salutary intimation, no less than for having faith (despite the depressing past experience) in Burke Mark II, which he consistently encouraged from the time its outline was made known to him, through every stage of composition and publication.

At a later stage, when I was looking for an American publisher, my first approach was to the University of Chicago Press, foremost in publication of Burke studies in America, and co-publishers (along with Cambridge University Press) of the ten volume edition of *The Correspondence of Edmund Burke* (see Notes on Sources and Introduction). Morris Philipson, Director of the Press welcomed the proposal with enthusiasm and brought it to fruition in co-operation with Christopher Sinclair-Stevenson.

The second group is made up of five people who read the entire manuscript. The first of these is my wife, who endured with me the protracted miseries of Burke Mark I, and later encouraged me, as her father had done, to return to Burke. She read and commented on every section of the book. Chapter 1, in particular, was reshaped as a result of a number of discussions with her and in all those parts of *The Great Melody* which have to do with Ireland, I am deeply indebted to her store of information as a Gaelic scholar, and to her insights into the hidden workings of Irish history (see below, section on Ireland). The indexes are our joint work.

John Silverlight has been a friend since my days on *The Observer*, London, when we were colleagues. I knew him then for a great sub-editor, and resourceful seeker after *le mot juste*. At Elaine Greene's suggestion, Christopher Sinclair-Stevenson asked John to be responsible for the copy-editing of *The Great Melody*, and a singularly happy and fruitful collaboration between author and copy-editor resulted. The difference between the manuscript as John received it, and the version which left his expert hands is like the difference in the appearance of our Springer spaniel, Greta, before and after clipping.

Owen Dudley Edwards's part in bringing me back to Burke is referred to in the Preface. He then read each section of the book, as I wrote it and provided detailed comment on all of it. His deep knowledge of both Irish and American history helped me with the first three chapters and his special study of Warren Hastings and Macaulay with the fourth, but the range of his historical erudition is such, that there is no area of this book's concern which he did not help to illuminate for me. Indeed his powers of psychological insight into the transactions of the past — especially in the large and murky zone where religion and politics overlap — helped me towards a better understanding of history itself. At a more mundane level, Owen saved me from publishing several clangers, on which certain historians would have been only too happy to pounce.

Ilsa Yardley has been a friend of ours since our Ghana days (1962–65). Ilsa read each section as it was completed. She then supplied me with what authors like to think of as 'constructive criticism'; meaning, unstinted praise, warmly and felicitously expressed. This was like oxygen to me, as I emerged from the scarcely-breathable atmosphere of Burke Mark I; I perked up no end, and got on with Mark II.

The fifth person who read the whole thing – and some of it several times over – in her case – is Kitty Quinn. I wrote the whole thing by hand – and rewrote much of it – and Kitty deciphered my difficult handwriting; with great patience, skill and good-humour and produced from it a text which could be read by other human beings. I also thank Clíona Ní Bhoēartúin for her part in producing the typescript and for coping efficiently and speedily with that same handwriting.

Then there are those who helped me specifically with certain areas of study.

Much the most difficult area is that of eighteenth-century Ireland (mainly Chapter 1 and large parts of Chapters III and VI). This area is difficult, for two overlapping reasons: First, many transactions in the Ireland of the Penal Laws were deliberately concealed or disguised: this was true not only in relation to the penalised Catholics, but also to Protestant transactions with Catholics, and – most particularly – to the lives and circumstances of recent converts (or 'converts') from Roman Catholicism to Anglicanism: a category to which Edmund Burke's father, Richard Burke, belonged (see Chapter 1). The second source of difficulty is that Edmund Burke himself, knowing himself to be politically vulnerable through his close connections with Catholic Ireland, did his best to cover his tracks in that area: mostly through extreme reticence, sometimes through misleading rhetoric (see Chapter 1). Whether baffled by these disguises, or simply incurious about Ireland, Burke's previous biographers have accorded no more than perfunctory treatment to Burke's Irish connections; in some cases one can almost hear the biographer's sigh of relief when he lands his subject onto the intelligible side of the Irish Sea.[1] I felt that an attempt to understand Burke's personality required greater effort than any previous biographer had made, to explore the pattern of Burke's relationship, through his family, with the bitterly-divided Ireland of the Penal laws. But I was also conscious of the difficulties (set out above) attending any such exploration. I needed help, most especially, in this particular area. Fortunately for me, this help has been accorded, generously and abundantly by several Irish scholars.

---

[1] There is a modern scholarly monograph, T. H. D. Mahoney's *Edmund Burke and Ireland* (Harvard, 1960). This is useful for the 'Irish' activities of the mature Burke, but no more satisfactory than the biographies, with regard to the nature of Burke's family involvement with the Ireland of the Penal Laws.

The first, and the earliest established of my helpers was my daughter Fedelma Simms. Fedelma has been associated with this project since its ill-starred beginnings ('Burke Mark I') when she did a good deal of research for me in the Blackwater Valley Co Cork. Although it had looked for years as if all that work was going to be wasted, Fedelma cheerfully volunteered her help again, when Burke Mark II broke out. The importance of her contribution, in relation to a particularly difficult and interesting area, is acknowledged in Chapter 1. After the shared tribulations of Burke Mark I, it was a great joy to share Mark II with her, and to feel we were getting somewhere at last. When I had finished the first draft of Chapter 1, I consulted Professor John A. Murphy of University College, Cork, who rendered me the signal service of putting me in touch with two scholars my debt to whom is acknowledged immediately below.

The first of these is Professor Kevin Whelan, of University College Dublin, a distinguished authority on the Ireland of the late eighteenth century: at present a growth area in Irish historiography. I showed him the first draft of Chapter 1 and he subjected the draft to detailed and helpful criticism, as a result of which I rewrote much of the Chapter, greatly to its advantage. I am, of course, alone responsible for any errors of fact or interpretation which may subsist in the amended Chapter (or elsewhere in the work).

The second person with whom Professor Murphy put me in touch, and who has given me valuable help, is Mr. Seamus Crowley of Mallow, Co Cork. Mr. Crowley is a notable local historian, steeped in the traditions of the Blackwater Valley. Through him I met another local historian, Father Robert Forde, and with these two I spent a number of instructive and delightful hours in the summers of 1990 and 1991 in the beautiful valley in which Edmund Burke lived as a child.

In that valley, I was hospitably received by a number of residents in places associated with Burke and the Nagles. My thanks are due, accordingly, to Michael T. Barry of Ballyduff Lodge, his wife Mairead and their son Tom; to Michael Barry of Monanimy Upper and his wife Helen; to Sister Joseph and Sister Bridie of the Presentation Order at the Nano Nagle Centre; to P. J. Walsh and his wife Linda at Carrigacunna Castle; to George Buckley and his wife Betty at Rockvale House, and to Klaus D. Richter at Monanimy Castle.

I am indebted to Professor Maurice O'Connell both in respect of his published work on eighteenth century Ireland, and for a number of penetrating comments in friendly correspondence.

I am grateful to Professor Aidan Clarke, of Trinity College, Dublin for putting me in touch with Daire Keogh, a young Irish historian specialising in the late eighteenth-century, who agreed to be my research assistant in revising the Irish parts of *The Great Melody*. Daire has helped me to revise Chapter 1 and also the Irish parts of Chapters III and VI. As well as being everything a good research assistant is supposed to be, Daire is also an excellent critic. He has helped me, not merely by enabling me to put in additional, relevant things, but also, on occasion, by getting me to leave things *out,* to the book's advantage. It has been a pleasure to work with him, and to have him become a friend to my family and myself.

My friends Eilis Dillon, Patrick Lynch and Muiris MacConghail all read Chapter 1 and made helpful and encouraging comments on it.

There are also collective debts. In the summer of 1991, I addressed a Conference of Eighteenth Century Irish Historians at Drumcondra, Dublin on 'Edmund Burke and Ireland.' I thank all those who attended, and in particular those who took part in the useful discussion that followed.

Finally – in relation to the Irish area – I should like to acknowledge a special indebtedness to the late Basil O'Connell, genealogist and antiquarian. O'Connell was a Nagle descendant, as well as a Nagle genealogist. He had a better 'feel' for the nature of Burke's Irishness than any other writer, and my own approach to that subject, in this book, owes correspondingly more to him.

Valerie Jobling read the Preface, the Introduction and Chapter 1 and supplied much useful criticism especially in relation to the footnotes. These are still not up to her exigent standards, but they are a lot better than when she found them. The improvement affected the footnotes of the entire book, and I am proportionately grateful for her help.

My elder son, Donal Cruise O'Brien discussed the book with me on a number of occasions and I benefited greatly from his comments. In particular, I consulted him about Chapter IV and he put me in touch with Andrew Grout, whose knowledge of Indian history and Indian historiography was of great assistance to me in relation to Warren Hastings. That my second son, Patrick, shares my interest in eighteenth-century is a constant source of satisfaction and pride. My daughter, Kate, herself writes professionally, and we are comrades in this, while the mysterious maturing of a detached and powerful intelligence in my youngest, Margaret, has provided an enlivening challenge throughout.

In relation to Chapters V and VI I am particularly indebted to the scholars who contributed to the great *Dictionnaire Critique de la Révolution Française* (Edited by François Furet and Mona Ozouf, Paris, 1988).

In the course of a stint (October–November 1991) as a Visiting Research Fellow at the Wilson Center for International Scholars in Washington, D.C., I gave a Public Lecture entitled 'Edmund Burke: Conservative and/or Liberal?' comparing, in particular, Burke's statements and activities concerning the American Revolution with those concerning the French Revolution. I found several comments made by scholars at the Wilson Center, – both in the general discussion that followed my lecture and in private conversations – helpful in the revision of the relevant Chapters of *The Great Melody*: II, III, V, VI. I thank all of my then colleagues at the Wilson Center and in particular the Director, Charles Blitzer, Jim Morris, who acted as moderater for my lecture, Michael J. Lacey and Alex Zwerdling.

In November, 1991, I delivered a Public Lecture at Harvard, at the invitation of Professor Harvey C. Mansfield – himself a notable Burkean scholar – of the Department of Government there. The Lecture was entitled 'Utopia and Revolution' and dealt with themes considered in the Epilogue of *The Great Melody*. I thank Professor Mansfield and his colleagues for a number of comments which have been helpful to me especially in the revision of the Epilogue.

My debt to Deirdre Levinson Bergson is acknowledged in the Dedication and in Chapter VI p. 534.

I wish here to convey my heartfelt thanks to the gentleman who presented *Letter to a Noble Lord* to Deirdre: Frederic Amory of Berkeley, California.

I am deeply grateful to Sir Isaiah Berlin, both for the correspondence which followed my review (in *the New York Review of Books*) of *The Crooked Timber of Humanity* and for allowing me to publish that correspondence as an Appendix to *The Great Melody*. As well as my general indebtedness (expressed in Introduction and Notes on Sources) to Burke's scholarly editors, I owe personal thanks to three of these: to the late Thomas Copeland for generous guidance while I was editing the Penguin Classics edition of *Reflections on the Revolution in France*: to R. B. McDowell, for teaching me how to read history (a great many years ago) and for leading me to Burke: to Paul Langford, for light shed in the course of conversation, as well as in his editorial work. Of course, none of these scholars bears any responsibility for any errors in *The Great Melody*.

Special thanks are due to a group of scholars at Edinburgh University: to Professor H. T. Dickinson for guidance over a wide range of British political history: to Dr Geoffrey Carnall and Dr Colin E. Nicholson for helping me to find my way in the India of Warren Hastings, and to Professor George Shepherdson, for his Burkean humanity and wisdom in relation to the Third World and much else. I thank John Ahtes, who helped me to conduct a graduate seminar on Burke at the University of Pennsylvania, for many penetrating observations and searching questions, and for his friendship.

My special thanks are due to the staffs of the Berkeley Library and of the Lecky Library at Trinity College, Dublin, where most of the research for *The Great Melody* was done. I am also greatly indebted to the staffs of the National Library of Ireland, the Library of University College, Dublin; the British Library; the National Library of Scotland; the Libraries of Dartmouth College, Hanover, New Hampshire; of Williams College, Williamstown, Mass; of the University of Pennsylvania; and of the Library of Congress, and of Sheffield City Libraries, home to the Fitzwilliam Burke Collection.

I owe a particular debt to Dr T. N. Mitchell, Provost of Trinity College, for finding space for the launching of the Great Melody, among the many competing claims arising around the celebrations of the College's Quarter centenary Year.

Finally, I respectfully thank the President of Ireland, Dr Mary Robinson, for her gracious interest in *The Great Melody*.

Note on Sources

INCOMPARABLY the most important sources, for this study, are the recorded words, both spoken and written, of Edmund Burke. I am deeply indebted, as all students of Burke must be, to those twentieth century scholars who have edited Burke. In the introduction I acknowledge my debt to the late Thomas Copeland, and the scholars who, under his General Editorship, completed the ten-volume Edition of Burke's *Correspondence*, which supplies the infrastructure for much of the present study. Here I wish to acknowledge a similar collective debt to Professor Paul Langford and the scholars who, under his general editorship, have been editing *The Writings and Speeches of Edmund Burke*. I am especially indebted to Paul Langford himself as Editor of Volume II, *Party, Parliament, and the American Crisis, (1766–1774)*; to P. J. Marshall, Editor of Volume V, *India, the Launching of the Hastings Impeachment*; and to R. B. McDowell, Editor of Volume IX, *The Revolutionary War, 1794–1797; ii: Ireland*.

Where a modern scholarly edition of a particular statement of Burke's was not yet available, I have used one of the nineteenth century editions: The Nimmo edition of 1899 in twelve volumes, which is the one I happen to own; it is an excellent reading edition. Like all the other nineteenth century editions it derives from the first, edited by French Laurence and Walker King, and completed in 1827.

The books and articles with reference to Burke which I have found most relevant – whether positively or negatively – to the present study as a whole are critically discussed in the Introduction. Books and articles found useful for individual chapters are cited in the footnotes and are listed in the General Index.

Facing page: Fanny Burney. 'Yet, at times I confess, with all that I felt, wished, and thought concerning Mr. Hastings, the whirlwind of [Burke's] eloquence nearly drew me into its vortex.' (p. 364)

Mrs Sheridan, 'the Saint Cecilia, whose delicate features, lighted up by love and music, art has rescued from the common decay'. (p. 361)

Preface

American colonies, Ireland, France and India
Harried, and Burke's great melody against it.
W. B. Yeats, 'The Seven Sages'

THE TITLE AND subtitle require some explanation, which is offered in this Preface.

About twenty years ago, I set out to write a biography of Edmund Burke. That biography, had it been completed, would have been on conventional lines, emphasising chronology, and without a sustained thematic dimension. The project soon got into difficulty. At first, I ascribed this to the distraction of other concerns at the time, but these were not the root of the trouble. The real trouble was that the Burke that interested me – Burke's mind and heart, at grips with the great issues of his time – seemed to get further and further away, the more closely I studied his career, along the lines I was then following. Also, and not merely through the usual effect of distance, Burke himself seemed to get smaller and smaller, until he became quite an inconsequential figure, hardly more significant than any of the other politicians of the time, and distinctly less significant than any of those who held major office.

This was largely due to the reductionist tendencies of most of the secondary sources I was consulting: a matter considered in my Introduction. But the chronological method which I followed at the time, really as a matter of routine, had the effect of confirming those reductionist tendencies. Burke was an exceptionally diligent parliamentarian and if you try to follow his political career, year by year, you will find that the exigencies of the parliamentary calendar, and the consequential frequent changes of theme, blur one's view of the person, within the parliamentary process.

So I got stuck. I couldn't, at that time, understand why I got stuck. I had already done some work on Burke – as editor of the Penguin Classics edition (1968) of *Reflections on the Revolution in France* – and had experienced no such frustration: quite the contrary. I can see now that the reason why working on *Reflections* had been so satisfactory was that I was looking at Burke's mind at work *on a single theme*, whereas in the kind of biography I later unsuccessfully attempted the themes were being switched around all the time, resulting in a blur, and loss of contact. Amid that blur and loss, the reductionist perspective on him came to seem almost plausible for a time: though I could never really reconcile it with the Burke I had been able to see and hear, while I worked on *Reflections*.

So I gave up on Burke, as I then thought, for good, and turned to an apparently quite unrelated subject. I wrote *The Siege: the Story of Israel and Zionism*. But while I was working on it, something kept nagging at me to go back to Burke, once I had finished *The Siege*. The nagging took a precise form. The two lines of Yeats, quoted at the head of this preface kept coming into my head and would not go away. At first my reaction was to wish that Yeats *would* go away, and his notion of the great melody along with him. I didn't treat Yeats seriously as an authority on Burke. Yeats, during the period of his greatest interest in Burke (around 1925) included him in a kind of Anglo-Irish Protestant aristocratic pantheon, along with Swift, Berkeley and Grattan. I knew Burke didn't really belong in that gallery, so I found it hard to believe that Yeats had a message for me, with a key to Burke.

After I had abandoned my original plan for a biography of Burke, I found myself being brought back to him, partly because of the incidence of relevant centenaries, commemorations and partly (as I now realise) because my friend Owen Dudley Edwards, of Edinburgh University, was tactfully determined to keep my interest in Burke alive.

The first relevant commemoration was that of the bicentenary, in 1976, of the American Revolution. I read a paper on 'Edmund Burke and the American Revolution' at a Bicentennial Conference in Ennis, Co. Clare.[1] In the process that came to shape the present study the interest of that paper lies in the status of those lines of Yeats. Clearly I felt their pull, but still wished to resist it. The paper opens: 'Let us begin by considering two-well known lines from W. B. Yeats's poem "The Seven Sages" (in *The Winding Stair and Other Poems*, 1933)':

[1] Later published in *America and Ireland, 1776–1976: The American Identity and the Irish Connection: Proceedings of the United States Bicentennial Conference of Cumann Merriman, Ennis, August 1976*, ed. David Noel Doyle and Owen Dudley Edwards (Greenwood Press, Westport, Connecticut and London); also by the Edinburgh University Student Publications Board in the *New Edinburgh Review's* collection: *Scotland, Europe and the American Revolution*, ed. Owen Dudley Edwards and George Shepperson (Edinburgh, 1976).

American colonies, Ireland, France and India
Harried, and Burke's great melody against it.

'What was *it*? I shall come back to that question. For the moment
let us note the implied acknowledgment of Burke's consistency; a
just acknowledgment of something that has been unjustly impugned.
In other ways, I think Yeats's lines somewhat misleading. The key
words, 'harried' and 'melody', suggest a Burke concerned to stir
emotions by his eloquence on behalf of the persecuted. He could do
that; he did it for the victims of the Irish Penal Laws, for the Begums
of Oudh and, most famously, for Marie Antoinette of France. He
knew well how to play on the emotions, but on the whole he used this
skill sparingly. The great bulk of his writings and speeches consists of
reasoned arguments. And nowhere is this more evident than in his
speeches aimed at averting the conflict in America.

'In all of Burke's great campaigns there was, as Yeats discerned,
one constant target. That target – Yeats's 'it' – was the abuse of
power. But the forms of the abuse of power differed in the different
cases mentioned, and Burke's manner of approaching the different
cases differs also.'

That is fair enough as far as it goes. Later in the paper my resistance
became more querulous. Having stressed, and slightly over-stressed,
the rational character of Burke's writings and speeches on the American crisis, I went on: 'This commonsense, down-to-earth Burke, concerned with practical interests and assessment of forces, may perhaps
seem, and indeed be, a less noble figure than the lamenting harpist
of "The Seven Sages". Yet if one has come to distrust the plangent
strain in politics, one turns with relief from that distorted Yeatsian
Burke, recognisable though some of the features are, to the real Burke
of the American Revolutionary period.'

Yet the final reference, in that paper, to those lines, is one of
acceptance: 'Burke, who had foreseen the disaster in America, in the
closing years of his life foresaw disaster in Ireland. That disaster
came in the year after his death, 1798. In that sense, Yeats was right.'

'Yeats was right.' I came to see that whatever reservations one
might have about Yeats's general interpretations of Burke, and whatever qualifications one might add to his metaphor about the melody,
Yeats was right about the main point. That is, he correctly identified,
and isolated for attention, the main areas on which Burke's creative
energies were concentrated throughout long and overlapping periods
of his career. That was why those lines had been nagging at my mind.

They were pointing me the way back, to find the Burke I had been looking for, and had lost.

I had accepted that, and was working accordingly, well before the next of the relevant centenary commemorations came round. These were the bicentenaries of the Impeachment of Warren Hastings (1988) and of the French Revolution (1989). I was invited by Owen Dudley Edwards, well ahead of time, to talk about Burke and Warren Hastings at a bicentenary commemorative conference on the Impeachment, held at Edinburgh University in February 1988. Up to now I had done a certain amount of work in relation to Burke on America, on France, and on Ireland, but had not yet seriously tackled the apparently formidable volumes of Burke on India. The Edinburgh commitment therefore obliged me to complete the Yeatsian quadrilateral, and this finally determined the agenda for the present study. My contribution to the conference is entitled 'Warren Hastings in Burke's Great Melody'[1], and contains no word of reservation as to the propriety of that metaphor.

For the Bicentenary of the French Revolution I reviewed, for the *New York Review of Books*, the great *Critical Dictionary of the French Revolution*, edited by François Furet and Mona Ozouf. This enabled me to see Burke in the perspective of modern French scholarship, which is far more favourable to Burke than was the dominant French historiographical tradition of the nineteenth century and the first half of the twentieth. I also contributed an essay, 'Nationalism and the French Revolution,' to a collection entitled *The Permanent Revolution: The French Revolution and its Legacy*.[2] This proved relevant to the consideration of Burke's struggle against what he continued to call 'Jacobinism', even after 1794. Finally, on the great day itself, 14 July 1989, I took part in a televised panel discussion in Paris, at the Invalides, set up by London Weekend Television. Through the great window we could see the gorgeous *défilé* organised by President Mitterrand, with all manner of songs and dances, ethnic spectacles, theatre and acrobatics. It was magnificent, but it wasn't the French Revolution. It was a wake. The tremendous thing that Edmund Burke had fought so fiercely, from a few months after its birth up to his own death, eight years later, was at last itself being

[1] Published in Geoffrey Carnall and Colin Nicholson (eds.) *The Impeachment of Warren Hastings, Papers from a Bicentenary Commemoration* (Edinburgh U.P. 1989).

[2] Ed. Geoffrey Best (Fontana Press, 1988). The collection is a useful one, but I have reservations about that title, as appears from this Preface.

laid to rest, in its own capital. On that same night in the same city, but away from the centre and the action, the true heirs of the French Revolution, the French Communist Party, in their own ceremonies in the Red *faubourg* of St. Denis, were doing their best to keep the tradition of the French Revolution alive. But nobody outside the dwindling and dispirited ranks of the faithful, was paying attention any longer to the true heirs of the French Revolution.

When I resumed work on a book on Burke, I found that the thematic approach suggested by Yeats's lines worked well for me. The day-to-day clutter, which accumulates in the path of a strictly chronological approach, fell away. The reductionist interpretation, sometimes plausible enough in the dark corners of the day-to-day, is seen in its actual tawdriness, in the steady light of Burke's consistent and disinterested commitment to great causes, from the beginning to the end of his political career. Each trivialising or demeaning hypothesis successively collapses, when tested in the context of the history of his conduct, in the long pursuit of each one of the four causes, and in their interrelations. I shall not labour these points. There is no need for this Preface to become a prospectus. The book is here, and the reader will make up his or her own mind, on reading it, as to whether the above claims are or are not made good.

I should like to make two further points about the propriety, respectively, of the title and the sub-title. The title, *The Great Melody*, should be understood primarily in a very broad sense, as implying the existence of a profound inner harmony within Burke's writings and speeches on the four themes. It should not be taken as implying passivity, merely elegant commentary, accompaniment. The melody is always 'against *it*' and is therefore a form of action, with varying fortunes. That action takes the form not only of rhetoric, but also of argument, aphorism, debate, logical and historical analysis; and all these are part of the Great Melody in the broad sense.

There is also a narrower sense, within the broad one, to which the poet's metaphor is felt to be peculiarly appropriate. In certain conditions, Burke's utterance, both in speech and in writing, attains to a glowing eloquence, unique in English literature and in the annals of oratory. He reserves that vein for special occasions, and he never overworks it. These utterances form, therefore, only a relatively small part, in terms of statistical proportion, of Burke's total utterances as these have come down to us. But it is natural for us to think of these moments of highest eloquence as also the highest expression of Burke's Great Melody (see 'Great Melody' in Thematic Index).

To the Great Melody, in that special and restricted sense, belong certain speeches over America, and over India, and certain writings about the French Revolution. On America, we have 'On American Taxation' (1774), 'On Conciliation with America' (1775), and three other speeches of the same order. On India, we have 'On Fox's East India Bill' (1783), 'On the Nabob of Arcot's Debts' (1785), two other speeches, and parts of the marathon eight-day speech opening (1788) and nine-day speech closing (1794) the Impeachment of Warren Hastings. On France, we have a number of passages in *Reflections on the Revolution in France* (1790); an *Appeal from the New to the Old Whigs* (1791); *Letter to a Member of the National Assembly* (1791); and *Letters on a Regicide Peace* (1796). *Letter to a Noble Lord* (1796) is in a special class of its own, but belongs in the general context of the French debate.

The attentive reader will have noticed that I have not proposed any of Burke's speeches or writings over Ireland as belonging to the highest category of the Great Melody. Burke attains his highest level of eloquence only in those conjunctures when he feels fully free to speak what he thinks and feels. For reasons examined in the present study, Burke never feels free over Ireland. During most of his life, with one startling exception, Burke's public statements concerning Ireland were few, guarded, cryptic, sometimes evasive. The startling exception is supplied by a passage in the Bristol Guildhall Speech (1780) in which, at a moment of great stress, his real feelings about the Irish Penal Laws gush out in an almost trance-like manner.[1] Ireland, in the Great Melody, is a brooding presence, expressed in haunted silences and transferred passions. Feelings which Burke represses over Ireland come out in other contexts, over the French Revolution to some extent, but especially over India.

Some readers may feel that I have been too lavish in my use of inference, concerning Burke's relation to Ireland, and the connection of that relation to the other branches of the Great Melody. However, without some audacity in the use of inference, to which I plead guilty, no adequate understanding of Burke's relation to Ireland is attainable. And given the tremendous tensions of his upbringing, in the Ireland of the Penal Laws, if you can't understand Burke's relation to the land of his upbringing, you can't understand Burke.

---

[1] In his early *Tract Relative to the Laws against Popery in Ireland* (1761) he analyses the Penal Code, and argues for its relaxation, but does not allow his feelings concerning it to show.

All previous biographies of him skim that relationship and founder on that rock.[1]

For adequate reasons he did his best to cover his tracks over Ireland. The student of Burke must uncover those tracks as best he may, often relying on cryptic remarks, strained silences, perceived constraints, together with a scrutiny of the actual Irish context of positions that he took up, or avoided, over Ireland. A good example, in this study, of such an inquiry concerns his attitude towards the Irish Volunteers and legislative independence for Ireland, in the early 1780s. A good liberal 'friend of Ireland' would be expected to be strongly in favour, both of the Volunteers and of legislative independence. Burke hung back, with muffled but unmistakable expressions of distaste, from both. The explanation offered in Chapter 1 does not go beyond the legitimate use of inference, respecting the basic data for the actual situation in Ireland, and Burke's relation to it. I would claim that the same applies to the general pattern offered here, concerning the role of Ireland within the Great Melody. But the reader must be the judge of that.

Then there is the question of the sub-title. Can this book properly be described as a biography? It is certainly not a conventional biography, but it is a complete biography, extending from the circumstances – key Burkean word – of the subject's birth in Ireland to those of his death in Beaconsfield, and taking in, in between, all the main events and circumstances of his education career and compositions. His personal life, apart from politics, was uneventful, his family relations happy, until the untimely death of the only one of his children who lived to maturity, Richard, three years before his own death. The centre of Edmund Burke's interests was political, and any biography of him has to be mainly political. The present one proceeds along the paths determined by its four themes, but it necessarily takes in, at every stage, the relation of his activities and utterances, concerning each theme, to their precise contexts in the British parliamentary politics of which he is part. British domestic politics are seen, however, always in their wider context of the momentous unrolling of international politics in the age of the American and French Revol-

---

[1] There are two monographs on Burke and Ireland: William O'Brien's *Edmund Burke and Ireland* (Dublin, 1924) and T. H. D. Mahoney's *Edmund Burke and Ireland* (Harvard, 1960). Both are of interest, but neither gives adequate attention to the nature of Burke's predicament, astride the great line of social and political division in the Ireland in which he was born and brought up. See especially the opening sections of Chapter 1.

utions. The idea is that British domestic politics must not be lost to view, but neither must Edmund Burke be lost to view, among the details of British domestic politics.

Within British politics, his relationships with major figures of the time are important and are explored in proportion to the perceived degree of their importance. His relationship with the Marquess of Rockingham and, through Rockingham, his growing influence over the Whig party, especially over American policy, are the main 'domestic' themes of the early part of his political career (1766–1782). Between Rockingham's death in 1782, which roughly coincides with the end of the American War, and the outbreak of the French Revolution, seven years later, Burke's main preoccupation is with India. In British domestic politics, this meant that Burke had to carry with him, first Charles James Fox, and then William Pitt the Younger – against inclination in both cases – in order to carry a majority in the House of Commons to vote for the Impeachment of Warren Hastings at the bar of the House of Lords.

The French Revolution brought a complete break with Fox, and an alliance with Pitt. After some years, under Burke's influence, and as the French Revolution unfolds in the manner foreseen by him, a number of the Whigs, headed by the Duke of Portland and Earl Fitzwilliam, leave Fox and join Pitt's Administration. The expanded Administration is shaken from the outset by Irish affairs, over which Burke and Pitt are opposed. Though deeply distressed by Pitt's handling of Ireland, Burke continues to support him, as indispensable to the conduct of the war against Revolutionary France. When, however, Pitt makes overtures towards peace with the Directory, Burke fiercely attacks this initiative in the last major political act of his political career, *Letters on a Regicide Peace* (1796). The peace initiative failed and the war continued, as Burke had insisted that it must, until the restoration of the French Monarchy, completed eighteen years after his death.

At every stage of his career, the influence of George III was of central importance, and Burke's relations to the king went through many 'transmigrations', to use a Burkean expression. It is argued here that the concluding stages of the American War involved a battle of wills between George, who wished to continue the war even after Cornwallis's surrender at Yorktown, and Burke, whose influence caused Rockingham to dictate terms of accepting office, by which the king must be prepared to accept the independence of America. After drafting an instrument of abdication, George accepted Rockingham's terms, which were Burke's terms, and the way to peace was open.

It is argued that Burke's influence over contemporary politics, both British and international, was more significant and pervasive, not merely in the above instances, but in several others, than many historians have supposed. It is also argued that Burke's analysis of the workings of the contemporary British political system, and particularly his theory of a 'double Cabinet' (the method by which George III exercised personal power, bypassing Cabinet and Parliament), is far from being as wide of the mark as one influential school of historians has claimed.

The purpose of the above résumé of some of the domestic aspects explored in *The Great Melody* is to show that a thematic biography need not be as limited in scope, or as rarefied, as a mere enumeration of the principal themes might suggest. A thematic approach would probably not be productive for most biographies. For Burke, having tried the conventional approach and then turned to the thematic, I am convinced by experience that the thematic approach is far more flexible, and far more illuminating.

Then there is the 'commented anthology' aspect. This follows necessarily from the choice of the Great Melody as governing concept. Under that sign, it is necessary that Burke's own voice, in all the variety of its inflections, be heard, frequently and at length. Summary and paraphrase, the regular resources of previous biographers, are of only marginal use for the purposes of the present study. This necessarily requires a large book, such as is before you. That in itself is no advantage. The relevant advantage, and it is no small one, is that much of the best of Burke, at present not readily accessible, or readily comprehensible out of context, is within these covers and situated, in every case, in its immediate context.

The 'commented anthology' aspect makes this an unusual book, in that it contains what it is about, and is about what it contains.

In a word, the basis and essentials of a Burke revival are here; especially in those pages where Burke himself is heard to speak. There are already signs of such a revival, especially in France, hitherto *partes infidelium* where Burke is concerned. France has a way of setting fashions, and I hope this good fashion will come round in time for the bicentenary of Burke's death, in 1997.

I wrote earlier of writing a preface, not a prospectus, but I find that the preface has in fact acquired a touch of prospectus. I don't correct this, because I don't feel that I am plugging 'my own book'.

There are two senses in which the book is not mine. Much of the text belongs to Burke himself. And the governing concept is that of W. B. Yeats, in those nagging lines to whose message I reluctantly but completely capitulated. Responsibility for the execution of that governing concept is mine, and on that aspect I have no comment to offer. As I complete this book I feel deeply grateful to the author of those lines, for pointing the way, for myself and my readers. The poet's eye detected that point of vantage from which we can descry, rising high above the confusion of woods and rocks in the valley, the central commanding range of Burke's political thought and action: a range with four majestic peaks, three of them shining clear, and one always partly shrouded in its native mists.

Introduction: Burke and Some Scholars

'Everyone is today aware of the fundamental difference between, on the one hand, those historians who paint portraits of entire societies or groups within them that are rounded and three-dimensional, so that we believe, whether rightly or mistakenly, that we are able to tell what it would have been like to have lived in such conditions, and, on the other, antiquaries, chroniclers, accumulators of facts or statistics on which large generalisations can be founded, learned compilers, or theorists who look on the use of imagination as opening the door to the horrors of guesswork, subjectivism, journalism, or worse.

'This all-important distinction rests precisely on the attitude to the faculty that Vico called *fantasia*, without which the past cannot, in his view, be resurrected. The crucial role he assigns to the imagination must not blind us – and did not blind him – to the necessity for verification; he allows that critical methods of examining evidence are indispensable. Yet without *fantasia* the past remains dead; to bring it to life we need, at least ideally, to hear men's voices, to conjecture (on the basis of such evidence as we can gather) what may have been their experience, their forms of expression, their values, outlook, aims, ways of living; without this we cannot grasp whence we came, how we come to be as we are now, not merely physically or biologically and, in a narrow sense, politically and institutionally, but socially, psychologically, morally; without this there can be no genuine self-understanding. We call great historians only those who not only are in full control of the factual evidence obtained by the use of the best critical methods available to them, but also possess the depth of imaginative insight that characterises gifted novelists. Clio, as the English historian G. M. Trevelyan pointed out long ago, is, after all, a muse.'[1] – Isaiah Berlin.

[1] 'Giambattista Vico and Cultural History' in *The Crooked Timber of Humanity: Chapters in the History of Ideas*, ed. by Henry Hardy (London and New York, 1990). The Vico essay was first published in the United States in 1983.

THE WHIG TRADITION

MY MAIN CONCERN in this Introduction is to consider how Burke's reputation in our own time has been affected by the attacks upon it by Sir Lewis Namier and other historians. But first it is necessary to say a word about how Burke's reputation stood in the nineteenth and early twentieth centuries before the Namierite assault began (in 1929).

By the middle of the nineteenth century, Burke's reputation was unique, in that he was venerated by both British political parties. Charles James Fox was a hero to the Liberals. William Pitt the Younger was a hero to the Tories. But both parties, with few exceptions, regarded Burke as a political sage, and drew on his wisdom. Karl Marx, who hated Burke, acknowledged this, describing him as 'the man who is held by every party in England as the paragon of British statesmen'.[1] There was some difference of emphasis in the respect accorded to Burke by the two parties. Tories tended to dwell on his statements about the French Revolution, and not on his statements about the American Revolution (not to mention India and Ireland). Liberals did not feel comfortable with his statements on the French Revolution: the issue on which he broke with the Whigs in 1791. Yet each party had its own reasons for not stressing the difference. Most Tories didn't want to appear as enemies of America; most Liberals didn't want to sound too friendly to the French Revolution.

---

[1] Leading article in the *New York Daily Tribune* No. 4597, 12 January 1856; reproduced in Karl Marx and Friedrich Engels, *Collected Works* (London, Lawrence & Wishart, 1980) Volume 14, p. 587.

In practical terms, Burke's influence was greater over the Liberals than over the Conservatives. Gladstone, when he was considering committing himself to Home Rule for Ireland, kept reading Burke and making extracts from him. 'We may easily imagine,' writes Gladstone's biographer John Morley, 'how the heat from that profound and glowing furnace still further influenced strong purposes and exalted resolution in Mr. Gladstone.'[1]

Although both parties laid claim to Burke, historians were not so evenly divided. For Liberal historians, Burke and his friends – the section of the Whigs led by the Marquess of Rockingham, and generally known as 'the Rockinghams' – were the direct precursors of the Liberal Party. Their commitment to political and constitutional issues, as distinct from the politics of place and preferment; their determination to act in a body; their willingness to make a stand on issues which they believed to be right, even when their stand was unpopular with parliamentary majorities, with the Court and with the country as over the American war; and their resolute defence of the Constitution against the encroachment of George III – all these considerations were believed to lead to the emergence of the nineteenth-century Liberal Party and also to the consolidation of the Constitution, as the nineteenth century (and also the twentieth century) came to understand it. This was what came to be known as 'the Whig interpretation of history', which was to be subjected to systematic oblique disparagement by Sir Lewis Namier and his followers. The authority of the Whig interpretation was successfully undermined by the twentieth-century campaign against it, but the interpretation itself has never been systematically refuted, and it remains, in my opinion, more persuasive than anything which twentieth-century historiography has offered in its place.

The most brilliant of the Whig interpreters was Thomas Babington Macaulay (1800–1859). Of the rise of the Rockingham Whigs, early in the reign of George III, he writes: 'If the new Whig statesmen had little experience in business and debate, they were, on the other hand, pure from the taint of that political immorality which had deeply infected their predecessors. Long prosperity had corrupted that great party which had expelled the Stuarts, limited the prerogatives of the Crown, and curbed the intolerance of the Hierarchy. Adversity had

---

[1] Morley, *Life of Gladstone* (London, 1903) Volume III, p. 280. For the nature of that influence see my Introduction to *Irish Affairs: Edmund Burke*, the Cresset Press edition (1988) of Matthew Arnold's selection of Burke's statements about Ireland.

already produced a salutary effect. On the day of the accession of George the Third, the ascendancy of the Whig party terminated; and on that day the purification of the Whig party began. The rising chiefs of that party were men of a very different sort from Sandys and Winnington, from Sir William Yonge and Henry Fox. They were men worthy to have charged by the side of Hampden at Chalgrove, or to have exchanged the last embrace with Russell on the scaffold in Lincoln's Inn Fields [in 1683]. They carried into politics the same high principles of virtue which regulated their private dealings, nor would they stoop to promote even the noblest and most salutary ends by means which honour and probity condemn. Such men were Lord John Cavendish, Sir George Savile, and others whom we hold in honour as the second founders of the Whig party, as the restorers of its pristine health and energy after half a century of degeneracy.

'The chief of this respectable band was the Marquess of Rockingham, a man of splendid fortune, excellent sense, and stainless character. He was indeed nervous to such a degree that, to the very close of his life, he never rose without great reluctance and embarrassment to address the House of Lords. But, though not a great orator, he had in a high degree some of the qualities of a statesman. He chose his friends well; and he had, in an extraordinary degree, the art of attaching them to him by ties of the most honourable kind. The cheerful fidelity with which they adhered to him through many years of almost hopeless opposition was less admirable than the disinterestedness and delicacy which they showed when he rose to power.'[1]

Macaulay went on to speak of Burke's accession to the Rockingham group in Parliament at the end of 1765: 'At this conjuncture Lord Rockingham had the wisdom to discern the value, and secure the aid, of an ally, who to eloquence surpassing the eloquence of Pitt, and to industry which shamed the industry of Grenville, united an amplitude of comprehension to which neither Pitt nor Grenville could lay claim. A young Irishman had, some time before, come over to push his fortune in London. He had written much for the booksellers; but he was best known by a little treatise, in which the style and reasoning of Bolingbroke were mimicked with exquisite skill[2] and by a theory of

---

[1] Essay, 'The Earl of Chatham', in the *Edinburgh Review* reprinted in Longman's *Complete Works of Lord Macaulay* (London, 1911) and in the later editions of *Macaulay's Critical and Historical Essays*. In his essay on Warren Hastings, Macaulay refers to Burke as 'the greatest man then living'.

[2] *A Vindication of Natural Society* (1756).

more ingenuity than soundness, touching the pleasures which we receive from the objects of taste.[1] He had also attained a high reputation as a talker, and was regarded by the men of letters who supped together at the Turk's Head as the only match in conversation for Dr. Johnson. He now became private secretary to Lord Rockingham, and was brought into Parliament by his patron's influence. These arrangements, indeed, were not made without some difficulty. The Duke of Newcastle, who was always meddling and chattering, adjured the First Lord of the Treasury to be on his guard against this adventurer, whose real name was O'Bourke, and whom his grace knew to be a wild Irishman, a Jacobite, a Papist, a concealed Jesuit. Lord Rockingham treated the calumny as it deserved; and the Whig Party was strengthened and adorned by the accession of Edmund Burke.'

Later in the century, another eminent historian in the Whig tradition, G. O. Trevelyan (1838–1928), Macaulay's nephew, gives Burke an even more prominent role within the Rockingham group, than Macaulay had done. Trevelyan is writing of the growth of the power of George III, at the time of the American crisis and of Burke as the leader of resistance to the royal abuse of power: 'The strong will, the imperious character, and the patient, unresting industry of the King, working through subservient Ministers upon a corrupt Parliament, had made him master of the State as effectively, and far more securely, than if his authority had rested on the support of an army of foreign mercenaries. The purpose to which he was capable of putting his all but unlimited authority was soon to be written in blood and fire over the face of the globe; but already there was a man who, from his reading of history, his knowledge of human nature, and his experience of what politics had become since the new policy began to be inaugurated, foresaw the consequences which could not fail to result from the establishment of absolute power.

That man was Edmund Burke, who for some time past had been looking about him in search of forces able to make good a resistance which he himself at any personal hazard whatever, was resolved to offer.'[2]

Burke was of central importance to the Whig interpretation of the

---

[1] *A Philosophical Inquiry into the Origins of our Ideas of the Sublime and Beautiful* (1757).

[2] G. O. Trevelyan, *The American Revolution* (New edition, 1905) Volume 1, section 'Burke and the Whigs', pp. 119–137. The first edition of *The American Revolution* appeared in January 1899. When I wrote (in Chapter III of this book) of a conflict of wills between George III and Edmund Burke, I was not aware that that view of the matter already had the sanction of an eminent Whig historian.

history of the late eighteenth century, not only by reason of his exceptional eloquence, industry and 'amplitude of comprehension', as discerned by Macaulay, and his leading role in resisting the encroachments of George III, but for a specific and functional reason. It was Burke who articulated the ideology of the Rockingham Whigs in a major tract: *Thoughts on the Causes of the Present Discontents* (1770). The Liberal historians of the nineteenth century took that ideology to themselves. Burke is thus not only a hero to the Whig interpretation of history: he is the actual founder of that school of interpretation. For that reason, when it came under attack in the twentieth century, he was in the front line.

Even in the nineteenth century, he had still plenty of enemies. Everything to the left of the Liberal Party was hostile to Burke, and faithful to Paine. The view from that quarter is best summed up in the passage from Marx's *Capital* which is quoted in the epilogue to this book. But even nearer the centre and within the broad Liberal family, there was a radical tradition, hostile to Burke, out of resentment of his defection from the Foxite Whigs in 1791, and for personal reasons. Among historians, this tradition is best represented by James Mill (John Stuart Mill's father) in his ten-volume *History of India*. Curiously, his view of the India of Warren Hastings is essentially the same as Burke's, and he documents a number of Burke's charges. But he gives Burke no credit for having resisted, in their day, the injustices which Mill reproves in retrospect. Burke, he writes, 'neither stretched his eye to the whole of the subject, nor did he carry its vision to the bottom. He was afraid. He was not a man to explore a new and dangerous path without associates. Edmund Burke lived upon applause – upon the applause of the men who were able to set a fashion; and the applause of such men was not to be hoped for by him who should expose to the foundation the iniquities of the juridical system. In the case of public institutions, Mr. Burke had also worked himself into an artificial admiration of the bare fact of existence; especially ancient existence. Every thing was to be protected, not because it was good, but, because it existed. Evil, to render itself an object of reverence in his eye, required only to be realized. Acutely sensible, however, to the spur of the occasion, he felt the abuses which crossed him in his path. These he has displayed with his usual felicity of language and these it is of importance with respect to the imitative herd of mankind to have stamped with the seal of his reprobation'[1]

[1] Mill, *The History of British India* (London, 1858) Fifth Edition, ed. H. H. Wilson, Vol. V, pp. 200–01.

This is the earliest example known to me of the extraordinary malevolence which Burke was – and is – capable of exciting, among people who never knew him. In this case, the malevolence is such as to lead a distinguished historian into gross distortion and flagrant injustice. There is no evidence in support of any of the charges made by Mill, in the first four sentences of the above diatribe, and there is a mountain of evidence against them. The wildness of Mill's charges is evident from the fact that Burke's contemporaries, many of whom did not let a week go by without slandering him, never thought of attacking him along those particular lines. He was never accused of skimping the subject of Warren Hastings's India; on the contrary, he was accused of going on about it to excess and exploring it in repulsive detail. No contemporary thought of him as being 'afraid', on the contrary the vice most commonly attributed to him was recklessness. If Burke 'lived upon applause', he was singularly perverse in his way of looking for it – by opposing the Irish Penal Laws, by opposing the attempts to tax the Americans, and then by opposing the Penal Laws against them and then the war itself; and by attacking the powerful East India Company.[1] So far from being unwilling 'to explore a new and dangerous path without associates,' he showed himself ready to do just that, repeatedly, over India, and he did it again, spectacularly, over the French Revolution. As for his alleged unwillingness to 'expose to the foundation the iniquities of the juridical system' in India, it should be sufficient to recall that he was censured by the House of Commons for having said, in the course of the impeachment of Warren Hastings, that Hastings 'murdered Nuncomar by the hands of Sir Elijah Impey' [Chief Justice of Bengal].

After the unbridled nonsense of the opening sentences of 'Mill on Burke', it is a relief to come to a charge that has at least some connection with the historical Burke. This is the charge against him of 'admiration of the bare fact of existence; especially ancient existence'. There is certainly something in that. It is not, however, true to say that, for Burke, 'Every thing was to be protected, not because it was good, but because it existed.' Protestant Ascendancy in Ireland 'existed' but he did not 'protect it'; he undermined it. It is, however, true to say that, for a long time (1767–1781), he was deterred from

---

[1] I don't mention here the attack on the French Revolution, because there the charge that Burke was seeking popularity, though untrue, at least came to possess a certain superficial plausibility.

serious criticism of the East India Company's system, out of respect
for its established existence, and a refusal to upset any established
system 'upon a Theory'. (The Company's original charter, for fifteen
years, was granted by Elizabeth I in 1600. It was subsequently
granted for ever by James I.) When, however, Burke had studied the
system sufficiently to convince himself that it was evil beyond repair,
he fought it relentlessly, from 1781 to 1794. The conclusion, in
which Mill condescends both to Burke and to the 'imitative band' of
mankind is revealing only of the extent of Mill's personal vanity,
possibly the root of most of his hostility towards Burke. The great
historian of British India may perhaps have felt obscurely that Burke
had unfairly got in first with an exposure of Warren Hastings's
regime, thus stealing the credit rightly due to James Mill. This, however, is a reductionist hypothesis, such as our study of Burke leads
us to distrust. A better explanation may lie in the gulf between Mill's
conception of history and Burke's. Mill was disposed to talk down
to history, and to talk at it, telling it how it should have behaved.
Burke, in contrast, viewed history with a blend of awe and horror,
seeing in it the mysterious and terrible workings of God's Providence.
Minds so differently constituted were not made to understand one
another.

Mill's attack, however, remained exceptional for its period. The
Whig interpretation held the high ground up to the First World
War, and even for a short time after it. The Eleventh Edition of the
Encyclopaedia Britannica – the last published before the Great War
– still carries a ten-page entry on Burke by John Morley, the leading
exponent of the Whig-Liberal tradition. His praise of Burke is discriminating and judicious: 'There have been many subtler, more original and more systematic thinkers about the conditions of the social
union. But no one that ever lived used the general ideas of the thinker
more successfully to judge the particular problems of the statesman.
No one has ever come so close to the details of practical politics, and
at the same time remembered that these can only be understood
and only dealt with by the aid of the broad conceptions of political
philosophy. And what is more than all for perpetuity of fame, he
was one of the great masters of the high and difficult art of elaborate
composition.'

Morley presents Burke as a central figure in the political life of the
time: 'The ministerial policy [of the first Rockingham Administration, 1766] towards the colonies was defended by Burke with
splendid and unanswerable eloquence. He had been returned to the

House of Commons for the pocket borough of Wendover, and his first speech [17 January 1766] was felt to be the rising of a new light. For the space of a quarter of a century, from this time down to 1790, Burke was one of the chief guides and inspirers of a revived Whig party. The "age of small factions" was now succeeded by an age of great principles, and selfish ties of mere families and persons were transformed into a union resting on common conviction and patriotic aims. It was Burke who did more than any one else to give to the Opposition, under the first half of the reign of George III, this stamp of elevation and grandeur.'

Morley also specifically endorses Burke's version of the political scene in Britain on the eve of the American war, and Burke's view of the role of the Court and of the Whigs: 'And he added a durable masterpiece to political literature in a pamphlet, which he called *Thoughts on the Cause of the Present Discontents* (1770). The immediate object of this excellent piece was to hold up the court scheme of weak, divided and dependent administrations in the light of its real purpose and design; to describe the distempers which had been engendered in parliament by the growth of royal influence and the faction of the king's friends; to show that the newly formed Whig party had combined for truly public ends, and was no mere family knot like the Grenvilles and the Bedfords; and, finally, to press for the hearty concurrence both of public men and of the nation at large in combining against "a faction ruling by the private instructions of a court against the general sense of the people".'

In his book *Edmund Burke: A Historical Study* (1879) Morley describes Burke as the inspiration of the Whig Party: 'With the usual insolent thanklessness shown by patricians in every age and country towards the greater plebeians who supply them with ideas and a policy, the party never offered him a seat in their cabinets. But for all that, he was their inspirer. To him they owed the whole vitality of their creed, the whole coherence of their principles, the whole of that enlightenment, that rational love of liberty, that antipathy to arbitrary ideas, on which rest their just claims to the gratitude of their descendants. Burke, from 1770 to 1790, was in the politics of the eighteenth century what Wesley was in its religion. He entered into the midst of the valley and found it full of dry bones. By his imagination, his reasoning, his enormous knowledge, above all, by his ardour and impetuosity of character, he brought the dead Whig principles up from out of the grave, and kindled a life in them, which has only just flickered out for ever in our own days.'

Morley is not an uncritical admirer. He was a declared agnostic; Burke a devout Christian. Morley is not in sympathy with Burke's position on the French Revolution, and deplores his attacks on what he calls 'atheism' and Morley calls 'scepticism' and 'freethinking'. But Morley is aware of the continuity of Burke's thinking on these matters, and even his dissent from Burke is marked by deep and discriminating respect, the result of long and careful study.

Perhaps the last and certainly the most notable, adherent, in the twentieth century, to the Whig interpretation in relation to Edmund Burke was Winston Churchill. In the essay on 'Consistency in Politics' (1932), Churchill offered Burke as his leading exemplar of that quality: 'No greater example in this field can be found than Burke. His *Thoughts on the Present Discontents*, his writings and speeches on the conciliation of America, form the main and lasting armoury of Liberal opinion throughout the English-speaking world. His *Letters on a Regicide Peace*, and *Reflections on the French Revolution*, will continue to furnish Conservatives for all time with the most formidable array of opposing weapons. On the one hand he is revealed as a foremost apostle of Liberty, on the other as the redoubtable champion of Authority. But a charge of political inconsistency applied to this life appears a mean and petty thing. History easily discerns the reasons and forces which actuated him, and the immense changes in the problems he was facing which evoked from the same profound mind and sincere spirit these entirely contrary manifestations. His soul revolted against tyranny, whether it appeared in the aspect of a domineering Monarch and a corrupt Court and Parliamentary system, or whether, mouthing the watch-words of a nonexistent liberty, it towered up against him in the dictation of a brutal mob and wicked sect. No one can read the Burke of Liberty and the Burke of Authority without feeling that here was the same man pursuing the same ends, seeking the same ideals of society and Government, at defending them from assaults, now from one extreme, now from the other. The same danger approached the same man from different directions and in different forms, and the same man turned to face it with incomparable weapons, drawn from the same armoury, used in a different quarter, but for the same purpose.'[1]

[1] Essay, 'Consistency in Politics' in *Thoughts and Adventures* (London, 1932) p. 40.

The detailed evidence accumulated in this book almost all tends, with only minor qualifications, to confirm that Churchillian interpretation.

By the time 'Consistency in Politics' was published in 1932, Burke's reputation was already entering a period of decline. The watershed year was 1929, the bicentenary of his birth.

The *Times Literary Supplement* celebrated the event on 10 January with an essay, 'The Bicentenary of Burke'. In it the Whig interpretation was still dominant. The *TLS* writer, like Morley and Churchill, had a deep sense of Burke's consistency: 'The view of the art and science of politics on which he condemned the French Revolutionaries is the same as that on which he condemned George III, and North; and it once more showed its truth by the event. If you ignore history and custom, he had said to North, you will lose America; and he lost it. If you ignore history and custom, in making a French Constitution, he said to the French Assembly, your Constitution will have a shorter life than the paper on which it is written; and it had.' That view of the matter would soon go out of fashion. That same bicentenary year saw the appearance over the intellectual horizon of a new star, baleful and blighting to the reputation of Edmund Burke. That star was L. B. (later Sir Lewis) Namier, with his book *The Structure of Politics at the Accession of George III* (London, 1929).

THE NAMIERITE ATTACK

Between the First and Second World Wars, the Whig version of the reign of George III and of Burke's role in it was subjected to such a subtle and sustained attack that it was made to seem untenable. The attack was spearheaded by Sir Lewis Namier (1888–1960). He was possibly the most influential British historian of the twentieth century. As far as the historiography of the late eighteenth century is concerned, he is incontestably the most influential of modern British historians. To say that the study of the late eighteenth century became a Namierite monopoly would be an exaggeration. But it would be true to say that, from about 1930 to about 1970, almost all of those who worked on the late eighteenth century in Britain were strongly influenced by Namier. American historians were also influenced by him, though less so. By the 1980s that influence was on the wane, but it remains considerable. Burke's reputation was severely damaged by the Namierite attacks of the mid-twentieth century, and is now slowly recovering.

We need not suppose that Namier set out with any particular animus against Edmund Burke. It is worth noting, however, that Burke and Namier both belonged socially to a common category: that of stigmatised gentry: in Burke's case Irish Catholic gentry under the Penal Laws; in Namier's case, Jewish gentry in anti-semitic Galicia. Such a community of condition can sometimes form a bond but alternatively it can produce an antipathy. In the Burke–Namier case, it certainly didn't form a bond. But the main reason Namier was against Burke was that Burke was in the way of what Namier was trying to do, and also in the way of how he was trying to do it. What he was trying to do was to substitute a new version of the reign of George III for the version offered by the Whig tradition. The principal contemporary witness for the Whig tradition was Edmund Burke. To overthrow the Whig tradition that witness had to be discredited. Specifically he had to be shorn of the aura of respect which, not merely the Whig tradition, but the whole nineteenth century mainstream of opinion had accorded to Burke. Namier never refuted, or even seriously set out to refute, the assessments of Burke by Macaulay, or G. O. Trevelyan or Morley. The method was more original and more effective. He wrote as if the refutation was an accomplished fact. In his demolishing asides, he assumes that only a simpleton could now believe that Burke should be taken seriously. And nobody wants to be taken for a simpleton.

The second reason for cutting Burke down to a size that Namier considered appropriate to him, was that Namier's method required such an operation for an historical figure whose actual stature was above the normal. Procrustes was the original Namierite. Linda Colley, in her respectful, but not hagiographical, book on Namier describes him at work on his chosen subjects for the *History of Parliament*: 'Namier himself deliberately chose to concentrate on biographies of MPs who were second- or even third-rate, or who were eccentric, or rogues, or in some cases insane. It was John Albert Bentinck (reputed "to have made some notable improvements in ships' pumps"), Bamber Gascoigne ("he was disliked, and was fully conscious of it"), and Edward Eliot ("it was his nature to hesitate and worry and tie himself into knots") he wrote about, and not Edmund Burke.' Linda Colley adds, concerning Namier's 'levelling attitude to the MPs he studied': 'Whatever their political importance or lack of it, all Members were equal to him because all were part of a sample – and, he believed, a representative sample – of the governing elite of the time.'[1] It was unfortunate for Burke that the historical period in which he lived and worked should have become the retrospective domain of a historian with these peculiar predispositions.

The first and decisive wave of the Namier assault on Burke and the Whigs came with the publication of Namier's *Structure of Politics at the Accession of George III* and, in 1930, *England in the Age of the American Revolution*. The attack is conducted with remarkable subtlety and economy, where Burke is concerned. It would be possible, I suppose, if you were not particularly interested in Burke, to read both books without noticing that he is the prime target. The references to him are few; that is part of the strategy. The rigorous historian – and Namier radiates rigour – does not takes Burke seriously, and lets this be known, *en passant*. There are just eight references to him in *Structure*. This might not be thought a meagre allowance, since he was not yet a member of Parliament at the time of the accession of George III. But the view of the politics of that period that Namier is concerned to refute was first formulated by Burke, partly retrospectively, in 1770, in *Thoughts on the Causes of the Present Discontents*. In the circumstances, one might perhaps expect a historian to examine in detail the thesis which he proposes to refute. But Namier proceeds otherwise. He treats the thesis as so absurd as not to require refutation. There is no explicit mention of *Thoughts on the Causes of the Present Discontents* in *Structure*. Namier simply assumes Burke's thesis to be so nonsensical that he need not waste time in examining it.

Of the eight references to Burke in the book, four are passing references, which need not detain us. The remaining four are worth looking at. Appropriately, Burke makes his first appearance between brackets in page 9 of *Structure* and with his case already prejudged. The brackets are like handcuffs: 'Yet Newcastle and Pitt (and Burke) are quoted by historians to prove the close oligarchic character of the eighteenth-century Parliament; and so widely accepted is this legend that it cannot be here ignored.' On the next page, we learn of Burke's lowly status among his associates: 'But if Burke was in a way looked down upon by his associates, this was due not so much to the contempt which the nobly born felt for his origin as to the

[1] *Sir Lewis Namier*, in the useful Weidenfeld series *Historians on Historians* (London, 1989) pp. 82–3.

admiration which he had for theirs: clearly no one can treat as an equal a man so full of respect and veneration.'

This is neat and sounds plausible, but it has been comprehensively refuted by the publication (1958–1978) of Burke's *Correspondence*, edited by Thomas Copeland, the scholarly publication of which began in 1958. Burke's closest associates, from the beginning to the end of his political life, were the Marquess of Rockingham and then, after Rockingham's death in 1782, Earl Fitzwilliam. Both consistently treated Burke in a friendly and respectful way, and both deferred to his judgment. Nor was he so full of respect and veneration as to prevent him from pressing his views strongly on Rockingham and Fitzwilliam and also on Charles James Fox and the Duke of Portland. After these introductory shots, we hear no more about Burke, for about 160 pages. Then we learn that Burke 'though exceptional in ability was not of a rare type'. Namier does not tell us in *Structure* what the 'type' was, but he had something to say on that, later. The last reference to Burke (page 258), like the first, links him firmly to 'legend'. We are told that the 'legend' about the early conflicts of the reign has its roots (among other places) 'in the literary afterthoughts of Edmund Burke and the latter-day Whigs'. So the picture of Burke that the reader of *Structure* acquires is that of a purveyor of a legend; a snob and toady despised by his associates, and a person of exceptional ability but of a commonplace type. The ability, it is implied, was literary rather than political, and went mainly into the creation of the legend. Note that this picture is built up exclusively by a few brief *obiter dicta*, which we are to take on Namier's authority, without specific reference to anything that was actually said or done by Burke.

In *England in the Age of the American Revolution* (1930), Namier gives Burke more of the same treatment. Here Namier is dealing, or purporting to be dealing, with a period and a subject within which all historians, before him, had considered Burke to have played a considerable part. Namier's Burke, on the other hand is a marginal figure, and of less interest than many other contemporary politicians who had seemed dim enough to pre-Namierite eyes (and also seemed dim to Namier himself, which was why he liked them). In this respect, the most eloquent section of *England in the Age of the American Revolution* is the index. 'Burke, Edmund MP' rates three lines, the same as 'Brudenell, James MP' and scores of others. As against that, 'Legge, Henry Bilson MP' got twelve lines. This same Legge is quite rightly referred to in the text (page 431) as 'the insignificant Legge'.

As the individual whose insignificance is acknowledged gets exactly four times the index entry allotted to Edmund Burke we can see how wonderfully Burke has shrunk, within the Namierised eighteenth century.

The longest entry in the index of *England in the Age of the American Revolution* – 180 lines – goes to the Duke of Newcastle, the first of that name. This is a rum feature of a rum book, for this Duke, who died in 1768, neither lived to see the American Revolution, nor played any part in the events that we now see as beginning to lead up to that event, from 1765 on. But then Namier is not in the least interested in the American Revolution. Out of the 418 pages of *England in the Age of the American Revolution*, only 53 have sustained connection with America. This is Chapter IV, 'The House of Commons and America', an inquiry into the American connections of various MPs. Debates and votes and alignments of political groups over America are not considered. Thus Burke's sphere of activity disappears from view. The rest of the book deals with the same period and subject as *Structure*. If accuracy in labelling had been a concern of author and publisher, *England in the Age of the American Revolution* should have been entitled *The Structure of Politics at the Accession of George III: Part II*. And if history books were subject to the same advertising regulations as are certain other commodities, *England in the Age of the American Revolution* would have had to be withdrawn from circulation because of its misleading description of its contents. Most of its entries on Burke I have noted as 'neutral' or 'mildly disparaging' but three are substantial. One of these develops the 'legend' thesis, making it a little more specific. Namier wrote: 'There never was a deliberate system of "double cabinets" as sketched by Burke in a polemical pamphlet, to which he himself might possibly have applied the phrase used by him on a different occasion: "By Gad, Madam, does any one swear to the truth of a song?" – but which has been often treated as if it were an impartial verdict on George III.' However, Namier's assertion has often been treated as if it were an impartial verdict on Burke. (The pamphlet, which Namier does not trouble to identify, was *Thoughts on the Causes of the Present Discontents*.) I shall come back to the question of the 'double Cabinet', to consider what Burke actually said, and whether what he said has been shown to be without foundation.

The book's second reference to Burke breaks new ground: 'It seems extremely doubtful whether Burke and his friends, if in power, would have succeeded in saving the First British Empire. Their ideas were no less hierarchical and authoritarian than those of George III and Lord North, and to them, too, trade was the soul of Empire; had Burke been in office during the American Revolution, we might merely have had to antedate his counter-revolutionary Toryism by some twenty years.' This passage is considered in Chapter III of this book. Here it is enough to say that the speculative innuendo in the damaging last sentence quoted above can be factually refuted. For Burke could have been in office during the American Revolution, had he chosen to be. In 1780 George III wrote that Burke would have been 'a real acquisition' to Lord North's Administration, provided he and his friends would abandon their 'Tenets'. This they were not prepared to do, and the most obnoxious of their 'Tenets' was their insistence that the king should not oppose a veto to the recognition of American independence. The attempt to enlarge the North Administration by the inclusion of the Rockinghams failed because of the Rockingham commitment to principle, over America. This transaction fits much better into the purportedly discredited 'Whig interpretation' than it does into the Namierite picture.

The book's third hostile reference to Burke, on page 179, is the most glancing and the most venomous: 'the men whose livery [Burke] happened to have taken'. Burke is coolly classified as a lackey; the opinions and activities go with the livery. Namier produces no argument, let alone evidence, in support of so drastic a verdict. We are to take it upon authority. Namier was known to have done a great deal of detailed research among eighteenth-century records. The reader would assume that this confident judgment is a summary of the results of his research. But of course it isn't. The evidence isn't there. Most of the present study is an accumulation of evidence to the contrary. Namier's researches were not concerned with Burke, but with people like Henry Bilson Legge. Burke was, for Namier, not primarily a subject of research, but a witness to be discredited. Namier's asides on him are a good example of the use of scholarly authority for purposes other than those which scholarship is supposed to be about. The object was, not to ascertain the truth, but to dominate a closed field of study, by ridiculing those who had previously dominated it. The personage whom the Whigs had venerated had to be held up as a negligible person: no more than the inhabitant of a 'livery'. This could not, indeed, be demonstrated, and Namier shrewdly makes no attempt at demonstration. Casual and repeated assertion – with the air of referring to something well known to all who had seriously studied the period – answered his purpose much better.

In what is perhaps the first sustained attack on Namier's method, the American political scientist Harvey C. Mansfield Jr. wrote: 'Namier's authority is in great part based upon his seeming care in his researches, since people suppose that those who are occupied with details are careful with details.'[1] This is not to suggest that Namier was not 'careful' with those details which did in fact occupy his attention. My complaint is that he abused an authority built on a reputation for attention to detail, in order to demolish a historical figure of whom he had made no detailed study.

It was the Namierite picture that prevailed, for most of the twentieth century. In those two books Namier, in an efficient, unobtrusive and apparently dispassionate manner, consigned Edmund Burke to the ash-bin of history, three layers of trash below the insignificant Henry Bilson Legge. Had that operation been attempted twenty years before, it would have caused a storm of controversy, and both Burke and the Whig interpretation would have been vigorously and ably defended. But between the eleventh edition of the *Encyclopaedia Britannica* and *The Structure of Politics at the Accession of George III* lay the chasm of World War I. In the bitter, cynical and disillusioned post-war climate, the mere fact that Burke had been a hero and sage to the leaders of Victorian and Edwardian England tended to discredit him in the eyes of the post-war generation. If you believed that the Eminent Victorians were frauds, as the war was believed to have demonstrated, what more likely then that any hero of theirs should have been a fraud also? Namier's operation was in tune with the *Zeitgeist*.

It wasn't only the *Zeitgeist*. Party politics had also changed, to Burke's disadvantage. The Liberal Party – the party of the Whig tradition – collapsed in the wake of the war. Its place was taken by the Labour Party and most Labour supporters – those that took an interest in history – were Tom Paine people (or tags-of-Tom-Paine people) and *ipso facto* anti-Burke, usually without reading him. Nor did the leaders of the Tory Party between the wars belong to a Burkean school. Baldwin, Chamberlain and their friends distrusted imagination and eloquence when applied to politics. Burke, from

---

[1] Mansfield, 'Sir Lewis Namier Considered', in *Journal of British Studies*, Volume II, No. 1 (May 1964) pp. 85–108.

their point of view, was an unsound outsider, like his admirer, Winston Churchill.

Namier understood this political context very well, and moved within it with ease. The theme and method of *England in the Age of the American Revolution* were of a nature to attract approval from Left and Right. The Right, and also the Court (see liii n. 1 below), liked the demolition of the Whig tradition, the rehabilitation of George III and the presentation of the opponents of the American war as no better than its supporters. The intellectual Left enjoyed the demolition of the author of *Reflections on the Revolution in France*, even when he was not being demolished in that specific capacity. Marxists, crypto-Marxists, and *marxisants*, all then rising in intellectual influence, appreciated Namier's method, with its scientific pretensions, its levelling tendencies and, as Linda Colley notes, its 'interest in the correlation between political decision-makers and their social and economic background.' So everything, from the Court to the Communists, smiled upon Namier's enterprise.

In these propitious conditions, those two books, despite the glaring flaws in the second, rapidly acquired canonical status, and the Whig interpretation was considered to have been conclusively refuted. In the 1930s the late eighteenth-century became a Namierite preserve, and this largely remained the case after the Second World War and up to Namier's death in 1960. It is true that certain English scholars, notably Herbert Butterfield, Alfred Cobban and Raymond Williams, preserved a fair and consequently a respectful approach to Edmund Burke, even during the heyday of Namierism. But they were isolated figures. Namierite writing held the inside track in historiography of the late eighteenth century. And its method, in demolishing Burke, was brilliant, especially in the hands of the Master himself. No one has ever discovered an antidote to the concentrated poison of a Namier aside.

The disparagement of Burke always remained a feature of Namier's own writings and of his closest associate John Brooke and to a lesser extent of other associated scholars. Damaging asides about Burke became a kind of signature tune of Namierite scholarship. For the most part, the asides were of the same type as those contained in the canonical Namier books. The disparagement was most effective, when conducted in an offhand fashion, as if referring to something self-evident. As N. C. Phillips shrewdly observed, Burke 'has suffered at the hands of the general historians, whose aspersions lose nothing in effect for being casual.'[1] I don't propose to collect the rest of the casual aspersions, since the method emerges as well established, from our examination of the canonical books. There are, however, a few instances where the aspersions exceed the limits of the casual and these deserve to be noted.

The high-water mark of Namierite offensiveness in relation to Burke was reached in the early and middle 1950s in two books, Richard Pares's *King George III and the Politicians* (Oxford, 1953), and John Brooke's *The Chatham Administration* (London, 1955). Pares, in his preface to the George III book declares himself 'indebted. . . . above all to Sir Lewis Namier for his corrections'. Perhaps in payment of that debt, Pares, near the beginning of his book, delivers the most offensive observation on Edmund Burke that has ever been framed; 'If we regard his social origins, we can only classify as an Irish adventurer the great Edmund Burke, the theorist and the high priest of snobbery, who had the grace to compare himself to a melon beside the ducal oaks, yet seems to have flattered himself, towards the end of his career, that such a melon might drop an acorn into the soil.' A footnote to this passage says that a peerage was 'a hope Burke had more than half entertained before his son's death'. (Earl Stanhope, Pitt the younger's biographer, believed that the peerage was actually offered, while Burke's son Richard was still alive.) Taking text and footnote together this passage is the academic equivalent of a brutal schoolboy jeer. What this historian wants to say to Burke is: 'You wanted to make your son a Lord, didn't you, and then he went and died on you, didn't he?' The thing is a flash from the depths lighting up the animus that had come to lie behind that steady accumulation of carefully casual Namierite aspersions. (To be fair to Pares, this regrettable passage is also an isolated one. Namier, who read this book and 'corrected' it, let that passage stand; if indeed he did not prompt it.)

John Brooke's *The Chatham Administration* (1955) has a preface by Sir Lewis Namier in which he calls Brooke 'my closest collaborator'. In *The Chatham Administration*, Brooke never sinks to the level of the author of the infamous 'acorn' passage, but he is more persistent and less off-hand in his attacks on Burke than had been previously the Namierite norm. He is also more inconsistent; any stick will do to beat Burke. Brooke rebukes Rockingham for being too much under Burke's

---

[1] 'Edmund Burke and the County Movement, 1779–1780', in Rosalind Mitchison (ed.) *Essays in Eighteenth Century History* from *The English Historical Review*, p. 301.

influence, referring to Rockingham's 'excessive admiration for Burke
. . . which frequently distorted his judgment'. That was on page 144.
But by page 309, it is Burke who is being rebuked for being too much
under Rockingham's influence. Commenting on a report by Burke of a
conversation with General Conway, a prominent former Rockingham
supporter, Brooke writes: 'Burke tied himself into knots in trying to
make sense of Rockingham's irritation and *malaise*. His master's
voice? Or his master's parrot?'[1]

'His master's parrot' is a good example of the cavalier way in
which a Namierite can treat the opinions of Burke's contemporaries.
No contemporary, and no scholar who has actually studied him,
thought of him as Rockingham's mouthpiece.[2] But Brooke and Namier didn't study Burke. They didn't need to, they had already made
up their minds and closed the case against him. Writing about the
imposition of the Townshend duties, in 1767, Brooke says: 'The
Rockinghams were silent on Jan. 26. Dowdeswell was in the House
and Burke was within handy distance, yet neither spoke against a
policy which threatened to undo all the good achieved by the repeal
of the Stamp Act. In both the pro-Americanism of the Rockinghams
was rather accidental than conscious, a shibboleth in British party
politics rather than a serious factor in imperial affairs.'[3]

This is a good specimen of a characteristic feature of the Namierite
campaign against Burke: the drawing of large and damaging conclusions from a supposed documentary silence. Both Brooke and
Namier knew very well that parliamentary reports for the 1760s
are extremely imperfect, yet Brooke can say 'neither spoke' with an
appearance of certitude when a damaging finding, in relation to
Burke, seems within reach. Actually it is virtually certain that Burke
did speak on this occasion. He is reported as having referred in the
following year, in the Commons, to the speech he had delivered in
the previous year against the imposition of the Townshend Duties,
and, as will be seen in Chapter II of this book, a draft of that speech
has now been found among his papers. And the conclusion towards
which Brooke was trying to move through a mistaken inference

[1] Brooke's anti-Rockingham and anti-Burke zeal was beginning to seem tedious
even to some former sympathisers, after 1955. Richard Pares, of all people, rebuked
Brooke on that score in his review of *The Chatham Administration* in the *English
Historical Review* (April, 1957).

[2] The editors of Burke's *Correspondence*, and the *Correspondence* itself, show
Rockingham as heavily under Burke's influence and a knowledgeable contemporary,
Shelburne, complained about this (see Chapter III, p. 203).

[3] *Monarchy and the Party System* (The Romanes Lecture) Oxford, 1952.

from a supposed silence, has been shown to be untenable. We now know that the Rockingham position in America was fully conscious, not accidental, and that it was indeed a serious factor in imperial affairs. The American war would have continued longer than it did, had it not been for the Rockingham factor (See Chapter III below, pp. 223–31).

John Brooke described Burke's theory of the 'Double Cabinet' as 'this hotch-potch'. Namier called it 'a product of Burke's fertile, disordered and malignant imagination'. But Burke himself, in the pamphlet under attack, implies that the term was already in common use, and used at court: 'The whole system, comprehending the exterior and interior administrations, is commonly called, in the technical language of the court *double cabinet*; in French or English, as you choose to pronounce it.'[1] 'The Double Cabinet' is neither a literal fact nor a 'hotch-potch' of legend. It is a metaphor.[2] The reality it refers to is the personal power of George III, exercised through channels other than the Cabinet responsible to Parliament. That there were such channels is a known fact. We know the names: Charles Jenkinson and John Robinson chief among them. We find them in confidential correspondence with the king, keeping him informed about the state of the House of Commons; and how Lord North is doing. It is true that we do not find them, in the preserved *Correspondence*, offering *advice* to the king, as distinct from confidential information. Since it's not on the record it can't have been given – that is the Namierite view of the matter. But this is another instance of the Namierite tendency to infer too much from documentary silence. In the nature of things, a confidential informant is likely to become a confidential adviser also. Jenkinson and Robinson were not the men to *offer* advice to their Sovereign. But we may be sure that if they were asked for advice, in the privacy of the closet, they would have given it. And we know that the royal power was applied, through them, to influence elections, by the use of bribes (see Chapter IV below, p. 335).

The belief that George III was exerting power, outside the Constitution, was not just a personal theory of Edmund Burke, nor was it confined to the Rockingham Party. Horace Walpole, who was hostile

[1] *Thoughts on the Cause of the Present Discontents* (1770): *Works*, 466.
[2] The best analysis of Burke's 'double Cabinet' metaphor is in Harvey C. Mansfield Jr's brilliant *Statesmanship and Party Government: A study of Burke and Bolingbroke* (Chicago University Press, 1965). Mansfield, a political scientist, refuses to treat the 'double Cabinet' literally, but takes its rhetoric seriously.

to Burke, and classed by Brooke as a reliable witness, believed in the
Double Cabinet. And in 1780 a majority of the House of Commons
endorsed Burke's general thesis by voting 233 against 215 for Dunning's Resolution, 'that the influence of the Crown has increased, is
increasing and ought to be diminished.'

Namier and Brooke, and some other members of the school they
founded, were guilty of historiographical hubris: they assumed they
knew more about late eighteenth-century England than did the
people who actually lived in it. As Finlay Peter Dunne's Mr. Dooley
remarked in 'On Heroes and History': 'The further ye get fr'm any
period the better ye can write about it. Ye are not subject to interruptions by people that were there'. The assumed superiority in information over 'the people that were there' is usually implicit: it
underlies, for example, the repeated assertions that Burke didn't
know what he was talking about, in his statements about what was
going on around him, in his own day. But Ian Christie, in *Myth and
Reality*, made the Namierite assumption explicit: 'It is the onlooker
(in this case the historian) not the player who sees most of the game.'[1]
This confidence rests on an undue reliance on things that happened
to get written down, on paper that happened to survive. The historian
is indeed obliged, willy-nilly, to rely on these things. But he should
not imagine that his access to these things necessarily enables him to
refute, from authority, statements made by people who lived at the
time. A written statement may be true or false, but its falsity cannot be
inferred merely from a lack of corroboration in the surviving documents. The system that Burke was describing was essentially a covert
system, and covert systems are generally designed to leave as little
documentary trace as possible (or a misleading documentary trace).

There is also a chronological bias. Namier, in his two most influential books, sticks very close indeed to 1760. The title of the second
book – *England in the Age of the American Revolution* – suggests
otherwise, but the title is misleading. As we have seen, Namier never
got as far as the American Revolution. Even in the last chapter, when
he talks about 'the war', he doesn't mean the American war; he means
the Seven Years War. Now, for a historian who wishes to minimise the
King's personal power, it is expedient to stick as closely as possible to
the period of the accession. The more the reign advanced – up to 1784
– the more that personal power became manifest. After the defeat of

---

[1] *Myth and Reality in Late Eighteenth Century British Politics and Other Papers*
(London, 1970).

Burgoyne at Saratoga (1777) it was George III's will which kept the American war going. And after Yorktown (1782) he would still have kept the war going, had not the Rockinghams, driving him to the verge of abdication, forced him to drop his veto on American independence. He had his revenge in the following year.

I don't understand how anybody can contemplate George's role in the dramatic political events of 1783–4 and still describe Burke's metaphor of the Double Cabinet as no more than 'a legend'. In December 1783, relying on information supplied by his confidential informants, George used threats based on his powers of patronage to defeat in the Lords a measure recommended by his official Cabinet. William Pitt, chosen by George, became chief Minister, although there was still a Commons majority favourable to the Fox-North Coalition. Pitt ruled for two months without a majority. During these two months, the king, through Charles Jenkinson, used his power of patronage to diminish the anti-Pitt majority. When that majority had dwindled to a margin of just one vote, he dissolved Parliament. In the ensuing elections, managed on George's behalf by Jenkinson and Robinson, with the help of Paul Benfield and the East India Company, wholesale bribery was used to defeat Pitt's opponents, and Pitt came back with the desired majority.

Namier, so far as I know, never wrote about the events of 1783–4. But John Brooke was obliged to refer to them, when he undertook to write a life of George III. Brooke passed rather lightly over all that, with no mention of the role of the informants/advisers, which might, if referred to, have seemed to corroborate Burke's 'hotch-potch'. On the subject of the constitutionality of George's proceedings in this crucial period, Brooke had this to say: 'It may be doubted whether the Crown can ever behave unconstitutionally.'[1] The momentum of the crusade against 'the Whig interpretation' was carrying this particular Namierite back towards the principles of Charles I.

By the 1950s the Namierite attacks on Burke were more direct and shriller than the more effective dead-pan detractions of the interwar period. The change of tone may be due to the fact that the Namierite view of the Rockinghams, including Burke, was beginning to lose credibility. In a 1954 paper, 'The Marquess of Rockingham and Lord North's Offer of a Coalition',[2] Ian Christie acknowledged that what

---

[1] Brooke, *King George III, with a Foreword by HRH the Prince of Wales (1972)*. The Prince's advisers might have done well to require the deletion of that sentence, before agreeing to the princely Foreword.

[2] *English Historical Review*, Volume LXIX (1954), pp. 388–407.

he called 'the traditional interpretation of Rockingham's conduct' – by which he meant, not the Whig interpretation, but the Namierite one – required 'modification'. 'The Marquess,' Christie stated, 'can be given more credit for consistency and for good faith towards friends than has hitherto been usually been conceded.' (See Chapter III below, pp. 214–18). Also signs of American impatience with some of the implications of Namierite reductionism were appearing. American historians had never quite shared the enthusiasm of the English Whigs for Burke and his friends, but the levelling tendencies of the Namierite approach to this most sensitive of historical periods were not congenial to Americans. As an American historian, Edmund S. Morgan, wrote: 'The deflation of Fox and Burke, and the other Rockingham Whigs, while accomplished with scarcely a glance in the direction of the colonies, nevertheless [deprived] the American revolutionists of a group of allies whose high-minded sympathy had been relied upon by earlier historians to help demonstrate the justice of the American cause.'[1]

The first two volumes of the *Correspondence of Edmund Burke*, edited by the late Thomas Copeland, came at the end of the decade: Volume I, edited by Copeland himself, came out in 1958; Volume II (Lucy Sutherland) 1960; Volume III (George H. Guttridge) 1961; IV (John A. Woods), 1963; V (Holden Furber, assisted by P. J. Marshall), 1965; VI (Alfred Cobban and Robert A. Smith), 1967; VII (P. J. Marshall and John A. Woods), 1968; VIII (R. B. McDowell), 1969; IX (R. B. McDowell and John A. Woods), 1970; X (Index) 1978.

By the time the final volume of this great edition was published, in 1970, the entire climate of Burke studies had been changed. This seems the appropriate point to salute the memory of Thomas Copeland, greatest and most generous of Burke scholars, and General Editor and moving spirit of the *Correspondence*. It should be noted that the enterprise which he brought to such a triumphant conclusion – and at such a rattling pace, as these things go – was not merely an international but an interdisciplinary one. In the nature of things, most of the participants were historians, but Copeland himself was a Professor of English, at the University of Massachusetts, and his

---

[1] 'The American Revolution: Revisions in need of revising', *William and Mary Quarterly*, 3rd series, XIV (1957), pp. 111–114. Ian Christie, in a conciliatory comment on this paper in the introduction to *Myth and Reality*, showed a willingness to moderate the Namierite interpretation, without, however, returning to the Whig tradition.

Advisory Committee included English scholars, political scientists and an economist, as well as historians. And, as we shall see, many of the most significant contributions to the subsequent (and consequential) revival in Burke studies were to come, not merely from professional historians but from Departments of English and Political Science and even Law.

Only the first two volumes of the *Correspondence* came out in the lifetime of Sir Lewis Namier. Romney Sedgwick, in reviewing Volume I for the *English Historical Review* (*EHR*, LXXV, 1960, p. 135) did his best to fit the volume into the Namierite interpretation. But as the volumes came out, year by year, readers could see increasingly for themselves how different the real Burke was from the trivialised opportunist Burke offered by the Namierised tradition, and how different were his relations with his principal associates from those of the toady depicted by Namier. Lucy Sutherland's Introduction to Volume II of the *Correspondence* is a transitional document. In it we see, I think, the editor torn between loyalty to the Namier tradition and what she actually sees, in the text she is editing.[1]

1960, the year of the publication of Volume II of the *Correspondence*, was also the year that Namier died. The active campaign against Burke did not survive the death of its prime mover. Several of the editors of individual volumes of the *Correspondence* were 'school of Namier' in a broad way, but none of them showed any of Namier's animus against Burke; nor would Thomas Copeland, as General Editor, have permitted the indulgence of any such animus. For the most part, the Clarendon Press, Oxford, edition of Burke's *Writings and Speeches* (1981–90), under the general editorship of Paul Langford continues in the tradition of Copeland, to whom the edition is dedicated. Fully in that great tradition are: Volume II: *Party, Parliament and the American Crisis 1766–1774*, edited Paul Langford (1981); Volume V: *India Madras and Bengal 1774–1785* edited P. J. Marshall (1981); Volume VI. *India, the launching of the Hastings Impeachment 1786–1788*, edited P. J. Marshall (1991); Volume IX: I: *The Revolutionary War 1794–1797* and II *Ireland*, edited R. B. McDowell (1991). For reasons considered below (pp. lix) and in Chapter V, Volume VIII, *The French Revolution 1790–1794*, edited by L. G. Mitchell (1988), is a regrettable aberration from

---

[1] See Chapter I, pp. 100–101. What is said in the text above, and in Chapter I, about Lucy Sutherland is only a personal opinion and may be wrong. Some people who knew her, as I did not, consider she was too strong-minded to have been overawed by Namier.

the high standards of this series. The Copeland edition of the *Correspondence* was an Anglo-American undertaking, published by the Cambridge University Press and the University of Chicago Press. It seems a pity that it was not possible to maintain the transatlantic co-operation for the *Writings and Speeches*. Had it been maintained, I don't believe that Volume VIII could have appeared in its present form.

Modern scholarship, from 1958 to 1991 has rendered untenable the contemptuous view of Burke which dominated the period from 1930 to 1960. Yet the damage that was done to Burke's reputation by Namier and Brooke, with some assistance from others, between 1929 and 1955 is not easily undone. A whole generation of history graduates – perhaps more than one generation – came down from the English universities imbued with the conviction that Burke's reputation had been grossly inflated as a result of a discredited 'Whig interpretation of history'. And the teaching of history in the schools was in the hands of such graduates. *The Structure of Politics at the Accession of George III* and *England in the Age of the American Revolution* are still accepted as authoritative. Slurs, long since refuted as a result of the great increase in our knowledge of Burke over the past sixty years and more, still appear in standard works authoritatively recommended to undergraduates, and they must have their effect. The young are only too inclined to believe that a person venerated by past generations has feet of clay. Only too ready, also, to take it on trust that an author esteemed by past generations is not worth reading.[1]

Some friends, who gently reproach me with excessive anti-Namierite zeal, have pointed out that it was 'Namierite scholarship that has put to rest the main accusation in the past against Burke: i.e. that he was sleazy, dubious in his financial transactions and was dragged in the wake of disreputable relations, especially over India'. I accept this, but with reservations. This was 'Namierite scholarship' in the sense that it was the work of people, primarily John A. Woods in the Introduction to Volume II of *Correspondence*, who had been influenced by Namier. But it was not scholarship in a Namierite context. Woods and Sutherland were working within the context of the editing of the *Correspondence*, an enterprise permeated by the spirit, not of Namier, but of Thomas Copeland. 'Namierite scholarship'

---

[1] I have heard it argued, in rebuttal of the charge that Namier was systematically unfair to Burke, that the fifteen-column entry on Burke in the *History of Parliament* (edited by Namier and Brooke) is generally fair, and even respectful. So it is. But the damage had already been done, in those poisoned asides.

within the context of the *Correspondence*, took on a different meaning
to what it had had in the writings of Namier himself and his close
associates from 1929 to 1955. Those earlier writings, where they
touched on Burke, grazing him and drawing blood, did more than anything else to create a climate in which more direct accusations of sleaz-
iness etc. could flourish. So there is poetic irony in the fact that it should
be 'Namierite scholarship', from the late 1950s on, which 'put to rest'
what an earlier form of 'Namierite scholarship' had fostered.

Namier's hostility to Burke, although no longer emulated by the
generality of modern scholarship, has a vestigial influence on modern
scholarly work. It shows itself in a disposition not to believe anything
Burke says, unless it receives a hundred per cent corroboration from
another source. Ninety-eight per cent corroboration will not do. John
Brooke had contended, on the basis of a documentary silence, that
Burke did not attack the Townshend Duties in 1767. Burke, in 1768,
referred in the Commons to the speech he said he had made in 1767
against those Duties. Paul Langford, in editing Burke's *Writings and
Speeches*, actually found a draft, in Burke's hand, of the speech Burke
said he had delivered. Yet Langford still leaves open the possibility that
Burke may have been lying in 1768. He may have been pretending – in
the presence of people who knew whatever he did or didn't say in 1767
– to have delivered a speech which in fact he only drafted, but did not
deliver. Such extraordinary rigour seems in the line of descent from
Namier. Burke is never to get the benefit of the doubt.

In general, the Namierite 'vestigial influence' is vague, diffuse,
finding expression in reservations rather than affirmatives. It is rare
to go further, but it can happen. The most striking illustration I
have found, after 1960, of a historian's putting trust in the Namier
interpretation of Edmund Burke, is contained in a passage in Alan
Valentine's *Lord North* (University of Oklahoma Press, 1967). He
writes in Volume II, page 104): 'But Burke's position was disin-
genuous. Although he was an Irishman and posed as an ardent friend
of his countrymen, he had drawn up Rockingham's protest against
taxing absentee Irish landlords, and since he had become a member
of the English Parliament for Bristol he was careful not to offend his
merchant constituents, who opposed Irish competition with their
own trade. What Burke condemned for Irish ears as too little, he
condemned for Bristol ears as too much. He proposed comprehensive
measures for conciliation of the Americans, but he made no equally
famous speech on concessions for the benefit of Irishmen.'

Only one of Valentine's charges against Burke is even plausible:

the one that concerns the taxation of absentee landlords. Even that is based on an unwarranted assumption that such taxation was in the interests of the Irish tenantry. It probably wasn't. Some of the best of the Irish landlords were wealthy men, resident in England, interested in the improvement of their holdings, both in England and in Ireland, and in the welfare of their tenants (see below, pp. 69–70). Burke's patron, Rockingham, was one such landlord. The worst landlords, resident or non-resident, were the most impecunious. The legislation in question could hardly have helped the Irish tenants, and Burke's opposition to it is reasonably founded. The rest of Valentine's argument is nonsense. Burke, so far from being 'careful not to offend his Bristol constituents' over Irish trade, gave them such serious offence that he lost his seat. He gave them offence knowingly, and he defended his position against their objections (see Chapter I below, pp. 71–86). When Valentine says, 'What Burke condemned for Irish ears as too little, he condemned for Bristol ears as too much' he cites a Burke letter of 11 April to his Quaker friend in Bristol, Richard Champion (1743–91), in which he says the relaxations on Irish trade with Britain were too little. Valentine assumes this 'too little' letter to have been written 'for Irish ears'. Unfortunately for Valentine, and for the Namierite hypothesis, Champion was not an Irish person at all but one of Burke's constituents. The letter Valentine quotes, in the edition from which he quotes it, carries the note '*Addressed*: to [Richard Champion Esq.] Castle Green, Bristol.' (See *Correspondence* III, 427).

For the rest, it is factually correct, but utterly misleading, to say that Burke 'made no equally famous speech for the benefit of Irishmen'. He did not, but he did more than anyone else to secure legislative redress for the benefit of Irishmen. The statement that he 'posed as an ardent friend of Ireland' is as absurd as it is offensive. There was nothing to be gained, in the eighteenth century, by posing as an ardent friend of Ireland; quite the contrary. Far from 'posing as a friend of Ireland' Burke was driven to dissimulate the depth of his commitment to Ireland and the cause of the Irish Catholics in particular. Valentine's interpretation of 'Burke on Ireland' is interesting only as an example of the grief that lies in wait for a historian who puts his trust in the Namierite asides as the key to a historical situation of which the trusting historian has made no deep study on his own account.[1]

---

[1] Valentine's book is useful about Lord North. In the passage quoted, the historian wandered too far west from his subject.

It is often reasonable to classify negative dispositions towards Burke, in post-1960 historiography, as vestigial Namierism. But there is one publication, as late as 1988, in which the antipathy towards Burke is more than vestigial. I am referring to Volume VIII, *The French Revolution 1790–4*, of *The Writings and Speeches of Edmund Burke* (Oxford 1989). This volume is edited by L. G. Mitchell. Mitchell's Introduction, from beginning to end, is a systematic belittling of Burke. Mitchell is not at all points a Namierite, since he appears to think highly of Charles James Fox, whom Namier despised. But his training was Namierite; his supervisor for his thesis at Oxford, J. B. Owen, was a devoted pupil of Namier's. Owen's piety towards his dead Master appears to have been impressively transmitted with respect to Burke, and Mitchell's assiduous intimations of Burke's worthlessness are obliquely conveyed in a deadpan manner reminiscent of the asides of that Master himself. Where Burke is concerned, L. G. Mitchell is the last surviving, fullblooded, Namierite demolition artist. It seems an odd choice to edit perhaps the most important volume in *The Writings and Speeches of Edmund Burke*. These *Writings and Speeches* are dedicated to the late Thomas Copeland, General Editor of the *Correspondence*. Having had the privilege of knowing Copeland, I do not believe he would have entrusted the editing of a volume of *Writings and Speeches* to a person who holds Burke in such low esteem as does L. G. Mitchell. If Burke is as worthless as Mitchell suggests, his *Writings and Speeches* are not worth editing.

In challenging 'Namier on Burke', I am not seeking to impugn Namier's scholarship in general. That scholarship was no doubt meticulous, when applied to his areas of predilection, which included people like Henry Bilson Legge and did not include Edmund Burke. Whether late eighteenth-century historiography has or has not benefited by Namier's activities is a moot point. He certainly unearthed a mass of detail. But may that contribution not be outweighed by the intrusion of a value system, within which Henry Bilson Legge is a more noteworthy figure than Edmund Burke? There is a relevant assessment by another historian, a colleague of Namier's at Manchester University, which Burkeans may tend to find acceptable. A. J. P. Taylor wrote: 'Namier took the mind out of history.'[1]

---

[1] Taylor, *A Personal History* (Hamish Hamilton, London, 1983) p. 113.

Fantasia

When I showed myself in an article in *The Times* to be impressed by Taylor's verdict, I received a courteous but distinct rebuke from G. R. Elton, which gave me pause. Yet Namier certainly took something out of history. What, exactly, did he take? While thinking that one over, I happened to read Isaiah Berlin's *The Crooked Timber of Humanity*, and found the passage quoted as the epigraph of this Introduction. There I discovered what it was that Namier had taken out of history: what Vico called *Fantasia*, rendered by Berlin as 'imaginative insight'. Not even Namier's greatest admirers would be likely to cite *The Structure of Politics at the Accession of George III* or *England in the Age of the American Revolution* as notable examples of *fantasia*.

Burke was himself one of the world's great masters of *fantasia*, and no historian who lacks that quality will ever do justice to Burke. Those who despise *fantasia* will be Burke's enemies, *ipso facto*. This century's historiography, as compared with that of the nineteenth, has set a relatively low value on *fantasia*, and this tendency has been most marked among British historians specialising in the late eighteenth century. I have an impression however that in the 1990s, the intellectual climate (among the minority interested in such things) is becoming more propitious to *fantasia* and therefore to Burke than has been the case in previous decades. In Britain his reputation among historians has been slowly recovering, after the blighted years, although with one serious relapse, in Volume VIII of *Writings and Speeches* quoted above. The recovery, so far, has been a cautious and somewhat negative affair, apparently confined to a desire – manifest in the editing of Volumes II and V of the *Writings and Speeches* – to avoid the anti-Burkean excesses which ran through the historiography of the middle third of the twentieth century. The methodology and general approach established in that period are still in the ascendant, at least in Britain, as far as the history of events are concerned. In the domain of the history of ideas, Britain has the greatest living master of *fantasia* in the person of Sir Isaiah Berlin. It is our misfortune, however, that he never turned his full attention to Edmund Burke. (But see Appendix, 'An Exchange with Isaiah Berlin).

In conclusion, I should like to consider America and France, two countries in which the intellectual climate seems more favourable, with regard to Burke and *fantasia* than is at present the case in Britain.

American historians were never as unsympathetic to Burke as leading British historians were from 1930 to 1960. But the Americans have sometimes not been altogether sympathetic either. There is a vein of condescension there, as towards a person who means well, but doesn't quite understand what is going on (see Chapter II below, pp. 111–12). In 1976, when I took part in a Bicentenary Conference at Norfolk, Virginia, I got some insight into the processes at work. Those American speakers who referred to Burke did so somewhat dismissively and with a touch of impatience. George III and Lord North, in contrast, were treated with consideration and respect. The general feeling seemed to be that those in England whose policies had done most to bring about the American Revolution deserved a place of honour at the festivities celebrating the bicentenary of that almost sacral event. Edmund Burke, in contrast, who had striven – almost sacrilegiously in the context – to avert the Revolution, by removing the British provocations, could have no such place.

There have been periods when Burke has been more or less fashionable in America. Thus in 1898 the speech 'On Conciliation with America' became required reading in American high schools. Presumably the idea was to promote better relations between America and Britain. The speech was dropped from the curriculum in 1932 for reasons unknown to me. Then there was another Burke revival, also connected with American politics and policies, in the 1950s and 1960s. Some American scholars, notably Peter J. Stanlis and Russell Kirk, drew upon Burke for arguments in the context of the Cold War, the Vietnam War, and the idea of America's imperial responsibilities. This revival produced some valuable detailed work, but as a whole the Burke of this revival was seriously distorted by its polemical and propagandist purposes, inflating the aspects of his career that suited those purposes, and deflating those that did not suit.

The use of Burke's authority to challenge Communism, and Western supporters of the Communist enterprise, was legitimate in a general way. There can be no doubt that he would have seen in Communism all the elements he did see in Jacobinism, as well as some new ones that he would also have detested. And he would have felt about Western pro-Communists just as he did about the pro-Jacobin British radicals of his own day. However, to offer him as implicitly approving of the Vietnam war was a misrepresentation. He did not feel about Asian peasants as he did about Jacobins in Paris or pro-Jacobins in London. Burke distinguished between rebellions which originated in 'wantonness and fullness of bread' and those that 'grew out of the bottom of human nature' (see Chapter VI, p. 573). Among the latter he included the incipient rebellion in Ireland in 1795–7, even though he knew that the potential rebels were pro-Jacobin and hoped for help from Jacobin France. This position would not suggest approval for the choice of Vietnam as a suitable place in which to fight Communism.

Even during the period of these political distortions, however, some American scholars were working on Burke, in an altogether disinterested way. Three such studies will be considered briefly here. The first to appear was Carl B. Cone's two-volume biography, published under the general title *Burke and the Nature of Politics* (University of Kentucky Press). The first volume appeared in 1957, with the subtitle *The Age of the American Revolution*; the second in 1964, subtitled *The Age of the French Revolution*. Although the late 1950s and early 1960s saw the peak of the 'cold war' exploitation of Burke, Cone wisely kept his distance from all that. *Burke and the Nature of Politics* is the fullest biography of Burke that exists, and Cone's comments and interpretations are judicious and dispassionate.

The second study in this category is Harvey C. Mansfield Jr's *Statesmanship and Party Government* already mentioned (see footnote p. xlvii above). This is among the best things ever written about Burke. Mansfield combines the skills of historian and literary critic with those of the political scientist. He takes words like 'legend' and 'rhetoric' which, in connection with Burke, have generally been used as terms of abuse, and fits them to Burke with care and respect, as in this passage concerning *Thoughts on the Causes of the Present Discontents*: 'The introductory part of the *Thoughts* consists of Burke's remarks on current opinions about the cause of distempers; his own analysis of the cause occupies the body of the pamphlet. This analysis identifies the cause as a "plan" or "project" by a "court cabal", a "certain set of intriguing men". But Burke is reluctant to identify the planners and concludes only that the court cabal has instituted a new system of policy. He supplies a vague narrative of the plan, which hints at occurrences known to all public men of the time, as through the new court system were a particular distemper, curable by something like a change in administration. Such a change would of course have re-established the Rockingham party in power, as an appropriate remedy for a particular distemper. But Burke's remedy is in fact a general recommendation of party, and he recommends the Rockingham party only as an example of a true party. The historians who think that Burke actually believed the new court system to be the instrument of a squad of plotters, ambitious in the ordinary way, reduce the generality of his suggested remedy and identify his motive as narrowly partisan.

'It can be shown, on the contrary, that Burke was proposing a constitutional remedy for a general danger produced by a new theory. This theory, not the malevolence of plotters, has created the new court system. The theory threatens the constitution by virtue of its plausibility to both the people and the public men. The "plan" is a rhetorical device contrived by Burke in accordance with the statesman's presumption that the people are good or good enough. Instead of attacking their gullibility, he represents the plausible theory by a "legend" (to use Namier's term) so that they can understand its evil intent and effect. The legend reads like a plot, in order to respect the statesman's presumption; yet the plot is never so specific that the Rockingham party can think to oppose it merely by replacing the present administration. The legend appears to be particular but only vaguely so. It is impossible if taken literally; yet it is carefully constructed for this delicate rhetorical effect' (*Statesmanship*, p. 30).

The third of these studies is Gerard W. Chapman's *Edmund Burke: The Practical Imagination* (Harvard U.P. 1967). Chapman's critique of Burke is thematically organised and in its structure it anticipates *The Great Melody*. In his Foreword Chapman writes: 'I have divided chapters to correspond with the five great issues or crises of his career – America, Ireland, Constitutional Reform, France and India – not for the sake of geographical neatness, but because these were the great political crises in his lifetime, and not to admit them in the organisation of the book would falsify things-as-Burke-encountered-them, the conscious horizons within which his thinking was carried out.'

Edmund Burke: The Practical Imagination came to my attention only after I had finished the basic draft of *The Great Melody* and the first contemplation of the structure of Chapman's book gave me a hollow feeling. What if the book I was writing had already been written, more than twenty years before, across the Atlantic? Fortunately, this turned out not to be so. The two books have not much in common except structure, and a shared respectful and non-propagandist approach to Burke. Chapman's is essentially a work of literary criticism; a perceptive exploration of Burke's use of words. He does not concern himself, to any great extent, with the political context, or immediate political impact, of Burke's utterances; he follows the language, the spirit and the ideas, and to great effect as in the following passages: 'Opaque, long-hardened words like *govern*, with its complicated fringe of meaning, constantly reawaken in Burke and startle one back into familiarity with them. "People must be governed," Burke said, "in a manner agreeable to their temper and disposition; and men of free character and spirit must be ruled with, at least, some condescension to this spirit and this character."

'One meets the curious paradox that in his behaviour during the American crisis, while turning to discover and accord with actual circumstances in a way that critics generally have called "liberal", Burke was really busying himself with, and urging conformity to, the *status quo*. The paradox is resolved by realising his assumption that change, novelty, growth, is often part of the *status quo* and indeed that the *status quo* itself is not made up primarily of "dead things" but of "principles" which are "living and productive". The presupposition of conserving the American colonies was a liberal view of their character and circumstances: nothing better shows the futility of trying to ticket (and dispose of) Burke by some neat little tag – more especially if "conservative" is to be made antithetical to "liberal" and both terms sent crabwalking down history in a narrow and jealous dialectic of change and resistance:

'"*Liberty*" is a curious plus word in Burke. At first reflection, one would suppose its meaning plain: liberty is the condition of doing as one pleases within certain limits, and these limits are the prevailing mode of justice. But the word often slips its legal formality and edges unannounced into a culture pattern. The abstract definition, whose worth is undisputed, presto robes itself in circumstances, without warning. The practical consequences of an idea grip his attention. As a politician, Burke is cautious about separating ideas from their envelope of suggestion, feeling, and intention, their unspoken relation to other ideas, their observable effects. Abstract essences splinter into existence and become moral essences, only to retract once more, as his thought moves, into abstract. And the quick grace of his flight between abstraction and circumstance, definition and practice, idea and behaviour, is sometimes deceptive, hard to follow. When he spoke of English liberty, he often confused conception and fact, and therefore he ended up with something like "cultural" liberty, broad and general as the air, a profound and present liberty which, long growing in a Whig-powered England, irradiated, as he hoped, all its dominions – a ruling and master principle latent in manners, habits, and old affections.'

Edmund Burke: The Practical Imagination is a seminal work; its influence on literary studies of Burke in America circa 1990, is palpable.

The 1980s and early 1990s have yielded further weighty American contributions to Burke studies. One of these is again from the pen of Harvey Mansfield Jr. in his Preface and Introduction to *Selected Letters of Edmund Burke* (University of Chicago Press, 1984). Mansfield, like Gerard W. Chapman, anticipated me in finding the need for a thematic approach to Edmund Burke. Mansfield organised his selection from the ten-volume *Correspondence* thematically, and illuminatingly, and explains his reasons for this approach: 'In place of their narrative history following on the flow of Burke's private pen, I have organised my selection around the grand themes of Burke's life. The result is a thematic Burke given to deliberation, reflection, and argument, rather than a contextual Burke known mainly for his whereabouts and his acquaintances.'

The introduction to Mansfield's *Selections* is full of insights, like this one with its lapidary conclusion: 'Even his prescient understanding of the character, importance, and future of the French Revolution is obscured by the extreme partisanship to which his understanding compelled him. He loses credit for his foresight because he acted on it.'

Mansfield is firm against the 'natural law' view of Burke's theoretical position, a view dear to the cold warriors of American Burke studies. He writes: 'It is striking that Burke was made the purveyor of a *Theory* necessary to healthy politics. If there is one recurrent theme in Burke's letters, speeches, and writings, it is his emphasis on the moral and political evils that follow upon the intrusion of theory into political practice. It is theory as such that he rejects; his emphasis on the evils of intrusive theory is not balanced by a compensating reliance on sound theory that men would need as a guide to their politics. Sound theory, to him, would seem to be self-denying theory.'

James K. Chandler's *Wordsworth's Second Nature: A Study of the Poetry and Politics* (Chicago, 1984) has three chapters devoted to Burke's influence on Wordsworth, which Chandler shows to be pervasive. Wordsworth, like Coleridge (below pp. lxix–lxx), struggled for years to shake off Burke's influence, but the influence is apparent even while he is resisting it. Wordsworth still supported the French Revolution as late as 1793, when he wrote his *Letter to the Bishop of Llandaff*. The poet reproaches the bishop for having drunk from 'Burke's intoxicating bowl'. The phrase, in its context recalls Voltaire's reference to Spinoza's 'enchanted Castle', words blurted out at a time when all the *philosophes* were bent on minimising their enormous intellectual debt to Spinoza.

It has commonly been assumed that Wordsworth fell under Burke's influence only late in life, when his poetic powers were in decline. Certainly that interpretation fits the long and somewhat bathetic 'retraction' passage from the 1850 edition of *The Prelude* that begins:

> *Genius of Burke! forgive the pen seduced*
> *By spurious wonders and too slow to tell . . .*

Chandler, however, shows that what he calls Wordsworth's 'affinity with Burke's thought and [his] debt to his writings' is apparent throughout the 'French' Books of *The Prelude* (Books ix and x) written at the height of the poet's powers. Chandler cites some clear Wordsworthian echoes of Burke but concludes that the influence goes far deeper than such echoes would suggest: 'Burkean assumptions tend to sink down into the France books, not to float near the surface. The central catastrophe of the France books – it is also that of the poem as a whole – is recounted under both its social and mental aspects from Burke's point of view. Burkean conceptions seem to underlie the very scheme according to which both social and mental events are narrated. Beginning, middle, and end, the story of this young Englishman's experience with France, has, I would argue, all been told before. Though verbal echoes can help to show that Wordsworth's story is such a retelling of Burke's, the real debt runs deeper.'

J. G. Pocock's 1989 Indianapolis/Cambridge edition of Burke's *Reflections on the Revolution in France* is a landmark in Burke studies in America. Its 40-page introduction is a subtle and generally respectful exploration of the political and intellectual context of *Reflections*. Pocock sympathetically examines what he calls Burke's conservatism, but at the same time he too distances himself from the cold war school of Burke studies. He points out, in his opening page, that Burke's 'conservatism' is 'part of the history of political conservatism' and does not belong with 'what is meant by the word in the contemporary United States, a blend of American patriotism, evangelical religion and free-enterprise values.'

I have only one cavil to make concerning this otherwise admirable Introduction. Pocock, unlike Mansfield, is significantly affected by what I have called the 'vestigial Namierism' so prevalent among late-twentieth-century British students of Burke. This means that he has a fairly poor resistance to reductionist hypothesis, and a disposition to disbelieve Burke, on a point where he cannot find independent corroboration. In two instances, this leads him into demonstrable error. The first concerns Warren Hastings. Pocock imputes to Burke in impeaching Hastings the motive of revenge for certain actions of George III and Pitt in 1783–4, actions which resulted in the removal of Burke and his friends from office, and their replacement by Pitt. Pocock writes that when Burke embarked upon the impeachment, in 1788, 'he was attempting to injure Pitt and the King by means of the Indian issue which had helped bring Pitt to power; but he had a case, and threw himself into it, for years to come, with the same moral passion as he was to display in his crusade against the French Revolution.'

Pocock here allows both for a reductionist motive and a more exalted one. But the reductionist hypothesis in this case is refuted by the chronology. It is true that the Impeachment began in February 1788, and is therefore subsequent to those transactions of the King and Pitt in 1783–4. But the actual impeachment, at the Bar of the House of Lords, come as only the climax to a parliamentary campaign sustained by Burke, virtually single-handed, against Hastings for seven years before the impeachment's opening. He first began to move against Hastings early in 1781, and in December 1782, in Parliament, he 'insisted not merely on Hastings's recall but on his trial and punishment' (see Chapter IV below, p. 311). From this 'vast task', as he then acknowledged it to be, he never afterwards desisted or faltered. And it is impossible that, in committing himself to the Hastings's impeachment, he should have been motivated by a desire for revenge for transactions which had not yet occurred. In short, a commitment publicly entered into in 1782 cannot be explained by reference to transactions of 1783–4, however neatly such an explanation may appear to fit a certain influential interpretation of Burke's character.

Curiously this same 'revenge theory' was offered by G. A. R. Gleig, Hastings's Victorian biographer, and was refuted by Macaulay, with the conclusive evidence of the date. He writes in his Warren Hastings essay (*Edinburgh Review*, October 1841): 'The idle story that [Burke] had some private slight to revenge has long been given up, even by the advocates of Hastings. Mr. Gleig supposes that Burke was actuated by party spirit, that he retained a bitter remembrance of the fall of the coalition, that he attributed that fall to the exertions of the East Indian interest and that he considered Hastings as the head and the representative of that interest. This explanation seems to be sufficiently refuted by a reference to dates. The hostility of Burke to Hastings commenced long before the coalition and lasted long after Burke had become a strenuous supporter of those by whom the coalition had been defeated'.

The second instance concerns the credibility of Burke and his wife Jane, in relation to the reaction of George III to *Reflections*. Pocock writes: 'There is a story that George III thanked Burke for pleading the cause "of all the gentlemen", but this rests on Jane Burke's account of what her husband had told her the king had said to him and is not much evidence of the dissemination of Burke's ideas.' Fortunately, there is other evidence, not so easily set aside, of George's favourable reaction to Burke's counter-revolutionary writings. On 6 May 1791 James Bland Burges, then Under-Secretary for Foreign Affairs, wrote to Burke to tell him officially of the king's reception of his latest counter-revolutionary pamphlet, *Letter to a Member of the National Assembly*: 'I lose no time in informing you that I have this morning had an opportunity of knowing, from the best Authority, that His Majesty has perused it with much attention, and that he expressed very great satisfaction at the whole of it, particularly those parts which relate to Rousseau, Mirabeau and the new Organisation of the Courts of Justice.' (Burke's *Correspondence* VI, 252–3). *Letter to a Member* is a continuation and development of the argument of *Reflections*. Anyone who read the one with 'very great satisfaction at the whole of it' would certainly have read the other with the same sentiments. There is therefore nothing in the least incredible about Jane Burke's account. No one could ever have imagined there was, who had not been conditioned to be suspicious about anything coming from Burke.

These and a few other blemishes in this otherwise valuable contribution to Burke scholarship are the results of the writer having unguardedly inhaled the faint but still toxic traces of Namierite reductionism which still linger in British scholarly work on Burke, and marginally affect American scholarship also.

Four recent American papers published in this decade are suggestive of a recrudescence of *fantasia* responsive to Burke's *fantasia*. Three, perhaps significantly, come from Departments of English, not Departments of History: the chapter 'Burke, Wordsworth and the Defense of History' in David Bromwich's *A Choice of Inheritance: Self and Community from Edmund Burke to Robert Frost* (Harvard U.P., 1989), A. C. Goodson's 'Burke's Orphics and Coleridge's Contrary Understanding' (*The Wordsworth Circle*, Summer, 1991) and James Engell's 'That Eye, Which Sees All Things: Burke as Poet and Prophet' (awaiting publication). Like Harvey Mansfield, whom they also resemble in other ways, all three writers reject or deprecate the classification of Burke as 'conservative'. Bromwich explores, with great alertness and subtlety, Burke's relation to the Enlightenment around the concept of 'prejudice': 'In the usual Enlightenment metaphor about nature and circumstance, prejudice appears as a circumstantial entity – it is added on, supplementary, and to be done away with when we please. Burke says that this metaphor itself is the contribution of reason, at a certain moment of human development, and that nothing about the nature of history can justify taking it seriously. Given the limitations of our research into the past, as also of our self-knowledge, it is false to suppose that we can see beyond the layers of prejudice that confront us. Neither history nor any other study can tell what human nature would be like without those layers. Beneath prejudice, more prejudice. It is easy to imagine how doubts of this sort could lead to skeptical conclusions; and Hume exemplifies one of them in his *Natural History of Religion*: if the revelations of divinity become more improbable the closer we get to their source, then such revelations are likely to be false, as a general rule. One can certainly imagine a similar argument applied to nature and the prejudices that constitute it. But Burke, having argued to this point in the Enlightenment manner, now offers an unexpectedly consistent defense of nature. All those habits, customs, and local superstitions you complain of (he says to the party of improvers), just *are* human nature. They are what we are. The thought of eradicating them is therefore something like a thought of self-destruction for the species.'

Goodson's paper is headed by a quotation from Thomas De Quincey: '[Fox] was helmsman to a party ... But Burke was no steersman; he was the Orpheus that sailed with the Argonauts; he was their seer, seeing more in his visions than was always intelligible even to himself; he was their watcher in the starry hours; he was their astrological interpreter. Who complains of a prophet for being a little darker of speech than a post-office directory? Or of him that reads the stars for being sometimes perplexed?'

Goodson is interested in what he calls 'Burke's dark interpretation, his orphic political understanding' and its effects on Coleridge and (partly through Coleridge) on De Quincey. Goodson quotes a Cambridge classmate of the young Coleridge as recalling: 'Ever and anon, a pamphlet issued from the pen of Burke. There was no need of having the book before us. Coleridge had read it in the morning, and in the evening he would repeat whole pages verbatim.' Goodson depicts Coleridge, not as a disciple of Burke, but as a mind at grips with him: 'Coleridge struggled with Burke: he did not yield to him.' The struggle is apparent in a passage quoted by Goodson, in which Coleridge, in the course of an effort to sustain a charge of inconsistency against Burke, delivers a towering tribute to Burke's consistency, of principle. 'I do not mean, that this great Man supported different Principles at different aeras [eras] of his political Life. On the contrary, no Man was ever more like himself! From his first published Speech on the American Colonies to his last posthumous Tracts, we see the same Man, the same Doctrines, the same uniform Wisdom of *practical* Councils, the same Reasoning and the same Prejudices against all abstract grounds, against all deduction of Practice from Theory. The inconsistency to which I allude, is of a different kind: it is the want of congruity in the Principles appealed to in different parts of the same Work, it is an apparent versatility of the Principle with the Occasion'. The point about 'apparent versatility of the Principle with the Occasion' was anticipated by Burke himself and is solidly answered in *An Appeal from the New to the Old Whigs* (see Chapter V, pp. 437–49). This essay is remarkable for a triple interplay of sympathetic minds: Coleridge's *fantasia* responding to Burke's, and the modern critic responding to both.

James Engell, in 'That Eye, which Sees All Things', places Burke at the 'crossroads of literature and power.' He goes on: 'Burke is a statesman and writer beyond familiar ideologies. Least of all is he susceptible to simplistic rubrics of our limited political vocabulary – I mean whatever unimaginative variations stem from the threadbare labels "liberal" and "conservative," "left" and "right". If there are still prophets in our secular age, Burke may be considered one. In power of language and vision this great rhetorician is a poet in the capacious sense of that word, a poet as Plato and Isaiah and Ezekiel are poets.'

A fourth paper, indicative of the present activity of American minds sympathetic to Burke, is John Faulkner's review of *The Writings and*

Speeches of Edmund Burke: Volume VIII. The French Revolution 1790–1794, with its uniformly derogatory Introduction. British reactions to that eccentric product were not uncritical, but were more respectful than was necessary. Faulkner does not fall into this trap. He describes his own review as 'severe'. So it is, justly. A good example of Faulkner's approach is his comment on a characteristic passage by L. G. Mitchell: 'Many of Burke's pamphlet opponents saw in the book not just extravagant views and polemic, but also the public apostasy of a man they had believed their friend. Thomas Jefferson was sent a copy of the *Reflections* by a London friend within days of its publication. After reading it, he commented that "the Revolution in France does not astonish me so much as the revolution in Mr. Burke."'[1] Faulkner comments: 'It is a well-chosen and witty quotation, but it is all readers get. If it is enough for Mitchell's purpose to cite a political adversary of Burke on the issue without committing himself or evaluating the validity of the comment he quotes, what are we to infer of that purpose? This is a tactic he often employs'. It is indeed. Faulkner goes on: 'Although Mitchell makes no judgment about the matter in his own voice, he is willing to let the opinion of Jefferson and the generalised "contemporaries" stand as the only view expressed on Burke's consistency in his introduction. As it happens, that view is highly dubious. Readers like Jefferson understandably based their expectations that Burke would join them in welcoming the French Revolution on the legislative positions he had taken concerning America fifteen years before, not on his ill-remembered grounds for taking them. In Burke's view, however, the colonists had deserved support, not because they had asserted abstract rights like those enumerated in Jefferson's Declaration of Independence (a document written only after fighting had begun), but for resisting the withdrawal of liberties which they had long enjoyed as British subjects.'

As we might expect from so sturdy a demolisher of the last of the unreconstructed anti-Burkeans, Faulkner is a firm friend to *fantasia*. He writes: '*Reflections* – and the more ambitious replies to it – are essays in political and moral imagination. Among other things, they are shaped by: partial information from favored informants; selective identification with certain groups and not with others based on assumptions which are almost always oversimplifications; analogies

---

[1] Jefferson to B. Vaughan, 12 May 1791, *The Papers of Thomas Jefferson*, ed. J. P. Boyd, (Princeton) xvii, p. 671.

of varying validity between France and Great Britain; and aspirations for and anxieties about the futures of both nations. British spectators to the unexampled events across the channel could hardly have reacted otherwise. By describing these writings as works of political imagination, I convey no slight and have no wish to consign them to some wholly subjective realm remote from analysis and criticism. Analysis of these works, however, would benefit from the recognition that politics itself is perpetually an imaginative activity – not merely in its often dismal electoral phases, but in the continual need to envision the consequences of one's own present actions and those of others. A similarly pervasive imaginative dimension is the human propensity to identify with others as individuals or in movements, which manifests itself in politics more than anywhere else. Neither Burke nor his major critics are very fully understood by merely identifying their positions and either verifying or assailing them. That may be necessary work, but, because close inspection so often discloses that the adversaries in this debate fail to engage each other's premises, it is frequently unrewarding. It will be helpful also to study such things as the imagined political worlds their writings imply and the experience which educates – or miseducates – their eyes when they observe. Burke, for example, may have been able to envision the rise of Bonaparte because of his awareness, born of experience and probably reading, of the likely consequences of a vacuum of authority. And *Reflections* is compounded of such transmuted experience at least as much as of information from abroad.' (*Eighteenth-Century Studies*, Volume 24. No. 4, Summer 1991).

In the *London Review of Books* (16 February 1989) R. W. Johnson wrote: 'Not surprisingly, Burke has always been ignored in France.' Always? *Reflections on the Revolution in France* was translated into French in December 1790. In the month following the English publication it sold 2,000 copies in its first two days, and was at the centre of a fierce controversy. Nor was Burke exactly ignored during the Terror, when mere possession of his book was enough to send its possessor to the guillotine. Nor, in the next century, did Michelet ignore Burke, when he called the book '*ce livre infâme*', and loudly and inaccurately denounced its author. Mr. Johnson should be more careful with his 'always'. In the same article he wrote: 'Men like Burke are always wise after the event, never before.' Never? For examples of Burke's almost uncanny ability to be wise before the event (see Chapter V, pp. 402–3, 436–7 and 449). Still, one is aware of the phenomena to which Johnson was loosely alluding. During the late nineteenth century, and much of the twentieth, the successively dominant schools of French historiography – those of F. V. A. Aulard, Albert Mathiez and Georges Lefèbvre – were all admirers of the French Revolution and consequently antipathetic to Burke. Their antipathy took the form of dismissing him briefly, or ignoring him. The tacit *consigne* was the same as that of the Namierites in England: 'Treat this man as if we had already refuted him.'

By the time, however, when the readers of the *London Review of Books* were learning how the French had 'always ignored' Burke, the school of French historiography now in the ascendant was already paying respectful attention to him. The attitudes of that school – far more critical of the French Revolution than any of its predecessors – are reflected in the great *Dictionnaire Critique de la Révolution Française*, edited by François Furet and Mona Ozouf, and published in Paris in 1988 (an English edition followed in 1989). The *Critical Dictionary* contains a respectful entry on Burke by Gérard Gengembre. Burke is the only English-speaker to be included among the seventeen thinkers in the section 'Historians and Commentators'. The only other non-Francophones to figure in the list are four Germans: Fichte, Hegel, Kant and Marx. Gengembre's essay concludes: 'Study of this penetrating foreigner's scrutiny of France remains profitable for anyone who would understand what was truly at stake in a Revolution from which the whole modern French political tradition ultimately derives.' The 'penetrating foreigner' bit is better in the original French: '*ce regard étranger, d'une clairvoyance pénétrante . . .*' Pity that English-speaking readers should miss that key-word 'clairvoyance'.

Burke's abiding significance is also implicitly acknowledged in the apparatus of the *Critical Dictionary*. Each entry is followed by a list of *renvois* (cross-references) to other entries. Readers are seventeen times referred to the 'Burke' entry. Nearly a third of entries in the section on *Idées* have cross-references to the Burke entry. These are the entries on '*Ancien Régime*', '*Contre-Révolution*', '*Liberté*', '*Lumières*', '*Régénération*', '*Révolution*', '*Révolution Americaine*' and '*Voltaire*'. In the section '*Historiens et interprètes*' nearly half the entries have cross-references to 'Burke'. These are the entries on 'Fichte,' 'Hegel', 'Kant', 'Maistre', 'Marx', 'Michelet', 'Taine' and 'Tocqueville'. Burke is thus securely integrated by French historians into the intellectual history of the French Revolution.

In Furet and Ozouf's recent massive collection, *The French Revol-*

ution and the Creation of Modern Political Culture, Volume 3 begins
with no fewer than five essays concerning Burke, three in English,
two in French.

1989 – the year of the Revolution's Bicentenary and the year when
an English-speaking audience was learning that the French 'always
ignored' Burke – saw the publication in Paris of a new, scholarly
edition of Burke's best-known work: *Réflexions sur la Révolution de
France* (Paris, Hachette). The volume is more than an edition of
Reflections; it also contains a 179-page anthology of Burke's other
utterances on the French Revolution, plus 192 pages of 'Notes and
commentary'. There is a perceptive 105-page introduction by Philippe Raynaud (also a contributor to the *Critical Dictionary*). This
introduction is in shining contrast to the introduction to the corresponding volume of the Oxford edition of the *Writings and Speeches*
(Volume VIII). Unlike L. G. Mitchell, Raynaud takes Burke seriously
and criticises him fairly, while acknowledging his basic greatness.
Raynaud offers the best and most succinct definition I know of
Burke's position at the time of the French Revolution: '*à la fois
libérale et contre-révolutionnaire*'. While finding Burke's position
'philosophically untenable', Raynaud at the same time acknowledges
that Burke's thought 'nonetheless unfolds themes and ideas which
are incapable of being eliminated (*sont . . . inéliminables*) from the
thinking of those who want to understand the political condition of
modern man'.

Raynaud's introduction ends: 'Whence comes, under these conditions, the persuasive force of the *Reflections*? Their charm comes
from the incomparable art with which Burke is able to evoke the
limits which the limited nature of man (*la finitude humaine*) sets to
political action: the impossibility of tearing without trauma, the
"veil" of conventions; the necessity, in which we find ourselves, of
comprehending the social bond on the basis of a "living world"
whose principles are never fully capable of being explained: the root-
edness of emancipation itself in the dependence which is the mark of
all education.'

Fantasia, there, responding to *fantasia*, deep unto deep.

As for myself, when I set out to write *The Great Melody*, starting
from a clue supplied by a poet, I was required, by the very nature of
my enterprise, not to set too tight a rein on such powers of imaginative insight as may have been granted to me. I proceeded accordingly
and, when I came to the point of revising my text for publication, my confidence in that approach was fortified by the discovery

of Isaiah Berlin's magisterial commentary on Vico's *fantasia*, and then by notable examples of the fruitfulness of that capacity, in relation to Edmund Burke, in the works of those French and American scholars from whom I have quoted.

'Richard Burke, with a considerable portion of talents from nature and cultivated, as may be well supposed, with the utmost care by his father who idolized him, was utterly deficient in judgement, in temper and especially the art of managing.' – Theobald Wolfe Tone (p. 473)

I
Ireland 1729–1780

'...we live in a world where every one is on the Catch, and the only way to be Safe is to be Silent. Silent in any affair of consequence, and I think it would not be a bad rule for every man to keep within what he thinks of others, of himself and of his own Affairs.' Edmund Burke, aged sixteen.'[1]

[1] Letter to Richard Shackleton, 15 February 1745/46, in *The Correspondence of Edmund Burke*, edited by Thomas W. Copeland in ten volumes (Cambridge University Press and University of Chicago Press, 1958–78) Vol I, p. 62. For individual volumes and their editors, see Introduction, p. lxiv. All my references to Burke's correspondence are to this edition.

William Fitz-Maurice Petty, First Marquis of Lansdowne (better known as Lord Shelburne), ob. 1815, from the original of Sir Joshua Reynolds. 'If Lord Shelburne was not a Cataline or a Borgia in morals, it must not be ascribed to anything but his understanding.' – Edmund Burke (p. 239)

BURKE'S FATHER

All Burke's biographers, from James Prior in 1826 to Stanley Ayling in 1988, state that Edmund Burke was born in Dublin, and that his father, an attorney, Richard Burke, was a Protestant and his mother, born Mary Nagle, a Catholic. The date of birth is now believed to have been New Year's Day 1729. It is not certain that he was born in Dublin; a local tradition (discussed below), affirms that he was born in the Blackwater Valley, Co. Cork. The description 'father a Protestant, mother a Catholic' is accurate as far as it goes but is probably seriously misleading, if left unqualified, as far as Burke's father's religion and social situation are concerned. The Penal Laws against Catholics were in full force at the time Burke was born. The position of his parents in relation to religion was therefore not a matter of solely theological or ecclesiastical significance, but one of profound importance for his social status, emotional and historical associations and psychology. It therefore requires much closer scrutiny than previous biographers have afforded it.

There is no doubt that Mary Nagle was a Catholic. The bare statement that Edmund's father, Richard Burke, was a Protestant is, however, inadequate. The name 'Richard Burke' appears on the Convert Rolls for 1722, two years before the marriage of Edmund's parents. None of the biographers considers the possibility that his father may have been the Richard Burke who conformed to the established church in 1722, seven years before Edmund was born. Yet, if that identification can be made, his family background is widely different from what the biographers' simple definition 'father a Protestant' suggests. Recent converts were in a class by themselves, and neither Protestants nor Catholics thought of them as simply Protestants. As T. P. Power writes: 'Conversions in eighteenth-century Ireland were largely induced by legal requirements and hence were nominal in nature. In the past it has been commonly held that catholics who conformed, particularly those of landed status, subsequently became fully integrated into the protestant establishment, subscribing to its beliefs and outlook. In turn this argument is used to explain the reduction in the percentage of land owners by catholics over the century. It also assumes that anglicans were keenly religious and that converts became so. Contrary to this viewpoint, it is apparent that conversion helped to maintain the catholic propertied interest, and that converts were not fully absorbed into the established order in church and state. Indeed converts came to constitute a hybrid group in Irish society. In this capacity, and contrary to Lecky's view that conversions were divisive, converts became a group through which many of the differences based on religion in Irish society were mediated.'[1]

In another paper, on conversions among the legal profession, in *Brehons, Sergeants and Attorneys: Studies in the Irish Legal Profession*, Power writes, of convert lawyers as a class: 'Thus these convert lawyers came to possess a dual capacity: they conformed officially and occasionally outwardly, but on the whole retained their catholic allegiance and connections.' Power also identifies Richard Burke as a member of this class of convert lawyers: 'Another example is Richard Burke, who conformed in March 1723 [this should read 1722], was admitted an Attorney in June 1723, and proceeded to establish a respectable legal practice. His son, Edmund Burke, following a period of study at Trinity College in the 1740s, entered the Middle Temple.' Power adds that in the case of Burke (and another case) 'eminence in the law in the first generation propelled the second generation into the mainstream of political life on the catholic side.'[2]

Now, I believe Power is basically right, in all three of those statements: But I am primarily concerned with the second: the identification of the name on the Convert Rolls with Burke's father. I believe that identification is right, but I can't make it with quite the certitude that Power appears to have, and the matter is absolutely crucial for Burke's biography. The late Thomas Copeland, dean of Burke scholars and editor of the monumental ten-volume edition of Burke's *Correspondence*, wrote in a Volume I footnote that Richard Burke 'seems to have conformed to the established church 13 March 1722,

---

[1] *Endurance and Emergence, Catholics in Ireland in the Eighteenth Century*, ed. T. P. Power and Kevin Whelan (Dublin, 1990) pp. 100–127.
[2] Edited by Daire Hogan and W. N. Osborough (Dublin, 1991) pp. 153–174.

about the time he began to practice law in Dublin.'[1] I quoted that sentence in the introduction to my Pelican Classics edition of *Reflections on the Revolution in France* (London, 1968). I sent the proofs of that introduction to Copeland, who wrote back (*inter alia*): 'Almost nothing is certain about [Burke's father]. Even his conforming in 1722. Some Richard Burke conformed then and it may have been him. But Richard Burke is not an uncommon name and the Conformity Rolls are our only evidence'.[2]

There is no evidence in the surviving Burke papers. He was always secretive (see Epigraph) about his Irish origins and Catholic connexions, which his enemies used against him, and he is known to have destroyed many of his papers. There are, however, several indications tending to confirm the hypothesis of conversion. James Prior, his first biographer, states that 'an ancestor of Mr. Burke's family is said to have been Mayor of the city of Limerick in 1646.'[3] John Burke, Mayor of Limerick in 1646, was certainly a Catholic, so since Burke's father was a Protestant, conversion must have occurred at some time in the post-reformation history of the Burke family. The late Basil O'Connell – leading Irish genealogist and antiquarian, and a collateral descendant of the Nagle family to which Burke's mother belonged – believed that the Burke who conformed was Edmund's father. O'Connell wrote: 'That Richard Burke, father of Edmund Burke, did conform has been the univocal tradition of the statesman's Nagle collaterals of whom the present writer is one.'[4] (see below p. 7). If that tradition had been no more than a rumour, it would have been unlikely to survive through the nineteenth century and first half of the twentieth. In those years, during which Catholicism reasserted itself in Ireland with increasing triumphalism, for a Catholic to have conformed to the Established Church came to be regarded as disgraceful, which had not generally been so in the eighteenth century. As Louis M. Cullen writes, 'In a period when so many of the surviving Catholic Landlords conformed, conversion to Protestantism was free from the abhorrence it often aroused in the nineteenth.'[5] The people whose names appeared in the eighteenth

[1] *Corr.* I, 274, n. 1.

[2] Copeland to author, 25 April 1968.

[3] Prior, *Memoir of the Life and Character of the Right. Hon. Edmund Burke* (London, 1826).

[4] O'Connell, *Edmund Burke (1729–1797) A Basis for a Pedigree*, Part II, pp. 115–22, reprinted from *Journal of Cork Historical and Archaeological Society*, LXI (1956).

[5] Cullen, *The Hidden Ireland: Reassessment of a Concept* (Mullingar, 1988).

century Convert Rolls came to be regarded by Catholics from the mid-nineteenth century on as 'perverts', a term to be pronounced in a whisper. So if one of Edmund Burke's 'Nagle collaterals' tells me that Edmund's father did conform, I have no hesitation in believing them. And indeed modern scholarship no longer seems to cling to the agnosticism on this point which tinged Copeland's letter to me (above p. 5). In his Introduction to Part II of Volume IX of the *Writings and Speeches of Edmund Burke* – proofs of which have come to hand just as the proofs of *The Great Melody* are going to press – R. B. McDowell refers (on page 407) to Burke's father simply as 'a Catholic who had conformed to the Established Church'. So be it.

O'Connell describes Richard as 'a fashionable lawyer acting in the Catholic interest'.[1] According to O'Connell and others he was involved, professionally (and no doubt sympathetically as well) in the greatest Irish *cause célèbre* of the first half of the eighteenth century: the Cotter Case.

James Cotter (1689–1720), of Ballinsperry, Co. Cork, was one of the few remaining large Catholic landlords of eighteenth-century Ireland. He was connected by marriage with Edmund's mother's family: James Cotter and Garret Nagle of Ballygriffin married two sisters. The Cotter family fortunes were the fruit of the gratitude of Charles II. James's father, Sir James Cotter (c. 1630–1705), had assassinated a proclaimed regicide, John Lisle, at Lausanne on 11 August 1664. Charles rewarded this exploit with promotion in the armed forces, a lucrative office in the West Indies, extensive grants of land in Co. Cork and a knighthood for the regicidicide. Sir James later fought for James II against William of Orange. James made him military Governor of Cork and he commanded the Jacobite forces in Cork, Limerick and Kerry. After Limerick surrendered on terms (1691), Sir James was adjudged to come within the Articles of the Treaty of Limerick and he was restored to his estates, to which his son succeeded.[2]

Young James's politics continued persistently and flamboyantly Jacobite, in the extremely hostile political environment of early eighteenth-century Ireland. He fomented riots at elections in the Tory

[1] 'Edmund Burke, Gaps in the Family Record', *Studies in Burke*, Volume IX, No. 3 (1968) pp. 946–949.
[2] See Brian O Cuív, 'James Cotter, a Seventeenth Century Agent of the Crown,' *Journal of the Royal Society of Antiquaries of Ireland*, Vol. LXXXIX (1959) pp. 135–9.

interest and generally set out to provoke the dominant Whig oligarchy. In 1718 he was arrested on a charge of raping a Quaker
woman. He was executed on 7 May 1720. Irish Catholics, on what
appear to be good grounds, regarded his conviction and execution
as a political judicial murder, on a trumped-up charge, designed to
intimidate Jacobite sympathisers, and Catholics generally, in the
south of Ireland. Cotter's fate became a theme of songs and ballads,
still being sung during Edmund Burke's childhood and youth and
even much later.[1]

While awaiting trial, James Cotter wrote four letters, seeking legal
advice, to Richard Burke, a lawyer, in Dublin. The editors of the
Cotter papers identify this Richard Burke as 'none other (than) the
father of the Rt. Hon. Edmund Burke, the famous statesman.'[2] Basil
O'Connell accepts the editors' identification of the Richard Burke of
the Cotter case, with Edmund's father. O'Connell comments: 'This
was the father of Edmund Burke, and this is the first time we hear
of him. We do not know where he was born, nor do we know the
names of his parents, though we think they came from Bruff, Co.
Limerick. As Cotter's lawyer, Richard Burke must have earned the
grave suspicion of the Establishment. Yet the connection is not, to
my knowledge, mentioned by Burke in his letters or in the conversation that has come down to us. It is surprising that this important
episode should until now have escaped us, and one is left with the
impression that it must have been a closely guarded family secret and
potentially dangerous.'[3]

I had at first some difficulty in accepting the identification of the
Richard Burke who was involved in the Cotter case, with the Richard
Burke who was Edmund's father. My difficulty was that the four
letters date from 1718–19, whereas the entry for Richard Burke in
the Convert Rolls is for 1722, and conformity to the Established
Church was a requirement for admission to the legal profession under
the laws then in force. I asked my daughter, Fedelma Simms, to
investigate the crucial question: 'Was Edmund's father the Richard
Burke who was Cotter's attorney?'. After spending some time in the

[1] There is no reference to the Cotter Case in Burke's surviving papers. But there
may well have been references among the many papers that he destroyed. (See *Corr.*
II, vii–viii). James Cotter's heir became a Protestant and kept the land.

[2] 'The Letters and Papers of James Cotter, 1689–1720', edited by William
Hogan and Seán Ó Buachalla: *Journal of the Cork Historical and Archaeological
Society* XVIII (1963) p. 75, n. 1.

[3] O'Connell, 'Edmund Burke, Gaps in the Family Record,' *Studies in Burke*, IX,
No. 3 (1968), pp. 946–949.

National Archives in Dublin, she came up with the answer: 'I think that he was. I believe that Edmund Burke's father was the only Richard Burke practising law in Ireland in the first half of the eighteenth century, and that he was practising in 1720. *The King's Inns Admission Papers 1607–1867*, by E. Keane, P. Beryl Phair & T. U. Sadlier, published in 1982 by the Irish Manuscripts Commission, and said by a librarian at the King's Inns Library to draw 'on all extant sources from between those dates', lists two Richard Burkes during the relevant period, and no Bourkes (the earliest Richard Bourke is 1796).

'The two Richard Burkes are respectively: Burke Richard attorney 26 June 1723, master, and Burke Richard attorney exchequer *c*.1734 d. 28 Nov. 1761. I think these are the same person. The Admissions Papers give three sources for this period: Public Record Office Lodge manuscript; Public Record Office Exchequer Petitions; and Royal Irish Academy Halliday Pamphlets Vol. 121. The Lodge manuscript lists one Burke Richard, giving just his death, 28 November 1761. This is presumably Edmund's father, whose will is dated 4 November 1761. The Exchequer Petitions are 222 surviving petitions for the period 1711–26, from clerks wishing to become attorneys. There is one dated 26 June 1723, which is presumably the source of the first entry in the *King's Inns Admission Papers*. It reads: 'The humble petition of Henry Brady – that your petitioner served Morgan Mahon deceased, who was an attorney of this honourable court, and Mr Richard Burke one of the attorneys of the said court as their clerk for four years, during which time your petitioner behaved himself faithfully and honestly, whereby your petitioner humbly conceives he is qualified to be an attorney of this honourable court. . . .'

To this appeal Richard Burke added the required confirmations: 'I do hereby certify that your petitioner hath served me as a clerk for near three years and that the contents of the above petition is true, dated the 26 day of June 1723. Rich Burke'. Richard Burke therefore was a qualified lawyer in 1720 at the time at least of Cotter's execution and two years before he conformed. There is no reason to believe that he was not a lawyer before this, and he must have served a four-year apprenticeship at some time to have become qualified, as, we have seen, did Henry Brady. That this is the source of the first entry seems to be confirmed by the fact that he is there described as 'master'.

'Vol. 121 of the Halliday Pamphlets, in the Royal Irish Academy, Dublin, is "An alphabetical list of such barristers attorneys and solicitors, as have taken the oath in the courts of Chancery, King's Bench, Common Pleas and Exchequer appointed by an Act of Parliament made in this kingdom entitled 'An Act for the amendment of the law in relation to Popish solicitors and for remedying other mischiefs in relation to practitioners in the several courts of law and equity', extracted from the rolls of the several courts to the end of the Hilary term 1734–5." Burke, Richard is listed in the section headed "a list of the attorneys of his Majesty's Court of Exchequer in Ireland who have taken the oath directed. . . ." That this is the source of the second entry in the *King's Inns Admission Papers*, seems to be confirmed by the fact that he is listed under the Court of Exchequer, but there does not seem to be any reason to believe that it is not the same man as the first, since we know Edmund Burke's father was practising in 1734.

'According to the *Admission Papers*, clerks had to serve twenty full terms with an attorney before becoming one themselves, but as we have seen in the case of Henry Brady, at the beginning of the eighteenth century, four years seems to have been enough (20 terms presumably meant seven years). The other papers looked at randomly give four years too. Therefore, if Richard Burke had had an apprentice for three years in 1723, he must have been a fully fledged attorney in 1720 and at the very least a clerk in 1716, which means he was at least semi-qualified to serve Cotter in 1718/19.'

It seems to me that this comes close to demonstration. If there was only one Richard Burke practising as an attorney, at the material time, this has to be Edmund's father. And it is hardly a coincidence that the 'Richard Burke' of the Lodge MS died a few weeks after Edmund's father made his will.

Basil O'Connell writes that after James Cotter's execution, 'a witch hunt followed for Catholic and Jacobite fellow-travellers, and Richard Burke conformed to the established church on 13 March 1722. Is it any wonder that Edmund Burke and his father were always so secretive about their religion? This again was an incident about which Edmund did not want publicity.'[1]

My first impression that Richard Burke, while still a Catholic, could not have practised as an attorney, rested on an unexamined and unwarranted assumption: that the laws in question were systematically enforced. But this was not so. The fact that the laws in question had not been effectively enforced was acknowledged in an

---

[1] O'Connell, 'Edmund Burke, Gaps in the Family Record' in *Studies in Burke*, Vol. IX, No. 3 (1968) p. 946.

Act of Parliament passed thirteen years after Cotter's execution. The preamble of the Act of 1733 specifically states: 'Whereas the laws now in force against Popish solicitors have been found ineffectual. . . .' The Act specifies that it applies to attorneys as well as solicitors. It seems that in early eighteenth century Ireland a Papist attorney who kept clear of controversy and confined himself to routine work could hope to be left alone. Against this, a modern writer who has made a study of this question holds that 'the penal laws still constituted a firm barrier against the admission to practice of Catholics'.[1] Yet the preamble to the 1733 act shows that the authorities in that year did not consider the barrier to be yet firm enough. By becoming involved in the Cotter case, Richard Burke broke the unwritten rules.

But even when he did conform, Richard was not yet out of the eerie wood of the Penal Laws. He had merely moved out of a legally proscribed category into a suspect one. And he was still vulnerable, even legally, after he was married, in 1724, thanks to his wife's remaining a practising Catholic. Under a Penal Law of 1697, a Protestant whose wife remained a Catholic was subject to the same disabilities as if he were a Catholic himself. And the Irish Parliament was still in the 1720s and 1730s trying to make life difficult not only for Papists, but for new converts, in the practice of the law. A 1733 statute (6 George II, cap. 20) provided that converts applying for admission to the legal practice would have to 'prove before the Lord Chancellor their having conformed as Protestants for two years before their admission'. If this provision had existed at the time of Richard's admission, he could not legally have been admitted. And he was vulnerable on yet another count: the education of his children. There were hostile rumours – probably based on fact but still only rumours – that Edmund had instruction in the Catholic religion as a young child, but at twelve he was sent to a school kept by a Quaker. However, it is known that Richard's daughter Juliana was brought up as a Catholic, and the 1733 Act disqualified any attorney 'educating any of his children or permitting any of his children to be educated in the papist religion'. Like many other provisions of the draconian Penal Code, the familial penalties seem to have been in practice almost wholly inoperative, and they were not invoked against Richard. The real penalty was social, in the suspicions entertained towards lawyers who were recent converts.

[1] Colum Kenny, 'The exclusion of Catholics from the legal profession in Ireland', *Irish Historical Studies*, vol XXV (Nov. 1987) pp. 337–357.

On 7 March 1727, five years after Richard Burke's conforming, and less than two years before Edmund's birth, Archbishop Hugh Boulter, the Church of Ireland primate during this period, addressed himself to this topic, in terms that suggest that the Burke family were among those he had in mind. 'We have had several who were papists, and on the road from London hither have taken the sacrament and obtained a certificate, and at their arrival here have been admitted to the bar. They likewise pretend that the children born after their conversion are not included in the clause [of the 1697 Act] about educating their children as Protestants, because they were not under fourteen at the time of their conversion: so that many of these converts have a papist wife who has mass said in the family and the children are brought up as Papists . . . Now this grievance is the greater here, because the business of the law from top to bottom is almost in the hands of these converts; when eight or ten Protestants are set aside, the rest of the bar are all converts; much the greatest part of attorneys, solicitors, deputy officers, sub-sheriff's clerks are new converts; and the new Protestants are every day more and more working out the business of the law, which must end in our ruin.'[1] Note the Archbishop's distinction between 'Protestants' and 'converts'. The Burke biographies all describe Burke's father simply as 'a Protestant' but in Richard Burke's own time the primate of the church to which he had conformed did not classify him as 'a Protestant', but merely as a most unwelcome and suspect 'convert'.

If, as I now unreservedly do, we accept the verdict of those Cork historians, that Edmund Burke was the son of the attorney who was caught up in the Cotter case, and conformed to the Established Church in the aftermath, then we have a picture of Burke's family background which is quite different from that offered by the previous biographies, and by other studies that take off from those biographies.[2] 'Father a Protestant' are the key words. If that description is accepted without qualification – and none of the biographies offers any – then Richard and Edmund Burke appear securely part of what became known towards the end of Burke's life as the Protestant Ascendancy. W. B. Yeats accepted him as a liberal member of the Ascendancy in this apostrophe in his poem 'The Tower' (1928):

---

[1] *Boulter's Letters* (Dublin and London, 1729). Boulter was a politician as well as a churchman: Chief Justice and Deputy to the Lord Lieutenant, as well as Primate. His observations on Catholic attorneys are primarily political.
[2] Including T. H. D. Mahoney's *Edmund Burke and Ireland* (Harvard, 1960).

> . . . people that were
> Bound neither to Cause nor to State,
> Neither to slaves that were spat on,
> Nor to the tyrants that spat,
> The people of Burke and of Grattan
> That gave, though free to refuse —

. . . 'That gave', *sc.* 'to Ireland'. Yeats, when he wrote those lines, was an aristocratic nationalist: a numerically limited category, under Irish conditions. It is important not to be diverted, by his occasional excursions into nonsense, from paying careful attention to the rest of what he says. I regret that for about ten years I allowed myself to be distracted, by such nonsense as is contained in the above lines, from the precise and piercing *sense* of the two lines which now supply the governing concept of this book (see preface).

In reality, the 'people of Burke' and the 'people of Grattan' were two distinct peoples, then in an adversarial relation to one another. Grattan's people were the Anglo-Irish, Protestant by religion, and of English origin. Burke's people were Irish Catholic gentry, of Hiberno-Norman stock long merged with Gaelic gentry. Conversions were important legally but, partly for that reason, did not bridge that gap, socially. Anti-Catholic writers such as the memorialist Sir Richard Musgrave simply ignored such conversions. Musgrave describes Burke as 'the son of a popish solicitor in Dublin'.[1] Edmund and his elder brother, Garrett, (c. 1725–1765), as we can now see, were the first of the family, on either side, to be brought up as members of the Established Church. This makes him a lonelier and more burdened figure than the one that earlier biographies present. The relation of his whole family to the Ireland of the Penal Laws was a tense, equivocal and secretive one.

The tendency of modern Irish historiography is to play down the importance of the Penal Laws. As Louis M. Cullen puts it: 'Overall, the impact of the Penal Laws has been exaggerated'.[2] I am sure that, with the qualifying adverb 'overall', this verdict is correct. The Laws,

[1] Musgrave, Sir Richard, *Memoirs of the different rebellions in Ireland, from the arrival of the English; also a particular detail of that which broke out the 23rd of May 1798 . . . with a concise history of the reformation in Ireland; and considerations for the means of extending its advantages therein.* (Dublin, 1801) p. 35.

[2] Louis M. Cullen, 'Catholics under the Penal Laws' in *Eighteenth Century Ireland (Dublin 1986)* Vol I, pp. 23–36 and 'Catholic Social Classes under the Penal Laws' in K. Whelan and T. Power (eds) *Endurance and Emergence* (Dublin 1990) pp. 59–85.

to the extent that they were actually applied around the time of Burke's birth, made little direct difference to the poor, who were the great majority of the Irish people. But the case of people like the Burkes and the Nagles, depressed gentry, trying to make their way back up again, was very different. The Penal Laws, and the Protestant domination which those laws enacted, stood in their way, not always directly or decisively, but always potentially. They permanently inhabited a zone of insecurity, in which habitual reticence was the norm, and dissimulation an occasional resource. Reticence in all that concerned his relationship to Catholic Ireland was a marked characteristic of Edmund Burke, throughout his political career. His occasional appearances in the persona of an English Whig, complete with a gallery of English Whig 'ancestors' may not have been a result of actual dissimulation, but if not, they were a flight from distressing and inconvenient reality into a decorous fantasy. From a single, uniquely revealing passage quoted later in this chapter (see below p. 82), in a special mode, in conditions of stress, in 1780 – he was speaking in Bristol Guildhall to his constituents – we know the depths of the horror that the Irish Penal Laws inspired in the mature Burke. He was over fifty and was living in England. But, in the nature of the situation, that horror must have been with him from his boyhood, as soon as he first realised the equivocal nature of his personal and familial relationship to the great divide between Catholic and Protestant which governed every aspect of the social, political and juridical life of eighteenth-century Ireland. The trauma of the Cotter case, the fear that followed it, and his father's conforming, must have cast a long shadow over the family home in Arran Quay, Dublin, even in the 1730s, when Edmund was growing up.

The story of Philoctetes, whose bow could never miss and whose putrid wound would never heal, is relevant here. The wound came early. I believe that it came with the humiliating discovery of his father's having conformed, out of fear, and, together with that discovery, the realisation that his own achievement would be based on the consequences of that act of conforming. The metaphorical 'bow', which the wounded Burke would use to deadly effect, as the wounded Philoctetes wielded his material one against the Trojans, took the form of a tremendous concentration of mental and spiritual energies in a life-long struggle, not merely against the particular form of oppression which had wounded him in Ireland, but also against abuse of power in America, in India, and at the end, above all, in France. That was Yeats's 'it' and the object of the Great Melody.

PLACE OF BIRTH

The view of all Burke's biographers is that he was born in Dublin, and the Matriculation Register of Trinity College, Dublin, does indeed describe him as *natus Dublinii*.[1] In the Blackwater Valley of Co. Cork there is, however, a strong tradition that Burke was born there. A local publication, *Edmund Burke, a Brief Study* (1980), by the committee of the North Cork Writers Festival, refers to the belief that he was born in Co. Cork and adds, 'this has not been proved, but the record of his year-old sister's baptism in Castletownroche (North Cork) raises Co. Cork suspicions'. A local historian, Seán O'Reilly, stated in a 1988 lecture that there was 'a very strong reason to believe nowadays, that [Burke] was born in the townland of Bally-water, Shanballymore, at the house of his uncle, James Nagle.'[2] Seán O'Reilly has since died, but when I visited the Blackwater Valley in 1990, with two other local historians, Séamus Crowley and Father Forde, I found that this tradition is accepted there. It was customary in certain areas for a married woman, expecting a child, to go to her mother's people, for the delivery. (This was almost required for the first child, but it also happened with other children.) As against that, there is the matriculation entry, for which the information must have been supplied by Burke himself. But the record and the tradition may not be irreconcilable. He knew that his background was suspect by the standards of the institution to which he was being admitted: Trinity College, Dublin, in the mid-eighteenth century; 'Shanbally-more', as place of birth, would cause eyebrows to be raised. That was in Papist rural Cork and simply not a place for a proper Protestant to be born in. If he actually was born there, Burke would probably have preferred, and thought it legitimate, to give the place of his father's residence at the time of his birth. He was secretive about his Catholic associations, as the conditions of the time required him to be.

---

[1] See Arthur Samuels, *Early Life, Correspondence and Diaries of Edmund Burke* (Cambridge, 1923) p. 1, also p. 20.
[2] Lecture to the Mallow Field Club, reported in *The Kerryman*, 27 December 1988.

PARENT'S MARRIAGE

Whether Burke was or was not born in Shanballymore, the connection of both his parents with that area is firmly attested. The marriage licence bond, dated 21 October 1724, between Richard Burke and Mary Nagle, describes the groom as *'Richard Bourke de Shanbally in Comit duff* [*Comitatus* = county] *Corc gen* [*generosus* = gentleman].' (*Sic,* but the book is signed 'Rich'd Burke'.) Garret Nagle, who signed the bond on behalf of the bride is described as being from the same place (*de ead.*).[1] That bond is an Anglican document, from the Church of Ireland diocese of Cloyne. There is no record of a Catholic marriage, but there must have been one. Mary Burke is known to have been a believing Catholic and could not have been content with the Anglican ceremony alone. Catholic marriages and baptisms were illegal under the Penal Laws and few records of any such marriages have been found for the early eighteenth century. For baptisms, Edmund's year-old sister appears to have been an exception (see p. 14 above.) There were some Catholic registers for the middle of the eighteenth century.[2]

MOTHER'S PEOPLE

We know very little about Edmund Burke's Protestant ancestry, which probably consisted of only one recent convert, his father, Richard. About Edmund's maternal Catholic relatives, in contrast, we know quite a lot. Shanballymore is in the heart of what is still known as 'the Nagle country', and Mary's people, a large extended family, were the leading Catholics in the area. A modern Irish historian, Kevin Whelan, describes the family as 'a well established sub-gentry Catholic family with extensive middleman holdings and a strong mercantile base in both Cork and France'[3]. 'Sub-gentry' is

[1] Samuels, *Early Life*. p. 2.
[2] Louis M. Cullen, *The Emergence of Modern Ireland 1600–1900*, (London, 1981) p. 133
[3] Whelan, 'The regional impact of Irish Catholicism 1700–1850', in W. Smyth and L. K. Whelan (eds) *Common Ground: Essays on the Historical Geography of Ireland presented to T. Jones Hughes* (Cork, 1988) pp. 252–271. See also K. Whelan's 'Catholic Mobilisation 1750–1855' in P. Bergeron et L. Cullen (eds). *Culture et Pratiques Politiques en France et en Irlande XVIe – XVIIIe Siècle: Actes Du Colloque De Marseille 28 septembre – 2 octobre 1988.*

accurate as concerning the position of the Nagles in the 1720s. The Catholics of Ireland were a defeated people; the Nagles shared in the consequences of that defeat and coped with it as best they could, sometimes by occasional conformity to the Church of Ireland (see below pp. 50–51). Mary Burke appears to have conformed shortly after her marriage but continued all her life as a practising Catholic.[1]

The Nagles were a family of Norman origin, with numerous branches near Castletownroche, in Co. Cork; the original name was de Angulo. A family of that name came to Ireland in the late twelfth century, and settled in Co. Meath. By the fourteenth century they were established in the Blackwater Valley; a son of the poet Edmund Spenser had married one of the family. The most eminent and notorious Nagle, in terms of the dominant conventions – Whig and Protestant – in Edmund Burke's lifetime, was Richard Nagle of Carrigacunna (fl. 1689), who had been James II's Attorney-General, and Speaker of the Irish House of Commons. Protestants regarded him as the most dangerous of James's Catholic advisers. Archbishop King, in *The State of the Protestants of Ireland under the Government of James II* (Dublin, 1691) says that Richard Nagle 'was at first designed for a Clergy-man, and educated among the Jesuits; but afterwards betook himself to the Study of Law, at which he arrived to a good Perfection, and was employed by many Protestants, so that he knew the weak Part of most of their titles'. King gives instances of the ways in which Nagle's 'Malice and Jesuitical Principles' deprived numerous Protestants of their estates and 'even put it out of the King's power to pardon them'. The second Earl of Clarendon wrote of Richard Nagle as 'a man of the best repute for learning, as well as honesty among that people', but later thought him ambitious, covetous and unreliable. He was in Ireland for the final collapse of the Jacobite cause there, and sailed from Limerick to France in 1691. At St Germain he was James's Secretary of State for Ireland.[2]

It would be a mistake, but how much of a mistake is uncertain, to think of the Nagles generally as adhering to Richard Nagle's ideas. Dean Swift, in the seventh of the *Drapier's Letters*, written a few years before Burke's birth, says that the Catholic gentry, and Catholics with any property generally, as well as the priests, were at that

---

[1] See Basil O'Connell, 'Burke's Reconciliation with his Father', *Burke News Letter* II, Vol. VIII, No. 2 (1966–7) pp. 714–715.

[2] J. S. Clarke's *The Life of James II*, Vol. II, p. 411, 'collected out of Memoirs writ of his own hand, with the King's advice to his Son and his Will, published from the original Stuart manuscript in Carlton House, London, 1816.'

time not Jacobites. So much is reasonably clear. Genuine loyalty to the Stuarts was a Scottish rather than an Irish affair; it was a Scottish family; the Irish did not rise in either the Fifteen or the Forty-five (although some of them would probably have done, had either Catholic Pretender landed in Ireland). James II had had the support of Irish Catholics, as a Catholic prince, rejected by Protestant England. Richard Nagle, in giving James the legal advice that his prerogative did not extend to the pardoning of Protestants who had acquired Catholic estates under Cromwell, expressed the conditional character of Irish Catholic loyalty. In this respect, at least, the Catholic gentry were indeed 'true Whigs'. Personal loyalty to James had been largely extinguished by his precipitate flight after the Battle of the Boyne in 1690. A vein of popular sentiment in favour of the Stuart pretenders found expression in songs and poems (but not in action) even in the nineteenth century. But the heroes, in terms of that tradition, were those who had lost everything: not those who, like the Nagle relations among whom Burke was brought up, had managed to keep their small estates by lying low – 'dastard gentry' was the description of such people used by a Jacobite correspondent of Swift's. There are Jacobite 'emigré' Nagles, like Richard of Carrigacunna, in James II's time, and reputed Jacobites like Garret of Ballygriffin and (possibly) Cambrai, and his brother Joseph in Burke's own time. Garret Nagle was mentioned in a House of Commons Report in 1733 – when Edmund Burke was four years old – as being 'the person who manages the Pretender's affairs in Munster, and Joseph as being Garret's agent there'.[1] This Garret Nagle was the father of the educational pioneer, Nano Nagle (1718–1784), foundress of the Presentation Order of nuns. Edmund Burke gave discreet support to Nano in her educational and charitable work.[2] There were Whig and Protestant Nagles – though the Protestantism was always dubious – like Edmund Nagle who became an admiral in Hanoverian service. And there were the Nagles who lived at home, as quietly as possible. One has the impression that all three sets of Nagles managed to get on pretty well together, recognising the differences of opportunity and necessity. In particular, the Nagles of the Blackwater Valley maintained close ties with the Nagle families established in France, and

[1] National Library of Ireland; Pamphlet 130, vol. 17; see also O'Connell, 'The Nagles of Ballygriffin', *Irish Genealogist*, vol. 3, no. 2 (1957) pp. 67–73, and the *Journal of the Irish House of Commons*, 1731–7.

[2] See T. J. Walsh, *Nano Nagle and The Presentation Sisters* (Dublin, 1959) p. 127.

were well informed about French affairs.[1] Edmund Burke's interest in France, an interest which impinged on Europe in the 1790s, went back to his boyhood in the Blackwater Valley.

Although the eighteenth-century Nagles had come down in the world, and were threatened by the Penal Laws, and by their Protestant neighbours, it would be quite wrong to think of them as hopelessly downtrodden, like say, the poor Catholics of the North-West. Munster was different and Munster Catholics of the Nagle class were resilient. Kevin Whelan, in the paper already quoted (see above p. 15), describes them perfectly as part of 'that fusion of long-established rural Catholic families, with close ties to the towns, and links with the Continent and the new world, which backboned Irish Catholicism in the late eighteenth century. Prosperous, self-confident, well educated, well connected, aware of external ideas and motivations but firmly rooted in a stable – indeed, in some respects, archaic–rural society and culture'. Within that collective description, we can already discern some of the lineaments of the maturity of Edmund Burke.

FATHER'S ANCESTORS

The nature of Burke's family connections, through his mother, stands out fairly distinctly. On his father's side the picture is less clear, but seems to be similar. The Burkes, like the Nagles, were a Hiberno-Norman family (originally de Burgo) and most of them remained Catholics. Richard Burke is believed to have been descended from a Limerick branch of the family, which had settled in Cork, probably in the late seventeenth century. According to a nineteenth-century writer on Burke, 'Tradition affirms that [Edmund Burke] was a scion of a respectable branch of the house of Clanrickarde [Burke] long settled in the counties of Galway and Limerick'. The same writer goes on: 'The greater part of the Limerick estates of the Burke family having been lost in the civil commotions of the seventeenth century [Edmund's] great-grandfather returned to a property he possessed in County Cork and settled there in the neighbourhood of Castletown

[1] For the French Nagles, see M. Raphael Consedine, *Listening Journey: A Study of the spirit and ideals of Nano Nagle and the Presentation Sisters* (Victoria, Australia, 1983) pp. 11–12.

Roche, a village about five miles from Doneraile.'[1] The area of Cork which Edmund's great grandfather settled in is in the mid Blackwater Valley, the Nagle country, and there was some intermarriage between Burkes and Nagles. Seán O'Reilly, in the lecture already quoted (see above p. 14), says that James Nagle, the owner of the house in which Edmund Burke is locally believed to have been born, was married to a Burke, a cousin of the statesman's father.

An ancestor of Edmund is believed to have been the John Burke who was Mayor of Limerick in 1646 (see above p. 5). That was a time when Irish Catholics were divided between those who were prepared (on certain conditions) to support the Royalists, and those who held it to be sinful to give any allegiance to a heretical Prince (Charles I). John Burke belonged in the former category and, as mayor, he proposed that Limerick should accept a 'peace' offered by Charles's viceroy, the Earl of Ormonde, under which all Catholics who rallied to the crown, would enjoy equal rights with all other subjects. For this proposal John Burke was savagely assaulted by a fanatical mob incited by friars. They cried 'Kill the rogues and traitors!' A priest cried: 'Kill all and I will absolve you!'[2] Three years later the moderate Catholics and fanatical Catholics alike went down in common ruin under the sword of Cromwell. The position adopted by that unfortunate ancestor is consistent with the position of the mature Edmund Burke in Irish Affairs: rejection of all religious and political fanaticism; acceptance of the link between Ireland and the British Crown; requirement that all Catholic disabilities be removed.

EARLY EDUCATION

One of the most marked features of Burke's mind, as it developed, is a sense of the contrast between social realities, on the one hand, and on the other, abstract systems claiming to govern such realities. His Ireland must have been, in that respect, a good school. At the age of six, he was sent by his parents to live with his maternal uncle, Patrick Nagle, in Ballyduff, at the foot of the Nagle Mountains, in Co. Cork. This was the county in which Edmund was born, accord-

---

[1] Peter Burke, *The Wisdom and Genius of the Rt. Hon Edmund Burke* (London, 1853) Parts X and XI.
[2] *Irish National Archive: Carte Papers 18: p. 213.*

ing to local tradition. It is said that he was sent there as a child, for the sake of his health, and indeed he was a sickly child, and the city of Dublin in the eighteenth century was an unhealthy place. But there was also probably another reason, not less important. As a devout Catholic, Mary Burke must have wanted her son to get the basics of a Catholic education, in spite of the ostensible and constrained conformity of the Burke family. Indeed it would be extremely surprising if he had not been privately baptised a Catholic over and above his public Anglican baptism. For getting a Catholic basic education, the move to Ballyduff was highly advantageous. Dublin, in those days, was the capital of an Ireland that was officially entirely Protestant, since the law presumed no such person as an Irish Roman Catholic to exist, except for the purpose of punishment. The law was very strong in Dublin, much less strong in rural Co. Cork. Throughout Ireland, in theory, the Penal Code still prohibited and penalised Catholic education, the presence of Catholic priests and attendance at Mass. But in practice the authorities had never, since Cromwellian times, seriously attempted to enforce the provisions of this religious side of the anti-Catholic laws. The provisions that were rigorously applied from 1691 on were those that pertained to wealth and power: those that made it advantageous for a Catholic landowner, or relative of a Catholic landowner, to become a Protestant; those that denied Catholics access to the franchise, Parliament, the military profession and – somewhat less rigorously – the legal profession.

Places like Ballyduff in the 1730s were openly Catholic, as far as the profession and practice of the Catholic religion were concerned. Protestant neighbours were vigilant and repressive, as in the Cotter case, about what they perceived as subversion: social, agrarian or political. But they did not attempt what would have been the daunting and dangerous task of interfering, or asking the Government to interfere, with the religious life of their far more numerous Catholic neighbours, even though that religious life was wholly contrary to statutes still theoretically in force. So there was never any danger that a party of red-coats would be sent down to Ballyduff to stop little Edmund from attending Mass, with his uncle. I feel sure that he did attend Mass regularly. Patrick Nagle would have assumed, if he was not directly told, that his sister Mary would want her son to get as much as possible of a Catholic upbringing, which could be achieved with much more security in Ballyduff than in Dublin. He would also assume that Richard Burke must have no serious objection to Edmund's being brought up a Catholic, or he would not have allowed him to be sent to Ballyduff for five years. Whilst there he attended a hedge school conducted by a teacher named O'Halloran, under the walls of the ruined castle of Monanimy, formerly a Nagle stronghold. Monanimy Castle is on an escarpment, rising above the North Bank of the Blackwater, about a hundred yards from the river. Looking South-east across the river from the grounds of his school, the young Burke could see, less than a mile away, on the other side of the river, the forfeited demesne lands and woods of his Jacobite kinsman, Sir Richard Nagle of Carrigacunna, James II's Attorney-General.[1] Behind those lost Nagle lands he could see the range of hills known – both then and now – as the Nagle Mountains.

The Blackwater Valley is one of the most beautiful regions in Ireland; Edmund Spenser lived there and it is the landscape of *The Faerie Queen*. The view from the ruins of Monanimy is described by Nano Nagle's biographer: 'The landscape has lost nothing of the sylvan glory and pastoral splendour which once held captive the soul of Spenser. The prospect northwards from Monanimy castle looks across the Ballyhoura hills to the country of FitzGibbon, the White Knight of Irish history. To the east the peaks of the Galtee mountains strain to link up with the Knockmealdown mountains of Waterford. Southwards are the undulating hills, known as the Nagle mountains at the base of which stands the graceful seventeenth-century castle of Sir Richard Nagle of Carrigacunna. Less than a mile from Carrigacunna on the western side is a dark belt of trees which shelters the house of the Nagles of Shanballyduff – the home of Edmund Burke's uncle Garret Nagle.'[2] For young Edmund, the view from his school must have had complex and powerful associations.

Hedge schools were Catholic institutions, in their general ethos, and were the only places where Catholics could get an education. They were illegal, for that reason, and were conducted in the open air, originally so that master and pupil could disperse more promptly, should the relevant law be enforced, as it sometimes had been in the very early years of the Penal Code, and might still be again to vent some personal spite. The mid-Blackwater-Valley in which Burke was brought up from his sixth to his eleventh year was different, in the early eighteenth century, from the anglicised East Coast, not only in religion, but in language. The vernacular of the Nagle country was

[1] Today, at least, Carrigacunna Castle is screened from view, at the level of the entrance to Monanimy Castle, by the woods of Carrigacunna demesne. But Carrigacunna Castle can be clearly seen from the roof of Monanimy.

[2] Walsh, *Nano Nagle and the Presentation Sisters* (Dublin, 1959) p. 24.

Irish (Gaelic). Edmund's Nagle relatives spoke Irish, although they also spoke English, and probably some French as well. In the hedge school, which prepared children for the real world, English would have been the medium of instruction, but at times of recreation the language would have been Irish. During this period, therefore, the young Burke was living in a culture quite distinct both from that of the English Pale in Ireland, that area in which traditionally the English writ had run since its earlier pacification, and where he had all his later schooling and where his parents lived. It was even more distinct from that of southern England, where he spent his maturity and old age. Such an experience, in his early boyhood, could not fail to leave an abiding mark on the personality. In later life, when so deep an early involvement with Catholic Ireland would have been compromising, Burke did not refer in any utterances that have been preserved to these early experiences, mentioning only the safely Protestant later phases of his education. What I refer to later as the 'Catholic layer' or 'Irish layer' in Burke's psyche is generally a somewhat elusive matter, but some speculation may be relevant. Did his early schooling amount to instruction in the Catholic faith? Was it – I asked Owen Dudley Edwards, of Edinburgh University, who knows more than I do about Catholicism, and about Catholic education in particular – from Jesuits, as later hostile rumours had it? He agreed that Edmund must have had some Catholic education but not from a Jesuit: 'The real likelihood is that he had some education while at hedge school from an "itinerant friar", probably a Dominican or Franciscan and almost certainly not a Jesuit.' He added this profound observation: 'The most likely deposit this might have had on his mind would be fear of damnation, associated with schism or apostasy. In cool, calm reflection this would be set aside: later in moments of darkness, doubt, depression, disorder, it could rise high in the imagination.'[1]

To pursue the question of that deposit would take us too deep into unverifiable speculation, but I wish the reader to be aware of the existence of such possibilities, with a bearing on the Burkean psyche.

[1] It is virtually certain that the Nagles, like other Catholic families, who managed to hold on to some land, would have had a clandestine priest, either a secular or a regular, living under their protection. Indeed, local tradition maintains that the young Burke was taught by Father William Inglis (1709–1778), an Augustinian, whose verse in Irish (Gaelic) shows a lively interest in Jacobite politics at home and overseas. For further detail on Father Inglis see Risteard Ó Foghludha, *Cois na Bríde* (Dublin, 1937).

To be brought up in Ballyduff, and to love his Nagle relatives, as Burke did, was to share directly in a considerable part of the experience of the Irish, Gaelic-speaking Catholic people and to be at least somewhat affected by Irish Catholic interpretations of history, and aspirations for the future. The forms of these prevailing among the Nagles were 'Catholic Whig', accepting the Revolution of 1688 and the Protestant Succession as at least *faits accomplis*; but bitterly resenting the broken Treaty of Limerick, the Penal Laws, and the Protestant Ascendancy, and looking for the rehabilitation of the Catholic Irish within a revised 'Revolution settlement'. Those views, which generally were to be those avowed by the mature and successful Burke, were suspect in the world in which he had to make his way as a young man, both in Ireland and England.

What is certain is that on the linguistic and cultural side, where reasons for concealment were less imperative than on the religious side, the continuity is clear. Burke all his life retained an interest in the Irish language and its literature. He played an important part in the preservation of its monuments, and in rendering them accessible to scholars. In 1765 he discovered in the library of his friend Sir John Sebright at Beechwood, in Hertfordshire, some important early manuscripts in Irish. Realising their value, he borrowed them and sent them for evaluation to the Librarian of Trinity College, Dublin. Sebright later presented them to the college library. They are recognised as being the main foundation of the Library's collection of Irish manuscripts.[1] Thus it was through Burke that an important part of the source material for the great scholarly advances of the nineteenth century in this field was made available.

LATER SCHOOLING

At the age of twelve, in 1741, Burke was moved out of this Catholic environment to the boarding school kept by a Quaker, Abraham Shackleton, at Ballitore, Co. Kildare, much nearer Dublin and in more 'settled' country. Presumably his father thought it was time for him to be preparing for a career, as a Protestant. The school was

[1] *Catalogue of Irish MSS in the British Museum*, Introduction to Vol. III. See also W. D. Love, 'Edmund Burke and the Irish Historiographical Controversy' in *History and Theory* II, pp. 180–198; and W. D. Love, 'Edmund Burke, Charles Vallencey and the Sebright MSS', in *Hermathena* XCV (1961) pp. 33–35.

well chosen. At Ballitore, Burke received a good classical preparation for Trinity College, Dublin. The atmosphere was Protestant but not strictly 'Ascendancy', since the Shackletons were dissenters, and Shackleton, a pacifist, was as remote as possible from any tendency to 'polemical theology'. The contrast between Ballyduff and Ballitore was not a collision; many people of various denominations and of considerable note sent their children to Ballitore. Paul Cullen, later Roman Catholic Archbishop of Dublin, and Cardinal, was a pupil there in 1812. It is clear that Abraham Shackleton was a man of independence and integrity, and that the school was run on his principles rather than on conventions dominant in the society from which he drew his pupils. In a published advertisement for the school he stated that he declined, from conscientious motives, 'to teach that part of the academic course which he conceives to be injurious to morals and subversive of sound principles, particularly those authors who recommend in seducing language the illusions of love and the abominable trade of war'.

In April 1744 Burke sat, successfully, for entrance to Trinity College, Dublin. The earliest letter that survives from his pen – to his friend at school and university, Richard Shackleton, Abraham Shackleton's son – tells of his examination, in Horace, Virgil and Homer by an 'exceeding good humour'd cleanly civil Fellow. N.B. I judge by outward appearances'. It also tells of the cleanly Fellow's comments: 'He was pleased to say (what I would not say after him unless to a particular friend) that I was a good Scholar understood the authors very well and seem'd to take pleasure in them (yet by the by I dont know how he could tell that) and that I was more fit for the College than three parts of my Class . . .'[1]

Most of what we know of Burke's life as an undergraduate in Trinity, and all we know of the early working of his mind, comes from a single series of sixty letters to Richard Shackleton, written between April 1744 and January 1748–9. Thomas Copeland says that Shackleton 'was an unusually intelligent and serious boy, steadier and more settled than Burke was ever to become.' On the series of Burke's letters to Shackleton, Copeland remarks, with justice, that they are disappointing, to those hoping for precocious revelations of genius. 'Critics', he writes, 'often speak of their eagerness to witness the trial flights of genius. Burke's sixty undergraduate letters, thirty-

---

[1] *Corr.* I, 1–3. The 'cleanly civil Fellow' was Dr Pellissier, who became Burke's tutor, and was later to be Vice-Provost.

five of them written before his seventeenth birthday, are the rare case
of the critics being given their hearts' desire. Alas for romantic hopes!
The undergraduate letters are an entirely creditable series, but they
are not much more vivid or interesting than other people's undergraduate letters. They do not record much of their writer's experience, perhaps because he had had very little. They do not give proof
of a precocious sensitivity to language, being in fact rather carelessly
written. What is most remarkable in them, a ranging energy of mind
that was always a characteristic of Burke, is not in its adolescent
phase an unusually winning virtue.'[1] Yet, though Burke's genius by
no means shines out in these adolescent letters, it is quite clear from
them that certain habits of mind, and certain attitudes or prejudices,
which were to prove lifelong, were already formed. There is already
here the Burkean emphasis on *circumstances*, the awareness that the
nature of things is a sturdy adversary: 'How little avails this freedom
[of man's will] if the objects he is to act upon be not as much disposd
to obey as he to Command, what well Laid and better executed
Scheme of his is there but what a Small Change of nature is sufficient
to defeat and entirely abolish.'[2] He is conscious already of the need
'to touch with my own hands', to have to do with substance rather
than abstraction: 'Your office of a Schoolmaster throws you amongst
the antient authors who are generally reputed the best, but as they
are commonly read and taught the only use that seems to be made
of em is barely to learn the language they are written in, a very
strange inversion of the use of that kind of learning! to read of things
to understand words, instead of learning words that we may be the
better enabled to profit by the excellent things which are wrapt up
in em'[3]. He is already very distrustful of human nature, and of those
who are confident in their own virtue: he expresses himself about
the 'inner light' in terms which must have been somewhat wounding
to his Quaker friend: 'I dont like that part of your letter wherein you
say you had the Testimonies of well doing in your Breast, whenever
such motions rise again endeavour to suppress em, it is one of the
Subtilest Strategems that the Enemy of mankind uses to delude us,
that by lulling us into a false peace his conquest may be the easier'[3].
Clear traces there of that 'deposit' of Catholic instruction, acquired
in the Ballyduff years!

[1] *Corr.* I, Introduction, xv.
[2] 25 January 1744/45: *Corr.* I, 39.
[3] To Richard Shackleton, 25, 31 July 1746: *Corr.* I, 68; 1 November 1744: *Corr.*
I, 36.

Copeland writes of the tentativeness and uncertainty that characterise much of this body of letters, in which the adolescent Burke tries on various styles and manners, devotional, facetious, oriental, romantic, and so on. The greater part of the letters does consist of 'exercises' of this kind, not very remarkable. What is striking, however, is that those passages – not many in number – which reflect attitudes and convictions which were to be lasting with him, are already marked by a greater maturity, vigour and determination, even testiness, of expression than the matter which surrounds them. The reader who cares to look through the hundred pages these letters take up in the *Correspondence* will, I think, agree that these extracts are well above the general level of the letters. Yet the extracts were selected only as being those which illustrated the continuity of Burke's thinking, not for any other merit of their own. It is also striking that, while he 'tries on' so many styles he does not 'try on' any systems or sets of ideas which are in any degree at variance with the bent of mind revealed in these particular passages.

It is not likely that Burke would have expressed himself with the same freedom to anyone else as he did to Richard Shackleton, whether in 'trying on' various styles for exercise, or in revealing his lasting attitudes. For a very young man he already knew only too well the need to be on one's guard. He hopes that a 'misfortune' of Richard's may do him some good in that it 'will give you a little experience and teach you more Caution and reserve in trusting your acquaintance.' There follows the passage already quoted as the epigraph of this chapter, but it is so central to the inner Burke that it is worth quoting again: '. . . we live in a world where every one is on the Catch, and the only way to be Safe is to be Silent. Silent in any affair of Consequence, and I think it would not be a bad rule for every man to keep within what he thinks of others, of himself, and of his own Affairs'. The keeping of this rule may well account for the large gaps which exist in our knowledge especially of Burke's early career. The learning of the lesson that 'to be Safe is to be Silent' has, I think, to be imputed to the peculiarity of Burke's situation as an Irish Protestant with the closest possible Irish Catholic connections. It is clear, that, although Richard was two years older than Edmund, Edmund considered himself to have more experience in the need for distrust, and that this opinion was well-founded.

Copeland says that Burke's early letters 'do not record much of their writer's experience, perhaps because he had had very little'. The passage above suggests another possible reason: that the experience he had, in the socio-religious border-zone in which he was brought up, was of a kind about which he felt it safest to be silent. It is probably not entirely a coincidence that the passage was written during the Forty-Five Jacobite rebellion, and probably not a coincidence either that Burke's first explicit reference to that rebellion comes in his next letter to Richard dated 26 April 1746, ten days after Culloden: 'This pretender who gave us so much disturbance for some time past is at length with his adherents entirely defeated and himself as some say taken prisoner, this is the most material or rather the only news here, tis Strange to see how the minds of people are in a few days changed, the very men who but awhile ago while they were alarmd by his progress so heartily cursed and hated those unfortunate creatures are now all pity and wish it could be terminated without bloodshed. I am sure I share in the general compassion, tis indeed melancholy to consider the state of those unhappy gentlemen who engag'd in this affair (as for the rest they lose but their lives) who have thrown away their lives and fortunes and destroy'd their families for ever in what I beleive they thought a just Cause.'[1]

Although loyalty to the Stuart cause was much less strong in Ireland than in Scotland where loyalty was sustained by national sentiments, all Catholics had strong reasons for wishing for a restoration of the Catholic dynasty. Deep down, Burke may well have shared that wish, but he knew that it was worse than useless to indulge a hope for something that was not going to happen. It would be surprising if the young Burke had not thought a good deal, during the course of that rebellion, about what might happen in Ireland, and to the Nagles, should it succeed; or should it look like succeeding, spread to Ireland, and then fail. For someone of Burke's temperament and political instinct, with the Nagle experience behind it, the hypothesis of apparent success, Irish involvement, and then failure would, I think, have been more vivid than any idea of a Jacobite restoration. If so, it is no wonder that he was setting so much store by caution and silence. In his actual reference, politic though it is, to the defeat of the Young Pretender, I believe there is discernible a note of relief. But it is not quite the orthodox relief of an ordinary Whig. The people someone in Burke's position had reason to be frightened of, at the time, *were* Whigs – 'the very men who but awhile ago while they were alarmed by his progress so heartily cursed and hated those unfortunate creatures. . . .' Their alarm must have been itself

[1] *Corr.* I, 62–63.

alarming, to one who could not freely curse and hate along with them, and whose own background was suspect. It is notable also that Burke was moved by the fate, not particularly of those who had only their lives to lose, but of the gentry who also lost their fortunes and destroyed their families for ever, as the Jacobite branches of the Nagles had been destroyed.[1]

Copeland finds in these letters signs of the unhappiness Edmund is experiencing at home: 'The Burke household was divided on the religious issue: the father and sons were Protestants, the mother and daughter Catholic: both parents were nervous and irritable. One feels in many passages of Burke's letters to Shackleton that he is clinging to his friend as part of a more peaceful world than he knew in his own home'. The last comment is perceptive: the earlier part may be a little misleading. To what extent could such a family really be said to be 'divided on the religious issues'? Both Burke's parents had been brought up as Catholics. Richard's conformity can hardly, in the circumstances, have been a matter of religious conviction. In these conditions there could be and probably often was, not so much a 'division on the religious issue' as an agreement to be seen to diverge. Catholic women might even be encouraged by their religious advisors to acquiesce in the nominal conformity of their spouses to the Established Church, subject to certain safeguards, such as secret Catholic baptism of the children, in order to ensure the economic and social survival of a family which would at least be under strong Catholic influence, as the Burkes, including the Protestant Edmund – or 'Protestant' Edmund – most certainly were. We know little about such relationships, which had to be conducted under the sign of 'safety in silence'. Burke's relations with his father were indeed strained, and it is certainly possible, in the circumstances, that religion, or the social consequences of religious associations and tendencies, may have contributed to the strain. A prudent attorney in Dublin of the mid-eighteenth century might reasonably, and without any strong theological convictions of his own, have feared the impact of an inconveniently pious Catholic mother on the career of a promising son.[2] But one way or another, whether there was a genuine religious

---

[1] The branches are those of David Nagle of Carrigoona and Ballygriffin and of Pierce Nagle of Annakissey, as well as of Richard of Carrigacunna, all maternal kin of Burke's.

[2] In a letter on Burke in 1766 (see below p. 63) Shackleton was to write: 'Richard Burke was more concerned to promote his children's interest in the world, than to trouble himself about controversial parts of religion, and therefore brought his sons up in the profession of that which he thought the public road to preferment, viz, the religion of the country, established by law.'

division, or only a distribution of roles, with ostensible conformity for the males, the conditions of such a home must have been exceedingly trying: not just the internal atmosphere, whatever it was, but the objective conditions, and ever-present social and economic threat; the nearness of an underworld, and the need to pretend it was not near. It is not surprising that Edmund turned to Richard Shackleton for the security and innocence of his situation, while at the same time talking down to him, yet with a kind of envy, for his lack of knowledge of suspicion, danger, dissimulation, and other manifestations of the evil in the heart of man. Edmund more than once cautioned Richard about the evils of schism.[1]

Arthur P. I. Samuels, the writer who has most closely examined Burke's early years, refers to 'his views strangely formed so early in life' on the crime of schism. Commenting on a letter of 15 October 1744 – in which Burke says that 'Men should not for a small matter commit so great a crime as breaking the unity of the Church' – Samuels infers from it that 'he seems from the first to have had that strong affection for the Established form of religion which he always retained. This attitude of combined loyalty to his own Church and wide toleration towards other creeds will be found reproduced in his letters and speeches in after life'.[2] This view of Burke's religious outlook has on the whole been adopted by subsequent biographers and commentators. Yet the basis for it all is rather shaky. The letter from which Samuels infers that Burke 'from the first' had 'a strong affection towards the Established form of religion' does not once mention 'the Established form of religion', Anglicanism or the Church of Ireland. Burke refers simply to 'the Church', its unity, and the crime of breaking it.

What did Burke mean by 'the Church'? The view that he meant 'the established form of religion', in Britain and Ireland, can only be accepted with very serious qualifications, extensions and restrictions. He had little enough reason to regard the Established Church in Ireland with 'strong affection'. His father probably conformed to that Church out of fear; his mother, his wife and her father, and his Nagle relatives all were stigmatised beings under the laws which upheld the Establishment, laws which he later so bitterly denounced. And where exactly would he have acquired such a strong affection for the Established Church? Not at his mother's knee; not from his

[1] *Corr.* Vol I, 32–4.
[2] Arthur Samuels, *The Early Life, Correspondence and Writings* (Cambridge, 1923) pp. 56–58.

father whom he feared rather than liked (and whose relation to the Established Church was at best one of prudential conformity); not in the Blackwater Valley, most certainly, and hardly at his Quaker School in Ballitore, though he did attend Church of Ireland services while there. Granted his background, and the suspicions in which it involved him personally, his relation to the established form of religion must necessarily have been fraught with tension. This does not perhaps altogether exclude the possibility of 'strong affection' developing at some stage, but it does exclude the kind of comfortable and tolerant ensconcement in Anglicanism which has been too often taken for granted as his position.

The young Burke does not make it clear what he meant by the Church. If in fact he meant anything significantly different from 'the established form of religion', then he had adequate reasons for leaving room for ambiguity, reticence and occasional dissimulation. Samuels invokes his later speeches and writings with reference to religion. I shall consider these in their place. It is enough to say here that I interpret them as implying that his loyalty went to what he calls 'Christianity at large', meaning a concept of the Catholic Church which embraced both Rome and the Anglican community and did not embrace either Dissent or the peculiarly 'Protestant' tendencies within the Churches of England and Ireland. On this view, Rome was not 'another creed' which he was prepared to tolerate but an integral part of the Church in which he believed, and about whose unity his views were 'strangely formed' so early. For Dissent, his attitude was indeed one of toleration, but this toleration was somewhat grudging and irritable, surprisingly so for one educated at Ballitore: not so surprisingly for one raised among Catholics in the Blackwater Valley. The short shrift he gave poor Richard Shackleton over the 'inner light' showed where the limits of toleration lay.

It is in this sense, I believe that his references to 'the Church' in that early letter should already be understood. On this view, his sensitivity to the 'great crime of schism' can readily be accounted for. Schism was not just something he read about in church history: it was part of his life. His family, as well as the people of his country, was cut in two. He himself was threatened by the internal schism of divided loyalties, or a division between inner loyalty and outward conformity, or some blend of these. His powerful and ingenious will copes with this threat under the sign of 'Christianity at large' and loyalty to a Church menaced, rather than actually riven, by schism. Both in youth and in his maturity Edmund Burke was a person of strong emotions and affections, and also an ambitious and practical person. The concept of a Church without schism – later of 'Christianity at large' – was big enough to shelter both persons and give them room to move. Without denying his mother's people, he was free to move, and indeed climb, in the world of their enemies – and ultimately to help that people.[1]

TRINITY COLLEGE, DUBLIN

Burke's university career was distinguished[2]. As the Irish historian Lecky[3] says, 'he appears to have found [in Trinity] an amount of intellectual activity considerably greater than that which Gibbon a few years later found at Oxford (*History of England*, Vol. III, p. 182). He became a Scholar of the House in his Senior Freshman year in June, 1746. Between then and taking his degree in January 1748, and for a short time after that, he busied himself to some purpose with the debating club which he founded and with a miscellany paper, *The Reformer*, which he also founded and largely wrote. Both were moralistic, preoccupied with improvement in taste and knowledge, earnest, determined, talented, a bit priggish, with the air of a rising middle class about them. Both also were exercises and preparations for success in the world. Both carry the imprint of Burke's will and purpose; the specific imprint of his quality of mind is generally not much more discernible in them than in the 'exercise' portions of his letters to Shackleton.

The club, founded on 21 April 1747, was a small one: the seven members included, as well as Burke, his room-mate William Dennis

[1] Compare Marx's radically different method of resolving an essentially similar dilemma. His father, whose father was a rabbi, had left Judaism for socially-acceptable Lutheranism. But where Burke sought to reconcile the creed his father was born in with the one to which he had conformed, Marx denied and derided both Judaism and Lutheranism, and religion in general. See my essay, 'Burke and Marx', *New American Review*, Vol. I, no. 1 (1966).

[2] Samuels shows that Burke's academic career could hardly have been more distinguished than it was, in the conditions of the day, and refutes the contrary view of earlier biographers, at least one of whom was, in Samuels' pleasant phrase, 'inspired by a stimulating ignorance of the conditions of academic distinction in Trinity College' (Samuels, *Early Life*, p. 135).

[3] For Lecky see p. 54, n. 1. below. This remarkable discussion of Burke's early life and views on reform (*Ibid.* 181–220) was found insufficiently Irish for inclusion in Lecky's *History of Ireland*.

and Andrew Buck. The others were his old friend Richard Shackleton, Matthew Mohun, Joseph Hamilton and Abraham Ardesoif. (Dennis and Buck both became Church of Ireland clergymen.) It was a group if not entirely of intimates, or even altogether like-minded people, at least of mutually acceptable people, an exclusive club, significantly different from a modern college debating society, such as the TCD College Historical Society, which claims descent from it and has preserved its records. The preamble to its laws begins: 'The Improvement of the mind being the proper employment of a reasonable creature . . .' It goes on to make it clear that the members are conscious of the club as a training ground for success in life, so that 'when years draw us further into the cares and business of life, we would be thereby enabled to go with more ease through the Duties of it; and more largely to contribute to the good of the public and to the increase of our private interest'.[1]

The club's business included the reading of prepared papers, reading aloud of suitable poetry, with a preference for the speeches from *Paradise Lost*, and debating on set themes. Little more than a week from its foundation, the Club experienced a certain conflict between freedom of debate and the concept of training for success in life. This was the third meeting of the Club; Burke acted as secretary for this and the following meeting. In the course of a debate on 'whether the woollen or linen manufacture be best for Ireland', it happened that 'some expression' was 'drop'd with some warmth concerning the conduct of the English in denying us a free commerce'. Andrew Buck then argues that no subjects shall be set 'which in the discussion of the question will make us show any dislike to his majesty or his ministry' and 'that questions related to the government of our country are ticklish points and not fit to be handled'. Burke argued against this, holding 'that to restrain us in considering what would be more useful to our country would take away a most considerable part of our improvement and that there is no danger of our showing any disloyalty to his Majesty'. A long debate followed. Further consideration of the question was adjourned to the next Committee meeting. 'When it came up again at a meeting on 8 May, Buck, who received 'thanks for his diligence in promoting the good of the society', proposed a new Law: 'No questions relating to the

---

[1] The laws were apparently the work of Andrew Buck, but were approved by Burke. The laws and minutes are printed in Samuels, *Early Life*, pp. 223–295.

Government of our country which may possibly affect our loyalty to be handled in this Assembly'. Burke's minutes record simply that the new Law 'was carried'; we do not know whether a debate occurred, or what the voting was. The minutes do record a debate, however, on another proposal by Buck, 'to restrain us from throwing any personal reflection on each other'. Burke opposed this, saying that 'we act here not in our real but certain personated characters, and that any reflection on Mr Buck of this Society does not hurt him as Mr Buck of the . . . , that confining us will destroy our Oratory and consequently the Society, as it only flourished in Great States which he confirmed by examples. This law were it to pass would take away our Spirit by reducing our speeches to dry logical reasoning, as otherwise it is almost impossible to condemn bad actions without also condemning him from whom they proceed'. Buck and Hamilton were for the motion: Burke and Mohan against. The motion was defeated by the casting vote of the chairman, William Dennis.

The incident is interesting, both for the pressure brought to bear on Burke, and for his response to that pressure. Buck's introduction of a 'loyalty' test of subjects for debate – a sanction drawn from the real world outside of the 'let's pretend' world of the Club – must have been disconcerting, unwelcome and even a little frightening. Someone with Burke's background was not in a good position to argue about loyalty, as conceived by the Protestant Ireland of his day.[1] In the first phase of the argument he had had to accept defeat: the constitution of the Club is modified in a very important way, or what appears as such, against his will. But he shifts his ground, and wins on the new ground: the question of personalities. And in the course of this debate he re-established what Buck had shaken: the fictitious, or Pastoral, nature of the proceedings of the Club: 'We act here not in our real but certain personated characters'. If there was felt to be something doubtful or dangerous about his contribution to the previous debate, or any debate, the 'personated character' would cover it. At no time in his life was Burke a stranger to what he was to describe in *Reflections on the Revolution in France* as the 'politick well-wrought veil'. Yet through the veil, at this moment of difficulty, and no doubt of emotion, we get one of those rare, early glimpses of the 'permanent' Burke, in his rejection of any-

---

[1] Protestant Ireland itself, of course, conceived of loyalty in different ways, but the different ways all included suspicion of Papists.

thing that would have the effect of 'reducing our speeches to dry logical reasoning', and his assertion that 'it is almost impossible to condemn bad actions without also condemning him from whom they proceed'.

In spite of the new Law, the question of loyalty came up again. Within less than a fortnight, Dennis was ordered to speak 'in favour of lenity for the Rebels of the Forty-Five'.[1] In doing so he seems to have sailed nearer the wind that was expected of him, arguing 'that their ill success in the Fifteen and the Union [1707] was yet a greater incitement to rebel as they believed the Union the destruction of their liberty – and as they had acted with regard to their country and urged by so strong motives they deserved lenity'. The minutes continue:

'Mr Burke accuses Mr Dennis of disaffection, says he had spoke more like a Rebel than a well wisher to the Government and desires him to clear himself of the Charge.'

'Mr Pres [Buck] likewise disapproves of his speech and orders him to be censur'd. Mr Burke speaks against the censure, but desires to accuse him.'

The distinction between 'censure' and 'accusation' is interesting. I take it that Burke's 'accusation' would have been felt to be part of the game, but that the president's 'censure' would have been felt to be something more serious, an intrusion of the real world and a recognition of danger. Eventually the President, withdrawing his own censure and Burke's accusation, ordered Dennis to speak again. Dennis 'begg'd to be excused if he spoke ill, for the confusion he was in had almost render'd him incapable', and spoke generally in favour of Mercy, without repeating his political arguments.

'Mr Burke, Answers tho' Mercy was amiable yet Justice was to be excuse'd, to punish adequately and stop a crime which otherwise might taint the whole Nation. That the rebels having thro' a weak judgement join'd with the Stewards ought to suffer, particularly as they continued it till death [sic] they deserve'd the strictest rigour of

---

[1] It is odd that Andrew Buck, as President, should have ordered this subject, which clearly involved a danger of contravening the Law of 8 May.

the Law. That no mercy should be shown to him that is an enemy to his country, and he who rebels is liable to all the mischiefs such a crime brings upon him.'

'Mr Pres. recaps the whole, tells Mr. Dennis he never spoke so bad and determines in favour of Mr Burke.'

Samuels comments that the view expressed here by Burke is 'merely the expression of a rhetorical view in fictitious debate', and that Burke's real opinion on the subject of mercy to the rebels is expressed in his letter to Shackleton on 26 April 1746,[1] after Culloden. This may be accepted, but it is hardly the whole story. Burke indeed was speaking in his 'personated character' and entirely in line with his own principle, not merely attacks the argument but also the 'personated character' of his opponent condemning 'him from whom the bad actions proceed,' and saying that 'he had spoke more like a Rebel than a well-wisher to the Government', a frightening enough charge in 1747. But then it becomes clear that, even in the make-believe, it is permissible to personate certain characters, but not others. The unhappy Dennis may well have been merely repeating a line of argument he had heard from Burke in their rooms (which resembles rather closely the argument by which Burke, later in life, justified Irish 'rebels' (see below Chapter VI, pp. 573–4). Dennis now avows his confusion and is forced to try again, dropping his best arguments, and then is reproved for speaking badly. Burke triumphs, in his personated character. In his real character he had also scored a success, ruthlessly compensating for his set-back over the 'loyalty law', vindicating his own principle of 'personated characters', and perhaps reducing any doubts about his own loyalty which the earlier transaction may have raised. Over the 'let's pretend' politics falls the shadow of the real politics of the time; and under the 'let's pretend' we can faintly make out a real political response to the shadow of real politics. As a preparation for 'the cares and business of life', the proceedings of the Club at this date were relevant enough. Perhaps they were felt to be all too relevant. It may be significant that the most 'ticklish' debates all occurred in the first month of the Club's life. Later the discussions took a more academic turn, and where politics are touched on, it is in a 'harmless' fashion, as in a Burke panegyric on Chesterfield's Lord Lieutenancy.

---

[1] Samuels *Early Life*, p. 24, n. 1. See also above p. 27.

In Burke's next enterprise also, early in the following year, he avoids the kind of points which had proved 'ticklish' in the Club. The miscellany called *The Reformer* does not concern itself with specific political reforms. The Penal Laws which Burke so passionately resented, as he was to show later, are not touched on here, no doubt wisely, for he was not yet strong enough to attack them effectively, and had he attacked them prematurely, might never have become strong enough.

The Reformer sets out to reform taste, arguing, on no very clear grounds, that the reform of taste provides the first and surest method of reforming morals. Inevitably it imitates Addison, skilfully enough. Its tone, like the club's, is middle-class but unlike the club, and unlike everything else in Burke's subsequent career, it is also provincial, making use of the typical argument that the citizens of the province enjoy exceptional virtue and good sense, which are menaced with corruption by the ephemeral and immoral productions of London – for which the author was to leave as soon as he could. The thirteen numbers of *The Reformer* (28 January to 21 April 1748) are exercises again – even the exploration of a blind alley can be an exercise – but less interesting, and less revealing than the debates of the Club. Burke is, however, consistent with himself in seeing morality as dependent on religion, and both as menaced by the two great enemies, 'infidelity and blind zeal': . . . 'the first gives rise to the Free-thinkers, the latter to the Sectarians'. These were the apparently opposing forces which, towards the end of his life, he was to see as joined in an unholy alliance, in the English response to the French Revolution. The explosion of *Reflections* was fitted to an exceptionally long fuse.

It was Richard Burke's intention that his son should follow in his footsteps. At 18 Edmund was accordingly enrolled as a student of the Middle Temple. He left Dublin at twenty-one to begin his studies; his bond in the Middle Temple is dated May 1750. Not long after his enrolment he had written to Shackleton, apparently about their friend William Dennis: 'Don't you think had he money to bear his charges but twere his best course to go to London? I am told that a man who writes, can't miss there getting some bread, and possibly good. I heard the other day of a gentleman who maintained himself in the study of the law by writing pamphlets in favour of the ministry.'[1] (To a modern reader this seems a curiously cynical reflec-

[1] *Corr.* I, 101. There is a biographical irony here in view of Burke's later sufferings at the hands of writers paid to be in favour of the Ministry.

tion to put in a letter to the unworldly Shackleton. But possibly neither Burke nor Shackleton found it cynical.) Burke may have seen the school of 'personated' characters' as fitting its graduates for such employment. At any rate it is clear that he saw not only law but writing and politics, or a combination of the two, as outlets for talents, and London, not Dublin, as the place of scope. A century and a half later another Irishman of genius, chose 'silence, exile and cunning'. Burke knew the uses of all three. For him, as for James Joyce, this triad was a set of means to set him free from Ireland; and never fully set him free.

THE MISSING YEARS

Hardly anything significant that pertains to Ireland is known about Burke's life for nine years after his graduation. As Thomas Copeland writes in his introduction to the collected *Correspondence* (page xvii): 'The well-recorded period of Burke's youth ends when he takes his B.A. at Trinity in January 1748. There is a single short letter written in the following month, and after that Burke's whole surviving correspondence for the two last years he remained in Ireland consists of two sentences and part of a third which biographers have quoted from letters now lost. . . . We have six letters – two of them highly uninformative poetic epistles – to tell us of his activities in his first two-and-a-half years in England. Then between the autumn of 1752 and the summer of 1757 comes the darkest period of all. To illuminate those five years there remains a single letter, which happens to be torn and incomplete.[1]'

Since we have so little to go on for this period, a piece of rather conversational gossip seems worth recording here: in Musgrave's *Memoirs* (p. 36, footnote) he writes that a year after Burke had gone to the Temple an apprentice of Richard Burke noted that Edmund 'seemed much agitated in his mind and that when they were alone, he frequently introduced religion as a topic of conversation'. The apprentice believed Burke 'was become a convert to P — [Popery]'. Burke's father was 'much concerned' at this report and had his brother-in-Law Mr Bowen make 'strict enquiry about the conversion of his son'. Bowen reported that Edmund had indeed converted. 'Mr

[1] *Corr.* I, Introduction, xvii.

Burke became furious, lamenting that the rising hope of his family was blasted, and that the expense he had been at in his education was now thrown away.' Musgrave continued that it was 'possible that Mr Burke, in the spring of life . . . might have conformed to the exterior ceremonies of Popery, to obtain Miss Nugent, of whom he was very much enamoured; but it is not to be supposed, that a person of so vigorous and highly cultivated an understanding, would have continued under the shackles of that absurd superstition'.

Because of Musgrave's obsession on the subject of Catholicism, he is often treated as an unreliable witness. However, another Irish memorialist of the period, Jonah Barrington, writes: 'Sir Richard Musgrave who (except on the abstract topics of politics, religion, martial law, his wife, the Pope, the Pretender, the Jesuits, Napper Tandy and the whipping post) was generally in his senses, formed during those intervals a very entertaining addition to the company'.[1] And although Basil O'Connell finds Musgrave obnoxious, he does not assume him to be always unreliable. Richard Burke's reported reaction to his son's reported conversion (or regression) to Catholicism has a ring of truth. And destruction of relevant correspondence by Burke himself could account for some of what is missing in 'the missing years'.

In the spring of 1757 Edmund Burke married Jane Nugent, the daughter of a well-known Irish Catholic physician, Christopher Nugent, a friend both of Burke and Dr Johnson. Musgrave characteristically describes him as 'a most bigoted Romanist bred at Douay in Flanders.' Jane Nugent appears to have conformed at one time to the Established Church, as did Burke's mother, but Jane, again like Mary Burke, practised the Catholic religion throughout her married life.[2] No record of the marriage has been found. If it were a Catholic marriage, as Jane, like Mary, would have insisted, it could not have been legally solemnised in England or Ireland. It may have been a Catholic marriage in France. Unfortunately the Paris parochial registers were destroyed in 1871.[3] 'Occasional conformity' seems to have

[1] *The Ireland of Sir Jonah Barrington*, ed. H. Staples (London, 1968) p. 245.
[2] R. B. McDowell (Introduction to Part II of Vol. IX of *Writings and Speeches of Edmund Burke*, p. 407) says that Jane's mother was 'a strong Presbyterian' who brought up Jane as 'a Protestant'. In the circumstances I doubt the authenticity of that Protestant education. In any case we know, from the unimpeachable testimony of Richard Shackleton, and Burke's reaction to it (see below pp. 63–66), that Jane Burke was a practising Catholic.
[3] The marriage is discussed by Basil O'Connell in 'Burke's Reconciliation with his Father,' *Burke Newsletter*, Vol. VIII, No. 2 (1966–67) pp. 714–715.

been more tolerable for women than for men, but the Catholicism of a wife or daughter could cast doubt on the Protestantism of a husband or father. In any case, the marriage of Edmund Burke and Jane Nugent, over its forty years, was to prove an extremely happy one.

In the late 1750s Burke published two books, which were well received: *A Vindication of Natural Society* (1756) and *A Philosophical Enquiry into the origin of our Ideas of the Sublime and Beautiful* (1757). Neither work has any overt connection with Ireland, but Burke's Irish formation has a bearing on both. A *Vindication* – a work with a qualified 'anti-Enlightenment' tendency – will be considered in Chapter VI below. *The Sublime* appears as an implicit rejection of the limitations of Burke's Quaker education. Abraham Shackleton had refused to teach 'those authors who recommend in seducing language the illusions of love and the abominable trade of war'. Burke found the origin of 'the beautiful' in love, and the origin of 'the sublime' in war. (Shackleton would have been delighted at Tolstoy's reaction, more than 140 years later, to his pupil's book. Tolstoy, having read Burke on the *Sublime and Beautiful*, agrees, in *What is Art?* (1895), that the Sublime does indeed mean war, and the Beautiful does mean sexual love, but Tolstoy goes on to lay it down that both the Sublime and the Beautiful are therefore to be rejected.)

IRISH CONCERNS IN EARLY POLITICAL CAREER

By the early 1760s Burke is laying the foundations of his political career in London. Sometime in 1759 he became an assistant to a well-known parliamentarian of his own age, William Gerard Hamilton (1729–1796). In April 1761 Hamilton became Chief Secretary for Ireland, and asked Burke to accompany him as his private secretary. Burke accepted. As private secretary to the Chief Secretary, he had an officially minor but significant role in the government of Ireland, from 1761 to 1764, when Hamilton was dismissed. Burke was in Dublin for sessions of the Irish parliament in the winters of 1761 and 1762. His principal objective as far as he could influence policy, was to improve the condition of the Catholics. In the autumn of 1761, while the Irish Parliament was in session, he is said to have been already at work on a *Tract Relative to the Laws against Popery in Ireland.*[1] The *Tract* was not completed, nor was any part of it published during his lifetime, but fragments of it occupy some seventy pages in the collected Works, where they are dated 1764.

The *Tract* is in the main a synopsis, and at the same time an indictment, of the Penal Code, as it existed in the 1760s, a period when the Code stood in full rigour on the statute book, but was no longer being generally enforced with the same degree of severity as had prevailed earlier in the century. Burke had clearly been studying the Code closely, no doubt in order to advise Hamilton and Lord Halifax, the Lord Lieutenant or viceroy, and to engage in discussion with other members of the administration and of the Irish Parliament. He was to return to this subject in later life – it's not too much to say that it obsessed him, and understandably so, throughout his life. He was to write about it during the American Revolution, during the French Revolution and the period of the incubation of the Irish Rebellion of 1798. But the *Tract* is important, as Burke's first investigation of the Penal Code. Unlike all Burke's later comment on the Code, it acknowledges, formally, that some measures of exclusion of Catholics are just and necessary. This acknowledgement occurs in the context of the pernicious economic and social effects of the Penal Code, through the barriers which the Code sets up against the acquisition of property by most of the people of Ireland. Burke writes: For 'they [Catholics] are not only excluded from all offices in Church and State, which, though a just and necessary provision, is yet no small restraint in the acquisition [of property], but they are interdicted from the army and the law, in all its branches.'[2] Without expressly arguing in favour of the admission of Catholics to the Armed Services and the Law, he goes on to offer some extreme examples of the 'scrupulous severity' in that particular with which the laws are enforced.

It is hard to credit that Burke ever really thought that the exclusion of Catholics from all State offices (whatever about the Anglican Church) was 'just and necessary'. Nothing in the rest of his writings suggests such a belief, and his later writings on the Penal Code are incompatible with it. I infer from this passage that the Tract was

---

[1] For the dating see Carl B. Cone, *Burke and the Nature of Politics; The Age of the American Revolution* (University of Kentucky Press, 1957) p. 43. Copeland, however, seems to imply that it was written a few years later. Also T. H. D. Mahoney, *Edmund Burke and Ireland* (Harvard, 1960) p. 15.

[2] Fragments of a *Tract Relative to the Laws against Popery in Ireland,* (Works, 1899 ed., VI, 311).

prepared to be shown to someone, probably Hamilton, who did believe that the exclusion of Catholics from State offices was just and necessary. Presumably Burke hoped that the concession, in that phrase, would make Hamilton more willing to listen to the rest of his argument. While Burke generally argued from deep and strong conviction, he was not above the occasional tactical adjustment, if it might serve to carry the rest of his argument. He himself was later to acknowledge publicly that 'an economy of truth' was permissible in certain circumstances.[1] For the rest, the *Tract* is made up of powerful arguments against various aspects of the Penal Code. It stresses that the victims of the code are the majority of the people of Ireland:

> The happiness or misery of multitudes can never be a thing indifferent. A law against the majority of the people, is in substance a law against the people itself; its extent determines its invalidity; it even changes its character as it enlarges its operation: it is not particular injustice, but general oppression; and can no longer be considered as a private hardship which might be borne, but spreads and grows up into the unfortunate importance of a national calamity. Now as a law directed against the mass of the nation has not the nature of a reasonable institution, so neither has it the authority: for in all forms of government the people is the true legislator; and whether the immediate and instrumental cause of the law be a single person or many, the remote and efficient cause is the consent of the people, either actual or implied; and such consent is absolutely essential to its validity.[2]

Burke points out that those in Ireland who most fiercely condemn the bigotry of the French monarchy in matters of religion are the first inclined to practise it themselves.

> For my part, there is no circumstance, in all the contradictions of our most mysterious nature, that appears to be more humiliating than the

---

[1] 'Falsehood and delusion are allowed in no case whatever: But, as in the exercise of all the virtues, there is an oeconomy of truth. It is a sort of temperance, by which a man speaks truth with measure that he may speak it the longer'. (*First Letter on a Regicide Peace: Works*, V, 340.) More than two centuries later that phrase 'an economy of truth', was to have an eerie echo in a sensational security case. On 23 November 1986 the British Cabinet Secretary, Sir Robert Armstrong, seeking to prevent publication in Australia of the book *Spycatcher*, by the former M.I.5 officer Peter Wright, said of his own testimony, in an Australian court, 'It contained a misleading impression, not a lie. I was being economical with the truth.'

[2] *Works*, VI, 320.

use we are disposed to make of those sad examples, which seem purposely marked for our correction and improvement. Every instance of fury and bigotry in other men, one should think, would naturally fill us with an horror of that disposition: the effect, however, is directly contrary. We are inspired, it is true, with a very sufficient hatred for the party, but with no detestation at all of the proceeding. Nay, we are apt to urge our dislike of such measures as a reason for imitating them and by an almost incredible absurdity, because some Powers have destroyed their country by their persecuting spirit, to argue, that we ought to retaliate on them by destroying our own.[1]

Having shown the Code to be ineffective in its declared objective, of penalising Papists into becoming Protestants, he finds the lapidary phrase: 'Ireland, after almost a century of persecution, is at this time full of penalties and full of Papists.' He takes on the Protestant argument, that any suffering the Catholics may endure is their own fault, because they are free to escape all penalties, simply by becoming Protestants:

Now as to the other point, that the objects of these Laws suffer voluntarily; this seems to me to be an insult rather than an argument. For besides that it totally annihilates every characteristick, and therefore every faulty idea of persecution, just as the former does; it supposes, what is false in fact, that it is in a man's moral power to change his religion whenever his convenience requires it. If he be beforehand satisfied that your opinion is better than his, he will voluntarily come over to you, and without compulsion; and then your Law would be unnecessary; but if he is not so convinced, he must know that it is his duty in this point to sacrifice his interest here to his opinion of his eternal happiness, else he could have in reality no religion at all. In the former case, therefore, as your Law would be unnecessary; in the latter, it would be persecuting; that is, it would put your penalty and his ideas of duty in the opposite scales; which is, or I know not what is, the precise idea of persecution.[2]

To one who, like myself, believes that Richard Burke was a convert to the Established Church, this passage has a poignant ring. If Burke *père* was indeed a convert, it would be virtually impossible, in the conditions of the time, for Edmund not to have known of so momentous a fact. If so, Richard had failed, in Edmund's view, in his 'duty . . . to sacrifice his interest here to his opinion of his eternal happi-

[1] *Works*, VI, 331.
[2] *Works*, VI, 334–5.

ness.' And Edmund's political career, then just beginning, was open to him only by virtue of that failure. Here he is writing in the persona of a strong but fair-minded Protestant, the better to expose the absurdity and injustice of the anti-Catholic Code: 'We found the people hereticks and idolaters; we have, by way of improving their condition, rendered them slaves and beggars: they remain in all the misfortune of their old errors, and all the superadded misery of their recent punishment.'[1]

I think I detect an autobiographical note in a passage which rehearses and comments on some habitual arguments of Irish Protestants in defence of the Penal Laws:

> The great prop of this whole system is not pretended to be its justice or its utility, but the supposed danger to the State which gave rise to it originally, and which they apprehend would return if this system were overturned. Whilst, say they, the Papists of this Kingdom were possessed of landed property, and of the influence consequent to such property, their allegiance to the Crown of Great Britain was ever insecure; the publick peace was ever liable to be broken; and Protestants never could be a moment secure either of their properties or of their lives. Indulgence only made them arrogant, and power daring; confidence only excited and enabled them to exert their inherent treachery; and the times, which they generally selected for their most wicked and desperate rebellions, were those in which they enjoyed the greatest ease and the most perfect tranquillity.
>
> Such are the arguments that are used, both publicly and privately, in every discussion upon this point. They are generally full of passion and of error, and built upon facts which in themselves are most false.[2]

'Whilst, say they, the Papists of this kingdom. . . .' How often, and with what a sinking heart, Burke must have listened to discourse that started off with something like that! He would not have been likely to hear such language in his home or in the Nagle Country; hardly any in that Quaker school at Ballitore, where Abraham Shackleton would have sternly discouraged any expression of religious bigotry. But he would have been bound to encounter bigots (though not only bigots) in the Trinity College of the 1740s, and later in political discussions in Dublin. He must have had to listen to people talk in that vein, and to reply to them, on the basis of assumptions common to Protestants in general – and not of the Catholic assump-

[1] *Works*, VI. 341.
[2] *Works*, VI, 355.

tions which were in fact so much nearer his heart and mind.

For a person in his predicament, straddling the great divide between Protestant and Catholic in eighteenth-century Ireland, and listening to a Protestant bigot's views about Papists, the most insistent and painful question must always have been: does he know? Does he know, that is, of Burke's close Catholic connections? If he did not know, the situation was relatively harmless; just a common-or-garden bigot, blathering on in the usual vein. But if he did know, then he was listening to a personal enemy, obliquely taunting him, menacing him with some hint of exposure. His position was closely comparable to that of a person of Jewish origin, brought up as a Christian, and having to listen, from time to time, to fellow Christians holding forth about 'The Jews', in hostile and contemptuous terms. But Burke's predicament was even worse than that analogy would suggest for, say, contemporary Britain. To complete the Jewish analogy, we would need to have the 'person of Jewish origin' listening to conversation of that type, in a country whose entire legal system was saturated in anti-semitism. Taking account of that predicament, I am more impressed than many writers about Burke allow themselves to be, by the courage and the selfless subordination of very real political ambition which he showed in taking up the cudgels against the powerful enemies of his people (or, at the very least, of his mother's people). Political courage is an expensive commodity, and he was to pay a heavy price for it in parliamentary terms nearly twenty years later.

The tenor of the Halifax-Hamilton Administration of 1761–2 was an exceptionally mild and enlightened one. Some of the credit for that should go to the private secretary to the Chief Secretary, that is to Burke. The main problem to which that Administration had to apply its collective mind was that set by the 'Whiteboy' disturbances in Munster in the early 1760s. The Irish Protestant landlord oligarchs insisted that these disturbances were essentially seditious in nature, and of Jacobite and French inspiration. 'French inspiration' was a particularly heavy imputation in 1761–2, for Britain and Ireland were then at war with France. The 'Jacobite-French' interpretation of Whiteboyism had, and was meant to have, a tendency to involve the Irish Catholic gentry – the natural leaders of their people in political matters at this time – in suspicions of responsibility for instigating the disturbances. A social and economic interpretation on the other hand, identifying the disturbances as essentially agrarian in character, tended to exonerate the Catholic gentry, most of whose economic interests were opposed to those of the impoverished Whiteboys.[1] The Administration resisted the pressures of the Protestant oligarchy, and adopted the 'social and economic' interpretation (which modern historians accept as generally correct). As Carl B. Cone writes: 'While in Ireland, Burke witnessed the Whiteboy outrages. These marked the beginnings of the agrarian disturbances that remained a baneful feature of Irish life for another century and a half. Against the protests of angry Protestants and frightened Francophobes, Lord Halifax steadfastly refused to consider the disorders of the early 1760s as either sectarian or political in nature. So did Sir Richard Aston, Chief Justice of the Common Pleas in Ireland. After making a judicial circuit of the embroiled counties, Aston wrote to Hamilton that the disturbances in which "Papist and Protestant were promiscuously concerned" were not caused by "disaffection to his Majesty, his government, or the laws in general," but arose mainly from bad economic conditions.'[2]

But although the Administration rejected the Jacobite-French interpretation, the Irish legal system was affected by it, especially in Munster, through the influence of Protestant landlords in the courts of law. To Burke's disgust a number of suspected Whiteboys were hanged: We find him writing to a friend Charles O'Hara (of whom more later) in August 1762 about 'the unfeeling Tyranny of a mungril Irish "Landlord" and "the Horrors of a Munster Circuit".'[3] I am not sure what Burke means by 'a mungril Irish Landlord', but I suspect that the reference is to the perceived inferior 'stock', or breeding of most of the Protestant landlords. Catholic gentry, like the Nagles, who could trace their line back to Norman and medieval origins, looked down on landlords of Cromwellian and Williamite origin as social upstarts. The realities of political power usually made scions of the Catholic gentry keep this theory of social precedence to themselves. (It might at first sight seem surprising that Burke should write so candidly in this line to O'Hara, who was himself a Protestant landlord, and a member of the Irish Parliament. But there was a special bond between Burke and O'Hara (see below pp. 55–57). A

---

[1] The 1762 *Annual Register*, founded four years earlier by Burke and the writer, publisher and bookseller, Robert Dodsley, had an entry on 'Rioters . . . called Levellers . . . likewise called Whiteboys, from their wearing shirts over their other cloaths, the better to distinguish each other by night.' (Dodsley is also credited with having suggested to Dr Johnson that he should compile a dictionary).

[2] Cone, *Burke and the Nature of Politics*, p. 46.

[3] *Corr.* I, 147: letter dated by the editor 'ante 23 August 1762'.

footnote to that letter links 'the horrors of a Munster Circuit' to Burke's concern for his Nagle relatives: "Burke was strongly interested in the agrarian disorders which broke out in southern Ireland in the early 1760s, and which were punished by a number of hangings, partly from a belief of the government that they were an organised Jacobite rebellion. (See an unfinished paper printed in *Corr.* [1844] I, 41–5)[1]. Among Burke MSS at Sheffield (Bk 8a) is a letter of William Fant to the Lord Lieutenant of Ireland (a document one is surprised to find among Burke's private papers), dated 18 October 1761 and endorsed in Burke's hand, 'First information of the forged Plot, from Fant who himself first r[ai]sed the White Boys.' Fant describes a meeting in June 1760 at which he thought he had seen the Pretender disguised as a woman. Burke's concern over the contents of this letter is not hard to explain. Fant's charges touched some of his maternal relatives: 'Hugh Massy Ingoldsby who is since that dead the Nagles and Hennesys were the Promoters of the Meeting.' The *Corke Journal* of 5 April 1762 and the *Dublin Journal* of 6–10 April 1762 report the imprisonment of a 'Garret Nagle', one of a group of men arrested 'on suspicion of their aiding and assisting of the clan called White Boys"'.[2]

The position taken by the Halifax-Hamilton administration towards the 'Jacobite-French' theory was identical with Burke's own, and I infer that he himself made a considerable contribution to the working out of that position. Some readers may be surprised at that inference, granted his modest status, within the Administration in question. Those historians who like to 'cut him down to size', tend to equate his political importance to the importance of the positions and offices he happened to hold, which was never great. But this is a serious mistake. His political importance reached its greatest height during the last seven years of his life, when he held no post at all and belonged to no party (See chapter VI). That importance derived from the capacity of his understanding, drawing on a mass of information, and expressed through an unexcelled mastery of English prose, both in speech and writing. His contemporaries were well aware of these gifts, even though they sometimes disparaged his use of them. As Copeland puts it in an essay: 'Even Burke's enemies granted him genius however deranged'. Burke was the only one of Samuel Johnson's contemporaries of whom Johnson stood in awe. Copeland ends

[1] *Corr.* [1844] is a reference to the nineteenth-century edition of Burke's *Correspondence*.

[2] *Corr.* I, 147–8, n. 5.

the essay: 'His ultimate and no doubt highest tribute will not come as a surprise to anyone who has worked long on Burke and known him well. It was paid on a day when Johnson was ill and not quite up to his usual exertions: Mr Burke having been mentioned, he said, "That fellow calls forth all my powers. Were I to see Burke now, it would kill me".'[1]

Lesser mortals were less inclined to stand in awe, and the lesser they were, the less in awe they stood. But William Hamilton was intelligent enough to understand Burke's unique combination of gifts. It was as an adviser, not as an amanuensis, that Hamilton employed him. So it is probably not a coincidence if a major policy, pursued by the Administration in which Hamilton was Chief Secretary, followed, on this point, the lines which we know Burke would have advised. It is possible, however that Hamilton while taking his advice, at least in the matter of the Whiteboys, during his term as Chief Secretary, came to resent the intellectual superiority of his adviser, and to chafe under his advice. In April–May of 1765 the two men quarrelled irrevocably, and with great mutual bitterness. The merits of the quarrel, which ended Burke's employment by Hamilton, need not detain us here. It is of interest, however, that the rift between them appears to have originated, at least in part, in a feeling on Burke's side that Hamilton had let him down, on a matter of concern to Irish Catholics. Rough notes written by Hamilton, apparently in April 1765, on Burke's conduct are published in the *Correspondence*. One note reads: 'Speech against R. Cath: B:' This reference is clarified by the following editorial footnote: 'Perhaps a bill brought into the Irish Parliament in 1762 to allow Roman Catholic nobles in Ireland to enter the military service of Portugal. According to Francis Hardy's *Memoirs of the Earl of Charlemont* (2nd ed. London, 1812, I, p. 130), the Bill was moved by Hamilton and 'supported by a torrent of eloquence which bore down all before it, but being strongly opposed by the Irish Protestants ... this measure, which undoubtedly might have been carried, was finally given up by government' (*ibid.* 132). Burke's feelings on such a Bill, and especially on its abandonment would be a likely cause of disagreement with Hamilton.[2]

Hamilton's slip of memory here is interesting, and possibly what we would now call Freudian. He remembers a speech 'against' a

---

[1] 'Johnson and Burke' in *Edmund Burke* (1950) p. 303.
[2] *Corr.* I, 190, n. 1. See also Mahoney, *Edmund Burke and Ireland*, p. 14.

Roman Catholic Bill, implying in the context that this was a cause of Burke's resentment against him. But what he had actually done was to make a powerful speech, no doubt inspired by Burke, *in favour* of the Bill in question. And what Burke appears to have resented was Hamilton's backing away, under Irish Protestant pressure, from the policy declared in Hamilton's own speech. In his rough, angry and almost incoherent notes, Burke appears as an untrustworthy and un-English figure. Two linked terms, clearly intended in the context as terms of abuse, are repeated. In the middle of the notes are the words 'a Jew and a Jesuit'. And the last words are: 'Jew-Jesuit'.

Burke soon acquired a new and more lasting patron. On 11 July 1765 he became private secretary to Charles Watson Wentworth, second Marquess of Rockingham (1730–1782), who was just then forming a government, which was to last for a year. He was leader of that section of the Whigs, which Burke regarded, not without reason, as the most high-minded and principled element in Parliament. Throughout Rockingham's life, which ended in 1782, Burke remained a loyal Rockingham Whig, and the chief ideologist and publicist for that party. But the relationship came near to foundering, within its first week, because of his Irish connections, as interpreted by his enemies. On 16 July, he quotes Macbeth to his actor friend David Garrick: 'So far at least, I thank God, the designs of my Enemies, who not long since made a desperate Stroke at my Fortune, my Liberty, and my reputation, (all! Hell kite! all at a Swoop,) have failed of their Effect; and their implacable and unprovoked malice has been disappointed.'[1]

According to the *Memoirs* of the Earl of Charlemont, who may well have heard the story from Burke himself, the Duke of Newcastle warned Rockingham that Burke was a dangerous person to be associated with. He was an Irish Papist; educated by the Jesuits at St Omer, a Jesuit himself and sent into England as a spy. He was able to satisfy Rockingham that the allegations were unfounded. Rockingham refused his offer of resignation, and the episode was closed. Unfortunately, we don't know what exactly he said, in his explanation to Rockingham. One could say that he probably 'practised an economy of truth'. But it would be wrong to overwork that phrase, to pass over with a quip one of the most painful episodes in his career. He

---

[1] *Corr.* I, 211. Rather surprisingly, this dramatic statement receives no annotation. The Newcastle episode is, however, the subject of a note later (p. 216, n. 4).

did allow room for that 'economy', but not much room, and much less than most politicians allowed themselves in his day (or allow themselves now). He had an acute sense of personal honour, and he was being questioned by one whom he respected, about matter of deep and intimate concern to him, over which he observed habitual reticence. Fortunately for him, Newcastle's specific 'Jesuit' charges were unfounded. He had not been educated by the Jesuits of St Omer, and indeed had never been near St Omer, at this period of his life. He was in a position to deny that one flatly, which presumably satisfied Rockingham. But Rockingham might not have been so easily satisfied if he had understood the full extent, the strength and depth, of Burke's connections with Catholic Ireland.[1]

Newcastle's specific charges were false, except perhaps for the 'Irish Papist' one, but what he was clumsily driving at came near the bone. Burke may not actually have been a crypto-Catholic, but in the eyes of strong Protestants in eighteenth-century Britain and Ireland, he was as near to being a crypto-Catholic as made no difference. And in Irish affairs he was wholeheartedly on the Catholic side, against the Protestant Ascendancy (as it was later designated). The charges probably date from his period as private secretary to William Hamilton. His Catholic connections must have attracted attention, in the context of Hamilton's resistance to the Munster Protestant landlords' interpretation of the Whiteboy disturbances as a French and Jacobite plot, in which the Irish Catholic gentry were implicated. In that context it would be natural for Burke's Catholic connections to become exaggerated, and for 'the Jesuits of St Omer' to make their appearance. Hamilton seems to have accepted these allegations retrospectively in the course of a bitter quarrel: hence the 'Jew-Jesuit' theme. He was probably the source of the rumours which reached Newcastle, and also the source of more widely diffused rumours, which proved meat to the caricaturists of the time.[2]

---

[1] The St Omer story stuck: we find Michelet repeating it, in the following century.

[2] William O'Brien, in *Edmund Burke as an Irishman* (Dublin, 1924) p. 102, states that 'it cannot be doubted' that the rumours were set in motion by Hamilton. It can be doubted, but it's probably a good guess. O'Brien would not have known about those 'rough notes'. However, Owen Dudley Edwards comments, in a letter to the author: 'I would argue [Hamilton] was less likely to start the rumours (which make him look at the very least a fool who had allowed himself to be manipulated by a subversive) than to confirm them (if Newcastle asked about it)'.

IRISH CONCERNS IN AND OUT OF PARLIAMENT
1766–1767

Burke was elected to Parliament for the Borough of Wendover in December 1765, and attracted public attention with the brilliance of his first speech (it was on America – see below pp. 107–8) in January 1766. Throughout his career, the cartoonists were to portray him in the garb of a Jesuit; that was how you knew it was Burke. That he was an Irish Jesuit didn't help. John Wilkes said that Burke's oratory 'stank of whiskey and potatoes'. The whiskey bottle and the potato joined the Jesuit cassock on those cartoons; there were no inhibitions about ethnic stereotypes in those days. Understandably, after the quarrel with Hamilton, and Newcastle's intervention, Burke was nervous about his Irish connections. In October 1765, between his appointment as Rockingham's private secretary and his election to Parliament, he uncharacteristically refused to grant a favour. This one was sought by his beloved uncle and almost foster-parent, Patrick Nagle. Admittedly, it was an unusually risky favour. Nagle wanted Burke to help a relative, Garrett, known as Garrett Atty,[1] Patrick's nephew and Edmund's cousin, out of a legal difficulty. It was quite a large legal difficulty: he had abducted a Protestant heiress, Elizabeth Forward, or fforward, niece to the Protestant oligarch, John Hely Hutchinson. Under the Penal Code, the abduction by a Catholic of a Protestant heiress was a capital offence. The terms in which Burke explains his inability to help are revealing of how he saw the delicacy of his own position, in relation to his Irish connections, at the outset of his political career in England: 'I am sincerely concerned for the match that Garrett Atty was so unfortunate as to make, and did from the beginning expect no better Issue of it, in a Country circumstanced as ours is; Assure my Uncle, that there is no one Step on earth in my power that I would not gladly take to give ease to his mind, which must be cruelly agitated; I most sincerely pity him; but I believe, when he reflects, how newly, and almost as a stranger I am come about these people, and knows the many industrious endeavours, which malice and envy, (very unprovoked undeed) have used to ruin me, he will see, that so early a request to suspend the operation of the Laws, upon my bare word, against the finding of a jury of the greatest County of the Kingdom, and that upon the most unpopular

---

[1] Atty is a diminutive for Athanasius, here possibly a patronymic.

point in the world, could have no other effect, than to do me infinite prejudice, without the least possibility of succeeding in the object I aimed at.'[1]

In the event, Garrett Atty was lucky enough to escape being hanged. In the course of escaping, he conformed to the Established Church. For good measure, he conformed twice, within a period of less than seven months: once on 2 June 1765 and again on 19 January 1766. Other Nagles conformed about the same time. Garrett Nagle of Clogher, Cork, Gent, conformed on 22 December 1765.[2] We don't know exactly why this last Garrett Nagle conformed, but we may reasonably infer, from the conditions of the time that he did so under some form of political, sectarian and legal pressure. He was a son of Edmund Burke's uncle, Patrick Nagle, and so Edmund's first cousin. He was also 'agent' for the small estate in Clogher which Burke nominally owned,[3] under one of those complicated collusive arrangements which were common in eighteenth-century Ireland. A relative who was a Protestant, or had at least conformed to the Established Church, acquired an estate, ostensibly for himself, but in reality for his Catholic relative, who was legally debarred from acquiring landed property, in his own right. A 'bigoted' Protestant, like those who were conducting the anti-Catholic drive in Munster, would regard a Protestant who engaged in the sort of arrangements which Burke had with Garrett Nagle of Clogher as something even worse than an avowed Papist: a spurious convert and a devious traitor to the Protestant cause.

All this brought the anti-Catholic drive in Munster, in the period 1765–6, uncomfortably close to the door of Edmund Burke MP, at the outset of his political career in England.

The other Nagle who conformed at this time was less close to Burke, but more prominent, and had a narrower shave with the law. This was James Nagle of Garnavilla, gentleman, of Co. Tipperary, who conformed to the Established Church on 22 December 1765, and was tried and acquitted more than a year later, on a charge of 'High Treason for being concerned with the deluded people called

---

[1] *Corr.* I, 216. An editorial note says that 'Burke's phrasing is discreet'. His Irish enemies might have employed harsher epithets if they could have seen the phrase 'the match that Garret Atty was so unfortunate as to make', used in reference to the abducting of a Protestant heiress by a Catholic cousin of the writer.

[2] 'The Nagles of Garnavilla' by Basil P. O'Connell in *The Irish Genealogist*, Vol. 3, No. 1 (1956) pp. 17–24.

[3] *Corr.* 217, n. 1.

the Whiteboys'. James Nagle is described as 'a gentleman grazier in a big way'.[1] It is unlikely that a person of this description had anything to do with the Whiteboys, just as it is unlikely that the Whiteboys had anything to do with such a hifalutin enterprise as High Treason. Graziers, as James Donnelly Jr. writes, were actually a particular target of the Whiteboys who cherished 'intense popular resentment against the keeping of land from tillage'.[2] The real targets of the wave of prosecutions – Donnelly calls it 'this unsavoury crusade' – were neither Whiteboys nor Jacobites, but Catholic gentry, and wealthy Catholics in general. Whiteboyism was a pretext, and Jacobitism hardly even that. Paradoxically, one of the reasons for the drive against the Catholic gentry was that 'the Jacobite threat' had begun to lose credibility. In the first half of the eighteenth century, that threat had seemed quite credible. True, Irish Catholics had not risen in either of the Jacobite rebellions, but some of them certainly might have if the rebellions had prospered. A Catholic family like the Nagles had its Jacobite connections and there was no knowing what people like the Nagles might do in the event, for example, of a major French landing in Munster. That was enough to keep the Jacobite threat alive throughout the Seven Years War with France. And the Jacobite scare seemed to most Englishmen, of that time, a solid argument in favour of maintaining the Protestant interest in Ireland, which by the end of the century would become known as 'the Protestant Ascendancy'. However after 1763, and peace with France, the Jacobite threat, the political stock-in-trade of the Protestant interest, was no longer credible to members of the British ruling class. Even Catholicism no longer seemed much of a threat. Englishmen of the governing classes knew that the France of the mid-1760s was hardly a hot-bed of Catholic fanaticism. It was at this time that the France of Louis XV expelled the Jesuits (1766). The Pope himself, a little later, had dissolved the Jesuit Order, as an international body, thus liquidating what had been the spiritual and political general staff of the Counter-Reformation. In France, in England and even in Rome, what was left of the spirit of the Wars of Religion seemed to be yielding ground, and at a rather brisk pace,

[1] O'Connell, *Irish Genealogist*, article already cited.
[2] See James S. Donnelly's masterly article, 'The Whiteboy Movement, 1761–5', *Irish Historical Studies* XXI, No. 81 (March 1978) pp. 20–54. Donnelly shows that the Whiteboys were mostly a movement of labourers and craftsmen, with some priests and farmers, and finds that the insistent claim that rich Catholics were involved was a fabrication of the Protestant side.

to the spirit of the Enlightenment. In Ireland, however, the pace was not quite so brisk. Indeed, what the progress of the European Enlightenment set in motion in Ireland, at first, was a relapse into what looked like the old religious fanaticism. It wasn't really religious fanaticism, by this time, but a clash of interests and a clash of castes. But the castes were identified by their religious heritages, culture and traditions.

The great event of the mid-1760s, as far as Ireland was concerned was the withdrawal, by Clement XIII, in 1766, of papal recognition from the House of Stuart, in the person of the contemporary Jacobite Pretender – and leader of the Forty-Five – Charles Edward (Bonnie Prince Charlie). In Ireland, the breach between the Papacy and the Pretender came as a great relief to most of the resident Catholic gentry. It meant that these could now declare loyalty to the Hanoverian Crown without equivocation, and without embarrassing and obscure explanations of the divergence between their religious allegiance, on the one hand, and their political allegiance, on the other. They could abjure the Pretender's claims and go on to argue that the severance of the Roman link between Catholicism and Jacobitism deprived the Penal Laws against Catholics of whatever justification they might once have had. Later, this argument, aided by the general tendencies of the Enlightenment, found hearing in England and, with much help from Burke, led to the gradual lifting of the disabilities against Catholics. But in Ireland, the immediate effect of these emerging tendencies was to put the Catholic gentry and clergy in greater danger than ever. The Protestant oligarchy was frightened by the nascent resurgence of the Catholics – the great majority in the island. The frightened minority sought in its turn to frighten the natural leaders of the majority: the Catholic gentry and clergy. They needed not only to frighten the Irish Catholic gentry and clergy, but also to asperse their loyalty, for it was apparent that Catholic loyalty, now becoming increasingly credible, was a far worse and more insidious danger, than Catholic disloyalty had been, at any point in the eighteenth century, to the Protestant oligarchy.

The renewed Whiteboy disturbances provided an occasion both for frightening leaders among the Catholics and for aspersing their loyalty. The case made by the Protestant oligarchs, in relation to these disturbances of the mid 1760s, was essentially the same as that made in relation to the similar earlier disturbances. The Whiteboys, so the case went, were not what they appeared to be: poor agitators engaging in sporadic agrarian disturbances. They were really part of a deep-laid conspiracy, led by members of the Catholic gentry and some of their clergy, in concert with foreign powers. The story looked a lot thinner in the mid-1760s than it had earlier because there was no longer a war on, and the Jacobites were no longer a threat. Perhaps because the story had been less convincing than before, the repression inspired by it was fiercer. The most noted victim of the repression in its worst phase, that of 1766, was a Catholic priest, Father Nicholas Sheehy. Father Sheehy, who was distantly related to Burke, had been acquitted in Dublin on 10 February of charges of inciting to riot and rebellion. He was then conveyed to Clonmel where he was convicted on a different charge of instigating to murder. He was hanged, drawn and quartered in Clonmel on 15 March. W. E. H. Lecky calls Sheehy's second trial 'one of the most scandalous ever known in Ireland'. In Catholic Ireland, Sheehy is generally regarded as a martyr. J. A. Froude, who viewed such cults with foreboding, wrote that Father Sheehy 'was raised on the spot to an honoured place in the Irish martyrology. His tomb became a place of pilgrimage – a scene at which the Catholic Celt could renew annually his vow of vengeance against the assassins of Ireland's saints. The stone which lay above his body was chipped in pieces by enthusiastic relic hunters.'[1]

On 3 May another member of the Sheehy family, Nicholas's cousin, also Edmund, was executed on similar charges. Understandably Burke took a keen interest in these proceedings. Thomas Copeland writes that among the papers at Sheffield 'are a printed letter of Sheehy, dated the day before his execution, and MS copies of: a petition of Edmund Sheehy (executed 3 May); the substance of another petition of Edmund Sheehy; Edmund Sheehy's last speech

[1] James Anthony Froude (1818–94) was a fine writer but his views were distorted by his highly idiosyncratic judgment, as evidenced by *The English in Ireland in the Eighteenth Century*, the source for this quotation (New York, 1888, Vol. II, p. 31). William Edward Hartpole Lecky (1838–1903), of Scottish descent, born near Dublin, educated at Trinity College, was one of the most generous-minded of Irish historians. He is perhaps best remembered for his five-volume *History of England in the Eighteenth Century* (London, 1878–92) one purpose of which was to refute what he described as the anti-Irish calumnies of Froude; portions of this work were later published as *History of Ireland in the Eighteenth Century* (1892). See also Philip O'Connell, 'The Plot against Father Nicholas Sheehy', *Irish Ecclesiastical Record* CVIII, fifth series, 1967, pp. 372–84. See also Maurice Bric, 'The Whiteboy Movement, 1760–1780', *Tipperary History and Society*, W. Nolan ed. (Dublin, 1985) pp. 148–185. Basil O'Connell writes in the article in *The Irish Genealogist* already cited: 'It is now known that Father Sheehy's sister married a Richard Burke, and we believe that this Richard was a first cousin of Edmund Burke.'

declaring his innocence; the last declaration of James Farrell (executed 3 May); the last declaration of James Buxton (executed 3 May); a letter written by James Buxton while in Kilkenny Gaol, asserting that he had been urged to give evidence against certain Roman Catholic gentlemen (including Burke's relative James Nagle), for which evidence he might have had his pardon.'[1]

Shortly after learning of Father Sheehy's execution, Burke had written in April, with savage irony, to Charles O'Hara: 'I find you go on in Ireland plotting; alarming; informing; seizing; and imprisoning as usual; What surprises me is to find by one or two of your Letters, that you are a little giving way to the ingenious Bon ton of our Country. I see it is impossible totally to avoid it. You seem to think, that if they do not discover the cause of their distemper by the dissection of Sheehy, they will leave off Their villanous Theories of Rebellions and Massacres. *Sic notus Ulysses?* [Is that how well you know Ulysses?] I hear they intend to poke in the Bowels of a few more for further discoveries. Why had I a connection of feeling or even of knowledge with such a Country!'[2] In a similar vein he had written to O'Hara more than three years before: 'For my part this same people of Ireland, their notions and their inclinations have always been a riddle to me. Why they should love heavy Taxation; why they should abhor a civil and covet a military establishment I cannot, I confess, in the least conceive. . . . The Truth is this military servitude is what they have grown up under; and like all licentious, and wild, but corrupt people, they love a Jobb better than a Salary; It looks more like plunder. . . . But I hate to think of Ireland, though my thoughts involuntarily take that turn, and whenever they do meet only with objects of grief or indignation.'[3]

The correspondence with Charles O'Hara (c. 1715–1776) of Annaghmore, Co. Sligo, is of special interest as regards Burke's relationship to Ireland. As we shall see throughout this study he was almost always on his guard where Ireland was concerned, not only

---

[1] *Corr.* I, 249, n. 4. The Irish historian Thomas Bartlett inclines to the view that Burke was thinking of writing about the Sheehy case as Voltaire had written about Calas, judicially murdered in France for political-sectarian reasons in 1762. This seems quite likely as Calas had been rehabilitated the year before the execution of the Sheehys, but Burke did not proceed with the idea. It would have been much more dangerous for him to take up the case of the Sheehys than it was for Voltaire to take up that of Calas.

[2] *Corr.* I, pp. 248–9.

[3] *Corr.* I, 161–2.

in public, but also, until his last years, in private letters. The copious correspondence, from 1759 to O'Hara's death in 1776, is unique in the insight it affords into Burke's thinking and feeling about Ireland. But it is coded, it needs to be read with a key. He writes in the persona of a gentleman who has 'grown out of Ireland' and now lives in a larger world. The 'Ireland' he refers to in these letters is always official Ireland, Protestant Ireland. O'Hara was a member of the (all-Protestant) Irish Parliament and Burke, with an undertone of banter, affects to treat O'Hara as representative of the Irish Protestant oligarchy. The correspondence is set in a Version of Pastoral. Burke writes as a member of the Enlightened Parliament of Great Britain, addressing a member of the Benighted Parliament of Ireland. One might expect O'Hara to take offence, but he does not, for it is all a game. O'Hara, on his side, affects to look down on the contending Protestant and Catholic factions equally, and gently mocks Burke for his pro-Catholic zeal.

The key to the correspondence is the unspoken bond between the two men. The bond is that both belonged to a special and suspect category – old Catholic gentry conforming to the Established Church. It is true that there was also a big difference. Charles's ancestor, Tadc O'Hara, had had the foresight to conform as early as 1616, and so the family had kept their large estates in Co. Sligo intact, during the decades in which the Burkes and Nagles had been battered and reduced in circumstances, as gentry of the losing side. A stranger would have seen O'Hara, in the mid-eighteenth century, as a secure member of the Protestant oligarchy. Yet he was not fully accepted as such, even after more than a century of conformity on the part of his family. Thomas Bartlett writes: 'Wealthy (though debt-ridden), well-connected, fervent patron of the turf, socially at ease with Lord Rockingham or with the tenants of his estate, intimate correspondent of Edmund Burke, and interested in "improvement" at a local level and "enlightenment" at the national level. Charles O'Hara personified the independent country gentleman of the eighteenth century. Or he appears to, for an important caveat has to be entered here: Charles O'Hara was never MP for Sligo county or Sligo borough. He was forced to go elsewhere for a seat in Parliament. Representation of one's county at some level was an indication of one's weight and local social standing. Charles's failure in this respect may be taken as an indication of the family's low status compared to the more prominent families of Ormsby, Gore, Cooper and Wynne. This low status may be attributed to the family's Gaelic origins or Catholic connections'.[1] That was the nature of the bond between O'Hara and Burke. Charles's mother, like Edmund's, was one of the Catholic gentry (Eleanor Mathew). The Mathews, the Burkes, the Nagles, the Cotters, the Sheehys were all intermarried, a close connection of Catholic gentry, some of whom had conformed to the Established Church, but were still suspect.

In his letters to O'Hara, Burke affects to treat the Protestant oligarchy as constituting 'the people of Ireland', thus taking its claims to be just that, with a feigned literalness. He also calls them 'the wild and corrupt people'. There was a bond of Gaelic origin between O'Hara and Burke, but there was also a strain on the bond. The O'Haras had kept their land, and although they were suspect, they also had common interests – as Burke did not – with those who suspected them. O'Hara was also of a more cautious temperament than Burke, and more affected by the tone of the more liberal section of the Irish Protestant Parliament, which was not all that liberal, by Burke's standards. In this particular matter O'Hara advised Burke to 'keep his cool', as we would now say, on matters about which Burke had no intention of being cool: the threatening and framing of Catholic gentry and clergy in Munster, under the pretext of suppressing the Whiteboys. Burke in the April 1766 letter, replies to O'Hara's advice with a bleak and acrid irony which, although it may be taken as playful, must have been wounding, in some degree. Burke uses the word 'you' in contexts which would associate O'Hara with the misdeeds of the persecuting section of the Protestant oligarchy. In the circumstances, it seems rather remarkable that the friendship between the two men survived, as it did. But the bond held, O'Hara knew his friend, and his close Catholic connections in Munster, well enough to make allowances for Burke's affliction, anger and anxiety, over the threat to his relatives, and also to his budding political career in Britain, in those dark days.

BURKE IN OPPOSITION
1767

The first Rockingham government fell in July and Burke shortly afterwards went to Ireland where he spent the next three months. It

[1] Thomas Bartlett, 'The O'Hara's of Annaghmore c1600–c1800: Survival and Revival' in *Irish Economic and Social History*, Vol IX (Dublin, 1982) pp. 34–52.

is probable that, in this rather protracted stay, he took counsel with his Nagle relatives about the Whiteboy threat, but any such discussions have left no trace, unless we count a letter to Patrick Nagle, after Burke's return to England in October. He wrote: 'I received your Letter in favour of Mr James Nagle [then awaiting trial; see above p. 51]. His Case is undoubtedly a very severe one. But the Plot is laid deep; and the persons concerned in it are very determined and very wicked, as far as I can judge, by the enquiries I have been capable of making into this affair. *To attempt even in the slightest manner to take it out of the Course of Law would be very idle; it would aggravate instead of alleviating the mischief, and would furnish a new handle to those, who are already willing to use every method to oppress the innocence of their Neighbours* [author's italics]. All I can do is by my advice. The Counsell which these Gentlemen have had are certainly men of Ability and Character, whom by all means they ought still to retain. But they ought to add to them some man of longer Standing in the Profession, and who by being a member of Parliament will have weight, both in the Court, and in representing the affair above, for very obvious reasons. Mr Harward is a man of great honour and spirit, perfectly well acquainted with every thing which relates to Criminal Law, and in every respect the fittest man they can possibly choose. It is the Course I would advise you to take if you were in the same Circumstances. I am thoroughly convinced of the innocence of these Gentlemen, but far from sure, that their lives are not in the greatest danger. They ought to Neglect no means, nor grudge any Expense they can go to. I did hear indeed with an astonishment, which I can scarcely express, that this measure had been originally proposed to them, and that they rejected it on account of the Charge. If that consideration, in such a Case, has any weight with them, I have nothing to say, but to lament their fate, as that of men whose avarice has betrayd their lives, Characters, and fortunes too, into their hands of their most bitter Enemies; and whose weakness will make it impossible to take a single step in their favour. You will (without sending him my Letter) take some method of conveying these sentiments from me to that Gentleman, whose Condition, I sincerely pity.'[1] On the phrase 'without sending him my letter', Thomas Copeland comments: 'Burke is conscious of the dangers to himself should this letter fall into unfriendly hands.' Indeed a

[1] *Corr.* I, 275–77.

sense of being in personal danger seems to pervade this letter from Burke to his uncle. Basil O'Connell comments: 'The letter seems to have been written as if this was the first that Burke had heard of the matter. But surely in Ireland his relatives must have taken the opportunity of consulting this important man of affairs about the dangers which surrounded them. One wonders whether Burke is being naïve.'[1] Burke was not being naïve, he was being prudent, and laying the basis of a defence, if that became necessary. It is rather clear that this is essentially a 'show' letter, to be used in a future emergency, (but concealed for the present) perhaps incorporating advice already given to the Nagles, but primarily designed to be kept by Patrick Nagle and produced by him, if any attempt were made to implicate Edmund Burke in the Whiteboy 'conspiracy'. In that respect, the key sentence is the one I have italicised. And there is some reason to believe that some such effort was being made, and that rumours to that effect were being spread, in the course of the 'great fear' of 1766.

MALICIOUS RUMOURS

In his *Memoirs of the Rebellions in Ireland* etc, Sir Richard Musgrave gives some indication of the kind of rumours current about Burke in the Ireland of 1765–1766. He asserts that Burke's younger brother Richard was there on Edmund's behalf between October 1765 and the following January to distribute money to the Whiteboys.[2] Basil O'Connell, a modern, pro-Catholic scholar, describes Musgrave, generally speaking, as 'biased, vindictive and inaccurate.' Here, however, O'Connell inclines to believe the assertion. He writes: 'I am assured by probably the best authority to express an opinion – Professor T. W. Copeland – that it is physically impossible that Dick Burke was in Ireland between October 1765 and January 1766. None the less Musgrave must have had some reason for thinking that he was, and this becomes therefore an essential part of the investigation'. O'Connell believed that the evidence which convinced

[1] O'Connell, *Irish Genealogist*, Vol. 3, No. 1 (1956) p. 21.
[2] Musgrave *Memoirs*, p. 38.

Copeland that Richard Burke could not have been in Ireland at that time was planted by Edmund in order to protect his brother: 'Strange things were happening to the Nagles in Ireland. The Nagles were taking precautions to protect themselves, and to qualify themselves against seizure of their estates. An investigator of experience would begin to wonder whether the unexpectable [*sic*: probably a misprint for "unexceptionable"] documentation providing an alibi for Richard is or is not valid.'

It would be quite understandable that Burke should be more concerned, during the 1766 crisis, with preparing the groundwork for a future defence of his Nagle relatives and possibly of himself, than with regard to strict historical accuracy. His October letter to Patrick Nagle about the defence of James Nagle of Garnavilla is significant in that context. At the same time, Musgrave's allegation, in so far as it implies support for Whiteboyism, is extremely improbable. The Burkes and the Nagles had no interest in fanning the flames of Whiteboyism; quite the contrary. It was Whiteboyism, interpreted by the Protestant Munster landlords and magistrates as a Jacobite conspiracy headed by the Catholic gentry, that was putting Nagle estates, and Nagle lives, in danger. If indeed, as is not improbable, Richard Burke was engaged in some kind of covert activity in Ireland, on Edmund's behalf, in 1765–6, that activity was almost certainly directed, not at stimulating Whiteboyism, but at protecting Nagle property, and Nagle lives. And even Musgrave allows that the Burkes may have been actuated by motives of charity and humanity. This is magnanimous by the standards of the time. Most Munster magistrates of the period would have assumed that if Burke was helping his Nagle relatives, who were part of the leadership of the Jacobite–Whiteboy conspiracy, then he personally was part of that conspiracy.

The conspiracy-theorists were, however not altogether wide of the mark. Burke was primarily concerned with the fate of the Nagles, more generally with the Penal Code, and more particularly with the threats to his own career. However, he had also some sympathy with the actual Whiteboys. He had written to a trusted Irish friend in Dublin in April 1763: 'I see by Williamsons last Paper that they are reviving the Rebellion Stories; and have produced a second song, indeed more plausible as to the manner than the former; they assert it was proved on the Trial of Dwyer at Clonmel; for God's sake let me know a little of this matter, and of the history of these new levellers. I see that you have but one way of relieving the poor in

Ireland. They call for bread, and you give them "not a Stone", but the Gallows.'[1]

Musgrave's allegations against Burke were, I believe similar in nature to those made by the Duke of Newcastle to Lord Rockingham (above pp. 48–9). That is, they may have been distorted and exaggerated in form, but they contained a significant kernel of truth. The Munster landlords whose surmises and gossip are reflected in the Newcastle and Musgrave allegations, correctly perceived Burke as a powerful, determined and well-placed enemy to their system and their interests. So, why was the Protestant oligarchy, with so much at stake, and holding almost a total monopoly of wealth and power in Ireland, unable to mount a successful attack on Burke, who was at this time a junior politician, and vulnerable through his Irish Catholic family connections and commitments? There are four main reasons, I believe. The primary one is that the tone of the Irish oligarchy with its anachronistic hysteria about Jacobite plots, had become distastefully archaic to the Enlightenment ethos of the British ruling classes of the 1760s. Second, Burke's lifelong discretion and reticence served him well; his enemies were never able to find anything remotely resembling what would now be called a 'smoking gun'. Third, in the absence of a 'smoking' gun, an attack on Burke would turn into an attack on Rockingham, and bring down on the oligarchy the wrath of an important section of the British ruling class. The fourth reason is that, from 1767 on, the Irish oligarchy had more pressing problems to deal with than Burke's influence over Rockingham.

After the fall of the first Rockingham government in the summer of 1766, the Rockingham Whigs were to remain in opposition for sixteen years. Some of the former Rockinghams took office under other administrations. Overtures were made to Burke, and his political career could have been much more brilliant than it was, had he chosen to abandon Rockingham, in or after 1766.[2] That is the course which Burke would certainly have followed, had he been a venal opportunist, as some historians suggest that he was. Instead he remained loyal to Rockingham, whose principles and character he admired, and so remained with him in the wilderness. Consequently he ceased to attract the same degree of animosity from the Irish Protestant oligarchy as he had experienced from 1761 to 1766. The

[1] Letter to John Ridge, 23 April (1763) in *Corr.* I, 168–9. Compare Burke's position in relation to a later movement, somewhat similar to the Whiteboys, that of the Defenders in the 1790s. See Chapter VI, pp. 572–3.

[2] For the offer to Burke see *Corr.* I, 279.

Nagles and the rest of the Catholic gentry also ceased to be under the alarming pressures they had experienced in 1765 and 1766. The oligarchy itself came under pressure, from a quarter which had nothing to do with the Rockinghams or Burke. Lord Townshend (1724–1807) became Lord Lieutenant in 1767 and ruled Ireland in a more substantial sense than any of his predecessors had done. Unlike them, he resided in Ireland and set himself, successfully, to curb the autonomy of the Protestant governing caste, which hated him proportionately. By the end of the Townshend Viceroyalty, as a modern historian puts it, 'the oligarchy had been broken'.[1] From 1767 on, Burke was more visibly preoccupied with America than with Irish affairs. There was a certain interaction between the two concerns which will be considered in Chapter III, 'American Colonies, Ireland'. But independently of America, Ireland continued to preoccupy Burke – to haunt him, would not be too much to say – throughout his life, even if the fires of persecution were never again to come as near to him as they did in 1765–66, through his Irish connections.

Burke and his Nagle relatives must have been hugely relieved by the advent of Townshend's 'direct rule' and the curbing of the Protestant oligarchy. But you would not infer as much from Burke's surviving references to the subject. In letters to Charles O'Hara he is mildly sarcastic about Townshend. In his persona as a good Rockingham Whig, he is almost obliged to be anti-Townshend who, in the Rockingham view, is controlling the Irish Parliament by the same arts as those by which the King was controlling the English Parliament, through the Duke of Grafton, then acting head of the Ministry in London. So Burke, writing to O'Hara is anti-Townshend, *ex officio*, as it were, while showing that he entertains no such personal animosity as he does towards Grafton: 'You are in a glorious situation, God bless you, in Ireland. You have a Lord Lieutenant that knows how to keep up the dignity of Government. His Grace of Grafton does as much for it here to the full; with this difference; that with the mobbish meanness of your Government you have something cheerful, something convivial, something that *looks like* good humour. Here with the same want of dignity and decorum, we have an harsh, unsocial, gloomy austerity of manner, that makes our domination

[1] See the article, 'The Townshend Viceroyalty of 1767–72' by Thomas Bartlett in *Penal Era and Golden Age: Essays in Irish History 1690–1800*, edited by Thomas Bartlett and D. W. Hayton, Ulster Historical Foundation (Belfast, 1979) p. 111. But the oligarchy was able to stage a come-back in the 1790s. See Chapter VI below, pp. 511–21.

not only contemptible, but disgustful and odious.'[1] A year later, he refers to 'your merry Lord Lieutenant and his melancholy Country.'[2] In fact Ireland was very much less a 'melancholy' Country, for the people about whom Burke cared most, in 1769 and 1770 than it had been in 1765–66. But he had always been reticent, as regards his personal connections with the Irish Catholic community, and after the 'great fear' of 1765–66, he had reason to be even more reticent than before. To show too much regard for a viceroy who was hated by Protestant Ireland might suggest dangerous associations. As the editors of the first two volumes of the *Correspondence*, Thomas Copeland and Lucy Sutherland, have pointed out, 'Burke not only took little care to preserve his correspondence but destroyed much of it, in particular that part which concerned his private and family affairs, about which he was almost morbidly sensitive.'[3]

He had reason to be careful, even into the 1770s. In April 1770, on the floor of the House, a country gentleman, Sir William Bagot, said of some debating point of Burke's; 'Such an idea, such a picture, where cou'd it be formed? I should only think it came from one bred at St. Omer's'. It was the old 'Jesuit' smear. Lord John Cavendish, on behalf of the Rockinghams, rebuked Bagot, who then apologised. This did not save him from a stinging retort from Burke, who avoided calling his antagonist a liar, but only by the nicest of margins: '. . . he thought Gentlemen above the Invention of a Lie would scorn to adopt the dirty falsehood that a Newspaper was probably paid for propagating'.[4] Just over a week after that scene in the Commons, the *London Evening Post* published an article based on particulars innocently supplied four years earlier by Burke's old school friend, Richard Shackleton. It is improbable that this was a coincidence. Certain particulars quoted in the article, would create among many Protestant readers an impression of 'no smoke without fire'. Of Burke's mother, Shackleton had written: 'She was of a *Popish family*; I cannot say whether she legally conformed to the Church of England, but she practised the duties of the *Romish religion* with a decent privacy.' He describes Burke's wife Jane as 'a genteel, well-bred

[1] *Corr.* II, 97; letter of 24 October 1769.
[2] *Corr.* II, 177; letter of 31 December 1770.
[3] *Corr.* II, vii, viii.
[4] Burke's 'kinsman', Will Burke, reported on this episode to Edmund's old Trinity College friend, William Dennis, on 3–6 April 1770 (*Corr.* II, 126–9). Will says Edmund gave the House 'an account' of his education. It would be interesting to know exactly what he said. I would think it unlikely that Monanimy was mentioned.

woman, of the Roman faith, whom he married neither for her *religion*, nor her *money*, but from the natural impulse of youthful affection.'[1]

Shackleton had supplied the information in May 1766 in response to a letter from a Quaker correspondent in Dublin, requesting some information, at the request of 'a particular friend' of a 'Kinsman' of the correspondent. The 'particular friend' asked to be advised of the family Connections Religion (if any) and General Character of Edwd [sic] Bourk [sic] Secretary to the Marqu of Rockinham [sic], this enquiry is not made with any Design to prejudice E. Bourk but as he apprehends quite the Contrary therefore I request thou will give me Such an Answer as thou thinks proper and Post per return'.[2] The unworldly Shackleton supplied the information requested in this peculiar letter. Thomas Copeland writes: 'Having no suspicion whatever that the facts he had to relate might be used maliciously, Shackleton wrote a most complimentary short sketch of his friend.' Later that year, Burke got word of the inquiry, and was sufficiently concerned to ask Shackleton about it: 'I am given to understand that you have received at some time a letter from England, some way relating to me. Have you ever received such a letter?'[3]

No reply to this inquiry appears to have been preserved, and there appear to have been no immediate repercussions. Now, in 1770, when it all came out in public, Burke was furious. The episode temporarily strained the friendship, and it revealed Burke's extreme sensitivity to any public discussion of his Catholic family connections (see above pp. 3–15). Replying to a letter from Shackleton, he wrote:

> I confess a little weakness to you. I feel somewhat mortified at a paper written by you, which some officious person has thought proper to insert in the *London Evening Post* of last Night. I am used to the most gross and virulent abuse daily repeated in the papers – I ought indeed rather have said, twice a day. But this abuse is loose and general invective. It affects very little either my own feelings, or the opinions of others, because it is thrown out by those that are known to be hired to the Office

---

[1] Tn to Letter of 14–17 April; *Corr.* II, p. 129. Lucy Sutherland writes of 'a good deal of abuse of Burke in the Press by ministerial writers' about this time; *Corr.* II, 139, n4. This was after the publication of Burke's pamphlet. *Thoughts on the Cause of the Present Discontents* in April 1770 (see *Works* I, 433–537). The reaction suggests that Burke's 'Double Cabinet' theory may not have been as fanciful as some historians have supposed (see Introduction pp. li–liii).

[2] *Corr.* I, 271 n. 1

[3] *Corr.* I, 270–71; letter of 19 October 1766.

of my Enemies. But this appears in the Garb of professed apology and panegyrick. It is evidently written by an intimate friend. It is full of anecdotes and particulars of my Life. It therefore cuts deep. I am sure I have nothing in my family, my Circumstances, or my Conduct that an honest man ought to be ashamd of. But the more circumstances of all these which are brought out, the more materials are furnished for malice to work upon: and I assure you that it will manufacture them to the utmost. Hitherto, much as I have been abused, my Table and my bed were left sacred, but since it has so unfortunately happend, that my Wife, a quiet woman, confined to her family Cares and affections, has been dragged into a Newspaper, I own I feel a little hurt. A Rough public man may be proof against all sorts of Buffets, and he has no business to be a publick man if he be not so. But there is as natural and proper a delicacy in the other Sex, which will not make it very pleasant to my Wife to be the daily subject of Grubstreet, and newspaper invectives; and at present, in Truth her health is little able to endure it.[1]

In his reply, the deeply wounded Shackleton attains an eloquence which his Quaker principles would have suppressed, under ordinary circumstances. The letter also gives a vivid impression of how Edmund Burke, in an angry mood, appeared to a quiet friend. Shackleton wrote: 'My dear Friend, if I may take the liberty still to call thee so, I have received thy Letter written in the vexation of thy spirit, cutting and wounding in the tenderest parts, and ripping open a Sore which I thought was long ago healed. I know nothing in the world about the publication of that unfortunate paper, but what thou tells me; nor who could be the Publisher of it. I have used thee and thy family grossly ill. I acknowledged it as fully as I could. I am covered with Grief, Shame, and Confusion for it. It was done in the Simplicity of my heart: I mean the writing of it. The giving a Copy of it I will not call Indiscretion, but Madness and Folly. With the same Simplicity I before let thee Know how I came to write it, and why I gave a Copy of it. When I had given it to my Friend, and he had given a Copy to his Friend, it very probably circulated out of the power of either of us to recall. It passed like money through the hands of People, good and bad, friends and enemies: and because the matter was Gold though bunglingly coined, and possibly still more defaced in the circulation, it was too precious to be lost. I am sure I had no more thoughts of it's spreading as it has done, nor of it's ever being published, than I have of the Publication of this Letter. If what has been published

[1] *Corr.* II, 129–33; letter of 19 April 1770.

varies at all from the Copy which I sent thee, or if I can do any thing by way of atonement or amendment, grant me this last favour of putting it in my power to do it. . . . I said thy letter cut and wounded me: it did indeed effectually. It was dictated by a perturbed mind: it was calculated to punish and fret me; and it has obtained its end. Thy family, thy circumstances, thy conduct, thy bed, thy board; I am indirectly or directly charged with defaming and vilifying them all; not indeed as a false friend, but as a very foolish one. I could bear even all this, whether deserved or not, from thee. Thou art so used to lay about thee, and give and take no Quarter with thy Enemies, that it is unsafe for thy friends to be near thee. If there be any of the language of Friendship in thy Letter, it is only like oil, to make the edge more keen: if the voice be any where like Jacob's the hands are Esau's. Thou art grown a rough publick man, sure enough – I say I could bear even this from thee; (for I know both my own heart and thine,) and if the affair lay only between ourselves, there might some time be an end of it. But thy mention of my interfering in thy dom-estick connexions and dragging the Partner of thy bed and the soft-ener of thy busy Scenes of life into a News-Paper is wounding to the last degree. Whatever thou art pleased to think of me, I have, Perhaps, and (for aught I know) ever had as great delicacy in these matters as any man. Look into that ill-advised, impertinent Paper which I stupidly wrote, and see is there any thing that offends against the nicest delicacy.'[1]

Burke's reply of 6 May 1770 is worthy of himself and of Shackle-ton. It also gives some idea of the stress Burke is under at this time:

> My dear friend, I am now in the place, from whence I was weak and blameable enough to write you a very angry, a very Cruel, and in all respects a very improper Letter. I will not be more dilatory in making all the amends in my power for the offence, than I was in offending. So I write immediately on the receipt of your Letter. But let my apology be, if it be one, that a Spirit, not naturally over patient had about that time ten thousand things to mortifye it; and this coming on the back of them did for a while put me beside myself. I assure you I am so concerned for what you have felt that I could not bear to read through your description of it. A little triffling mere imprudence, at worst, did by no means deserve any thing like a reproof; much less so harsh an one. As to my Wife you needed to make no apology at all to her. She felt nothing but goodwishes and friendship to you, and is by no means liable to those Spurts of Passion to which I am unfortunately but too subject.

[1] *Corr.* II, 133–5; letter of 28 April 1770.

Burke, while reconciled and magnamimous, is also characteristically wary, for he adds;

> burn the Letter I wrote which deserves no better fate; and may I beg since it is one of the drawbacks on those who get a little consideration in the world, that every little matter relative to them, how unfit soever for the publick Eye, is dragged before it by one means or other, that you would commit to the same flames any other letters or papers of mine which you may find and which you think liable, through some accident to be so abused. It is hardly credible how many people live by such publications and how hard it is altogether to escape their interested diligence.[1]

The exchange in the House with Sir William Bagot apart (and the altercation with his friend Richard) Burke felt, on the whole, that he had come reasonably well out of what had been a stormy parliamentary session for him personally, principally through his Irish connections. He wrote to Charles O'Hara on 21 May 1770: 'After saying so much of the general State of things you will expect I should say a word of myself. I must say, that the Session ended well for me, I thank God. I have no doubt that a plan had been formed, by general calumny of every kind, as well as by personal attacks in Parliament, to reduce my little consideration to none at all. So it has happend, that (notwithstanding I find every thing which goes through the Irish Channel is very unfavourably reported for me) the malice of my Enemies has not overpowerd me; on the contrary it has been of service to me.'[2] In June he writes to O'Hara in a lighter vein, but still with a touch, though only a touch, of that Burkean 'edge' which had cut Shackleton so deeply. As we have seen, the 'edge' shows in the jocular affectation of casting O'Hara in the role of a persecutor of Papists: 'You need not doubt of the pleasure I should have had in being of your Party on the Lake of Killarney. Killarney with all its Beauties would not have been necessary, to make a party with you a pleasant one to me. It must have been pleasant to you who have a Taste for improvements in a Country, and in mankind, to see the judicious and humane plans of my Lord Kenmare.[3] He was always a publick spirited man. I have seen him once or twice; and he seemd to me to have a great deal of well cultivated sense. But he is a Papist,

---

[1] *Corr.* II, pp. 135–6.
[2] *Corr.* II, 137–40.
[3] Thomas Browne, fourth Viscount Kenmare (1726–95), a leader of the Irish Catholics at this time: for his role in the 1790s (more conservative than Burke's) see Chapter VI.

And you know that such a man cannot and ought not to be endured in your Country, no more than the honest Anabaptist at Lisbon. I remember they were going to fall upon him as well as upon others on the Treasonable Plot of the White Boys. Mais cultivons Notre Jardin – in spite of blind Sons, disagreeable wives, party rage, ignorance, and bigotry – If we wait until these evils cease to be the lot of the best as well as the worst men, we shall have no Cabbages.'[1] Burke had clearly been reading Voltaire's *Candide*.

There is also a certain deceptive affectation of treating Irish affairs as parochial, something for someone like O'Hara to attend to, but a bit below the level of Burke's attention. 'As to your proceedings in Ireland, I begin to feel every day less and less, any interest in them; I thank God it is so; for otherwise, I should have uneasiness on what side soever I lookd.' In November he writes: 'What is your Government, if Government at all it be doing? Their scheme seems to me the destruction of the Grants.[2] Never certainly was there more abuse in any practice – but a reformation might, and I think would, unless conducted with care and sobriety greatly retard the improvement of *your* Country – I was going to say ours – but I have not much more interest in it, than that it furnishes some matter of reproach against me to the Scotch writers in pay of the Ministry, without any one in that Country thinking himself concerned in supporting me. It is bad to be loaded with the local prejudices against a Country without getting any thing by those in favour of it.'[3]

Less 'interest', but also less uneasiness. Burke, as became clear later in the decade (below pp. 75–85), was still deeply interested in Ireland, and in particular in the disabilities of the Irish Catholics. But he needed, in the early 1770s, to keep his distance from an Ireland which had come frighteningly close in 1765–66. Detachment and even dissimulation were desirable, both in the interests of his personal career and in order to help Ireland, and specifically the Catholics, as he signally did in 1778 (below p. 78) in the persona of a disinterested and liberal observer of the Irish scene. Even as late as November 1771, and even in England, Burke was still suspected of sympathy with the Jacobite cause, almost extinct though it was. In a very long letter to Dr. William Markham (1719–1807; at the time he was bishop of Chester), dated '*post* November 1771', Burke defended

---

[1] *Corr.* II, 143; letter of 20 June 1770.
[2] 'Grants to individuals and organisations out of public funds' were cut by Lord Townshend as a matter of economy. *Corr.* II, 287, n. 6
[3] *Corr.* II, 287–8.

himself on that score: 'My passions are not to be roused either on the side of partiality or on that of hatred, by those who lye in their cold lead quiet and innoxious in the Chapel of Henry 7 in the Churches of Windsor Castle or La Trappe[1]. . . . My Lord in charging us with indiscretion, together with the word stuarts, you have coupled the revolution; If I were to guess at a charge of indiscretion, from the Credit and fortunes of Men, I should on this occasion suppose we had spoken too favourably of that Event. But do you mean the contrary? And under this and the foregoing words seriously intend to insinuate a charge of Jacobitism? Then be it so – I am afraid that our Enemies who do not allow us *common* Virtues, will hardly agree with you in giving us the credit of so amazing, and *supernatural* a fidelity; that at the Expense of fame and fortune, and every thing dear to Man, we should choose to be attached to a person [The Jacobite Pretender] when He is deserted by the whole world and by himself. When He has, as I am told, not so much as a single Scotch, English, or Irish footman about him. Truly we never were so wonderfully dazzled with the splendours of actual royalty, as to be captivated with what is not even the shadow of it; nor ever was so in my time.' Burke defended – quite boldly in the context – his personal view that the Irish (Catholic) Rebellion of 1641 was not unprovoked. 'Indeed I *have* my opinion on that part of history, which I have often delivered to you; to every one I conversed with on the Subject, and which I mean still, to deliver whenever the occasion calls for it. Which is "That the Irish Rebellion of 1641 was not only (as our silly things called Historys call it), not utterly *unprovoked* but that no History, that I have ever read furnishes an Instance of any that was so *provoked*." And that "in almost all parts of it, it has been extremely and most absurdly misrepresented."'[2]

Burke needed to rid himself of that shadow of suspicion before he could render efficacious aid to the Irish Catholics. From the late 1760s to the late 1770s, we find him primarily preoccupied with his parliamentary responsibilities, with his Bristol constituency, and with the affairs of America. As it happened, however, the topic of Ireland spilled over into all three contexts. In the main, Burke's activities in relation to Ireland constitute a strong refutation of Namier's sneer about 'the men whose livery he happened to have taken' (see Introduction p. xlvi). Over Ireland, he almost always acted on his own

[1] Burke seems to have believed that James II was buried at La Trappe, which was not the case (see *Corr.* II, 281, n. 2).
[2] *Corr.* II, 282, 284–5.

personal initiative and he pushed disinterestedness to the verge of political suicide as we shall see (below pp. 71–78). However there is one Irish issue on which his conduct may appear vulnerable. This is the matter of a tax on absentee landlords, mooted in 1773. As mentioned earlier, Burke was nominally the owner of a small estate in Ireland at Clogher, Co. Cork (see above p. 51). Much more significantly, Rockingham owned large estates in Ireland, and stood to lose heavily by the passage of the Bill. It may therefore seem plausible to infer that the opposition to the Bill, by Rockingham and Burke, was dictated by their material interests, in particular, Rockingham's. This would fit neatly into the Namier view. That Burke's opposition to the Absentee Tax was compatible with his leader's material interests is obvious. But was opposition to the Absentee Tax compatible with the general principles on which Burke acted concerning the relationship between Ireland and Britain? I find that opposition to the Absentee Tax entirely consistent. His guiding principle was the exact reverse of that of the father of Irish Republicanism, Theobald Wolfe Tone. Tone wanted 'to break the connection with England, the never failing source of all our political evils.' Burke wanted to strengthen that connection by making it more equitable, both in general by abolishing restraints on trade between the two countries, and specifically, in relation to the majority of the Irish people, by dismantling the Penal Code. He thought that objective much more likely to be achieved through the British Parliament, than through an Irish Parliament, made up of Protestant resident landlords. He did not want Members of Parliament who had estates in both kingdoms – as had both Rockingham whom Burke loved, and Shelburne (see below pp. 233–242) whom he detested – to be forced to choose between one or other kingdom as their place of residence. In general, he thought that what Ireland needed was the removal of existing restraints and penalties, rather than the introduction of new ones; and the strengthening, not the weakening, of relations between the two kingdoms. Burke's writings on the Absentee Tax have the ring of conviction, and are animated by the same spirit as animates the rest of his writing about Ireland. To Rockingham, he wrote on 29 September 1773: 'I never can forget that I am an Irishman. I flatter myself perhaps; but I think, I would shed my blood rather than see the Limb I belong to oppressed and defrauded of its due nourishment. But this measure tends to put us out of our place; and not to improve us in our natural situation. It is the mere effect of narrowness and passion and if it should take effect would bring on the Natural consequence of these causes. Perhaps this Country by dispositions and actions of a similar Nature has taught this Lesson to a scholar more docile than informed. These are the sentiments which I entertain, in common, I believe, with your Lordships friends. But I am not at all certain, that it will affect people in the same manner even in England. There is a superficial appearance of Equity in this Tax, which cannot fail to captivate almost all those who are not led by some immediate Interest to an attentive examination of its intrinsick merits.'[1] Characteristically, Burke does not dissemble the existence of 'Interest', but finds it conducive to 'attentive examination' which exposes the weaknesses of the proposed Absentee Tax. Responding both to the force of the 'attentive examination' and to the weight of the 'Interest' behind it, the Government – after the measure had been defeated in the Committee of Ways and Means of the Irish House of Commons in November 1773 – dropped the proposed tax, and Burke did not have to return to the matter.

MEMBER FOR BRISTOL
1774–80

In 1774 Edmund Burke was elected Member for Bristol. This was a great step forward in his political career, and a great enhancement of his parliamentary status. Hitherto, he had been member for the insignificant pocket borough of Wendover. Now he was the representative of a great and thriving port, the second city in Great Britain. If he had been the unprincipled opportunist whom some historians depict, or even if he had been just an average politician, he would have nursed his new and prestigious constituency with the utmost care and would have avoided any course which would run counter to the perceived interests of his constituents, or offend their prejudices. He failed to follow this prudent and obvious political course. He put free trade principles, in relation to trade between Ireland and Britain, ahead of the perceived interests of his most powerful constituents in April 1778. And then he went on in the following

[1] *Corr.* II, 468. See also letter to Sir Charles Bingham, 30 October 1773, *Corr.* II, 474–81. Owen Dudley Edwards adds: 'To me Burke on the absentee tax and in his general relations with Rockingham is reflecting some of the anger about resident but rapacious and absolutely unimproving landlords, Rockingham himself being a great improver' (letter to the author).

month to offend their prejudices, by helping to bring about the first legislative measure which relaxed the Penal Code against Catholics. At the beginning of April British reverses in America (see below pp. 184–5) and France's entry into the war led to various proposals for dealing with the crisis. One set of proposals, supported by Burke, concerned trade with Ireland and these were approved in Committee.[1] They provided for the direct importation of Irish goods, except woollens, into the colonies, and of colonial products, except tobacco and indigo, into Ireland; the exportation of Irish glass; and the abolition of duties on cotton yarn, sailcloth and cordage imported into Britain from Ireland.

Realising that this measure would not go down well in Bristol, Burke wrote to one of his most prominent constituents and supporters, Samuel Span, of the Society of Merchant Adventurers: 'It is found absolutely necessary to improve the portion of this Empire which is left so as to enable every part to contribute in some degree to the strength and welfare of the whole. Our late misfortunes have taught us the danger and mischief of a restrictive coercive and partial policy. The trade in some degree opened by the resolutions is necessary, not so much for any benefit thereby derived to Ireland as to satisfy and unite the minds of men at this juncture by the sense of a common interest in the common defence. If nothing of this kind should be done I apprehend very serious consequences. Ireland may probably in some future time come to participate of the benefits which we derive from the West India Trade. But Ireland being a Country of the same nature with this can never be beneficial to this Kingdom but by pursuing several, if not all, of the objects of commerce and manufacture which are cultivated here. The world I apprehend is large enough for all, and we are not to conclude that what is gained to one part of it is lost of course to the other. The prosperity arising from an enlarged and liberal system improves all its objects: and the participation of a trade with flourishing Countries is much better than the monopoly of want and penury. These opinions I am satisfied will be relished by the clear understanding of the Merchants of Bristol who will discern that a great Empire cannot at this time be supported upon a narrow and restrictive scheme either of commerce or government'.[2]

Constituents generally don't care to be addressed in such a way

---

[1] *Corr.* III, 426.
[2] Letter of 9 April 1778 in *Corr.* III, 426.

by their parliamentary representative, and it seems that Span was no exception. His reply of 13 April strikes an ominous note, with respect to Burke's prospects in the next election: 'Mr Burke's Letter of the 9th Instant, transmitting copy of the Resolutions of the Committee of the House of Commons on the Trade of Ireland, was this day read at a general Meeting of this Society –; The City are greatly alarmed at the Measure, and intend to oppose it all in their power, and We are sorry that We are likely to be deprived of so able an Advocate as Mr Burke –. Ireland has many local Advantages over us, and their Dutys are not in some instances (particularly Sugar) above one fourth of ours, the difference between English and Irish Money considered –; The Revenue in England will likewise be greatly diminished, and then Additional Taxes will be laid on –; It strikes us at present that it would be much better for this Kingdom that an Union should take place rather than this very prejudicial measure, and then We should be on a more equal footing –; The interest of Your Constituents and of the English Manufactures call for Your Strenuous opposition to this Plan.'[1]

Burke replied to Span, on 23 April 1778, in a long, earnest, and impressive letter. He took up Span's point about a union between Britain and Ireland:

> You tell me, Sir, that you prefer an union with Ireland to the little regulations which are proposed in parliament. This union is a great question of state, to which, when it comes properly before me in my parliamentary capacity, I shall give an honest and unprejudiced consideration. However, it is a settled rule with me, to make the most of my *actual situation*; and not to refuse to do a proper thing, because there is something else more proper, which I am not able to do. This union is a business of difficulty; and, on the principles of your letter, a business impracticable. Until it can be matured into a feasible and desirable scheme, I wish to have as close an union of interest and affection with Ireland as I can have; and that, I am sure, is a far better thing than any nominal union of government.[2]

He tries to get Span to see that Bristol, as well as Ireland, can benefit from increased Anglo-Irish trade:

> If I thought you inclined to take up this matter on local considerations, I should state to you, that I do not know any part of the kingdom so

---

[1] *Corr.* III, 429.
[2] *Corr.* III, 434.

well situated for an advantageous commerce with Ireland as Bristol; and that none would be so likely to profit of its prosperity as our city. But your profit and theirs must concur. Beggary and bankruptcy are not the circumstances which invite to an intercourse with that or with any country; and I believe it will be found invariably true, that the superfluities of a rich nation furnish a better object of trade than the necessities of a poor one. It is the interest of the commercial world that wealth should be found everywhere.

He ends with a notable declaration of the duty of a public representative:

I have written this long letter, in order to give all possible satisfaction to my constituents, with regard to the part I have taken in this affair. It gave me inexpressible concern to find, that my conduct had been a cause of uneasiness to any of them. Next to my honour and conscience, I have nothing so near and dear to me as their approbation. However, I had much rather run the risk of displeasing than of injuring them; – if I am driven to make such an option. You obligingly lament, that you are not to have me for your advocate; but if I had been capable of acting as an advocate in opposition to a plan so perfectly consonant to my known principles, and to the opinions I had publicly declared on a hundred occasions, I should only disgrace myself, without supporting, with the smallest degree of credit or effect, the cause you wished me to undertake. I should have lost the only thing which can make such abilities as mine of any use to the world now or hereafter; I mean that authority which is derived from an opinion, that a member speaks the language of truth and sincerity; and that he is not ready to take up or lay down a great political system for the convenience of the hour; that he is in parliament to support his opinion of the public good, and does not form his opinion in order to get into parliament, or to continue in it. It is in a great measure for your sake, that I wish to preserve this character. Without it, I am sure, I should be ill able to discharge, by any service, the smallest part of that debt of gratitude and affection which I owe you for the great and honourable trust you have reposed in me.[1]

Statements should always be read in context and in this case, it is the context that proves the sincerity of the principle that is being asserted. Any politician, then or now, can utter noble principles that cost him nothing. But Burke, under pressure, is holding firm to a principle which brings him no material or career advantage, and

[1] *Corr.* III, 435–6.

which he knows may be about to cost him the greatest prize of his political career to date, his seat as Member of Parliament for Bristol. The principles he maintains, under Span's pressure, are those which he had declared on his election for Bristol in 1774:

Certainly, Gentlemen, it ought to be the happiness and glory of a representative to live in the strictest union, the closest correspondence, and the most unreserved communication with his constituents. Their wishes ought to have great weight with him; their opinions high respect; their business unremitted attention. It is his duty to sacrifice his repose, his pleasure, his satisfactions, to theirs, – and above all, ever, and in all cases, to prefer their interest to his own.

But his unbiased opinion, his mature judgement, his enlightened conscience, he ought not to sacrifice to you, to any man, or to any set of men living. These he does not derive from your pleasure, – no, nor from the law and the Constitution. They are a trust from Providence, for the abuse of which he is deeply answerable. Your representative owes you, not his industry only, but his judgement; and he betrays, instead of serving you, if he sacrifices it to your opinion.

Burke was distressed, but not daunted, by Span's threat. To a more friendly correspondent, John Noble (1743–1828), Burke writes on the very next day:

You are so good as to say, that you wish to see me Member for Bristol at the next general Election. I most sincerely thank you; and beg leave to add this friendly wish, to the innumerable obligations which I have to you already. To represent Bristol, is a capital Object of my Pride at present. Indeed I have nothing external, on which I can value myself, but that honourable situation. If I should live to the next general Election, and if being a Member of Parliament, at that time, should be desireable to me; I intend to offer myself again to your approbation. But far from wishing to throw the memory of the present business into the Shade, I propose to put it forward to you; and to plead my conduct on this Occasion, as a matter of Merit, on which to ground my pretentions to your future favour. I do not wish to represent Bristol, or to represent any place, but upon Terms that shall be honourable to the Chosen and to the Choosers.[1]

In the summer of 1778 the first measure relaxing the Penal Code passed through the British Parliament (and later through the Irish

---

[1] *Corr.* III, 438.

Parliament). Burke did not introduce it; he probably feared that its prospects would be damaged by its being introduced by the notorious 'Jesuit'. It was introduced by Sir George Savile (1726–84) a shrewd and influential Yorkshire country gentleman, and a close friend of Rockingham. Burke, who would have been Rockingham's accepted authority about Irish matters, drafted the Bill, and did a lot of lobbying for it, with other groups, and even with Lord North. Its essence – which received the Royal Assent on 3 June and became known as the Catholic Relief Act – was the relaxation of the restrictions upon the ownership of property by Catholics, and the abolition of the threat of forfeiture to Protestant relatives and informers. It repealed one of the earliest and most effective of the Penal Laws (11 and 12 Will. III c.) On the day it passed, Burke wrote a letter explaining the strategy behind it:

> Some people, who heartily agreed with us in the principle of our proceedings, were of opinion, that, in an affair like this, involved in a Multitude of penal regulations and disabilities, we ought not to have satisfied ourselves with the repeal of a Single Act of Parliament, whilst we suffered grievances to continue under other unrepealed Acts, which were of as harsh an Nature as those, to which we had given a remedy. I admit this larger plan would have been theoretically preferable, and was most suitable to the firm and systematick mind of the Attorney general, who recommended it. But it was too large for the time; and it would inevitably have entangled us in the speculations of every rash and busy Mind. In a popular Assembly we should never have found an End to a work of this kind. It was necessary to come with simplicity and directness to the point, and to repeal that Act, which, with the least apparent cruelty had the most certain operation; leaving those Laws, which from their very savageness and ferocity, were more noisy than effective, to wait for a time of greater leisure. Neither was the choice of this method wholly blind and without a principle; for it affirmed that *property* was to be encouraged in the acquisition, and quieted in the holding, whatever might become of religious toleration; and *disabilities* were to be removed though penalties might remain; as the latter however unjustifiable and opposite of Christian Charity and protestant principles, did not so directly sap the foundation of the national prosperity.[1]

---

[1] To Unknown [*circa* 3 June 1778] *Corr.* III, 455. The 'Unknown' may have been Sir Lucius O'Brien, who helped to carry a similar measure through the Irish Parliament.

The Attorney General referred to in this letter is almost certainly Edward Thurlow (1731–1806; he was Attorney General until that same 3 June, when he became Lord Chancellor). It happens that Thurlow has left a striking record of what it felt like to be lobbied by Burke, on the subject of the Penal Laws. To Burke himself, Thurlow wrote, after talking with him: 'I am ashamed to confess how much emotion your display of the Popery Law in Ireland raised and how much it unfitted me to form any *judgement* upon them. If one so . . . phlegmatic as myself feels in that Is it impossible that all your knowledge may not find a formidable adversary in your Feeling.'[1]

Burke's management of the first repeal of a Penal Law was conducted mainly behind the scenes, but it attracted the favourable attention of the Irish Catholic Committee which, at its November meeting in Dublin, voted to present him with five hundred guineas. He civilly declined the offer, and urged the Committee to use the money 'to give some aid to places of education for your own youth at home, which is indeed much wanted'.[2]

His activities on behalf of the Irish Catholics also attracted less favourable attention from other quarters. Inevitably the passage of the Catholic Relief Act aroused great resentment among fervent Protestants. Although Burke's vital role in the preparation and passage of that Act had been discreet, he had already marked himself out as a champion of Catholic Relief by presenting to the Commons the petition of the Scottish Catholics in March, 1779.[3]

The Gordon Riots, in the first week of June 1780, came about when Lord George Gordon, accompanied by a crowd of some 60,000, brought to the House of Commons the petition of the Protestant Association for the repeal of the Act. Lord George at intervals addressed supporters outside the House while the petition was debated within. Burke's responsibility for the measure was known to the petitioners, many of whom became rioters. A witness, Lord Frederick Cavendish, noted Lord George's 'inflammatory Speeches' to his supporters, 'Particularly against Burke'. His life was threatened, on several occasions during the riots, and witnesses attested his courageous conduct. He was not injured physically but he was

[1] *Corr.* IV, 9, n. 2.
[2] Letter of 14 August 1779, to Dr John Curry, *Corr.* IV, 118–120. Curry was a distinguished scholar and an old friend of Burke's. They shared a strong interest in Irish history. But Curry was writing on behalf of the Catholic Committee and Burke was replying in the persona of a benevolent Protestant.
[3] See Mahoney, *Burke and Ireland*, pp. 92–3.

injured politically. Most Englishmen condemned the rioters, but some also blamed those whose imprudent sponsorship of the measure had 'provoked' the riots. And some of the people who were thinking along these lines lived in Bristol, where Burke was about to face an election in the Autumn of the same year.

Between the riots of June and the elections in September we find him writing to a Bristol hosier, Job Watts: 'You tell me besides, that religious prejudices have set me ill in the Minds of some people. I do not know how this could possibly happen, as I do not know, that I have ever offerd either in a publick or private capacity, an hardship or even an affront to the religious prejudices of any person whatsoever. I have been a steady friend, since I came to the use of reason to the Cause of religious toleration, not only as a Christian and a protestant, but as one concernd for the civil welfare of the Country in which I live, and in which I have for some time discharged a publick Trust. I never thought it wise, My dear Mr Watts, to force men into Enmity to the State by ill Treatment, upon any pretence either of civil or religious party; and if I never thought it wise in any Circumstances, still less do I think it wise when we have lost one half of our Empire [America] by one idle quarrel, to distract, and perhaps to Lose too, the other half by another quarrel, not less injudicious and absurd. No people ought to be permitted to live in a Country, who are not permitted to have an Interest in its Welfare, by quiet in their goods, their freedom, and their conscience.'[1]

Next day, 11 August, writing to another constituent, John Noble, Burke refers sardonically to 'the rout made about my Conduct relative to the late *acts of scanty and imperfect toleration*'; [The Catholic Relief Acts – in Britain and in Ireland] and asks if the Act 'was of a nature so distasteful to any of my Constituents why did none of them express their dislike of it untill two years after it was passed?'[2] The answer is of course that the Gordon Riots of June 1780 had given a new and lurid salience – which had been lacking in 1778 – to Burke as an agent for the promotion of Catholic interests. And this view of Burke mingled, in a manner most awkward for him, with the perhaps more deep-seated resentment of his promotion of Irish Trade.

Obviously, we can never be quite certain that the Irish issues were the principal causes of the loss of support in Bristol which led Burke to withdraw from the contest in September. John Morley, Glad-

---

[1] *Corr.* IV, 260–2.
[2] *Corr.* IV. 263.

stone's biographer and the leading nineteenth-century authority on Burke, thought that they were. 'He had lost his seat in Bristol in consequence of his courageous advocacy of a measure of toleration for Catholics and his even more courageous exposure of the enormities of the commercial policy of England towards Ireland.'[1] Burke himself in his '*Speech at Bristol, in the Guildhall, Previous to the Election*' discusses 'matters which have been at various times objected to me in this city': 'These charges, I think, are four in number: my neglect of a due attention to my constituents, the not paying more frequent visits here; my conduct on the affairs of the first Irish Trade Acts; my opinion and mode of proceeding on Lord Beauchamp's Debtors' Bill; and my votes on the late affairs of the Roman Catholics.'

The two 'Irish' charges are the ones that concern us here. This Bristol speech occupies fifty-six pages in the edition of Burke's works that I am using. Of these the 'Irish' charges together take up forty-three pages, very unevenly divided: six pages on Irish trade and thirty-seven on 'the late affairs of the Roman Catholics'.[2] It is clear, at least, that Burke himself attached far more importance to the 'Irish' and in particular the 'Catholic' charges against him than to the others. The attention he gives to the 'Catholic' charges might appear excessive, since Burke himself, in opening up the subject, acknowledges that he had found very little (overt) anti-Popery in Bristol:

> Nothing now remains to trouble you with but the fourth charge against me, – the business of the Roman Catholics. It is a business closely connected with the rest. They are all on one and the same principle. My little scheme of conduct, such as it is, is all arranged [arraigned?]. I could do nothing but what I have done on this subject, without confounding the whole train of my ideas and disturbing the whole order of my life. Gentlemen, I ought to apologize to you for seeming to think anything at all necessary to be said upon this matter. The calumny is fitter to be scrawled with the midnight chalk of incendiaries, with 'No Popery,' on walls and doors of devoted houses, than to be mentioned in any civilized company. I had heard that the spirit of discontent on that subject was very prevalent here. With pleasure I find that I have been grossly misinformed. If it exists

---

[1] Entry on Burke, *Encyclopaedia Britannica*, Eleventh Edition (1910–11). Morley understates Burke's services to Catholic Emancipation. It wasn't just 'courageous advocacy'; Burke played a leading part in repealing the Penal Laws.

[2] *The Works of the Right Honourable Edmund Burke in twelve Volumes*, London 1899, Vol. II, pp. 367–423. For editions of the *Works*, see 'Sources'.

at all in this city, the Laws have crushed its exertions, and our morals have shamed its appearance in daylight. I have pursued this spirit wherever I could trace it; but it still fled from me. It was a ghost which all had heard of, but none had seen. None would acknowledge that he thought the public proceeding with regard to our Catholic dissenters to be blamable; but several were sorry it had made an ill impression upon others, and that my interest was hurt by my share in the business. I find with satisfaction and pride, that not above four or five in this city (and I dare say those misled by some gross misrepresentation) have signed that symbol of delusion and bond of sedition, that libel on the national religion and English character, the Protestant Association. It is, therefore, Gentlemen, not by way of cure, but of prevention, and lest the arts of wicked men may prevail over the integrity of any one amongst us, that I think it necessary to open to you the merits of this transaction pretty much at large; and I beg your patience upon it; for, although the reasonings that have been used to depreciate the act are of little force, and though the authority of the men concerned in this ill design is not very imposing, yet the audaciousness of these conspirators against the national honour, and the extensive wickedness of their attempts, have raised persons of little importance to a degree of evil eminence, and imparted a sort of sinister dignity to proceedings that had their origin in only the meanest and blindest malice.[1]

'Several were sorry it had made an ill impression upon others.' Overt anti-Catholicism had become unfashionable in late eighteenth-century Britain. People of substance, like those who came to the Guildhall to listen to Edmund Burke, did not want to be associated with riff-raff, like the supporters of Lord George Gordon. At the same time, some of the respectable citizens of Bristol were disposed to blame Burke, for having provoked the Gordon Riots, by an untimely and unnecessary zeal for removal of Catholic disabilities. Again, a Jewish analogy is possible. Overt anti-semitism is unfashionable, in late twentieth-century Britain (and America), just as overt anti-Catholicism had become unfashionable in late eighteenth-century Britain. But coded anti-Catholicism was acceptable then, just as coded anti-semitism is acceptable now. Modern anti-semitism often appears in the respectable guise of an exceptionally sensitive anti-anti-semitism. The speaker opposes a given course of action, not on anti-semitic grounds, but quite the contrary; because the course of action in question might provoke anti-semitic reactions, and that is what the speaker wants above all things to avoid. An anti-anti-

[1] *Works* II, 388–9.

Catholicism of that type was the impalpable and invisible force against which Edmund Burke struggled and lost in the Bristol Guildhall in September 1780. That was 'the ghost which all had heard of but none had seen'.

Accurately, but disingenuously, Burke disclaimed having proposed or seconded the Catholic Relief Bill of 1778: 'I will now tell you by whom the bill of repeal was brought into Parliament. I find it has been industriously given out in this city (from kindness to me, unquestionably) that I was the mover or the seconder. The fact is, I did not once open my lips on the subject during the whole progress of the bill I do not say this as disclaiming my share in that measure. Very far from it. I inform you of this fact, lest I should seem to arrogate to myself the merits which belongs to others.'[1] Burke had indeed neither proposed, nor seconded, the Catholic Relief Bill, nor had he spoken in favour of it. All the same, he had been the guiding spirit who had shaped the measure, and organised its passage:[2] Lord George Gordon's 'Protestant Association' suspected as much, and that was the factor which had raised Edmund Burke 'to a degree of evil eminence' which some of his constituents did not care for. They may not have realised the full extent of his responsibility for the passage of the Catholic Relief Act, but his support for it was avowed and defended by him. And that, for some of his constituents, appears to have been enough. In retrospect from the autumn of 1780, to have voted for the Catholic Relief Bill of 1778, was to have a share in the responsibility for the Gordon Riots of June 1780. A Bristol merchant, thinking of himself as a moderate, could look with disfavour on the extremism of Lord George Gordon, on the one hand, and of Edmund Burke on the other, thus bracketing the Member for Bristol with a half-crazy incendiarist. This view of the matter must have been high among the factors which convinced Burke that he could not win, and so induced him to withdraw from the contest in Bristol. Even on the day of his withdrawal, Burke still had some warm friends in Bristol. One of these, Richard Champion, thus described the proceedings for Rockingham. 'I never was present at a more moving Scene. There were, My Lord, very few dry Eyes in Court. When he finished, it was not so much a Plaudit, as a burst of Affectionate Regard. A general Silence succeeded, and we all returned with him to the Town House, with the same degree of Solemnity, as if the people had lost their best

[1] *Works* II, 396.
[2] See Morley, *Burke* (London, 1902) p. 137.

friend and were following him to the Grave. The Streets were crowded with people, who though of different parties, and of different descriptions, universally joined in the solemn and silent tribute of affectionate Regard.'[1]

In justifying his support for repeal, Burke gave his constituents an extensive review of the character and history of the Irish Penal Laws. The culminating part of this review consists of the following semi-autobiographical paragraph, concerning their impact:

> In this situation men not only shrink from the frowns of a stern magistrate; but they are obliged to fly from their very species. The seeds of destruction are sown in civil intercourse, in social habitude. The blood of wholesome kindred is infected. Their tables and beds are surrounded with snares. All the means given by Providence to make life safe and comfortable, are perverted into instruments of terror and torment. This species of universal subserviency, that makes the very servant who waits behind your chair the arbiter of your life and fortune, has such a tendency to degrade and abase mankind, and to deprive them of that assured and liberal state of mind, which alone can make us what we ought to be, that I vow to God I would sooner bring myself to put a man to immediate death for opinions at once, than to fret him with a feverish being, tainted with the jail-distemper of a contagious servitude, to keep him above ground an animated mass of putrefaction, corrupted himself, and corrupting all about him.[2]

This is the closest glimpse we get of the festering wound of Philoctetes (above p. 13).

In that extraordinary Swiftian passage, Burke is not simply inveighing against bad laws. He is talking, surely, about something that has touched him personally and caused him deep personal anguish. The emphasis on contamination – 'corruption', 'infection', 'contagious' – is significant. For the mass of Roman Catholics, those who openly adhered to their religion and neither conformed nor pretended to conform to Anglicanism, could not reasonably be described as 'corrupted' or 'infected'. They were simply oppressed, in a straightforward manner. Where the Penal Laws had a clear tendency to corrupt and infect, was among those who either conformed or pretended to conform to the Established Church, for

---

[1] *Corr.* IV, 280–1, letter of 11 September 1780.

[2] Guildhall speech at Bristol, September 1780. *Works* II, 395–6. Mahoney, in his paraphrase of this speech in *Burke and Ireland* (pp. 103–108) does not advert to this remarkable passage.

reasons of worldly ambition, social acceptability or fear. It was these who had best reason to know the corrupting potential of these laws. As we have seen, Burke's father almost certainly belonged in the category of whose who conformed, mainly for reasons of fear. Edmund himself had benefited from his father's decision, and his own consequent Anglican baptism. Without that, he could not have become Member of Parliament, for Bristol or anywhere else. And Burke's beloved wife belongs in the category of those who had once pretended to conform, in her case presumably for the sake of her husband's career. It is also reasonable to assume that her husband advised her to do so. When Burke speaks of 'infection' and 'corruption' in this context, he necessarily has his own family and personal situation most uncomfortably in mind. He loathes the Penal Laws, not merely for being unjust, but because of the false position in which the combined effects of the laws, and fear and worldly ambition, have placed the Burkes. This is what 'frets him with a feverish being.' and is clearly fretting him right there in the Guildhall, in the probably perplexed presence of the discontented burgesses of Bristol.

Burke's constancy in the cause of Ireland is all the more remarkable because of the horror which the condition of Ireland inspired in him, and because of the shame which he felt at the false positions imposed on his family by the Penal Laws and the need to dissimulate. A lesser person, circumstanced as he was, would have turned his back on Ireland altogether, and this would have been wholly to the advantage of his political career in Britain. It would have freed him from the 'Jesuit' albatross, which he carried round his neck throughout his political career. It would almost certainly have saved his seat at Bristol, whose retention would have enhanced his consequences in the House of Commons. Above all, by 'living down' his Irishness, and never saying or doing anything that could remind anyone of its existence, Burke would have become a more 'normal' person in the eyes of his English contemporaries, and therefore eligible for high office to which his talents, untainted by perceived Irishness, would have entitled him. Edmund Burke chose otherwise. He often spoke in the persona of an Englishman, but he never dropped Ireland altogether, which was the only way he could have induced Englishmen to take him seriously as one of themselves. Specifically, he failed to drop the cause of the Irish Catholics, the most compromising and the most disabling, by far, of all his Irish associations.

As we shall see, his Irish connections influenced him, in varying degrees, on other major issues of the day – America, France and

India. We have to ask ourselves the question; For what reason did Burke, to the detriment of his career in Britain, continue to cling to an Ireland which inspired in him the most lively sentiments of shame and horror? My own guess is that he needed to do so precisely in order to exorcise the shame and the horror, for the sake of his kinsfolk, of himself, and especially of his beloved son Richard, by leading the dismantling of the Penal Laws. The evidence in support of that general motivation appears in the first section of this chapter.

I believe there was also a special and more intimate motivation, which cannot be proved but is probable. This is that Burke, who often uses spectral metaphors, was haunted by the need to expiate a particular transaction. That transaction was the conversion – or apostasy – of his father, Richard (see above pp. 3–19). He did not refer to that transaction, or to any such transactions, in the 'contamination' passage of his Guildhall speech. In fact he never in any document that has been preserved directly refers to this specific transaction.[1] But he does refer to this *category* of transactions, in the course of a private letter to his son and in a tone very similar to that of the 'contamination' passage in the Guildhall speech. The letter to his son was written early in 1793, and thus belongs chronologically in Chapter VI of this book. I am, however, taking it into account here, at the close of Chapter I, because I think it sheds light on the 'contamination' part of the Guildhall speech. He is writing to Richard about Protestant domination in general as applied to Ireland, and specifically about the Oath of Conformity: 'Let three millions of people but abandon all that they and their ancestors have been taught to be sacred, and to forswear it publicly in terms the most degrading, scurrilous, and indecent for men of integrity and virtue, and to abuse the whole of their former lives, and to slander the education they have received, and nothing more is required of them.'[2]

The Oath of Conformity is that required by 2. Anne, c, 3: 'An Act to prevent the further growth of Popery (1704). This is what Burke called 'the ferocious act of Anne'. The Oath runs:

> I [Richard Burke] do solemnly and sincerely, in the presence of God, testify and declare, that I do believe, that in the sacrament of the Lord's Supper, there is not any transubstantiation of the elements of bread and wine into the body and blood of Christ, at or after the consecration

---

[1] It is known that Burke destroyed many of his private papers; see *Corr.* II, vii.
[2] *Works*, VI, 387–412; unfinished letter begun early in 1792; see *Corr.* VII, 65, n. 5.

thereof by any person whatsoever, and that the adoration or invocation of the Virgin Mary, or any other saint, and the sacrifice of the Mass, as they are now used in the Church of Rome, are superstitious and idolatrous.

Had Richard Burke, Edmund's father, and grandfather of young Richard, taken that oath, and so in Edmund's opinion, foresworn all that the Burke and Nagle ancestors had been taught to believe sacred? I believe that Edmund Burke's father did take that oath, and that Edmund's strong, painful and complex feelings about that trans-action had an important bearing on his life, and in particular on the later development of his political activity and thought. The taking of the Oath of Conformity was essentially a required act of submission and ritual humiliation, designed to deter conversions, rather than bring them about. The conforming party 'made his appearance at a public service in a place of Protestant worship and before the assembled congregation read his renunciation'[1]. Edmund Burke was a proud man, with a strong sense of family honour. He praised in *Reflections on the Revolution in France* those who 'felt an insult like a wound'. I infer – as probable from the 'contamination' passage in the Guildhall speech, and from the letter to his own son, twelve years later – that Burke felt his father's conformity as a stain on the family escutcheon which had to be wiped out. To most of us in the late twentieth century, the notion of a stain on an escutcheon may seem quaintly archaic and somewhat absurd. But for an eighteenth-century gentleman – especially a 'marginalised' gentleman closely linked to a conquered and outcaste people, as Burke was – a stain on the escutcheon was no laughing matter but something to brood over. He did a lot of brooding, and had a lot to brood over.

In another aspect of the family relationships, Burke, in undermin-ing the Penal Laws, may have been expiating the insult to his mother's faith, which his father had been obliged to inflict, in order to make possible his son's career. To discharge that debt, Edmund was in honour bound to subordinate that career, to a significant and costly degree, to the service of his mother's people. Finally, there was the

---

[1] 'The Irish Convert Rolls' by Francis Finegan SJ in *Studies*, Vol. XXXVIII (1949) pp. 72–82. The writer describes the person so conforming as 'a pervert'. Burke's hedge school companions at Monanimy may well on occasions have treated him as 'son of a pervert'. Eighteenth-century Catholic adults were inclined to be charitable about such a transaction, but an angry schoolboy will pounce on any vulnerable point.

question of his own son Richard, the apple of his father's eye. The Penal Code had, in different ways, 'ensnared the soul and body' of Burke's mother and father, and of himself. To save his son from that snare, he had to weaken, and if possible destroy, the Penal Code.

The idea of chivalry was important to Edmund Burke. Contemporaries sometimes saw him as Don Quixote, and the comparison is apt, within limits. The difference is that the foes whom Burke had to fight were real and not imaginary. If, as appears to be the case, he saw himself as a man with a dragon to slay, the dragon was real enough, as the Gordon Riots are there to testify. And he did deal the brute some swingeing blows, notably in the Catholic Relief Act of 1778 and in the removal of most of the remaining Catholic disabilities in 1793 (see below Chapter VI, p. 497). Burke thus rendered, at serious cost to his own political career, services to the Irish Catholic people: services which most of that people seem now to have almost entirely forgotten. But the services inspired by his experiences of Ireland were to extend to the world.

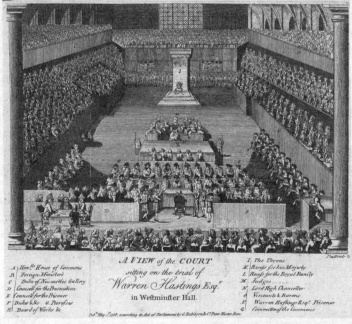

'The place was worthy of such a trial. It was the great hall of William Rufus; the hall which had resounded with acclamations at the inauguration of thirty Kings . . .' – Macaulay (p. 359)
Note: Burke is seated on the left hand side of table Q (in foreground) with Fox on his left.

II
American Colonies

'. . . It seems extremely doubtful whether Burke and his friends, if in power, would have succeeded in saving the First British Empire. Their ideas were no less hierarchical and authoritarian than those of George III and Lord North, and to them, too, trade was the soul of the Empire; had Burke been in office during the American Revolution we might have had to antedate his counter-revolutionary Toryism by some twenty years' –

SIR LEWIS NAMIER, *England in the Age of the American Revolution*, p. 45.

Mary Wollstonecraft. 'Reading your *Reflections* warily over, it has continually struck me, that had you been a Frenchman, you would have been, in spite of your respect for rank and antiquity, a violent revolutionist.' (p. 413)

Yeats's Metaphor and Burke's Pronouncements on America

The metaphor of the Great Melody does not seem to fit so closely to Burke's speeches and writings on America as it does to those on France and India (Ireland is in a category of its own; see Chapter I, *passim*). There are two reasons for this: first, in the pre-war stages of the American crisis, his emotions are not as directly involved as in the other two causes. Ross Hoffman, the American historian who made the first close study of Burke's American concerns (especially for the period 1770–1775) says 'there is not in him a trace of sentimental pro-Americanism – and his indignation at ministerial mismanagement of the colonies had always been a great deal warmer than his sympathy for their grievances'.[1] This seems to be true for the pre-war stages of the crisis, with which Hoffman is primarily concerned. But the *Correspondence*, from 1775 on, shows that Burke's emotions were strongly aroused, on the side of the colonists, once fighting broke out.[2]

Hoffman goes on: 'Conciliation of the colonies was to Burke a means rather than an end – a means of preserving the British Empire in North America. The tranquillity and prosperity of the Empire formed the object of his American politics, not the vindication of natural justice.' But Burke was not interested just in 'preserving' the British Empire; he was interested in seeing that it was run for the benefit of its inhabitants generally, and not just for the benefit of

[1] Hoffman, *Edmund Burke, New York Agent: with his letters to the New York Assembly and intimate correspondence with Charles O'Hara 1761–1776* (Philadelphia, 1956) p. 181.

[2] See below pp. 149–171 and 202–234. The modern edition of the *Correspondence* was not of course available in 1956, when Hoffman's book was published.

those represented in the Parliament of Great Britain (or in the Parliament of Ireland). And he was interested not only in the 'tranquillity and prosperity of the Empire' but also in its freedom; by which he meant that the full benefits of the British Constitution should be extended to all the subjects of the Crown. For Burke, conciliation was a means not merely of preserving the Empire but of extending its freedom. And when, with the outbreak of the revolutionary war, it came to a stark choice between the preservation of the Empire and the freedom of the Americans, he and his friends openly chose the freedom of the Americans. They did so at the cost of isolating themselves from the rest of Parliament and from the great majority of the English people, for the duration of the war.

Hoffman's mental picture of Burke in relation to America is seriously flawed by a misunderstanding of Burke's relationship to England and to Ireland: a misunderstanding that is widely shared. Burke, Hoffman writes, was 'a thoroughly Briticized Irishman who had become an English country squire, a passionate patriot for his adopted country and an ardent upholder of its empire'.[1] If, as Hoffman puts it, Burke had been 'thoroughly Briticized', he would not have put his seat at Bristol at risk, and lost it, by activities on behalf of Irish Catholics which he well knew to be deeply distasteful to many of his constituents. Nor was he 'a passionate patriot' for his adopted country (see Chapter I *passim*). He often speaks in an exalted vein about the merits of British institutions, in the persona of an Englishman, but I do not know of any statement by him which could be correctly described as an expression of passionate English patriotism. His Irish Catholic connections, and the emotions surrounding these, which strongly affected him throughout his life, precluded that. The 'passionate patriots' of England, in his day, were passionately anti-Catholic, as their kind had been since the days of Elizabeth. To such 'patriots', Catholics were aliens of the worst kind, agents of a hostile foreign power, Jesuits. The Gordon rioters, among whom Burke risked his life in 1780, were passionate patriots. And he was reminded, almost every day, in the London press and in the caricatures, how he himself appeared, in the eyes of the passionate patriots of England. Even a not-very-passionate patriot, Horace Walpole, ridiculed the idea that Burke could be any kind of patriot.[2]

[1] Hoffman, *Edmund Burke etc.*, p. 73.
[2] 'The patriot remonstrance by an Irishman, from a papist family [Burke], was deservedly ridiculed' (Walpole, *Memoirs of the Reign of King George III*, Vol. III, p. 260).

And how could a passionate patriot of England, an ardent upholder of its empire, have opted, as Burke did, in favour of American independence and against the preservation of the empire, when it came to the moment of truth, in 1778? The passionate patriots and ardent upholders, throughout the period, were passionately in favour of crushing the American rebels, and preserving the empire by force, from 1775 to 1782. To such people Burke and his friends appeared as little better than traitors, throughout the course of the American revolution.

I believe that in the beginning of the crisis his feelings were ambivalent, both towards the English and towards the Americans. His feeling towards the English have been explored in Chapter I and will be further explored. His feelings towards the Americans were rather similar, and had similar connections with his personal and family experience. His most positive feeling towards the Americans was not initially affection but admiration. He admired American energy, audacity, ingenuity and hardihood, and he celebrated these qualities in major speeches. He was warning the English that if they used force against the Americans, they might be taking on an adversary which would eventually prove too much for them.

Burke has much less to say about his negative feelings towards Americans. To do so would have hindered rather than helped what he was trying to do. He was trying, during the early phases of the pre-revolutionary process, to persuade the English not to provoke Americans into rebellion; during the later pre-revolutionary phases, he was trying to dissuade the English from using force against the Americans; during the actual revolutionary war he was trying, with little hope up to 1778, and no success up to 1782, to persuade the English to concede independence to the Americans; *de facto* independence up to 1778; *de jure* independence from then on.[1] At no stage of this prolonged effort would it have been helpful or relevant for him to give expression to negative feelings about America. Yet these negative feelings existed, especially in relation to two great regions of pre-revolutionary and revolutionary America: the Southern colonies and New England.

Burke hated slavery, and he argued against seating representative Americans in the British Parliament, on the ground that this would mean the seating of slave-owners. This was at the beginning of the

---

[1] It may be said that the 'success' of 1782 had everything to do with the surrender of Cornwallis at Yorktown and nothing at all to do with Burke's arguments. This is not altogether true; see Chapter III below, pp. 220–232.

pre-revolutionary process, in 1765. The cry of 'no taxation without representation' had been raised in the course of the American resistance to the implementation of the Stamp Act (see below pp. 97–8) and the seating of Americans in the British Parliament had been offered as one possible solution. In his *Annual Register* he wrote against the seating of slave-owners in the Commons: 'Common sense, nay self-preservation, seem to forbid, that those, who allow themselves an unlimited right over the liberties and lives of others, should have any share in making laws for those, who have long renounced such injust [sic] and cruel distinctions.'[1] Ross Hoffman aptly comments on this statement: 'Burke's feelings towards American slave-owners thus were not unlike his feelings towards the 'bashaws' who as a master class ruled the people of his native Ireland.'[2]

Feeling as he did about American slavery, Burke must have felt uncomfortable with the copious American revolutionary rhetoric about freedom. Especially so, when the rhetoric came from the slave-owners, as in the case of the momentous 'Virginia resolves' (i.e. resolutions) of 29 May 1765, which opened America's campaign of defiance against the Stamp Act.[3] He favoured repeal of the Act on rational grounds, but he is unlikely to have been impressed by an assertion of the importance of 'American freedom', coming from Virginia's House of Burgesses. Burke's friend Samuel Johnson – who disagreed with him on the American question – was sarcastic on the subject of the freedom-loving slave-owners. Burke did not join in the sarcasm, which was a weapon in the armoury of those who wished to repress the free Americans. But he certainly felt the force of Johnson's point.

The second matter which must have helped to keep Burke at a certain emotional distance from the Americans, before the outbreak of the war, was American anti-Catholicism. In general, America in this period was more anti-Catholic than Britain. And the revolutionaries exploited and fanned anti-Catholicism, especially in the pulpits of New England, for their own political purposes. In 1774–5, on the

[1] *Annual Register* (1765) p. 37. This must have been written before Burke's election to Parliament in December. He does not seem to have returned to this subject in Parliament, but then he didn't have to. No one there was seriously thinking of seating any Americans, whether slave-owning or not.

[2] Hoffman, *Edmund Burke*, p. 34. This hardly seems quite consistent with Hoffman's picture of a 'thoroughly Briticized' Burke.

[3] See L. H. Gipson, *The British Empire before the American Revolution* (New York, 1939–70) Vol. X and more especially his *The Coming of the Revolution 1763–1775* (New York, 1954) pp. 86–89.

eve of war, the American leaders were seeking to legitimise their own recent revolutionary loyalties putting them in line with England's Glorious Revolution of 1688. This was entirely the reason for casting George III in the role of James II, the last Roman Catholic king of Great Britain. It was rather difficult to pretend that the strongly anti-Catholic George was really a Catholic, but the emerging revolutionaries found a plausible argument in the Quebec Act of 1774, which recognised and tolerated Catholicism as the religion of Canada. Most Americans resented that, and accepted the revolutionary argument that the Act was part of a great British and Catholic conspiracy against the freedoms and religion of American Protestants. In that way, revolution became a religious duty as well as a political cause.[1] The anti-Catholic paroxysm of the 1774–75 phase of the American revolution has been generally forgotten. The amnesia is understandable; this aspect would be hard to handle in the classrooms of modern urban America. In any case, the anti-Catholic phase of the revolution was short-lived. Once serious fighting began, George Washington sternly discouraged any manifestation of anti-Popery in the army. He wanted recruits, whatever their religion, and he wanted allies, whatever their religion.

On 21 October 1774, the Continental Congress issued an 'Address to the People of Great Britain' condemning Parliament for establishing in Canada a religion which had deluged England with blood and 'disbursed impiety, bigotry, persecution, murder and rebellion through every part of the world.'[2] Burke must have read that address with disgust. This was the language of the enemies of his people. The American revolutionaries apparently wanted the Catholics of Canada to be submitted to the same treatment as was endured by the Catholics of Ireland. Burke's party, the Rockingham Whigs, had opposed the Quebec Bill in Parliament, not of course on 'anti-

[1] See Alan Heimert, *Religion and the American Mind: From The Great Awakening to the Revolution* (Cambridge Mass, Harvard University Press, 1966); Carl Bridenbaugh, *Mitre and Sceptre: Transatlantic Faiths, Ideas, Personalities and Politics, 1689–1775* (New York, Oxford University Press, 1962); Edward Frank Humphry, *Nationalism and Religion in America, 1774–89* (Boston, 1924); Charles H. Metzger SJ, *The Quebec Act* (New York, United States Catholic Historical Society, 1936); Conor Cruise O'Brien, *God Land: Reflections on Religion and Nationalism* (Harvard University Press, 1988).

[2] Having addressed the British Parliament in the above manner, the Continental Congress, five days later, assured the Catholics of Canada of Congress's liberal disposition towards them. The bigoted ranting of the 'Address to Parliament' was probably as calculated as the liberalism of the address to the Canadians.

popery' grounds, but mainly because of its enlargment of the powers of the Crown. (Opposition to that enlargement was a central pre-occupation of the party throughout the period.) Opposing the Bill in Parliament, Burke said: 'Give them English liberty, give them an English constitution – and then, whether they speak French or English, whether they go to mass or attend our own communion, you will render them valuable and useful subjects of Great Britain. If you refuse to do this the consequence will be most injurious: Canada will become a dangerous instrument in the hands of those who wish to destroy English liberty in every part of our possessions.' By 'those who wish' etc. he was referring to the king's confidential advisers; by which he meant, in reality, George himself (see Introduction, pp. xxxv–xxxvi).

Some four years earlier Burke had been appointed London agent for the New York Assembly, to which he now reported on the passage of the Quebec Act. Although he himself had opposed the measure, he wrote in a manner intended to reconcile his American audience to its passage. Hoffman writes: 'The whole tone of his letter breathed a hope that New York might find cause for satisfaction rather than for grievance in the Quebec Act. On the subject of the French Catholic establishment – politically the most inflammatory feature of the law – he said not a word.'[1] That pregnant silence is his only comment on the anti-Catholic agitation which swept America at the eve of the Revolution. And this is very characteristic. While he showed high courage in his personal efforts to remove the disabilities of Catholics in Ireland and England, he was, as we have seen, very guarded about his personal connections with Catholicism.

Unless there was some practical purpose to be served, he avoided, for prudential reasons, any utterance which might suggest, or betray, a Catholic or pro-Catholic orientation on his part. Thus, he eschewed an appearance of sensitivity to manifestations of anti-Catholicism – rather as nineteenth century European Jews played down manifestations of anti-semitism (as did Theodor Herzl before his conversion to Zionism). This caution has misled many writers on Burke into underestimating the importance of his Catholic connections. I know of only one direct reference by him – and that not a public one – to the prevalence of religious intolerance in America. This was during

[1] Hoffman, *Edmund Burke*, p. 149. Hoffman also notes Burke's long delay in submitting his report. The Bill was proposed on 13 June and he did not send his report until 2 August. The delay may be indicative of how emotionally fraught the subject-matter was for him.

an earlier and milder phase, two years before the frenzy that followed the Quebec Act. In 1772 militant American dissenters were denouncing an alleged plot to introduce Anglican bishops into the American colonies: Anglicanism being seen, by American Congregationalists and Presbyterians in the eighteenth century, as a creeping form of Popery. Burke was writing privately to a leading member of the New York Assembly, John Cruger, about the defeat in the Lords of a measure carried in the Commons for the relief of dissenters. This gave him an opportunity, and a practical reason, for referring to American intolerance. He explains to Cruger, in effect, how a display of intolerance by American dissenters had given members of the House of Lords a pretext for exercising their own form of intolerance: '. . . . I have no doubt that in time [the relief measure] will be carried, and that this spirit of intolerance will vanish away by degrees both on our side of the water and on yours.'[1]

However, besides that comment there are also those two pregnant Burkean silences. The first (already mentioned) was in his August 1774 report to the New York Assembly on the passage of the Quebec Act. A major theme of the Commons debate had been denunciation of the Act, led by William Pitt, later Lord Chatham, as a breach of the Reformation, of the Glorious Revolution, and of the King's Coronation Oath: all highly congenial themes, to the Americans in 1774. But his report does not mention any of that. He is not going to say anything that could feed the flames of anti-Popery in America. The second Burkean silence, in the same connection, was noted and correctly interpreted by an unfriendly but acute contemporary, Horace Walpole (1717–1797). This was on 16 November 1775, when Burke introduced his motion for repeal of anti-American legislation. Walpole commented: 'Mr. Burke made his conciliatory motion and spoke for three hours and a half – in general ill. It was remarkable that in his proposed repeal he did not mention the Quebec Bill – another symptom of his old Popery.'[2]

This awareness of the prevalence of religious intolerance, on both sides of the Atlantic, may possibly account for the consistently cool and cerebral tone of Burke's speeches and writings on America, before the Penal Acts of 1774–5 and the outbreak of war (see below

---

[1] Hoffman, *Edmund Burke*, p. 208. Burke is able to rebuke American religious intolerance here, without exposing his Catholic feelings, because the intolerance in question had been aimed at Anglicans, in this instance, and not directly at Roman Catholics.

[2] Walpole, *Last Journals* (London, 1910) Vol 1, p. 494.

pp. 137–159). His emotions are not so much detached from the contest as almost evenly distributed between the parties. So the passionate outbursts which occur in speeches and writings on France, India and (more rarely) Ireland are absent from those on America, up to the war. His speeches on America are more 'chaste from flights', to use a phrase of Horace Walpole's. Yet too much should not be made of the difference. Passionate outbursts, in the other areas, do occur, but they are rare, as they would need to be. For the most part the tone of his utterances on the other three themes of the Great Melody is similar, though not identical, to that of his writings and speeches on America. But once the war had actually broken out, in 1775, his correspondence shows him as having shed his reservations: he is now fully committed on the American side. When the Americans are resisting British aggression, he can forget, for the duration, his reservations about some of their attitudes about Papists and slaves. From this point on, Burke's statements on America are fully in harmony with the other parts of the Melody. He knows which side he is on.

Despite the existence of a certain limited contrast between America and the other three causes, Yeats was right to include 'American colonies' in his metaphor. The four themes were linked in Burke's own mind. At the beginning of his parliamentary career, as we shall see, he consciously linked America with Ireland, and hoped to use one to help the other. Later, he linked India with Ireland, and France with India. He believed his positions on all four issues to be consistent: he rejected, for example, the view that his position on the French Revolution was incompatible with his position on the American Revolution. Burke would have appreciated Yeats's 'it'. The enemy, in all four cases was, Burke believed, essentially the same. 'It' can be defined most simply as abuse of power.

The second objection to the Great Melody, especially as applicable to America, is that since Burke's positions on political matters were part of a collective position, that of a political party, they cannot be allowed the status of a 'Melody' freely created by one person.

This objection is valid, in relation to some, but few, of Burke's political utterances. It is applicable to his early statements on India (1766–1773) and I do not include any of these statements in the canon of the Great Melody. The Indian part of the Melody begins only in 1783 and lasts until 1794. Throughout this period he is not 'speaking for his party', but speaking out of deep personal conviction which he imposes on his party, to its growing discomfort and eventual discomfiture. On Ireland, his public utterances are few, often cryptic and always guarded, not mainly for party reasons, but influenced by that factor among others. The Melody as a whole is powerfully affected by Ireland, but indirectly, mainly through India. The public statements dealing directly with Ireland are generally not part of the Melody. There is one exception: the passage in his Bristol Guildhall speech of November 1780 (see Chapter I above, p. 82). Some of the letters on Ireland also belong in the Melody, notably the one quoted in Chapter VI (see Thematic Index, 'Great Melody').

Over America, it might be expected that, as with India, the early speeches at least would be dominated by considerations of party. Burke's parliamentary debut coincided with the opening phase of the American crisis, and such a very new MP would normally take a lead from his party (especially as Burke was private secretary to the party leader, Rockingham). In fact, however, as we shall see, Burke had made up his mind on the main issue of the day – the fate of the Stamp Act – before his party did. With one party-dominated exception, in 1770, considered below (pp. 131–135), his American speeches are all conviction speeches and several belong in the Great Melody, beginning with the one on the Declaratory Bill, delivered in his first parliamentary session.

Already before his election to Parliament, Burke had questioned the wisdom of passing the Stamp Act. 'This sullenness in the colonies should alone, one would imagine, have prevented the laying of any additional burden on them.' This position, adopted by him as a private citizen, was consistent with his position as an MP, supporting the Rockingham Administration in its repeal of the Stamp Act.

The Stamp Act was a measure adopted in 1765 by Parliament, on the recommendation of the Administration of George Grenville (1712–70), who was shortly afterwards replaced by Rockingham. The object was to raise revenue in the colonies, and relieve the burdens on British taxpayers. The Act extended to the colonies the system of stamp duties, on all legal documents etc., already in force in Britain. Parliament saw this at the time as a simple matter of getting the colonists to bear their fair share of the expenses of Empire. But the colonists, having borne their fair share, as they believed, in the Seven Years War (1756–1763), which ended French power in North America, were in no mood to accept from the British Parliament fiscal innovations, about which they had not been consulted, but with which they were to be burdened. No longer under threat by the French, the Americans no longer felt a need for British government. The Stamp Act shifted the mere passive absence of felt need into positive rejection and resistance.

The Americans raised the cry of 'No taxation without representation' and also raised mobs to destroy the stamps and menace, and sometimes molest, the would-be collectors of the Stamp Duty and those officials who tried to protect the collectors. These measures were effective. It became quite impossible to collect the Duties. Equally effective was a boycott of British goods, to last until the repeal of the Stamp Act. The boycott was organised by the same leaders who had organised the resistance to the Act. Some of these leaders were later prominent in the actual American revolution, to which the Act was the earliest prelude.

By the beginning of 1766, when Burke took his seat, British trade in America was at a stand-still. The question of the hour was: whether to repeal, or not to repeal, the Stamp Act. Writing to his friend Charles O'Hara eight days after his election and before the Rockinghams had decided what to do about the Act, Burke acknowledges the overwhelming importance of the American issue, and states his own intention of voting in accordance with his own opinion, irrespective of what his party may think:

> There are wonderful materials of combustion at hand; and surely, since this monarchy, more material point never came under the consideration of Parliament. I mean the Conduct which is to be held with regard to America. And there are difficulties in plenty interior and exterior. Administration has not yet conclusively (I imagine) fixed upon their plan in this respect, as every day's information from abroad may necessitate some alteration. In the mean time the Grenvillians [devisers and supporters of the Stamp Act] rejoice and Triumph as if they had gained some capital advantage, by the confusions into which they have thrown every thing. With regard to myself and my private opinion, my resolution is taken; and if the Point is put in any way in which the affirmative or Negative become the Test of my Vote I shall certainly vote according to them; though some of my very best friends should determine to the Contrary. You will think me ridiculous; but I do not look upon this as a common question. [1]

Paul Langford, General Editor of the modern scholarly edition of Burke's *Writings and Speeches* and editor of the volume from which that extract is taken, finds that 'Burke had arrived at his clear verdict

---

[1] *Corr.* I, 229.

for repeal of the Stamp Act before his friends. . . . and essentially independently of them . . .'[1]

I have no doubt that Burke meant what he said in that letter, and would have done what he said he would do – as he did a quarter of a century later, over the French Revolution. Fortunately, he was spared being split from his party at the outset of his career, over the American question, because his party reached a decision – to repeal the Act – which was in conformity with his own views. The Rockingham Administration's Bill for the repeal of the Act received its First Reading in February. Next month Burke is writing happily to O'Hara, telling him of his work on the revision of the commercial laws: 'This you see will find me at least as much Business as the Evidence on the Stamp act; but it is a Business I like; and the Spirit of those I act with is just what I could wish it, in things of this Kind.'[2]

Could he, having entered Parliament a bare two months earlier, have influenced his party's decision to adopt a line which he personally intended to follow anyway, whatever his party wished to do? Most twentieth-century British historians would have answered the question with a decided No. Burke, in their view, was too low in the political and social hierarchy to have a serious influence over party policy on a major issue. Lucy Sutherland writes of him at this stage (and many historians would agree with her) that he was of 'far too slight consequence to be a deciding factor in the policy of the party, but though he can claim no credit as a commercial reformer, in the working out of the ministerial policy he rose from obscurity and appeared, not yet as the prophet of the system, but instead, rather surprisingly, as one of its most practical organisers. By the end of the ministry, in spite of his occasional rashness he had become, together with Dowdeswell [1721–1775], the Chancellor of the Exchequer, the most noted man of his group. It was indeed said in the last months of the ministry that Burke, "not . . . Lord Rockingham's right hand, but . . . both his hands", was a metaphysical visionary. But his success in organising commercial propaganda, in keeping in touch with commercial leaders, in encouraging every sign of public support, for popularity, he remarked, "is current coin, or it is nothing," show that practical vigour, which, in the most fortunate periods of his political career, was the complement of his speculative

[1] *The Writings and Speeches of Edmund Burke*, Vol II: *Party Parliament and the American Crisis 1766–1774*, pp. 26–27.
[2] *Corr.* I, 240.

genius. It was this which compensated in part for his lack of political finesse and judgment, and won him his place in the Rockingham connection, more than his much greater intellectual claims.'[1]

Burke is here depicted as an industrious drudge, whose intellect, however 'remarkable', was politically irrelevant. Certainly he worked hard. But where is the evidence that his intellect was irrelevant? Elsewhere, and covering a slightly later period beginning in 1768, Lucy Sutherland acknowledges Burke's 'growing importance in the councils of his party' but adds that 'the belief of some of his earlier biographers (reinforced as they were by the occasional sallies of contemporary satirists) that he dominated his leader, inspired the party and controlled its destinies in the House of Commons, gains no support from his correspondence.'[2]

There are some contradictions here, and some questionable assertions. If Burke was indeed 'of far too slight consequence to be a deciding factor in the policy of his party,' how come that when the Rockingham Administration ended only four months later, in July 1766, Burke, with one other, William Dowdeswell, Chancellor of the Exchequer, no less, 'had become the most noted man of his group'? This was a noteworthy achievement, and must surely have conferred more 'consequence' on him than Sutherland acknowledges. If a contemporary could see Burke as 'not . . . Lord Rockingham's right-hand but . . . both his hands', why should we, many generations later, assume that Burke had little influence over Rockingham?

An American historian takes a very different view of Burke's importance at the outset of his parliamentary career. G. H. Guttridge writes: 'Nothing in the history of the new administration was of greater permanent significance' than Burke's appointment as Rockingham's private secretary in July before he became an MP. Guttridge adds that Burke, after his election, in December 1765, 'soon became the driving force of the ministry'.[3] It is true, as Sutherland says, that the large claims for Burke's influence made by early biographers – and by some contemporaries – have 'no support from the correspondence' (but no contradiction either). But this does not prove that

---

[1] L. Sutherland, 'Edmund Burke and the first Rockingham Ministry' in *English Historical Review* LXVI (January 1932) pp. 46–72.

[2] *Corr.* II, Introduction, xi. Lucy Sutherland is the editor of this volume.

[3] G. H. Guttridge, *English Whiggism and the American Revolution* (University of California Press, 1963) p. 22. The Namierite radiations lose some of their intensity by the time they reach the Pacific. For contrasts between British and American historiography, in relation to Burke, see the Introduction to the present study.

the earlier biographers, and contemporaries, were necessarily wrong. When Parliament was in session, and urgent political choices had to be made, the Rockinghams met regularly. They didn't have to send letters to one another. They talked. Such influence as any one of them exerted over the others, other than the influence conferred by higher social standing, had to be exerted in conversation. And we know, on high authority, that Burke's conversational powers were extraordinary. Dr. Johnson, his fellow member of The Club [1], stood in awe of him: not a sensation any other contemporaries are known to have inspired in Samuel Johnson. Would a person who impressed Johnson to that extent not be likely to have been heard with close attention by his own political associates, even so early in his political career?

The Sutherland picture of Burke is a restrained but classic exercise in Namierite reductionism. Burke's 'intellectual claims' (*sic*) are acknowledged but disconnected from his political environment. A kind of posthumous lobotomy is performed. Burke, minus his mind, turns into a hard-working dogsbody, good for performing organisational tasks. Sutherland invests Burke with something called 'speculative genius' – an exalted attribute, but detached from reality – while arbitrarily divesting him of an essential intellectual quality: judgment. But surely his judgment in relation to the processes that led to the American Revolution, has stood the test of time? What more important matter was there for the exercise of political judgment than America? Which of his leading political contemporaries can be considered as possessed of better judgment than he showed in relation to America? Chatham? George Grenville? Charles Townshend? Lord Hillsborough? Lord Mansfield? Lord George Germain? Lord North? George III?

Years afterwards, at a time when his own judgment was diverging momentously from Burke's – over the French Revolution, in 1791 – Charles James Fox (1794–1806) paid a memorable tribute to Burke's influence over him. He said that 'if he were to put all the political information which he had learnt from books, all which he had gained from science, and all which any knowledge of the world and its affairs had taught him, into one scale, and the improvement which he had derived from his right hon. friend's [Burke's] instruction and

[1] The Club was founded by Johnson on Joshua Reynolds's suggestion – another of the nine original members was Goldsmith. Later members included Boswell, Garrick, Charles James Fox, Richard Brinsley Sheridan and Adam Smith. It met at the Turk's Head, in Soho.

conversation were placed in the other, he should be at a loss to decide to which to give the preference.'[1] Johnson and Fox, two of the leading spirits of the age, are telling us about someone whom they knew well. I think their impressions of Burke are likely to be considerably more reliable than the retrospective definitions of historians with an axe to grind, and a person to cut down to size with the same.

There is no direct evidence that Burke played a significant part in the most important decision of the first Rockingham Administration: the decision to repeal the Stamp Act. But there are good grounds for inferring that he probably did play such a part. He had motive, means and opportunity for doing so.

Motive: As we know from the letter to Charles O'Hara of 31 December 1765, Burke had by then not only made up his mind on the policy to be adopted but had determined to follow the line he thought right 'though some of my very best friends should determine to the contrary'. The 'very best friends' were of course the Rockinghams, who did not make up their minds what to do about the Stamp Act, until a week or so later. It was most important for Burke that they should make up their mind in the way that he had already made up his. It was important in terms of the issue itself, on which he held clear and strong views, but also for his political future. If the Rockinghams decided against Repeal, while he held out for it, he would be likely to lose his patron, Rockingham, together with the whole Rockingham connection. Nor would it be easy, after such a break, to acquire a new patron and a new connection. Outside Parliament, a person who broke with his political friends over a point of principle, might perhaps be esteemed. In Parliament he would not. Such people were not trusted. Burke was ambitious, in the early stages of his career, though he was at no time prepared to subordinate everything else to his ambition. His only hope of reconciling his ambition with his principles, early in 1766, lay in talking the Rockinghams round, especially the Marquess himself. It would be surprising if he didn't have a good try even though there is no documentary confirmation that he did.

Means: Burke's formidable persuasive powers were backed by a wealth of information, acquired as a result of his formidable capacity for hard work. Nobody in his party could quite match that combi-

---

[1] Quoted in Loren Reid, *Charles James Fox* (London, 1969) p. 259.

nation. (Dowdeswell, who led the party in the Commons, came the nearest).

Opportunity: Burke's main opportunity consisted in his position as Rockingham's private secretary, giving him privileged access to his party leader, at all times during the parliamentary sessions. He was Rockingham's adviser, more than his amanuensis. And Rockingham needed him for information too. Rockingham was a high-minded nobleman, but intellectually indolent ('weak' and 'ignorant' according to Horace Walpole), so he needed help in finding what to be high-minded about. Shortly after Burke became his secretary, Charles O'Hara, who at that time knew Rockingham better than Burke did, offered some advice: 'You have pride to deal with, but much softened by manner: and exceeding good sense, but you must feed it, for it cant feed itself.' [1] I am sure that Burke did feed Rockingham's good sense, and to a lesser extent that of Rockingham's principal followers. And I believe that the feeding process made a significant contribution to the Rockinghams' decision to repeal the Stamp Act. Burke's American biographer, Carl B. Cone, assigns to him a leading role in the formation of the party's American policy. After referring to the letter to O'Hara quoted above, Cone writes: 'This important statement shows that Burke had decided, earlier than the Rockingham chieftains, in favour of repeal of the Stamp Act and passage of a Declaratory Act.' [2] Cone also cites a letter written by William Dowdeswell, on 10 January 1767, acknowledging the Rockingham policy on America as originating with Burke. [3]

In order to accept the validity of Yeats's metaphor in regard to America, however, we don't have to accept that Rockingham policy on America was largely shaped by Burke. It is enough for us to be convinced that, in his statements on America, he is speaking out of the depths of his personal convictions, and not in constrained conformity with the policy of a party. And this is clearly so. Once the decision to repeal the Stamp Act had been taken, Burke tells O'Hara that 'the spirit of those I act with is just what I would wish it . . .' and this remained so (with just one brief and partial exception in 1770) over the following sixteen years, through the years of incubation of the American Revolution, and the years of the revolutionary war. From the moment of the decision on the Stamp Act, in

[1] *Corr.* I, 214.
[2] Cone, *Burke and the Nature of Politics*, Vol I (1957) p. 87.
[3] *Ibid.*

February 1766, to the end of 1782, the Rockinghams, at every critical juncture, favoured conciliation as against coercion. And that was also Burke's personal position, even before it became that of his party. As Ross Hoffman says, his 'American politics remained unchanged from the time he argued for the repeal of the Stamp Act until he opposed the ministerial and parliamentary measures of 1774–5 that plunged the empire into a civil war.'[1] They also remained consistent throughout that war, until 1782, when George III accepted defeat, by calling on Rockingham to form an Administration. In his speeches on America, Burke speaks for himself, as well as his party.

This is not to say that he never deferred to collective decisions of his party. From 1766 to 1774 the Rockinghams in opposition were largely though not entirely inactive on the affairs of America, for reasons discussed in the next section. Burke either agreed with this policy or acquiesced in it. Some of his silences may have been constrained. On one occasion, in introducing the Rockingham-Grenville resolutions of 1770, he acts as a spokesman for an inter-party consensus, and is not speaking out of the fullness of his own personal convictions (see below pp. 131–135). With the exception of the early Indian Speeches (1767–1773), this is the only example of its kind in Burke's career. There is just one other lapse from the level of the Great Melody in its broader sense. This is the passage about Ireland in 'On Conciliation with America' (see below pp. 151–154). Here the rhetoric rings for a moment hollow, and the assertions are at variance both with the historical realities to which they allude and with Burke's known personal convictions.

With those two exceptions – interesting in themselves but constituting a tiny proportion of Burke's voluminous contributions to the debate on America – his American statements are consistent with one another and clearly reflect his personal convictions. There are four major recorded statements on America: 'On the Declaratory Bill (1766), 'On American Taxation' (1774), most of 'On Conciliation with America' (1775) and 'A Letter to the Sheriffs of Bristol' (1777). There is also a major but imperfectly recorded speech, 'On Military Employment of Indians' (1778). All these are examined later. Here it is enough to say that in them, and in the numerous minor statements and interventions in debate, we hear the voice of Edmund Burke, as clear and as spontaneous as we hear it in the impeachment

[1] Hoffman, *Edmund Burke*, p. 189

of Warren Hastings and in his writings on the French Revolution and clearer than we usually hear it on the affairs of Ireland. On America, the tone is calmer, at least in the pre-war phase, but the voice is unmistakably the same. I conclude that the Great Melody metaphor is as valid for America as for the other three causes to which Yeats applied it.

NARRATIVE: 1766–1778

There have been too many short, glib, general assertions by historians, usually disparaging, such as Sir Lewis Namier's in the epigraph to this chapter, about Burke's attitude towards the American crisis. To find out what that attitude really was, we have to pay attention to what Burke said and did, in the different phases of the developing crisis, both before and during the war. This requires a chronological approach. It also requires copious quotations from Burke.

On 23 December 1765 he was elected MP for Wendover, a pocket borough belonging to lord Verney, a patron friendly to Rockingham. Next day Burke wrote to Charles O'Hara: 'This is only to tell you in a few words that yesterday I was elected for Wendover, got very drunk, and this day have a heavy cold.'[1] (Getting drunk seems to have been practically mandatory on candidates in such elections. Burke was not habitually a heavy drinker.) On 14 January the new MP took his seat for the opening of the new session. Thanks to American resistance to the Stamp Act, Parliament was meeting at a time of major crisis in both countries. The American boycott had brought the western ports of Great Britain to a standstill, as is described in this account based on contemporary newspaper reports: 'After the first of January, piers where American ships docked were forsaken. An unwonted, almost uncanny stillness, hung over the waterfront of the western ports, in place of the bustle and stir of other days. Vessels with shrouded sails rose and fell with the tide, and pulled on their hawsers in vain attempts to be free. Here and there a solitary deck hand half hidden by the mist, crawled about among the rigging, making a mooring more secure. Ships returning from Philadelphia or Boston, laden with hats which patriotic Ameri-

---

[1] *Corr.* I, 223–4. An eye-witness at Wendover, writing on the same day, tells of '... Empty Bottles, broken Glasses, Rivers of Wine, Brooks of Brandy'

cans had refused, only intensified the general gloom. Dock labourers earned a few shillings, then returned to their mugs of ale at the tavern where shipwrights and caulkers soused away their idle hours.'[1]

The parliamentary debate on 14 January was one of the most dramatic and momentous of the entire eighteenth century. Formally, the debate was about the King's Speech which, since the Rockingham Administration had not yet made up its mind on what to do about the Stamp Act, was non-committal. William Pitt the Elder (1708–78) had come to demand the repeal of the Act. His presence was an event in itself, for he had been absent because of illness from Parliament all the previous year: the year in which the Act was passed. Pitt was the hero of the nation, having led it to victory in the Seven Years War. He was also the greatest parliamentary speaker of his time. George Grenville, the author of the Stamp Act, and a tenacious and formidable politician, was there to defend his brainchild against Pitt, and to attack the Rockingham Administration for its weakness, in failing to impose the Stamp Act on the refractory colonists. A striking feature of that great debate was the agreement by the rival protagonists that the issue at stake was enormously important and that revolution in America was a serious possibility, if Parliament took the wrong decision. They were divided only over what the right decision was. Pitt thought it right to repeal the Stamp Act. Grenville thought it right to impose the Act by military force.

Pitt said he rejoiced that the colonists were forcibly resisting taxation by a Parliament in which they were not represented, and he compared the resisting colonists to those who had carried out England's own Glorious Revolution. He called the American resistance to the Stamp Act 'a subject of greater importance than ever engaged the attention of this House! that subject only excepted, when near a century ago it was the question whether you yourselves were to be bound or free!'[2] Grenville neatly took up an understatement of the Rockingham Administration's. The King's Speech had referred to what was happening in America as 'disturbances'. Grenville said that

[1] Dora M. Clark, *British Opinion and the American Revolution* (Yale University Press, 1930) p. 38.

[2] *Parliamentary History*, xvi, 98. The view that the American Revolution was a continuation of England's Glorious Revolution became the received doctrine of the American revolutionaries in the following decade. Mainly because of the speech quoted above, Pitt was far more popular in America than any other member of the British Parliament. Burke never, before the war, went so far 'on the American side' as Pitt did here. However, when war came, Pitt opposed American independence up to his death, while Burke and Rockingham accepted it in 1778 (see below p. 205).

'the "disturbances" began in July [16 July 1765 was the date on which the Rockingham Administration succeeded Grenville's] and now we are in the middle of January; lately they were only "occurrences", they are now grown to "disturbances, to tumults and riots". I doubt [suspect] they border on open rebellion; and if the doctrine I have heard this day [in Pitt's speech] be confirmed, I fear they will lose that name to take that of revolution. The government over them being dissolved, a revolution will take place in America.' [1]

That day's debate was the first major one concerning the process which was about to lead to revolution in America. Less than a year before, Parliament had passed the Stamp Act without a division and almost without a debate. Yet by January 1766 the Act has become the central issue of British politics. One British statesman (Pitt) foresees revolution in America if the Stamp Act is not repealed; another (Grenville) foresees revolution in America if it is not imposed by force. As the Stamp Act was repealed, and the American Revolution did occur, Grenville's argument might appear to have been vindicated by history. But that would be an erroneous inference. The Act was repealed, but in 1767 the attempt to find a revenue in America by fiscal innovation was renewed (see below pp. 119–127). The colonists resisted and a later Administration decided, in accordance with Grenville's prescription, to put down American resistance by military force. The results were as predicted by Pitt, ten years before. Sadly, the fatal taxes were imposed by an Administration presided over, though not controlled, by Pitt himself, now Earl of Chatham.

On 12 January, three days after the opening of the Stamp Act debate, Burke made his maiden speech. No published record of the speech as delivered exists and there is no draft since it was impromptu. Our only information about the speech – or rather speeches, for he spoke more than once that day – is in a letter written next day to Charles O'Hara:

That day I took my first trial. Sir William Meredith [a senior Rockingham] desired me to present the Manchester petition [of merchants against the Stamp Act]: I know not what struck me, but I took a sudden resolution to say something about it, though I had got it but that moment, and had scarcely time to read it, short as it was; I did say something, what it was, I know not upon my honour; I felt like a man drunk. Lord

[1] *Parliamentary History*, xvi, 101. The quotation marks round 'disturbances' and 'occurrences' are mine. A modern reporter would so render what was clearly Grenville's inflection.

Frederick Campbell made me some answer to which I replied; ill enough
too; but I was by this time pretty well on my Legs; Mr. Grenville
answered; and I was now heated, and could have been much better, but
Sir G. Savill [another Rockingham] caught the speaker's eyes before me;
and it was then thought better not to proceed further, as it would keep
off the business of the day. However I had now grown a little stouter
[braver], though still giddy, and affected with a swimming in my head;
So that I ventured up again on the motion, and spoke some minutes,
poorly but not quite so ill as before. All I hoped was to plunge in, and
get off the first horrors; I had no hopes of making a figure. I find my
Voice not strong enough to fill the House; but I shall endeavour to raise
it as high as it will bear. [1]

'Mr. Grenville answered' is interesting. We would not expect a
former head of Administration to reply to an argument of a maiden
speaker. Clearly something that Burke said had struck home to the
author of the Stamp Act, and leading advocate of punishing resistance to it. Burke was, from the beginning, an unusually aggressive
debater. For the close of the year that saw his parliamentary debut,
Horace Walpole notes: 'Burke, an adventurer, was to push his way
by distinguishing himself as a formidable antagonist.' [2] Burke's own
antagonist was Grenville, whose arguments the new MP treated with
a kind of casual contempt that must have been particularly galling,
coming from very 'junior' to very 'senior' both socially and politically. Burke replies, to Grenville's demand for strong and early
action, and his complaint that Parliament should have convened
sooner: 'Nothing shews a more weak undetermined unsystematic
spirit than to fall into a little hurry of weak premature, undigested
measures either of force or of Policy and not to rest steadily. Parliament met when it did because Parliament could do nothing then that
it cannot do now.' [3]

In 1774, four years after Grenville's death, Burke offered the
House, in his great speech 'On American Taxation' (see below
pp. 138–144), a not unkindly posthumous portrait of George Grenville:

No man can believe, that at this time of day I mean to lean on the
venerable memory of a great man, whose loss we deplore in common.

---

[1] *Corr.* I, 232–3.
[2] Walpole, *Memoirs*, p. 265; for November 1766.
[3] *Writings and Speeches* II, 45. This is from the earliest of Burke's draft speeches.
These sentences immediately preceded the 'Theatre of a Civil War' sentence (see
below p. 111).

Our little party differences have been long ago composed; and I have acted more with him, and certainly with more pleasure with him, than ever I acted against him. [1] Undoubtedly Mr. Grenville was a first-rate figure in this country. With a masculine understanding, and a stout and resolute heart, he had an application undissipated and unwearied. He took public business, not as a duty which he was to fulfil, but as a pleasure he was to enjoy; and he seemed to have no delight out of this House, except in such things as someway related to the business that was to be done within it. If he was ambitious, I will say this for him, his ambition was of a noble and generous strain. It was to raise himself, not by the low pimping politics of a court, but to win his way to power, through the laborious gradations of public service; and to secure to himself a well earned rank in Parliament, by a thorough knowledge of its constitution, and a perfect practice in all its business.

Sir, if such a man fell into errors, it must be from defects not intrinsic, they must be rather sought in the particular habits of his life; which, though they do not alter the ground work of character, yet tinge it with their own hue. He was bred in a profession. He was bred to the Law, which is, in my opinion, one of the first and noblest of the human sciences; a science which does more to quicken and invigorate the understanding, than all the other kinds of learning put together; but it is not apt, except in persons very happily born, to open and to liberalise the mind exactly in the same proportion. Passing from that study he did not go very largely into the world; but plunged into business; I mean into the business of office; and the limited and fixed methods and forms established there. Much knowledge is to be had undoubtedly in that line and there is no knowledge which is not valuable. But it may be truly said, that men too much conversant in office, are rarely minds of remarkable enlargement. Their habits of office are apt to give them a turn to think the substance of business not to be much more important than the forms in which it is conducted. These forms are adapted to ordinary occasions; and therefore persons who are nurtured in office do admirably well, as long as things go on in their common order; but when the high roads are broken up, and the waters out, when a new and troubled scene is opened, and the file affords no precedent, then it is that a greater knowledge of mankind, and a far more extensive comprehension of things, is requisite than ever office gave, or than office can ever give.

This is a splendid passage in a splendid speech, but there is something that staggers the mind in the Olympian condescension of that final

[1] I doubt whether this was true: see below, pp. 129–135. The editor suggests (p. 431, n.3) that the first and more complimentary paragraph of this assessment may never have been delivered, but inserted in the published version.

sentence. The speaker clearly implies that he himself possesses those lofty qualities in which Grenville was deficient. Burke was right, both about himself and about Grenville, but his self-confidence is disconcerting. Burke's personality combined deep-seated existential insecurity, derived from his ambiguous religious and national status, with an intellectual self-assurance that was sometimes overwhelming. Contemporaries who disliked him (Walpole, Grenville, General Henry Conway and others, not to mention William Hamilton), being unable to cope with the intellectual self-assurance, got back at him through his vulnerable side: social status. 'Irish adventurer' became a stock epithet for Burke in his own day. Later it was to be handed on as a legacy to his twentieth-century enemies from his eighteenth-century ones.

The reports of parliamentary speeches for this period are sparse (reporters were not admitted to the public gallery until 1783). Fortunately Burke's drafts of several speeches are now available. They were published for the first time in 1981 in Volume II of the modern edition of *Writings and Speeches*. They confirm Burke's consistency. The editor, Paul Langford, states: 'The drafts of speeches in 1766 and 1767 on America ... clearly vindicate Burke's claim to have formulated his view of the imperial constitution long before the great American speeches of 1774–5.'[1]

The Great Melody metaphor hardly applies to Burke's earliest recorded speech, in the draft form which is alone available. It is sound and no more, except for the last sentence. Burke had good reasons for holding himself in. He had to show that he could make a competent contribution to debate, before he could hope to be heard as an orator. Also, he had as yet no theme for oratory; in mid-January, the Rockingham party had still not quite made up its collective mind. Burke was nudging them in the direction of repeal; to anticipate their decision might have put them off. His line in this early speech, which I have highly compressed, was to defend the Administration against Grenville's charges that it should have acted immediately to repress the riots that followed the news of the passage of the Stamp Act. Burke showed that the Grenville Administration had altogether failed to foresee the resistance to the Act, and had therefore failed to provide the forces needed to repress it, if repression was the proper course. To send reinforcements was impossible, once winter had set in. As Parliament was meeting in the depths of winter

---

[1] *Writings and Speeches* II, 40.

there was time for due deliberation, whatever might be its outcome. He ended: 'There is time enough God knows, to open the Theatre of a Civil War.' That last sentence was the solitary harbinger of eloquence to come.

Horace Walpole noted in his *Memoirs* for January 1766: 'There appeared in this debate a new speaker, whose fame for eloquence soon rose high above the ordinary pitch. His name was Edmund Burke, an Irishman, of a Roman Catholic family, and actually married to one of that persuasion.' [1] Clearly in Walpole's opinion, Burke was a man who could bear watching, both for negative and positive reasons. And Walpole was to keep a beady eye trained on Burke, over the next thirty years.

So, Burke had made an impressive parliamentary debut. He had surpassed the high expectations of such friends as David Garrick and Samuel Johnson; he had won the praise of Pitt; even Horace Walpole, in the ranks of Tuscany, could scarce forbear to cheer. And that was while he was still speaking for a party which had yet to make up its mind on the subject under debate.

By the end of January the Rockinghams had made their decision, the one Burke had been looking for. This set him free to deploy the full range of his eloquence for a cause he strongly believed in. But before coming to his important American speeches of February 1766, it is necessary to consider the policy he was defending, the objections to it, and the reasons for it. What the Rockinghams decided, on Burke's advice, was to precede repeal of the Stamp Act with a Declaratory Act, affirming parliament's legislative supremacy over the colonies. The combination came to be severely criticised. Two American historians have even found that the repeal of the Stamp Act, in the circumstances, was 'almost as fruitful of evil consequences as the passage'. [2] This seems rather drastic. What was already clear in 1766 was that if the Act could be made to operate at all in the colonies, it could only be done by the lavish application of military force. What is clear is that if the Act had not been repealed in 1766,

---

[1] Walpole, *Memoirs of the Reign of George III*, edited by G. F. Russell Barker (London and New York, 1894) Vol. II, pp. 193–4. In the 'contents' section of this edition, this entry is listed as 'First Speech of Edmund Burke'. However, Burke's first speech was on 17 January and Walpole's entry is for 27 January. I think that by 'this debate', Walpole is referring to the continuing debate over the Stamp Act, in which Burke intervened several times.

[2] Edmund S. Morgan and Helen M. Morgan, *The Stamp Act Crisis: Prologue to Revolution* (University of North Carolina Press, 1953), p. 269.

the American Revolution would have started in that year, instead of ten years later.

Burke and his party believed that the repeal of the Stamp Act could not be carried unless accompanied by a solemn expression of Parliament's legislative superiority over the colonies (which is what the Declaratory Act was). [1] The party might have been split over repeal, had waverers not had the Declaratory Act to reassure them. So that Act was necessary, if the Stamp Act was to be repealed. [2] Some have suggested that while the repeal of the Stamp Act had a soothing effect in the short run, the accompanying Declaratory Act was productive of great evils in the longer term; this appears to be the position of the writers of the book just quoted. What was certainly productive of great evils was the domineering mind-set of George III, of most of the membership of both Houses of Parliament, and probably of the people of England, towards the colonists. That attitude was antecedent to the Declaratory Act, and would have still prevailed, had the Act never been passed. Even with the addition of the Act, repeal could probably not have carried had it not been for the crisis in British commerce caused by the American boycott. The Rockinghams did more than any other group to force that crisis on the attention of Parliament and Burke, as usual, did more than any other Rockingham. He was the link between Rockingham and the merchants, and indefatigable in the preparation and presentation of merchant petitions. Both by his activities behind the parliamentary scenes and in Parliament itself, he deserves much of the credit for the only successful measure of conciliation passed by Parliament after the dispute with the Americans began. That the success did not prove lasting was not his fault or that of his friends. The Rockinghams did, indeed believe, as Namier says (see epigraph), that 'trade was the soul of the empire'. But this conviction did not lead them, as he implies, in the direction of coercing the Americans: quite the contrary. And the Rockinghams opposed coercion of the colonists not only in 1766, when British merchants were on their side, but also consistently in the later years, with little or no merchant support.

Burke spoke in Parliament on the Declaratory Resolution, on 3

[1] The Act follows the wording of the 1719 Dependency of Ireland Act and I suspect the actual form of the Declaratory Act was suggested by Burke. He is more likely than any other Rockingham to have been familiar with that precedent.

[2] The Duke of Grafton said so, and so did twenty-eight merchants who wrote to Rockingham on the subject. D. M. Clark, *British Opinion and the American Revolution* (London, 1930) p. 90.

February. As his friends had by then made up their minds, and to his satisfaction, he was now able to speak in terms of the general principles which should govern Parliament's approach to the colonies. He made a strong impression. That speech, Paul Langford writes, with others which followed shortly after, 'established him immediately as a major figure at Westminster.'[1] Its central theme, like that of those to come, was that Parliament should content itself with affirming the principle of legislative supremacy, and should refrain from any further practical exercise of that supremacy, through any new legislation or taxation. Burke was certainly speaking for himself. Was he also speaking for his party? They did not challenge him on it, but on one occasion four years later, they were to show themselves wobbly, for parliamentary tactical reasons, on the principle of non-intervention in America. For the rest they opposed, in succession over the years, taxation, coercion and the war. The Rockingham Administration fell in July 1766, and its successors governed, or rather tried to govern, the colonies according to completely different principles. The Rockinghams did not get back into office again until 1782, after Yorktown, when the bankruptcy of American policies pursued by their successors, in those sixteen years had been conclusively demonstrated, at a heavy cost in life and treasure.

In his speech on the Declaratory Resolution Burke said (in part) according to the surviving draft:

This speculative Idea of a right deduced from the unlimited Nature of the supreme Legislative authority, very clear and very undeniable, but, when explained proved and admitted little to the purpose.

The Practical, executive, exertion of this Right may be impracticable, may be inequitable and may be contrary to the Genius and Spirit even of the Constitution which gives this right at least contrary to the principles of Liberty.

This Practical Idea of the Constitution of the British Empire to be deduced from the general and relative Situation of its parts. The purposes for which they were formed. The Law of England and examples of other Countries not applicable here. It must be governed upon principles of Freedom. There is not a more difficult subject for the understanding of men than to govern a Large Empire upon a plan of Liberty. . . .

Besides the abstract point of right there is in every Country a difference between the Ideal; and the practical constitution – They will be confounded by Pedants, they will be distinguished by men of sense; they may

[1] *Writings and Speeches* II, 45–46.

not follow from the rules of metaphysical reasoning but they must be rules of Government. The practical Exertion of many clear rights may by change of times and circumstances become impossible, may be inequitable; may clash with the genius of the very constitution that gives them or at least may clash entirely with Liberty; and those who are not for governing with an attention to the circumstances of times, opinions, situations and manners, they will not govern wisely, they cannot govern long, because the powers they impiously attempt. . . .

Neither I apprehend will it be sufficient to resort for rules of the present practical constitution of the British Empire to our old Laws and Law Books; to resort to contracted Ideas, operating in dark times, on a Limited object; not in the broad daylight of Science, for Governing a Tract of the world, that our Ancestors so far from knowing how to Govern did not know it existed in the Universe.

'Govern America as you govern an English Corporation which happens not to be represented in Parliament.'[1] Are Gentlemen really serious when they propose this? Is there a single Trait of Resemblance between those few Towns disseminated through a represented County, and a great a growing people spread over a vast quarter of the Globe, almost from the Polar Circle to the Equator, separated from us by a mighty Ocean, neither actually or by a possibility a part in our Government. The rule of their Constitution must be taken from their Circumstances, not by oppressing them by the weight [of a] gross dead body, but by applying as far as the rules of subordination will permit the principles of the British Constitution – The eternal Barriers of Nature forbid that the Colonies should be blended or coalesce into the mass of the particular constitution of this Kingdom. We have nothing therefore for it, but to let them carry across the ocean into the woods and desarts of America the images of the British constitution; the Penates of an Englishman, to be his Comfort in his Exile, and to be the pledges of his fidelity and to give him an interest in his Dependency on this Country.[2]

Nothing could be more at variance with the 'authoritarianism' attributed to Burke by Namier (see epigraph) than the tenor of this first major speech on America and of his later pronouncements, right up to the end of the American War. They are all strongly and consistently anti-authoritarian – he found all authoritarianism abhorrent, morally, politically, philosophically and temperamentally. Yeats's 'It'

---

[1] The quotation marks around this sentence have been supplied for the sake of clarity–C.C.O'B.

[2] *Writings and Speeches* II, 47–50. These excerpts are taken from Burke's drafts, but we know from shorter contemporary published accounts that he did speak at this time along these lines.

was authoritarianism. Burke hated it in the Irish Protestant Ascendancy; in Warren Hastings; in the Jacobins; and in the politics towards America of Grenville, North and George III. The only way in which you can find Edmund Burke guilty of authoritarianism is by choosing to ignore everything he ever said, as a result of arbitrarily deciding that he didn't mean any of it. Which sums up the Namier approach to Burke. If Parliament had followed Burke's advice, as given here and elsewhere, there would have been no American Revolution. (Which doesn't of course mean that America would still be in the British Empire.) Some Americans resent his attempt to deprive them of their Revolution, and they disparage him accordingly (see Introduction p. lxi).

He again spoke four days later, opposing Grenville's demand for enforcing the Stamp Act forthwith. This was an effort to pre-empt repeal, and it was a dangerous one, because of the mood of exasperation in the House at the colonists' insubordination. The motion was a tactical one, and Burke's speech in reply was also tactical; not an oration but a debating speech. As Paul Langford says: 'Burke's remarks are evidence of his early attention to the precise requirements of a parliamentary situation; they were addressed not to the substantive questions of principle involved, but rather to the imprudence and impropriety of Grenville's manoeuvre.' Burke desperately needed to influence votes, which he did not need to do in the Declaratory Resolution, whose passage was automatic. For his purpose, the most effective part of the speech was probably the conclusion, aimed at gaining time, and forcing attention on the plight of English merchants rather than on the misbehaviour of the American colonists: 'Before we do determine, we must have our preparatory grounds before us. Our merchants object to it as having brought them to the brink of ruin. Let us hear them. Let us consider the subject in its full extent before a single resolution if possible should reach America.' [1] The tactics worked. Langford notes: 'In a crucial division Grenville's motion was negatived by 274 to 134 votes and the way for relief of colonial grievances opened.' The Declaratory Bill and the Bill repealing the Stamp Act both received the royal assent on 18 March 1766. The work of the first Rockingham Administration in relation to America was now substantially complete.

The session came to an end on 6 June. There was much opposition bitterness, especially against Burke. Thomas Bradshaw, a parliamen-

[1] *Writings and Speeches* II, 51–52.

tary supporter of the Administration, and soon to be Secretary to the Treasury, reported that people were saying the King's Speech must have been written by Burke, because it was 'so impudent'. George Grenville, more bitter than anyone, raked up Burke's Irish past (as seen by the more intransigent members of the Irish Protestant oligarchy) and that of his kinsman Will Burke. Grenville sarcastically questioned the sanity of the Rockingham leadership in designating 'for their men of busyness and of confidence in the two great offices of the Treasury and the Secretary of State, the two Mr. Burkes, whose Whig pedigree, history and qualifications for this unlimited trust may be learnt from those who have been lately in Ireland.'[1] The point of bringing in Will Burke (1728–98) was that he represented another chink in Burke's armour, in addition to the Catholic one. Will's financial reputation was dubious and his finances were entangled with Edmund's own, in ways that sometimes brought Burke near to the brink of disaster. The sneer at the Whig pedigree is a reference to Burke's Jacobite connections, through the Nagles.

After the end of the session, the king dismissed Rockingham, and called on Lord Chatham to form a new Administration. What George III liked about Chatham was that he, like George, was opposed to 'connection'. 'Connection' meant acting like a political party. When a connection formed an Administration, it meant that its members acted in concert, in a manner approaching what would later be known as 'cabinet responsibility'. The Rockinghams formed a 'connection' on principle. The king felt their connection interfered with the exercise of his proper authority. Chatham believed in 'measures not men' – a piece of cant, in Burke's view – and drew his ministers from every faction represented in Parliament. The king believed that an Administration so composed would leave more scope for the exercise of his personal authority than had existed under the Rockinghams. George was right about that, but the consequences of his enlarged power were to prove unfortunate for his realm. (See Introduction, pp. lxi–lxiii).

A few days after the Rockingham Administration's dismissal, Burke wrote a pamphlet, *A Short Account of a Short Late Administration*, celebrating the Administration's achievements. The pamphlet included the sentence: 'The Passions and Animosities of the Colonies, by judicious and lenient Measures, were allayed and composed, and

[1] Cone, *Burke and the Nature of Politics*, Vol. I (1957) p. 98. Grenville had probably been talking to William Hamilton, the oracle of those who resented Burke's 'impudence'.

the Foundation laid for a lasting Agreement amongst them.'[1] He must have regretted the complacency of that wording, before the 1767 session was well under way. Yet he could, and did, reasonably argue that, if succeeding Administrations had not foolishly adopted policies quite contrary to those of the Rockinghams, the 'foundation' laid in 1766 would indeed have endured.

The news of the repeal of the Stamp Act was greeted with rejoicing in America, and the Declaratory Act was ignored. Burke's name was among those toasted in America both on the news of their repeal, and on the anniversary celebrations of that event up to 1770.[2] It was only when, after new duties had been imposed, unrest began to turn to revolution, in the mid-1770s, that the Declaratory Act began to look more significant to Americans than the repeal of the Stamp Act, and the names of Burke and his friends ceased to be 'relevant', to use a term dear to more modern militants.

1767

'None of the politicians in 1767 was thinking of America' –
JOHN BROOKE.[3]

The repeal of the Stamp Act brought the disturbances in America to an end, for the time being, and restored commerce between Britain and the colonies. But some disputed issues remained. One was in New York, whose Assembly had refused to make the appropriations for barrack supplies, thus defying the 1765 Mutiny Act, which required colonial legislatures to provide, at their own expense, facilities for imperial troops, Charles Townshend (1725–67),[4] the new Chancellor of the Exchequer, was the driving force at this time of the Administration nominally headed by Chatham. He had opposed repeal of the Stamp Act, and was now determined to quell insubordination in the colonies and to raise a revenue there. Townshend decided to make an example of New York. He introduced resolutions condemning the Assembly and approving the making of a Bill to

[1] *Writings and Speeches* II, 55–56.
[2] Hoffman, *Edmund Burke*, p. 101.
[3] *The Chatham Administration* (London, 1956) p. 332.
[4] Townshend was younger brother to George Townshend, the fourth viscount and Lord Lieutenant of Ireland (see Chapter I, pp. 61–2).

suspend it. The Rockinghams, now in opposition, were uncertain as a body about what to do about the new administration's American measures. Paul Langford notes: [1] 'In the midst of a highly confusing political situation, the Rockinghams were embarrassed by their conflicting desires to oppose the ministry without alienating friends such as Conway who remained in it, and to co-operate with their colleagues in opposition, the Bedford and Grenville parties, without betraying the American principles, which they had espoused in 1766. It is clear that Dowdeswell in particular, while not wishing to support Townshend, was deeply disturbed by the conduct of the colonists, as indeed were most of the friends of America, not excepting Chatham and Shelburne.'

On 13 May 1767, Burke spoke against the proposal to suspend the New York Assembly. The speech is fully in line with the policy of non-interference in American affairs he had laid down in his Declaratory Act speech. He now makes a forceful, unequivocal attack, showing no trace of the 'conflicting desires', which we know to have afflicted the Rockinghams collectively at this time, on the subject of America:

> It is with unaffected Sorrow of heart I see the Business of America come again before the House. Because every such Event affords a new, a convincing, and surely a most humiliating proof of the utter insufficiency of publick Debate to discuss, and of parliamentary regulation to settle anything upon a subject of so very intricate and so very delicate a policy.
>
> The proposition which is made to you is liable to every objection which can be brought against an executive plan as violent, unjust; and ineffective. 1st. Objection. That the enforcing penalties not essentially connected with the Act. It is collateral to it; it is foreign to it. It proceeds in Effect by an interdict of all Government – nor tends except by a side Wind to its execution. It touches another object – for if the Colonists are satisfied to dispense with any New Provincial Laws, that act is utterly destitute and falls to the ground. And then after you have made this Law to enforce your Last: you must make another to enforce that – and so on in the endless rotation of Vain and impotent Efforts – Every great act you make must be attended with a little act like a Squire to carry his Armour. And the power and wisdom of Parliament will wander about, the ridicule of the world.
>
> 2dly. It is not penal as all Laws ought to the immediate offender but falls equally heavy on the innocent and guilty – upon the factious and

[1] *Writings and Speeches* II, 57–8. Although Dowdeswell was the Rockinghams' leader in the Commons, Burke was clearly not taking a lead from him on America.

the moderate. Nay it falls heaviest on the best for few but the good, the sober and the industrious greatly feel the want of Laws. . . .

3dly. It falls even upon that Government which it would avenge and support – Government has an Interest in subsidies and Laws as well as the Subject – If you put a stop to them you stop the Machine and then your Method of executing your Laws is by weakening and destroying all the Executive power you have in the Country. Miserable as your power is, until I see a revenue for its support, I will not wantonly throw away the support you have, how do you enforce your act? by suspending their Legislature – observe that during this suspense of their authority; you suspend your own.

It would be particularly hard to reconcile this speech, in its political context, with the Namierite view of Burke as a party hack, possessing the knack of dressing up the party line in fancy language. As Paul Langford says: 'Burke's attack on the resolutions went further than most of his friends would have gone.'[1]

Townshend's proposal for suspension was easily carried. As it happened, it did no harm, because the New York Assembly, before word of the proposal reached them, had decided, after all, to comply with the Mutiny Act. On 15 May, however, Townshend introduced new revenue duties, which were to renew the revolutionary process in America that had been halted in the previous year by the repeal of the Stamp Act. Did Burke oppose Townshend's new duties when they were introduced? If he did not, that would tend to confirm the view of him as an opportunist. Also, he would have been lying on 8 November 1768, when he said: 'With regard to when this was laid before the House, I expressed the little opinion I had. I shall prove a true Prophet that you will never see a single shilling from America.'[2]

Paul Langford, commenting on that statement in the course of a general disparagement of the Rockinghams in relation to America, said he could find 'no contemporary confirmation' of Burke's claim to have spoken in 1767 on the Townshend duties.[3] In the circumstances, however, the lack of 'contemporary confirmation' – in the shape of a published version of the speech, dating from 1767 – should surely not be allowed much weight, as against Burke's statement, on the floor of the House of Commons, in 1768, that he did make such

[1] *Writings and Speeches* II, 57–8. The quotations are from Burke's draft; a brief account in Walpole's *Memoirs*, Vol III, p. 26, shows that the speech was delivered and establishes the date.

[2] *Writings and Speeches* II, 96.

[3] Langford, *The First Rockingham Administration, 1765–6* (London, 1973) 'Townshend Duties'.

a speech. As already noted, Parliamentary reporting was notoriously incomplete, and whether a published report exists or not is largely a matter of chance. Against Langford's comment, Burke's statement in the House that he did make such a speech, has high evidential value. No sane Parliamentarian would tell his fellow Parliamentarians he had made a certain speech, in the same Parliament, as recently as the previous year, if he had not in fact made it.

Burke could afford even less than other MPs to run such a risk. He had enemies, and suspicious critics, constantly on the watch for things which might be to his discredit. Horace Walpole, one of the critics, had retired from the Commons early in 1768, but he was still attentive to parliamentary business, and likely to pick up and puncture a false claim. George Grenville, one of the enemies, was still an MP and very attentive both to American business and to anything Burke might be up to. If he had ventured a false claim about an American speech, Grenville would have pounced on it and demolished it. Burke's enemies in the newspapers, very active in this period, would have been happy to spread the news of that demolition. It did not occur.

The 1768 statement is virtually self-confirming. But as it happens, we now do have 'contemporary confirmation', dating from 1767, and we owe this to none other than Paul Langford. After becoming General Editor of *The Writings & Speeches Of Edmund Burke*, he discovered Burke's draft of this speech. In *Writings & Speeches* II (pages 61–4) Professor Langford publishes the draft as 'Speech on Townshend Duties, 15 May, 1767'. But he is still not quite convinced that the speech was actually delivered. In a note preceding the published draft, Langford acknowledges that the draft was prepared for the Townshend debates. He goes on: 'It is less easy to be sure that the remarks outlined here were actually delivered, however. Technically the House was considering the resolutions concerning the New York Assembly, approved in Committee on 13 May, and it is known that Burke spoke to them [on 15 May]. . . . It is reasonable to suppose that he made his prepared observations on American policy generally, but no report records sufficient of his speech to make certainty possible. The point is particularly important since in 1768 Burke was to insist that he had opposed Townshend Duties from the beginning, a claim which gains credence from this draft.' Scholarly caution is required of an editor, but surely that good quality is here being pushed to excessive lengths. The lingering doubt casts a gratuitous slur on Burke's character. When it is intrinsically most improbable, from the context, that Burke could have been lying, and when the only positive evidence available goes a long way to confirm the truth of what he claimed, it seems ungenerous to suggest, on the basis of no more than a gap in the evidence, that Burke may still have been lying. I do not suggest that Professor Langford is now personally biased against Burke; he clearly is not. But he was trained within a historiographical tradition – that of Namier – according to which Burke is never to get the benefit of the doubt even when, as here, the doubt, if it exists at all, is infinitesimal.

The speech on the Townshend duties opens:

I confess I feel myself not a little affected to find again before [us] an American Tax upon a principle of supply – as tending in my opinion further to unsettle America, and to weaken the opinion they ought and I hope will have of the Constancy Equity and wisdom of Parliament . . .

You did it [repealed the Stamp Act] solely from an opinion, that a General Tax upon the Colonies was not suitable to their circumstances at that time and not consistent with the principles of Commercial Policy on which they were founded.

You examined Merchants from every part of your extended Dominions, you examined Tradesmen in every part of your extensive Manufactures – The examination was long and in Detail –

What facts are now before you from whence you can infer a difference in their Circumstances or a Change in your own policy – None! It is not whether it be a breach in the Act of Navigation – but whether it be a breach in the true policy of this kingdom – an emulation between Ministers who should be the readiest in finding out American Taxes.[1]

Burke's draft, which at this point takes the form of rough notes, includes the words 'The Taxes – well chosen'. As Langford says, this is 'apparently somewhat at odds with his condemnation of new taxes'. In the context it seems clear that what Burke meant was: 'There shouldn't be any new taxes, but if there have to be some, these ones seem well chosen.' For reasons examined by Langford, it would have been harder for Burke to attack the specific taxes proposed, on glass, paint etc., than to object to new taxation in principle. His leader in the Commons, Dowdeswell, when Chancellor of the Exchequer, had 'entertained very similar plans' to those of Townshend and had indeed passed them to Townshend. Burke would not

[1] *Writings and Speeches* II, 61–64.

be restrained by Dowdeswell from making his opposition to new taxes clear in principle, but neither was he prepared to antagonise Dowdeswell unnecessarily by attacking the specifics of the new taxation. I believe this episode is characteristic of the extent to which Burke was prepared to allow his American speeches to be affected by tactical party considerations. It is a quite limited extent.

The Rockinghams did not divide the House over the Townshend Duties. Probably they were themselves divided over them. Neither Burke nor Dowdeswell would have wished to advertise a division in their ranks. In any case there was now no chance of defeating the Duties, which were extremely popular in Parliament. The country gentlemen looked to the new revenue from America to relieve their tax burden; the placemen – members holding lucrative posts, usually sinecures, at the pleasure of the monarch – saw the prospect of jobs for their relatives. (Placemen were commonly known as 'king's friends'. Burke was in the habit of referring to them as 'the Household Troops'.)

Most parliamentarians were probably thinking about their own affairs, and how America might be used to their advantage, rather than about American affairs in themselves. But that does not justify John Brooke's sweeping generalisation, quoted in the epigraph to this section, 'None of the politicians in 1767 was thinking of America.' The momentum of Namierite reductionism here carries this distinguished historian into a fantasy of omniscience: he imagines he can see into the minds of all the British politicians of 200 years ago, and know what each one of them was thinking about, or at least what each was not thinking about, in 1767.

That generalisation, extravagant though it is, is not random or unmotivated. It has a definite function within a concerted strategy. The Namierite revolution was being consolidated in the 1950s, when Brooke wrote *The Chatham Administration*, and the demolition of the Whig historical tradition was still in progress, though losing momentum. The Whigs had exalted the Rockinghams, and especially Burke, so it was important to cut the Rockinghams, and especially Burke, down to size. The generalisation serves that purpose very neatly. Whig historians had praised the Rockinghams, especially Burke, for the wisdom, consistency and far-sightedness of their views on America. But if 'none of the politicians', including the Rockinghams and including Burke, had been 'thinking about America' in the crucial year 1767, that would seriously detract from their reputation, and from Burke's, concerning America. The introduction of the

Townshend duties is recognised as a crucial event in the lead-up to the American Revolution. If none of the politicians, not even Burke, was thinking about America in the year those duties were imposed, then the wisdom etc. attributed to Burke appears as largely fraudulent. But if the Brooke verdict is accepted, important consequences follow for later years also. If Burke failed to oppose the duties at the time of their imposition, then his later attacks on the Government, in relation to those duties, can be made to appear merely factious and opportunistic. As is duly done in *The Chatham Administration*.

I am not primarily concerned here with the collective reputation of the Rockinghams. I am concerned with Burke. Where he is concerned, Brooke's generalisation is false. We know, from the two 'American' speeches of 1767 that Burke was thinking about America in that year. We know from his own draft for the speech of 15 May, that he was thinking about America at the time of the imposition of the duties. We also know, from the same draft, that his thinking about America, at that moment, was consonant both with his earlier and later thinking about America. In short, the evidence on this crucial point confirms the traditional Whig view of Burke, and invalidates the demeaning interpretation favoured by Brooke and other Namierites. The fact that Burke was indeed 'thinking about America' in 1767 as well as in all the other years of the crisis does not mean that he was not thinking about other matters as well: about parliamentary contingencies and tactics; hopes and fears for the future; personalities of friends and foes. All these affect him to a degree and moderate or stimulate the flight of his eloquence.

His speech opposing the Townshend Duties lacks the cutting edge of his replies to Grenville over the Stamp Act. One reason for this is personalities. They mattered a lot to Burke. He did not like George Grenville, but he did like Charles Townshend (1725–1767), whose secretary he nearly became in 1765.[1] Burke's 1774 posthumous portrait of Grenville, in his speech 'On Taxation', is respectful, perhaps more respectful than Burke felt. But his posthumous portrait of Townshend in the same speech is warmed by admiration and affection. He begins by referring to Townshend's rise to leadership in Chatham's declining years:

For even then, Sir, even before this splendid orb was entirely set, and

[1] A Namierite would hold that, if Burke had become Townshend's secretary, he would have supported the Townshend Duties. I believe that Burke would either have dissuaded Townshend from imposing those duties, or resigned from his service.

while the Western horizon was in a blaze with his descending glory, on the opposite quarter of the heavens arose another luminary, and, for his hour, became lord of the ascendant.

This light too is passed and set for ever. You understand, to be sure, that I speak of Charles Townshend, officially the reproducer of this fatal scheme; whom I cannot even now remember without some degree of sensibility. In truth, Sir, he was the delight and ornament of this house, and the charm of every private society which he honoured with his presence. Perhaps there never arose in this country, nor in any country, a man of a more pointed and finished wit; and (where his passions were not concerned) of a more refined, exquisite, and penetrating a judgement. If he had not so great a stock, as some have had who flourished formerly, of knowledge long treasured up, he knew better by far, than any man I ever was acquainted with, how to bring together within a short time, all that was necessary to establish, to illustrate and to decorate that side of the question he supported. He stated his matter skilfully and powerfully. He particularly excelled in a most luminous explanation, and display of his subject. His style of argument was neither trite and vulgar, nor subtle and abstruse. He hit the house just between wind and water. – And not being troubled with too anxious a zeal for any matter in question, he was never more tedious or more earnest, than the pre-conceived opinions, and present temper of his hearers required; to whom he was always in perfect unison. [1] He conformed exactly to the temper of the house; and he seemed to guide, because he was always sure to follow it.

I beg pardon Sir, if when I speak of this and of other great men, I appear to digress in saying something of their characters. In this eventful history of the revolutions of America, the characters of such men are of much importance. Great men are the guide-posts and land-marks in the state. The credit of such men at court, or in the nation, is the sole cause of all the publick measures. It would be an invidious thing, (most foreign I trust to what you think my disposition) to remark the errors into which the authority of great names has brought the nation, without doing justice at the same time to the great qualities, whence that authority arose. The subject is instructive to those who wish to form themselves on whatever of excellence has gone before them. There are many young members in the house (such of late has been the rapid succession of public men) who never saw that prodigy Charles Townshend; nor of course know what a ferment he was able to excite in every thing by the violent ebullition of his mixed virtues and failings. For failings he had undoubtedly – many of us remember them; we are this day considering the effect of them. But he had no failings which were not owing to a noble cause; to an ardent, generous, perhaps an immoderate passion for Fame; a passion which is

[1] There is an implicit contrast here with Burke's own parliamentary style and how Parliament sometimes received it.

the instinct of all great souls. He worshipped that goddess wheresoever she appeared; but he paid his particular devotions to her in her favourite habitation, in her chosen temple, the House of Commons. Besides the characters of the individuals that compose our body, it is impossible, Mr. Speaker, not to observe, that this house has a collective character of its own. That character too, however imperfect, is not unamiable. Like all great public collections of men, you possess a marked love of virtue, and an abhorrence of vice. But among vices, there is none which the house abhors in the same degree with obstinacy. Obstinacy, Sir, is certainly a great vice; and in the changeful state of political affairs it is frequently the cause of great mischief. It happens, however, very unfortunately, that almost the whole line of the great and masculine virtues, constancy, gravity, magnanimity, fortitude, fidelity, and firmness are closely allied to this disagreeable quality, of which you have so just an abhorrence; and in their excess, all these virtues very easily fall into it. He, who paid such a punctilious attention to all your feelings, certainly took care not to shock them by that vice which is the most disgustful to you. [1]

Burke was not so constituted as to be able to deploy, against a man whom he liked and admired, the cold and cutting condescension which had enraged George Grenville (see above p 108). Affection for Townshend was the first reason for Burke's relatively restrained approach to 1767 Resolutions. The second reason was more pressing. There was another personality, relations with whom also counselled moderation. This was William Dowdeswell, whom Burke respected and worked with closely; their partnership was at the heart of the Rockingham opposition in the Commons. On the question of the Duties, Dowdeswell agreed with Townshend, not Burke. For Burke to oppose the Duties at all must have strained the relation with Dowdeswell; to be really scathing about them might have strained that relationship to breaking point, which would have been a disaster, both for the Rockinghams and for Burke.

There was a third reason, of a more general order, making for moderation. Burke knew that the Townshend Duties would carry, and that they would probably be resisted in America. But he also knew that, if he specifically predicted resistance, he would later be accused of having stimulated what he had predicted. Grenville had made precisely that charge against the Rockinghams over the Stamp Act. So when Burke delivered his warning against the Duties, he did so quietly. But that the warning was delivered quietly is less significant than that it was delivered.

[1] *Writings and Speeches* II, 452–3.

1768–1773

Throughout this period the Rockinghams, including Burke, maintained their opposition to the policy of taxing the colonists, but they did not emphasise that opposition. This is not surprising because, as an issue for mobilising opinion against the Administration – which, after all, is what an opposition must try to do – the Rockingham policy on America was absolutely unsaleable. The policy of raising revenue in America was as overwhelmingly popular in Britain as the resistance of the Americans was overwhelmingly unpopular. The king, the great majority in Parliament, and the mass of the people were all agreed, both about the taxes and about the Americans. Nor were the merchants generally demanding the repeal of the Townshend Duties as they had demanded the repeal of the Stamp Act. The Duties were not quickly followed by any such commercial crisis in Britain as had almost immediately followed the Act.[1] Although there was a downturn in British exports to the American colonies in 1768, it was followed by a steep rise. In 1771 British exports attained by far their highest recorded level: twice the average levels of 1763–66. After that exports fell steeply, reaching zero in 1776. Merchants were uneasy, and some petitioned. But they did not collectively at any stage come out in favour of a repeal of the Townshend duties. No significant body of British opinion favoured that.

In these forbidding circumstances, it is to the credit of the Rockinghams, and of Burke in particular, that they held, with just one brief lapse, in 1770 (see below pp. 131–135) to the sound principles first laid down by Burke in 1766, in his speech on the Declaratory Act. In Parliament Burke reaffirmed those principles repeatedly; he also published a powerful assertion of them in a pamphlet. But his letters show him and his friends generally preoccupied with other topics. Burke seems, during most of this period to have averted his mind from this dismal topic of America. The statement 'none of the politicians in 1767 was thinking of America' was not true, in any year of the prolonged crisis, but it was nearer the truth for Burke in 1768 than in 1767, the year for which it was intended, with malice aforethought against Burke.

[1] Above pp. 105–106. See 'Chart of trade between England and the Thirteen Colonies in America' (1763–1781) in Dora M. Clark, *British Opinion and the American Revolution* (London, 1930) p. 49.

The references in the *Correspondence* to American affairs, in this period, are few and short. In September, after colonial resistance to a circular letter issued by Lord Hillsborough (1718–1793), the new Secretary of State for the Colonies (see below p. 142), Burke writes to Charles O'Hara about the Administration (then in the hands of the third Duke of Grafton (1720–1811) after Charles Townshend's death, in 1767). 'The affairs of America prosper ill in their hands. Lord Hillsborough has taken a step which has influenced and united all that Country. In short they proceed wildly, by fits and starts, without order or System.' [1]

In autumn 1769 Burke is out of humour with the colonial disturbances. 'America,' he writes to Rockingham, 'is more wild and absurd than ever.' [2] He had warned against the 'unsettling' effects of the Townshend Duties, but the actual process of unsettlement was deepening the isolation of the Rockinghams, perceived as friends of the outrageous colonists. There are no further references to America in Burke's political correspondence for 1768–1773. But a letter on 1 September 1769 shows him thinking about America, and not unfavourably, and also giving some reasons for his not having too much to say on the subject. He is writing to an acquaintance, a soldier of fortune who had gone to America: 'It was extremely kind of you to remember your friends in our dull worn out Hemisphere, among infinite Objects of Curiosity, that are so exuberantly spread out before you, in the vast Field of America. There is indeed abundant matter, both natural and political, to give full scope to a mind active and enterprising like yours; where so much has been done, and undone; and where still there is an ample range for wisdom and mistake. Either must produce considerable Effects in an affair of such extent and importance. It will be no light mischief, and no trivial Benefit. When one considers, what might be done there, it is truly miserable to think of its present distracted condition. But as the Errors which have brought things into that state of confusion are not likely to be corrected by any influence of ours, upon either side of the Water, it is not wise to speculate too much on the Subject. It can have no Effect, but to make ourselves uneasy, without any possible advantage to the publick.' [3]

Burke's view that it was 'not wise to speculate too much on the subject', did not prevent him, in practice from making public state-

[1] *Corr.* II, 14.
[2] *Corr.* II, 77.
[3] Letter of 1 February 1774 to General Charles Lee: *Corr.* II, 517–518.

ments on America, when stimulated, provoked, or required by Parliamentary business. On 8 November 1768 he delivered a powerful speech on the address, analysing the disastrous effects of the Townshend Duties (*Writings and Speeches* II, 94–99). In August, 1768 he published a reply to a pamphlet in praise of George Grenville.[1] The reply began:

> I look upon it as one of the principal Misfortunes attendant on Mr. Grenville, that he has not only Enemies, but the very worst kind of Enemies; I mean Friends of very active Zeal, guided by no Sort of Judgement. Upon the Arrival of every Piece of News, whether true or false, of disturbances, whether great or small, in America those persons never fail to take the Opportunity of putting the Public in Mind of that Gentleman. They will never suffer us to forget by whose Means it happened, that those Colonies, who were once not only submissive but most affectionate to their Mother Country, who were contented within themselves, obedient to our Government, and most beneficial to our Commerce, are now become totally estranged, discontented, disobedient, riotous, and, one of them, [Massachusetts] almost rebellious.[2]

In the same article Burke delivers a general attack on the taxation of America: an attack, he was to develop in the pamphlet, *Observations on a Late State of the Nation* (February 1769):

> North America was once indeed a great strength to this nation, in opportunity of ports, in ships, in provisions, in men. We found her a sound, an active, a vigorous member of the empire. I hope, by wise management, she will again become so. But one of our capital present misfortunes is, her discontent and disobedience. To which of the author's favourites this discontent is owing, we all know but too sufficiently. It would be a dismal event, if this foundation of his security, and indeed of all of our public strength, should, in reality, become our weakness; and if all the powers of this empire, which ought to fall with a compacted weight upon the head of our enemies, should be dissipated and distracted by a jealous vigilance, or by hostile attempts upon one another. . . .
>
> Taxes for the purpose of raising revenue had hitherto been sparingly attempted by America. Without ever doubting the extent of its lawful power, parliament always doubted the propriety of such impositions. And the Americans on their part never thought of contesting a right by which they were so little affected. Their assemblies in the main answered

[1] William Knox's *State of the Nation*, October 1768.
[2] *Writings and Speeches* II, 87: Article Signed 'Tandem' in *The Publick Advertiser* of 4 August 1768.

all the purposes necessary to the internal economy of a free people, and provided for all the exigencies of government which arose amongst themselves. In the midst of that happy enjoyment, they never thought of critically settling the exact limits of a power, which was necessary to their union, their safety, their equality, and even their liberty. Thus the two very difficult points, superiority in the presiding state, and freedom in the subordinate, were on the whole sufficiently, that is, practically, reconciled; without agitating those vexatious questions, which in truth rather belong to metaphysics than politicks, and which can never be moved without shaking the foundations of the best governments that have ever been constituted by human wisdom. By this measure was let loose that dangerous spirit of disquisition, not in the coolness of philosophical enquiry, but enflamed with all the passions of an haughty resentful people, who thought themselves deeply injured, and that they were contending for every thing that was valuable in the world. [1]

In that pamphlet – which was widely acclaimed – Burke may have been trying to fend off an emerging commitment that cannot have been to his liking, politically or personally. This was a drift in the direction of an alliance between the Rockinghams and Grenvilles (George Grenville's personal following in Parliament). The idea of such an alliance was a monstrosity in terms of America: an alliance between the author of the Stamp Act, and the authors of the repeal of the Stamp Act. Grenville still maintained the wisdom of the Stamp Act, as the Rockinghams maintained the wisdom of the repeal. In terms of America, the idea of such an alliance made no sense at all. But in terms of purely domestic British politics it made some sense. The Grenvilles and the Rockinghams were in *de facto* alliance against the refusal of the Administration, [2] and its parliamentary majority, to allow the elected member for Middlesex, John Wilkes, to take his seat in parliament. Unlike opposition on the American issue, opposition on the Wilkes issue attracted a significant body of support outside Parliament. In the circumstances it is not altogether surprising that the Rockinghams, smarting from their own isolation and unpopularity, should have been tempted to fudge the American issue in order to coalesce with the Grenvilles.

This development cannot have been congenial to Burke, either politically or personally. Apart from the American issue, he must have remembered Grenville's sneer in the House in June 1766 at his Irishness and his Catholic connections (see above p. 116). In his

[1] *Writings and Speeches* II, 187–9.
[2] *Corr.* II, 26, 85, 93, 115, 169.

correspondence one can sense something of his embarrassment, and concern, over the rapprochement with Grenville. In May 1769 he writes to Charles O'Hara: 'You probably hear that there is a perfect coalition between us and Grenville; but there is nothing more than good humour towards one another, and a determination to act with Joint Forces against this New, usurped, and most dangerous power of the House of Commons, in electing their own Members.'[1] Burke here is clearly trying to limit the alliance to an *ad hoc* one, over Wilkes. He did not succeed. In October 1769 we find him reporting to Rockingham in a conversation, about a wider parliamentary opposition alliance then being mooted including 'the three brothers', (in fact, kinsmen) Chatham, George Grenville, and George Nugent Grenville, third Earl Temple (1753–1813). Burke's report shows him trying to discourage this development, in his conversation with Tommy Townshend, an intermediary between Chatham and Rockingham: 'we talked, as all the world does, of the Union of Parties in opposition, as a thing very happy and certain. I threw out a good many doubts of the possibility of a cordial or safe union for us, under the direction of the Brothers; or of their even consenting to act with us under any other direction.'[2]

Rockingham's reply must have been disconcerting. Rockingham dismisses indeed the notion of the wider alliance, but he comes down in favour of an exclusive alliance with Grenville: 'In many respects amongs the three Brothers – I think G: Grenvile [*sic*] the best for us. The use of him in the House of Commons would be of service, and I think notwithstanding his character of obstinacy &c—He would sacrifice some things, to be really and confidentially united with us.' As if to soften the blow, Rockingham adds: 'I don't mean that in the present moment any thing could be done on this Line – I only think that we might, in regard to communication of ideas of what would be right to do, when Parliament meets – in regard to concerting plans of the operations in the House of Commons &c &c – our manner towards him might be very civil and good Humoured.' The softener is offset, however, by an intimation that the rapprochement with Grenville is approved by a consensus of the Rockingham leadership: 'I have wrote my thoughts so fully and freely in this Letter

[1] *Corr.* II, 26–7.
[2] *Corr.* II, 88. This Townshend (1733–1800) is perhaps best remembered through Goldsmith's couplet on Burke in *Retaliation*, 'Though fraught with all learning yet straining his throat/To persuade Tommy Townshend to lend him a vote.'

that I must beg you would not shew it to anybody except you should see the D: of Richmond – and Lord John Cavendish. I have kept a copy to shew Dowdeswell. I think by what I know of our friends – they would agree in these sentiments.'[1]

The united front came into being early in 1770. Burke had great affection and respect for Rockingham and was obviously disinclined to differ from him on a major question on which he had taken a decision. But the consequence of acquiescence in the alliance was that for the brief time it lasted, in the first half of 1770, he was no longer free to speak his own mind or take initiatives on America. This temporary occultation of his mind in relation to America affairs occurred at a most unfortunate time. Lord North (1732–1792), who had become head of the Administration in the previous autumn, decided to try to restore calm in the colonies, by repealing most of the Townshend Duties.

On 5 March 1770 North moved their repeal – all but the one on tea. In the Commons three speakers urged the repeal of the Tea duty as well. Everything they said conformed with the principles Burke had laid down in his speech on the Declaratory Act, and had often reaffirmed since then. In that debate, however, he was silent. But George Grenville spoke, and what he said may have been the reason why Burke was silent. Having reproached the Administration with inconsistencies, Grenville added: 'I cannot on the one hand suppose that a partial repeal of the present tax will reduce the colonies to temper [i.e. calm], nor on the other by forcing government into a total repeal, can I suppose we have sufficiently provided for the dignity of the nation.'[2]

Less than two years before, Burke had savagely attacked the cant of those who argued that it was necessary to collect the taxes in the colonies in order to preserve the dignity of the nation: 'When they had the peace,' after the repeal of the Stamp Act, 'they began to pine, and whine for their dignity, for some little thing that would give them back their dignity.'[3] Under the political stresses of 1770, however, Burke was obliged to give a respectful hearing to this sort of thing, when it fell from the lips of Grenville. The main significance of the speech was that it constituted a veto, in terms of the Grenville –Rockingham alliance, on calling for a repeal of the Tea Duty. And it was of course the attempt to collect the Tea Duty that was to

[1] *Corr.* II, 89–95.
[2] *Parliamentary History*, xvi, 871.
[3] *Writings and Speeches* II, 96.

keep the colonies plunged into turmoil over the next five years, until turmoil evolved into revolution. On the principles laid down by Burke from 1766 on, the repeal of the Tea Duty was as clear a necessity in 1770, as the repeal of the Stamp Act had been in 1766. But Burke was now silenced on that particular topic, by the alliance.

Rockingham and Grenville reached agreement, probably in April 1770, on a set of resolutions on America to be introduced in Parliament. The most important, and the only one put to a vote, was the second, 'That a principal Cause of the Disorders which have lately prevailed in North America, had arisen from the ill-judged and inconsistent Instructions given, from time to time, by Persons in Administration, to the Governors of some of the Provinces in North America'.[1]

Basically, all that the Rockinghams and the Grenvilles could agree upon, in relation to America, was charging the Administration with inconsistency. The inconsistency lay in following toughness with leniency: Grenville was in favour of the toughness; Rockingham of the leniency. The two leaders were therefore themselves inconsistent in their reasons for charging the Administration with inconsistency. Of the eight resolutions, some were obviously 'Rockingham', others 'Grenville', and of course they clashed. Thus the third resolution was 'Rockingham': 'That the directing the Dissolution of the Assemblies of North America, upon their Refusal to comply with certain Propositions, operated as a Menace injurious to the deliberate Capacity of these Assemblies, and tended to excite Discontent, and to produce unjustifiable Combinations'. The fifth resolution was 'Grenville': 'That it is unwarrantable, of dangerous Consequence, and an high Breach of the Privilege of this House, to promise to the Assemblies of North America the Interposition or Influence of His Majesty, or his confidential Servants, with this House, in any Manner which may tend to create an Opinion in those Assemblies, that such Interposition or Influence, must necessarily bring on a Repeal of any Duties or Taxes laid, or to be laid, by Authority of Parliament.'[2]

Of the eight resolutions, I reckon four as 'Grenville', two as 'Rockingham' and two as 'neutral'. In the Grenville-Rockingham partnership, Grenville was clearly the predominant partner. None of the resolutions mentioned the Tea Duty. Two of the 'Grenville' resol-

---

[1] *Writings and Speeches* II, 332.
[2] *Writings and Speeches* II, 333.

utions were incompatible with everything that Burke had been saying about American Taxation over the past four years:

That it is highly derogatory from His Majesty's Honour, and from the Freedom of Parliamentary Deliberation, to pledge the Faith of the Crown to the said Assemblies, for the repealing, or laying on, or continuing, or not laying of, any Taxes or Duties whatsoever;

That to give Assurances in His Majesty's Name, distinguishing certain Principles of Taxation, and disclaiming an Intention to propose any taxes within the said Description, in order to establish and justify unwarrantable Distinctions, has a Tendency further to disturb the Minds of His Majesty's Subjects in America, and to weaken the Authority of Lawful Government.

Yet it was Burke who was assigned the unenviable task of introducing these resolutions. Having accepted out of loyalty to Rockingham, he duly introduced them, on 9 May 1770. His speech was a polished professional performance and won applause at the time – 'a fine speech,' said Horace Walpole. It was certainly adroit, as shown in the handling of the repeal of the Stamp Act, that delicate issue for the Grenville-Rockingham alliance. Burke allowed for both of the conflicting points of view:

The consequences of this act appeared in two Views one immediate – the other remote – It brought present peace. It might encourage to future disturbance. The first was certain, the Latter was contingent and problematical.' Then Burke passes on to the Townshend Duties, not quite so awkward an issue for the alliance: 'In the next session – it was not thought Right to leave this matter to its natural operation; We begin to tire of the Tranquillity which we enjoyed. It was said We purchased peace by dignity, and now we must purchase dignity at the hazard of peace. At all hazards, America must be taxed again – and reasons given for it which – independent of the taxation, unpopular enough in itself were calculated to irritate them much more than the Taxation. Thus after we had been in Harbour we had got to Sea again on this New Traffick for Dignity. We were on a Rotten bottom. The Winds began to blow. [1]

The trouble with that was that neither the resolutions Burke was introducing nor his own speech made any mention of the only one

[1] *Writings and Speeches* II, 326–327.

of the Townshend Duties that was still in force: the Tea Duty, now the centre of the whole controversy. Burke could not allude to this, since Grenville wanted to keep the Tea Duty, precisely for reasons of 'dignity'. The very evil Burke was denouncing existed within the alliance on whose behalf Burke was speaking. And Burke was speaking on behalf of the alliance, not just the Rockingham end of it. Perhaps the strongest passage in the speech makes what is essentially a 'Grenville' point: that the Administration ought not to have introduced duties without also providing the means for their enforcement:

> At three thousand miles distance, if your Scheme be not wonderfully well arranged indeed, you ought to consider maturely before you leave nothing to immediate discretion to present circumstances. You ought to have looked into all the consequences of that Scheme. To be sure the matter ought to have been well considered before the authority of Government was committed upon such a Measure. They ought to have considered how they could get another assembly – how they could manage the new men so as to prevail on them to disavow the former or how they could contrive to govern without any assembly at all. Had you been in the Cabinet you would have asked every one of these questions? If you had no satisfactory solution upon them you would have desisted from the Scheme. Because if ever there was in all the Proceedings of Government a rule that is fundamental, universal, invariable it is this that you ought never to attempt a measure of authority you are not morally sure you can go through with. For by doing otherwise you risque the whole stock and fund of Government at a single cast of Chance. Its Providence you forfeit in not foreseeing the difficulties it was to engage in its wisdom in not providing against them; Its Powers in not overcoming them. All is lost. All the Machines of Government shown to be without force –.

The alliance did not call for a division on any of the resolutions, except the second, the 'inconsistency' one which was negatived by 199 votes to 79. The others were negatived without a division. Had the division taken place on any of the others, they would have been defeated by even wider margins, since they would have split the Rockinghams from the Grenvilles. The fruits of the alliance are not impressive even in the narrow parliamentary context for which the alliance was created.

That speech of 9 May 1770 causes me some distress, the kind one feels when an admired person is constrained to descend for a time from the intellectual and moral level which he normally inhabits. In that speech, and in that speech alone, over all the sixteen years of the American crisis, Burke actually appears in the role in which hostile historians would cast him for his whole career: that of a party spokesman, dressing up in fine language, policies laid down for him by others. Ross Hoffman comments on the speech: 'No doubt Burke wished to maintain the Empire – which certainly was not yet collapsing – but his immediate aim was to use America as a stick to beat the ministers, for his speech was a mixture of the fundamentally unfusable opinions of the Grenvilles and Rockinghams on America.'[1] Hoffman's comments are fully justified. But by failing to advert to the singularity of this speech – its wholly exceptional character in the long series of Burke's American statements – he gives a misleading impression of Burke's general approach to America, greatly exaggerating the 'party factor.'

Normally, Burke influenced Rockingham more than Rockingham influenced him. But Rockingham under the potent influence of Grenville was a different Rockingham. Burke was now feeling, through Rockingham, the pressure of an imperious alien will, and of a system of ideas essentially inimical to his own. I suspect that he could not have submitted to that pressure for long. As it was, he didn't have to. On 13 November 1770 George Grenville died. The alliance died with him. The repealer of the Stamp Act was no longer the prisoner of the author of the Stamp Act. The time of occultation was over.[2]

It is remarkable that for nearly four years, between May 1770 and March 1774, American affairs did not again come to the attention of Parliament. The Administration had no occasion to bring them there, and the Opposition knew that whenever it might raise them, it would receive another drubbing in terms of parliamentary votes, without striking any sympathetic chord in any significant sector of British public opinion. Throughout this period, the public was profoundly indifferent to American affairs. As Burke wrote to Rockingham on 2 February 1774: 'Your Lordship remarks very rightly on the supineness of the publick. Any Remarkable Highway Robbery at Hounslow Heath would make more conversation than all the disturbances of America.'[3] Burke, however, did not cease 'thinking about America'. Indeed, as London agent for the New York

---

[1] Hoffman, *Edmund Burke*, p. 69.

[2] Burke himself does not seem to have been conscious that occultation had occurred. Twelve days later he wrote a cheerful letter to O'Hara claiming to have emerged with 'credit' from his performance. We all deceive ourselves at times and a great man may have greater powers of self-deception than the rest of us. And perhaps that is the way occultation works.

[3] *Corr.* II, 524.

Assembly, he was paid for thinking about it. New York was one of the more 'moderate' of the colonies and so appreciated his efforts, as over the repeal of the Stamp Act, to avert the threat of revolution. But he is frank, in his 1772 letter to John Cruger (1710–1791), Speaker of the New York Assembly (see above p. 95), about the inability of himself and his friends to do much for America under present conditions: 'The strength of Opposition remains nearly the same as ever – unexerted indeed, but unimpaired. You know that everything in political conduct depends upon occasions and opportunities. In the present state of things it has been thought advisable to be less active than formerly. Since it has appeared upon a multitude of trials and upon a great variety of matters that there is a determined, systematical, and considerable majority in both houses in favour of the Court scheme [to coerce America], an unremitted fight would only serve to exhibit a longer series of defeats. It was therefore thought advisable to attend to circumstances and to pitch only upon those where the advantage of situation might supply the want of numbers, or where though without hope of victory, you could not decline the combat without disgrace. This was, during the last session, the measure of our conduct.'[1]

On 16 December 1773, however, an event occurred which was to bring the parliamentary dead calm to an end: the Boston Tea Party, that conspicuous act of defiance to which the North Administration decided to respond by a series of coercive measures. This created one of these situations where, in Burke's opinion, 'you could not decline the combat without disgrace.' As it happened, the Boston Tea party linked the American crisis with the next in sequence of Burke's great global preoccupations, for the tea was the property of the East Indian Company. On this imperial conjuncture of 1773 one of Warren Hasting's biographers, Sir Alfred Lyall, wrote with insight: 'It is useful to recollect that the tea thrown into Boston harbour in December 1773 belonged to the East India Company, and had been allowed free export by way of helping them commercially; for the incident fixes important dates, and marks a curious point of connection between eastern and western complications. And while it is remarkable that a petty concession to the Indian trading company should have been the signal for rebellion in the American colonies, such an electric

---

[1] Letter to John Cruger: 6th May 1772; in Hoffman, *Edmund Burke, New York Agent*, p. 208.

reverberation across the horizon illustrates the tempestuous condition of the whole political atmosphere.'[1]

1774

The first of the North Administration's coercive Measures after the
Tea Party was the Boston Port Bill, which proclaimed the closure of
the port until Bostonians accepted the tea duties and paid compensation for the Party. When it was introduced in the Commons, in
March 1774, Burke spoke in opposition to it. He conceded that the
perpetrators of the Tea Party might properly be punished, but he
argued strongly against the collective punishment of an entire city:

> You can't pursue this Example, if other Towns should do the like. Have
> you considered what to do if this Example should not operate as you
> wish? Would you put a total proscription to the whole Trade of America.
> Virginia does not mean to pay our Taxes, as its asserted. If we stop the
> Trade there We lose £300,000 per annum revenue, as well as a great
> loss by many other means. I do not say punishment ought not to be
> inflicted on America and I think it might and on the offenders too. If
> punishment is not just but rigorous its a double Cause of Complaint. To
> make a place Situate on the Sea Coast, as an Island place is the heaviest
> punishment that can be. Every punishment is unjust that is inflicted on a
> party unheard. This distance of the party is no argument for not hearing.
> Its a devilish doctrine that every person is punishable where a riot is
> committed, even though it should be out of his power to prevent it. We
> punish the Governed for the faults of the Governors.[2]

Or, as Burke puts it elsewhere: 'We whip the child until it cries, and
then we whip it for crying.'

The Rockinghams did not divide the House on the Bill. Burke
explains why in a letter to the Committee of the New York Assembly:
'The popular current, both within doors and without, sets strongly
against America. There were indeed not wanting some persons [i.e.
the Rockinghams] in the House of Commons who disapproved of
the Bill and who expressed their disapprobation in the strongest and
most explicit terms. But their arguments upon this point made so

[1] Lyall, *Warren Hastings* (London, 1889) p. 52.
[2] *Writings and Speeches* II, 405.

little impression that it was not thought advisable to divide the House. Those who spoke in opposition did it more for the acquittal of their own honour and discharge of their own consciences, by delivering their free sentiments on so critical an occasion, than from any sort of hope they entertained of bringing any considerable number to their opinion, or even of keeping in that opinion several of those who had formerly concurred in the same general line of policy with regard to the Colonies.'

'The acquittal of their own honour and the discharge of their own consciences . . .' Burke's own conscience and sense of honour were exigent. Neither can have been entirely happy with his 9 May 1770 speech on America, or with the long Rockingham silence that followed it. A sense of release from oppressive constraints may do something to account for the splendour of Burke's eloquence in the two famous speeches. 'On American Taxation' in 1774 and, in the next year, 'On Conciliation with America'.

With Grenville gone, Rockingham had again become open to Burke's influence; Rockingham was also temperamentally disinclined from coercive measures. Both factors probably contributed to the resumption of active opposition on American issues, in spite of the fact that the party knew such opposition to be even more hopeless, politically speaking, than it had been in 1770. The Rockinghams now took the decision from which they had flinched in 1770 (see above pp. 131–135). They decided to call for the repeal of the one remaining Townshend Duty, on tea. This decision set Burke free once more to speak on America with the full force of his mind; as he had been able to do in 1766 over the Declaratory Resolution and as he had not been able to do in 1770 when introducing the hotch-potch of the Rockingham-Grenville resolutions. [1]

On 19 April, speaking in support of a motion for the repeal of the Tea Duty Burke delivered the speech which was later published as 'On American Taxation'. It was part of his strategy, in all his American pronouncements after his maiden speech, to review the past history of the question, showing that non-taxation of the colonists, as exemplified by the repeal of the Stamp Act, had been a wise policy, and that taxation, as exemplified by the Townshend Duties, had been proved to be unwise. Immediately before Burke rose Charles Cornwall, a member of the North Administration, had tried to pre-

[1] Compare, in Chapter IV (p. 316) the release of Burke's energies, once he had decided, after 1781, to commit himself fully to the cause of India and to ignore the justifiable misgivings of his party colleagues.

empt this type of argument by affirming that it was the present, not the past, which should be of concern to the House. Burke's reply, which had to be impromptu, is remarkable both for its concentrated and polished argument and for the sudden stinging epigram of its conclusion:

> He asserts, that retrospect is not wise; and the proper, the only proper subject of enquiry is, 'not how we got into this difficulty, but how we are to get out of it'. In other words, we are, according to him, to consult our invention, and to reject our experience. The mode of deliberation he recommends is diametrically opposite to every rule of reason, and every principle of good sense established amongst mankind. For, that sense and that reason, I have always understood, absolutely to prescribe, whenever we are involved in difficulties from the measures we have pursued, that we should take a strict review of those measures, in order to correct our errors if they should be corrigible; or at least to avoid a dull uniformity in mischief, and the unpitied calamity of being repeatedly caught in the same snare.

Burke is *debating*, not just delivering, a 'fine harangue,' as Walpole said. And perhaps the most remarkable feature of 'On American Taxation' is the way in which the impromptu debating points are made to fit into and embellish a pattern of which the general lines were clearly thought out in advance. The phrase 'a dull uniformity in mischief' is both an effective reply to Cornwall's particular objection and a devastating characterisation of the policies towards America pursued by every British Administration since 1766. To be able to reply to an objection on the floor of the House, in such a way that the reply blends into the texture and pattern of the prepared part of the speech and becomes indistinguishable from it, is a sure mark of deep personal conviction. No party hack, however clever, could pull off a trick like that, in any age. In much the same way Burke takes another particular objection of Cornwall's and, in carefully replying to it, moves by a series of logical steps through to a powerful attack on the whole record and present position of the Administration:

> He desires to know, whether, if we were to repeal this tax, agreeably to the proposition of the Hon. Gentleman who made the motion, the Americans would not take post on this concession, in order to make a new attack on the next body of taxes; and whether they would not call for a repeal of the duty on wine as loudly as they do now for the repeal of the duty on tea? Sir, I can give no security on this subject. But I will do all

that I can, and all that can be fairly demanded. To the *experience* which the Hon. Gentleman reprobates in one instant, and reverts to in the next; to that experience, without the least wavering or hesitation on my part, I steadily appeal; and would to God there was no other arbiter to decide on the vote with which the House is to conclude this day! [1]

When Parliament repealed the Stamp Act in the year 1766, I affirm, first, that the Americans did *not* in consequence of this measure call upon you to give up the former parliamentary revenue which subsisted in that Country; or even any one of the articles which comprise it. I affirm also, that when, departing from the maxims of that repeal, you revived the scheme of taxation, and thereby filled the minds of the Colonists with new jealousy, and all sorts of apprehensions, then it was that they quarrelled with the old taxes, as well as the new; then it was, and not till then, that they questioned all the parts of your legislative power; and by the battery of such questions have shaken the solid structure of this Empire to its deepest foundations. [2]

Burke can also move in the other direction: from a general attack on the Administration down to particular observations of the previous speaker, and then back again, using Cornwall's remarks to refuel the general attack. In linking the personal with the general in the following passage Burke also delicately suggests the venality which underlay so much of the support for the Administration. Cornwall had been a strong supporter of the Rockinghams but had defected from them in the previous year. He was rewarded by becoming a Lord of the Treasury. Hence the reference to 'his new friends' in the speech, which gives a good idea of the undulating continuity of Burke's oratory:

It is then, Sir, upon the principle of this measure, and nothing else, that we are at issue. It is a principle of political expediency. Your act of 1767 asserts, that it is expedient to raise a revenue in America; your act of 1769, which takes away that revenue [3], contradicts the act of 1767; and, by something much stronger than words, asserts, that it is not expedient. It is a reflection upon your wisdom to persist in a solemn parliamentary declaration of the expediency of any object, for which, at the same time,

---

[1] Burke is here referring to the Crown's influence through the 'placemen'. In 1774, however – at any date from 1766 to 1778 for that matter – the Administration would have had a majority even without this factor, because the policy of taxing the Americans, and of coercing them when they resisted taxation, was then extremely popular with the British public.

[2] *Writings and Speeches* II, 410–11.

[3] This was the measure that dropped all the Townshend Duties, except on tea.

you make no sort of provision. And pray Sir, let not this circumstance escape you; it is very material; that the preamble of this act which we wish to repeal, is not declaratory of a right, as some gentlemen seem to argue it: It is only a recital of the expediency of a certain exercise of a right supposed already to have been asserted; an exercise you are now contending for by ways and means, which you confess, though they were obeyed to be utterly insufficient for their purpose. You are therefore at this moment in the awkward situation of fighting for a phantom; a quiddity; a thing that wants, not only a substance, but even a name; for a thing which is neither abstract right, nor profitable enjoyment.

They tell you, Sir, that your dignity is tied to it. I know not how it happens, but this dignity of yours is a terrible incumberance to you; for it has of late been ever at war with your interest, your equity, and every idea of your policy. Shew the thing you contend for to be reason; shew it to be common sense, shew it to be the means for attaining some useful end; and then I am content to allow it what dignity you please. But what dignity is derived from the perseverance in absurdity is more than ever I could discern. The Hon. Gentleman has said well – indeed, in most of his general observations I agree with him – he says, that this subject does not stand as it did formerly. Oh, certainly not! Every hour you continue on this ill-chosen ground, your difficulties thicken on you; and therefore my conclusion is, remove from a bad position as quickly as you can. The disgrace, and the necessity of yielding, both of them, grow upon you every hour of your delay.

But will you repeal the act, says the Hon. Gentleman, at this instant when America is in open resistance to your authority, and that you have just revived your system of taxation? He thinks he has driven us into a corner. But thus pent up, I am content to meet him; because I enter the lists supported by my old authority, his new friends, the ministers themselves. The Hon. Gentlemen remembers, that about five years ago as great disturbances as the present prevailed in America on account of the new taxes. The ministers represented these disturbances as treasonable; and this House, thought proper, on that representation, to make a famous address for a revival, and for a new application of a statute of Henry VIII. [1] We besought the King, in that well-considered address, to enquire into treasons and to bring the supposed traitors from America to Great Britain for trial. His Majesty was pleased graciously to promise a compliance with our request. All the attempts from this side of the House to resist these violences, and to bring about a repeal were treated with the utmost scorn. An apprehension of the very consequences now

[1] The statute of 1543 (35 Hen. VIII c.2) regulating treasons outside the realm of England. The Chatham Administration had obtained parliamentary approval in the 1768–9 session for using this statute against rebellious colonists.

stated by the Hon. Gentleman, was then given as a reason for shutting the door against all hope of such an alteration. And so strong was the spirit for supporting the new taxes that the session concluded with the following remarkable declaration. After stating the vigorous measures which had been pursued, the Speech from the Throne proceeds:

'You have assured me of your firm support in the prosecution of them. Nothing, in my opinion, could be more likely to enable the well-disposed among my subjects in that part of the world, effectually to discourage and defeat the designs of the factious and seditious, than the hearty concurrence of every branch of the Legislature, in maintaining the execution of the laws in every part of my dominions.'

After this no man dreamt that a repeal under this ministry could possibly take place. The Hon. Gentleman knows as well as I, that the idea was utterly exploded by those that sway the house. This Speech was made on the ninth day of May, 1769. Five days after this Speech, that is, on 13th of the same month, the public Circular Letter a part of which I am going to read to you was written by Lord Hillsborough Secretary of State for the Colonies. After reciting the substance of the King's speech he goes on thus:

'I can take upon me to assure you, not withstanding insinuations to the contrary from men with factious and seditious views, that His Majesty's present administration have at no time entertained a design to propose to parliament to lay any further taxes upon America, for the purpose of RAISING A REVENUE: and that it is at present their intention to propose the next Session of parliament to take off the duties upon glass, paper and colours, upon consideration of such duties having being laid contrary to the true principles of Commerce.

'These have always been, and still are, the sentiments of His Majesty's present servants; and by which their conduct in respect to America has been governed. And his Majesty relies upon their prudence and fidelity for such an explanation of his measures as may tend to remove the prejudices which have been excited by the misrepresentations of those who are enemies to the peace and prosperity of Great Britain and her Colonies; and to re-establish that mutual confidence and affection, upon which the glory and safety of the British Empire depend.'

Here, Sir, is a canonical book of ministerial scripture; the general epistle to the Americans. What does the gentleman say to it? Here a repeal is promised; promised without condition; and while your authority was actually resisted. I pass by the public promise of a Peer relative to the repeal of taxes by this House. I pass by the use of the King's name in a matter of supply, that sacred and reserved right of the Commons. I conceal the ridiculous figure of Parliament, hurling its thunders at the gigantic rebellion of America; and then five days after prostrate at the feet of those assemblies we affected to despise; begging them by the intervention of our ministerial sureties, to receive our submission; and heartily promising amendment. These might have been serious matters formerly; but we are grown wiser than our fathers.[1]

That last sentence has a foretaste of the Burke of *Reflections*, sixteen years later.

Burke's mastery of cumulative argument appears in the above passage. He was also the master of the pithy retort. The Marquis of Carmarthen, earlier in the debate, had said that 'the Americans are our children and how can they revolt against their parent?' Burke replied: 'They are "our children"; but when children ask for bread we are not to give a stone.'[2]

Much comment on this speech acknowledges the power of Burke's oratory but fails to recognise that its power derives in great part from the force of its reasoning, and from the depth of conviction that underlies the reasoning. Several commentators, at the time and since, have suggested that, fine speech though it is, it recommends no policy. But it does recommend a policy, both through its general tenor and in the following specific passage:

Again, and again, revert to your old principles – seek peace and ensue it – leave America, if she has taxable matter in her, to tax herself. I am not here going into the distinctions of rights, nor attempting to mark their boundaries. I do not enter into these metaphysical distinctions; I hate the very sound of them. Leave the Americans as they antiently stood, and these distinctions, born of our unhappy contest, will die along with it. They, and we, and their and our ancestors, have been happy under that system. Let the memories of all actions, in contradiction to that good old mode, on both sides, be extinguished for ever. Be content to bind America by laws of trade; you have always done it. Let this be your reason for binding their trade. Do not burthen them by taxes; you were not used to do so from the beginning. Let this be your reason for not taxing. These are the arguments of states and kingdoms. Leave the rest to the schools [of metaphysics]; for there only they may be discussed with safety. But if, intemperately, unwisely, fatally, you sophisticate and poison the very source of government, by urging subtle deductions, and consequences odious to those you govern, from the unlimited and illimitable nature of

[1] *Writings and Speeches* II, 418–420.
[2] *Writings and Speeches* II, 459.

supreme sovereignty, you will teach them by these means to call that sovereignty itself in question. [1]

The motion for the repeal of the Tea Duty was defeated by 182 to 49. As Paul Langford observed: 'Considering that Rockingham had taken particular pains to rally the forces of his party for that day, this represented a crushing defeat for the opposition.' [2] There must have been some among the Rockinghams who felt that the margin of defeat vindicated the previous practice of keeping quiet about America.

Burke, however, persevered. In April he spoke against the Massachusetts Bay Regulation Bill, the second and toughest of North's coercive measure: it removed the appointment of the Massachusetts Council from popular to royal control and dealt similarly with juries. Burke rose late at night, at 11.45, and spoke for an hour and a quarter; he had a rough ride. One report shows him feeling the pressure: 'I do feel myself what with the weight upon me, and the temper of the House under a difficulty to go on. I shall endeavour to contract as narrowly as I can to comply with the temper of the House and with my own weakness, to comply with the temper of the House (a great noise) my respect to the House absolutely makes me silent: my respect to my duty absolutely pushes me on. First the magnitude of the subject, my mind saturated with it I scarce know where to begin or where to end. I will jump into the middle of it.' Another report shows him as defiant: 'The House being noisy, several members going out soon after which he got up and said I find, Sir, I have got my voice and I shall beat down the noise of the House.' [3] The reports are compatible, for different phases of the ordeal, and both can be accepted.

The Massachusetts Bay Regulation Bill was overwhelmingly

---

[1] *Writings and Speeches* II, 458. As regards 'binding their trade', Carl B. Cone, *American Revolution*, pp. 261–2, suggests that, if the Tea Duty had been repealed, the colonists' next objective would have been the repeal of the Navigation Acts restricting trade with the colonists. True enough. But the logic of Burke's general position would require that he would demand the abandonment of the Navigation Acts also, once it was clear that the Americans opposed them. He was always a free-trader by instinct and became one in principle after the publication of Adam Smith's *The Wealth Of Nations*, in 1776. (Burke said that 'in its ultimate results' it was 'probably the most important book ever written'.)

[2] *Writings and Speeches* II, 463. The Rockinghams, without support from the rest of the Opposition, could normally muster about seventy votes.

[3] *Writings and Speeches* II, 464.

carried, by 239 votes to 64 and the other excise acts were carried by similar margins. 'Within doors' opposition on American issues was both futile and unpleasant. But outside the doors there were, for the first time since 1766, signs that some people were attending favourably to what Burke was saying. At the end of June he received an inquiry from Dr. the Rev. Thomas Wilson (1703–84), Rector of St. Margaret's, Westminster, as to whether he would stand as candidate for Bristol if his friends there were strong enough to nominate him. The main reason, though not the only one, why Burke had attracted support in Bristol was that he was known there as 'an able opponent of many odious measures – especially those injurious to American trade.'

Bristol was the principal port for the American Trade and although its merchants seemed on the whole to have shared in the general merchant acquiescence in the Townshend Duties, some seemed to have taken alarm at North's coercive measures. Burke replied cautiously, expressing willingness, but not eagerness, to stand.[1] This correspondence was eventually to lead, after a number of vicissitudes, to Burke's winning Bristol, in the general election of 1774. His new position, as member for the second greatest commercial city of Great Britain, greatly enhanced his prestige and influence in Parliament, and his authority in the councils of the Rockinghams. As for the drearily reductionist hypothesis, consistent with the Namierite view of Burke, that the speech 'On American Taxation' may have been no more than a smart wheeze for winning a seat in Bristol, there is no evidence for such a suggestion. The circumstances in which he was to sacrifice the seat six years later refute it.

He did not at first entertain much hope for Bristol, though he needed to find a seat. His patron, Lord Verney, being in financial difficulties, was compelled to sell Wendover to someone else. Burke understood the necessity for this, and it did not alter his regard for Verney. As the American editor of Volume III of Burke's Correspondence, George H. Guttridge, in the preface (p. xi) observes 'It is characteristic of his deep loyalty that even in this predicament, when he talked of retiring from politics, his letters showed as much concern for Verney's political future as for his own.'

In September Burke wrote a long and unusually personal letter to Rockingham. He writes in a despondent vein, which is also unusual, about America, about British politics, and about his own situation.

[1] *Corr.* III, 3.

In America, he correctly foresees a long-drawn-out struggle but, perhaps because of his mood, he underestimates the capacity of the Americans to sustain such a struggle: 'I agree with your Lordship entirely, that the American and foreign affairs will not come to any crisis, sufficient to rouse the publick from its present Stupefaction, during the Course of the next Session. I have my doubts whether, those, at least of America, will do it for some years to come. I don't know, whether the London Papers have taken in the Pensylvania instructions to their Representatives. Lest they should not, I send your Lordship the Philadelphia Paper which contains them. It is evident from the Spirit of these instructions, as well as by the measure of a Congress, and consequent Embassy, that the affair will draw out into great Length. If it does, I look upon it as next to impossible, that the present Temper and unanimity of America can be kept up; Popular remedies must be quick and sharp or they are very ineffectual.'[1]

In British politics the scene is equally bleak: 'But in the present Temper of the Nation, and with the Character of the present administration, the disorder and discontent of all America and the more remote future mischiefs, which may arise from those Causes, operate as little as the division of Poland. The insensibility of the Merchants of London is of a degree and kind scarcely to be conceived. Even those most likely to be overwhelmed by any real American confusion are amongst the most supine.'[2]

As regards his personal situation, Burke mentions his troubles at Wendover (but not the Bristol possibility, which he seems to have considered at an end by this time): 'In this difficulty which is super-added to others, though sometimes when I am alone, in spite of all my Efforts, I fall into a melancholy which is inexpressible; and to which if I gave way, I should not continue long under it, but must totally sink. Yet I do assure you, that partly and indeed principally, by the force of natural good Spirits, and partly by a strong sense of what I ought to do, I bare up so well, that no one who did not know them could easily discover the State of my Mind or my Circumstances. I have those that are dear to me, for whom I must live as long as God pleases; and in what way he pleases. Whether I ought not totally to abandon this publick station for which I am so unfit, and have, of course, been so unfortunate, I know not. It is certainly

---

[1] *Corr.* III, 30.
[2] *Corr.* III, 31.

not so easy to arrange me in it, as it has been hither to. Most assuredly I never would put my feet within the Doors of Saint Stephen's Chappel without being as much my own master as hitherto I have been, and at Liberty to pursue the same Course.'[1] (The use of the expression, 'my own master', in a letter from Burke to the leader of his party, is interesting, with the implied assumption that his leader agrees with this view of the matter. By this time, of course, Burke and Rockingham knew one another very well indeed and trusted one another completely. 'Livery' indeed!)[2]

Early in October Burke got his nomination for Bristol. He expected it so little that before it arrived he had set out for Malton, a borough offered to him by Rockingham. On learning of the nomination, Burke chose to fight for Bristol. It was a hard-fought campaign and, like all his enemies, his opponents automatically attacked him on his weak side: his Irish Catholic connections. Ironically, one of the reasons which had initially commended him to his Bristol supporters was the anti-Papist zeal attributed to him there (Horace Walpole would have been amused). Dr. Wilson, in making the original tentative offer, had said that 'the Quebec Affair' had aroused the Bristol Quakers and Dissenters, 'making the time especially favourable for such an intervention as he proposed.'[3]

Almost all the commotion in America ÷ and all the commotion in Britain – against the Quebec Act of 1774, had been anti-Papist in character. Since Burke had voted against the Quebec Bill, these Quakers and Dissenters of Bristol made the simplistic assumption that he was a sound anti-Papist. But he had made it clear in his speech of 10 June that his opposition to the Bill was not on anti-Catholic grounds. Probably, no one in Bristol had read that speech. So, in July, and from a distance, Burke had looked like a good Protestant to some of his Bristol supporters. By October and in the throes of a contested election, his opponents were busy trying to clear up that misconception.

His younger brother Richard (1733–1794), who acted as his election agent, was so worried about the 'Saint Omer & Popery' stories that he sought the help of Burke's Quaker friend, Richard Shackleton. The faithful Shackleton promptly came to the rescue with the following, addressed to William Fry, a prominent Quaker preacher in Bristol: 'I this day (and not before) was informed that Edmund

[1] *Corr.* III, 35.
[2] 'The men whose livery [Burke] happened to have taken.' (Namier).
[3] *Corr.* III, 3.

Burke had offered himself a candidate to represent your city in Parliament. . . . Having had a particular intimacy with Edmund Burke from our early youth . . . I think then thou mayst with great truth assure our friends there, and anyone else in thy freedom, that Edmund Burke is a man of the strictest honour and integrity; *a firm and staunch protestant*; a zealous advocate (not an enthusiastic brawler) for that which rightly deserves the name of liberty.' [1]

The words 'a firm and staunch protestant' and the emphasis given to them were probably suggested by Richard Burke. Shackleton would not have meant those words to imply that Burke was a bigoted anti-Papist. He knew that Burke was not like that, and would not have lied, even to protect his friend. All the same, that was what the words did mean, in the context of the Bristol election, and they must have helped Burke's chances with the Quakers of Bristol. Not for the first time, Ballitore and its Quaker school are being used to filter out, from Burke's public past, his unacceptable associations with Catholic Ballyduff and the hedge school under the ruins of Monanimy Castle.

The strain he was under during the election, partly by reason of the rumours, is reflected in the furious letter he wrote, on the eve of the poll, to a Bristol merchant who had refused to support him because of some story the merchant had heard from one George Prescott: 'I should still presume to solicit the favour of your Support, if I thought you had been an absolute Stranger to George Prescott. In that case it might be very natural, that you should give some momentary Credit to a Story from him. But as it is universally known that he is the lowest and most infamous of mankind, and one whose cowardice alone protects him from the punishments his daily false-hoods and habitual villainies so richly deserve, pardon me Sir, for thinking, that his choice of me for an object of his Slander, ought rather to pass with you for a presumption in favour of my moral Character, than to do me any prejudice in your opinion.' [2] (I am impressed, in that long sentence, by the flawless syntax standing up

---

[1] *Corr.* III, 65.

[2] *Corr.* III, 70. Prescott was a Quaker, who had had some financial dealings with Burke, so the 'slander' probably had to do mainly with money. However, if Prescott hated Burke as cordially as Burke hated him, the 'St. Omer' factor would probably have been dragged in as well. Burke added a postscript in his letter to the merchant: 'If you can condescend to converse with Prescott, you will be pleased to show him this letter.' It looks as if Burke is here trying to provoke Prescott into a duel. If so, nothing came of it. The Shackletons would not approve an attempt to provoke a duel. Nor would Burke, once he had calmed down.

under the elemental strain of one of Burke's rare but torrential storms of rage.)

Despite the rumours Burke was duly elected MP for Bristol on 2 November, three days after writing that letter. Presumably his 'American' services had outweighed his 'Irish' associations. But some of the 'Quakers and Dissenters' who voted for him must have regretted their decision four years later when their 'firm and staunch protestant' discreetly piloted the first Catholic Relief Act through the Parliament of Great Britain. As recounted in Chapter I, they had their revenge in the general election of 1780. At the end of 1774, however, Burke is at the height of his political career. Not only did his victory at Bristol greatly enhance his political status, but the fatal illness of William Dowdeswell, long-time leader of the Rockinghams in the Commons, left Burke effectively as the leader there, though not nominally. With Bristol behind him, and fortified by his success – and by the support it demonstrated for his position on America – he could once more turn his attention actively to American affairs.

1775

On 5 January Burke wrote Rockingham another long letter in a very different vein to that of the dismal one in September. He is now confident, all business, eager for the fray. He says that 'the season for action is drawing near,' and goes on: 'For these two last Sessions, indeed for the three last, the publick seemd to be so perfectly careless and supine with regard to its most essential Interests, that so much exertion on our part, would rather have indicated a restlessness of Spirit, than a manly Zeal. I concurred intirely in the reasonableness of our remaining quiet; and taking no further part in Business than what served to mark our dissent from the Measures which have been unfortunately in Fashion. It was all that we could then do. Even at this time, I do not see all that Spirit against Ministry, which I should have expected to rise among the people on the disappointment of every hope that had been held out to them. However it seems to be rising; and perhaps nearly as much, and as fast, as a Spirit wholly unmanaged can rise.'[1]

The 'managing' in question, Burke writes, must be supplied by the

---

[1] *Corr.* III, 88.

Rockinghams: 'If your Lordship should see things in this Light you will of Course perceive too, the necessity of proceeding regularly and with your whole Force; and that this great Affair of America is to be taken up as a Business.'[1] He then describes how such a campaign could be organised. It is not worth while entering into his details, because Rockingham's style of leadership did not change. It was not that he would dismiss Burke's advice: he did try to take it. But Rockingham was simply not capable of conducting a political campaign 'as a business', and neither were his aristocratic associates. If Burke wanted anything done from the opposition benches, he would have to do it himself; so he did.

Burke's letter is important as showing that he was now personally anxious to see much greater opposition activity on the American question. That anxiety, and frustration following on it, seem to have put a strain on his health at this time. At the end of January his Bristol Quaker friend Richard Champion notes in a letter, that American affairs have taken 'a bad aspect' and he goes on: 'Mr. Burke takes it so to heart that he is much fallen away and is far from well.' By mid-March Burke is physically on the mend, but again in a mood of deep despondency, in sharp contrast with his buoyancy in early January. He writes to one of his New York correspondents: 'I have been busy in these matters so as to have, for some short time an ill effect on my health, partly by attendance, partly by vexation. I have acted, to the best of my Judgement, with fair intentions towards the Mother Country and Colonies. I am now in better health. Despair of success will abate my Efforts, and preserve I hope my little remains of strength.'[2]

Although Burke was unable to induce the Rockinghams to be more active on America than it was in their nature to be, they were at least now consistently taking a policy lead from him on American affairs, in the Commons. On 22 March he introduced a series of resolutions on America;[3] his speech was later published under the title of 'On Conciliation with America'. In America it became, and long remained, the most famous of all his statements; it was on the syllabus of the American school-system from 1898 to 1933. Unlike the 1770 Grenville-Rockingham resolutions (see above pp. 131–35), which were the product of an inter-party pact, the 1775 resolutions

[1] *Corr.* III, 88.
[2] *Corr.* III, 137 and n. 5; letters of 31 January and 14 March 1775.
[3] The resolutions were seconded by Lord John Cavendish (1732–1796), nominally now the Rockinghams' leader in the Commons.

are clearly Burke's work, at least in the main, accepted from him by the Rockinghams. They are comprehensive and far-reaching. If passed, they would have repealed the Tea Duty and all the recent penal acts, known in America as 'The Intolerable Acts'. [1] The resolutions would also have acknowledged the right of Americans to tax themselves, and not to be taxed by the Parliament of Great Britain. The resolutions were thus a serious effort to get to the root of the matter and avert an impending war. The war broke out, at Concord, Massachusetts, just four weeks after those resolutions were rejected.

'On Conciliation with America' is more of a set speech than 'On American Taxation'. This is a result of the difference in the parliamentary context of the two speeches. In 'On American Taxation', Burke is intervening in a debate (on the unsuccessful 1774 motion to repeal the Tea Duty), answering previous speeches, thinking on his feet. In 'On Conciliation' he is moving a set of resolutions; there are no previous speeches. A speech in the first role is necessarily partly extemporary: the second role permits full advance preparation. The first role is more lively; the second more stately. The first affords Burke the opportunity to demonstrate, under stress, his exuberant intellectual agility. But it's not just a question of modes. 'On American Taxation' is all in Burke's own voice; in a part of 'On Conciliation', however, he is speaking in a persona that does not belong to him; a sort of collective persona, appropriate to the Rockinghams, on whose behalf he is introducing the resolutions. In the following passage he is arguing himself out of his own personality and actual ancestry and into the 'frame of mind' of a proper English Whig:

> In forming a plan for this purpose, I endeavoured to put myself in that frame of mind which was the most natural and most reasonable, and which was certainly the most probable means of securing me from all error. I set out with a perfect distrust of my own abilities, a total renunciation of every speculation of my own, and with a profound reverence for the wisdom of our ancestors, who have left us the inheritance of so happy a Constitution and so flourishing an empire, and, what is a thousand times more valuable, the treasury of the maxims and principles which formed the one and obtained the other. [2]

[1] The resolutions repealed the penal acts, not the Quebec Act (above pp. 93–5) which was not a penal act, although the Americans included it among 'The Intolerable Acts', mainly because it tolerated Papists. It does not seem probable, however, that they would have gone to war, just because the Quebec Act was still on the Statute Book.

[2] *Works* II, 145.

When 'On Conciliation' was published, in the summer of 1775, some copies must have found their way into the Nagle Country in the Blackwater valley of County Cork. Did anyone smile, I wonder, at the phrase 'the wisdom of our ancestors'? Such Whiggish ancestors as Richard Nagle of Carrigacunna, James II's Attorney General? So thoroughly, so almost hypnotically, does Burke renounce 'every speculation of my own' and enter into the frame of mind of an English Whig, in this section of his speech, that he even offers us an idyllic view of Ireland, as it might appear to a Whig constitutional lawyer, who had never visited the place, and who accepted the penal laws as perfectly in order:

> It was not English arms, but the English Constitution, that conquered Ireland. From that time, Ireland has ever had a general Parliament, as she had before a partial Parliament. You changed the people, you altered the religion, but you never touched the form or the vital substance of free government in that kingdom. You deposed the kings; you restored them; you altered the succession to theirs, as well as to your own crown; but you never altered their Constitution the principle of which was respected by usurpation, restored with the restoration of monarchy, and established, I trust, forever by the glorious Revolution. This has made Ireland the great and flourishing kingdom that it is, and, from a disgrace and burden intolerable to this nation, has rendered her a principal part of our strength and ornament [1]

Burke here temporarily talks himself out of existence. The metaphor of the Great Melody is not at all applicable to this passage, or to a few other phrases in this great, but flawed speech. When he was moving a set of resolutions, on behalf of himself and his friends, as distinct from making a personal statement in a debate, he seems to have felt a need to hold himself in, to some extent, and to avoid the idiosyncratic. 'On Conciliation' struck precisely the right note as far as the Rockinghams were concerned. From a letter written by the third Duke of Richmond (1735–1806), on receiving the published version of the speech, one can see the sort of thing the Rockinghams liked to hear from Burke, and the sort of thing that made them nervous: 'Since I saw You I have read Your last Speech and cannot too strongly express my admiration of it. It is so calm, so quiet, so reasonable, so just, so proper, that one cannot refuse conviction to every Part. At other Times, wit, or strong Pictures, or violent

[1] *Works* II, 147.

Declamations may be proper. There may be a season for Poetry, but in the present awful moment, the grave sober language of Truth and cool Reason is much better timed. And You appear in this speech, not that lively astonishing orator that some of Your works shew You to be, but the most wise, dispassionate, and calm Statesman.'[1]

But if 'On Conciliation With America' is less thoroughly Burkean than 'On American Taxation', it is the finest example of one of Burke's manners: that of polished *gravitas*. It contains, for example, some of the best specimens of the Burkean aphorism:

> Terror is not always the effect of force, and an armament is not victory. If you do not succeed, you are without resource: for, conciliation failing, force remains; but, force failing, no further hope of reconciliation is left. Power and authority are sometimes bought by kindness; but they can never be begged as alms by an impoverished and defeated violence.
>
> I do not know the method of drawing up an indictment against an whole people.
>
> Man acts from adequate motives relative to his interest and not on metaphysical speculations.
>
> Magnanimity in politics is not seldom the truest wisdom; and a great empire and little minds go ill together.[2]

'On Conciliation' also contain one of the finest examples of the Burkean oratorical set-piece:

> Pass by the other parts, and look at the manner in which the people of New England have of late carried on the whale-fishery. Whilst we follow them among the tumbling mountains of ice, and behold them penetrating into the deepest frozen recesses of Hudson's Bay and Davis's Straits, whilst we are looking for them beneath the arctic circle, we hear that they have pierced into the opposite region of polar cold, that they are at the antipodes, and engaged under the frozen serpent of the South. Falkland Island, which seemed too remote and romantic an object for the grasp of national ambition, is but a stage and resting place in the progress of their victorious industry. Nor is the equinoctial heat more discouraging to them than the accumulated winter of both the poles. We know, that, whilst some of them draw the line and strike the harpoon on the coast of Africa, others run the longitude, and pursue their gigantic game along the coast of Brazil. No sea but what is vexed by their fisheries. No climate that is not witness to their toils. Neither the perseverance of Holland,

[1] *Corr.* III, 170–171.
[2] *Works* II, 118–19; 136; 170; 181.

nor the activity of France, nor the dexterous and firm sagacity of English enterprise, ever carried this most perilous mode of hard industry to the extent to which it has been pushed by this recent people, – a people who are still, as it were, but in the gristle, and not yet hardened into the bone of manhood. [1]

The core of the case is contained in this passage, near the conclusion:

My hold of the colonies is in the close affection which grows from common names, from kindred blood, from similar privileges, and equal protection. These are ties which, though light as air, are as strong as links of iron. Let the colonies always keep the idea of their civil rights associated with your government, – they will cling and grapple to you, and no force under heaven will be of power to tear them from their allegiance. But let it be once understood that your government may be one thing and their privileges another, that these two things may exist without any mutual relation, – the cement is gone, the cohesion is loosened, and everything hastens to decay and dissolution. [2]

The resolutions were negatived without debate, by 270 votes to 78. [3] Burke had expected no other result:

I have this comfort, – that, in every stage of the American affairs, I have steadily opposed the measures that have produced the confusion, and may bring on the destruction, of this Empire. I now go so far so to risk a proposal of my own. If I cannot give peace to my country, I give it to my conscience. [4]

Richard Burke, writing to Richard Shackleton on the day the speech was delivered, gives an impression of its impact, which was quite distinct from its capacity to influence the vote: 'He began at half past three, and was on his Legs, untill six O Clock. From a Torrent of Members rushing from the House when he sat down, I could hear the loudest, the most unanimous, and the highest strains of applause. That such a performance even from him was never before heard in that house.' [5] Richard Burke goes on to make a

---

[1] *Works* II, 117.
[2] *Works* II, 179.
[3] The size of the minority indicates a full Rockingham turn-out, plus a few others.
[4] *Works* II, 176.
[5] *Corr.* III, 139.

comment, which shows the family to have been worried by the extent to which American affairs had been preying on Burke's mind, since the drift to war had begun, with the passage of the penal acts, at the end of 1774: 'In short by what I can learn, he has done himself infinite Credit – I know that he has discharged his conscience of a load that was on it. I do not use the word Conscience, other than in its ordinary acceptation; believe me America was not on his mind only as a Politician, it hung on his Conscience as being accountable for his Actions and his conduct. That is now satisfyd – may he be satisfyd – it will be highly necessary that he should, to his health and to his peace.' [1]

In May the Second Continental Congress met in Philadelphia, set up a Continental Army, and appointed George Washington as Commander-in-Chief. The battle of Bunker Hill followed on 17 June, with heavy British casualties. George III declared the colonies to be 'in open rebellion'. In July, before the news of Bunker Hill had reached London, Burke writes to Richard Champion in Bristol: 'Things are come to a Crisis in America. I confess to you that I cannot avoid a very great degree of uneasiness in this most anxious interval. An Engagement must instantly follow this Proclamation of [General] Gage's. If he should succeed, and beat the raw American Troops, which from his superiority in discipline and authority as well as his present considerable Numbers, I think he probably will; then we shall be so elevated as to throw all moderation behind us and plunge ourselves into a War which cannot be ended by many such Battles, though they should terminate in so many Victories. If we are beat, America is gone irrecoverably.' (*Corr.* III, 179–80)

By August Burke is beginning to see the possibility of an eventual American victory; 'The Spirit of America is incredible,' he writes to Rockingham. 'God knows they are very inferior in all human resources. But a remote and difficult Country and such a Spirit as now animates them may do strange things. Our Victories can only complete our ruin.' He is deeply distressed by the almost universal acquiescence, on the British side, in the prosecution of the war against the colonies. He sees it as acquiescence rather than support, but the political effect is the same: 'No man commends the measures which have been pursued, or expects any good from those which are in preparation; But it is a cold Languid opinion; like what men discover in affairs that do not concern them. It excites to no passion; It

[1] *Corr.* III, 140.

prompts to no Action.' He sees no allies in Britain. The old allies of the days of the repeal of the Stamp Act – the merchants – are no longer available. Out of his Bristol experience, he warns that 'we look to the Merchants in vain. They are gone from us, and from themselves. They consider America as lost, and they look to administration for indemnity. Hopes are accordingly held out to them, that some equivalent for their Debts will be provided. In the meantime the leading men among them are kept full fed with Contracts, remittances and Jobbs of all descriptions. And they are indefatigable in their endeavours to keep the others quiet with the prospect of their share in those emoluments, of which they see their advisers already so amply in possession. They all, or the greater Number of them, begin to snuff the cadaverous Haut Gout of a Lucrative War. War indeed is become a sort of substitute for Commerce.'[1]

Burke's admonitions take on an almost frantic tone: 'I shall therefore make no apology for urging again and again how necessary it is for your Lordship and your great friends, most seriously to take under immediate deliberation what you are to do in this Crisis. Nothing like it has happened in your political Life. I protest to God, I think that your reputation, your Duty, and the Duty and honour of all who profess your Sentiments, from the highest to the lowest of us demand at this time one honest, hearty effort, in order to avert the heavy calamities that are impending, to keep our hands from blood, and if possible to keep the poor, giddy, thoughtless people of our Country from plunging headlong into this impious War.'

Rockingham's long reply shows him as anxious to live up to Burke's expectations from him, but not capable of actually doing so. He writes about presenting some kind of memorial or address, but goes on: 'I have no conception that we can do anything by a constant attendance on Parliament – and occasional debates – at any rate, I think we should shew fully our adherance to our opinions of the impending ruin of this country – if the violent measures are continued towards America, and after we have done so, once or twice after this next meeting of Parliament I think we should abstain from going to either House of Parliament, when the American affairs are the subject of debate.'[2] Burke seems to have hoped for more. He had indeed advocated secession from parliament, but implies that this should be accompanied by an extra-parliamentary effort to gain support:

[1] *Corr.* III, 179–80; 187; 190; 191.
[2] *Corr.* III, 192–3; 205–6.

'. . . All opposition is absolutely crippled, if it can obtain no kind of support without Doors.'[1] But Extra-parliamentary exertions, however, were never wholly congenial to the Rockinghams although they were to attempt them, not without success, at a later stage of the war (see below pp. 209–213).

Having failed to galvanise Rockingham, Burke does his best with the next most important member of the party, the Duke of Richmond. 'I am perfectly sensible of the greatness of the difficulties', he writes to Richmond near the end of September, 'and the weakness and fewness of the helps in every publick affair which you can undertake. I am sensible too of the shocking indifference and newtrality of a great part of the Nation. But a Speculative despair is unpardonable where it is our duty to Act. I cannot think the people at large wholly to blame; or if they were, it is to no purpose to blame them. For God's sake my dear Lord endeavour to mend them. I must beg leave to put you in mind, without meaning, I am sure, to censure the body of your friends much less the most active amongst them, but I must put you in mind, that no regular or sustained endeavours of any kind have been used to dispose the people to a better sense of their Condition. Any Election must be lost; any family Interest in a Country would melt away, if greater pains infinitely greater were not employed to support them, than had ever been employed in this End and object of all Elections, and in this most important Interest of the Nation and of every individual in it. The people are not answerable for their present supine acquiescence. Indeed they are not. God and nature never made them to think or to Act without Guidance and Direction. They have obeyed the only impulse they have received. When they resist such endeavours as ought to be used, by those who by their Rank and fortune in the Country, by the goodness of their Characters, and their experience in their affairs, are their Natural Leaders, then it will be time enough to despair and to let their Blood lie upon their own heads.'

Richmond's influence with the Irish Parliament was considerable and Burke wanted him to use that influence to get that Parliament to come out against the war: 'Ireland is always a part of some importance in the general System; but Ireland never was in the situation of real honour and real consequence in which she now stands. She has the Ballance of the Empire and perhaps its fate for ever, in

---

[1] *Corr.* III, 217–220. The reference to the 'people of our Country' points in the same direction.

her hands. If the parliament which is shortly to meet there, should interpose a friendly mediation; should send a pathetic Address to the King, and a letter to both houses of Parliament here, It is impossible that they should not succeed. If they should only add to this, a suspension of extraordinary grants and supplies for Troops employed out of the Kingdom, in Effect employed against their own rights and privileges, they would preserve the whole Empire from a ruinous War, and with a saving rather than expense prevent this infatuated Country, from establishing a Plan which tends to its own ruin by enslaving all its dependencies. Ministry would not like to have a contest with the whole Empire upon their hands at once.'[1] Nothing came of the idea – Irish, American and British politics did not begin to interact seriously until 1778, after Burgoyne's defeat at Saratoga (see below Chapter III).

I have the impression that Burke's mind is by now so powerfully affected by the American war that he is clutching at straws rather than fall into 'a Speculative despair'. The conclusion of this letter to Richmond shows how deeply his emotions have become engaged, on the side of America. He is referring to the Administration's efforts, which eventually failed, to raise a body of Russian troops to fight the American colonies: 'I beg pardon for this long and unmanaged letter. I am on thorns. I cannot at my Ease see Russian Barbarism let loose to waste the most beautiful object that ever appeared upon this Globe.'[2]

Frustrated in his efforts to galvanise his party leaders, Burke had to fall back on new parliamentary initiative of his own. Foredoomed though any such initiative was, in terms of parliamentary votes, he could still hope that it could have some impact on the country as 'On American Taxation' had had, at least in Bristol. He introduced his 'Bill for composing the present Troubles in America' on 16 November. It contained substantially the same set of measures as were contained in his March Resolutions, but embodied them in somewhat more explicit form. The speech introducing his Bill was in a low key, analytical and businesslike, rather than oratorical. The most remarkable part of it was a prediction whose accuracy was to be demonstrated three years later. The 'predatory war' waged by the government, he said, 'did not lead to a speedy decision. The longer our distractions continued, the greater chance there was for the inter-

---

[1] *Corr.* III, 217–220.
[2] *Corr.* III, 217–9.

ference of the Bourbon powers, which in a long protracted war, may be considered not only as probable but in a manner certain. That he was very sure this country was utterly incapable of carrying on a war with America and these powers [France and Spain] acting in conjunction'. [1]

Exposing the fallacy of the ministerial policy of forcing the Americans to consent to terms, he argued that 'if the ministers treated for a revenue, or for any other purpose, they had but two securities for the performance of the terms: either the same force which compelled these terms: or the honour, sincerity, and good inclination of the people. If they could trust the people to keep the terms without force, they might trust them to make them without force. If nothing but force could hold them, and they meant nothing but independency, as the Speech from the throne asserted, then the House was to consider how a standing army of 26,000 men, and 70 ships of war, could be constantly kept up in America. A people meaning independency, will not mean it the less, because they have, to avoid a present inconvenience, submitted to treaty. That after all our struggles, our hold in America is, and must be, her good inclination. If this fails, all fails . . .'

Cogent reasoning, which fell on deaf ears. In the debate that followed, the first ministerial speaker, a King's friend, Welbore Ellis (1713–1802), gave the standard ministerial answer to the case for conciliation. He urged that 'the greater disposition Great Britain showed towards conciliation the more obstinate, rebellious, and insolent America would become.' [2] Burke's Bill was negatived by 210 votes to 105. The defeat was immediately followed by Lord North's American Prohibiting Bill, forbidding 'all traffic and intercourse with the American colonies.' On that disheartening note, the session of 1775 ended, so far as American business was concerned.

1776

The first months of 1776 went badly for the British in America. General Sir William Howe (1729–1840), who had been sent to punish Boston, was now cooped up there, surrounded by the bitterly

[1] *Parl. History*, xviii, 958–966
[2] *Parl. History*, xviii, 970–1; 982.

hostile population of Massachusetts and besieged by Washington's forces. In mid-March Howe withdrew to Halifax, in Nova Scotia. For several months all the thirteen colonies were 'clear of redcoats'. On 20 February, with Howe still besieged in Boston, Charles James Fox, now in alliance with the Rockinghams, proposed a 'Motion for an Enquiry into the Causes of the ill Success of British arms in North America.'[1] Burke spoke in support.

Fox was a fairly recent convert, and a brilliant acquisition, to Rockingham Whiggery and it was Burke, more than anybody else, who had converted him. According to the biographer quoted earlier, Fox, after 'listening attentively' to his 1774 speech 'On American Taxation', became his 'pupil' (see above pp. 101–2). Fox himself later declared that he had learned more from Burke 'than from all his books and studies'. From now on, in relation to much American business, and in the Commons, Burke plays second fiddle to a first violin he himself had trained; the relationship, so far as I know, is unique in political history. It is Fox who applies to each new situation the Burkean principles, and it is Burke who backs him up with the necessary historical facts or figures. Thus, after Fox had eloquently proposed the motion on 20 February, Burke, according to the *Parliamentary History*, 'showed from the records of parliament and from history, that nothing was more frequent than enquiries of the kind now proposed; and observed, at no time within the course of his reading, did he ever recollect a period at which such a proceeding was more absolutely necessary than the present.'[2]

There is no sign that Burke resented this relationship. On the contrary, the two men were on terms of warm friendship and it took the impact of the French Revolution to destroy that friendship in May 1791.[3] Fox would not have taken the lead without Burke's approval – indeed it was probably Burke's idea that Fox should do so. The policies that Burke believed in would carry more weight with Parliament and public when advocated by a well-connected Englishman – and the only contemporary orator in his class – than by an Irish adventurer. Taking a second place to Fox, in this context, is another measure of Burke's commitment to the policies in which

[1] *Parl. History*, xviii, 1143–55; 982.
[2] *Parl. History* xviii, 1154.
[3] In 1775–76 Fox was so close to Burke that a friend, Lady Sarah Lennox (1745–1826), wrote of him: 'He had left off all his fine acquaintances last year and lived quite with Mr. Burke.' The friendship was, however, seriously troubled by Indian affairs in the late 1780s (see Chapter IV).

he believed. Policies consistently came ahead of considerations of personal advantage or advancement.

Throughout the spring and summer mobilisation was going ahead for the American war. Burke is distressed, for both sides, but his emotions are now definitely engaged on the side of the Americans. 'The worst about Canada is certainly true,' he writes to Rockingham in June, 'And much more of the same bad kind, not very improbable.' The 'worst' had been a British victory, and the retreat of the American forces from Canada. Next month he writes: 'I received your Letter before I was up this morning, and not having passed a good Night, I tried to sleep after it; but the hurry and Bustle of the March of the first division and second division of Pennsylvania Troops of the fortification of Boston, and all the Din of War, disturbed me in such a manner, that I courted sleep in vain.'[1] That letter was written on the day of the Declaration of Independence, 4 July 1776.

The war was now going against the Americans. General Howe, having landed his forces on Staten Island early that month, defeated Washington in the Battle of Long Island, and Washington retreated into Pennsylvania. In Britain, the supporters of the war triumphed. Burke wrote to Richard Champion: 'I have as yet heard it imperfectly. Three thousand of the Provincials are killed or are prisoners. A total rout of all that were on Long Island, of which the King's troops are entire masters. They say they have burnt the camp and all on it, on account of the dirt and infectious filth of which it was full. They say further, that numbers were drowned on their flight to New York. The Provincials must evacuate that place; they say they are eat up by epidemical distempers. The number of the killed, &c., on the Provincials' side is said to be three thousand; on the King's side three hundred Hessians, and not above fifty English.'[2]

Parliament resumed late in October. Ministerial speakers urged that, since the Americans had declared independence, there could be no negotiating with them. Burke held that the delay, on the British side, in starting serious negotiations with the Americans had been at the root of all the trouble:

By this delay you drove them into the declaration of independency . . . and now they have declared it, you bring it as an argument to prove, that there can be no other reasoning used with them, but the sword. . . . In order to bring things to this unhappy situation, did not you pave the

[1] *Corr.* III, 272; 278.
[2] *Corr.* III, 293.

way, by a succession of acts of Tyranny; – for this, you shut up their ports; – cut off their fishery; – annihilated their charters; – and governed them by an army. Sir, the recollection of these things being the evident causes of what we have seen, is more than what ought to be endured – This it is, that has burned the noble city of New York; that has planted the bayonet in the bosoms of my principals; – in the bosom of the city; where alone your wretched government once boasted the only friends she could number in America.'[1]

Burke, clearly in a towering passion, now falls into one of those extravagances which occasionally embarrassed his friends. The king had ordered church services and a public fast in support of the American war. Burke comments: 'Till our churches are purified from this abominable service, I shall consider them, not as the temples of the Almighty, but the synagogues of Satan.' Extravagant, no doubt, but an extravagance that reveals a furious commitment, such as no man can simulate.

1777

The opening weeks of 1777 were the nadir for friends of America in Britain. On 15 January Sir George Savile (see Chapter 1, p. 75) reports to Rockingham: 'We are not only patriots *out of place*, but patriots out *of the opinion of the public*. The repeated successes [of British arms], *hollow* as I think them and the more *ruinous* if they *are real*, have fixed or converted ninety-nine in one hundred.'[2] Earlier in January Burke writes to Rockingham: 'The affairs of America seem to be drawing towards a Crisis. The Howes are by this time in possession of, or able to awe, the whole Middle Coast of America, from Delaware to the Western Boundary of Massachusettes Bay; the Naval Barrier on the Side of Canada is broken; a great Tract of Country is open to the supply of the Troops; The River Hudson opens away into the hearts of the Provinces; and nothing, in all probability can prevent an early offensive Campain. What the Americans have done, is, in their Circumstances, truly astonishing. It is indeed infinitely more than I expected from them. But having done

[1] *Parl. History*, xviii, 1442–44.
[2] Quoted in George Thomas Keppel, Earl of Albemarle, *Memoirs of the Marquis of Rockingham and his Contemporaries* (London, 1852) Vol II, p. 305.

so much, for some short time I entertained an opinion, that they might do more. But it is now evident, that they cannot look standing Armies in the Face.'[1]

That last opinion was based on information available in Britain at that time. In America, it had already been disproved. Crossing the Delaware, on Christmas Day, Washington had captured Trenton, from the Hessian regulars who occupied it, and won another victory at Princeton on 2 January.

Burke discusses Benjamin Franklin's recently begun mission to Paris, and mentions an idea of his own about a possible Rockingham mediation. He writes: 'If the Congress could be brought to declare in favour of those Terms [the Rockinghams'] for which 108 Members of the House of Commons voted last year,[2] with some Civility to the Party which held out those Terms, it would undoubtedly have an Effect to revive the Cause of our Liberties in England, and to give the Colonies some sort of mooring and anchorage in this Country. It seemed to me, that Franklin might be made to feel the propriety of such a Step; and as I have an acquaintance with him I had for a Moment a strong desire of taking a Turn to Paris. Everything else failing, one might obtain a better knowledge of the general Aspect of things abroad than I believe any of us possess at the present. The Duke of Portland approved the Idea. But when I had conversed with the very few of your Lordships friends who were in Town and considered a little more maturely the constant Temper and standing Maxims of the Party, I laid aside the design; not being desirous of risquing the displeasure of those for whose sake alone I wished to take that fatiguing Journey at this Severe Season of the Year.'[3][4]

In Burke's dropping this project, it is tempting to see an example of his excessive deference to the Rockingham aristocrats. Against this, Burke's mission would only have been of interest from Franklin's point of view, if he could speak for the most significant section of the British opposition. In any case, he would not have proposed such a mediation, had he known of Trenton and Princeton. Still, there is a sense of loss at being deprived of a dramatic set-piece: Edmund Burke and Benjamin Franklin, in diplomatic negotiations in Paris, in the winter of 1776–7. Their reports on that conversation,

[1] *Corr.* III, 309.
[2] This was a slip (Freudian?): the voting was 210–105 (see above, pp. 158–59).
[3] The Duke of Portland referred to is the third duke (1738–1809), who became leader of the Rockingham Whigs after Rockingham's death in 1782.
[4] *Corr.* III, 309–310.

to London and to Philadelphia would have made marvellously instructive and entertaining reading, but it was not to be. Most of the rest of the long letter to Rockingham consists of unavailing exhortations: the work of what Burke would, a little later, ruefully call a *flapper* (defined in the OED as 'person who arouses the attention or jogs the memory'). As Burke wrote to a friend: 'I believe you know that my chief employment for many years has been that woeful one, of a flapper. I begin to think it time to leave it off. It only defeats its own purpose when given too long and too liberally; and I am persuaded that the men who will not move, when you want to teize them out of their inactivity, will begin to reproach yours, when you let them alone.'[1]

His mood was not improved by outbreaks of arson in his constituency of Bristol, followed by rumours that the fires were caused by some of those 'friends of America', of whom their MP was notoriously one.

At this time the Rockinghams were staying away from Parliament, finding opposition hopeless as long as the British appeared to be winning in America. In April, partly in order to justify to his constituents the policy of abstention – through temporary and partial secession – Burke published *A Letter To The Sheriffs Of Bristol*. The tactical part about secession in *A Letter* need not detain us here; the policy ended shortly after appearance of the tract, once the news of the American victories at Trenton and Princeton had arrived to shake ministerialists and hearten the opposition. It is for Burke's thinking, at a time when the American cause seemed at its lowest ebb, that the tract is important. With the speeches on the Declaratory Act (1766), 'On American Taxation' (1774), and most of 'On Conciliation with America' (1775), *A Letter to the Sheriffs of Bristol* completes the quartet of his major pronouncements on America. Taken together, they make up the heart of the American part of Burke's great melody; although the melody is enriched by a great number of occasional speeches, and by the sharp metallic notes of Burke's devastating debating replies.

A Letter differs from the others in that it is written, not spoken. The difference is not so great, since most of Burke's fully recorded speeches are highly structured, as if on parade, with each subordinate clause firmly in line. Still, there is a difference in texture. *A Letter* is even more tightly argued than his other statements. In all the parts directly addressed to America, it is in Burke's central style: grave,

[1] *Corr.* III, 389.

sober, aphoristic, energetic. The stately-courtly manner, prominent in *On Conciliation*, appears only in a complimentary flourish about the Rockinghams. There are no jokes. Burke's anger, though lowering as often on the horizon, is under control; no 'synagogues of Satan' here.

The tract – which was sent to the Sheriffs with copies of the penal Acts against America – begins:

> It affords no matter for very pleasing reflection to observe that our subjects diminish as our laws increase. . . . I think I know America, – if I do not, my ignorance is uncurable, for I have spared no pains to understand it: and I do most solemnly assure those of my constituents who put any sort of confidence in my industry and integrity, that everything that has been done there has arisen from a total misconception of the object: that our means of originally holding America, that our means of reconciling with it after quarrel, of recovering it after separation, of keeping it after victory, did depend, and must depend, in their several stages and periods, upon a total renounciation of that unconditional submission which has taken such possession of the minds of violent men.

There is a wealth of painful experience behind the next two paragraphs:

> When any community is subordinately connected with another, the great danger of the connection is the extreme pride and self-complacency of the superior, which in all matters of controversy will probably decide in its own favor. . . .
>   They have been told that their dissent from violent measures is an encouragement to rebellion. Men of great presumption will hold a language which is contradicted by a whole course of history. *General* rebellions and revolts of an whole people were never *encouraged*, now or at any time. They are always *provoked*. [Burke's emphasis]. [1]

Burke harks back to the repeal of the Stamp Act in 1766, and cites a relevant declaration of Congress, which has been ignored by the many historians who depreciate the importance of that measure:

> The Congress has used an expression with regard to this pacification which appears to me truly significant. After the repeal of the Stamp Act, 'the colonies fell,' says the Assembly, 'into their ancient state of

---

[1] Long afterwards, in the debates over the French Revolution, Fox was to use this quotation against Burke (see Chapter V, p. 423).

unsuspecting confidence in the mother country.' This unsuspecting confidence is the true centre of gravity-amongst mankind, about which all the parts are at rest. It is this unsuspecting confidence that removes all difficulties, and reconciles all the contradictions which occur in the complexity of all ancient puzzled political extablishments. Happy are the rulers which have the secret of preserving it.

Burke goes on, with reference to the Declaratory Act which accompanied the repeal:

If this undefined power has become odious since that time, and full of horror to the colonies, it is because the unsuspecting confidence is lost, and the parental affection, in the bosom of whose boundless authority they reposed their privileges, is become strange and hostile.

Burke refutes the claim that there is a contradiction between his support for the Declaratory Bill, in 1766, and his advocacy of the denial of parliament's power to tax the colonists, in 1775:

It will be asked, if such was then my opinion of the mode of pacification, how I came to be the very person who moved, not only for a repeal of all the late coercive statues, but for mutilating, by positive law, the entireness of the legislative power of Parliament, and the cutting off from it the whole right of taxation. I answer, Because a different state of things requires a different conduct. When the dispute had gone to these last extremities, (which no man labored more to prevent than I did,) the concessions which had satisfied in the beginning could satisfy no longer; because the violation of tacit faith required explicit security. The same cause which has introduced all formal compacts and covenants among men made it necessary: I mean habits of soreness, jealousy, and distrust. I parted with it as with a limb, but as a limb to save the body: and I would have parted with more, if more had been necessary; anything rather than a fruitless, hopeless, unnatural civil war. This mode of yielding would, it is said, give way to independency without a war. I am persuaded, from the nature of things, and from every information, that it would have had a directly contrary effect. But if it had this effect, I confess, that I should prefer independency without war to independency with it; and I have so much trust in the inclinations and prejudices of mankind, and so little in anything else, that I should expect ten times more benefit to this kingdom from the affection of America, though under a separate establishment, than from her perfect submission to the crown and Parliament, accompanied with her terror, disgust, and abhorrence.

Bodies tied together by so unnatural a bond of union as mutual hatred are only connected to their ruin.[1]

By summer 1777, after the heartening news of Trenton and Princeton, the opposition is back in business. There are no more parliamentary set pieces from Burke this year; he knows better than to attempt a repeat of 'On Conciliation'. Rather, he follows through from the thesis of 'On Conciliation' – which he leaves Fox to reassert – by crushing interventions in debate. Thus, in a debate on the Budget in May, Charles Jenkinson, the king's closest political confidant and a *bête noire* of Burke, had argued that 'if America was to remain a part of the British Empire, she ought most certainly to bear a proportionate share of the expence of general protection.' Burke retorted: 'it would be extremely difficult for him to shew, that the surest steps towards conquering America, or inducing the colonies to come to terms of accommodation, would be to apprize them that, conquer or submit, they must pay the expence of conquest, or of the measures previously taken to induce them to submit to unconditional obedience. On the contrary, experience, every thing in America, and out of it, contradicted such an absurd expectation.'[2]

That summer Burke was preoccupied with America to the exclusion of almost everything else, and conscious of the forces impelling France towards intervention in America. To Philip Francis (1740–1818)[3], in India, Burke writes: 'the affairs of America, which are as important [as Indian affairs], and more distracted, have almost entirely engrossed the attention which I am able to give to any thing. I wished, and laboured to keep war at a distance; never having been able to discover any advantage which could be derived from the greatest success; I never approved of our engaging in it, and I am sure it might have been avoided. The ministers this year hold out to us the strongest hopes of what they call a victorious campaign. I am, indeed, ready enough to believe, that we shall obtain those delusive advantages, which will encourage us to proceed, but will not bring matters nearer to an happy termination. France gives all the assistance to the colonies which is consistent with the appearance of neutrality. Time is to shew whether she will proceed further, or whether America can maintain herself in the present struggle without a more

[1] *Works* II, 189; 209–11; 216; 217; 234; 235; 236.
[2] *Parl. History*, xix, 251.
[3] For Burke's relations with Philip Francis, author of the *Junius* letters, see Chapter IV *passim*.

open declaration and more decided effort from that power. At present, the Ministers seem confident that France is resolved to be quiet. If the Court of Versaille be so pacific, I assure you it is in defiance of the wishes and opinions of that whole nation.'[1]

The 'delusive advantages' duly materialised, shortly before disaster struck. In July Burgoyne captured Ticonderoga on his southward march from Canada, towards, as he believed, a junction with Howe, the isolation of New England, and comprehensive victory. In September, Howe, who was not giving much thought to a junction with Burgoyne, won the battle of Brandywine and entered Philadelphia. Burke wrote to Richard Champion: 'The worst of the matter is this: that let Howes success be what or where it may, it will be sufficient to keep up the delusion here, and to draw in parliament deeper and deeper into this System of endless hopes and disappointments.'[2]

In November, shortly before news of Brandywine reached Britain, Burke appealed to Parliament to take advantage of her position of relative strength to attempt accommodation. This was clearly a powerful speech, but the Parliamentary History gives only part of it: 'If it were possible, we would give a detail of a speech, which in the course of almost two hours, commanded the attention, excited the laughter, and sometimes drew tears from the sympathising few. . . . but we must. . . . touch only on that pathetic supplication which he made to the House to seize the present happy moment to attempt an accommodation, when neither elated with insolent victory, nor debased with abject defeat, we could, without dishonour to ourselves, make such proposals to our colonists, as they could, without dishonour, accept. . . . Shall we give them no alternative but unconditional submission? A three years war has not terrified them, distressed as they are, from their great purpose. Let us try the power of lenity over those generous bosoms.'[3]

The chance, which would not have been taken, was already lost. Burgoyne's army had surrendered at Saratoga on 17 October, but the news did not reach England until 2 December, the day before the Commons convened. On 3 December, Lord George Germain (1716–1785), the disastrous Secretary of State for the Colonies, had 'a piece of very unhappy intelligence to report.' The ensuing angry and excited debate brought Burke into personal danger. He had attacked North's Solicitor-General, Alexander Wedderburn (1733–1805),

[1] *Corr.* III, 348–9.
[2] *Corr.* III, 377.
[3] *Parl. History*, xix, p. 431, 18 November 1777.

calling him 'counsel' to the despised Germain. [1] During Wedderburn's reply, Burke laughed loudly. Wedderburn exclaimed that 'if
the gentleman did not know manners, *he as an individual* would
teach them to him.' Burke made a sign to Wedderburn to follow him
out of the House, and a duel was averted only by the intervention
of Fox and other friends. On learning that it had been averted, Rockingham wrote: 'My dear Burke,

> My heart is at ease
> Ever yours Most affectionately,
> Rockingham [2]

The entry of France into the war, an event long foreseen by Burke,
was now inevitable. In the Commons, on 10 December, he spoke of
'our natural and avowed enemy the French, negotiating the treaty –
perhaps not negotiating but even perfecting a treaty by which
America will be irrevocably lost to this country.' [3]

1778

On 6 February Burke proposed in the Commons a 'Motion relative
to the Military Employment of Indians in the Civil War with
America'. This was no side issue; it referred to the principal cause of
Saratoga. Burgoyne's proclamation explicitly threatening the use of
his Indian allies against the settlers, many of whom hitherto had been
neutral, caused them to embody as militia and rally to the aid of the
revolutionary army, in overwhelming the British forces. There is a
copy of that proclamation in the museum at Bennington, Vermont,
and even today its unctuous ferocity can still chill the blood. Burgoyne threatened to use the Indians, not just against the rebels, but
against any settler families who should fail to assist his army. That
was the threat that doomed his army. As reported in the *Parliamentary History*, Burke said: 'the fault of employing [Indians] did not
consist in their being of one colour or another; but in their way of

---

[1] Wedderburn was a former Rockingham ally, considered as having defected for
the sake of office. Later, when the Whigs split over the French Revolution, Wedderburn (as Lord Loughborough) became an ally of Burke.
[2] *Corr.* III, 406–8.
[3] *Parl. History*, xix, 590–1.

making war: which was so horrible, that it not only shocked the manners of all civilised nations but far exceeded the ferocity of any other Barbarians that have been recorded either by ancient or modern history.' On the claim that 'great care had been taken to prevent that indiscriminate murder of men, women, and children, which was customary with the savages', he comments that if so, 'their employment could have answered no purpose; their only effective use consisted in that cruelty which was to be restrained' and he attributed the fatal catastrophe at Saratoga 'to the cruelties exercised by these barbarians, which obliged all mankind, without regard to party, or to political principle, and in despite of military indisposition, to become soldiers, and to unite as one man in the common defence.' [1]

Horace Walpole, in his *Last Journals*, provides a more vivid impression of the speech and its impact: 'The 6th was memorable for the chef-d'oeuvre of Burke's orations. He called Burgoyne's Talk with the Indians the "sublimity of bombast absurdity", in which he demanded the assistance of seventeen Indian nations, by considerations of *our Holy Religion*, by regard for our constitution; and though he enjoined them not to scalp men, women, or children alive, he promised to pay them for any scalps of the dead, and required them to repair to the king's standard. . . . Seventeen interpreters from the several nations, said he, could not have given them any idea of his reasons – but, added Burke, the invitation was just as if, at a riot on Tower Hill, the keeper of the wild beasts had turned them loose, but adding, "my gentle lions, my sentimental wolves, my tender-hearted hyenas, go forth, but take care not to hurt men, women, or children." He then grew serious; and as the former part had excited the warmest and most continued bursts of laughter even from Lord North . . . and the Ministers themselves, so he drew such a pathetic picture of the cruelties of the King's army, particularly in the alleged case of a young woman on whose ransom, not beauty, they quarrelled and murdered her, – that he *drew iron tears* down Barré's [2] cheek, who implored him to print his speech, and said, with many invectives against the Bishops, that it ought to be pasted up on every church under *their* proclamation for the Fast, and that he himself would paste it upon some. Governor Johnston said he was now glad that strangers were excluded, as, if they had been admitted Burke's

---

[1] *Parl. Hist.* xix, 695, 697, 698.
[2] The reference is to Colonel Isaac Barré (1726–1802), MP for Wycombe, a strong opponent of the American war.

speech would have excited them to tear the Ministers to pieces as they went out of the House.'[1]

The comment of a modern historian on this episode is itself something of a *chef d'oeuvre* – an appropriately small one – in Namierite reductionism. Professor A. S. Foord writes that '[Burke's] motion to deny payment was lost, 56 to 21, but his oration against arming "the savages of America to butcher, torture, scalp and murder old men, women, children, and infants at the breast" put him in the morally and sentimentally impregnable position so dear to a Rockinghamite.'[2]

On 17 February the Commons debated Lord North's Conciliatory Propositions to the Americans. Ironically, the Propositions were in substance identical, as Fox pointed out in the debate, to those put forward by Burke in 1775: repeal of the Tea Duty and the Penal Acts: dropping of the right to tax. Offered then, those propositions would probably have led to peace; offered in 1778, after Saratoga, they were hopeless. There is a description in the *Annual Register*, probably by Burke himself, of the scene in Parliament, when North had finished his appeal: 'A dull melancholy for some time followed this speech. It had been heard with profound attention, left without a single mark of approbation to any part from any description of men, or any particular man in the House. Astonishment, dejection and fear overwhelmed the whole assembly.' The 'fear' was due to the general belief that North would never have made such an offer, reversing his (or rather George III's) whole policy of the last three years, unless he had had word that a French-American treaty was well on the way to conclusion, meaning that war with France would follow.

On 16 March, seconding a 'Motion for all Communications touching a Treaty between France and America', Burke demanded 'a discovery of the councils, and of the persons who gave them, by which [Britain] had been reduced from the pinnacle of honour and power to the lowest ebb of wretchedness and disgrace.' Next day George III publicly acknowledged being informed of the conclusion of 'a Treaty of Amity and Commerce between the court of France and certain persons employed by his Majesty's revolted subjects in America.'[3]

The British Ambassador was withdrawn from Paris. Great Britain

[1] *Last Journals* II, 104–5.
[2] A. S. Foord, *His Majesty's Opposition* (Oxford, 1964) p. 355.
[3] *Parliamentary History* xix, 908–26.

and France were now in a state of war. The British Isles were under threat of invasion. The British Government had now to give some urgent attention to the affairs of that island in which a French invasion would be likely to find a welcome. Burke would now be simultaneously involved in the political affairs of America and his native Ireland.

Charles James Fox. 'But he has put to hazard his ease, his security, his interest, his power, even his darling popularity, for the benefit of a people whom he has never seen.' – Edmund Burke (p. 329)

III
American Colonies,
Ireland

CINCINNATUS in Retirement.
falsely supposed to represent Jesuit-Pad driven back to his native Potatos. see Romish Common-Wealth.

'Throughout his career, the cartoonists were to portray him in the garb of a Jesuit; that was how you knew it was Burke. That he was an Irish Jesuit didn't help. John Wilkes said that Burke's oratory "stank of whiskey and potatoes".' (p. 50)

IRELAND
1778–1780

From the very beginning of Burke's parliamentary career, Ireland and America were connected in his mind. On 31 December 1765, shortly after his election for Wendover, he wrote to his friend Charles O'Hara: 'One thing however is fortunate to you, though without any merits of your own, that the Liberties, (or what shadows of Liberty there are) of Ireland have been saved in America.' He presumably meant that America's resistance to the Stamp Act had averted a possible decision by the British Parliament to tax Ireland. What exactly he may have meant by 'the Liberties of Ireland' or 'what shadows of Liberty there are' is a puzzling question, and one which seems to have puzzled Burke himself.

On 4 March 1766 we find him writing to O'Hara: 'Could not Ireland be somehow *hooked* into this system?'[1] By 'this system', he seems to be referring specifically to a revision of the Commercial Laws, affecting North America and the West Indies, which the first Rockingham Administration, with Burke's energetic assistance, was then working on. (He later dropped the idea of including Ireland in the commercial revision[2].) But he refers, virtually in the same breath, to his exertions over the repeal of the Stamp Act. Clearly what is attracting him, in this exhilarating dawn of his parliamentary career, is the idea of stimulating some kind of benign and freedom-laden interaction between the affairs of his native Ireland and those of the rest of the British Empire, and especially of America.

[1] *Corr.* I, 229; 240.
[2] *Corr.* I, 247.

In 1775 Burke again had such an interaction in mind (as was noted in Chapter II, see above pp. 157–8) when he tried, in vain, to get the Irish Parliament to declare itself against the American war by a 'pathetic address' to the king and by a 'suspension of extraordinary grants' for troops employed overseas. This bid failed; the Irish Parliament probably assumed at this time, as did most people in Britain, that the American rebellion would be speedily snuffed out.

Some interaction between America and Ireland did set in, with the outbreak of the American war, but it was limited and of limited interest to Burke. Only one set of people in Ireland was passionately interested in the outcome of the American war; and this was not the set of people with which Burke had emotional ties. The strongest Irish partisans of America were mainly the Dissenters, most of them in Eastern Ulster (what is now Northern Ireland).[1] Many of these Dissenters had emigrated to America, mostly to Western Pennsylvania where they became known as the Scotch-Irish. As a body they were pro-Revolution and made up an important part of Washington's armies. Most of their kin in Ireland made the American cause their own.[2] A minority of radicals belonging to the Established Church agreed with the Dissenters on that point. Many Protestants, who were neither Dissenters nor radicals, were understood to 'sympathize more or less' with the Americans.[3] Lord Midleton a young Whiggish peer, wrote from Cork: 'We are all Americans here except such as are attached securely to the castle or are papists.'[4] (Yet Irish-Protestant 'pro-American' sympathisers, at the level of the Irish Parliament, were not reliable, in a practical way, as Burke had found when he appealed to the sympathies in question, in 1775).

Support in Ireland for the American cause was mainly a Protestant affair. Taking note of that, Catholic leaders, especially the Hierarchy and gentry, sought to take advantage of the situation, through declarations of loyalty to the Crown and contributions to the war-effort. The implicit message was: 'The people you have treated as disloyal are the ones who are loyal, in the present emergency, while the people you have treated as loyal are now the disloyal ones. So isn't it time

[1] R. B. McDowell, *Ireland in the Age of Imperialism and Revolution, 1760–1801* (Oxford 1979) pp. 244–55.
[2] Not quite all of them; see McDowell, p. 244.
[3] McDowell, p. 241.
[4] *Ibid.* The 'castle' is Dublin Castle, seat of the British Administration in Ireland.

you removed disabilities imposed on us for our supposed disloyalty?'[1]

Burke understood these tactics well; years afterwards, during the French Revolution, he was to use similar arguments himself, to the advantage of the Catholics. In general the dispositions of the different sets of Irish people, over the American war, were most uncomfortable for him. The people whose interests he had most at heart, the Catholics, supported the war he opposed; or at least those who claimed to speak for them did, without reported contradiction. The people who were most fervently anti-Catholic at this time in both Ireland and America, were also the most fervent opponents of George III's war, of which Burke too was a fervent opponent. In the Great Melody, the passage 'American Colonies, Ireland' is the most intricate and is interspersed, as we shall hear, with haunting Burkean silences.

This analysis of Irish responses to the American War applies to the period between the beginning of the American War, in 1775, and Burgoyne's surrender at Saratoga, in 1777. During this period, British politicians, from George III down, noted with moderate gratification the assurances of Catholic loyalty. They were not unduly alarmed by support for the Americans among Dissenters, who were a minority, and unlikely to stage an insurrection on their own. The insurrection most to be feared was one by the great majority of the population, the Catholics.

Assurances of loyalty by the 'leadership' might perhaps be taken with a grain of salt. They were not disinterested, and there was no guarantee that the Catholic masses – peasants and unskilled workers – would in fact follow the lead of their putative leaders, in any emergency. The really reassuring factor, from a British point of view, was the complete absence of any signs of enthusiasm for the American cause, on the part of any substantial section of the Catholic population. Since the British Parliament was not preoccupied with Irish affairs, Burke was under no obligation to take up positions about them, and probably felt no great inclination to do so, given the uncongenial alignment of forces in Ireland, with regard to America.

However, after the news of Saratoga had reached Britain in 1777,

---

[1] The leadership overstated the extent of Catholic loyalty. Gaelic poems have survived, celebrating Washington's early victories. The Catholic Hierarchy, which stressed its loyalty at this time, had no legal existence. Recruitments of Irish Catholics for British service in the American war were illegal, but occurred.

Ireland became overnight a matter of acute concern to the people and Parliament of Great Britain. The interaction of 'Ireland' and 'America' had begun in earnest. But it proved to be a more disconcerting kind of interaction than Burke had visualised at the beginning of his parliamentary career. The Franco-American Treaty, the principal consequence of Saratoga, was concluded in March 1778. Britain and France were now at war and the British Isles were exposed to an imminent threat of invasion that summer and, even more in the next. Army and Navy were heavily committed to the war in America. The Treasury was depleted for the same reason. England itself was in danger, and everything available, in soldiers and ships, had to be committed to its defence. The Royal Navy would try to repel a French landing in any port, but if the French succeeded in landing in force in Ireland, the Government had little available to resist them. Irishmen themselves would have to do most of the resisting. Some Irishmen.

This was the emergency that led to the creation of the armed force known as the Irish Volunteers, as they became known in 1779. The Volunteers were to dominate Irish politics for the duration of the war with France. They were also to have a powerful effect on British politics, and to bring about two important pieces of legislation, of great concern to Burke.

His relationship to the Volunteers deserves careful examination, which it has never received, not altogether surprisingly: clues to the relationship are not easy to pick up. Burke himself never, so far as I can find, alluded to them directly. There is no entry under 'Irish Volunteers' in the General Index to his *Correspondence* although there are three other entries under 'Irish', all inconsequential. A casual reader might assume that he had no particular interest in the Volunteers. Yet for anyone who has tried to follow his involvements closely, this Burkean silence, interspersed as it is with cryptic and sombre asides, has something familiar about it. We are in the presence of something Burke cares about so deeply that he doesn't want to talk about it at all. This is the dark side of the Burkean moon.

With the lucidity of fascinated malice, Horace Walpole put his finger on the nub of the matter where Burke was concerned. In October 1779, when the Volunteer movement was at its height, Walpole wrote: 'The Irish have 28,000 men in arms . . . I dare to say that Mr. Edmund Burke does not approve of these proceedings, for the 28,000 are all Protestants.'[1] Burke must have watched the emergence of the Volunteers, with the deepest foreboding, though hardly a trace of this has survived in his recorded utterances. The 1778 situation bore an ominous resemblance to the Whiteboy disturbances in 1766, the year of persecution, in which some of Burke's Nagle relations had come close to the gallows (see Chapter I above, pp. 50–55). Now, as before, a French invasion of Ireland was expected; although with much greater reason. As in 1766, it was expected that if the French did land in force, there would be an Irish Catholic rising in support of them. And as in 1766, Protestant vigilantes were on the look out for 'papist whiteboys' who might be in league with the French.[2] That vigilante movement was at the origin of the Irish Volunteers. And the Volunteers themselves, at their inception, were not merely exclusively Protestant in composition; they were militantly and triumphantly Protestant. Their red-letter days, on which they held their great winter and summer parades, were 4 November (birthday of William III) and 12 July (Battle of the Boyne). These were the days – one of them still is in Northern Ireland – on which Protestant Ireland annually celebrated its decisive seventeenth-century victory over its Irish Papist enemies, and their French allies (1689–1691). And the Volunteers of 1778 were clearly looking forward to yet another victory over precisely the same combination of enemies.

To Burke, that pattern of association was, of necessity, profoundly uncongenial. And the pattern carried within it a possibility of dire import to those whom he loved in Ireland: might not the Protestant vigilantism of the Irish Volunteers turn into a bloody witch-hunt against the Irish Catholic gentry as had happened with the Protestant vigilantism of 1766? That question must have lain heavily on the heart and mind of Edmund Burke in the summer of 1778.

Generally we should avoid saying what a historical figure 'must have' thought or felt about something, when there is no explicit record that that person did in fact so think or feel about a particular topic at the time in question. In this case, however, we do know what

---

[1] H. Walpole, *Corr.* Vol. 28, p. 469. Weirdly, the same Walpole, four years later, was to refer to the Volunteers as 'a popish army'. It is true that by 1783, unlike 1779, some Catholics were being admitted to the Volunteers. But in 1783, as in 1779, they were an overwhelmingly Protestant force. In 1782–3, however, some of their leaders were making overtures to Catholics, and this must have misled Walpole. But in 1779, he has got it right.

[2] McDowell, *Ireland etc.*, pp. 255–6.

Burke thought and felt. The initial pattern of the events of 1778 and 1766 are so strikingly similar that I believe the inference that Burke's thoughts and feelings were the same on both occasions is inescapable. Why, it may be asked, do we know his thoughts and feelings for 1766, but have to infer them, for 1778? Because the person in whom he confided in 1766 was dead by 1778. Charles O'Hara, who died in 1776, was the only person, before 1790, to whom Burke communicated, in writings that have survived, anything of his feelings about relations between Catholics and Protestants in Ireland.

There is just one reference in Burke's correspondence to the arming of Irish Protestants, in the summer of 1778. He is writing to Garret Nagle of Ballyduff, his first cousin, to express his satisfaction at the passage by the Irish Parliament of measures modelled on the 1778 British Catholic Relief Act (see Chapter I above, pp. 75–77). He refers to the possibility of what would now be called 'backlash' from some Protestants, in the wake of this measure: 'If some anger appears in many upon this occasion; remember, it is pleasanter to endure the rage of disappointment, than the insolence of Victory. There will be much arming, much blustering, and many pretended fears and apprehensions on this occasion. But I recommend it to you, and all you converse with, to bear all such things with good humour and humility.'[1]

The association between the 'much arming' of the summer of 1778 and anti-Catholicism is significant.

In the event there was no return in the 1770s and 1780s to the persecution of 1766. Partly, this was due to the fact that the Catholic leadership supported the Irish Volunteers. Catholic leaders before France's entry into the war had been emphasing their loyalty, in contrast to the disloyalty of the 'pro-American' Protestants. Many Protestants were still pro-American – and would soon appear to emulate the Americans – but they were strongly opposed to an occupation of Ireland by America's European ally, Catholic France. (In reality, the France of the late 1770s was only nominally Catholic, but anti-Papists still thought of it as Papist). The Protestants possessed almost everything that was worth possessing in eighteenth-century Ireland, and they stood to lose it all, if the French landed in force and if large numbers of Irish Catholics rose in their support. So the determination professed by the Irish Volunteers to resist a French landing was absolutely sincere. In point of resistance to the

[1] *Corr.* IV, 19.

French, if not in other respects, George III possessed no more loyal body of subjects than the Protestants of Ireland, in 1778–1780. On the other hand, the sincerity of Irish Catholic professions of loyalty to the Crown, as against the French, was open to serious question. After all, if what Protestants feared were to come to pass, Catholics would be the gainers. In the circumstances, the Catholic professions of loyalty, and offers of assistance to the Volunteers – and, in a very few cases, enlistment in the Volunteers – have to be seen as largely tactical.[1] The Catholic gentry seem to have judged it prudent to assume either that the French would not land at all, or that they would not land in sufficient force to overthrow the existing system. On either assumption, by far the most prudent course for the subject people was to demonstrate their solidarity with their Protestant neighbours, as against the threatened French invasion.

The leaders of the Irish Volunteers knew the feelings of their Catholic 'fellow countrymen' well enough to have little belief in their professions of loyalty to the Crown, and still less in their expressions of enthusiasm for an Irish armed force which was, at its inception, exclusively Protestant and which publicly celebrated Protestant victories over Catholics. That being so, local Volunteer commanders at first rebuffed Catholic overtures. We are told that Catholics 'subscribed generously towards the buying of arms and equipment, and in other ways offered their services, only to have them refused, sometimes ungraciously.'[2] At some point, however, probably at a higher level, second thoughts prevailed. The Volunteers remained to the end

---

[1] For examples of 'Catholic loyalty' and its limits see Maurice R. O'Connell, *Irish Politics and Social Conflict in the Age of the American Revolution*, (Philadelphia, 1965). This is the most illuminating book that exists on the politics of Ireland in this period. (Maurice O'Connell – like his eighteenth-century cousins, another Maurice and Richard – belongs to the Derrynane O'Connells, the family that produced the great 'Liberator', Daniel O'Connell (1775–1847). However, more recent work has also to be taken into account, including contributions, concerning the Volunteers, to the Irish journal of military history, *The Irish Sword*. See Peter Smyth, 'Our Cloud-Capt Volunteers: the Volunteers as a military force' (I.S. XIII, 1978, pp. 185–207); Pádraig Ó Snodaigh, 'Some Police and Military Aspects of the Irish Volunteers' (*ibid* pp. 217–229); K. P. Ferguson, 'The Volunteer Movement and the Government' (*ibid* pp. 208–216). See also P. D. H. Smyth, 'The Volunteers and Parliament, 1779–84, *Penal Era and Golden Age: Essays in Irish History, 1690–1800*, edited by Thomas Bartlett and D. W. Hayton (Belfast, 1979) pp. 113–136.

[2] Rev. Patrick Rogers, *The Irish Volunteers and Catholic Emancipation*, (London, 1934). Father Rogers appears to assume that Catholic support for the Volunteers was entirely genuine and that those Protestants who rejected it were acting out of mindless bigotry. I cannot fully share either assumption but the book is a useful, informative study.

overwhelmingly Protestant in character, and exclusively Protestant in command structure, but some Catholics, hand-picked by Protestant officers, were allowed to enlist. Volunteer statements became more conciliatory. Officially, Catholic support for the Volunteers became welcome. With that welcome, the possibility of a 1766-style witch-hunt against Catholics receded.

There is no record of the reasons for the shift in official Volunteer attitudes towards Catholics; in the conditions of eighteenth-century Ireland, the reasons for such shifts were unlikely to be recorded. But the nature of the general context in which the shift occurred is known, and certain reasonable inferences can be made from it.

The danger to the established order in Ireland was far greater in 1778, with its real threat of invasion, than it had been in 1766, with its fantasy threat. Three years after the triumphant conclusion of the Seven Years War, with the conquest of Canada and India, English power, and authority over Ireland, looked invulnerable. In 1778, after Burgoyne's defeat by the unaided Americans at Saratoga, England looked very vulnerable indeed. To a conquered people, as the Irish Catholics were, the news that their conquerors have undergone a defeat, at the hands of some of their former subjects, is inherently exciting. Before Saratoga, Irish Catholics seem to have shown little interest in America; they may well have been put off by the enthusiasm of Irish Protestants for the American cause. But after Saratoga, and especially after the entry of France into the war, it would have been impossible for Irish Catholics not to have taken a keen interest in the course of the war. Most of them probably hoped for a French victory. They did not say so, for that would have put their lives in danger, to no good purpose. Nor did they contradict their social betters, and supposed leaders, when these gave assurances, on their behalf, of total loyalty to the Crown, and support for their Protestant fellow-subjects, embodied in the Irish Volunteers.

Irish Catholics, when beyond the reach of Protestant power, could indulge in more candid discourse. Maurice O'Connell, the historian, quotes Richard O'Connell, an officer in the French army at this time, as saying: 'Would to God that we were, at this moment 200,000 strong in Ireland . . . I would kick the members (of parliament) and their Volunteers and their unions and their Societies to the Devil! I would make the Rascally spawn of Damned Cromwell curse the hour of his Birth!'[1]

[1] O'Connell, *op. cit.*, p. 81.

Even in Ireland an O'Connell, in the remote family fastness of Derrynane in Co. Kerry, could afford to give the Irish Volunteers the cold shoulder, provided he did so discreetly. Richard O'Connell's cousin Maurice was invited by a Protestant neighbour to help to establish a Corps of Volunteers in the borough of Iveragh. His reply is masterly, in its use of the style and vocabulary of absolute loyalty and submission to constituted authority, in order to convey a complete refusal of any practical support: 'I am fully convinced that the Roman Catholic gentlemen of Iveragh would readily unite with their Protestant neighbours ... to form a Corps did they think such a measure would meet the approbation of the Legislature. They would, in common with every Catholic of standing in Ireland, be exceedingly happy by every means in their power to give additional weight and strength and security to the kingdom; but what can they do while the laws of their country forbid them the use of arms? Under such circumstances, I look upon it to be their duty to confine themselves to that line of conduct marked out for them by the Legislature, and with humility and resignation wait for a further relaxation of the laws, which a more enlightened and liberal way of thinking, added to a clearer and more deliberate attention to the real interests and prosperity of the country will, I hope, soon bring about.'[1] The O'Connell cousins were clearly less remote from one another in spirit than might be imagined from their contrasting epistolary styles. The two letters, taken together, make a good example of the influence of political and social contexts on forms of expression.

Irish Protestants were well aware that they were widely regarded as the 'Rascally spawn of Damned Cromwell', even among the Catholic upper class, currently offering support for the Irish Volunteers, whose members were drawn from the spawn in question. Yet there were sound reasons why the Volunteer leadership should take the proffered Catholic support at face value. For while Catholic and Protestant interests were generally opposed, there was an area in which Protestant interests overlapped with those of Catholics who had something to lose. This would become apparent in the event of a French landing in limited strength. Protestants were aware that their Catholic supporters would desert them in the event of a massive French invasion, capable of overthrowing the Ascendancy. But in the much more likely event of a limited French landing, most of the Catholic support for the Volunteers – support which came from the

---

[1] O'Connell, *op. cit.*, p. 81–2.

Catholic upper class – could probably be relied on. It would be in the Catholics' own vital interest to prevent a hopeless rising, followed by a bloody repression, in which they and their families might perish. In that event, the Catholic clergy, gentry and merchant class would be useful, if reluctant and uncongenial, allies. So Catholic support was acceptable. Each side was making use of the other, for its own ends.

On the surface, the politics of Ireland in 1778 presented a spectacle of unprecedented harmony. Protestants were arming for the defence of their country, and 'Catholics' – those who were being heard from, that is – were supporting their Protestant defenders. For the rest, the political conjuncture in Britain was more favourable than ever before to the two Irish causes closest to Burke's heart: Free Trade and Catholic Emancipation. Frightened by possible disaffection in Ireland, in the context of the threatened invasion, the North Administration decided, though it later temporarily changed its mind, on a limited relaxation of the restrictions on trade with Ireland. It also decided on a limited measure of Catholic relief, which did go through, in 1778. Burke spoke in the Commons, in April and May, in support of the Irish Trade Bills, explicitly linking these to events in America: 'Ireland was now the chief dependency of the British Crown, and it particularly behoved this country to admit the Irish nation to the privileges of British citizens.' Burke's point here is that America is as good as lost. [1]

The Irish Trade Bills were unpopular in Britain, and a backlash set in. Burke writes: 'A strong opposition was forming against the Irish Bills. . . . A general alarm was spread, through most of the trading and manufacturing parts of the kingdom . . . It ran like an infection every where and took such absolute possession of the mind, that the recent, and immediately sore-felt example of America, with respect to any general application of cause to effects, was totally forgotten.' [2] The 'infection' had spread to Burke's own constituency of Bristol. He acknowledged in the Commons that his support for the Irish Trade Bills might result in his being 'deprived of his seat . . . his conduct being disapproved by many of his chief friends and supporters, as well as by all who had opposed him at his election'. Burke adds: 'He should not blame [his constituents] if they did reject him: the event would afford a very useful example, on the one hand

[1] *Parl. History*, xix, 1103.
[2] *Parl. Hist.*, xix, 1114–5, 9 April 1778: quoting *Annual Register*.

of a senator inflexibly adhering to his opinion against interest and against popularity; and, on the other, of constituents exercising their undoubted right of rejection; not on corrupt [grounds], but from their persuasion that he whom they had chosen had acted against the judgment and interest of those he represented.'[1] Support for the Irish Trade Bills might not, in itself, have lost Burke his seat. What sank him, as recounted in Chapter I, was the combination of two Ireland-related issues: the Trade Bills and the Catholic Relief Act. More frightened, in 1778, by the 'general alarm' in Britain than by anything in Ireland, the North Administration decided in effect to drop the Trade Bills, by voiding them of all substance. This was a decision they were to regret, and to rescind, in the following year.

Burke first publicly adverts to the existence of the Volunteers, though without naming them, when speaking on 12 March 1779 in the Commons on a Motion 'respecting the state of Ireland': 'Were there not at this very time 11,000 land-forces actually under arms in Ireland without any kind of subordination to the government or any part thereof? . . . Not that he blamed those soldiers. Both the officers and the men, he was sure, deserved every compliment that could be paid them. But was it possible for that House to sit down tamely under such a fact? For his part, he was determined not to sit down before he had sifted the matter to the bottom. With respect to the influence of the noble lord [North], if it produced anything at all, it was one eternal scene of anarchy and confusion. But what alas! was that compared with the anarchy that the noble lord had raised through the whole continent of America?'[2]

In expressing alarm about the 'anarchic' potential of the Irish Volunteers, Burke seems to have been alone at this date. Most people in authority in Britain and Ireland seem to have found their assumption of a new role in 1779 reassuring. But then he had adequate reasons of his own, which he was not about to acknowledge explicitly, for not being reassured by the thought of large bodies of armed Irish Protestants patrolling the countryside, for whatever declared purpose, under no form of outside supervision or control.

The great expansion of the Volunteers began in May. There had been 11,000 of them when Burke first took alarm, in March. By July there were 18,000; in October at least 25,000, according to official estimates.[3] Unofficial estimates, towards the end of the year, went

[1] *Parl. Hist.* xix, 1123.
[2] *Parl. Hist.* xx, 271.
[3] O'Connell, *op. cit.*, p. 148.

higher: 40,000, 60,000. As they expanded, they added to their original role – of defenders of Ireland against French invaders – a new,
political role, that of armed reformers, whose immediate aim was
Free Trade: principally, the removal of the burdensome restrictions
on Irish exports to Britain. In Dublin, the Lord Lieutenant, the Earl
of Buckinghamshire (who had been hearing that the Volunteers had
begun to 'moulder away') became alarmed when he found, late in
May, that 'on the contrary, within these days, intelligence has
reached me, that additional companies are forming; and it has been
asserted, that this arises from the insinuations which are daily circulated in the public prints, that the idea of their numbers may conduce
to the attainment of political advantages to their country.'[1] What
the Lord Lieutenant had just discovered was that, although he still
possessed office, he no longer had power. He was dependent, for the
defence of that part of the king's realms, on a force not under his
control, with a political programme of its own, as well as the muscle
to back that programme.

And the Volunteers were needed for the defence of Ireland even
more acutely than in the previous summer: Spain entered the war as
France's ally, though without recognising the United States. In early
June the French fleet, with twenty-four ships of the line, left the port
of Brest, unhindered by the British Navy, to rendezvous with the
Spanish fleet. The rendezvous was achieved, but only on 23 July near
Corunna. The combined fleet outnumbered British ships in home
waters. The British Isles were now in greater danger of invasion than
at any time since the Spanish Armada.[2] It was thought that the
enemy fleet might be bound for Ireland, in which case the fate of the
Empire would be in the hands of the Irish Volunteers. In late July
Burke thought that the fleet – 'the greatest Force ever got together'[3]
– was bound either for Ireland or the West Indies. The French had
indeed made contingency plans for a landing in Ireland, but the
Spaniards had ruled that out, because it would mean a long war for
which Spain was not prepared. The objective of the combined fleet
was the occupation of a port in southern England, followed by a
dictated peace. In August the fleet lay off Plymouth. London was
believed to be in imminent danger; we find Burke thanking his friends

[1] Letter to Weymouth, 23 May 1779, quoted in O'Connell, *op.cit.*, p. 148.
[2] See A. Temple Patterson, *The Other Armada: The Franco-Spanish Attempt to Invade Britain in 1779* (Manchester, 1960).
[3] *Corr.* IV, 107.

the Champions, for offering his wife Jane 'asylum' in Bristol.[1] About a week later the danger was over, at least for that year. The great fleet returned to Brest and never put to sea again. There had been no naval engagement. The enterprise had been defeated by disease.[2]

With the threat of invasion out of the way, for 1779 at least, the Volunteers were free to concentrate their abundant energies on political agitation, in the last months of the year. For Burke this was a most uncomfortable period. He had expressed some of his reservations about the Volunteers in his 'anarchy' speech in March. But his political friends had difficulty in understanding what his reservations were about. From the view point of a typical English Whig, the Irish Volunteers were a thoroughly admirable body. That the Volunteers were true Whigs, their pious observation of the Whig festivals of 12 July and 4 November amply attested. Their patriotism was demonstrated by their voluntary enlistment to resist the French. The Irish Volunteers were a standing demonstration that Whigs could be pro-American and anti-French at the same time: a point it was important to make, and difficult to get across, once the French had become the allies of the Americans. If the Volunteers were admirable in themselves, so also was their political agitation. Their objective, free trade, was also a Whig objective; its most eloquent advocate in the British Parliament was Burke. In defying unconstitutional and corrupt practices in Britain and Ireland, under the governmental system of George III and his secret advisers, the Irish Volunteers were acting in the best Whig tradition.

Charles James Fox became an enthusiast for the Volunteers, along the above lines, at this time: 'The Irish associations [i.e. the Volunteers] had been called illegal; legal or illegal, he entirely approved of them.'[3] We find Burke anxiously trying to restrain similar tendencies in Rockingham. In a letter of 9 May 1779, in which the Irish Volunteers are never directly mentioned, Burke tries to keep Whig support in Parliament for Free Trade, altogether separate from the agitation, backed by implicit threats, which the Volunteers were conducting in Ireland. The subject of the letter is a draft motion prepared for Rockingham's consideration, by another hand. The key word, which Burke wants to keep out of the motion, is 'danger'. The original draft, on which Rockingham accepted Burke's revision, had

[1] *Corr.* IV, 126.
[2] Patterson, *The Other Armada*, pp. 210–12.
[3] Speech of 25 November 1779: *Parl. Hist.* xx, 1226–47.

referred to 'dangerous Associations not to import or use any British commodities', a reference to a boycott campaign by the Volunteers. Burke strikes that out. The draft also said that 'the spirit of discontent' might 'take a deep Root and endanger the Safety of his Majesty's kingdoms already too far engaged in a Civil as well as a foreign War'. He strikes that out too. He tells Rockingham that all this is 'highly indiscreet and dangerous'. He goes on: 'The Troubles in Ireland ought to be seriously looked into, as all National discontents ought to be; and on the question of removing them, the course of equity, Justice, and moderation is far preferable to that of ill Temper and rigour. But in God's Name where is the Necessity that Parliament should lose all appearance of Grace and dignity in the manner of making its concessions? Fallen we certainly are; and a pompous language ill becomes our Condition; but still there is a decorum, even in the humility of decayed greatness, which ought never to be parted with; it is a possession which fortune cannot take away; and I do not see why we should wantonly throw it out of our hands.'[1]

Burke's concern, here for the 'dignity' and 'decorum' of Parliament is paradoxical. He had mocked that line of argument – 'mumping and whining for their dignity, for some little thing that will give them back their dignity.' – when it had been used against the American colonists (see Chapter II above, p. 131). But at that time he wanted Parliament to make concessions to the American colonists. He clearly does not want Parliament to be seen making concessions to the Irish Volunteers. Something very important for Burke is involved here. It was to the British Parliament, and specifically to the English Whigs that he looked for the emancipation of the Irish Catholics. The first measure towards that end had just come from the British Parliament, in 1778, and the Irish Parliament had only reluctantly and partially followed suit. If the power of the Irish Volunteers – the armed power of an exclusive, dominant caste – were to be substituted for the ultimate authority of Britain, the Irish Catholics would be trapped, at the mercy of the caste whose interest it was to keep them permanently disfranchised. So for Burke it was of the utmost importance that the British Parliament should not be seen to yield to the authority of the Volunteers.

Rockingham accepted the amendment to the Motion, but clearly did not understand what Burke was talking about. As an Irish land-

---

[1] The important draft letter from Burke to Rockingham is annotated in *Corr*. IV, 70–72.

lord, Rockingham was a supporter of the Volunteers. He armed and equipped his tenants at Shillelagh, Co. Wicklow, as a corps of Volunteers. [1] The idea that the Volunteers might pose some kind of threat to the Catholics is one that probably never occurred to him and Burke, in writing to him, never alludes to such a possibility.

Burke, while getting 'danger' out of the Motion, had realised that Rockingham was, in any case, going to talk about it in his speech, introducing the Motion in the Lords. Burke tries to get him to take it easy: 'Not that it would not be proper too for your Lordship to touch upon the danger; but to touch it with a light and delicate hand . . .' [2]

The attempt to manage Rockingham's speech goes almost comically astray. On 11 May, two days after Burke's letter, Rockingham introduced the Motion on Irish trade in the Lords. He spoke, unfortunately for Burke, not once but three times. The first speech was clearly prepared by Burke, for the *Parliamentary History* says: 'The Marquss of Rockingham rose and entered into a long, computative and authentic detail, showing the comparative ability of Ireland to bear burdens.' In the same speech, Rockingham 'pointed out the danger of irritating the people, lest, by being driven to extremities, they might, in act of despair, be forced into resistance.' That might perhaps pass for a light and delicate touch, although Burke would not have used 'the people' in that particular context. But Rockingham went on. In a second intervention he said: 'As an additional argument, why it was necessary and prudent in the King's service to agree to associations now on foot in that kingdom; and desired to know if they had been informed of their nature and extent. This, he said, was matter truly alarming, if the British Government meant to adhere to their former system of oppression and injustice and therefore it highly behoved members if they were obstinately bent to throw every part of the empire into a flame, to seriously investigate the degree of resistance they were likely to meet.' Then a third intervention: 'He remembered the American war commenced in address and petitions; that when those were turned a deaf ear to, they were followed with non-importation agreements.' [3]

[1] *Corr.* IV, 186, n. 2. The Shillelagh Volunteers were 'rechristened the Rockingham Volunteers'.

[2] *Corr.* IV, 70.

[3] The comment on this speech by a modern historian is unexpected. R. B. McDowell writes: 'In the Lords, Rockingham, influenced by Burke, took a very moderate line' (*Ireland in the Age of Imperialism and Revolution*, p. 265). McDowell goes on to paraphrase Rockingham's first intervention to which McDowell's comment is indeed applicable. But there is precious little moderation or influence of Burke in Rockingham's second and third interventions.

Rockingham had done the very opposite to what Burke was trying to get him to do: he had magnified the importance of the Irish Volunteers, and thereby enhanced it. The two men were essentially at variance over the Irish question, during this period, although Rockingham never seems to have realised this. As he showed in that address to the Lords, he saw the Irish volunteers as resisting 'a system of oppression and injustice', which he seems to have assumed to be affecting the Irish in general. But Burke saw the Volunteers as *representing* a specific system of injustice, which weighed on one section of the Irish: the Catholic majority. It seems, however, that Burke at this time was incapable of conveying to Rockingham and the other Whigs what he felt about all this. The fact is that, in relation to Ireland and to Catholicism, Burke had been playing a part, before his fellow Whigs and before the public. We see him playing that part to a pitch of extravagance in the 'Ireland' section of his speech 'On Conciliation with America'. There he goes so far as to speak in the persona of a descendant of the English Whigs of the Glorious Revolution, whereas he was in fact a descendant of Irish Jacobites of the same period. [1]

To contrast the idyllic picture of Ireland offered in 'On Conciliation with America' with the corrupt and corrupting Hell described in Burke's 1780 speech, see Chapter I above (p. 82), in a moment of emotion when his defences temporarily broke down, is to measure the gulf between the ostensible feelings of Burke's assumed persona, and his real feelings about Ireland in the period of the American Revolution. He did not again carry dissimulation to such lengths. Normally it was a question of minimising the importance of his Catholic connections and of taking care to be taken for a normal Anglican. That meant keeping the Catholic side of his feelings, and habits of viewing Irish affairs, under careful control. The keeping up of these particular pretences with Rockingham must have been especially delicate and trying. As noted earlier, Rockingham had to question him about his Catholic connections at the very beginning of their relationship. Rockingham found Burke's answers satisfactory. I doubt if Burke did. I feel sure that the answers were factually accurate. I also feel sure that Burke made himself sound more Protestant than he actually felt: that was habitual with him during this period. When asked about his education he would have volunteered the

---

[1] Not all the Nagles risked their lives and fortunes for James II. But they would all, or almost all, have shared in the general Catholic hope for the Victory of the Catholic King.

acceptable Protestant parts: Ballitore; Trinity College, Dublin. Unless specifically asked about his earlier education which he probably was not, he would not have offered Ballyduff and Monanimy, the submerged Catholic layer.

Burke's incapacity to communicate seriously with Rockingham and the other Whigs on the subject of Ireland didn't matter much in his first twelve years as an MP, because Ireland was not then a matter of pressing concern in British politics. But in 1778, under the French invasion threat, Irish affairs shot to near the top of the British political agenda, and remained there for four years. His colleagues now engaged in animated discussion over Irish affairs, about which they knew little. Burke, in contrast, knew far more than he could tell, for he had schooled himself over many years to tell as little as possible about this painful and dangerous subject. It was with Rockingham in particular that communication broke down. As an Irish landlord, Rockingham supported the Irish Volunteers, or, in his words, 'justified the association,' without thinking very deeply about them, both in their capacity as defenders of Ireland against French invasion, and in their most recent capacity of Whigs protesting against unjust laws. When Burke urges the need for a 'light and delicate touch' concerning the results of the activities of these admirable people, Rockingham can't see what Burke is talking about. When Burke warns against the danger of crying 'Danger!' Rockingham cries 'Danger!' at the top of his voice. Burke can't get his message through, because the mask he was in the habit of wearing, in these particular matters, had become also a gag. In other matters, and notably over American affairs, Burke's influence over Rockingham remains great, even decisive, right up to Rockingham's death in July 1782. [1] But over Whig policy towards Ireland his influence was limited up to 1782. In relation to this subject he became a tongue-tied and irritable passenger in a vehicle which he felt to be travelling in the wrong direction.

In 1779, on William III's birthday, the Volunteer campaign mounted to a climax in a great parade through Dublin. R. B. McDowell writes that 'On 4 November the Dublin Volunteers corps (one of them commanded by the duke of Leinster) paraded in College Green before an immense crowd of spectators. The pedestal of King William's statue was decorated "with labels in large capital letters",

---

[1] John A. Woods, editor of Volume IV of the *Correspondence*, writes: 'It was Burke who influenced Rockingham most profoundly over Irish affairs' (*Corr.* IV, xiii). The fate of Burke's advice on the motion on trade with Ireland shows both the reality of that influence and its limits.

one of which read "A short money bill" and another "A free trade or else". There were 900 men on parade and the precision of their firing, it was said, was not surpassed by any army in Europe. Ten days later there was a cruder display of public feeling when some thousands of artisans, assembled it was rumoured by printed hand bills, beset the parliament house demanding a free trade, and a party of rioters, trying to find the attorney-general, stormed his house in Harcourt Street and swept through the Four Courts'. [1]

The Irish agitation was now led by Henry Grattan (1746–1820), a young member of the Irish Parliament, who worked in concert with the commander of the Volunteers, the Earl of Charlemont (1728–1799). Grattan was one of the most admired orators of the day. His best-known speeches resemble the more ornate of Burke's, but he lacked Burke's range and variety, as well as his intellectual power. He was, however, a skilful and audacious politician, especially in this quasi-revolutionary phase of his career (1779–1782). The Irish Volunteers, by the end of 1779, were said to number 50,000 men. The British Government had no force in Ireland that could match that, and no force elsewhere available for Ireland. Grattan and the Volunteers were masters of the Irish scene. He could now dictate to the Irish Parliament, to which he laid down the law in terms which prefigure the imperious and absolute language of the French Revolution, ten years later, stylistically and conceptually. (There is a common source, in Rousseau.) An MP, according to Grattan, 'was the servant of his constituents, whose commands he was bound to obey, as the servants of the Crown were the Royal Authority. If a member deviates from the intentions of his constituents, they were authorised to associate against him to reprobate his proceedings – and never trust him with their rights again'. [2]

This was just the doctrine that Burke had so resonantly rejected in his famous speech to the electors of Bristol in 1774 (see Chapter I above, pp. 74–5). On the face of it, Burke and Grattan were agreed over the question of the hour: Free trade for Ireland. But basically, they were antagonists, both over the general direction of Irish policy, and in their general political philosophy. In any case, Grattan was using the term 'constituents' in a somewhat specialised sense. When Grattan spoke of 'constituents . . . authorised to associate against' a 'deviating' member 'to reprobate his proceedings', he was, in the

[1] McDowell, *op. cit.*, p. 267.
[2] O'Connell, *Irish Politics*, p. 176.

context of the brute realities of the time, threatening the violence of the (largely Protestant) Dublin mob, backed by the Irish Volunteers, against any parliamentarian who might dare to vote against Free Trade. The Irish Parliament understood and capitulated. An amendment to the address, demanding Free Trade, was carried unanimously on 12 October 1779. As the Irish Parliament was normally subservient to the Administration of the day, this vote is symptomatic of a near-revolutionary situation in Ireland during the 'Free Trade' crisis.

The centre of the political storm over Ireland then shifted to the British Parliament, which met on 25 November. Burke spoke 'on the address', and on the question of Free Trade (he was the first speaker for the party). He was clearly under heavy stress. The Parliamentary History records that Burke was 'suffering from a violent cold and hoarseness' and 'sat down once or twice and would have declined speaking, had he not been previously solicited by the unanimous sense of the House to proceed.' Burke went on to link Ireland to America:

... However the noble lord [North] ... might pretend to disunite the American war from the present affairs of Ireland and the temper and disposition of the people there, his lordship would find the mad, cruel and accursed American war, written in the most legible characters, in every single cause, circumstance and step which had contributed to call further, the spirit, the resentment and resolution of the Irish nation, whether already in actual existence, or in embryo, ready to burst forth in tenfold mischief, or in a storm strike the nation and, shake it to its very foundations. ...[1]

'*The spirit, the resentment and resolution of the Irish nation.*' ... This rings false. The Irish Volunteers did think and speak of themselves as the embodiment of the Irish Nation, and the English Whigs accepted that from the Volunteers, at face value. The English Whigs were accustomed to forgetting about the Irish Catholics. Burke could never forget about them; he could only pretend to, sometimes, as here. He knew that what the Volunteers represented was the Protestant Nation which was not, for him, the Irish Nation. He is expressing here, not his personal opinion or feelings, but the general attitude of the Rockingham Whigs on this question, an attitude with which he personally was at variance. And something of Burke's revulsion at hearing himself speaking in this unnatural way can be discerned in the remainder of his remarks.

[1] *Parl. Hist.* xx, 1134.

'*Whether already in actual existence, or in embryo . . .*' This phrase, which must have puzzled Burke's audience, appears as an attempt to qualify the phrase 'the Irish nation', in its context so foreign to Burke's real thoughts and feelings. The immediate objective of the Volunteers – Free Trade – was common to both Catholics and Protestants. The Catholic gentry, denied other outlets, made up a significant portion of the merchant class. Catholic merchants were fully behind the Volunteers, in the demand for Free Trade. Thus, if Burke gagged at the notion of the Volunteers as representing 'the Irish nation' already in actual existence, he could grasp at the idea of the Volunteer demand for Free Trade as 'embryo' of something yet to be born: the real Irish nation, made up of both Catholics and Protestants. Burke did cherish a hope that such a nation might come into being in his time. He wrote to Edmund Sexton Pery, Speaker of the Irish House of Commons, in August 1778, to congratulate him on the progress of the Catholic Relief Bill in the Irish Parliament: 'You are now beginning to have a Country and I trust you will complete the Design'.[1] Hence 'embryo'.

. . . Ireland with 42,000 men in arms. Why not apply to Ireland the kind of measures that were used in America? Ministers dare not . . . the danger of the present awful moment made insolence and arrogance give way to pride [*sic*] and humiliation.

America has pointed out to (Ireland), not the rule of her conduct, but her just claims upon this country. The people of Ireland have reasoned fairly and justly: the colonies, they know have been offered the most that their own most sanguine expectations could aspire to, a free trade with all the world, America, for her revolt, has had a choice of favours. This reward of rebellion . . . Though an Irishman by birth, he was urged, he said, from real sentiment, to express his warmest gratitude to this country, which had raised him from a humble situation, from obscurity to a seat in the national great council: and declared that he must be the most ungrateful and worthless man existing if he ever forgot the profusion of favours she had heaped upon him; he would not say totally unmerited, but infinitely beyond anything his most sanguine expectations ever held out to him . . . He was induced, from every consideration which struck him, to believe, that what ever measure would serve Ireland essentially would and must in the end serve England: but, if ever any concessions on the part of his native country should be insisted upon, derogatory to the interest and prosperity of this country, he would be one of the first men in this House, in the character of a British senator,

[1] *Corr.* IV, 15.

to rise and oppose in the most peremptory and decisive manner, any proposition tending directly or indirectly to any such point.[1]

'*Why not apply to Ireland the same measures that were used in America?*' This question, which must have startled all Burke's auditors, and shocked some of them, could be interpreted as the surfacing of a repressed wish to destroy the organisation of the armed Protestants and to liberate the Catholics of Ireland.

'*Though an Irishman by birth* etc.'. The rather strained and fulsome passage that follows has been interpreted, along with other similar passages in his writings and speeches, to Burke's disadvantage. He has been seen as turning his back on his native country, to fawn on its oppressors. But this is a complete misreading. The 'Ireland' on which Burke here turns his back is not his 'native country' but the Ireland of its oppressors: the exclusively Protestant Nation, armed and embodied in the Irish Volunteers. The England whose interests he prefers to those of the Protestant Irish Nation, is the enlightened England, whose best representatives were the Rockingham Whigs. The British Parliament, influenced both by the Enlightenment and the American War and guided by Burke, had given Catholics a significant measure of emancipation in the previous year. It was to the British Parliament that Burke looked to complete that work, overruling expected opposition from the forces represented in the Irish Volunteers. There are false and inconsistent passages in this difficult and troubled speech, but this passage is not among them, though some of its expressions are strained. In expressing his preference for England, as against official 'Ireland' he is speaking out of his deepest and most abiding loyalties, not the least of which is his loyalty to his own people.

'*But if ever any concessions* etc.' Burke is here looking ahead, and delivering a warning. He foresees, correctly, that the next demand from the Irish Volunteers will be for independence for 'Ireland' – Protestant Ireland, that is. He is serving notice that he will oppose any such demand. Nominally, he is opposing on purely British grounds 'concessions ... derogatory to the interest and properity of this country [England]'. I have no doubt, however, of his real grounds for opposition, for these are inherent in the situation. A fully independent parliament in Ireland would have been a Protestant Parliament, whose interests would be incompatible with Catholic enfranchisement. Burke's hopes for his people would be extinguished at least

---

[1] *Parl. Hist.* xx, 1205–12.

for his lifetime. He is nowhere more profoundly Irish than in this extravagantly 'British' passage. As he clutches round him his toga as 'a British senator', he is articulating, in Aesopian language, the hopes and fears of the Nagle country in the Blackwater Valley, and the rest of Catholic Ireland.

On 15 December North's Administration caved in before the demand for Free Trade, backed by the Irish Volunteers, now almost in full control in Ireland. After North had announced his concessions, Burke was silent. As he was spokesman on Ireland for the Rockingham Whigs, he was being silent on behalf of his party as well as of himself. In Ireland, where the granting of Free Trade was greeted with general enthusiasm, Burke at this time got an extremely bad Press, which was overwhelmingly Protestant and unreservedly pro-Volunteer. The *Dublin Evening Post* of 23 December 1779 condemned 'the almost unaccountable conduct of Opposition upon that day [15 December], the day on which Lord North introduced in the British Commons the bill to give freedom to export wool and glass – our Countryman Burke endeavoured to raise every obstacle to prevent their being carried through the House – but finding every means ineffectual, stole away mute, and was followed by the whole squad.'[1]

Burke, who had put his seat at Bristol at high risk, through his support for Free Trade with Ireland, was understandably exasperated by the outcry against him in Ireland, merely for having silently accepted the Government's belated concession. He wrote a long letter to an Irish MP explaining and justifying his conduct in parliament on Free Trade with Ireland. As regard the contentious matter of his silence on the day of the concession, he writes: 'But, it seems, I was silent at the passing the resolutions. Why, what had I to say? If I had thought them too much, I should have been accused of an endeavor to inflame England. If I should represent them as too little, I should have been charged with a design of fomenting the discontents of Ireland into actual rebellion.'[2]

[1] O'Connell, *op. cit.*, p. 198. Possibly Burke had tried to raise some procedural points, but these have left no trace. He had apparently asked whether the concessions on trade were fully acceptable to the Irish Parliament: apparently he thought 'amendments of their Constitution' would be required as well, and that was the ground on which he was prepared to make his stand. Actually, the Constitutional issue was not formally raised in the Irish Parliament until four months later (below p. 197). The *Dublin Evening Post* is described by O'Connell (p. 312) as 'the most interesting of the [Dublin] journals with the best news coverage and largest format'.

[2] Letter to Thomas Burgh, *Works* VI, 230. About the same time he had also to write to a Bristol constituent defending himself for having supported free trade with Ireland (*Corr.* IV, 223–5).

Burke was a sufficiently skillful parliamentarian to have coped with that difficulty. His real difficulty lay elsewhere, in having to reconcile his satisfaction with the attainment of free trade, in itself, with his repugnance and foreboding at this revelation of the apparently irresistible power of the Irish Volunteers. There was much there to be silent about. George III having studied reports about the Irish Volunteers concluded that 'there is an end of all Government in that Country.'[1] For once Burke was in full agreement with his royal adversary.

Early the next month, when Burke is speaking on a Motion respecting the State of Ireland, the same embarrassment as showed in his speech on the address appears again.

1780–1781

On 19 April 1780 Henry Grattan formally launched the struggle for the legislative independence of Ireland. He introduced the Resolution: 'that His most excellent Majesty by and with the consent of the Lords and Commons of Ireland are [sic] the only power competent to enact laws to bind Ireland.'[2]

This was the move Burke had been dreading: a proposal for legislative independence, perhaps to be followed by full independence, for an exclusively Protestant Irish Parliament. But the threat, though now explicitly formulated for the first time, did not immediately become pressing. In his son's *Memoirs* (p. 39) Grattan is quoted as saying 'I brought on the question [of legislative independence] the 19th April, 1780 – *That was a great day for Ireland – that day gave her liberty!*' One might think from this language that the resolution was at least carried by the Irish Parliament in 1780, but this was not so: Grattan is rhetorically anticipating developments of two years later. The resolution of 19 April was actually defeated in the Irish Commons, through a negative amendment, by 136 votes to 97.[3]

In October the same assembly had voted unanimously in favour

[1] *Correspondence of King George III*, Vol. V, p. 506, No. 2863: The King to North.

[2] *Memoirs of the Life and Times of the Rt. Hon. Henry Grattan*, by his son, Henry Grattan (London 1849) Vol II, p. 39.

[3] O'Connell, *op. cit.*, p. 231.

of free trade. But then free trade was a cause that aroused enthusiasm among Irish people of all classes, and both castes. The Dublin mob was so aroused by the economic benefits it thought would follow from it that any legislator who voted against it would have been in serious danger of being lynched; hence the unanimous vote. Now, members could vote as they pleased, over legislative independence, without fear of unpleasant consequences to their persons. The Dublin mob 'showed no sign of being excited over the debate'. [1] Legislative independence, unlike free trade, was divisive, both in terms of caste and class. Catholics, being excluded both from Parliament and from the franchise, had no reason to support such a measure, unless it were accompanied by a measure removing the relevant Catholic disabilities, which was not the case. The dominant Protestant caste was divided along class lines. The landlords, although accustomed, in theory, to reject the British Parliament's assumed right to legislate for Ireland, did not think it expedient, in practice, to assert legislative independence, as that vote showed. At the other end of the class spectrum, lower-class Protestants, excluded by the property qualification from the franchise, could hardly get more excited about the question than the Catholics were. So, in practice, support for the cause of legislative independence was confined, with few exceptions, to the Protestant middle-class, embodied in the Irish Volunteers. [2]

The Protestant middle-class was by far the most dynamic class in Ireland, and its support for legislative independence would in time be sufficient to bring that cause to victory; or at least the appearance of victory. But it was not sufficient, under the circumstances of that time. Grattan looked to the American War for the furtherance of his cause. To the objection of a parliamentary opponent that it was wrong to put forward such a measure while England was at war, he replied that 'war was the only time for obtaining concessions from England; it was while she was weak that she would grant Ireland her freedom.' [3] He was right about that, as far as free trade was concerned, and he was eventually to be proved right in the case of legislative independence also. But not in 1780–81. The war did not

[1] *Ibid.* p. 231.

[2] The class-conflicts of the early 1780s in Ireland – much more complex than the above summary can show – are brilliantly analysed by O'Connell in the chapter 'The failure of radicalism in 1780'.

[3] O'Connell, *Irish Politics*, p. 225. Grattan here anticipates Theobald Wolfe Tone's famous 'England's difficulty is Ireland's opportunity.'

help Grattan's case, in those years, because the British appeared to be beating the Americans (see below p. 209).

Since the Irish Parliament had thrown out the resolution for Irish legislative independence, the issue did not come before the British Parliament, and so in direct form to Burke's official attention. But due to a subtle and astute move on the part of Grattan's patriot party, the issue did come to the British Parliament, from Ireland, in an indirect form. The form it took was the Irish Mutiny Bill, passed 2 June and transmitted to London for approval on 3 July. This was the first Irish Mutiny Bill. Ever since the Glorious Revolution of 1688 there had been annual Mutiny Bills, in the British Parliament, designed to ensure the continuity of parliamentary control over the armed forces. It had long been assumed that the British Parliament's Mutiny Act covered all the Crown forces, in whatever parts of His Majesty's dominions these might be stationed. In 1780, however, the opposition in the Irish Parliament successfully challenged that assumption. The idea of an Irish Mutiny Bill – 'a political stroke of almost Machiavellian cleverness,' as Maurice O'Connell calls it – was probably prompted by the course of the debate in the Irish Parliament in April on Grattan's Resolution for legislative independence. All those who spoke in that debate, even those who voted against Grattan, denied the right of the British Parliament to legislate for Ireland; that was a normal part of Irish parliamentary rhetoric. But if – so the Irish opposition argued – the British Parliament had no right to legislate for Ireland, then the Mutiny Act did not apply to the British forces stationed in Ireland, and these therefore escaped all legal control.[1] Frightened by the thought of a lawless soldiery, the British Parliament decided to be on the safe side and pass an Irish Mutiny Act.[2]

Grattan had failed to carry a Resolution explicitly challenging the right of the British Parliament to legislate for Ireland. But he and his friends had now succeeded in bringing about the passage of an Act of the Irish Parliament which implicitly challenged that right.

The British Administration had initially tried to use its influence over the Irish Parliament to defeat the Irish Mutiny Bill (it was an Act in Ireland but a Bill in Britain) because of its implicit challenge to the authority of the British Parliament. However, in the event the

[1] Those forces then numbered about 12,000 men, and were outnumbered by the Volunteers. But the British regulars, far more disciplined than the politically ebullient volunteers, were considered indispensable for the secure defense of property.

[2] O'Connell, pp. 215–6, 307–8.

Administration was itself constrained to accept defeat. As a consequence, the word 'Ireland' was omitted from the British Mutiny Bill for 1781. In the Commons, on 20 February 1781 Burke pounced on the implications of this partial abdication of the British Parliament. America, he argued, was already lost, through the follies of government, and now Ireland was being lost too. He spoke in elegiac vein: 'Mr. Burke said so many and such great revolutions had happened of late, that he was not much surprised to hear the right hon. gentlemen treat the loss of the supremacy of this country over Ireland as a matter of very little consequence. Thus one star, and that the brightest ornament of our orrery [America], having been suffered to be lost, those who were accustomed to inspect and watch our political heavens, ought not to wonder that it should be followed by the loss of another:

> So star would follow star, and light light
> Till all was darkness and eternal night'. [1]

Charles James Fox, who was clearly disturbed by the implications of what Burke was saying, intervened to say that 'it was not his purpose to attack the claim which they [the Irish] had set up to legislative independency.' This only made matters worse from Fox's point of view. The intervention provoked Burke to move from his relatively harmless elegiac vein to an expression of determination to oppose legislative independence for Ireland: '. . . It became him to be firm and to look on the preservation of what yet remained as their first duty.' [2]

Burke was now committed to supporting American independence while opposing the independence of his own country, Ireland. This puzzled contemporaries, including friends like Fox. It is among the puzzles which some twentieth-century historians 'solved' by assuming Burke's motivations to be purely opportunistic and venal, thus accounting for all departures from consistency of principle. But in fact his position, on the two kinds of independence, is perfectly consistent in principle. He supported independence for America because he saw it as a genuine case of a people demanding its freedom. Grattan's demand for 'independence' for 'Ireland' is bogus: it means freedom, not for a people, but for a dominant caste, setting it free

---

[1] *Parl. Hist.* xxl, 1293–1305: 'Debate in the Commons over the omission of the word "Ireland" from the Mutiny Bill.'
[2] *Ibid.*

to perpetuate its domination over the disenfranchised and oppressed Catholic majority of the people of Ireland.

The distinction is tenable. Yet Burke's position remained a puzzle, for he never explicitly articulated this distinction in a parliamentary debate. More than that, he distracts attention from it. During that debate of the omission of the word 'Ireland', he said that 'he thought himself called upon not to decline giving his opinion on a subject in which local attachments might be supposed to interfere with his duty.'[1]

This was misleading: Burke's strongest 'local attachments' did not, as he implies, join him to those in Ireland who were demanding legislative independence, but to the unwilling subjects of those who were making that demand. His picture of himself as an impartial imperial legislator in the Roman style, deaf to all local considerations, and bound by no ties of personal affection to any particular group of people, is most unlike the real Burke. This is a *persona* he assumes at times of stress, as in the 'Ireland' passage of 'On Conciliation with America'.

Burke's burning resentment of the Irish Protestant supremacy over Catholics, and of the Penal Laws that codified that supremacy, was lifelong – already in 1761, well before his parliamentary career began, he was working on his *Tract Relative to the Laws against Popery in Ireland*. However, from 1765, when he became Rockingham's private secretary (and, later that year, an MP), his resentment finds no explicit recorded expression except for the explosive, emotional outburst in the 1780 Bristol Guildhall speech.

The contrast between that speech and some of his earlier public statements, especially the 'Ireland' portion of 'On Conciliation with America' (see above pp. 150–4), is stark. The constraint and artificiality of his public position stands out in sharp relief. A truthful man in other respects, and with an acute sense of personal honour, Burke at this time, and in this respect, was living a lie. It must have been a torment to him. The pressure from Ireland, though perceptible, was not very great in 1781. But a new Irish crisis was in the making, and would break once the news reached the British Isles, at the end of the year, of Cornwallis's surrender to Washington, on 17 October.

[1] *Parl. Hist.* xxl. 1305.

AMERICA
1778–1780

Between Saratoga and Yorktown, the parliamentary struggle over
America consisted essentially of a battle of wills between George III
and Edmund Burke. And the same is true of the months between the
news of Yorktown and the yielding of the King, through his acceptance of the Second Rockingham Administration. [1]

In the heyday of Namierite reductionism in relation to Burke,
around the mid century, the above statements would have been
received with derision by virtually all historians specialising in the
history of the British Parliament of the late eighteenth century. Even
today, in what might be called the post-Namierite period, when the
relevant historians are both better informed about Burke and more
respectful towards him, these statements may still be received with
polite scepticism. At first sight they may seem improbable in that
George and Burke appear as incommensurate entities, which indeed
they were in some important respects. In terms of eighteenth century
values, George was the star, around which the whole system
revolved, while Burke was no more than an occasionally visible
moon, revolving around the minor planet, Rockingham, at a great
distance from the star. But there is another way of looking at things.
In terms of intellect and imagination, it is Burke who is the star and
George, at best, a moon, though that is a minority point of view.
There are, however, politically relevant ways in which the two entities are commensurate, and alike. They are alike in 'strength of will,
intensity, and continuity of purpose' (as the Irish politician John
Dillon has described the principal leadership qualities of Charles
Stewart Parnell). They were both deeply committed, on opposing
sides, on the great questions of the day. They both identified the
same two political issues as the vital ones, and they identified the
relationship between them in the same way. The issues were the
American War and what would now be called Cabinet responsibility.
Burke and his friends were determined to bring the American War
to an end, at the first opportunity. George was determined to prosecute the American War to a victorious conclusion, despite every
set-back. Burke's view of the Constitution was what later became

[1] Below, pp. 223–234.

the accepted one: that the monarch must do as advised by Ministers, collectively responsible to Parliament. George's view was that ministers could advise the monarch, but that once the monarch had made up his mind, even in a manner contrary to the advice offered, the ministers must comply with the monarch's decisions. The test case, for the constitutional question, was the American War. George saw that if the Rockingham party were ever to form an administration, he would be under pressure to end the American War unless, that is, Rockingham could be persuaded, before joining or forming an administration, to drop his opposition over America. The attempt was tried, but it failed completely. Rockingham not merely refused to give the necessary assurances but demanded that the king, before Rockingham would accept a share in administration, should drop his attempt to assert a royal veto on America independence (see below pp. 214–18).

Let us now look more closely at their respective positions. It is to Rockingham, not to Burke, that George refers in his *Correspondence*, when he is complaining about factious opposition to the Royal will. But 'Rockingham' refers to someone so strongly under Burke's influence that he is virtually controlled by him. Historians have claimed, not quite convincingly, that Burke's influence over Rockingham was insignificant, in the early years of their relationship. (See Chapter II above, pp. 99–101). There is no dispute however, over the extent of his influence over his nominal leader, during the last four years of the American War and of Rockingham's life. John A. Woods, the editor of the relevant volume of Burke's *Correspondence* (IV. 1778–1782), writes: 'In this period Burke was exercising a decisive and almost unchallenged influence upon Lord Rockingham'.[1]

Burke's decisive influence over Rockingham was also acknowledged by contemporaries, sometimes ruefully. Lord Shelburne, who next to Rockingham was the most important Whig leader, wrote: 'There is no dealing with Mr. Burke, he is so violently attached to his own opinion that there is no arguing with him, and has got so

[1] *Corr.* IV, xii: The late Dr. Woods, a Namierite by training and a Burkean by conversion, added a 'word of caution': 'We cannot always know when Burke was overruled, or how often he was a sponsor of other men's ideas.' As far as the American crisis was concerned, there was only one brief period in which Burke was clearly 'overruled'. This was in 1770, in the days of the Grenville-Rockingham alliance, (see Chapter II above, pp. 132–5). After Grenville's death in that year Rockingham fell again under Burke's influence, and after the death of William Dowdeswell, in 1775, Woods writes, 'Burke had no serious rival, though it was a few years before his ascendancy became obvious.'

much ascendancy over Lord Rockingham that I protest I see no method of doing anything.'[1] Isaac Barré (see Chapter II above, p. 170), a follower of Shelburne, although, unlike Shelburne, personally friendly to Burke, wrote to the Duke of Richmond (a rather wayward follower of Rockingham) '. . . I love Burke, I admire him even in his wanderings, but when those wanderings come to be adopted seriously and obstinately by men of far higher description [i.e. social standing] than himself, they then become alarming indeed.'[2]

These complaints, coming from the Shelburne camp, are significant in relation to the battle of wills over the American war. Lord Shelburne was the leader of the smaller of the two Whig factions in opposition; he had ten followers, Rockingham 70. Shelburne had been a Chatham follower, but after Chatham's death in May 1778, he was making overtures to Rockingham in order to establish a common front of the two factions, leading eventually to a Rockingham–Shelburne Administration. Shelburne and Barré felt that this desirable development was being blocked by Burke. They were right about this. Personally, Burke disliked and distrusted Shelburne (see below pp. 234–42). The mere dislike might not have impeded political partnership, but the distrust did, for it was a political distrust, although other factors also entered into it. Shelburne had been a member of the chaotic Chatham Administration (1766–1770) under which, or under part of which, the Townshend duties had been imposed on the Americans, thus leading to the renewed American resistance out of which the American War developed. Shelburne's membership of the Chatham Administration, which ousted Rockingham's in 1766, would in itself have been a reason for distrusting him. But there was a more pressing reason, which was decisive: major divergence between Shelburne, on one side, and Burke and Rockingham on the other, over American independence.

Shelburne, like his former leader, Chatham, while favouring a generally conciliatory approach to America, opposed the granting of independence, even after Saratoga, and even, for a while, after Yorktown. Burke had hoped, up to Saratoga, that American independence might be avoided, and America kept within the British Empire, through the concessions he had unsuccessfully proposed before the Declaration of Independence (1776): essentially, the end of all

[1] *Corr.* IV, xiii.
[2] Lord Fitzmaurice, *Life of William, Earl of Shelburne* (London, 1912) Vol II, p. 68.

attempts to tax Americans, and the repeal of all the penal Acts against them. In 1775 these concessions had a good chance of being accepted by the Americans but were withheld. After Saratoga, North's Administration offered the Americans precisely the same concessions only to have them contemptuously rejected. By then nothing less than independence would do. After that offer and its rejection Burke concluded that recognition of American independence had become 'a necessity'. Speaking on the Army Estimates, in December 1778, he told the Commons how reluctantly he had reached that conclusion: 'With regard to acknowledging the independency of America, gentlemen looked at the position in a wrong point of view, and talked of it merely as a matter of choice, when, in fact, it was now become a matter of necessity.... It was incumbent on Great Britain to acknowledge it directly. On the day that he first heard of the American states having claimed independency, – it made him sick at heart; it struck him to the soul, because he saw it was a claim essentially injurious to this country, and a claim which Great Britain could never get rid of: never! never! never! It was not, therefore to be thought that he voted for the independency of America. Far from it. He felt it as a circumstance exceedingly detrimental to the fame – and exceedingly detrimental to the interest, of this country. But when, by a wrong management of the cards, the gamester had lost much, it was right for him to make the most of the game as it then stood, and to take care that he did not lose more.... The language [of the North Administration was] the language held by those who had gained the estates of minors by dice and hazard. "You lost your estate at the gaming table – go there again; there it is, that you must look for another estate".' Burke went on to justify the American decision to accept an alliance with France: a bold argument indeed to advance in the British Parliament at a time when Britain was at war with France, as well as with the American colonists. The fact that Burke was able to offer that argument, without rebuke from his leader, or remonstrance from any of his party colleagues, is evidence of the authority he had achieved over both leader and party, in the formulation of policy over the American War.

For Rockingham to have accepted a close alliance with Shelburne would have meant the abandonment, or at least the dilution, of the policy of accepting the necessity of recognising American independence, which Burke had laid down on behalf of his party in the speech on the Army Estimates. A Rockingham-Shelburne alliance would have involved, at best, fudging the American question, as the Rockingham-Grenville alliance had fudged it in 1770. But Shelburne was worse from Burke's point of view than Grenville. Shelburne's opposition to the recognition of American independence made him a supporter of George III on the main question of the day. So it was essential to fend off any Rockingham-Shelburne alliance if Burke's policy was to hold. The fending off of Shelburne was an important victory within the larger conflict: the war of wills with George.

That war was conducted largely, but not exclusively, through Rockingham. Burke had a capacity not only to win Rockingham over to his own opinion but to instil into Rockingham, over the vital question of America, his own deep commitment to his opinion. Isaac Barré's reference to Rockingham's having 'seriously and obstinately' adopted Burke's 'wanderings' is relevant here. Rockingham had been regarded as a rather vacillating politician. But there is nothing vacillating about him, when fully under the influence of Burke, over the American War. In the two indirect negotiations with George III, in 1780 and 1782, Rockingham shows a steely inflexibility over the question of independence for America, which is without parallel in the parliamentary history of the period. It is almost as if Burke had not only convinced Rockingham, over American policy, but had hypnotised him into a total incapacity to deviate from that policy by a hair's breadth, even under pressure from a king.

The main channel through which Burke's will carried on its war with George's was Rockingham. But Burke also challenged George directly, in the Commons, in leading the struggle for 'Economical Reform', directed against the king's influence over Parliament, through holders of sinecures. And the struggle for Economical Reform and against the king's influence was linked in Burke's mind with the American war. The idea was to bring down North's Administration and force the king to accept one led by Rockingham; also to accept recognition of American independence.

Burke and his friends had sometimes exaggerated the extent of the royal responsibility for the American crisis. The crisis had began, not in 'the closet' (the king's private apartments in which he exercised his personal influence over Ministers) but in the minds of members of the Commons, and the fatal early decisions had been extremely popular in that House. Grenville – whom George detested, for personal reasons which had nothing to do with America – had started it, in an effort not to please the king but to balance the nation's books. Charles Townshend had imposed his fatal duties in a quest for popularity in the Commons – as Burke himself had noted (see Chapter II above, pp. 124–5). As long as the crisis remained confined to matters of taxation – roughly, up to 1774 – the Americans themselves directed their protests against Parliament, not against George. They even, on occasion, appealed to him, over the heads of his Parliament. As the crisis developed, however, George came increasingly to feel that his personal dignity was at stake, through the defiance of his subjects. He strongly supported (and probably prompted) the Penal Acts – the passage of the Boston Port Act gave him 'infinite satisfaction.'[1] Before that, an unfinished memorandum, perhaps of 1773, shows the depth of his resentment against the party of Rockingham and Burke for their encouragement of the Americans: 'Perhaps no one period in our History can produce so strange a circumstance, as the Gentlemen who pretend to be Patriots, instead of acting agreeable to such sentiments, avowing the unatural doctrine of encouraging the American Colonies in their disputes with their Mother Country; this so plainly shews that Men not measures decide their opinions, that it is not necessary to deduce the total want of principle which this motley tribe by their conduct....' (unfinished).[2]

The actual coming of the war, and the Rockingham Whigs' continued support for the Americans, inevitably aggravated this resentment. Once war began, the king was determined that the only tolerable end to it would be the unconditional surrender of the revolting colonists. And after Saratoga his will becomes the main force that sustained the war, which was by this time no longer popular, though opposition to it was not popular either. The effort to tax the Americans, which had been the source of the popularity of the American measures, had clearly failed, and was explicitly abandoned by North after Saratoga. The war itself, especially after the entry of the French, then of the Spaniards, then the Dutch, was costing far more than could conceivably have been raised by taxing the Americans.

---

[1] *The Correspondence of King George III*, edited by Sir John Fortescue (1928) Vol III, p. 97. No. 1448: King to Lord North, 22 April 1774.
[2] *Corr. Geo III*, Vol. III, pp. 47–48, No. 1361; dated by the Editor '(?1773)'. 'Measures not men' was the device of Chatham and Shelburne; Burke detested both men and despised 'measures, not men' as cant.

After Saratoga it would have made sense for Britain to cut her losses in America, and concentrate on fighting her other enemies at sea. But the king was bent on beating the Americans. North's heart is not in the struggle; he begs repeatedly to be allowed to resign, but the king will not let him. [1] During 1777 North had been confident that the Americans would be looking for peace-terms 'before Winter', [2] and he was correspondingly unnerved by Saratoga, 'this most fatal event'. George was not unnerved. His editor, commenting on this period, praises 'the extraordinary courage and firmness of the King at the most critical moment.' [3] Writing to North on 11 June 1779, the king, remembering the history of the American crisis, registers the unwisdom of the attempt to tax the Americans, but expresses his determination to resist independence, and expounds what would later be called a 'domino' theory: 'The present Contest with America I cannot help seeing as the most serious in which any Country was engaged . . . whether the laying a Tax was deserving all the Evils that have arisen from it, I should suppose no man could alledge that without being thought more fit for Bedlam than a seat in the Senate; but step by step the demands of America have risen – independence is their object . . . ; that [this] country can never submit to; should America succeed in that, the West Indies must follow them; Ireland would soon follow the plan and be a separate State . . . then this Island would be reduced to itself, and soon would be a poor Island indeed.' [4]

Writing to North again, the king expresses hope for the future of the war, and his relish for the use of the Indians against the settlers, and lays down his conditions for admission to his administration: 'The different papers from America shew very clearly that had not Spain now thrown off the mask [Spain's entry into the war] that we should have soon found the Colonies sue for pardon to the Mother Country; I do not yet despair that with the activity Clinton is inclined to addopt *and the Indians in the Rear* [my italics – C.C.O'B] that the Provinces will even now submit. . . . before I will ever hear of any Man's readiness to come into Office, I will expect to see it signed under his hand that He is resolved to keep the Empire entire and

---

[1] On 14 November 1778, for example, North speaks of 'the misery he feels from continuing in office because it is his Majesty's pleasure that he should continue there.' *Corr. Geo. III*, Vol. IV. p. 219, No. 2450.

[2] *Corr. Geo III*, Vol. III, 450, No. 2009; 4 June 1777.

[3] *Corr. Geo. III*, Vol. IV, p. xxvii.

[4] *Corr. Geo. III*, Vol. IV, p. 35, No. 2649.

that no troops shall be consequently withdrawn from thence nor Independence ever allowed.'[1]

In that last, critically important sentence, the person George had in mind was Rockingham, the leader both of parliamentary opposition in general and specifically of opposition to the war in America. Before taking Rockingham into his Administration, the king insists on an undertaking never to grant independence to America. As against that, as we shall see, Rockingham, guided by Burke, opposes his own insistence, that before he himself agrees to enter Administration, the king must explicitly drop his veto over American independence. That was what the battle of wills was about.

After Saratoga the war, concentrated in the Southern states, appeared to go well for the British. British troops overran large parts of Georgia and South Carolina. This phase culminated in Britain's greatest victory of the American war: the capture of Charleston, with 3,000 American prisoners, in June 1780.

It would therefore, have been unprofitable, at this time, to concentrate opposition activity on America. In late 1779 an opportunity presented itself for challenging and perhaps reducing, the king's influence – without raising the unpopular American issue. Burke took this opportunity with both hands.

As we have seen, Burke had repeatedly urged on Rockingham the need for extra-parliamentary agitation, in support of parliamentary opposition in the extraordinary conditions brought about by the American war. Rockingham had agreed in principle, but failed to follow through. Toward the end of 1779, however, the discontent of landowners over high taxation – a discontent which first manifested itself in Rockingham's own county of Yorkshire – converted him to extra-parliamentary action. On 3 November 1779 Rockingham writes to Burke, in an unusually energetic letter: 'It matters not whether it has *as yet* been declared at the Market Cross in every Town in England, that the System of Government has *misled*, and that the corrupt *Influence of the Crown* has enabled the Ministers to carry into execution the Measures by which this Country has been ruin'd:-I now believe that the above is the general Predominant opinion of the Nation, and I think the Means of power, and the

---

[1] *Corr. Geo. III*, Vol. IV p. 369–10, No. 2674; 22 June 1779. '*And the Indians in the Rear*': the king had long urged the use of greater ferocity in crushing the Americans. In a letter written before Saratoga he had recommended 'the mode of war best calculated to end this combat as most distressing to the Americans', the 'mode' meaning the Indians (*Corr. Geo III*, Vol. III p. 485, No. 2072; 28 October, 1777).

means of corrupt influence in the Crown must soon submit to be *shorn*. NB I much prefer the shears to the Hatchets.'[1] N. C. Phillips, who has made a valuable study of Burke's relation to that movement,[2] comments: 'So the pupil gave his instructions to the tutor and soon the shears were being sharpened.'[3]

The plan was to mobilise the general discontent in the country through the organisation of petitions in such a way as to apply pressure on the 'county members' –, almost the only ones, in the eighteenth-century parliaments, who had to pay attention to their constituents. As a result of that pressure, Burke hoped to win majorities for the measure of 'Economical Reform', which he would introduce in Parliament in the following Feberuary. If the measure was carried, the resulting abolition of sinecures would reduce the influence of the Crown. The defeat of North's Administration and its replacement by a Rockingham one would come within reach. 'It is natural', Phillips writes, 'to suppose that after fourteen years in the wilderness the Rockinghams were aiming at office; but their immediate and ostensible purpose was the reduction of the influence of the Crown.'[4] The words 'office' and 'ostensible' are misleading. As was noted in my Introduction, Rockingham and Burke could have had office – certainly in 1780, and probably on other occasions in the previous fourteen years – if they had been prepared to drop what George called their 'tenets', and adopt those of the king. This they refused to do, because they wanted office in order to give effect to certain 'tenets' – notably recognition of American independence – which were obnoxious to the king. Reducing the influence of the Crown, far from being an 'ostensible purpose', was something basic to their hopes of attaining not just office but real power, through which they could give effect to the 'tenets' opposed by George.

As Phillips says: 'It was Burke, who, in the critical few months

[1] *Corr. IV*, p. 163. Rockingham's semi-jocose reference to the 'Hatchets' implies that he sees his 'shearing' of the influence of the Crown as a means of averting a possible revolution in England. For the revolutionary possibilities of this period, see Herbert Butterfield, *George III, Lord North and the People* (London, 1949) *passim*.

[2] N. C. Phillips, 'Edmund Burke and the County Movement, 1779–80' in Rosalind Mitchison (ed.), *Essays in Eighteenth Century History from the English Historical Review* (London, 1966) pp. 301–325.

[3] *Ibid.* p. 305.

[4] Phillips *op. cit.*, p. 305. Phillips adds that Burke and his friends had 'come to believe their own propaganda' about the influence of the Crown. It is hard to see how anyone can read George III's *Correspondence* and regard the influence of the Crown as 'propaganda', but a number of historians have succeeded in doing just that (see Introduction pp. xxxviii–xli, and Chapter IV, pp. 331-336).

between December and April, bore the heat and burden of the day for his party.' He both prepared the Plan for Economical Reform, a huge and complex task, and led the parliamentary struggle for it. He introduced it in the Commons on 11 February 1780. The opening words of the full title are significant: 'Plan for the Better Security of the Independence of Parliament and the Economical Reformation of the Civil and other Establishments.' His speech occupies seventy-two columns in the *Parliamentary History*, and it made a great impression on the minds, though not quite so great an impression on the votes, of the Members. 'Lord North, when Burke had finished, paid Mr. Burke very great compliments, which he said was one of the most able he had ever heard.'[1] Sir Nathaniel Wraxall records the general impression: 'Whatever opinion might be entertained respecting the necessity or the eligibility of those proposed regulations in the royal household, only one sentiment pervaded the House and the nation on the unexampled combinations of eloquence, labour, and persever-ance which had been displayed by their enlightened author. They covered with astonishment and admiration even those who from principle or from party appeared most strenuous in opposing the progress of the Bill itself through every stage. The very rejection which had attended many clauses of it, and the address with which others were finally evaded or eluded, had conduced to raise him in the national opinion.'[2]

We are concerned here with the 'county movement' and 'Economi-cal Reform' issues only in so far as they relate to the battle of wills with George III, and so to the American war. In his speech Burke avoided direct references to America, and even his indirect references to the war are extremely cautious; he was after all looking for votes, for Economical Reform, even from habitual supporters of the Ameri-can war. The only substantial direct link between his proposals and America is the proposal to abolish the post of Secretary of State for the Colonies, then held by the extremely unpopular Lord George Germain, on the grounds that the American Colonies were already lost. Yet even though he soft-pedals America in the speech, America remains central to the strategic objective he is aiming at. That objec-

---

[1] *Parl. Hist.* xxi, 72.
[2] Wraxall, *Historical Memoirs of my Own Time* (London, 1884) Vol. II, p. 27. Wraxall (1751–1831) had a colourful career that included three years' service in the East India Company, wide travel in Europe, and a confidential mission from Queen Caroline-Matilda of Denmark to her brother George III. He entered Parlia-ment in 1780 as a follower of North, but went over to Pitt.

tive is to move towards a Rockingham Administration, and peace with America, through an attack on the corrupting influence of the Crown. If Burke's proposals had carried, George III would have lost about sixty placemen. That loss would have rendered the North Administration far more vulnerable, and the monarch's will that much less formidable.

Burke lost his parliamentary engagement, but narrowly. North, a master of parliamentary tactics – which was why his master, George III, insisted on keeping him on – succeeded in defeating the Plan, piecemeal, by removing most of its sections in a series of divisions. But the margin of victory for the Administration was much narrower than had been usual in the period of the American war. The king, who followed the progress of 'Mr. Burke's *Extraordinary* Bill' [1] with close attention was dismayed by the narrowness of the margin, in one division: 'Lord North Cannot be surprised at my having read with some astonishment that the Majority was so small this Morning, in a question which if it tended to anything was to circumscribe the power of the Crown to shew it[s] Benevolence to persons in Narrow Circumstances; it shews what little dependence can be placed on the momentary whims that strike Popular Assemblies'. [2]

Burke would have been pleased if he could have seen that comment: it showed he was getting close. In his speech introducing the Plan, he had referred, in a parody of the courtly style, to royal resentment as a thing of the past: 'Gentlemen who are, with me, verging towards the decline of life, and are apt to form their ideas of kings from kings of former times, might dread the anger of a reigning prince . . . in putting forward such a Plan.' But the defeat of the Plan rebounded into a defeat for the king. On 6 April 1780 Dunning's Resolution, 'that the influence of the Crown has increased, is increasing and ought to be diminished', [3] was carried by 233 votes to 215. John Dunning (1721–83) was a follower of Shelburne's, but an admirer of Burke's. In introducing his Resolution he explicitly linked it to the Plan and paid tribute to Burke: 'He could not pass over in silence what must remain as a monument to be handed down to posterity of the uncommon zeal, unrivalled industry astonishing abilities and invincible perseverance of the hon. Gentleman.' In the parliamentary context, Dunning would certainly have discussed the

---

[1] *Corr. George III*, Vol. V, p. 35, No. 295: King to Lord North, 21 March 1780.
[2] *Corr. Geo. III*, Vol. V, p. 20, No. 2945: King to Lord North, 22 Feb. 1780.
[3] *Parl Hist.* xxi, 340–367.

wording of his motion with Burke, who was leading for the Rocking-hams at the time, and the wording may be Burke's in whole or in part. North reported the passage of the Dunning Resolutions (there were two others calling for the production of documents etc) to the king in a letter dated 'April 7; 2 O'clock a.m.: Sir – It has happen'd as I expected, & the House of Commons have come to three resolutions on the motion of Mr. Dunning by a considerable Majority

Ayes. 233

Noes. 215

If I had not for four years past apprized your Majesty that this event would happen & if I had not made it my constant prayer that I might be allow'd to quit your Majesty's Service, I should feel very unhappy now at what has happen'd & may further be expected. I humbly submit once more to your Majesty that it is absolutely necessary that I should be permitted to retire at the end of the Session, & some other arrangement take place. [1]

The king, as usual, refuses North permission to resign. He ends by saying that the Resolutions 'can by no means be looked on as personal to him [Lord North]; I wish I did not feel at whom they are *personally levelled.*' [2]

In the early summer of 1780, Burke and his friends could look to the future with brighter hopes than at any time since 1766. The defeat of the Economical Reform proposals had been a set-back, but there were reasons for expecting better results at a second attempt in the autumn. Government majorities had been much smaller than usual; the passage of Dunning's Resolution had been a symbolic triumph, and a tonic to supporters in the country. It looked as if a massive renewal of the petitioning 'county movement' might exert sufficient additional pressure as to carry Burke's Economical Reform Plan by the end of 1780. The first week of June, however, dashed these hopes. The Gordon Riots had started with the presentation of a petition to Parliament. In the aftermath of the riots, the idea of petitioning became comprehensively discredited throughout the country. The 'county movement' fizzled out. The Burke-Rockingham strategy against the power of George III had lost its extra-parliamentary motive force.

It seemed that, once more, nothing could help the opposition, except news of a major British defeat. The news that actually came,

---

[1] *Corr. Geo. III*, Vol. V, pp. 39–40, No. 2986.

[2] *Corr. Geo. III*, Vol. V, p. 40, No. 2987; 7.50 a.m. on 7 April. The added emphasis on the last two words is the king's.

in that grim June in the life of Edmund Burke, was of the fall of Charleston, the greatest British victory of the war. The Administration, naturally, used the news to proclaim that a victorious end to the war was in sight. The luckless opposition was now politically worse off than it had been at the beginning of the arduous, skilful and effective campaign which had culminated in Burke's Plan for Economical Reform. Burke's 'invincible perseverance', praised by Dunning, seemed harnessed, like his other great gifts, to the perpetual, fruitless labour of Sisyphus. Yet the king and Lord North were somewhat less confident than they appeared in the summer of 1780. North, in particular, had been deeply shaken by the effectiveness of the opposition, in the spring. To avert the resumption of such attacks, he now, with the king's approval, tried to bring Rockingham and others, including Burke, into his Administration. The attempt failed – as a result of the intransigence of both Rockingham and George – but it is worth close examination, for the light it sheds on the real positions of both parties, and also for the exposure, through modern scholarly investigation, of damaging misinterpretations of the basic positions of Rockingham and Burke.

Ian Christie, in his study 'The Marquis of Rockingham and Lord North's offer of a Coalition',[1] finds that what he calls 'the traditional interpretation of Rockingham's conduct' requires 'modification in the light of information now available from the Fitzwilliam papers [at Sheffield]. The Marquis can be given more credit for consistency and for good faith towards friends and associates than has hitherto been usually conceded.' This is interesting, as much in relation to Burke as to Rockingham. The 'traditional interpretation' here is based on a malicious contemporary account by Horace Walpole: an account which strongly influenced the Namierite portrayal of both Burke and Rockingham. Christie's revision of this 'traditional interpretation' is the more impressive, in that Christie, himself, when he wrote it, was a member of the Namier school, then near its zenith of historiographical authority. He acknowledges, in a footnote, his indebtedness to papers 'to which I have had access under the direction of Sir Lewis Namier, in the course of preparing material for the *History of Parliament*.'[2] In these circumstances, the publication by a Namierite of a paper which demolishes a key part of the Namierite case against Burke is an edifying example of scholarly integrity.

---

[1] *English Historical Review*, Vol. LXIX (1954) pp. 388–407.
[2] Christie, *ibid*. p. 388, n.i.

Walpole's account of the 'Coalition' affair deserves to be quoted in full, for its acceptance in 'the traditional interpretation' is basic to the reductionist Namierite version of Burke. I have italicised the direct references to Burke but, in reality, the whole of this narrative is about him. Walpole, who merely despised Rockingham but was obsessed by Burke, writes: 'Soon after the negotiation with General Conway had been attempted and failed, another (which displayed the King's duplicity and indifference to his Ministers) was begun with Lord Rockingham. In the other North was to have been the sacrifice, in this he was the negotiator and was to be preserved. He engaged Frederick Montague, his old friend, but once in opposition to him, to sound the Marquess on what terms he and his friends would unite with the Court. Lord North said he was not absolutely authorised by the King, but would answer for his Majesty's acquiescence, though his Majesty would wish that he, Lord North, should remain at the head of the Treasury. This seemed to preclude all success, as Lord Rockingham's point had ever been the Treasury; but *Lord North seemed to have learnt from Burke that that would no longer be an obstacle, and, in fact, it looked as if Lord Rockingham in this treaty was solely led by Burke, and consulted no others of his friends.*

'Accordingly, Lord Rockingham's answer was that he himself desired no place nor anything but a seat in the Cabinet. The terms he demanded (for show) were that something should be done to give some satisfaction on the Middlesex election, something likewise on the Contractors' Bill, that some part of Burke's reforming bill should be adopted, and some of the Crown's influence diminished by taking away the votes of excisemen, Ec. His Lordship demanded that the King should not declare that he would never consent to the independence of America, though his Lordship, on his side, wished that his Majesty should grant independence to America. As to places, Lord Rockingham desired that the Duke of Richmond and Fox should be Secretaries of State, T. Townshend Chancellor of the Exchequer, *and that Burke should have a good place*, and some others; and that Admiral Keppel should be at the head of the Admiralty.

'Nothing could be more futile and pitiful than these demands. They were most inadequate to the language held by the Opposition and to Lord Rockingham's late remonstrance. They were far below the demands not only of the associations but of the committees, which last Lord Rockingham had subscribed; they discovered no general views, aimed at reforming no capital grievances, and still less specified complaints against anybody. They were not more honourable to his party than beneficial to the nation, and were by their silence singularly disrespectful to Lord Camden, Lord Shelburne, and the Duke of Grafton, even the last of whom was as able a man as his Lordship, and yet the Duke was very far from a great man. *The demands were so timid, so insignificant, so unmanly, that they had the appearance of being managed only to facilitate Burke's throwing himself into all the measures of the Court, and did not even preserve the dignity of a man courted to be an apostate.* The Court treated the Marquess with the contempt he had so justly incurred. The answer was that something might be done on the Middlesex election and the Contractors' Bill, and on Burke's reform, but it would be unjust to deprive excisemen of their votes; that as the Duke of Richmond did not go to Court, nothing could be done for him till he did; that Charles Fox was too young yet for Secretary of State, though he might be so hereafter; Admiral Keppel might command the fleet, but he could not be at the head of the Admiralty; but a more specific rejection of Lord Rockingham and his terms was the immediately bestowing Greenwich Hospital on Sir Hugh Palliser.

'Lord Rockingham then first notified the transaction to the Duke of Grafton, who very properly disdained to make an answer.'[1]

Lord Edmund Fitzmaurice, biographer of Burke's enemy Shelburne, quotes Walpole's account, and improves on the denigration: '[Rockingham's] reply [to North's overture] showed a practical desertion of everything for which the Opposition had been struggling during the past year. Even the independence of America was abandoned' [sic].[2] If that had been true the king, as his own papers show (below p. 217), would have accepted Rockingham, and Burke, into his administration. But it wasn't true. Christie quotes, from Rockingham's papers, his own account of his position, to be conveyed to the king through his emissaries. Rockingham stipulated 'that peace was in every respect most desirable – that a fundamental obstacle to peace must exist if his Majesty had, or continued to have, a decisive objection against acknowledging the independency of America at any rate or risk: I therefore desired to premise that if any new administration were to be formed, that it should be known, whether his Majesty would put a *veto* on the acknowledgement of the independency of Am: and *on the other hand* I stated that what seemed

---

[1] *Last Journals of Horace Walpole*, Vol. II, pp. 324–5.
[2] *Life of William, Earl of Shelburne* (London, 1912) Vol. II, p. 62. Even Walpole had not claimed that 'the independence of America was abandoned' by Rockingham.

requisite was, that it should be understood both by H.M. and his ministers that the *ultimatum* upon that business must, and was, to depend on the circumstances of, and at, the time.' That wording sounds to me like the result of careful rehearsal with Burke.[1]

Christie comments: 'The question uppermost in Rockingham's mind was America, a fact which does not emerge from Walpole's narrative. To this matter the marquis addressed his first observations and the demand for the abandonment of the King's veto on American independence was vital.' North, in conveying Rockingham's reply to the king, seems to have drastically toned down Rockingham's message about America, since the king describes this as 'evasive', which it certainly was not. North had reasons for toning down the message, for he desperately wanted the negotiations to succeed, thus averting the threat of any more 'Dunning Resolutions', and he knew they could not succeed, if the king received the Rockingham message *en clair*. So he garbled it. Even garbled, it would not do for George. He commented on 3 July 1780 that 'the Dependency of America need not also be mentioned as it could not at the present hour be necessary to be taken into consideration' (meaning that the British seemed to be winning). He further comments that 'the evasive [*sic*] answer on America can by no means answer my expectations. . . . it is absolutely necessary, if any coalition is to be attained, that those who come into Office must give Assurance that they do not mean to be hampered by the Tenets they have held during their opposition [!] I fear I am not wrong in suspecting that those gentlemen wish to bring at least part of their Tenets with them.'[2]

The 'assurances' sought by Rockingham from the king, and by the king from Rockingham, were almost grotesquely incompatible, and both were unobtainable. The coalition idea died. On Rockingham's share in these strange 'negotiations', Christie concludes: 'On all points, Rockingham was consistent, he yielded nothing.'[3]

In George's letter there is one sentence of high significance for Burke's career. Discussing who might be admitted to the coalition (if coalition occurred), the king notes: 'Mess Townshend and Burke would be real acquisitions.' This is rather remarkable, since George regarded Burke's Economical Reform Bill as having been personally levelled against himself. Clearly he was more impressed by the desir-

---

[1] 'The Marquis etc.' p. 396 in E. H. R. Vol. LXIX (1954).
[2] *Corr. Geo. III*, Vol. V., p. 96, No. 3099.
[3] 'The Marquis etc.' in E. H. R. Vol. LXIX (1954) p. 404.

ability of acquiring Burke's talents – minus his 'tenets' – than he was swayed by any personal rancour.

That sentence, in George's own handwriting, ought to put paid to the theory that Burke's political activities were motivated just by personal ambition. He simply didn't need to thrash around for sixteen years in opposition in order to force himself into office. He could have had office for the asking, at any time. George appreciated, needed, and would have been happy to use, Burke's parliamentary skills; and would have richly rewarded him. All he had to do was to convey to North that he was prepared to drop his 'Tenets' and adopt the king's. The sentence also makes nonsense of Namier's claim that 'had Burke been in office during the American Revolution we might have had to antedate his counter-revolutionary Toryism by some twenty years'. [1]

North, having failed to widen the basis of his Administration by bringing in the Rockinghams, decided on a parliamentary dissolution, in hope that the ensuing elections, influenced by the favourable war news, would bring him additional parliamentary support. In the event, the parliamentary balance was unchanged but Burke lost his seat at Bristol. (See above Chapter I, end.)

So, the king's will prevailed, and North, who had seemed to waver about the American war, at least in private conversation, was now fully committed to it. In October, after his defeat at Bristol, Burke wrote to the Duke of Portland: 'I hear, that the Ministers who in their conversation had given up the American War, and seem'd to have come to that late ripe Wisdom, which belongs to men of no foresight, are now like men that never can be taught Wisdom even by time and suffering [and] are going to plunge into it deeper and deeper.' [2]

That same election saw the first sign of a rift between Burke and Fox who, unlike Burke, was re-elected for his Westminster seat. In his electoral campaign, he made a bid for what might be called 'the Gordon vote'. He publicly declared: 'I never have supported nor ever will support any measure prejudicial to the Protestant religion, or tending to establish Popery in this Kingdom'. Once Fox was safely re-elected, however, his conscience smote him. It is revealing of the relationship then existing between the two men that, in this distress

[1] See Chapter II epigraph; Namier, who made a special study of *The Correspondence of George III*, must have known the sentence in question. He chose to ignore it.
[2] *Corr. IV*, 314.

of conscience, Fox asks Burke to be his judge: 'If anyone were to think that I had given up in the smallest degree the great cause of Toleration for the sake of a point of my own I should be the most miserable man in the world . . . Pray judge me severely and say whether I have done wrong.'[1] No reply by Burke has been preserved. It would have been in character for Burke to have reassured a friend, in conversation, over a lapse which troubled him. But it would also be in character for Burke to forgive the lapse, but not forget it. He must have remembered this one ten years later when Fox first gave public expression to his enthusiasm for the French Revolution, whose anti-Catholic character was linked in Burke's mind with the Gordon Riots (see Chapter VI below).

On 23 January 1781 Burke was returned to the new Parliament as member for Rockingham's borough of Malton. He at once resumed his attack on the king's influence by preparing a Bill for the Regulation of the Civil List Establishments. He introduced it on 15 February, almost exactly a year after introducing his Plan for Economical Reform, and he stressed the identity of purpose of the two measures. He began by having the Dunning Resolutions read out. 'It remained,' he said, 'for the present parliament to accomplish and fulfil what the others had but begun that the resolutions . . . might not stand upon the Journals, public monuments to their [parliament's] disgrace.' Having set out the financial savings which would result from the Bill, he added: 'What he valued more than all this saving was the destruction of an undue influence over the minds of sixty members of parliament in both Houses.'[2] But the Gordon Riots had taken their toll; the new measure, not being supported by a great flow of petitions as the old one had been, was easily defeated. Fox commented: 'The design [of the Bill] was very wise and proper, but, like every other design of that description it had failed by means of that very influence which it was calculated to prevent'.[3]

In May a motion to restore peace with America was defeated 72–106, which shows that it was supported only by the Rockinghams. In June Burke introduced a petition on behalf of the American prisoners: 'Mr. Burke ascribed the ill usage of those poor men to the rancour that had pervaded our whole system of politics with regard to America, and contended that it would be as pernicious to our

[1] Loren Reid, *Fox* (London, 1969) p. 117.
[2] *Parl. Hist.* xxi, 1223–1229 records the debate on the Bill.
[3] *Parl. Hist.* xxi, 1338.

cause as it was inhuman in its nature'.[1] The Motion was lost. Burke was right about the 'rancour': the American War was taking on a nastiness that neither side would like to recall. And the prime source of the rancour was the king's determination that his rebellious subjects must be made to suffer, to the greatest possible extent, as through 'the Indians in the rear.'

For the king 1781 was a good year, almost to its close. Yet he had doubts about whether 'the Nation is equally determined with myself' to pursue the American War. On 3 November, three weeks before the news of Yorktown reached London, he quotes a British general's opinion that 'Lord Cornwallis will certainly leave the Chesapeak and return to Charles Town, after having beat La Fayette.' However, he is clearly bracing himself to receive bad news, for he ends his letter to North with the words 'duplicity [which he ascribes to his enemies] can never withstand any disasters, but those who act on other motives [himself] ought ever to support any misfortune from the consciousness of the rectitude of intentions.'[2]

In the last week of November, a few days before Parliament resumed after the summer recess, the news reached London of the surrender of Cornwallis and his army, to Washington, at Yorktown.

After Yorktown

Summary accounts of the American Revolution generally end with the defeat of Cornwallis at Yorktown. The impression is given that British recognition of American independence followed the defeat automatically. This was not so. On 25 November, two days after the news arrived, the king opened Parliament. In his speech he treated the event as a serious, but local, set-back to British arms: 'The events of war have been very unfortunate to my army in Virginia, having ended in the loss of my forces in that province.' He added: 'I retain a perfect conviction of the justice of my cause.' Burke, rightly, interpreted the speech as conveying a determination to continue the war: 'Victories gave us hopes, defeats made us desperate, and both instigated us to go on.'[3] The stupid obstinacy of an intent to persist

---

[1] *Parl. Hist.* xxii, 607.
[2] *Corr. Geo. III*, Vol. V, p. 297: No. 3439.
[3] *Parl. Hist.* xxii, 719.

with the war after Yorktown, suggests to Burke one of his Aesopian zoological metaphors. Formally, and by constitutional convention, Burke's target is the king's chief Minister, Lord North. But the use of the word 'prerogative', at the opening of the metaphor, shows that the real object of Burke's ridicule is George himself. 'Oh, says a silly one, full of his prerogative of dominion over a few beasts of the field, there is excellent wool on the back of a wolf, and therefore he must be sheared. What! shear a wolf? Yes. But will be comply? have you considered the trouble? How will you get this wool? Oh, I have considered nothing, but my right: a wolf is an animal that has wool; all animals that have wool are to be shorn, and therefore I will shear the wolf.'[1]

The Commons address, drafted by ministers, left the question of future American policy open, but George decided to treat the carrying of the Address, by 218 votes to 129, as constituting, in the circumstances, a mandate to continue with the war. He wrote to North: 'Lord North's account that the Address was carried this morning by a considerable majority is very pleasing to Me as it shows the House retains that spirit for which this Nation has always been renowned, and which alone can preserve it in its difficulties; that some principal Members have wavered in their sentiments as to the measures to be pursued does not surprise me; many men choose rather to despond on difficulties than see how to get out of them.

'I have already directed Lord G. Germain to put on paper the mode that seems most feasible for conducting the War, that every Member of the Cabinet may have his propositions to weigh by themselves, when I shall expect to hear their sentiments separately, that we may adopt a Plan and abide by it; fluctuating Counsels, and taking up measures with[out] connecting them with the whole of this complicated War must make us weak in every part; with the assistance of Parliament I do not doubt if measures are well concerted a good end may yet be made to this War, but if we despond certain ruin ensues.'[2]

On 12 December a Motion for putting an end to the American War, on which Burke spoke, was defeated by 220 votes to 179. The rise in the opposition vote showed that the country gentlemen, who had supported the Administration up to now, were now beginning to desert it. In the debate, North, for the first time since Yorktown,

---

[1] *Parl. Hist.* xxii, 722.
[2] *Corr. Geo. III*, Vol. V, pp. 303–04; 25 November 1781.

gave an indication of future policy: 'that it would not be wise or right to go on with the American war as we had done, that was to say, to send armies to traverse from the south to the north of the provinces in their interior parts, which had been done in a late case, and which had failed of producing the intended and the deserved effect.'[1] As usual in his parliamentary statements, North was reflecting, in a diffuse and diluted way, the view of his master. George wrote that 'though Internal Continental Opperations [*sic*] in North America are not advisable, the prosecution of the War can alone preserve us from a most ignominious Peace.'[2]

That was how matters stood on the eve of the Christmas recess. When Parliament resumed, after members had had the opportunity of learning the views of their constituents and neighbours, the pressure on the Administration drastically increased. On 27 February 1782 the House debated a Resolution moved by General Henry Conway 'against the further Prosecution of Offensive War with America'.[3] After a pro-Administration amendment had been defeated (215–234) the 'original question' – that is Conway's resolution – was carried without a division. North reported the passage of Conway's Resolution to the king 'with the utmost concern'.[4] North could see a vote of no confidence beginning to loom up. George himself remained firm. He told North that 'the basis of Public Measures [was] founded on keeping what is in our present possession in America.' The remainder of the king's policy-outline shows him still cherishing some chimerical notions about Americans; and 'attempting by a negotiation with any separate Provinces or even Districts to defend them from France[!], even upon any Plan of their own, provided they remain separate States.' But the idea of 'keeping what is in our present possession' was, at least, not chimerical (see below p. 230). The possessions included New York.[5] The House submitted to George an address reflecting its resolution. He replied on 4 March: 'You may be assured that, in pursuance of your advice, I shall take such measures as shall appear to me to be most conducive to the restoration of harmony between Great Britain and the revolted colonies – and that my efforts shall be directed against our European enemies, until such a peace can be obtained as shall consist with the

---

[1] Christie, *End of North's Ministry 1780–82* (Macmillan, 1958) p. 272.
[2] *Corr. Geo. III*, Vol. V, pp. , 313–314, No. 3469.
[3] *Parl. Hist.* xxii, 1064–65.
[4] *Corr. Geo. III*, Vol. V, p. 374, No. 3535; 28 February 1782.
[5] *Corr. Geo. III*, Vol. V, p. 375, No. 3537; 28 February 1782.

interest and permanent welfare of my kingdom.' Observing that the king's reply 'was not quite so explicit as he could have wished', Conway moved a second Resolution 'declaring the Advisers of the further prosecution of Offensive War in America to be Enemies to the King and Country.'[1] Because of the dramatic and memorable wording, the passage of this Resolution is sometimes seen as the breaking point in the parliamentary struggle over whether to persist with the American War after Yorktown. But again this was not so. Nobody now really favoured 'the prosecution of Offensive War in America'. North was certainly not so advising; and if challenged he could have pointed to his speech of 12 December. The king having renounced 'Internal Offensive Operations', would live comfortably with both the Conway resolutions in themselves. All he wanted was 'the prosecution of the War', without adjective. The Conway resolutions would not prevent him from doing this. Conway had explained the object of his first resolution as being 'to order his ministers to renounce the war on the continent of America, for the impracticable object of reducing the colonies by force.'[2] That formula was not incompatible with the king's position. North had reported the passage of Conway's second Resolution to the king, without comment.[3]

The Conway resolutions were purely declaratory and, although they weakened North's position, they did not render it untenable. What rendered it untenable in North's opinion, which was decisive on the point, was a motion that was actually not carried. This was the motion proposed by Lord John Cavendish on 8 March declaring 'that the calamities and expense of the times have proceeded from want of foresight in the ministers'.[4] Unlike the previous resolutions, this was a motion of no confidence. Both the identity of the mover, and the wording of the motion, are significant. Cavendish was a leading Foxite and nominal leader of the Rockingham party in the Commons; the real leader was Burke, as had been abundantly proved in the two previous sessions. All the previous resolutions had been moved by members not belonging to the Rockingham party. By now Burke was by far the most experienced as well as the most astute and energetic parliamentarian of the opposition, and there can be no

[1] *Parl. Hist.*, xxii, 1086.
[2] Christie, op. cit., p. 320.
[3] *Corr. Geo. III*, Vol. V, p. 376, No. 3539; 4 March, 1782.
[4] *Parl. Hist.* xxii, 1114–1150; *Corr. Geo. III*, Vol. V, p. 381; No. 3546, King to North.

doubt that he was in charge of parliamentary strategy and tactics for the Rockinghams, during these momentous weeks. It is characteristic of him to encourage others, holding similar views to his own, on particular questions, to take the parliamentary lead for certain purposes: thus Fox, on American questions from 1774 on; Savile on the Catholic Relief Bill; Dunning on the Motion of 6 April, 1780, and Conway on the Resolutions of February and March 1782 against 'Offensive War'.

When it came to the crucial motion, however – the one aimed at bringing down the North Administration – the Rockinghams flew their own flag: the name of their own nominal leader in the Commons. They were clearly establishing their claim to the succession. The wording of the Motion also bolstered that claim. Their accusation of 'lack of foresight' carried weight because the foresight of Burke and his friends, shown in their unheeded warnings about the disastrous course of American policy, was only too well known to the House.

The Motion was so worded as to catch as many votes as possible, since it recorded an opinion almost universally held. It did not refer directly, as previous Motions had done, to the corrupting influence of the Crown, but Burke was on hand to make that point in a speech, in a context in which it would go home. It was his practice, in critical debates, to 'mark' a particular speaker on the other side, and rise to speak after him. In this case, the speaker was Charles Jenkinson (1729–1808), who moved the Administration amendment – 'that the other orders of the day be now read' – designed to defeat the Cavendish Motion. As the king's confidential personal agent in the Commons, Jenkinson was the principal agent of the system which Burke aimed to destroy. (Jenkinson's own peerages were still to come. George later rewarded him, for his assiduous services and absolute obedience, by creating him Baron Hawkesbury and Earl of Liverpool.) Burke had alluded to the system in one of the February debates: 'What had the American War produced? What but peerages and calamities? What but insults and titles?'[1] Answering him now Burke said: 'There was no man in that House, unless he had a place, a contract, or some such motive to speak, that attempted to defend [North's Administration].' Burke liked to make that particular charge come to life, by using it in answering a member who was a notorious example – and in this case agent and beneficiary – of the corrupt

---

[1] *Parl. Hist.* xxii, 1039.

system in question. The Jenkinson amendment carried, but only by a margin of ten votes: 226–216.[1] So narrow a margin was almost equivalent to a defeat. North wrote to George: 'After such division Lord North is obliged to repeat his opinion that it is totally impossible for the present Ministry to conduct His Majesty's business any longer.'[2]

The King asked for time, and got the Lord Chancellor, Edward Thurlow, to sound Rockingham about 'forming an Administration, upon a broad bottom and public views'. Thurlow reported to George III Rockingham's conditions for entering an administration. The report began 'On Thursday, March 14, the Marquis came to the Lord Chancellor and said: "The King must not give a Veto to the Independence of America".'[3]

From the style alone, I am confident that these words – the words that were to end George's hopes of carrying on a 'defensive' war against America – are Burke's. Rockingham, left to himself, before he fell under Burke's 'ascendancy', would either have set no precondition at all, which is probable, or he would have wrapped up his precondition in such courtly phraseology that the king would be able to wriggle out of it. The formula actually used makes its meaning absolutely plain, at the cost, in terms of the conventions of the time, of pushing discourtesy to the verge of treason. George may well never before have read, or heard, a sentence beginning with the words, 'The King must not.' The substance of that curt message must have been as startlingly obnoxious as the style. Parliament, even after Yorktown, was not calling for the independence of America; the topic had not been mentioned in any of the resolutions carried or even proposed; it had not even been a theme of debate. Nor was the king at all prepared for any such demand, coming from Rockingham. He had laid down that precondition before, in the abortive negotiations of 1780, (see above pp. 214–18), but North had apparently so toned down Rockingham's message that George thought Rockingham 'evasive' about America. But the message received through

---

[1] *Parl. Hist.* xxii, 1114–1150.
[2] *Corr. Geo. III*, Vol. V, p. 381, No. 3545.
[3] *Corr. Geo. III*, Vol. V, p. 392, No. 3564; King to Thurlow, 18 March 1782. Other conditions followed: enactment of Burke's full programme of Economical Reform and full power for the Marquess to form an Administration excluding all persons who had been considered as *obnoxious Ministers*, or those who were deemed as belonging to a set of secret systems.

Thurlow is so far from being evasive that it is designed to preclude evasion on the part of the king.

George did his best to resist. He wrote to Thurlow: 'The King feels the indignity offered to His Person by such propositions and cannot direct any further conversation to be held with the Marquis. . . . H.M. cannot offer up his Principles, his Honour and the interests of his good subjects to the disposal of any set of Men.'[1] On the same day, however, North, who knew that the days of his Administration were numbered, warned the king, in language of unprecedented firmness and gravity, that, as a constitutional monarch, he has no choice; 'Your Majesty is well apprized that, in this country, the Prince on the Throne cannot, with prudence, oppose the deliberate resolution of the House of Commons . . . There are no persons capable or willing to form a New Administration, except Lord Rockingham and Lord Shelburne with their parties.'[2]

For a few days, while the North Administration lingered on, George still hopes that Rockingham's demands will somehow go away. Just after North's warning, the king must have told Charles Jenkinson to find out whether Rockingham is really serious. Jenkinson reports Rockingham as 'still insisting on the several conditions he had mentioned before.'[3] George's mind, as he later avowed to North, was 'truly tore [sic] to pieces.' Rather than send for Rockingham, the king seriously contemplated abdication. His draft instrument of abdication, found among his papers, read: 'His Majesty during the twenty one years He has sate on the Throne of Great Britain, has had no object so much at heart as the Maintenance of the British Constitution, of which the difficulties He has at times met with from His scrupulous attachment to the Rights of Parliament are sufficient proofs.

'His Majesty is convinced that the sudden change of Sentiments of one Branch of the Legislature has totally incapacitated Him from either conducting the War with effect, or from obtaining any Peace but on conditions which would prove destructive to the Commerce as well as essential Rights of the British Nation.

'His Majesty therefore with much sorrow finds He can be of no further Utility to His Native Country which drives Him to the painful step of quitting it for ever.

[1] *Corr. Geo. III*, Vol. V, p. 393, No. 3564.
[2] *Corr. Geo. III*, Vol. V, p. 395, No. 3566.
[3] *Corr. Geo. III*, Vol. V, p. 401, No. 3571.

'In consequence of which Intention His Majesty resigns the Crown of Great Britain and the Dominions appertaining thereto to His Dearly Beloved Son and lawful Successor, George Prince of Wales, whose endeavours for the Prosperity of the British Empire He hopes may prove more Successful.'[1]

On consideration, George swallowed his pride, accepted North's advice, and decided to call on Rockingham and Shelburne. Shelburne was a consolation, from the king's point of view; he had been opposed to American independence, and was still not committed to it, and he habitually addressed the king in the soothing language of a courtier. But it was Rockingham, as the leader of far the largest section of the opposition, who had to be First Lord of the Treasury, that is to say Chief Minister. And Rockingham, before accepting office, again spelt out the conditions on which alone he will accept it and he demands that the king will confirm his acceptance of those conditions. They are set out in a letter to Shelburne, which he sends on to the king: 'Lord Rockingham . . . desires to explain clearly to His Lordship his opinion that such a Cabinet should be formed as is suitable to the execution of the very important Measures which Lord Rockingham had the honour of submitting to His Majesty, through the Lord Chancellor.

'Upon Lord R— —m's being assured that His Majesty consented to these Measures, and that He shall have this consent confirmed to him by His Majesty himself, Lord R— —m is willing to state to Lord Shelburne his Ideas of a Cabinet likely to concurr in the Principles of those Measures, and therefore fit for the Execution of them.'[2]

Burke's drafting there, surely: not the spontaneous letter of a marquess to an earl, to be shown to a king, but a document drafted by the man of business of a marquess, to make dead sure that his principal does not get cheated. Burke's radical distrust of Shelburne shows in the almost insulting, but vitally necessary, provision 'that he shall have this consent confirmed to him by His Majesty himself' (The king had been trying to deal with Rockingham, exclusively through Shelburne.) George now accepted Rockingham, on Rockingham's terms, though he still hoped to evade these. On 27 March 1782 North's Administration resigned, and on the same day the second Rockingham Administration was sworn in, with Rockingham as First

[1] *Corr. Geo. III*, Vol. V, p. 425, No. 3601. This document is undated but ascribed to March 1782.

[2] *Corr. Geo. III*, Vol. V, pp. 407–08, No. 3575; 24 March, 1782.

Lord of the Treasury, and Shelburne and Fox as Secretaries of State. [1]

In the next few weeks, George honoured the condition which had brought him to the verge of abdication, and ceased to impose a barrier on the negotiation and conclusion of peace with America on the only basis on which peace was available: recognition of the independence of the United States of America. As we shall see, however, the king tried for a while, through Shelburne, to evade the conclusion of peace.

Considering what was at stake over the king's acceptance of Rockingham's precondition about American independence, historians have shown a singular lack of interest in that historical crux. In some cases, this may be accounted for by the general Namierite tendency to disparage anything connected with Burke and Rockingham, and also to assume that material interests are always more important, to eighteenth century politicians, than any 'issues of principle'. For Ian Christie, for example, the parliamentary struggle at this time was 'openly, not a struggle over war or peace, but a struggle for power, between the opposition, covetous for office and the ministers intent on keeping their places'. [2] The statement may sound very realistic, but it is demonstrably untrue, as appears from the battle of wills between Rockingham and George. Rockingham was so little 'covetous for office', and so committed to the issue of 'war or peace', that he laid down a precondition for the acceptance of office which, when laid down on a previous occasion, had denied him office (see above pp. 214–218). And it was also the issue of 'war or peace' which was of supreme importance for the king. In his book Christie manages to ignore this also. Having listed Rockingham's conditions of acceptance, he makes no comment about the vital stipulation on American independence, but ascribes George's resistance wholly to a difference of opinion about ministerial appointments: 'Such a defiance of the royal prerogative of choosing ministers was wholly revolting to

---

[1] *Corr. Geo. III*, Vol. V, p. 419, No. 3590.

[2] *The End of North's Ministry 1780–82* (1958), p. 344. This book is the principal Namierite study of the theme and period here under review. Something regrettable seems to have happened to Ian Christie between 1954 and 1958. In his 1954 study, 'The Marquis of Rockingham and Lord North's offer of a Coalition', Christie did more than anyone to refute the demeaning generalisations, which he himself serves up again in *The End of North's Ministry* as if he had never read, let alone written, his 1954 paper. Clearly in the intervening years, he had been brainwashed by Namier. The description of Rockingham, in the 'Coalition' study, is not compatible with the generalisations in the book. See above pp. 214–218.

George III'[1]. But the subject of the king's draft instrument of abdication is not 'the royal prerogative of choosing ministers'; it is policy over America (see above p. 226). This crude application of Namierite assumptions is demeaning, not only to Burke and Rockingham, but also to the king. George III was a serious person, with a conscience, even though the results of his seriousness and his conscience were unfortunate, as far as America was concerned.

The Namier school apart, even general historians, free from levelling assumptions and having no particular axes to grind, have generally missed the significance of the Rockingham precondition and its acceptance by the king. American historians, understandably, tend to close the substantive story in October 1781 at Yorktown, the decisive military victory, after which, inevitably, in an American perspective, there were no more major military engagements, and Britain recognised the independence of America. British historians tend to close the substantive story, in February–March, 1782 with the passage of the two Conway 'anti-war' resolutions and the subsequent loss of a parliamentary majority for North's Administration. After that, inevitably, the incoming Administration negotiated peace. In reality there was no 'inevitability' about it, in either case. Militarily, Yorktown, like Saratoga, had been a major defeat for the British, but the war had continued after Saratoga, and could have continued after Yorktown; Burke feared that it would. Politically, Yorktown didn't make British recognition of American independence inevitable either. After Yorktown, as after Saratoga, George was determined to refuse to recognise American independence. Nor was the king on a collision course with Parliament over American independence. Parliament had not advised the king to recognise American independence, nor had it even advised the conclusion of an early peace with America. The only advice it had offered George was to avoid 'the Prosecution of Offensive War on America'. This advice he was spontaneously inclined to accept.

The North Administration was wrecked by the direct impact of Yorktown on British opinion, but that impact hardly registered on the reserve of authority commanded by the king. He had still valuable cards to play – if Rockingham, guided by Burke, had allowed him time to play them. Critical historians are likely to ask for documentary evidence for that 'guided by Burke'. There is no such documentary evidence. Burke and Rockingham were both at Westminster

[1] Christie, *End of North's Ministry*, pp. 350–351.

during the post-Yorktown parliamentary crisis, and did not need to exchange letters. Historians agree that Burke, in the last years of the American War, possessed 'decisive influence' over Rockingham (above p. 203). It is reasonable to assume that Burke would have exerted all the influence he possessed, in the most critical conjuncture of the entire political careers of his party leader and himself, and that Rockingham would have responded. Hence, in shorthand, 'guided by Burke'.

Consider the likely course of events, if Rockingham had agreed to form an Administration, without that precondition on American independence. George would have approved a King's Speech which promised an immediate end to 'offensive war', and declared an intention to negotiate a peace. This would have satisfied Parliament. But if Rockingham had proposed to include a reference to the recognition of American independence, the king, unbound by any previous agreement, would certainly have refused. Rockingham would have been in no position to force George's hand. He had no parliamentary mandate to advise the king to recognise the independence of America, and if he had tried to get one, he would have failed. The Americans were at least as unpopular in Britain, in Parliament as in the country, after Yorktown as they had been before. A king who, while renouncing 'Offensive War', resisted recognising the independence of America, would have been seen as a Patriot King, in line with the mood of his people.

If Rockingham, in office, had tried conclusions with George, on that issue in 1782, he would have fallen. He would have been replaced by an Administration, probably headed by Shelburne, pledged to the pursuit of 'peace' but not committed to the recognition of American independence. (It was Shelburne who, as Secretary of State, conducted the peace negotiations with the Americans. But that was after George's will to continue the war had been broken by Rockingham, not Shelburne.) The Americans, after Yorktown as after Saratoga, and *a fortiori*, would have refused negotiations unless their right to independence was recognised, and the war would have dragged on. It could have dragged on for years, for the fortune of war changed, in Britain's favour, shortly after George's acceptance of Rockingham's precondition. On 12 April 1782, at the Battle of the Saints, in the West Indies, Rodney defeated and captured the French admiral, the Comte de Grasse. It had been French command of the sea, off the Chesapeake, which had made possible the victory of the land forces of Washington and Rochambeau at Yorktown.

Rodney's victory gave a correspondingly great boost to British morale. It also, by altering the balance of force at sea, favoured the kind of war that George had wanted to continue. He duly tried to use the victory to retract recognition of America's right to independence. He wrote to Shelburne, who was just about to become head of the Administration as a result of Rockingham's death: 'He must see that the great success of Lord Rodney's Engagement has again so far roused the Nation, that the Peace which would have been acquiesced in three months ago would now be matter of complaint.'[1]

Shelburne, not surprisingly, concurred. As L. G. Mitchell puts it, with reference to the opposition by Chatham, Shelburne's former leader, to the recognition of American independence: 'The naval victory at the Saintes had merely strengthened Shelburne's Chathamite prejudices against unconditional independence.'[2] That is a misleading formulation; Mitchell does not quote the relevant letter (quoted above) addressed to Shelburne, which establishes *the king's* position, after the Battle of the Saints. (One of the more mysterious phenomena in late-eighteenth-century English historiography is the strong tendency, among certain historians, at every critical conjuncture, to fail to perceive the massive, political presence of an intervening king.)

It is not at all likely that Shelburne (second earl of that name, later first Marquess of Lansdowne, 1737–1805), amid the intense political pressures of the summer of 1782, was musing on the supposed political philosophy of his own deceased leader. George III was alive and kicking, and still wanting the war to continue. Shelburne, a courtier to his fingertips, did his best to comply with his royal master's wish. The key to Shelburne's conduct is contained in the following dialogue (on 23 March 1783) recorded by Boswell: *Boswell* 'How then, Sir, did [Shelburne] get into favour with the King?' *Johnson*: 'Because, Sir, I suppose he promised the King to do whatever the King pleases.'[3]

Conformably to the division at the heart of the Rockingham-Shelburne Administration, the British negotiations with the Americans in Paris were also divided into two sections led by the two

[1] *Corr. Geo. III*, Vol. VI, p. 70, No. 3825.
[2] *Charles James Fox and the Disintegration of the Whig Party, 1782–1794* (Oxford, 1971) p. 19.
[3] *Boswell's Life of Johnson*, ed. G. D. Hill, rev. L. F. Powell (Oxford, 1934) Vol. IV, p. 174.

Secretaries of State: Fox, whose agent was Thomas Grenville, and Shelburne, whose agent was Richard Oswald. On 23 May 1782 the Cabinet had decided to offer unconditional independence to the Americans. Fox instructed Grenville to inform the Americans of the Cabinet decision. Shelburne did not inform Oswald, who thus could not confirm Grenville's account. The Americans knew that Oswald's silence might be more significant than Grenville's words, since Oswald's master, Shelburne, was close to George, while Grenville's master was anathema to him. The negotiations stalled, and the state of war continued. Shelburne's prevarication over the war was high among the reasons for the resignation of Fox and Burke on 4 July, after Rockingham's death. The basic reason was Shelburne's subservience to the king, but Shelburne's conduct in relation to the American war was the prime example of that subservience.

After the resignation of Fox and Burke, followed by the defection of most of the parliamentary support on which the Administration had been based, Shelburne was in an exceedingly weak parliamentary position which, paradoxically, put him in a much stronger position vis-à-vis the king. George desperately needed Shelburne because he was desperately afraid that the Rockinghams, headed by the odious Fox, might come back. Shelburne, hoping to strengthen his parliamentary position, was able, without loss of favour, to persuade the king to accept the independence of America, and the Provisional Articles of Peace were signed. On 5 December 1782 the king signified his capitulation, in his address to Parliament: 'Finding it indispensable to an entire and cordial reconciliation with the Colonies [*sic*], I did not hesitate,' he said, not quite accurately, 'to go the full length of the powers vested in me, and offered to declare them Free and Independent States . . .'[1]

At every stage in George's long rearguard action after Yorktown, it was pressure from the Rockinghams that induced him to concede, and in 1783, it was dread of a Rockingham come-back – now under Fox – that induced his capitulation. By a final irony, however, it was actually the document that embodied the king's capitulation which brought about the defeat of Shelburne, and the return of Fox. When the Articles of Peace were made known to Parliament, in March 1783, an amendment to them was proposed by Lord John Cavendish, and carried (224 to 208) by a coalition of supporters of Fox and supporters of North. This division had nothing to do with America.

---

[1] *Parl. Hist.*, xxiii, 206.

The Fox-North Coalition in which Burke played a crucial part (see below Chapter IV, pp. 312–14) which arose out of it went on to conclude peace with America in terms which did not materially differ from the Provisional Articles. George, having capitulated over America, to avoid becoming a prisoner of his enemies, Fox and his friends, now found himself a prisoner of those enemies, in alliance with his former trusted servant. It was an abominable predicament from which the king would soon contrive a dramatic escape. But by then America was no longer an issue.

After this review of the king's rearguard action, it will be useful to look at the crucial moment in the political termination of the American War: Rockingham's laying down of terms for acceptance of office, in March 1782. On the eve of forming his Administration, Rockingham had far more leverage over George, than he would ever have once it was formed. North had advised the king, in effect, that he could not reject Rockingham – after Parliament's peace resolutions and the near-miss of the No Confidence resolution – without precipitating a constitutional crisis. George, after toying with, and discarding, the idea of abdication, flinched from the constitutional crisis and accepted the terms which Rockingham, not Parliament, had laid down for him. The issue was more important even than the securing of an early end to the American War. The nature of royal authority was at stake. By accepting the preconditions, George was accepting the view of his legitimate authority, which Burke, twelve years before, had laid down on the Rockinghams' behalf. The king was beginning to assume the character of a constitutional monarch as the Rockinghams, and not George himself, understood the Constitution. And that was also the sense in which later generations were to understand the constitution. The king's acceptance of the Rockingham preconditions is a more significant milestone in British constitutional history than it is generally perceived to have been. It took a first-class political mind to identify the precise ground on which the royal authority could be successfully challenged and the precise time at which alone the thing could be done. There was only one such mind in the Rockingham party, and it was not Lord Rockingham's.

As for George, the loser in that long battle of wills, he remained bitter for many months over the loss of so substantial a part of the vast dominions he had inherited at his coronation in 1760, but he eventually consoled himself with the following Royal Reflection: 'I cannot conclude without mentioning how sensibly I feel the dismemberment of America from this Empire, and that I should be miserable

indeed if I did not feel that no blame on that account can be laid at
my door, and did I not know that knavery seems to be so much the
striking feature of its Inhabitants that it may not in the end be an
evil that they become Aliens to this Kingdom.'[1]

A FELLOW-IRISHMAN
1782–83

In the second Rockingham Administration, formed in March 1782,
Burke became Paymaster-General. It was a minor post, but probably
the one he wanted and had asked for. It was lucrative and he needed
the money. What mattered more to him, he got a minor Treasury
post for his beloved son Richard. Burke never seems to have craved
major office – he didn't need to. As long as Rockingham lived and
was First Lord of the Treasury, his policies were shaped by his confidential adviser. Whatever power Rockingham possessed was in
Burke's hands. This should have meant that once Rockingham took
office Burke was the effective head. In practice, this was not the case,
for Rockingham himself was not really in control of the Administration. The time when Rockingham, guided by Burke, had really
wielded power, and to tremendous effect, was during the four days
before the formation of the Rockingham Administration. In office,
Rockingham could proceed with the policy already laid down – the
policy of the preconditions – but that was all. The king, having been
forced to comply with Rockingham's demands during the parliamentary crisis, naturally wanted no further advice from him, and shut
him off from access. George communicated with the Rockingham
Administration, not through its head, as with North, but through a
Secretary of State, Shelburne. It was Shelburne, in consequence, who
was in control of patronage. Patronage was not absolutely everything
in the eighteenth-century Parliaments – as some Namierites sometimes seem to imply – but it was a great deal. For many parliamentarians, it was Shelburne, not Rockingham, who was the effective
head of the Rockingham Administration.

Burke deeply distrusted Shelburne, and with good reason. On the
eve of the formation of the new Administration, Shelburne was sig-

---

[1] *Corr. Geo. III*, Vol. VI, p. 154, No. 3978: King to Lord Shelburne (draft), 10
November 1782.

nalling to George his intention of siding with him against Rockingham, his leader-to-be. A letter beginning, 'I was with Lord
Rockingham till very late last night', ends by expressing the hope
'that I shall have been able to keep things within the bounds prescribed by Your Majesty'.[1] Shelburne was widely distrusted, and
was more disliked than any other contemporary politician, partly
because of his oily manners. His biographer and kinsman, Fitzmaurice, lists among Shelburne's 'liabilities' an 'overstrained affectation of extreme courtesy and a habit of issuing unnecessary
compliments in conversation'.[2] Clearly a man one would go round
corners to avoid. Burke's feelings towards Shelburne, however, are
far stronger than the normal antipathy experienced by contemporaries: the loathing verges on the obsessive (see below p. 239). And
as always, when Burke's feelings are stronger than one might expect,
and there is a hint of obsession in the air, there is an Irish connection.

They were both Irish: common Irishness is always a bond of some
kind, but not always a bond of affection. Both were jeered at by
some English people, for their Irishness, and the same stereotype
was applied to both: Shelburne was labelled 'the Jesuit of Berkeley
Square'. Yet the 'Jesuit' taunt – which came near the bone for Burke
– was far wide of the mark for Shelburne. William Petty (1612–87),
the founder of the Shelburne family fortunes, acquired his enormous
wealth and vast estates in Co. Kerry through services to Oliver Cromwell. In his *Memoirs* Shelburne refers to his own family as the only
acceptable feature of Ireland: 'Good-breeding within my own family,
which made part of the feudal system, but out of it nothing but those
uncultivated undisciplined manners which make all Irish society so
justly odious all over England.'[3]

How Burke would have snorted, could he have read the words
'good-breeding within my own family which made part of the feudal
system', coming from Shelburne! Feudal Cromwellians! Burke would
not have been likely to use Richard O'Connell's phrase, 'dastardly
spawn of damned Cromwell', but there is a definite whiff of that
sentiment in Burke's feelings about Shelburne. The Irish Catholic
gentry were intensely proud of their Norman blood – both Burke
and Nagle are Hiberno-Norman names – and regarded the great
Cromwellian landlords as upstarts who had usurped the lands of

[1] *Corr. Geo. III*, Vol. V, p. 412, No. 3581; Shelburne to George III, 26 March
1782.
[2] Fitzmaurice, *Shelburne*, Vol. I, p. 390.
[3] Fitzmaurice, *Shelburne*, Vol. I, p. 8.

their betters. But there is more than atavistic resentment to it. In the here-and-now of the 1780s Burke was aware of Shelburne as an anti-Papist. Shelburne wore his anti-Popery discreetly, as 'good-breeding' required, in the Enlightened social climate of the late eighteenth century, but both Papists and anti-Papists were well aware of his feelings. It was widely alleged, at the time of the Gordon riots, that Shelburne had instigated them, and Burke believed him fully capable of such an act (see below p. 239). Whether Shelburne instigated the riots or not, he was certainly popular with the rioters. His biographer puts his position at the time of the Gordon Riots in the most favourable possible light. Fitzmaurice writes that he 'was accused not only of having consented, but of having been an actual party to some of the excesses of the mob; and the fact of his being one of the few Peers who, on the evening of the 2nd. of June, had reached the House of Lords without molestation, gave a colourable pretext for slanders, to which judges on the Bench did not scruple by their language to give an importance which they otherwise would have lacked. The natural explanation of the favour with which Shelburne was regarded by the Protestant mob lay in his being known, like Grafton, to hold, notwithstanding his advocacy of religious toleration, views respecting the Papal powers similar to those which had influenced the statesmen of the Revolution; but were now beginning to lose their force, with the altered policy of the Roman Curia, since the Pontificate of Ganganelli.'[1] When Burke and Rockingham were demanding that the military be called out for the protection of those under attack by the rioters, Shelburne, in the Lords, opposed this measure, ostensibly on constitutional grounds.

Burke's feelings about Shelburne and his feelings about the Irish Volunteers and Irish legislative independence are linked by suspicion and detestation of dissimulated anti-Popery. The volunteers' movement for legislative independence had faltered in 1781, as we have seen, but it regained momentum early in 1782, once the political impact of the American victory at Yorktown began to be felt. But before we can examine the enigmatic matter of Burke's relation to this movement, in 1782–3, we must first consider his rapidly chang-

---

[1] Fitzmaurice, *Shelburne*, Vol. II, 58. Lorenzo Ganganelli reigned as Pope Clement XIV from 1769–1774, and is best known for his dissolution of the Jesuit Order in 1773. However, it was his predecessor Clement XIII, Pope from 1758–69, who was responsible for the policy change which most affected the Catholics of Britain and Ireland. On the death of the Old Pretender ('James III') in 1766, Clement XIII rejected the Stuarts and recognised George III (see Chapter I, p. 53).

ing fortunes in British politics in this period. The constant factor, the one which accounts for the principal changes, is his detestation of Shelburne and determination to destroy him politically. That detestation had, as already noted, deep, emotional, Irish roots. But there were also solid, rational, political grounds for suspecting and detesting Shelburne. Shelburne was a courtier-politician to his finger-tips, as his correspondence with George III amply demonstrates. [1] If the royal influence, which Burke had done so much to curtail, was about to be restored, Shelburne was the chosen and willing agent of that restoration. Just as he concealed religious bigotry behind a façade of Enlightenment, so he also concealed Tory sensibility behind a façade of Whig principles. In whichever light Burke contemplated Shelburne, he saw a whited sepulchre.

From its beginning, the second Rockingham Administration was poisoned for Burke by Shelburne's presence in it. This appeared in Burke's Commons speech of 20 March on assuming office, surely one of the strangest statements ever offered to a Parliament by a member of an incoming Administration.

Mr. Burke said, that that was not a moment of levity or exultation: he regarded it with a calmness of content, a placid satisfaction; he looked forward with fear and trembling; but the present was a moment of great awfulness and every gentleman who expected either to form a part of the new administration or intended to support it, ought to question themselves, examine their own hearts and see, whether they had been acting upon principles, which were strictly right, and upon which they could continue to act in power, as firmly as they had continued to act upon them, while out of power. If, upon such an examination, any gentleman found he could not, that man, be he who he might, ought not to accept of power. The present, he farther said, was that peculiar period of men's lives, when their ambitious views, that had lain secretly in a corner of their hearts, almost undiscovered to themselves, were unlocked when their prejudices operated most forcibly, when all their desires, their self-opinions, their vanity, their avarice, and their lust of power, and all the worst passions of the human mind. . . . There was a certain fatality attending human nature, which very often defeated the best purposes; for the greatest virtues were generally accompanied with very great defects; independence and public spirit were attended with indolence and supineness. . . . [2]

The trouble of Burke's mind, so evident in the above speech, stems

[1] *Corr. Geo. III*, Vols. V and VI, *passim.*
[2] *Parl. Hist.* xxii, 1224.

from the extreme ambivalence of his feelings towards the Rocking-ham—Shelburne coalition, then in process of formation. His conflict-ing feelings about his relation to the English ruling class found symbolic expression, from time to time, through the creation of con-trasting pairs of angel-figures and devil-figures, represented by emi-nent contemporaries. In the early 1780s the reigning angel-figure was, as it had been since 1765, Rockingham. From 1780 on the devil-figure was Shelburne. So the coalition now taking shape, a coalition of which Burke himself was part, was an angel-devil coalition. Burke's evident distress is understandable. The part of the speech that is aimed at Shelburne – 'all the worst passions of the human mind' and so on – is not surprising. But the concluding refer-ence to what are obviously Rockingham's 'worst defects . . . indol-ence and supineness' is startling, even shocking. It is as if a cult, which had lasted seventeen years, is coming to an end. The Angel had been contaminated, by supping with the Devil.

In the daylight world, out of which Burke wanders for a few minutes in that parliamentary soliloquy, he knew that Shelburne's partnership was dictated by parliamentary arithmetic. The Rocking-ham Administration, with a small shaky majority, needed the ten votes Shelburne could deliver. As a politician Burke could understand that. But spiritually the thought of being in political partnership with Shelburne was a contamination which Burke could scarcely bear.

At the beginning of July Rockingham unexpectedly died. Burke had lost a friend and leader, whom he still loved and respected although he had become somewhat disenchanted with him in the last months. But he had also lost the medium through which he had exercised commanding influence, only three months before. Rocking-ham had been the Archimedean lever with which Burke had moved the king, and broken his will to pursue the American War. Burke had indeed very strong influence over Charles James Fox, who was to become the leader of the Whigs in the Commons in succession to Rockingham, but it was not the same as the continuous, close-knit controlling influence that he had attained over Rockingham in the last seven years of Rockingham's life. Burke's party-political career had now passed its peak. He soon began to move into the role of political prophet, over India, France and Ireland, which occupied most of his latter years.

Soon, but not immediately; in the eighteen months immediately following Rockingham's death, Burke is extremely busy politically in a brisk and brilliantly conducted feud with Shelburne, whom the king now made head of the Administration. Burke immediately resigned, as did Fox. John Morley wrote that Burke resigned out of loyalty to Fox, but he would have resigned anyway, even if Fox had not done so, on learning of Shelburne's appointment: it was psychologically impossible for Burke to serve under Shelburne. [1] His resignation entailed heavy financial sacrifice. It also – which distressed him far more – nipped in the bud his son Richard's political career. All of which must have fanned the rage against Shelburne.

That rage leaps out in Burke's resignation speech of 9 July 1782, in which he makes explicit the angel-devil contrast which had been implicit in his speech of 20 March:

> On the late change of ministry, the people, he said, looked up to the Marquis of Rockingham as the only person who must be at the head of affairs, as the clearness of his head, and the purity of his heart, made him universally beloved . . . But as fate had so ordained it, as to take that great and virtuous statesman from us, the first step his Majesty's ministers should have done was to seek out some person like him in sentiment and integrity; but unfortunately for the country it had turned out just the reverse; they had pitched on a man, of all others the most unlike to him. . . . He was a man that he could by no means confide in, and he called heaven and earth to witness, so help him God, that he verily believed the present ministry would be fifty times worse than that of the noble lord, who lately had been reprobated and removed [Lord North]. He would ask the gentleman [Conway] whether if he had lived in the time of the immortal Cicero, he would have taken Cataline upon trust for his colleague in the consulship, after he had heard his guilt so clearly demonstrated by that great orator? Would he be co-partner with Borgia in his schemes after he had read of his accursed principles? If Lord Shelburne was not a Cataline or a Borgia in morals, it must not be ascribed to anything but his understanding. [2]

In other words, Shelburne was too stupid to be a first-class villain.

The Cataline and Borgia passage seems excessive to us, but may not have seemed so to many of Burke's auditors. The whiff of brimstone, which Burke detected as emanating from Shelburne's person, was also perceptible to other contemporary nostrils. Walpole also compared Shelburne to both Cataline and Borgia. Burke's reference

[1] Burke at first favoured fighting Shelburne *within* the Ministry but then agreed to resignation. See L. H. Cannon *The Fox–North Coalition: Crisis of the Constitution, 1782–4* (Cambridge, 1969) pp. 21–4.

[2] *Parl. Hist.* xxiii, 180–183.

to 'guilt so clearly demonstrated' is presumably to the judicial observations attributing to Shelburne complicity in the Gordon Riots (see
above p. 236).

Burke and Fox, now on the opposition benches, were in partnership, bent on the destruction of a detested former colleague (who sat
of course in the other House, luckily for him). Their opportunity
came in March 1783, when Burke and Fox joined forces with Lord
North to drive Shelburne from office. He soon afterwards left political life, for ever.

The Administration which took over from Shelburne's was nominally headed by the Duke of Portland, but is known as the Fox-
North Coalition. Burke served in it, again as Paymaster.
Contemporaries were shocked, or affected to be shocked, by the
opportunism in this sudden reconciliation of old adversaries. In later
generations also the coalition has had a bad press. Burke's Victorian
admirers were distressed by their hero's having stooped to accepting
office from the hands of this shady combination. John Morley wrote
that the coalition 'was not only a political blunder, but a shock
to [Whig] party morality, which brought speedy retribution'.[1] A
transaction condemned on grounds of morality, even by writers such
as Morley, fits neatly into the picture painted by Burke's twentieth-
century detractors: of Burke as venal and unscrupulously ambitious.
(His resignation from Shelburne's Administration fits less con-
veniently into that picture.) He always maintained that his acceptance
of office in the Fox-North Coalition was consistent with his principles
and past record. I believe this can be shown to be so. He believed
that in 1783 the man who represented a danger to the country and
the Constitution was Shelburne, not North. In his resignation speech,
Burke had described a Shelburne Administration as fifty times worse
than North's. Nobody had fought harder against North, in the days
when North was pursuing policies laid down for him by the king,
primarily the prosecution of the American War. But in 1783 the
vehicle of the corrupting Royal influence was no longer North but
Shelburne who, by grace and favour of the king, had usurped and
corrupted the Rockingham Administration. What was important
now was to drive Shelburne from office. If North was prepared to
assist in that, so much the better. The memory of battles fought and
won should not be allowed to distract from the task of winning
the battle that needed to be won. The king drew up yet another

---

[1] Article on 'Edmund Burke' in *Encyclopaedia Britannica*, Eleventh Edition.

'abdication', on learning of the Fox-North coalition, thus unconsciously ratifying the continuity of Fox-North in 1783 with Rockingham in 1782.

The continuity of principle in Burke's opposition to Shelburne is quite genuine. But the hostility to Shelburne does not, of course, derive solely from continuity of principle. Well before he was aware of Shelburne as a vehicle of royal corruption he had been aware of Shelburne as a 'bad man'. Like George III,[1] he believed that 'bad men' should be driven from office, even though he and his sovereign did not until much later, agree on who the bad men were. To 'Measures, not men,' the pompous maxim of Shelburne, and of his master, Chatham, Burke opposed a maxim of his own: 'The power of bad men is no indifferent thing.'

In this matter there is a continuity of feeling, as well as of principle. Burke had long hated Shelburne, even – or especially – when they were colleagues under Rockingham. He had never hated North; even in the years of strong political opposition, the two men were personally on friendly terms, and sometimes terms of banter. Burke regarded North as a good but weak man, under the domination of a more powerful mind and will than his own. The symmetry between George's relationship with North and Burke's with Rockingham is remarkable. I suspect – though I know of no evidence, either way – that the idea of the Fox-North Coalition may have germinated in the 'joking Relation' between North and Burke during the opposition to Shelburne. The North-Shelburne comparison in Burke's resignation speech may suggest that the idea was present in his mind even then. Long afterwards a contemporary, Lord John Townshend (1757–1833), recalled Burke's attitude as decisive in the run-up to the Fox-North Coalition: 'If Burke had been adverse we must have Dropped all idea of the thing, as he had the greatest sway, I might almost say command, over Lord Rockingham's friends, with the exception of the Duke of Devonshire.'[2] The Fox-North Coalition had three heads; not just two.

Burke was closer to North than Fox was. Burke was also passionately motivated towards destroying Shelburne politically. The Fox–

---

[1] 'I . . . look on all who will not heartily assist me as bad men as well as ungrateful Subjects.' King to North, *Corr. Geo. III*, Vol. VI, p. 151, No. 3973; 4 November 1782.

[2] *Corr.* V, 75, n. 55. The editors of this volume advise that this statement 'must be treated with great caution'. I suggest that Townshend may actually be understating Burke's role in the formation of the Fox-North Coalition.

North Coalition was the efficient instrument of that destruction. This may have been a coincidence, but I doubt it. A letter from Burke to his old friend Richard Shackleton, immediately after the formation of the Coalition, reflects his sombre but real satisfaction at the political destruction of Shelburne: 'We have demolished the Earl of Shelburne; but in his fall he has pulled down a large piece of the Building. He had indeed undermined it before. This wicked man, and no less weak and stupid, than false and hypocritical, had contrived to break to pieces the body of men, whose integrity, wisdom, and union, were alone capable of giving consistency to public measures, and recovering this Kingdom from the miserable State into which it is fallen. To destroy him was a necessary preliminary to everything that could be devised beneficial for the public.'[1] How the idea that Burke not merely joined in the infamous Fox-North coalition, but actually may have invented it, would have horrified Burke's Victorian admirers! But it was for the Victorian admirers, not for Burke, that the Fox-North coalition was infamous. For him the coalition was a providential instrument for ridding the body politic of infamy, in the person of Shelburne.

The Fox-North Coalition fell in December 1783. The successor William Pitt (see Chapter IV below, p. 331), unlike North, was the effective head of his Administration, not under the control of the king. Rockingham had prepared the way for the role of Prime Minister in the modern sense, though the term was not yet in use. Shelburne had become head of the Administration by compliance as a court favourite. So William Pitt the Younger (1759–1806) was the first Prime Minister as we know the position today.[2] But he owed more to Rockingham and Burke for the king's acceptance of this than he probably realised. In forcing the acceptance of their 'preconditions' in 1782 they had 'broken in' George III as a (more or less) constitutional monarch. He later got a bit frisky again under Shelburne's permissive handling, but was again temporarily reduced to submission – after a second threat of abdication – by the Fox-North Coalition. In terms of Burkean values, the termination of Lord Shelburne's political career and the continuance of the reduction of George III to constitutional submission, were the two great achievements of the Fox-North Coalition, and justified its coming into being.

[1] *Corr.* V, 71–2: letter of 3 March 1783.
[2] 'Prime Minister' came into use in the middle of the last century. It was officially recognised only in 1905.

IRELAND
1782–1783

'Will no one stop this madman Grattan?'
—EDMUND BURKE

The agitation of the Irish Volunteers for legislative independence acquired a new momentum in early 1782, as a result of Cornwallis's surrender at Yorktown. A Catholic Relief Bill – modelled on the 1778 British Catholic Relief Act, which Burke had guided through Parliament – was then going through the Irish Parliament. Resolutions welcoming this development were drawn up by Henry Grattan, and carried at a great Convention of Volunteers at Dungannon in February. The Resolutions read:

Resolved, that we hold the right of private judgement in matters of Religion to be equally sacred in others as in ourselves.

Resolved, therefore, that as men and as Irishmen, as Christians and as Protestants, we rejoice in the relaxation of the Penal Laws against our Roman Catholic fellow-subjects, and that we conceive the measure to be fraught with the happiest consequences to the union and prosperity of the inhabitants of Ireland.[1]

The liberalism of the Dungannon Resolutions was not of a nature to win Burke over to the Volunteer movement. It probably reminded him of Shelburne's liberalism. The very wording of the second resolution is a reminder of the exclusively Protestant direction of a Volunteer movement, which was aiming at independence for an exclusively Protestant Parliament. Burke's inhibitions about his Catholic associations, and his tongue-tied incapacity to communicate the nature of his reservations about the Volunteers and their objective, had permitted Rockingham and Fox to commit themselves to the cause of legislative independence for Ireland. It was the second Rockingham Administration which carried legislative independence through the British Parliament in an Address declaring 'no body of men competent to bind this nation [Ireland] except the King, Lords and Commons of Ireland.'[2] Thus the British Parliament at length ratified the proposition which Grattan had put to the Irish Parliament on 19 April 1780. Grattan himself believed that Burke had been among

---

[1] Rev. Patrick Rogers, *Irish Volunteers etc.*, p. 70.
[2] *Parl. Hist.* xxiii, 35–48, 17 May 1782.

those who had tried to stop him at that time. In his *Memoirs* of his father, the younger Grattan wrote that those who had hitherto appeared as friends of Ireland, the Whigs, 'were deterred, some by influence, other by threats, and many by offers and blandishments held out to them, of every kind and description – title, place and pension. At length, recourse was had to Edmund Burke: even He had been applied to; and he had written to Ireland, condemning these extremes, as they were called, and advising them to stop; Mr. Grattan quoted:

Will no one speak to this madman?
Will no one stop this madman Grattan?

'Such were the feelings and expressions of Mr. Burke, who, though an Irishman, spoke in the phraseology of what he called his *"better and his adopted country"*. Such was the language applied to those who struggled for the liberties of their country.'[1]

Grattan, like so many others, and in so many instances, attributes a perceived anomaly in Burke's conduct to a base motive. Grattan genuinely thought of himself as struggling for 'the liberties of his Country,' which he was brought up to think of as a Protestant country, and he could not understand Burke's resistance to liberties which did not include liberty for Catholics.[2] The Address, recognising the legislative independence of Ireland, was moved by Fox, who declared that 'he would rather see Ireland totally separated from England, than kept in obedience only by force.' Burke spoke in this debate, but without reference to the specific content of the Address. His language is unusually vague, diffuse and emollient: 'Mr. Burke said, that it was not on such a day as that, when there was not a difference of opinion that he would rise to fight the battle of Ireland; her cause was nearest his heart; and nothing gave him so much satisfaction, when he was first honoured with a seat in that House, so that it might be in his power, some way or other, to be of service to the country that gave him birth. . . . He was a friend to his country, but gentlemen need not be jealous of that, for in being the

---

[1] *Memoirs of the Life and Times of the Rt. Hon. Henry Grattan* by his son, Henry Grattan (London, 1839–46) Vol. II, p. 36.

[2] John A. Woods, editor of the relevant volume of Burke's *Correspondence*, includes the 'madman' sentences in the canon of the *Correspondence* (IV, 231) but comments that 'the phraseology of the extract hardly sounds as if it came from his pen'. It sounds like something he might have said, rather than written (as Grattan said it was). But, however it may have been communicated, I have no doubt it represented Burke's real feelings, when legislative independence for Ireland was first mooted.

friend of Ireland, he deemed himself of course the friend of England; their interests were inseparable. He spoke also of his friendship to the natives of India, whom he did not know, and who could never know him, and by proving himself their friend, he was convinced that he must prove himself also the friend of England.'[1]

Burke's acquiescence in the passage of a measure to whose original introduction he had been so vehemently opposed may appear tame. I think, however, that there is no basic contradiction. What had alarmed Burke about Grattan's proposal in 1780 was its tendency. It seemed to be heading in the direction of the breaking of the connection with Britain: real independence for the Irish Protestant nation. But what was actually passing through the British Parliament was very much less than that. 'Legislative independence of Ireland' – if it went no further than that – was largely a sham, as Burke well knew. The British Parliament could at any time withdraw the legislative independence it was now granting, as it was to withdraw it eighteen years later. In the meantime, the British Government maintained its control over the Irish executive and thus exercised a powerful influence, to say the least, over legislative processes also.

So Burke could accept 'legislative independence', though without enthusiasm. There was no need for him to be dismayed by Grattan's glittering language, based on the Rockingham Administration's concessions to Ireland. As a working parliamentarian, Burke understood the dependent relationship which that hollow rhetoric concealed. He was determined, however, that his friends should proceed no further along the road of concessions to the Irish Protestant version of the Irish nation. Burke's influence over Rockingham policy, for the future, is clearly discernible in a letter written by Fox (before legislative independence had been conceded) as Secretary of State, to Richard Fitzpatrick, the new Chief Secretary in Dublin: 'My opinion is clear for giving them all they ask, but for giving it them so as to secure us from further demands, and at the same time to have some clear understanding with respect to what we are to expect from Ireland in return for the protection and assistance which she receives from those fleets which cost us such enormous sums, and her nothing.'[2] Fox's enthusiasm for 'Irish independence' had been brought under control.

In Ireland, Henry Flood – Grattan's great rival – disparaged the

[1] *Parl. Hist.* xxiii, 33: 17 May 1782.
[2] O'Connell, *Irish Politics*, p. 343: letter of 28 April 1782. 'Ireland' here is of course Protestant Ireland.

concessions won by Grattan and demanded that the British Parliament 'renounce for ever any right to legislate for Ireland'.[1] With this demand, Flood gained in popularity over Grattan in the second half of 1782. From Burke's point of view Flood was now the dangerous man, Grattan, the safe one. The concession demanded by Flood would be a long step from the sham independence of 'Grattan's Parliament' in the direction of real independence. From Burke's point of view sham independence was the most the exclusively Protestant Parliament of Ireland could safely be trusted with. He therefore did his best to help Grattan, against Flood, by maximising the importance of the concessions already granted, in order to stave off the demand for further concessions. In a Commons debate in December 'on the affairs of Ireland', Burke 'spoke of the repeal of the Dependency of Ireland Act of 1719, on which the Declaratory Act of 1766, on America, was modelled, and declared that however mistaken motives to the contrary have been since excited and fomented in Ireland [by Flood], the repeal of that Act was meant by those who proposed it, to be considered as a total dereliction on the part of this country of all claim to the right of legislative, or judicial power over Ireland, in every case whatsoever.'[2] This was helpful to Grattan, and may have been requested by him, as authoritative confirmation of his claims concerning the nature of the legislative independence accorded to Ireland by the British Parliament under the Rockingham Administration. When Burke was back in office, in the Fox-North Coalition, we find him advising the new Chief Secretary that the success of the new Lord Lieutenant, Lord Northington, 'will depend not only on Grattan's formal assistance but upon his cordial and earnest support'.[3] The 'madman' of 1780 had become a prop and stay by 1783.

In 1783 a new tendency appeared among the Irish Volunteers, which outdid Flood in 'extremism', just as he previously had outdone Grattan. The new tendency was to put pressure on Grattan's Parliament to widen the franchise, so as to include the middle-classes.[4] To give this demand more credibility, and widen the basis for its support, spokesmen for the tendency (the most eminent was the brilliant and eccentric Frederick Augustus Hervey, Earl of Bristol and Bishop of Derry) asked that the franchise reform include Catholics,

[1] O'Connell, *op. cit*, 333.
[2] *Parl. Hist.* xxiii, 325; 19 December 1782
[3] *Corr.* V, 92.
[4] Rogers, *op. cit.*, p. 117.

provided they possessed the property qualifications of the proposed new franchise law. The Hervey concessions were not as radical as they may sound. It has been reckoned that if Grattan's Parliament had been reformed in the way Hervey intended only some 300 to 500 Catholics would have been enfranchised.[1] On that basis, the Irish Parliament might have remained exclusively Protestant and would certainly have remained overwhelmingly Protestant. The people whom the Hervey proposals really aimed at emancipating were middle-class Protestants. These were generally more enthusiastic for 'the Protestant nation' than the landlords were, and their representation in the Irish Parliament would have increased the pressure for real independence for that nation. Burke's reservations about franchise reform were by no means modified by the emergency of the Hervey tendency. Quite the contrary. The Fox-North Administration, of which Burke was a key member – almost as important as its eponymous leaders – which held office throughout most of 1783, strongly opposed the radical tendency in the Irish Volunteers. It would have been impossible for the Coalition to take the strong and clear position it did take without Burke's agreement. I believe that the Coalition took the line it did, not merely with his agreement but actually under his influence (see below p. 249).

Some of the Irish reformers were also proclaiming the merits of incorporating Catholics (as private soldiers only) into the Irish Volunteers. A pamphlet called *Thoughts on the Conduct and Continuation of the Irish Volunteers* (1783) stated: 'The Protestant would not have ventured to clasp the Catholic [except] to an armed bosom. Volunteering has done what the law could not do. The Catholic who wishes to bear arms proposes himself to a Protestant corps. His character is tried by his neighbours; he is admitted to an honour and a privilege: he receives a reward for his good conduct; a reward by which the giver is benefited, and which the receiver holds no longer than he deserved it.' Patrick Rogers, who quotes the passage in his book on the Volunteers and Catholic Emancipation, comments (page 79): 'The writer considered himself as a liberal Protestant . . . and, judged by the standards of the age, no doubt he was. Yet . . . he spoke of his Catholic fellow-Volunteers much as a Spartan citizen would have spoken of certain well-behaved Helots who were likely to prove useful to him. To shoulder a musket as a private Volunteer was still an honour and a privilege, and one which would be accorded

[1] Rogers, *op. cit.*, p. 120.

the fortunate Catholic only as long as he pleased his benefactor.'

Burke has left no statement on the radical, and putatively ecumenical, phase of the Volunteer movement. We know that later, in the 1790s, he was deeply suspicious about Protestant radical attempts to exploit Catholic discontent: attempts which he believed, quite rightly, to be potentially disastrous for the Catholics concerned. From the stand taken in November 1783 by the Administration, of which Burke was part, against the radical Volunteers, I infer that his sentiments on this subject were the same as those which he expressed in a letter in the next decade (see below Chapter VI, pp. 570–71).

A great National Convention of the Irish Volunteers was announced, to open in Dublin on 10 November. The 1779 National Convention had demanded Free Trade, and won it, with little delay. The 1780 Convention had demanded legislative Independence and that too had been conceded, at least in form, in 1782. The radicals now hoped that the 1783 Convention would demand parliamentary reform, giving the vote to the Protestant middle-class, plus a few Catholics. If the Convention approved that demand, it was expected that the Irish Parliament – which, unlike the British Parliament, was open to serious pressure from the Irish Volunteers – would concede the reform demanded. Real independence, for Protestant Ireland, would be likely to follow.

The Fox-North Administration was alarmed by these developments. As Secretary of State, Fox was the relevant Minister. He wrote two letters on the eve of the Convention, one to General Burgoyne, of Saratoga fame and now commanding the British forces in Ireland, and one to Lord Northington, the Lord Lieutenant.

To Burgoyne: 'If either the parliamentary reform in any shape, however modified, or any other point claimed by the Bishop of Derry and his Volunteers be conceded, Ireland is irrevocably lost for ever, and this would be my opinion if I were as fond of the measures themselves as their most enthusiastic admirers. The question is not whether this or that measure shall take place, but whether the Constitution of Ireland, which Irish patriots are so proud of having established, shall exist or whether the government shall be purely military, as ever it was under the Praetorian bands.'[1]

To Northington: 'Unless they [the Volunteers] dissolve in a reasonable time, Government, and even the name of it, must be at an end. . . . If they are treated as they ought to be – if you show firmness,

---

[1] Quoted in Rogers, *op. cit.*, p. 120.

and that firmness is seconded by the aristocracy and Parliament – I look to their dissolution as a certain and not very distant event; if otherwise, I reckon their [the Volunteers] Government, or rather Anarchy, as firmly established as such a thing is capable of being . . . Volunteers, and soon, possibly, Volunteers without property, will be the only Government in Ireland, unless they are faced this year in a manful manner. . . . All other points appear to me to be trifling in comparison of this great one of the Volunteers.' [1]

Coming from Fox, these robustly anti-Volunteer sentiments are remarkable. In 1779 he had been enthusiastic for the Volunteers, making Burke uneasy; Fox had also strongly supported the demand for legislative independence (see above p. 200). From then on, however, he adopts Burke's line of 'no further concessions', and by 1783 he is urging the dissolution of the Volunteers. It looks as if Burke must have been working on him, and finally brought him round. However that may be, it seems certain, that he would have consulted Burke, the acknowledged expert on Irish affairs, about Irish despatches with such major implications as these had for the Fox-North coalition policy. So even if the despatches were not instigated by Burke they were almost certainly sanctioned by him.

Burke and Fox need not have been so worried. The National Convention was a fiasco. Unlike 'Free Trade' and 'Legislative Independence', Parliamentary reform including a Catholic franchise was deeply divisive. Apart from the eccentric Bishop of Derry, none of the Irish leaders was in favour of this one. Grattan, who theoretically favoured Catholic enfranchisement, was in practice opposed, at this time, to any further measure of parliamentary reform. Flood and the nominal commander of the Volunteers, Charlemont, were in favour of parliamentary reform, but opposed to any franchise for Catholics. And that also seems to have been the position of most of the delegates.

After the Convention had heard conflicting reports about what the Catholics wanted – there were of course no Catholic delegates present – the Convention did not vote about a franchise for Catholics, but simply sent to the Irish Parliament 'Resolutions . . . which proposed the grant of votes to Protestant freeholders and leaseholders exclusively.' [2] As the Convention's proceedings showed the Irish Volunteers to be deeply divided over this question, the Irish Parlia-

[1] O'Connell, *op. cit.*, p. 337.
[2] Rogers, *op. cit.*, p. 126.

ment felt it could safely defy its Resolutions. They were defeated by 158 votes to 49.

After the Convention, the Lord-Lieutenant sent a report to Fox. This report has given great satisfaction to generations of Irish nationalist historians as a classic example of British 'divide and rule' Machiavellian policy. Northington wrote about his own preparations for the Convention: 'The next step was to try by means of our friends in this assembly to perplex its proceedings and to create confusion in their deliberations, to bring this meeting into contempt and to create a necessity of it dissolving itself.'[1]

Fox may possibly have been impressed, as the Lord Lieutenant clearly intended him to be, by the zeal and cunning with which he had acted in the spirit of his instructions. Burke, to whom Fox would have shown Northington's report, would have hardly been impressed. Dublin Castle's capacity to manipulate the Irish Volunteers had not been a conspicuous feature of the previous five years. If the Volunteers were split, the split was much more likely to be spontaneous than artificially generated. Burke, unlike Fox, knew the sort of people who attended that Convention – he could envisage the Munster Delegates with particular clarity – and the failure of the Volunteer delegates to support even a very limited measure of Catholic enfranchisement would not have surprised him in the least. In retrospect, after the debacle of the 1783 Convention, Burke would have been ironically grateful to the Bishop of Derry, for introducing that Catholic apple of discord, thus inadvertently scuppering a potentially dangerous movement for franchise reform.

On the failure of the 1783 Volunteers' Convention, their last, Theobald Wolfe Tone wrote: 'The government seeing the Convention by their own act separate themselves from the great mass of the people who could alone give them effective force, held them at defiance; and that formidable assembly, which, under better principles, might have held the fate of Ireland in their hands, was broken up with disgrace and ignominy, a memorable warning that those who know not to render their just rights to others, will be found incapable of firmly adhering to their own.'[2]

It is worth noting that, in this impressive statement Tone does not put the blame on Dublin Castle or the British Government. It was 'by their own act' that the Volunteer delegates separated themselves

---

[1] Report of 17 November 1783 quoted in Rogers, *op. cit.*, p. 121.
[2] Quoted in Rogers, *op. cit.*, p. 129.

from 'the great mass of the people.' But later generations of Irish nationalists did not see it that way. It suited them to take North-ington's words at their face value, and put the whole blame for the fiasco on British intrigue. Exonerated, the Irish Volunteers soon became, in nationalist retrospect, idealised as well. By the mid-nineteenth century, they had become role-models for physical-force nationalists. The Irish poet and journalist Thomas Davis (1814–45) wrote with reference to the eloquent, pacific Daniel O'Connell:

> And vain were words till flashed the swords
> Of the Irish Volunteers!

The almost-exclusively Protestant character of the Volunteers was lost sight of in a nationalist mythology, the great majority of whose devotees were Catholics. Also lost sight of was the fact that the Volunteer movement had come into being, spontaneously, in order to help the British defend Ireland, against the French, and to put down Whiteboys, potential rebels. All that mattered, in that retro-spect, was those flashing swords, and the victory they won in the shape of 'Grattan's Parliament'. That institution, too, was idealised in retrospect, and its exclusively Protestant composition to the end was glossed over. (In 1982, Charles J. Haughey's Government hap-pily celebrated the bicentenary of a parliament into which neither he nor any of his colleagues would have been admitted, and for which none of them would have been allowed to vote. The reason why nationalists idealise Grattan's parliament is that the British got rid of it, in 1800.)

In the nationalist retrospect Burke's hostility to the Volunteers would appear as treacherous: an Irishman siding with England against Ireland. Burke, who had to deal with contemporary realities, not retrospective fantasies, did not see it that way. He and Tone, who deeply disagreed about so much, had one basic objective in common. Both men wished, and strove hard in their different ways, to bring about the end of the Penal Laws. Tone tried to achieve this, first by agitation in Ireland, later by revolutionary action breaking the connection with England. In contrast Burke tried, with some success, to utilise the connection with England for the benefit of all the Irish, Catholic and Protestant, as well as England. His approach to both the Irish and American questions was the same.

From 1765 to 1775 he tried to stay the movement towards Ameri-can independence through timely concessions and the renunciation of imprudent British pretentions. Only in 1778, when all that had failed, did he reluctantly decide that American independence would have to be recognised. And in 1782 he and Rockingham succeeded in imposing the acceptance of that conviction on George III. So with Ireland. In 1778 he had achieved – at considerable cost to himself, his seat at Bristol – the Catholic Relief Act. (Later, in 1793, he was to achieve another far-reaching measure, bringing Catholic Emancipation near to completion – see below Chapter VI, p. 497.) But though his approach to the two questions was identical, he saw the circumstances – always a key concept with him – as vastly different. With the awkward exception of slaves and slave-owners, the Americans were a people, fighting for their freedom. The Irish Volunteers were merely a *caste*, which denied to a majority of the Irish *people* the freedom they demanded for themselves. Burke saw in the Volunteer movement a potential for breaking the connection with England in a particular way, creating an independent Ireland, dominated by a caste which could not let go, thus perpetuating the Penal Laws. Wolfe Tone would have detested that as much as Burke did, but he doesn't seem to have seen the danger. (In any case that particular danger had passed by the 1790s, the period of Tone's greatest activity.)

If Tone's ideal had been realised and a mass-movement, unifying Catholics and Protestants, had come into force, and if the members of that movement had risen in arms to demand the independence of Ireland, I believe that Edmund Burke, as with America, would have reluctantly counselled the recognition of Irish Independence. But Tone's ideal was not realised, though nationalist fantasists pretend that it was, in 1798; nor has it been realised since. Northern Ireland today is a monument to the unreality of Tone's visions, of centuries ago, while the Republic of Ireland, supposedly dedicated to Tone's ideals, is homogeneously Catholic.

We can conceive of Burke's recognising Irish Independence in the imaginary conditions postulated by Tone. But in the real conditions of his time, he would never have recognised the form of Irish Independence that threatened to materialise: genuine sovereign independence for a Parliament dominated by the Irish Volunteers. Rather than recognise the kind of independence that seemed to be emerging in 1783, the Fox-North Coalition, advised by Burke, would have been prepared to use force: the threat is implicit in Fox's use of the word 'dissolution' in his letter to Northington. And in 1783, with the American War over, the use of force, by Britain, was a practical option, as it had not been in 1779. General Burgoyne could have had a victory at last. As it was, the Volunteers dissolved themselves. The purpose for which they had originally embodied had disappeared, through the end of the war with France. The political purposes on which they had agreed – Free Trade, which was real, and a version of 'legislative independence' which was largely spurious – had been secured. There was nothing left, on which they could agree, that could arouse the old enthusiasm.

The Irish Volunteers disappear from history in 1783, but they left two things behind them: a memory and a residue. The memory, being vague and confused, was exploitable for the purposes of physical-force nationalism, as we have seen with Thomas Davis's 'vain were words' dig at Daniel O'Connell.

The exploitation of the memory was long after Burke's day. But the residue became potent in Burke's day and was to plague him. The residue consisted of those – mainly Dissenters – who had hoped to enlist Catholic support for a radical programme. This was the seed-bed of the Irish Jacobins, with whom Burke would have to contend in the following decade (see below Chapter VI).

George III. 'Between Saratoga and Yorktown, the parliamentary struggle over America consisted essentially of a battle of wills between George III and Edmund Burke. And the same is true of the months between the news of Yorktown and the yielding of the King . . .' (p. 202)

Warren Hastings. 'We have brought before you the chief of the
tribe, the head of the whole body of Eastern offenders, a captain-general
of iniquity, under whom all the fraud, all the peculation, all the
tyranny in India are embodied, disciplined, arrayed and paid.' –
Edmund Burke (p. 369)

IV
India 1767–1790

'I have no party in this business, my dear Miss Palmer, but among a set of people, who have none of your Lillies and Roses in their faces; but who are the images of the great Pattern as well as you and I. I know what I am doing; whether the white people like it or not' –
     EDMUND BURKE TO MARY PALMER, 19 JANUARY 1786.

Engraved by Freeman.

Sir Philip Francis. 'I decline Controversy with you; because I feel myself overmatched in a competition with such talents as yours.' – Edmund Burke (p. 411)

Burke Under Restraint

Burke's active concern with Indian affairs lasted even longer than his concern with America. The concern with India was first recorded in 1767, the year he entered Parliament, and it lasted almost until his death, thirty years later. But the record of his concern with India is greatly different from that of his concern with America. On America Burke is remarkably consistent, from 1766 to 1782, as we have seen in Chapters II and III. But on India there is no such overall consistency. There is some internal consistency, indeed, in Burke's statements from 1767 to 1773, and there is complete consistency in the statements from 1781 to 1795. There is no consistency however, but a great area of contradiction, between these two sets of statements. Up to 1773 we find Burke, again and again, defending the East India Company against ministerial attempts to control it. From 1782 on we find him insisting that the East India Company be brought under parliamentary control, and then that the Company's most powerful figure – 'servant', in theory – Warren Hastings, Governor-General of Bengal, be impeached.

Both in Burke's time and since, into our own time, hostile writers have tried to account for this inconsistency as they do for each one of the perceived anomalies in Burke's career: by the hypothesis that venality and personal ambition were Burke's main motives throughout his political life. As there are many such anomalies in Burke's career, a writer who never considers any possible explanation for any of them, other than this discreditable one, can build up what may look like an impressive 'pattern', against Burke. But when one takes account, in each case, of other possible explanations, which in turn interrelate, a much more complex and subtle pattern appears.

The basic difference between 'Burke on America' and 'Burke on

India' is that Burke found his way – his own personal way – very quickly over America but only very slowly over India. As Lucy Sutherland, the editor of volume II of Burke's *Correspondence*, wrote when commenting on a letter of November 1772: 'This and the rest of Burke's correspondence on East India affairs at this time make it clear that the attitude adopted by the Rockingham group was not the result of reliance on his knowledge of and opinion on these matters, and that he himself began with no clearly defined views on the right line to adopt, nor any particular inside knowledge of the Company's concerns. Nor is there any suggestion that Burke felt that he had personal issues at stake.'[1]

The reason for the difference in pace, in Burke's finding his way, may lie partly in the unparalleled urgency of American affairs at the very beginning of Burke's career in 1766, and again by the mid 1770s; and partly in the existence of a collective Rockingham orthodoxy over India which it did not have on America. When Burke took his seat in the Commons, the Rockinghams did not have an American policy. Their customary touchstone – resisting the influence of 'the Court' – was hardly relevant to America in 1766, though it later became so (see above, Chapter II). Indeed the 'anti-Court' tendency, left to itself, might conceivably have led the Rockinghams in 1766 to align themselves with George Grenville, and keep the Stamp Act. Grenville, after all, had been forced out of office by George III's personal influence, and so might have appeared a natural ally. Burke had already made up his mind against the Stamp Act, and I believe he helped the Rockinghams make up their collective mind in the same way as he had done (see Chapter II above, pp. 99–103). Thus, in the case of the party's American policies, Burke had been 'present at the creation', and he was increasingly seen as a main guiding influence over the further development of those policies. On India, however, there was a definite Rockingham 'line', laid down without Burke's participation, and accepted by him, for six years. The essentials of the line were that ministerial efforts to regulate the East India Company were to be regarded with intense suspicion. The motivating force behind any such proposals was deemed to be a desire, on the part, not merely of ministers, but of persons connected with the Court, to get their hands on the vast patronage and loot of India. If they did get their hands on that, and on the plenitude of power that went with it, England would be on its way back to absolute

[1] *Corr.* II, 382.

Monarchy. So 'Hands Off the East India Company' became a Rockingham slogan, and was never entirely disavowed during Rockingham's life, though it ceased to be followed in practice after the
Madras crisis of 1776 (see below, pp. 304–7).

This view of the matter was not just paranoid fantasy, as
some historians imply (see Introduction, pp. xxxvi–xxxviii). Any
Ministerial effort to regulate the East India Company would involve
an extension of Ministerial patronage, and would be seen by any
opposition as devised solely for that purpose. Burke himself was
later to have painful experience of that, over his own legislation,
commonly known as 'Fox's East India Bill' in 1783. Nor was
'Court' interest in the East India Company an imaginary factor.
Ironically, in view of the long effort by Burke and his friends to
keep 'the Court' out of India, it was the King's personal political
agents, Charles Jenkinson and John Robinson (1727–1802), in
alliance with members of the East India Company, who were to
destroy Fox's Bill – and 'the Fox-North' Coalition Government,
of which Burke was part – in 1783, and helped William Pitt to
power in Britain, and to authority over India, in 1784 (see below
pp. 333–335).

The Rockingham line over India in the 1760s and 1770s was not
senseless, as has sometimes been suggested, but it did lack balance,
in an important way. Inherent in it was a strong tendency to magnify
a threat to India, from Ministers and 'the Court', and to minimise
abuses, already luxuriantly established there, by Company 'servants'.
After Burke had made a study of the Company, in 1781, he soon
emerged as the most determined, passionate and eloquent enemy of
that oppressive system. But the system was at least as oppressive, in
the 1760s and 1770s, when Burke was defending the Company, as
it was in the 1780s, when he was passionately denouncing both the
system of oppression (for the working of the system, see below
pp. 281–6) and the Company which discreetly colluded with it, and
profited from it.

Some difficult questions arise here. In the six years 1767–1773,
can Burke's acute, attentive mind really have failed to see that very
serious abuses were going on in India, under the Company's rule? If
so, why did he fail? And if he did see it, how could he fail to speak
out against such abuses if he really had the horror of them, which
he later proclaimed? To answer these questions requires a closer look
at what Burke had to say about India between 1767 and 1773. But
first a qualification. I am not dealing with these particular speeches

under the rubric of the Great Melody. The Indian part of the Great Melody – the part where we hear the personal voice of Edmund Burke at full power – begins with the great speech on Fox's East India Bill in 1783, and continues through the opening and closing speeches in the Impeachment of Warren Hastings (1788–1794). The speeches considered in the next section are on a lower level: they are almost entirely the speeches of an able politician, forcefully expressing the collective views of his party. All the same, these speeches are of significance for our understanding of Burke, partly because of their mainly, though not totally, antithetical relation to the Indian part of Burke's Great Melody. But the deepest significance of this set of speeches, on my interpretation, is that remorse for them was to lend poignancy and intensity to the Great Melody when, belatedly, it made itself heard.

1766–1773

Burke's first recorded speech on Indian affairs came on 16 May 1767, although it appears from the draft that he had already spoken several times in Parliament in a similar sense. On 25 November 1766, for example, he opposed a motion for a Committee of Enquiry into the Company's affairs (*Corr.* I, 281, n4). The *Parliamentary History*, however, contains no Burke speeches on India for 1766. The 1767 speech was opposing the East India Dividend Bill, which levied an annual sum of £400,000 on the Company and restricted the Company's right to declare a dividend. Burke at once takes high Rockingham ground:

> You are going to restrict by a positive arbitrary Regulation the enjoyment of the profits which should be made in Commerce. I suppose there is nothing like this to be found in the Code of Laws in any Civilised Country upon Earth – you are going to cancel the great line which distinguishes free Government.[1]

He is not known to have spoken on Indian affairs again until nearly two years later, when the arrangement of 1767 expired, and the Government presented a new 'East India Settlement', on similar lines to the earlier one. Burke adheres to his earlier line, but awk-

[1] *Writings and Speeches* II, 65.

wardly, and without the earlier confident resonance. Lord Clive had spoken before him, and Burke was clearly taken aback by part of what he had to say.[1] He had begun by speaking in glowing terms of the potential of Britain's Indian Empire – of which he himself was the founder – but he went on to demand 'sweeping reforms of the Company, with rigorous central control of the officials both in London and in India.'

This was precisely the policy which Burke and his friends were to follow energetically when in office fourteen years later. But in 1769, what Clive demanded ran clean contrary to established Rockingham policy. And Clive's authority, in an Indian debate, at that time, overshadowed that of all other living persons. In this distressing situation for a debater, even Burke is driven to dither. He opens by asserting that 'the Committee are bound by the Noble Lord's arguments', and goes on to resist the Noble Lord's recommendations. He eulogises Clive, and then tries to dissent from the views of the person eulogised. These are difficult rhetorical feats to bring off, and Burke duly fails to bring them off. The following passage from this speech is the weakest I know of, in the entire canon of Burke's oratory:

> It is plausible to continue the power in it's Directors; but is a matter of serious consideration. – Without entering into that Act [a statute proposed by Clive, making the Court of Directors of the Company responsible to Parliament, rather than to the stockholders] they have their dark side, as well as their bright side. This Company is grown under such Directors, it is become a great, a glorious Company. Men continually watched by their constituents, it works them into vigour. The body has not been so fluctuating, some have been changed. They may be formed into a body against their country. They are apt to form themselves into cabals. I do not say this in opposition to the Noble Lord. But I hope whenever the Committee sit upon that, they will not be too quick in adopting that idea.[2]

I infer from the uncharacteristic confusion and irresolution of these remarks that Burke is shaken by Clive's ideas, and that he is beginning to have serious doubts about the Rockingham line. Burke does not have occasion to return to Indian affairs until more than three years later. He spoke on the East India Select Committee on 13 April

[1] Robert, Lord Clive (1725–1774), who had just been made an Irish peer, sat in the Commons as Member for Shrewsbury. His argument is summarised in a note in *Writings and Speeches* II, 220.
[2] *Writings and Speeches* II, 221.

1772. It was a polished performance. There are elements, in it, of both the old Rockingham line and the Clive doctrine, laid down three years before. It is not easy to make 'Rockingham' and 'Clive' compatible, but Burke, at least, manages to combine them effectively, in a smooth and skilful piece of polemical advocacy. The matter immediately under discussion was a private member's motion calling for an inquiry into the Company's affairs. As the motion was supported by the North Administration, Rockingham principles dictated opposition to the motion, and Burke duly supplies this, in a confident, scornful, debating style:

> He liked to see his way before him, and would never plunge himself into any Business without knowing how he was to get through it. He would not beat the Cover, merely to see what Game might start out; Neither would he consent to go barking and questing about the East India Company or any other Corporations, in order to drive them into the Toils of administration.

That debate, says Paul Langford, the editor of Volume II of *Writings and Speeches*, offered Burke and his friends 'a new opportunity to renew their defence of the Company originally undertaken in 1766–67 . . .' This is fine, as far as it goes, but the principles on which Burke now 'defends the Company' are radically different from those on which he had defended it in 1766, and half-defended it in 1769. He now embraces, in principle, the Clive doctrine which he had half-opposed in 1769. He blames the North Administration for not having taken that advice, and then he uses the culpability he imputes to the Administration, in that matter, to exonerate the Company and its servants for any irregularities they may have committed, in an inherently irregular situation:

> When discretionary power (said he) is lodged in the hands of any man, or class of men, experience proves, that it will always be abused. This was the case with the East-India company. That charter, which was well enough calculated for the purposes of a factory, becomes totally insufficient upon the acquisition of extensive territories. Hence unlimited authority fell necessarily into the hands of their governors. The directors, attentive to the extension of their trade, had not time, nor perhaps capacity, to make general regulations sufficient for the good government of so great an empire: and, had they been possessed of both these requisites, yet they wanted the power to exert them. Else why have they now applied for a new charter? The thing speaks for itself. They could only act within their charter, and send to their governors directions, and direc-

tions that were not binding in law, no competent authority having been delegated to them by the legislature. Does it not follow from this, that they were obliged to leave their governors a discretionary power? But how was the governor to keep in awe the company's servants, who knew that he did not derive his authority from law, and that they could not be punished for disobedience beyond the ditch of Calcutta? In order to preserve some kind of subordination, he was forced occasionally to act the despot, and to terrify the refractory by the arm of power or violence. This, I believe, you will find to be the genuine source of that arbitrary conduct charged upon the late governors in Bengal. Where no laws exist, men must be arbitrary; and very necessary acts of government will often be, in such case, represented by the interested and malevolent as instances of wanton oppression. Suppose some examples of real tyranny to have occurred, does it thence follow, that the governors were culpable? Is it not possible, that they were misinformed? In such a multiplicity of affairs, and in a government without laws, some enormities must have been committed. But who are the blameable persons? Not the company, nor the company's servants, who have not done what experience tells us is above the reach of humanity, and what they had not legal right to do; but those who did not, upon the acquisition of such vast territories, compose for their use a comprehensive and well-digested code of laws, for the rule of every man's conduct. Had the ministry, upon a former occasion, adopted this plan, as they were advised, we should not now be debating this point, nor should we have heard that the neat revenues of Bengal are sunk to less than two hundred thousand pounds. In fact, administration is, in this case, the only culprit. The East-India company is not punishable for not performing what no body of men in their circumstances ever did or will perform. It is the men who are at the helm of affairs, and who neglected, or wanted capacity and inclination, to make the proper arrangements, that ought to be the objects of public and parliamentary vengeance.[1]

Warren Hastings could have used that line of argument, to great effect in his defence, in the following decade, when he was being impeached by Burke. But then Hastings might never have been allowed to be impeached if Burke had been heeded: towards the end of the speech from which I have just quoted he argued for 'a general amnesty or act of oblivion' for the Company's servants in India. A few months later, in August, Burke received an offer from the East India Company. Laurence Sulivan, its powerful deputy Chairman – and chief protector of Warren Hastings – urged Burke to accept the appointment of head of a Commission of three supervisors to be sent

---

[1] *Writings and Speeches II*, 371–3.

out to investigate and correct abuses in their Indian Presidencies.[1]

It is interesting, and altogether characteristic of the Company, that a person who had recently argued for 'a general amnesty and Act of oblivion' for the Company's servants should have been asked to lead a Commission 'to investigate and correct abuses' committed by the servants in question. Quite clearly what was intended was a white-wash. Lucy Sutherland comments: 'It was tempting financially to a man in his position.' This is something of an understatement. If Burke had accepted this invitation, and then done what the Company expected of him, he could have returned from India a wealthy man, with wealthy and powerful friends. The individual depicted by his detractors would have been angling for such an offer – quite a plaus-ible hypothesis – and would have greedily gobbled it up. Burke turned it down.

The series of Burke's early Indian speeches was now drawing to a close. Several broke no new ground, and simply continued to put all the blame on the North Administration: 'They pretended reformation, and they meant nothing but plunder.' His next major speech came on 5 April 1773. It contains one highly significant pass-age, revealing the real state of his feelings at this time, towards the Company he had been defending. The speech – on North's East India Resolutions – was clearly an impassioned one. A newspaper report of it begins: 'Mr. Edmund Burke next arose, and with a vehemence uncommon amongst our modern Orators, he arraigned, as usual, the conduct of Administration.'[2] The report refers to Burke as speaking 'with the *verbum ardens*, or glowing expression of the ancients.' For most of the speech, as noted, the *verbum ardens* is directed against the Administration, which was then that of Lord North. But then it suddenly takes a different and startling turn, with the following warning that

> the East-India Company tied about their necks, would, like a mill-stone, drag them down into an unfathomable abyss; that it was well if it dragged not this nation along with them, for that, for his part, he always had had his fears, and would now venture to prophecy his apprehensions, that this cursed Company would at last, viper, be the destruction of the country which fostered it in her bosom.

If the Company was a viper, it was one that Burke had been fostering

---

[1] *Corr.* II, 319.
[2] *Writings and Speeches* II, 390–9, quoting *General Evening Post*, 8 April 1773.

in his own bosom. That is the nature of the horror he is experiencing, as he 'prophesies his apprehensions.' The peroration of this strange speech may be seen as an attempt to bring together Burke's warnings about the Administration with the loathing which he has just acknowledged himself to feel towards the Company:

> . . . as to the East-India Company, he foresaw it would be the *destruction of this country*, but that for his part he would sooner have the Company itself totally overthrown; he would sooner see it fall to ruin about his ears, than have *the base of the English Constitution undermined, or a single pillar which contributed to the support of so excellent a structure receive the slightest fracture, or defaced in the minutest part*.[1]

To that he added, according to another report, 'I have eased my conscience.' I have no doubt he had.

Burke did not again, in this period, attack the East India Company. That 'viper' passage remains isolated: a strange and lonely harbinger of the tremendous barrage which he was to unleash against the Company ten years later.

On 10 June 1773 Burke found himself again defending what he had called 'this cursed Company'. The circumstances of this speech, on the East India Regulating Bill, were rather special. It was North's major Indian measure of the 1770s. It was also a peculiarly obnoxious measure, in terms of what was still the general Rockingham doctrine of non-intervention in Company affairs. Paul Langford writes: 'It was the suspicion of many that the government was effectually asserting a large measure of control over the Company, and such suspicions were naturally exploited by those in opposition who had consistently denounced parliamentary intervention in the East India Company's affairs. Dowdeswell led the attack on the third reading and Burke spoke late in the subsequent debate.'[2]

Dowdeswell was then the leader of the Rockingham party in the Commons, and Burke would be expected to back him up, on such an important occasion. Party discipline was nothing like as tight, in the late eighteenth century, as it was later to become, but it did exist, among the Rockinghams in particular, in the form of an expectation of at least loose conformity to a general consensus, where one had taken shape, as over the East India Company. Burke, as we have

[1] *Writings and Speeches*, II, 390–3.
[2] Topnote to report of 'Speech on East India Regulating Bill': *Writings and Speeches*, II, 393–396.

seen, had deviated, in some of his earlier speeches, significantly from the Rockingham consensus, not just by the outburst against 'this cursed Company', but substantially on 13 April, 1772 when he accepted the principle of comprehensive statutory regulation of the Company's affairs. He foreshadowed then what would, eleven years later, under his influence, become his party's policy, and find expression in 'Fox's East India Bill'. But in 1772–73, what Burke had advocated, under Clive's influence, was directly opposed to party policy. We do not know how much attention may have been paid to Burke's restiveness over the party's position on the East India Company, but I believe that William Dowdeswell, at least, must have noticed something, and have been worried about Burke's position, in the major debate on the Regulating Bill: an occasion on which the Rockinghams would wish to show a united front.[1]

The report of the speech on the East India Regulating Bill opens: 'Mr. E. Burke got up next, and made an apology to the House for his having been silent hitherto concerning this momentous and important business.' This is an unusual parliamentary opening, and implies an unusual parliamentary context. Under normal conditions, an MP who apologised for 'having been silent hitherto' would be laughed at for his self-importance. Burke's opening implies that his silence had been the subject of comment, and had worried his friends. There was nothing unusual in his speaking late – that was his usual position. But on this occasion he seems to have hung back so long as to excite speculation that he might not be going to speak at all. Such speculation would have been unlikely unless Members, on both sides, were aware that Burke was having difficulty with the Rockingham line on the Company. He was being watched, both by friends and foes; he often was. He might well have hoped to avoid speaking at all. The prospect of fostering that viper, yet once more, must have been exceedingly distasteful. Yet he held his nose, as it were, did his duty by his Party, and defended the East Indian Company. As might be expected, it was hardly an inspiring defence. He referred to 'the affairs of the India Company, which he in his opinion, deemed not improperly managed; nor that the abuses complained of either at home or abroad, were existing in the manner represented.' Later, as if feeling that that formula might sound a bit grudging, to the ears of his friends, he adds that 'if the House, would but allow a short

[1] Burke's 'heretical' speech of 13 April 1772, in which he adopted Clive's position on regulating the Company, was made on a relatively insignificant parliamentary occasion – a Private Member's Motion.

time, these disorders, few as they are, would be able to correct themselves; that the Company surely had done great things, and would still do greater, if they were suffered to go on.'

The preamble to North's Bill had referred to abuses committed by the Company's servants in India. Burke comments that certain Company servants, whom he names, are '*blackened* in the *preamble* without cause.' Among those so *blackened* is Warren Hastings. That speech on North's East India Regulating Bill is the clearest example on record of Edmund Burke's toeing a party line; since we know him not to have been in agreement, in his heart, with that line. With one exception (in 1770, when he was proposing the Rockingham-Grenville American resolutions – see Chapter II above, pp. 131–5) all the other examples are from the 'Indian' speeches of 1767–73. Taken as a whole they show both that Burke was capable of toeing a party line, and that he had considerable difficulty in doing so consistently, when his heart was not in it.

Fortunately for Burke, he never again felt obliged to defend the East India Company, or to minimise abuses committed in India. For nearly four years following the debate on the Regulating Bill, he has nothing to say in public about India as he becomes more and more committed to American affairs. But he surely also welcomed the change of theme, from a then uncongenial subject, to one on which he could speak with an unconstrained mind and heart. I suggested in Chapter II that the soaring *élan* of the great American speeches of 1774–5 may derive in part from a sense of release, after six years of constrained silences, over America. But it may also derive, at least as much, from a sense of release from something much worse: six years of constrained utterances, over India. Overall; the years from 1769 to 1773 must have been most uncomfortable for him, since he was discouraged from talking about the subject on which he was in full accord with his party, while being encouraged to talk about the subject on which he felt in increasing disaccord with his party.

Burke did not again discuss India, after June 1773, until May 1777. But when he does return to the subject, it is in a radically changed context. He is now free to expose abuses and chastise the Company's masterful 'servants' (see below pp. 304–6). And this is the role which he will sustain, with dedication, for the rest of his career, even against the growing reluctance of his Party.

So, to return to the questions posed earlier, could he have failed to be aware of an oppressive system being operated by the Company's 'servants' in India?

He might, perhaps, have been unaware, in the beginning. But by February 1769 his obvious distress and confusion at having to try to resist Clive's demands for sweeping reforms of the Company shows him to be painfully aware that there was something badly wrong in India itself; and therefore something badly wrong in a Rockingham line that protected the Company and, along with it, the activities of its 'servants' in India. 'By 1772 parliamentary and public concern at the maladministration and corruption which allegedly disfigured the East India Company's rule in India had grown to unprecedented proportions.'[1] And in April 1773 Burke's loathing of the company, and disgust at having to defend it, breaks out in the cry against 'this cursed Company. . . . viper. . . .'. In the same passage, he acknowledges that this view of the matter is not altogether new to him – 'he had always had his fears . . .' So if we find, as we must, that Burke did see at least by 1772–3 that serious abuses were going on in India, then the second question – Why did he fail to see them – does not arise. What does arise is the third question: 'How could he fail to speak out against such abuses if he really had the horror of these which he proclaimed in the 1780s?'

The 'viper' outburst of April 1773 shows that Burke's feelings towards the oppression of India were already the same – though far from being so thoroughly based on evidence – as those which found powerful and sustained expression ten years later, and for twelve years thereafter. I believe those feelings failed to find similar expression in the 1770s because he failed to carry his party with him on policy towards the company; and that he did not then feel that it would do any good for him to speak out, until he *could* carry his party with him.

There is no direct evidence that Burke tried to persuade his party colleagues to change their line over India. Such an effort at persuasion, if it occurred, would be unlikely to have left a written record. Parliament was in session; party colleagues could talk to one another. There were no formal meetings on policy, and of course no minutes. If Burke wanted the party to change course, he would have talked to Rockingham, to William Dowdeswell, to Lord John Cavendish, and perhaps to one or two others. I believe he did so, early in 1772; that he initially got some encouragement, or thought he did; and acted on it with the 1772 speech accepting the Clive doctrine on the East India Company; but that he was then told, probably by

[1] *Writings and Speeches* II, 371, tn.

Rockingham himself, after consultation with a few others, that party policy must continue to be as before: Hands off the East India Company. [1]

I have reached this opinion by way of inference from the only relevant evidence we have: Burke's speeches for 1772–1773. The major piece of evidence here is that speech of 13 April 1772 (see above pp. 261–3). In terms of Rockingham policy on India, it was revolutionary. By accepting Clive's doctrine of statutory regulation of the Company's affairs, Burke was jettisoning the main plank of what had up to then been that policy. That Burke continued to believe in statutory regulation was to appear eleven years later, when he drafted the Fox East India Bill. But the approach indicated in the 1772 speech was never renewed in the 1770s. Burke returned to the previous policy of defending the Company's independence. That he did so with deep reluctance is apparent: his next speech, the 'viper' outburst, came a year later. Just for a moment, the impulse to rebel could not be repressed. After that it seems that he tried to get out of speaking on Indian affairs at all, but was persuaded to make one last, sad appearance, on 10 June 1773, in the role of a defender of the East India Company. He was able to avoid speaking on India again, with one minor exception, for the next four years. [2] Then, in 1776 a dramatic episode – the arrest and deposition of Lord Pigot, the newly-appointed Governor of Madras at the hands of his colleagues in the Madras Council – ended Rockingham enthusiasm for the independence of the Company (see below pp. 304–6). Burke was now free to speak his mind.

I have spoken earlier of Burke 'toeing a party line'. That expression is indeed more applicable to him in the early 1770s and on the topic of India, than it is for any other period, or any other topic. Yet even for this period, and even for this topic, the expression is a little misleading. In general the Rockingham party line was not something imposed on Burke; he had done more to shape it than anyone else, and he became its principal exponent. And the Rockingham line over India was not a deviation from the general line; it followed implicitly

---

[1] On the legitimacy and necessity of the use of inference in the study of Burke, see Preface, p. viii.

[2] *The Parliamentary History* records no debates on India for 1774 or 1776. There was one minor debate in April 1775 on a Bill to oblige the company to export English manufactures to India. Burke spoke, mainly to make an 'American point': 'While administration annihilates the American market she cooks up others in the East Indies' (*Parl. Hist.* xvii, 656–619).

from that line. If the encroachments of 'the Court' should be resisted, in general, then they should also be resisted in the specific case of India. In the abstract, statutory regulation of the Company might be an excellent idea. But in practice, any regulating that was done, between 1770 and 1782, would be done by Lord North, with, behind him in the shadows, the creatures of George III, manipulating things and men. Great though the abuses in India might be, under straight company rule, might they not get even worse, once the Jenkinsons and the Robinsons were let loose out there? Burke could feel the force of such arguments, and would have found it hard to counter them, when heard from the lips of his friends. But his heart revolted against them, as the 'viper' passage shows.

His silence over India, from 1773 to 1777 is comparable – but only to a limited extent – with his (relative) silence over America, from 1770 to 1774. In both cases, Burke was silent because he felt that, in the prevailing conditions, there was nothing that he could usefully say. On America, the silencing factor was the immense popularity, both in Parliament and among the people of Britain, of the policy of taxing America. On India, the silencing factor was Rockingham policy, a policy Burke found intellectually hard to challenge, but increasingly uncongenial, emotionally, to have to defend. To end each silence, a major new development was needed. Over America, the new development was the Boston Port Bill (see Chapter II above, pp. 137–8); over India, it was the arrest of Lord Pigot (see pp. 304–6 below).

The silences were comparable, but different in quality. The American silence came after Burke had been speaking out of profound conviction in 1766–69. When he resumed speaking about America, in 1774, he was speaking out of the same depth of the same conviction. Everything in *On American Taxation* (1774) is fully consistent with *On the Declaratory Bill* (1766). The Indian silence is far more fraught. Up to 1773 he had been defending the independence of the Company in most of his speeches; and even in the one speech (in 1772) where he temporarily abandoned that independence, he opposed any inquiry into abuses in India, and even called for a general amnesty for all persons who might be accused of such abuses. But when he breaks his silence, in 1777, he is found to be demanding inquiry into abuses, and punishment of offenders. The 1773–1777 silence is a chasm, separating two incompatible policies, propounded by the same person.

He must, in retrospect, have experienced shame and guilt whenever he came to think of the sort of things he had been saying about India earlier. He can hardly have avoided some remembrance of all that when, in 1781, he first settled down to a serious study of how India was being governed. Many of the abuses which he then identified, and subsequently exposed, were actually being perpetrated while Edmund Burke was still defending the Company's independence, opposing inquiry into abuses, proposing general amnesties for offenders, and protesting against the 'blackening' of Warren Hastings. Burke would have tried to suppress such memories; he was never one to acknowledge past errors. But the memories were still around, and perhaps the more potent for being suppressed. I believe that those haunting memories do much to account for the elemental fury of Burke's Indian speeches of the 1780s, and above all for the concentrated, compulsive venom of his attack on Warren Hastings.

Hastings had committed terrible crimes in India; so the Burke of the 1780s passionately believed (see below p. 308 and ff. *passim*). But the Burke of the 1770's had been a partner in that guilt, for he had condoned those crimes, had sought to conceal them, and protect the perpetrators. In punishing Hastings, Burke is also punishing himself. His party, too, was punished, for what they had made him do to India, up to 1773. Contemporaries noted, in 1783, his driving fury in pursuing his Indian concern, with reckless disregard for the risks thereby incurred, for his party and the government of which he was part. As a result, that government was overthrown and, in the subsequent general election, Burke's party and its allies lost 89 seats, and were consigned to opposition for the rest of Burke's life. Far from being dismayed by these drastic political consequences Burke, in the new Parliament, after the electoral catastrophe of 1783, immediately reasserted the primacy of his Indian concern, and managed to induce the remnants of his party to join him in pressing for Hastings's impeachment. In the early 1770s Burke may have had to toe the party line: but in 1784–1795, he makes the party toe the Burke line, over India.

His driving concern over India, in the 1780s is fuelled by a need to atone for a personal dereliction in the previous decade. But it is also fuelled by forces coming from deeper in the psyche. His concern for the suffering people of India clearly has something to do with his concern for his own suffering people: the Catholics of Ireland under the Penal Laws. Partly, and to an important extent, this is a matter of being able to empathise with another oppressed people, out of one's own experience of an oppressive system. But the forces at work are more complex than this, and more dynamic. It is not just a question of championing an oppressed people or sympathising with it. There is also a question of defecting from an oppressed people, and so betraying that people.

Edmund Burke came from an oppressed people but, as a privileged Protestant, he was part of an oppressive system, to the extent of his personal exemption from the Penal Laws. A person in that situation would necessarily feel some degree of guilt. I find Burke's to have been a high degree, especially since there is reason to believe that his privileged position derived from his father's apostasy from the Catholic religion. As far as Ireland was concerned, Burke responded to the situation, by a long, heroic, skilful and largely successful effort to demolish the oppressive system of which he was both beneficiary and victim: the Penal Laws (see Chapter I above, *passim*). This predicament led him to engage his energies against other systems which he regarded as oppressive.

With India, however, Burke, at the outset of his career found himself precluded, by Rockingham policy, from any intervention in defence of Indians. I believe that, as he looked back on that period, from the vantage point of his greater knowledge of, and involvement in, Indian affairs from 1777 on, he came to feel, at some level that, by defending the independence of the East Indian Company up to 1773, he had betrayed the oppressed people of India, just as his father had betrayed the oppressed people of Ireland, by abjuring their religion. Edmund Burke, in short, by betraying the Indians, had re-enacted the apostasy of his father. I believe it was that thought, combined with a compulsion to banish it, that drove him on in his Indian crusade from 1781 to 1795.

In the person of Warren Hastings, Burke is punishing not only himself, but also his father; and vindicating the peoples who were wronged by him and his father, as well as by Hastings. All this may seem somewhat feverish, and indeed there is something feverish about it. But the fever is in Burke himself. Where Ireland is concerned the clearest outbreak is in the Bristol Guildhall speech of 1780, but there are symptoms of the trouble, whenever Burke has to discuss Irish or Indian affairs.

Such matters, so far as they relate to Burke's motivation, are hardly susceptible of proof. But I believe, after studying Burke for a good many years, that the above observations comprise a good guess, which respects the contours of the known facts and relationships. In short: it fits.

AN INDIAN AGON
1773–1780

This section is an interlude; the scene is set in India, and Burke is not on stage. But the two protagonists in the struggle described here profoundly affected Burke's life. The struggle itself prepared the way for the impeachment of one protagonist. The other protagonist helped Burke to prepare the impeachment. The protagonists were Warren Hastings (1732–1818) and Philip Francis (1740–1818). The two men were brought together by a piece of legislation which Burke had opposed, lamely and reluctantly: Lord North's East India Regulating Act, of 1773. Under the Act, Warren Hastings became Governor-General of Bengal, of which he had been Governor since 1772. As Governor-General, Hastings had (vaguely defined) authority also over the two other main areas of British power in India: Bombay and Madras. But as well as elevating Hastings, the Act also hemmed him in. It provided him with a Council of four members (in addition to himself) and stipulated that decisions should be taken by a majority in Council.

One of the Councillors, Richard Barwell (1741–1804), was in Hastings's pocket. Or, as one of his biographers puts it: 'Barwell had by now entirely succumbed to Hastings's charm of manner and superior abilities and was prepared to give him his cordial support. Hastings seems to have facilitated matters by winking at his [Barwell's] irregular methods of acquiring a fortune.'[1] So, from Hastings's point of view, Barwell was 'safe'; the three other councillors named in the Act, were not. These were General Sir John Clavering (1722–77), Colonel George Monson (d.1775), and Philip Francis. Monson and Clavering have been aptly described as 'two third-rate politicians of considerable parliamentary influence'.[2] Francis, a man of remarkable ability, soon took the lead in the new Council. As he had the support of the other two newly-appointed councillors, he had the legal authority to over-rule Hastings. Burke was impressed by Francis's position at this time. He wrote to Rockingham: 'Francis will be here, by appointment, today [20 October 1773] . . . I find that this Mr. Francis is entirely [in the] interests of Lord Clive. Everything contributes to the Greatness of this Man,

[1] Penderel Moon, *Warren Hastings and British India* (London, 1947) p. 139.
[2] *Encyclopaedia Britannica*, Eleventh Edition: entry on Hastings.

who whether Government or the Company prevails will go near to govern India.'[1] 'Go near' turned out to be right.

The new Councillors arrived in Calcutta on 19 October 1774. Francis described their reception as 'mean and dishonourable'. Why was there no guard of honour? And why was there a salute of only seventeen guns, instead of twenty-one? One can visualise the arriving Councillors looking at one another uncomfortably, as the silence that follows the discharge of the seventeenth gun begins to get too long. And they had reason for dismay; it wasn't just a matter of hurt vanity, though that did come into it. The absence of a guard of honour and the truncated salutes were signals from the Governor-General, to all Calcutta, as well as to the Councillors themselves, that Councillors are persons of much less consequence than a Governor-General.

The new Councillors had a mandate to inquire into past abuses, and they now put this inquiry at the head of their agenda. Hastings obstructed the inquiry, and the struggle between Francis and Hastings began. It was to last for the next twenty-one years.

Superficially the protagonists in that epic struggle appear ridiculously mismatched. Warren Hastings was the absolute ruler of vast territories. Philip Francis, for all of Burke's tribute to his 'greatness', had at that time done nothing but serve in minor government posts. However, his pseudonymous writings, the *Letters of Junius*, were the talk of the British political world. The *Letters*, a brilliant series of political polemics, appeared in the *Public Advertiser* between 21 January 1769 and 21 January 1772. They were mainly directed against the Duke of Grafton's Administration from the point of view of a supporter of George Grenville, and the political argument is on a high intellectual level. But Junius's readers were less interested in political argument than in damaging personal allegations, couched in a tone of silky menace, which intersperse the argument and lend spice to it. Politicians read Junius with bated breath, in fear of what might be coming next.

The *Letters* are superbly written – some of the finest writers of the time, including Burke, are among those credited with the authorship. But the identity of the author remained in dispute until, in 1962, Alvar Ellegaård, on the basis of statistico-linguistic tests, established conclusively that Junius was Francis. One of the targets was the distinguished soldier Sir William Draper, (1721–87), conqueror of

[1] *Corr.* II, 472.

Manila and a personal friend of Francis's father, Dr. Philip Francis, an eminent classicist. Two others were John Calcraft (1726–1772) and Welbore Ellis (1713–1802), both benefactors of Francis. Francis's outwardly good relations with these two men tended to invalidate the hypothesis that he was the author. The politician and writer John Wilson Croker (1780–1857) dismissed the 'Franciscan' hypothesis on the grounds that if Francis was Junius, he must have been a 'monster of treachery,' which Croker thought was improbable. [1] One wonders what Croker would have thought had he known that a few days after ceasing to write his *Letters*, Francis had written to his printer, 'Having nothing better to do, I propose to entertain myself and the public by torturing that bloody wretch Barrington.' [2] And in 1787, when Francis, by now an MP, was attacked in the Commons for allowing himself to be included among the managers in the impeachment of Hastings (his personal enemy, so that he could not be impartial) Francis had no compunction in citing his victim Draper, now dead, as someone he had consulted and who had approved his conduct: 'Those who knew Sir William Draper, I am sure will acknowledge that there could not be a stricter and more scrupulous judge of point of honour than he was.' [3]

But though it was nearly two centuries before the authorship was established conclusively, people who studied Francis were pretty certain who Junius was. Joseph Parkes and Henry Merivale wrote: 'That Sir W. Draper was a personal friend . . . and known to his son, at the time when Junius was inflicting on him his severest stabs, is clear enough from the Doctor's letter which follows. But we know enough by this time, or shall know hereafter, of Francis, to be aware that this affords no reason for doubting the relationship.' [4] They go on to quote a letter by Dr. Francis to his son – whom he adored, and never dreamt could be Junius – telling him of Draper's distress after a personal attack on him by Junius: 'Poor Sir William! I am glad he is gone to Clifton where he may eat his own heart in peace. So sensible to friendship, what must he suffer in his feelings for his own Reputation! When he repeated to me some passages of his letter, I bid him prepare his best philosophy for an answer. But who is this

[1] *Quarterly Review*, Vol. XC (December 1851) pp. 91–162. The words quoted are on p. 97.

[2] Quoted by C. V. Everett in *The Letters of Junius* (London, 1927) p. 317.

[3] *Memoirs of Sir Philip Francis* (he was made KCB in 1806) three volumes, by Joseph Parkes and Henry Merivale (London, 1867) Vol. I, p. 224.

[4] *Memoirs*, Vol. I, p. 229.

Devil Junius, or rather legion of Devils? Is it not B – k's pen dipped in the Gall of Sa – ll's heart? Poor Sir William.'[1]

I am afraid that I can imagine Philip Francis finding his father's letter excruciatingly funny.

The idea that Burke was Junius, was one that had been put about by Francis himself, in order to put people off the scent.[2] But it is interesting that Dr. Francis realises that 'the Gall' of Junius is not characteristic of Burke, and must have come from some other source. Poor Dr. Francis might well have had a seizure if he had ever learned what that source actually was.

There is, both in Junius's public letters and even more explicitly in his letters to his printer, H. S. Woodfall, an unmistakable whiff of blackmail. It has been surmised that the blackmailer was handsomely rewarded, as the price of silence. That is the meaning of Byron's remark: 'He had his price, and was gagged and sent to India'.[3] A biographer of Lord Mansfield, the eminent political jurist who was one of Junius's prime targets, wrote: 'JUNIUS, from the acquittal of the printers [see below p. 279] till the beginning of the year 1772, when he made a treaty with the Government and for ever disappeared, exercised a tyranny of which we can form little conception, living in an age when the press is more decorous, and we are able by law to restrain its excesses' (John Lord Campbell, *The Lives of the Chief Justices of England*, London, 1849, Vol. II, p. 490).[4]

Now that we know that Junius was Philip Francis, we can see that the 'blackmail rewarded' hypothesis fits neatly into the known facts of the career of Junius – Francis (as Macaulay had guessed). The last

---

[1] *Memoirs of Sir Philip Francis*, Vol I, p. 229. 'Sa – ll' is Sir George Savile.

[2] See *Memoirs* I, 220, n. 1. Francis wrote to a friend, Macrabie, on 12 June 1790: 'Junius is not known, and that circumstance is perhaps as curious as any of his writings. I have always suspected Burke' (*Memoirs* p. 243). But in writing to George Grenville whom he championed – 'that able and honest Minister' – and by whom he hoped to be rewarded, Francis insinuates that Burke is *pretending* to be Junius: 'Mr. Burke denies [being] Junius as he would a fact which he wishes to have believed' (*Memoirs* 1, p. 219). Boswell writes in his *Life of Johnson* that in 1779, talking of 'the wonderful concealment of the author of the celebrated letters signed *Junius*; he [Johnson] said, "I should have believed Burke to be Junius, because I know no man but Burke who is capable of writing these letters; but Burke spontaneously denied it to me. The case would have been different had I asked him if he was the author; a man so questioned, as to an anonymous publication, may think he has a right to deny it".'

[3] Thomas Medwin, *Conversations of Lord Byron and Edward J. Lovell Jr* (Princeton, 1966) p. 202.

[4] *Memoirs of Sir Philip Francis*, Vol. I, p. 238, n.1.

letter in the series – Letter LXIX – appeared early in 1772. The last paragraph of Junius's last letter runs: 'The man, who fairly and completely answers this argument, shall have my thanks and my applause. My heart is already with him. – I am ready to be converted. – I admire his morality, and would gladly subscribe to the articles of his faith. – Grateful as I am to the GOOD BEING, whose bounty has imparted to me this reasoning intellect, whatever it is, I hold myself proportionally indebted to him, from whose enlightened understanding another ray of knowledge communicates to mine. But neither should I think the most exalted faculties of the human mind, a gift worthy of the divinity; nor any assistance, in the improvement of them, a subject of gratitude to my fellow-creature, if I were not satisfied, that really to inform the understanding corrects and enlarges the heart.' In this piece of moralising *à la* Joseph Surface, there are only six credible words: 'I am ready to be converted.'

Philip Francis gave up his War Office job and in the following year he accepted the offer of the lucrative and honourable post of a member of the new Council for Bengal, created by North's Regulating Act. This was a political plum. Two fellow-councillors who set out with him were being rewarded for political services. It seems probable that he was being rewarded for political *disservices*, and for the cessation of the same.

I believe that the decision to buy Junius off was probably taken by George III, the real head of the Administration for which Lord North was the parliamentary front. We know from Junius's correspondence with his printer that George III learned the identity of Junius, from David Garrick, early in November 1771, a few months before Junius wrote his last Letter. Garrick had somehow acquired the information from the printer. Junius sent a warning to the printer and a published threatening letter to Garrick:

'To H. S. Woodfall [10 November 1771]

(secret)

beware of David Garrick. he was sent to pump you, & went directly to Richmond to tell the king I shd. write no more.'[1]
'To Mr David Garrick [10 November 1771]

I am very exactly informed of your impertinent inquiries, & of the information you so busily sent to Richmond, & with what triumph & exultation it was received. I knew every particular

[1] John Cannon (ed.) *The Letters of Junius* (Oxford, 1998) p. 379.

of it the next day. Now mark me, vagabond. – Keep to your pantomimes, or be assured you shall hear of it. Meddle no more, thou busy informer! – It is in *my* power to make you curse the hour, in which you dared to interfere with   Junius.'[1]

I believe the 'blackmail rewarded' hypothesis is substantially correct, but that it needs to be qualified. There is often a whiff of blackmail in Junius's letters – a hint of further revelations, if the party attacked does not mend his ways – but I don't think the letters, at their inception, were a blackmailing enterprise. They started out, in part out of political conviction, and in part out of an expectation of reward. The political conviction was the general Whiggish one – shared by Burke – that the King's influence was increasing, and ought to be diminished. The expected reward was to come from George Grenville, all of whose political positions, including the Stamp Act, were championed by Junius. In 1769, many people expected that George Grenville, in alliance with the Rockinghams, would return to power. Francis shared that expectation. As Junius, he wrote to Grenville: 'Until you are minister, I must not permit myself the honour of being known to you.'

But on 13 November, 1770, George Grenville died, at the age of 58. This unexpected event, which liberated Burke (see above p. 135), left Junius without a practical objective. After Grenville's death, he was a power in the land, but lacked a purpose to which the power could be applied. He was exercising a kind of verbal reign of terror – 'a tyranny', as Lord Campbell wrote – over the highest ranks of society, and the terror extended even to the King. One of the characteristics which made Junius so talked about was the extreme audacity of his attacks on George III. The famous address to the King in Letter XXXV (19 December 1769) begins: 'Sir, – It is the misfortune of your life, and originally the cause of every reproach and distress, which has attended your government, that you should never have been acquainted with the language of truth, until you heard it in the complaints of your people.' The letter closes: 'The name of Stuart, of itself, is only contemptible; – armed with the Sovereign authority, their principles are formidable. The Prince, who imitates their conduct, should be warned by their example; and,

---

[1] *Letters of Junius* (ed. Everett) pp. 311–2. Francis sent the manuscript of this letter to his printer with instructions to have it copied, so that the letter which reached Garrick, would not be in Francis's hand.

while he plumes himself upon the security of his title to the crown, should remember that, as it was acquired by one revolution, it may be lost by another.' The printers of Letter XXXV were prosecuted, but the prosecution failed.

On 9 July 1771 Junius's attack on the King took the form of a letter to the Duke of Grafton. In it the whiff of blackmail is stronger still: 'The only letter I ever addressed to the King was so unkindly received, that I believe I shall never presume to trouble his Majesty, in that way, again. But my zeal for his service is superior to neglect, and like Mr. Wilkes's patriotism, thrives by persecution. Yet his Majesty is much addicted to useful reading, and, if I am not ill-informed, has honoured the *Public Advertiser* with particular attention. I have endeavoured therefore, and not without success, (as perhaps you may remember), to furnish it with such interesting and edifying intelligence, as probably would not reach him through any other channel. The services you have done the nation, – your integrity in office, and signal fidelity to your approved good master, have been faithfully recorded. Nor have his own virtues been entirely neglected. These letters, my Lord, are read in other countries and in other languages; and I think I may affirm without vanity, that the gracious character of the best of Princes is by this time not only perfectly known to his subjects, but tolerably well understood by the rest of Europe.'

In the final Junius *Letters* the verbal terrorism is stepped up. The antepenultimate *Letter* LXVII, of 22 November 1771, is a scurrilous and salacious attack, with plenty of scandalous detail, on 'the King's brother-in-law Col. Luttrell'. Junius pushes this distasteful matter under the King's nose: 'Yet I confess I should be sorry that the opprobrious infamy of this match should reach beyond the family. – We have now a better reason than ever to pray for the long life of the best of princes, *and the welfare of his royal issue.* – I will not mix any thing ominous with my prayers.'[1]

It seems that Francis decided, in late 1771, to go out of business as Junius, and cash in on the enormous nuisance-value he had accumulated. As might be expected, he sets about this with some subtlety. He arranges for the collection of his *Letters*, for publication in book form and, contrary to his usual secretiveness, allows word to go out that he will 'write no more'. Then, when Garrick joyfully carries this word to the king at Richmond, Francis sends Garrick a

[1] *Letters of Junius* (ed. Cannon) pp. 160; 251; 316–18.

letter that is venomous, even by the standards of Junius, and threatens more of the same. The message is clear: Junius, left to himself, cannot be relied on 'to write no more'. So better make sure of him, by an appropriate inducement. . . .

The inducement was the seat on the Bengal Council. No one has ever offered a plausible explanation of why such a plum should go to an obscure retired War Office clerk called Philip Francis. But the hypothesis that it went to him in order to close his mouth, would explain the transaction. Francis's grandson, H. R. Francis, writes that the family accepted that that is what took place: 'From the nature of the case, and from sundry fragments of evidence casually disclosed, I have drawn a general conclusion, which I know to have been that arrived at by my father and by his sister, Mrs. Godschall Johnson, the one, perhaps, of Sir Philip's daughters who most resembled him in keen political intelligence. It seems, I venture to say, in the highest degree probable that shortly after the retirement of Francis from the War Office – Junius having already ceased to write – some members of the Ministry learnt who Junius really was, and what was more important, how much of sympathy and covert support he had found from leading politicians, hostile or neutral, with whom they did not wish to come into violent conflict. On the approved principle, then, of building a bridge of gold for a flying enemy, they would naturally seek at once to effectually silence the hostile mouthpiece, and to conciliate Junius's most influential well-wishers. My belief is that this twofold object was attained about the date of Francis's last Letter from the War Office, and was attained by a promise, probably from Lord North, of a good appointment abroad after the shortest interval that might suffice to avert the immediate suspicion of a bargain, Francis on his part engaging to drop the role of masked pamphleteer, but never to remove the mask he had worn as Junius.'[1]

The Philip Francis who landed at Calcutta on 19 October, 1774, was a dangerous and unscrupulous man. But he was to find a man awaiting him there who was even more dangerous and unscrupulous than he was.

*　　　　*　　　　*

Warren Hastings, at the time of Francis's arrival, had an experience of India that spanned almost a quarter of a century, including a revolution in the character of the East India Company. He first came

---

[1] H. R. Francis, *Junius Revealed* (London 1894).

to India in October 1750, at the age of eighteen, as a 'writer', the lowest rank in the company's service. It was then a straightforward commercial company: selling British goods to the Indians, and buying the products of India with the money so obtained. The Nawab of Bengal was then in reality an independent prince, while owing nominal fealty to the Moghul Emperor. But in 1757, following Clive's decisive victory over the last fully independent Nawab of Bengal, at the battle of Plassey, the Company became, in effect, the sovereign power in Bengal. As its objectives remained purely commercial, it used its new found sovereign power to maximise profits. The 'Investment', as the moneys sent home to England were paradoxically known, was based on the land revenues of Bengal. The Company, collectively, had the incentive to squeeze the Bengalis as hard as possible. Individually, its servants each had an incentive to squeeze the natives still further, in order to accumulate the personal fortunes, which each had come to India to seek. [1]

In short, the Company's government of Bengal, under the Nawab's nominal authority, became a gigantic extortion racket, practised at the expense of the Indians. Hastings did not invent this system, and he even made some efforts to reform it, during the first of his two terms in India. But after the spectacular failure of his reforming efforts had brought his first term to a disastrous close, (see below, p. 282). Hastings returned to India as the practitioner-in-chief of the system he had once tried to reform. This was the Warren Hastings whom Burke, in the 1780s was to see as the personification of the evil system, and to impeach accordingly.

Clive had detected the abilities of Hastings and appointed him, in 1758, to the key post, within the system, of Company's Resident at the Court of the Nawab. The then Nawab, Mir Jafar (1691–1765), had been appointed by Clive, and accepted a subservient role. But, from 1760 on, a new Nawab, Mir Qasim (d. 1763), while accepting the Company's collective hegemony, sought to curb the individual depredations of the Company's servants. Henry Vansittart (died 1769), Clive's successor as governor, backed Mir Qasim in this, and was supported by Hastings, now a member of the Company's Council. But Hastings and Vansittart were in a minority. The majority on the Council, being made up of people who were doing very well out of the prevailing system, demanded that all the Company's

[1] A good analysis of this system can be found in A. T. Embree, *Charles Grant and British Rule in India* (London, 1962) pp. 31–2.

servants and agents should be entirely exempt from control by the Nawab's Government. Hastings vigorously opposed this demand, using language that would have earned the warm approbation of Edmund Burke:

'It is now proposed absolving every person in our service from the jurisdiction of the Government. This it is true will prevent their suffering any oppression; but it gives them a full licence of oppressing others, since, whatever crimes they may commit, the magistrate must patiently look on, nor dare even to defend the lives and properties of the subjects committed to his care, without a violation of our rights and privileges. Such a system of government cannot fail to create in the minds of the wretched inhabitants an abhorrence of the English name and authority, and how would it be possible for the Nawab, whilst he hears the cries of his people which he cannot redress, not to wish to free himself from an alliance which subjects him to such indignities?'[1]

Hastings's support for Mir Qasim made him very unpopular with his Company colleagues. This unpopularity was heightened after Mir Qasim, reacting to provocation by some of the Company's servants, massacred two hundred Europeans at Patna. The Company's forces defeated Mir Qasim at Buxar in October 1764. He was deposed, and his predecessor, the pliant Mir Jafar, was reinstated. The Company's system was now restored in Bengal, in its full rigour, and with full licence for its servants to rob the natives to their heart's desire.

Hastings's position had become untenable. In December 1764, after Buxar, he and Vansittart resigned and returned to England. Hastings was to spend the next four years in England, where he made valuable contacts among the Company's Court of Directors, and renewed his acquaintance with Clive. He seems to have convinced Clive that, if he were allowed to return to India, he would follow the line Clive had advised for him in 1758, which he had ignored. The line was one of severity towards the natives: 'These people will do nothing, through inclination,' Clive advised. 'Ten sepoys now and then will greatly expedite payment'. He added that nothing but fear will make the Muslims 'do justice to the Company's claims.'[2]

Before returning to Bengal as Governor, as he did in 1772, Hast-

---

[1] Penderel Moon, *Warren Hastings and British India* (London, 1947) pp. 51–2.
[2] M. E. Monckton Jones, *Warren Hastings in Bengal, 1772–1774* (Oxford, 1918) p. 95.

ings wrote to Clive: 'I cannot wish to profit by a surer guide than your counsel and your example.' [1]

The Warren Hastings who returned to India in 1772 as governor – and who was to be elevated to Governor-General next year – was a very different person from the reform-minded man who had stood out against the majority on Vansittart's Council. The new Hastings is a realist, who accepts the realities of British India. Never again will he challenge powerful Company servants, who were using their positions to accumulate fabulous personal fortunes. He did not take many bribes himself: his personal fortune, when he left India was modest, by Nabob standards. He was more interested in power than in money. But precisely because he was interested in power, he sought allies from among those who had power-bases in India: men like Richard Barwell (1741–1804) at Calcutta, and Paul Benfield (c.1740–1810) at Madras. And these were the people who were most successful in enriching themselves at the expense of the natives. Ambition and avarice go well together, as Burke was later to observe. Once the Barwells and the Benfields realised that the new governor represented no threat to their interests, they rallied to his support. So did the rest of the Company's servants, who hoped, in the course of time, to become Barwells and Benfields themselves. The Hastings who had been a pariah in British India at the end of his first term, became its hero in his second term; especially after the new Councillors had arrived, to challenge the Governor General's authority, which had become the shield of the Company's voracious 'servants'.

Hastings was an excellent servant of the East India Company, in that he was more interested in raising revenue for the Company, than for himself, and that he was highly efficient at raising revenue. His operations now ranged far beyond the borders of Bengal, westward up the Ganges valley, through Oudh and Rohilkhand and out to Benares. As Governor-General of Bengal, Hastings was responsible, at least ostensibly, to the Company's Court of Directors in Leadenhall Street. But in dealing with the territories he informally acquired, Hastings was responsible to no one. In these territories, he exercised arbitrary power, through his absolute control of a nominally sovereign prince, the Nawab of Oudh. He used this arbitrary power in order to extort as much money as possible from the Nawab's subjects. Then he leased out the Company's troops to the Nawab, at a

[1] Quoted in Moon, *Warren Hastings*, p. 83. Moon seems to think this is just polite. It seems to me a genuine statement of intent, and the registration of an understanding in virtue of which Hastings was able to return to Bengal as Governor.

stiff price, in order to annex Rohilkhand to the Nawab's territories, in theory; in reality to the territories of Warren Hastings. Later the same system was extended to Benares and its unfortunate Rajah Chait Singh. Hastings's admiring Victorian biographer, G. R. Gleig, a clergyman, describes Hastings's reasons for seizing this Rajah's property: 'As he held his province [Benares] on very easy terms, and was known to have accumulated a vast amount of treasure, Mr. Hastings was not visited by any compunctious misgivings as to the propriety as well as the justice of demanding that the English should at this juncture derive some benefit from his superfluity'[1]. The new domains were devastated, as well as being systematically looted.'

Hastings practised collective extortion from the natives of India, on behalf of the Company, and extended the area of its operation. He also connived at individual extortion, for private enrichment, by the Company's servants. He thus presided over a double system of extortion from the natives of India. Burke, when he came to denounce, and later impeach, Hastings, in the 1780s, used some exaggerated language, and was mistaken over particular incidents. But he was basically right in his analysis of the system over which Warren Hastings had presided, while Governor-General of Bengal.

Other views are on offer. M. E. Monckton Jones, for example presents the following idyllic picture: 'Warren Hastings was sent by the East India Company to their settlement at Calcutta as Governor in 1772, and by unsparing labour, coupled with imaginative insight into native needs, he converted the presence of the English from a bane into a source of healing and strength, first for Bengal itself, and then for the rest of an ever-widening British India. He made the economic, religious, and social rights of the people his first care, and built up the prosperity of the state upon the welfare of the cultivator.'[2] Monckton Jones does not provide detailed documentation of these benevolent transactions. Hastings's personal inclinations towards Indians were indeed benevolent. He was not a racist. He had a deep respect for Indian culture, Hindu and Muslim. He was a pioneering patron of Oriental scholarship, and in general an enlightened and cultivated person. The Monckton Jones version is, I

---

[1] For a detailed account of these transactions see Vols. III and IV of James Mill's ten-volume *History of British India* (fifth edition, 1858) edited with Notes and Continuation by H. H. Wilson. Hastings's admirers, including Mill's editor, deprecate the account, but have not been able to refute it. See below, pp. 286–8.

[2] Monckton Jones, *op. cit.*, p. 1.

believe, a good picture of how Warren Hastings would have liked to govern India, had he been free to follow his personal inclinations. But he was not free. By choosing to return to India, on Clive's terms, he had abjured the practice of benevolence. He was part of a system which was inimical to the interests of the Indians. He himself recognised this. In a letter to his personal secretary and confidant, Alex Elliot, he wrote, in February 1777: 'In my government I face an endless and a painful choice of evils. *The primary exigencies of the Company conflict with the interests of the Indian peoples who are subject to its authority*' (my italics).[1] That last sentence is a masterly summary of what Company rule in India represented, under the authority of the author of that sentence, Warren Hastings.

As a civilised human being, Warren Hastings might – and did occasionally – spare a sigh for the sufferings of the peoples of India. For example, he gives a moving description of the condition of Benares, after his minions had taken it over. 'From the confines of Buxar to Benares I was followed and fatigued by the clamours of the discontented inhabitants ... complete devastation in every village ... I have reason to believe that the cause existed principally in a defective, if not a corrupt and oppressive administration.' (Quoted in Mill's *History*, Vol IV, p. 355). On this Mill aptly comments: 'The arrangements for the government of Benares were his own; and for the effect of them he was responsible, but he enjoyed a happy faculty of laying the blame at any door rather than his own.') But as Governor-General of Bengal, he was required to satisfy 'the primary exigencies of the Company', by increasing and extending the sufferings of the peoples of India.

The grand system of extortion sometimes involved torture; mostly this arose spontaneously, out of the nature of the system. Hastings did not have to instruct his agents to use torture, if it seemed the only way to get money out of people reported to have some. Hastings's agents – the Indians to whom he farmed out the rents – were not the kind of people who needed such instructions. These agents – like Devi Singh whose atrocities were recounted by Burke (see below, pp. 371–4) – were interested in getting the money, by any means at all, provided the means got the money. Torture was an obvious resource, and they used it. Hastings would tell the House of Lords that he didn't tell anyone to use torture, and he probably didn't in most cases. He just told them to get the money. However, there

[1] Gleig, *Memoirs of Warren Hastings*, Vol. I, p. 184.

is one case with a documented link between Hastings and the use of torture: the case of the eunuchs of the Begums of Oudh.

So far we have conducted our (necessarily cursory) examination of the Hastings regime in India in the abstract, establishing its general nature. The story of the treatment of the eunuchs is a concrete instance, which provides an authentic whiff of the atmosphere of Hastings's India. As we look at the episode we get a bonus, from the nature of our principal narrative source, the fifth edition, edited by H. H. Wilson, of James Mill's ten-volume *History of British India*. This edition has the peculiar characteristic of embodying a series of attacks, by the editor, on large sections of the text he is editing. Almost all these attacks concern Warren Hastings. Mill is severely critical of Hastings, who is a hero to Wilson. After a while, this torrent of editorial expostulation against the text being edited begins to have a comic effect. It put me in mind of a dialogue between a priest and a school teacher, in an old French film:

Priest: 'Joan of Arc heard voices'.
Teacher: 'Joan of Arc *thought* she heard voices' and so on.

Comic effects apart, the reader benefits from this form of editing. The reader is put into the position of a juror, hearing both sides, and deciding on the merits. This is particularly helpful, in forming an opinion on so controversial a figure as Warren Hastings. When Mill produces evidence damaging to Hastings, and Wilson falls silent, we know that the defence has no case.

In January 1775 the Nawab of Oudh died. His son and heir was a minor. Warren Hastings put two of his own agents in charge of the boy with instructions to get him to demand from his mother and grandmother – the Begums of Oude – certain large sums of money they had received from the boy's father. Hastings claimed that, since the Begums were women, their possession of such sums was illegal under Muslim law. (This claim was false. [1]) The boy, having no choice in the matter, did as he was told and demanded the money, which was of course intended for the Company's benefit, not the boy's. The Begums resisted the demand. For a time, for reasons discussed below (see pp. 288–9), Hastings was not in a position to

[1] See Kabir-Ur-Rahman Khan, 'The Impeachment: Certain Issues of International Law'; in Carnall and Nicholson (eds) *The Impeachment of Warren Hastings* (Edinburgh, 1989). Hastings's interested version of Muslim law later became an article of faith for his admirers, such as Penderel Moon and Sir James Fitzjames Stephen.

exert full control. When he recovered it, he imprisoned the two eunuchs, men of business of the Begums. The eunuchs were then subjected to physical pressure, to get them to tell where the money was. Did this pressure amount to torture?

Mill: 'By the torture of one party, money was to be extorted from another. The cruel lessons of Eastern despotism were well acquired by English men'.

Wilson: 'This is quite unauthorised. No person was 'tortured'; and whatever punishments were inflicted were not the acts of Englishmen. Except as guards in the service of the Vizier, they had nothing whatever to do with the proceedings; and the severities adopted were the acts of the Nabob and his ministers. The orders for their enforcement were addressed to the officers on duty through the Resident, but they originated with the Nabob.' (Wilson's certitude that 'no person was tortured' is at variance with his agnosticism regarding 'whatever punishments were inflicted.' The insistence on the legal fiction of 'the independence of the Nabob' is also unattractive.)

Mill: 'To the officers guarding the eunuchs the following letter was addressed by the Resident, dated the 20th. of January, 1782. "Sir, when this note is delivered to you, I have to desire, that you order the two prisoners to be put in irons, keeping them from all food etc, agreeable to my instructions of yesterday (Signed) Nathaniel Middleton."' (Middleton [d.1807] was the Company's Resident at Lucknow, and thus Hastings's personal representative. Wilson does not contest this document's authenticity; his silence confirms it. The failure to expostulate, as he usually does, against the rest of Mill's narrative of this episode has the same implication.)

Mill: 'Before the 23rd. of February 1782, upwards of £500,000 had been received by the Resident for the use of the Company.' (Not contested by Wilson.)

Mill: 'The prisoners were removed to Lucknow, and cruelties inflicted upon them of which the nature is not disclosed, but of which the following letter, addressed by the assistant resident to the commanding officer of the English guard is a disgraceful proof. "Sir, the Nabob having determined to inflict corporal punishment upon the prisoners under your guard, this is to desire that his officers, when they shall have come, may have free access to the prisoners, and be permitted to do with them as they shall see proper".' (Not contested by Wilson. Nor does he comment on Mill's 'disgraceful proof'. Perhaps Wilson felt that, since Middleton's letter refers only to 'corporal punishment', and not to 'torture', it did not conflict with Wilson's earlier assertion that 'No person was tortured'.)

In a minute in answer to charges against Middleton, Hastings accepted full responsibility for Middleton's actions in this matter. Mill quotes the minute: '"I was pointed in my orders to Mr. Middleton, that he should not allow any negotiation *or forbearance* [Mill's italics], when he had once employed the Company's influence or power in asserting the Nabob's claims on the Begums" – Governor General's minute on Mr. Middleton's Defence, 21st. October, 1763.'[1]

It is hard to resist the inference, not only that torture was applied in this instance, in accordance with the spirit of the Governor-General's instructions, but also that torture was a routine resource of his general system of extortion. Yet Hastings's admirers, over the generations, have always resisted any such inference. G. R. Gleig finds no fault with Hastings's ethics: 'But as Mr. Hastings did not direct the means to be used in order to compel the surrender of these funds, so is he free from the responsibility whatever it may be, which attaches to their adoption' (*Memoirs*, Vol. II, 447–8).

When the new Councillors arrived in October 1774, most of the transactions described above were still in the future. But the Councillors had a mandate to inquire into past abuses, and they suspected that evidence of these might be contained in Hastings's correspondence with Middleton. This was a shrewd suspicion, and no doubt originated with Philip Francis, who, as Junius, was well used to investigating abuses. The Council demanded to see all the correspondence. Hastings, who had foreseen this demand, refused – on 17 September he had written to Middleton: 'I desire that you will hereafter make a distinction between such matters contained in your letters as you mean only for my private information and such as you propose, or have no objection to have produced, if required, on record.' (Gleig, *Memoirs*, Vol. 1, p. 447). So two sets of letters, one ostensible, the other real. This sort of thing was common practice in the Company, at every level. The majority in the Council then voted to recall Middleton, and replace him with a nominee of their own, John Bristow (1750–1802). They also began to hear witnesses into the conduct of the Rohilla War, in which Hastings had hired out Company troops to annex the territory of the Rohillas, a people who had been living at peace with Oudh, and with the Company.

---

[1] Mill, *History* Vol. IV, pp. 320; 320 n. 1; 321; 323.

Nominally, the result of the Rohilla War was an expansion of the domains of the Nawab of Oude. Actually, it was an expansion of the territory, beyond Bengal itself, over which Warren Hastings wielded absolute power.

The replacement of Middleton, and the investigation into the Rohilla War, signalled to all political Bengal, both British and Indian, that Hastings was no longer in control. Against that background, Francis and his colleagues, Clavering and Monson, let it be known that their doors were open to people having charges to make against Hastings. By February 1775 Hastings knew that his enemies on the Council were in close touch with an Indian whom he had been making use of in the murky politics of Oudh: 'the principal Theatre of his Iniquities', as Francis called it later. Hastings wrote: 'Nundcomar whom I have this long protected and supported, whom against my nature I have cherished like a serpent, is now in close connection with my adversaries.'[1]

Maharaja Nandakumar (c. 1720–75) was an astute Brahmin of business, whom Hastings at one time opposed, and later used. (He was known to Burke, Hastings and other contemporaries as 'Nunco-mar', the form I shall use here.) Two weeks later, at a meeting of the Council, Francis produced a letter from this Nuncomar containing charges of bribery against Hastings. Nuncomar asked permission to appear before the Council Board to produce evidence in support of his charges. Francis and his associates demanded that Nuncomar be heard. The Governor-General, naturally, declined to submit to this procedure, which would have meant acquiescence in his own trial, in a Council dominated by his enemies. He asked the Council: 'The Chief of this administration, your superior, gentlemen, appointed by the Legislature itself, shall I sit at this board to be arraigned in the presence of a wretch whom you all know to be one of the basest of mankind? I will not.'[2] The Governor-General and his supporter Barwell left the Council Board, while Francis and his colleagues listened to Nuncomar.

For over two centuries Hastings's biographers and other admirers have echoed his indignation at the willingness of Francis and his

---

[1] Letter of 25 February 1775 to the Company's Deputy Chairman, Laurence Sulivan, quoted in Mill, *op. cit.*, Vol. IV, p. 505. Interesting that the same imagery, with regard to Company transactions, is present to the minds of both Burke and Hastings (see above p. 264).

[2] Moon, *Hastings*, p. 153.

allies to listen to such a notorious scoundrel as Nuncomar. [1] Unfortunately for the admirers, this argument has a pronounced tendency to rebound against their hero. If Nuncomar was such a scoundrel, why had Warren Hastings 'long protected and supported him,' cherishing him 'like a serpent'? Hastings had made use of Nuncomar for several purposes, all having extortion as their aim. His principal use for Nuncomar was for the purpose of conducting, in 1772, what Hastings calls 'an enquiry' into the affairs of Mohammad Reza Khan, formerly chief minister of the Nawab of Oudh. Hastings accused this man of embezzlement, and ordered him to be imprisoned. He also ordered an inquiry into Reza Khan's affairs, and put Nuncomar, 'the basest of mankind', in charge of the enquiry. Hastings has left a candid statement of his reasons for doing so. 'It would be superfluous to add other arguments to show the necessity of pressing the enquiry by breaking Reza Khan's influence, removing his dependants, and putting the direction of all the affairs which had been committed to his care, into the hands of the most powerful and active of his enemies.' [2] He added: 'You will be pleased to recollect that the Charge was general, without any Specificates of Time, Places, or Persons. I had neither Witnesses nor Vouchers, nor Materials of any sort to begin with. For these I relied chiefly on the Abilities, Observation, and *active Malignity* of Mahraja Nundcomar' (my italics).

Reza Khan was imprisoned for two years, while the inquiry proceeded. Hastings then declared Reza Khan 'acquitted', for lack of evidence. It may seem odd that an inquiry entrusted by Hastings to Reza Khan's enemy, by reason of the fact that he was his enemy, should fail to come up with evidence that would satisfy Hastings of Reza Khan's guilt. Nuncomar himself, however, had an explanation. The charges were dropped, Nuncomar told Francis and his allies in the Council, because Hastings had taken a bribe to drop the charges. This was the most plausible of Nuncomar's allegations, and indeed hardly anything else could account for the phenomenon of such an 'inquiry', followed by such an 'acquittal'. To use the language of modern extortion, Hastings had 'put the frighteners' on Reza Khan, by setting Nuncomar on him, and it worked. Francis, in setting Nun-

[1] See for example, Moon, *Warren Hastings*, chapter 10, 'Discomfiture of Nandakumar'.

[2] Quoted in Mill, *History*, Vol. III, p. 379. Hastings often wrote in this vein of casual avowal of shocking transactions. If I had to debate with an admirer of Hastings, I could drown the admirer in quotations from his hero.

comar on Hastings, in 1775, was acting in very much the same way. If the word 'scoundrel' is to be used, it should not be confined as it generally is to the Indian partner, alone, in these transactions.

Nuncomar, it seems, had been let down by Hastings, over Reza Khan. Nuncomar was now to be let down by Francis, with lethal effect. Six weeks after he had formulated his charges, he himself was arrested. As Macaulay put it in a famous passage: 'On a sudden, Calcutta was astounded by the news that Nuncomar had been taken up on a charge of felony, committed, and thrown into the common jail. The crime imputed to him was, that six years before he had forged a bond. The ostensible prosecutor was a native. But it was then, and still is, the opinion of every body – idiots and biographers excepted – that Hastings was the real mover in the business' (*Edinburgh Review*, October 1841). There is no evidence that Hastings, personally, took any hand in this matter. He didn't need to. When a native made charges of this kind against the Governor-General, the whole of British India had to close ranks behind their chief, irrespective of what they might feel about him personally. His friends, who were numerous and powerful, intervened on his behalf against Nuncomar, as Lucy Sutherland has shown: 'They assured Nuncomar's private prosecutors that they would have State support for their action, they unofficially advised in the conduct of the case, and privately selected leading Counsel for the Prosecution.'[1] As Owen Dudley Edwards puts it: 'Macaulay overdid matters in calling Hastings "the real mover"; or, he overdid it if we think of Hastings only as a man, and not also as an institution.'[2] The whole weight of this formidable institution now descended to crush the unfortunate Nuncomar, as a deterrent to others: notably Francis and his allies.

The East India Company Act, which had created the new Council, also created a new Bengal Supreme Court, before which Nuncomar was brought for trial. The Chief Justice was Sir Elijah Impey, a friend of Warren Hastings since their schooldays at Westminster. The first critical decision was taken by the Chief Justice, before the trial proper, could open. This concerned the composition of the jury. Owen Dudley Edwards writes: 'Impey certainly had three colleagues on the bench, but as presiding judge he took decisions on which the whole question turned. Counsel for Nandakumar very reasonably

---

[1] L. S. Sutherland, 'New Evidence on the Nandakumar Trial', *English Historical Review*, LXXII (1957) pp. 438–65.

[2] 'Macaulay's Warren Hastings', Geoffrey Carnall and Colin Nicholson (eds), *The Impeachment of Warren Hastings* (Edinburgh, 1989) pp. 130–1; 135.

demanded that his client, who had pleaded not guilty, be tried by a
jury of his peers. Impey replied that a jury of Englishmen met this
requirement, on the ground that "a peer of Ireland tried in England
would be tried by a common jury". It was manifestly an utterly unfair
precedent. Nandakumar was not "in England": he was a Brahmin in
his own country. The Irish precedent was applicable in the context
of Ireland, to which, as in India, English law had been extended. An
Irish peer in 1775 would have been tried in Ireland under English
law as codified by the Irish Parliament with the permission of the
British Parliament, and would have had a jury of his peers. Impey's
precedent in fact showed his intentions. A jury of Brahmins would
have acquitted Nandakumar. He got a jury which would not.'

The second critical decision, also taken by Impey, was that English
law applied in Calcutta, to natives as well as Indians, so that, as
forgery was then a capital offence in England, it was also a capital
offence at Calcutta. A modern legal authority speaks of 'the easy
unconcern with which English law was admitted to India' and holds
that – even assuming the general applicability of English law to the
natives of Calcutta – the particular Act of George II, under which
Nuncomar was tried and convicted, 'was not applicable in India at
all'.[1] So it looks as if the law was being interpreted with a view to
a particular outcome, in a particular case, of immense importance to
all the Company's servants in India.[2]

Stephen's technique was to dwell on Impey's impeccable but essentially irrelevant *obiter dicta*, in the course of the trial, while looking
away from his questionable basic rulings; such as the decision that
an English jury satisfied the requirement of 'trial by his peers', for a
Bengal Brahmin. One of Hastings's more sensible defenders, of the
twentieth century, found the death-sentence on Nuncomar
'indefensible'.[3]

[1] J. D. M. Derrett, 'Nandakumar's Forgery', *English Historical Review*, LXXV
(1960) p. 237.

[2] Hastings's admirers, especially in the late nineteenth century, went to great
pains to contend that Nuncomar got a fair trial, and that Macaulay misrepresented
the whole affair. Sir James Fitzjames Stephen's *The Story of Nuncomar and the
Impeachment of Sir Elijah Impey* (2 vols. London, 1885) is the major effort along
these lines. Sir James's brother, Leslie Stephen, as editor of the *D.N.B.*, supervised
the entry on Warren Hastings which declared that 'the legality of Nuncomar's trial
is thoroughly proved by Sir James Stephen'. Modern scholarship does not sustain
this verdict. P. J. Marshall, in *The Impeachment of Warren Hastings* (Oxford, 1965)
p. 142, n. 2., finds that Stephen's argument to the effect that the prosecution had
no connection with political events 'is no longer tenable'.

[3] Moon, *Warren Hastings*, p. 165.

Once the basic decisions were in – British jury, general applicability of English law, capital punishment for forgery – Nuncomar knew that he was doomed, unless the majority in the Council, who had enticed him to his ruin, would now come to his aid. So Nuncomar sent the Councillors a petition. He also sent a pathetic personal appeal to Francis. Nuncomar's letter, dated 31 July 1775, begins: 'Most Worshipful Sir, – In the perilous and unhappy circumstances I am now reduced to at present, [I doubt not but what you are acquainted with.] I am now thinking I have but a short time to live.' It ends: 'As I entirely rely on your worship's endeavour to do me all the good you can, I shall not, according to the opinion of the Hindoos, accuse you in the day of Judgment of neglecting to assist me in the extremity I am now in.' [1]

We know that Francis opened the private letter, for it is preserved in his letter-book. But he did not open the petition. Instead, he sent it to be burned by the common hangman, and allowed it to be known that he had treated it in this way. And Nuncomar himself, thus abandoned, was now, as Hastings commented, 'in a fair way to be hanged.' [2] G. R. Gleig says that the majority in the Council 'might have suspended the execution [of Nuncomar] till a reference should be made to the Court of Directors (of the Company) at home.' [3] Gleig goes on to speculate that the Majority may have let the execution go ahead in order to use it later, to discredit Hastings. A simpler explanation (favoured by Owen Dudley Edwards) is that Francis and his colleagues were afraid for their lives, as they had reason to be. Any intervention in the Nuncomar case – even an attempt at a stay of execution – would be likely to be construed by the Impey court as contempt of court and interference with due process. A jail sentence would follow. A term in a Calcutta jail, guarded by the agents of Warren Hastings, was not an attractive prospect for Philip Francis. Francis was in deadly danger. In the following year Lord Pigot, who was a threat to the interests of Paul Benfield in the Carnatic as Francis was to Hastings in Bengal, was to be thrown into jail in Madras where he died less than a year later. Francis, facing the combination of Hastings and Impey, knew that his only hope was to send out, to all of British India, an unmistakable signal that he had abandoned Nuncomar to his fate, and was no

[1] Quoted in Sir James Stephen's *Story of Nuncomar* (London, 1885) Vol. I, pp. 234–5; also quoted in Parke and Merivale, *Memoirs of Francis*, Vol. II, p. 37.
[2] Gleig, *Memoirs*, Vol. I, p. 521.
[3] *Memoirs*, Vol. II, p. 4.

longer a threat to the power of Warren Hastings. Francis sent this signal, by letting it be known that he had handed over Nuncomar's petition to the common hangman. As Owen Dudley Edwards neatly puts it: 'Junius had no interest in posthumous publication.'[1]

As for Nuncomar, he was duly found guilty by his British jury, and duly sentenced to death by Sir Elijah Impey. The sentence was carried out immediately. For good measure, and in case anyone should miss the point, the defence witnesses, who were all Indians, were all prosecuted for perjury.

Hastings's familiars, in their private communications, made no secret of the connection between Nuncomar's death, and the stopping of the mouths of Hastings's accusers. John Stewart, Secretary of Bengal and a member of Hastings's official 'family', comparing Hastings's accusers to the *Delatores* (the denouncers/informers of Nero's reign) wrote: 'I do not . . . really believe the *Delatores* will come out very thick till they see how [Nuncomar's] ears hang on his head, that is to say, if he is not hung up head and tail and ears and all before the other is decided.'[2] 'The other' being, of course the charges against Hastings.

Stewart was writing before Nuncomar's execution. After the execution, another enthusiastic Hastings supporter wrote: 'With the life of [Nuncomar] has ended the prevalent spirit of informants and the litigants: the Blacks know not which way to look; everyone cautious and reserved. The change which the execution has worked is easily perceived and felt [by] the different ranks of the inhabitants in this settlement – and I hope they may continue in their timid disposition.'[3] Or, as Burke put it years afterwards: 'Mr. Hastings observes, that no man in India complains of him. It is generally true. The voice of India is stopped. All complaint was strangled with the same cord that strangled Nuncomar.'[4]

Burke and his friends, in 1787, tried to get the Commons to impeach Impey, but the attempt failed. Even more than the case against Hastings – which of course succeeded in the Commons – the case against Impey depended on legal interpretation. The lawyers in the House were naturally inclined to exonerate Impey, who had

[1] Carnall and Nicholson (eds) *Impeachment*, p. 136.
[2] Quoted in Lucy Sutherland, 'New Evidence in the Nandakuma Trial', in *Politics and Finance in the Eighteenth Century* (London, 1984) pp. 244–5.
[3] E. Sherwin to J. Graham, 25 August 1775, quoted in Marshall, *Impeachment*, p. 141.
[4] *Works* X, 30: speech in opening the Impeachment.

presided over the trial with a satisfactory appearance of decorum. Burke was censured by the Commons, years after the acquittal, for having said: 'Warren Hastings murdered Nuncomar by the hands of Sir Elijah Impey.'

The censure of the Commons has worn less well, after more than two hundred years, than Edmund Burke's eleven-word summary of the effect of Nuncomar's end.[1]

* * *

A less determined character than Philip Francis would have left India shortly after that decisive defeat, in the Nuncomar matter. But he stayed on for a further six years, even though he soon lost his only institutional asset, the majority on the Council. The death of Colonel Monson (25 September 1775) meant that the division in the Council was now 2-2, the issue being then resolved, in Hastings's favour, by Hastings's casting vote. Opposition to Hastings was now quite hopeless. Francis now offered a show of co-operation. Hastings accepted this, for some years, though of course he didn't trust Francis: 'Even the apparent levity of [Francis's] ordinary behaviour is but a cloak to deception.'[2] Yet, if Francis was willing to stay, accepting Hastings's dominant position, Hastings had good reason for not refusing this in the 1770s. His enemies, who had provided him with that hostile majority on Council, were still in the ascendant in North's Administration. The return of Francis, bearing a credible account of recent transactions, might well precipitate the recall of Warren Hastings. So why didn't Francis return, in 1775–6, and bring down Hastings that way? I suspect that the answer to that one lies in the Junius story. If, as I believe, there was a deal, through which he got a seat in the Council in exchange for silence, then it seems likely that a part of the deal would be an undertaking by him to remain in India, for a set period of years. To break that undertaking might be dangerous: there are, after all other ways of dealing with a blackmailer who, after being bought off, fails to adhere to the terms on which he was bought off.

[1] Impey was a stickler for decorum, and the pains he had taken in that regard continued to impress one late-Victorian commentator: 'Nuncomar's trial began before an English jury on June 8th., and lasted until the 16th; the heat must have been at its maximum in Calcutta, yet the judges wore their heavy wigs continually, that no forms might be wanting.' Sir Alfred Lyall, *Warren Hastings* (London 1883) p. 66.
[2] *Memoirs*, Vol. II, p. 224.

So Francis stayed on, in most uneasy subordination to Warren Hastings. Hastings probably knew that Francis, throughout that period, was enlarging a dossier for use against him. Presumably he thought that the longer Francis remained in India, the longer it would be before the dossier could be used against him. But after five years of this, and some symptoms of renewed intrigue by Francis, Hastings decided to provoke a duel, kill Francis if he could, and if not, frighten him into going home. The method chosen shows that Hastings was a man of honour, according to the standards of his place and time. The code of honour covered relations between gentlemen. Unlike Francis and Hastings, Mohammad Reza Khan and Nuncomar were not gentlemen, being Orientals, though they were persons of high status within their own societies, Muslim and Hindu respectively. During the ten years from Nuncomar's death to Hastings's resignation in 1785, Hastings was absolute master of British India, with agents at his disposal, who were accustomed to carry out his wishes, without hesitation or scruple. He could have arranged for the 'accidental' or 'natural' death of Philip Francis, without the slightest risk either to his person or to his official position. So the course he actually chose, the provocation of a duel, was an honourable one, in the circumstances. [1]

The occasion of the duel was an adverse vote by Philip Francis in the Council when, thanks to the temporary absence of Hastings's faithful Barwell, and Francis's influence over a new member, Wheler, Francis had briefly once more a majority in the Council. Hastings believed that Francis's vote violated an agreement entered into between the two men in the previous year. The sequel is well told by Sir Alfred Lyall, who clearly had access to the recollections of eye-witnesses: 'Hastings unquestionably believed that he had been tricked, and took his measures characteristically. He conveyed his wife to Chinsurah, at a short distance from Calcutta, and returning alone sent to the Council, a minute redolent with the bitterness and resentment distilled out of their long personal altercations. "But in truth", he said, "I do not trust to [Francis's] promise of candour;

---

[1] I am not sure that Hastings would never, in any circumstances, have given the nod for the murder of an inconvenient English gentleman. I have sometimes wondered about the deaths of Colonel Monson and General Clavering, Philip Francis's fellow-members of what was once the majority in the Council. Both died in India, and both deaths were convenient to Hastings. But both may well have died natural deaths. Englishmen often did meet untimely deaths in India, because of the climate, in the eighteenth century.

convinced that he is incapable of it, and that his sole purpose and wish are to embarrass and defeat every measure which I may undertake, or which may tend even to promote the public interests, if my credit is connected with them. Such has been the tendency and such the manifest spirit of all his actions from the beginning; almost every measure proposed by me has for that reason had his opposition to it. When carried against his opposition, and too far engaged to be withdrawn, yet even then and in every stage of it his labours to overcome it have been unremitted; every disappointment and misfortune have been aggravated by him, and every fabricated tale of armies devoted to famine and to massacre have found their first and most ready way to his office, where it is known they would meet with most welcome reception. To the same design may be attributed the annual computations of declining finances and an exhausted treasury; computations which though made in the time of abundance, must verge to earth at last, from the effect of a discordant government, not a constitutional decay. To the same design shall I attribute the policy of accelerating the boded event, and creating an artificial want, by keeping up a useless hoard of treasure and withholding it from a temporary circulation."

'Then came the homicidal provocation: "I judge of his public conduct by my experience of his private, which I have found void of truth and honour. This is a severe charge, but temperately and deliberately made."

'These words produced the effect intended; for after the meeting of Council at which the minute was read, Francis drew Hastings aside and read him a written challenge, which was accepted. 'On the second day following they met at a spot still well remembered in Calcutta tradition, taking ground at a distance of fourteen paces, measured out by Colonel Watson, one of the seconds, who said that Charles Fox and Adams had fought (1779) at that distance; although Hastings observed that it was a great distance for pistols. The seconds had baked the powder for their respective friends, nevertheless Francis' pistol missed fire. Hastings waited until he had primed again and had missed, when he returned the shot so effectively that Francis was carried home with a ball in his right side. The remarkable coolness of Hastings was noticed; he objected to the spot first proposed as being overshadowed by trees; and probably those were right who inferred from his behaviour that he intended to hit his man. That the single English newspaper then published in Calcutta should have made no mention of so sensational an incident as the Governor-General's duel, is good evidence of the kind of censorship then maintained over the Bengal press. But the editor had recently been in jail for a smart lampoon upon Hastings and Impey, a formidable pair of magnates to cut scandalous jokes upon in those days.' [1]

Elsewhere in his book, Lyall declared himself convinced by Sir Leslie Stephen's 'vindication' of Hastings's innocence in relation to Nuncomar. But Lyall's aside at the end of the above passage is telling us something different. 'The duel served Hastings well, since it removed the last and strongest of the three adversaries against whom he had been contending in Council since 1774. Such a mode of dealing with political opponents may be thought questionable; but governors and high officials of that period had to be as ready with the pistol as with the pen, for a challenge was often the resource not only of irritated rivals but of disappointed subordinates. Fox had met Adams, and Lord Shelburne, Colonel Fullerton; Lord Macartney was called out by General Stuart to account at twelve paces for some censure which he had passed on the general during his Madras governorship; and Sir John Macpherson, who held the Governor-Generalship for a time after Hastings, met an offended Major Brown in Hyde Park. Hastings sent Francis a friendly message, offering to visit him; but Francis declined any private intercourse with his adversary, and some months later he returned to England, where he prosecuted his feud against Hastings with pertinacious and inveterate malignity.'

Although Hastings knew that Francis was going home 'to prosecute his feud', he doesn't seem to have been worried about this. He probably thought his political position in London at this time too strong to be shaken by the likes of Philip Francis. This was a reasonable assumption, in 1780. Hastings's position had been alarmingly shaky, in the mid-1770's, when the North Administration sent him out those three hostile Councillors. But his political fortunes recovered dramatically in London, from 1778 on. This was entirely because of the dramatic weakening in Britain's world position, after Burgoyne's defeat at Saratoga, followed by the French alliance with America (see Chapter II above, pp. 171–2). As Gleig puts it: 'The minister who had lost America, did not care to risk the loss of India likewise, and therefore sought to represent matters as great and pros-

---

[1] Sir Alfred Lyall, *Warren Hastings* (London, 1889) pp. 110–2.

perous there by way of a counterpoise to the evils which had over-
taken the nation elsewhere.'[1]

Gleig's point is well taken, but there was more involved than Lord
North's public relations. From 1779 on, the loss of India was a real
threat, together with the loss of America. The French hoped that,
through a confederation of Indian military princes against the British,
they themselves might recover the position they had lost in India
more than twenty years before. The government was in no position
to send help to India. British shores were threatened with a French
invasion and Britain had almost lost control of Ireland. Hastings was
on his own. Whether or not Britain was to retain its hegemony in
India depended on him.

As Francis had found, Hastings was at his ruthless best, when in
a tight corner. He responded to the crisis created by the degenerating
American war, by going on the offensive in India, against the major
remaining native Indian military force, the Mahratta confederacy,
with its centre at Poona, in Western India.[2] Hastings chose his
military commanders well, and instructed them as to their objectives
with a lucidity not often found, in history, in relations between political leaders and military executants. In their terseness and clarity, his
military dispatches recall the style of Julius Caesar. Like Caesar, he
was also lucky. All his operations were successful and, by the time
he had done, there was no longer any military opposition to British
power in India. An important ingredient in Hastings's really formidable military success was his experience and skill as an extortionist.
That is how he raised the money to win the wars; no money was
forthcoming, or to be expected, from home; the traffic was always
the other way in the eighteenth century.

There is an honest case to be made for Warren Hastings, as distinct
from the more-or-less fraudulent ones advanced by H. H. Wilson,
the Stephen brothers, Monckton Jones and others. The honest case,
never publicly advanced, but always powerfully present – and near
the surface in Hastings's more sensible defenders, such as Lyall and

[1] *Memoirs*, Vol. II p. 469. Gleig, though he could be obtuse enough about his
hero's defects, was not the all-round figure of fun that Macaulay made him out to
be, in his *Edinburgh Review* essay.

[2] Francis, who had advised a defensive posture, because of the British Empire's
general weakness, as a result of the American war, convinced Burke that the Mahratta war was one of Hastings's crimes, and as a result this war was among the
charges in the impeachment of Hastings. As, by that time, the Mahratta war had
been won, and British India 'saved' thereby, the 'Mahratta' charge was the weakest
feature in the impeachment of Warren Hastings.

Moon – runs: 'He saved India, and to do that he had to raise the money. We don't give a damn *how* he raised the money, or what he may have done to the bloody Indians in the process. What matters is that he saved India *for us*.' What is astonishing is that Burke, with his very different ideas of what 'saving India' might mean, was able to carry the Hastings impeachment through the Commons, against the powerful undertow of that unpublicised argument. The Lords acquittal, essentially on the basis of that argument, is not surprising. But carrying the impeachment through the Commons is a strange business, and has to do with the strangeness of Edmund Burke.

We shall be looking at that later. But in 1781, while Francis was sailing home, no thought of impeachment could have crossed Hastings's mind. He had done the State some service, and he thought they knew it. North's Administration had made its peace with him in the East India Act of 1781 reappointing him, by name, as Governor-General. Hastings's achievement was, in some ways, greater than that of Clive. Clive had prevailed, at a period of unparalleled universal triumph for British arms, both in the Old World and the New. But Hastings had held out in the Old World, while the New World was being lost. At the nadir of England's imperial fortunes, he alone could show a record of victory. He had a right to look forward with confidence to a peerage, which had been Clive's reward, and then to a position, such as Clive's had been, of uncontested authority in England over Indian affairs.

That Francis could do him out of all that, and have him put on trial instead, would have been inconceivable to him. He believed he had taken the measure of Francis, when Nuncomar's petition was handed over to the common hangman. But Hastings had yet to take the measure of the ally Francis was about to enlist. I believe that, if Hastings could have foreseen what the conjuncture of Francis and Burke would do to him, Francis would not have been allowed to leave the India of which Hastings was absolute master. Francis would have left his bones in India, along with those of his former allies in the Council, Colonel Monson and General Clavering. As it was, he was able to sail from Calcutta towards his fateful rendezvous with Burke. Francis landed at Dover on 18 October 1781.

BURKE AND FRANCIS
1781–1785

Burke and Junius were not made to be soul-mates, not by any means. Burke was only eleven years older than Francis, but the gap between the two was much wider, in terms of outlook. Burke had grown up in the first half of the century, when Montesquieu and Locke were in the ascendant, and Enlightenment was felt to be fully compatible with tolerant forms of Christianity. Burke's Christian faith – though its exact form may be debated – was of profound importance to him. It underlay his thoughts and feelings about India, as is seen in the epigraph to this chapter, with its reference to Indians who are 'the images of the great Pattern.'

Francis, in contrast, had matured in the second half of a century of exceptionally rapid and momentous ideological change. He belonged to the militant Voltairean phase of the Enlightenment, contemptuous of Christianity. So contemptuous indeed as to call it 'priestianity', not a coinage to endear him to Burke, had it been used in his presence. [1] The religious difference did not prevent a close and long working alliance between the two men, over India, but it did operate, together with moral and political differences, to prevent the alliance from developing into a genuine friendship, despite efforts on both sides to make it so.

The moral gap between the two was related to the religious one. There are deists who, while rejecting the supernatural part of Christianity, cling to the ethical side. Francis was not a deist of that kind. He was what his French contemporaries called a *libertin*: a person so enlightened as to be superior to moral considerations. Junius, certainly, behaved as if he thought of himself in this way. Politically too, the differences are important. Junius had opposed the repeal of the Stamp Act, and therefore the whole Rockingham policy towards America, a matter of the greatest consequence to Burke. Even worse, Junius was 'school of Shelburne'; so close indeed that a modern scholar (C. W. Everett, editor of the 1927 *Letters of Junius*) believed that Shelburne actually was Junius. And Shelburne, for Burke, was an embodiment of evil, on a par with Warren Hastings himself. (Appropriately, Shelburne ordered a bust of Hastings, with an

---

[1] 'Early impressions in Lisbon explain Francis's hatred of superstition and priestly domination.' Parkes and Merivale, *Memoirs* Vol. I, p. 157.

inscription commemorative of the ingratitude of his countrymen, to
be set up in Lansdowne House.) [1]

Despite these weighty differences between Burke and Francis, a
powerful and complex emotional bond, less than friendship, but also
more, developed between them in the matter of punishing Warren
Hastings. Contemporaries didn't think so. They thought that Francis
was coldly manipulating, for his own ends, Burke's genuine indignation about the oppression of Indians. This opinion of the comparative motivations of the two men crystallised in two Commons
decisions, when the Managers of the Impeachment of Warren Hastings were being chosen in 1787. When Burke was proposed as Chief
Manager, the House did not divide; the choice was unanimous. But
when Burke then nominated Francis, as a member of his Impeachment team, his name was rejected by a large majority, much to
Burke's dismay, and Francis's mortification. In reality, their motivations were more similar than contemporaries supposed. The Francis
who had returned from India is no longer altogether the cool and
calculating Junius, but also a tormented, driven man, a man with a
mission. Contemporaries might see him as bent on revenge for personal injuries, but that is not how he saw himself. How he saw
himself appears in an extraordinary passage in a letter, written about
a month after his return from India, to his friend Sir John Day:
'Nuncomar is returned and, like Caesar's ghost with Ate by his side,
is now raging for revenge.' [2]

This suggests a soul in pain. He had brought back with him to
England Nuncomar's letter to him with its desperate appeal, and the
implicit contingent curse, in its last sentence (see above p. 293). If we
can imagine the real Nuncomar returning, and looking for revenge, it
is certainly on Francis, not Hastings, that he would wish to be
revenged. Nuncomar had attacked Hastings, and could hardly blame
him for striking back. But Francis had incited Nuncomar to take the
bold step that was to lead to his destruction. Then, when Nuncomar,
in the toils, called on Francis for help, Francis had not merely declined
to help, but spurned his appeal in the most spectacular fashion
imaginable.

Francis's conduct had been so outrageous as to arouse feelings of
guilt even in the bosom of Junius. His imagination copes with the
guilt by turning himself into the man he had incited and betrayed,

---

[1] Fitzmaurice, *Shelburne* II, 386.
[2] *Memoirs of Francis* Vol. II, p. 213; letter of 24 November 1781.

and then portraying that man as in quest of revenge on Warren Hastings. Not on Philip Francis, not at all –

Thou canst not say I did it.

The common factor, between Burke and Francis, over Hastings, is a genuine indignation, which is partly fuelled by a sense of personal guilt. Burke of course had not betrayed any individual, but he seems to have felt that he had betrayed the Indians collectively, through following the Rockinghams' party line, supportive of the Company, up to 1773. He may well have felt guiltier about this abstract offence than Francis felt about Nuncomar. Burke's conscience was a far more exigent force than Francis's can ever have been. Francis, while in India, had not shown any concern over the oppression of Indians. But once back in England, and clothed in the imagined robes of Nuncomar, he is in the grip of a genuine indignation, which feeds Burke's indignation. Francis knew the Indian system of extortion very well – he had been near the heart of it – and he is now 'debriefed' on it by Burke.

On India, Burke and Francis (who was no longer quite Junius, but had turned partly into Nuncomar) were in total sympathy. In the pursuit of Warren Hastings, they worked in concert, and with unbroken harmony, for the next nine years, until the impact of the French Revolution disrupted their personal relationship. Even after that they continued to collaborate on the Impeachment. But the relationship was always a somewhat strained one, when anything other than India was in question. There is something in Burke's surviving 'sociable' letters to Francis that sets the teeth on edge. The tone is different from anything else in Burke's correspondence. There is a touch of effusiveness, an affected jocularity, even in one or two letters, an affectation of rakishness, most uncharacteristic of him, and unbecoming to him. It is as if he is trying to take his tone from Francis, and not managing to bring it off.

I believe he was always distastefully aware that Francis was Junius, but that he tried to suppress that awareness, for the sake of the invaluable partnership, over India. The awareness shows, in the forced cordiality of these letters. Burke sensed that he was yoked, for a particular purpose, with an alien spirit. Significantly, the first sign that he knows that Francis is Junius comes only in the letter that breaks off their friendship – or attempted friendship – in 1790 (see below Chapter VI).

Even the partnership over India, well as it worked, has something disturbing about it. There is a hint of *folie à deux* in the shared guilt, and the compulsion to project all of it onto the person of Warren Hastings. Yet it is, at worst, no more than a hint. Curiosity about motivations should not obscure the fact that the system of extortion against which Burke and Francis campaigned so indefatigably really did exist in India, and that it was Hastings who presided over it, ably and ruthlessly. Burke, aided by Francis, did far more than anybody else to bring that system to an end; and also to establish the accountability of the rulers of India, and the principle that the welfare of its natives was a criterion of government. These were great public services and it took a quite extraordinary expenditure of energy to bring them about. It may be that so much energy could not have been generated without the driving force of guilt. Roger Casement who, in the early twentieth century, was to do for the Congo very much what Edmund Burke did for India in the eighteenth, was also a driven man.

*　　　*　　　*

As was seen in the first section of this chapter, Burke fell silent over Indian affairs in 1773, after that series of increasingly uncomfortable, guilt-ridden speeches in defence of the East India Company. He returned to Indian affairs in 1777, in a new situation, which had greatly relaxed the Rockingham inhibition about interference with the Company's affairs.

In 1775 the East India Company, in one of its periodical fits of attempting to restrain the excesses of its 'servants' in India, sent out Lord Pigot as Governor of Madras, with instructions of a reformist tendency. Pigot (1719–1777; he was the first baron of that name) was instructed to restore the Rajah of Tanjore to his territories, which had been annexed in 1773 in the name of the Nawab of the Carnatic (also known as 'the Nabob of Arcot'). The restoration of the Rajah of Tanjore was a perilous undertaking, comparable to setting Nuncomar on Warren Hastings. The Company's system worked in essentially the same way in the Carnatic, the region around Madras, as it did in Bengal. The Nawab of the Carnatic was as powerless as the Nawab of Oudh. In the Carnatic, as in Oudh, real power was in the hands of Europeans, who used their power for the purposes of extortion, and extended the supposed domains of the Nawab, so as to widen the basis of their system of extortion. In the Carnatic, the practitioners and beneficiaries of this system were the majority on Lord Pigot's Council, a group of speculators led by the notorious Paul Benfield (c. 1740–1810), who amassed one of the largest fortunes ever brought home from India.

Benfield and his friends saw Pigot's instructions over Tanjore as a threat to their interests. So, on 24 August 1776, they had Pigot seized by Company troops and thrown into jail in Madras, where he died two years later. In Madras, as in Bengal, the Company's 'servants' in India wielded more power than their putative masters, the Court of Directors, in Leadenhall Street, in London. When news of this event reached Britain, the Rockinghams began to organise a campaign for the release and rehabilitation of Lord Pigot, who had been a political supporter of theirs (his brother, Admiral Hugh Pigot, was a leading associate). Burke eagerly joined in this campaign. Yet, although the Rockinghams had changed course, it appeared that they did not wish to acknowledge that they had done so. In his 'Speech on Restoring Lord Pigot' (22 May 1777) Burke still pays lip-service to the old policy: 'Far from meaning to take away I mean to strengthen the authority of the Company – to preserve respect to its orders obedience to its Governors: Honesty in its Councils, and discipline in its armies, not to subject her to ministerial jobs, but to take her out of the bondage of Court Cabals'. However, while putting on record the formal continuity of policy, Burke was discreetly logging the actual change of course: 'I wished to see the Company free from Court influence that it might always be under publick Control.'[1]

The key words are 'public control'. Favoured by the new situation, Burke has managed to get back to the policy he had adopted – following Clive – five years before, but had been forced to abandon. The continuity of purpose, under difficult conditions is remarkable and it is matched by the deft and conciliatory style of execution. The Rockinghams are being turned around, while being encouraged to bask in the contemplation of their own consistency. There was one aspect that remained continuous: the emphasis on *Court influence, Court Cabals*. This was a Rockingham 'tenet' to which Burke was strongly attached. Nor – *pace* Sir Lewis Namier and his school – was it a fanciful tenet. The personal influence of George III, exercised mainly through his confidential political agents, Charles Jenkinson and John Robinson, was a potent force in the affairs of the Company, as well as in Parliament itself. Burke and his friends would feel the

[1] *Writings and Speeches* V, 36.

full weight of that influence, to their discomfiture, in 1783–4 (see below, pp. 330–336).

In general, Burke never abandoned his concern about 'Court influence'. But as soon as he had made up his mind about Indian affairs, he ceased to put a primary emphasis on Court influence. He had come to see that the immediate oppressors of India were not at Court or even in England, but in India itself. In 1777, however, he was still quite far from having made up his mind and seen his way clear. He knew the general direction in which he wished to proceed – 'publick control' – but that was about all. And the situation was now complicated by the appearance on the Indian scene, of his kinsman and close friend, Will Burke. Will was a goose whom Edmund took for a swan. He was not without abilities, and he seems to have been good company, and beloved by all the Burkes, but he was forever thinking up schemes and speculations which always ended in disaster. Edmund so doted on him that he backed him up in all his undertakings, to the misfortune of both Burkes.

Will now determined to go to India, to repair his shattered fortunes. He went out as the bearer of a message from Admiral Pigot to his imprisoned brother. This was not the most promising introduction, for the purposes of making money, in a Carnatic dominated by Lord Pigot's jailers. By the time Will Burke reached Madras, Lord Pigot was already dead, but Will did get to see the Rajah of Tanjore and was appointed by him as his agent in London. (Presumably he got some money for this, but it cannot have been much. The Rajah, like Will himself, was a loser.) As Warren Hastings backed 'the Nawab of the Carnatic' – which is to say, Paul Benfield – against the Rajah of Tanjore, it has inevitably been suggested that Burke's hostility to Hastings was a result of the financial interests of his kinsman. This is dismissed by modern scholarship.[1] But in the late 1770s, before Burke had identified Warren Hastings as his quarry, he was certainly affected by concern for Will's interests. He collaborated with him in preparing a curious and rather regrettable pamphlet, *The Policy of making Conquests for the Mahometans*.[2] There was no

[1] See, for example, *Corr*. V, 203–4, n. 6. There is also a theory that Burke's anger against Hastings and the Company was dictated by anger at the Burke loss of money in the 1769 crash of Company stocks. This is refuted by Burke's post-1769 speeches in which he continues to defend the Company, and even protests against the 'blackening' of Warren Hastings (see above pp. 262–7). But one should not spend too much time on swatting these pullulating insects of trivialising calumny.

[2] *Writings and Speeches* V, 41–124.

such policy; as Burke was soon to realise, the conquests in question were all planned by Britons, for their own benefit. The religious affiliations of the various native princes involved were irrelevant. I believe that this pamphlet was essentially Will Burke's, as part of his job as agent to the Rajah of Tanjore, and that Edmund, out of friendship, helped him to get his inadequate notions into more presentable shape.

Poor Will seems to have had some realisation that he was only getting in Edmund's way. In a letter to Edmund's son Richard he expressed dismay at the rumours that Edmund's Indian exertions were motivated by concern for Will's interests. 'Oh my God', he wrote, 'there is something sad and at the same time ridiculous, that the foreign papers . . . should consider me as the spur and motive of your father's Eastern exertions, when in fact, his alarms for me, are the only stay or reserve that hangs on his mind, in that noble walk of his.'[1]

By early 1781, well before Philip Francis's return, Burke was already beginning to grasp the nature of the system of extortion in India. The focus of his attention was still Madras, and not yet Bengal; but the system, in both places, was essentially the same. In October 1780, Burke had acquired a £1,000 holding of East Indian Company Stock, the minimum required for a vote in the Court of Proprietors, the supreme body in the affairs of the Company (it could overrule the Court of Directors, the executive body). Burke acquired the holding in order to have a say in the deliberations of the Court of Proprietors in the matter of Paul Benfield. Benfield had been recalled as a result of the scandal over Lord Pigot's death, and was now seeking reinstatement. When the Court of Proprietors met to consider the case, on 17 January 1781, Burke presented 17 'Heads of Objection' to Benfield. The first three charges read:

'That a Dealing by the Company's Servants in Money transactions with the Country Powers in India hath been prohibited by strict and repeated Orders from the Court of Directors and hath been productive of Mischievous consequences to the Revenues of the Company to those of the Country Powers in Alliance with the Company to the Trade, prosperity, population and safety of the Countries on the Coast of Coromandel.

[1] Marshall, *Impeachment*, p. 5. It's interesting that Will could see the nobility of the walk, because he himself had no sympathy at all with those for whose benefit the walk was undertaken. He told Richard Burke that he could not 'for the soul of me', feel as Edmund did about 'the black primates' (letter of 30 December 1785).

2nd. That Paul Benfield Esquire appears to have been a dealer in Money transactions, to an enormous extent, with one of the Country Powers in India, contrary to the Letter and spirit of the Company's Orders.

3rd. That the immense Magnitude of the Sums alleged by him to be due as aforesaid in the Year 1775 to the said Paul Benfield, furnishes a just Cause to doubt, whether the Money (if really advanced as pretended) could be acquired by lawful means, considering Mr. Benfield's Rank in the Service, the nature of his Trade, and the time of his residence in India.'

Burke tried to have witnesses examined in support of the charges, but the Court of Proprietors decided, by 109 votes to 90, not to hear witnesses. Burke protested against: 'sending Mr. Benfield again to India with such charges upon him, and refusing so much as to hear the grounds of those charges that had a tendency to drive thirty or forty millions of distressed people into absolute despair.' The Court decided to put the question of Benfield's reinstatement to a ballot of the shareholders. 'With the [North] government urging its supporters to vote for him, Benfield won his reinstatement by 368 votes to 302.'[1]

Defeated at Company level, Burke now threw himself into parliamentary investigation of India – Bengal indeed was now the focus of parliamentary interest. On 15 January 1781, North set up a Select Committee of the House to consider a number of petitions from Bengal. Government supporters were not interested in unprofitable things like petitions from Bengal, and the Select Committee consisted mostly of Opposition members. Burke joined it immediately, and soon came to dominate its proceedings. Three of the Committee's Reports are believed to have been written by him, including the Ninth Report on the economic exploitation of India and the Eleventh Report (November 1783), which is an indictment of Warren Hastings, over his acceptance of bribes. The establishment of the Select Committee is therefore an important stage in the long process that was to lead to the impeachment of Warren Hastings.

On 23 March we find Burke writing to Sir Thomas Rumbold, Lord Pigot's successor as Governor of Madras:

I feel, as a Member of this Community, and as a Member of the Community of Mankind at large, your Merit in discountenancing, as I under-

---

[1] *Writings and Speeches* V, 125–6, 132 editorial note.

stand you have done, the present ruinous Maratta War; and I shall ever acknowledge it as a publick Service. In condemning the perverse policy which led to that War, and which had before given rise to the still less justifiable War against the Rohillas, I do not speak from the smallest degree of prejudice or personal animosity against the respectable person (for such in many particulars he undoubtedly is) who was so unhappy as to be the author of both these Measures. I rather gave him my little Voice as long as I thought it justifiable to afford him the smallest degree of support. I was always an Admirer of his Talents; and the farthest in the World from being engaged in a faction against him. [1]

Most Englishmen would see the Mahratta War as a glorious episode in Hastings's career: through his complete victory, he ended serious native resistance to British rule in India, and so denied any possible foothold for the hostile French. Warren Hastings had, quite simply, 'saved India'. But 'Saving India' for Burke meant something quite different: having to do with the welfare of the Indian people. Burke, unfortunately for Hastings, did not contemplate Indian affairs with the feelings of a proper Englishman. Already, by April 1781, there are signs that, at a deep level in Burke's psyche, Ireland and India are beginning to fuse into one. His horror at the oppression of the Indians, and his horror at the oppression of the Irish Catholics became one horror. The tell-tale sign is a compulsive resort, in Indian speeches, to the imagery of physical corruption: the imagery which had dominated his Guildhall speech of 1780 on the Irish Penal Laws. This imagery, in relation to India, first appears in a speech on the establishment of a Secret Committee on Indian affairs. Burke attacks the idea of secrecy:

> Secrets of inefficacy, of treachery, or of corruption, were the bane of governments. He never knew of a state that had been ruined by the openness of its system; by its readiness to search into its distempers, and to lay bare its wounds; but he had heard and read of many that had been ruined by the timorous secrecy of their proceedings, by the concealments which they observed in their inferior branches and dependencies; by which corruption and disease were suffered to gather head, until, when they burst into eruptions, they were too formidable for remedy, and withstood all the powers of physic.

And again, later in the speech:

[1] *Corr.* IV, 344–45.

These are the mere pustules, the eruptions on the skin, and while you are intent on the examination of these, you neglect the real seat of the disease, which is in the blood, from the corruption of which these appearances have their rise. [1]

The appearance of this particular imagery, which recurs in later Burke speeches on India (see, for example, the great speech on the Nabob of Arcot's debts, below pp. 341–351) is a signal that Burke is now emotionally committed to the Indian cause, through a horror which has Irish, as well as Indian, sources. From now on, he will allow nothing to deflect him from his pursuit of those responsible for the oppression of India. Significantly, it is in this same speech where the imagery of physical corruption first occurs in an Indian context, that Burke gives his first hint that he is about to attack Hastings: 'Let us enter on this enquiry with a determined spirit to screen no delinquent from punishment, however high.'

In June–July 1781, he was able to carry through Parliament a major piece of Indian legislation, the Bengal Judicature Bill, designed to restrict the use of English law in Bengal. The occasion for it had been the extension – by Elijah Impey, in collusion with Hastings – of English law over the natives of Bengal. This was greatly resented, and gave rise to the petitions which had led to the creation of the Select Committee. The Committee, on 8 May, had reported adversely on the consequences of the extension of English làw. Burke, speaking on the Bill in Parliament on 27 June, 1781, said: 'The House had, in the report of the committee, an account of the proceedings of those Judges. They were arbitrary in the extreme. The incroachments which they made on the most sacred privileges of the people, the violation of their dearest rights, particularly in forcing the ladies before their courts; the contempt that was shown for their religious ceremonies and mysteries; and the cruel punishments inflicted upon them in case of their disobedience; new, strange, and obnoxious to them; all these things contributed in fact, to compel the British legislature to restore peace, order, and unanimity to the extensive territories of India, by giving them the laws which they approved.'

Burke went on to identify a common principle, applicable to the governance of countries as different from one another as the American colonies and India: 'We had suffered enough in attempting to enervate the system of a country, and we must now be guided as we

[1] Speech on Secret Committee, 30 April 1781: *Writings and Speeches* V, 136–7.

ought to have been with respect to America, by studying the genius, the temper, and the manners of the people, and adapting to them the laws that we establish.'

It is remarkable that Burke, as a private Member, and in opposition, should have been able to carry such an important measure through Parliament. Partly this was thanks to having acquired, through the Select Committee, considerable influence over the Commons. Almost all the Committee's members had become converts to Burke's views, and they spread the word, principally among the Rockinghams, of whom Burke became the *de facto* leader on Indian affairs from the summer of 1781 on. On the other side, North, around this time, was trying, as we have seen (see above pp. 218–9) to conciliate Burke and his friends in the hope of enlisting their support for his Administration. Also North probably didn't greatly care whether English law was extended to the natives of India or not. Finally, Burke had concluded a tactical working alliance with Henry Dundas, (1742–1811), North's specialist on India who, for reasons of his own, not resembling Burke's, was anxious to change the system of governing India. The Bengal Judicature Act of 1781, Burke's achievement, was the first parliamentary blow to the Hastings-Impey system in Bengal.

*   *   *

After Francis had returned from India, in October 1781, he became the Select Committee's principal witness. The long collaboration between Burke and Francis had begun. The collaboration was, however, to some extent disrupted, within about a month of its inception, by the news from America. The news of Yorktown, arriving at the end of November, 1781, changed the face of British politics. As recounted in Chapter III, Burke, in the first half of 1782 is principally preoccupied, first with peace with America, and then with the affairs of the short-lived Second Rockingham Administration (March–July 1782). Yet even in the aftermath of Yorktown we find Burke still working hard on Indian affairs. On 15 January 1782 Jane Burke describes him as having been 'full as busy since we came into the Country as he was in Town; he is trying whether he shall have more success in saving the East, then he had in his indeavours for the West; he has been drawing Acts of Parliament and bills, and reports ever since we have been here.'[1] He was probably working on the First

---

[1] *Writings and Speeches* V, 144 tn.

Report of the Select Committee, which was published on 5 February. This was a strong indictment of the corrupt bargain between Hastings and Impey, giving Impey jurisdiction over the Native Courts but making him removable (in that capacity) at Hastings's discretion. As P. J. Marshall points out, this arrangement was 'open to criticism; a royal judge intended to be an independent check on the Company was accepting a salaried post from it to preside over one of its own courts.'[1]

Resolutions highly critical of Impey, were passed in April by the Commons, under the influence of that first Select Committee Report. The Rockinghams were now in power, and Burke was directing the course of Indian policy. In May the House voted for the recall of both Hastings and Impey. The Court of Directors were prepared to comply with the Commons demand but the Court of Proprietors overruled the Directors on 19 June. The Court of Proprietors took the audacious constitutional line that the Company was not bound by decisions of the Commons alone; only by decisions of both Houses of Parliament. It is not likely that the Court would have taken so potentially dangerous a line unless they had definite indications of support, not only within the House of Lords but also from the king. We may suspect that Charles Jenkinson, the liaison between George III and the Company, had been at work. George bitterly resented what Rockingham had done to him over America, and a wish to frustrate Rockingham designs concerning the Indian part of his domains would have been instinctive with him.[2] In the Lords, George's influence was even stronger than in the Commons. The position adopted by the Court of Proprietors was the first warning sign of an impending confrontation between the two Houses, with the king making use of the Lords against the Commons. That confrontation took dramatic shape, at the end of 1783, with disastrous political results for Burke and his friends.

The momentum of the drive towards Indian reform was now sweeping Burke and his friends into dangerous constitutional waters, as he surely knew from the Company's unprecedented defiance of a Commons decision. But neither that nor any other consideration could now deflect him from his Indian purpose.

[1] *Writings and Speeches* V, 145 editorial note. Marshall's occasional criticisms of Hastings and his associates are generally cautious and understated, as this one is.
[2] There is no evidence of royal intervention. But the hypothesis that it may have occurred is credible, in the light of the spectacular royal intervention, with a similar tendency, in 1783–4 (see below, p. 330).

By the end of 1782, with American affairs no longer an issue in British politics, India becomes his constant and over-riding concern. It remains so until, in late 1789, his alarm at the impact of the French Revolution in Britain makes France his primary concern, with India an important secondary one. On 29 December 1782 we find him writing to Francis: 'I want you very much. I have undertaken a vast Task; but with your assistance I may get through it.' Also in December Burke, in the House, had defined the vast task when he had insisted not merely on Hastings's recall 'but on his trial and punishment.' [1]

It is often suggested that Burke's mind was poisoned against Hastings by the rancorous Francis. No doubt Francis was rancorous, but there is no evidence that he misled Burke, in any material particular (except perhaps about the Mahratta War) concerning Hastings. He didn't have to: he knew that the Company's practices regarding Indians were inherently repugnant to Burke. Burke's mind was already moving against Hastings on the basis of evidence available to him: mainly Hastings's dispatches and those of his subordinates. What Francis provided to Burke and his Committee was abundant corroboration of documentary evidence. The astute Francis knew that it was not in his interest to lie about Hastings, when the truth would serve his interests just as well, and would not break down under examination. What he did have an interest in disguising from Burke and his Committee, was his own role in India: the fact that he had favoured the expansion of the system of extortion to Benares, for example, and above all his treatment of Nuncomar. But he was not pressed on any of that: it was not his record that was under investigation. Burke may well have suspected that there was something unsavoury about that record, but Burke would not have wanted to think about that, any more than about Junius. His need of Francis, as a well-informed and determined ally, was too great, for Burke to be able to think about such matters.

In 1783, while continuing to move against Hastings, Burke is also moving along a broad front towards the reform of the Company system, to place it under 'publick control.' In March he was back in office again, as part of the Fox-North Coalition, which lasted until December. Burke made sure that Indian legislation would be the centre-piece of the new Administration's legislative programme. By August he had convinced Fox of the need for the measure and in that

[1] *Corr.* V, 60; 60 n. 1.

same month, Burke had begun drafting it, at Fox's house. This was the measure known in history as 'Fox's East India Bill'. It was Fox who introduced the Bill in the Commons, but it was entirely Burke's Bill, both in concept and execution, and it had been Burke who persuaded his colleagues to back it. The Bill provided for the punishment of abuses, the observance of Indian rights and customs, and much stricter control from London. As L. G. Mitchell points out, all this 'had been foreshadowed for years in the correspondence of Burke.'

The East India Company detested the whole idea, of course, and it had powerful friends. The Court of Proprietors' defiance of the Commons in June was a strong signal of danger ahead. Several of Burke's colleagues advised caution. He, however, was determined to go ahead and, by August, he had succeeded in getting Fox's approval for the plan of an East India Bill. A letter written apparently shortly before the decision to take the plunge over India shows Fox completely but probably not consciously under Burke's spell: 'If I had considered nothing but keeping my power, it was the safest way to leave things as they are or to propose some trifling alteration and I am not all ignorant of the political danger which I run by this bold measure; but whether I succeed or no, I shall always be glad that I attempted because I know I have done no more than I was bound to do in risking my power and that of my friends when the happiness of so many millions is at stake.'[1]

That was in August. But by mid-November, three weeks before the Bill was due to be introduced, Fox was beginning to be worried. Charles Jenkinson had attacked the plan of the Bill as 'injurious to the interests of the Crown'. Jenkinson was officially a supporter of Lord North – and consequently of the Coalition – but as George III's chief confidential political agent, he was a much more important figure in eighteenth-century political life than might be imagined from historians who have striven to minimise the personal influence of the king. Every contemporary parliamentarian knew that Jenkinson would never have referred to something as 'injurious to the Crown', without having first ascertained, from George in person, that the king himself looked on the matter in that light. The Coalition was now under notice that George, as well as the East India Company, was opposed to their Indian enterprise. King and Company,

[1] L. G. Mitchell, *Charles James Fox and the Disintegration of the Whig Party* (Oxford, 1971) p. 65.

like Hastings and Impey, were a formidable pair. It was now clear that the East India Bill, even if it passed the Commons, would run into serious trouble in the Lords. Some members of the Coalition, including Richard Brinsley Sheridan, probably with the support of Fox, now made overtures to Hastings's friends, to see if there was any way of buying them off. L. G. Mitchell writes in his book on Fox (p. 67), that Sheridan, 'with or without the knowledge of Fox and Burke, attempted to buy off the displeasure of the friends of Warren Hastings.' That form of words might be taken as indicating that Burke was privy to those overtures and approved of them (as was so with Fox). This was certainly not so with Burke.

On 15 November Hastings's London Agent, Major Scott, reported that it 'has become now the fashion with Ministers to speak handsomely of Mr. Hastings.' Three days later, however, any hope of conciliation was shattered. As P. J. Marshall puts it: 'On the day the [East India] Bills were presented, the Select Committee produced a report with the sole purpose of proving Hastings's personal corruption. The Eleventh Report was quickly put on sale to the public in an edition produced by Debrett and copies of it were later distributed "under Blank covers to several (if not at all) Members of the Upper House of Parliament".'[1] The Select Committee was dominated by Burke; the *Eleventh Report* is known to be his work: the timing of its publication and the publicity ensured for it also bear Burke's mark. The *Report* is a political land-mine, detonated by Burke on the day of the publication of the East India Bill in order to destroy the effort to do a deal with Hastings.

This drastic, and successful, intervention provides a measure of Burke's political autonomy in Indian affairs, by late 1783. He, not Fox or North, had laid down the Coalition's Indian policy, and by his coup with the *Report*, he made sure that there would be no deviation from the policy laid down by him. This was a bold stroke, because the negotiations attempted with Hastings had, at the least, the blessing of the party leader, Fox. But, where Indian affairs were concerned, it was Burke, with his power-base in the Select Committee, who dominated Fox and, through him, the Coalition. Fox was never Burke's leader, except in name (and in the Commons). Fox stood in awe of Burke, morally and intellectually, and Burke was well aware of this. He could call Fox to order – as he implicitly did with the *Eleventh Report* – but Fox never successfully called him to

[1] *Writings and Speeches* V, 334 tn.

order, though he was to try in 1791, over France (see below Chapter V).

Burke's colleagues had every reason to be worried about the dangerous course he had marked out for them. Before the end of the year, that course would bring down the Coalition, and many of his colleagues and allies would lose their seats in the following general elections. Burke could see the danger as well as anyone else, or better; of all men, he best understood the ominous implications of Charles Jenkinson's 'injurious to the Crown'. Yet, deliberately oblivious of all that, he drove his faint-hearted colleagues on remorselessly, towards the battle they dreaded. If, in punishing Warren Hastings, Edmund Burke was also punishing himself, he was not going to spare his colleagues either: the party that in the early 1770s had hemmed him in, and induced him to betray the suffering peoples of India, to whose interests he was now passionately committed, in heart, soul and mind.

Once committed to a cause, Edmund Burke could be as ruthless, in his own way, as Warren Hastings himself. And Burke was no less effective than Hastings, in imposing his will on those around him, when he felt a driving need to do so.[1]

We are now on the verge of that phase in Burke's career which caused Yeats to include 'India' in Burke's Great Melody. We are reaching this only at this late stage in the chapter, because Burke himself reached it only belatedly, after sixteen years of intermittent, but increasingly serious, involvement in Indian affairs. The Great Melody of 1783–1790, cannot, in my view, be properly appreciated without some awareness of the course of Burke's previous involvement; and especially of the significance of the earliest stages of his involvement, in which he took a position directly contrary to that which he later passionately adopted.

The *Eleventh Report* led in directly to the first speech which is clearly in the Great Melody canon, the speech on 'Fox's East India Bill' (1 December 1783). I would not include the *Eleventh Report* itself because, although it is entirely written by Burke, and played an

---

[1] Historians of the period have generally missed this. Burke held only a small office in the Fox-North Administration and historians have tended to assume that his importance, in the parliamentary politics of the time, roughly corresponded to his office. This tendency is reinforced by the habitual dreary round of trivialising assumptions concerning Burke's motivation etc. But when the record is examined, without recourse to such assumptions, it becomes absolutely clear that it was Burke, not Fox or North, who dominated the short life of the 'Fox-North Coalition' – just as 'Fox's East India Bill' was, in reality, Burke's East India Bill.

important part in his Indian strategy, it is written as a Report of a Committee, and thus lacks the spontaneity and personal style of his best speeches. But, as a committee report, it is exceptionally powerful, and seems to have influenced subsequent debates and votes in the Commons. It does a lot of damage to Hastings, mostly through its quotations from his own dispatches, and well-taken comments on these. Here is just one sample:

'The Company itself must suffer extremely in the whole Order and regularity of their public Accounts, if the Ideas upon which Mr. Hastings justifies the taking of these Presents receives the smallest Countenance. On his Principles, the same Sum may become private Property or public, at the Pleasure of the Receiver: It is in his Power, Mr. Hastings says, to conceal it for ever. He certainly has it in his Power not only to keep it back and bring it forward at his own Times, but even to shift and reverse the Relations in the Accounts (as Mr. Hastings has done) in what Manner and Proportion seems good to him, and to make himself alternately Debtor or Creditor for the same Sums.

'Of this Irregularity Mr. Hastings himself appears in some Degree sensible. He conceives it possible, that his Transactions of this Nature may, to the Court of Directors, seem unsatisfactory. He, however, puts it hypothetically:"If to you (says he) who are accustomed to view Business in an official and regular Light, they should appear unprecedented, if not improper!" He just conceives it possible, that in an official Money Transaction the Directors may expect a Proceeding official and regular. In what other Lights than those which are official and regular, Matters of public Account ought to be regarded by those who have the Charge of them, either in Bengal or in England, does not appear to Your Committee. Any other is certainly "unprecedented and improper"; and can only serve to cover Fraud both in the Receipt and in the Expenditure. The Acquisition of 58,000 Rupees, or near £6,000, which appears in the Sort of unofficial and irregular Account that he furnishes of his Presents, in his Letter of May 1782, must appear extraordinary indeed, to those who expect from Men in Office something official and something regular. "This' Sum (says he) I received while I was on my Journey to Benares." He tells it with the same careless Indifference, as if Things of this Kind were found by Accident on the high Road.'[1]

---

[1] The text of the *Eleventh Report* is given in *Writings and Speeches* V, 334–378. The passage quoted is on pages 356–7.

Or, in the language of two centuries later: 'It fell off the back of a lorry.'

Fox introduced his East India Bill on 18 November, with a fine Burkean speech – Burke spoke only briefly in the debate on the Second Reading. When the two men were in agreement – that is to say, when Fox agreed with Burke – Burke had always been happy to leave the speaking honours to Fox, even in the days when Fox had been only an ally of the Rockingham party and not, as now, its leader in the Commons. Burke reserved his remarks for a second debate – on whether the House should proceed to the Committee stage – on 1 December 1783. The main feature of the Bill was that it substituted a commission appointed by Parliament, and responsible to Parliament, for the Company's Court of Directors, responsible to the Company's Court of Proprietors. That is to say, it sought to end the Company's autonomy.

P. J. Marshall, in Volume V of *Writings and Speeches* (page 380), aptly summarises the general thrust of the speech: 'Speaking second in the debate, he met objections old and new, about chartered rights, the powers of the Crown, or the powers of ministers, with what he saw as the unanswerable case for reform at whatever price, the catalogue of the crimes of the East India Company.'

He begins by presenting himself in the unconvincing guise of a humble but diligent disciple of the putative author of the Bill:

> I asked myself, and I asked myself nothing else, what part it was fit for a member of parliament, who has supplied a mediocrity of talents by the extreme of diligence, and who has thought himself obliged, by the research of years, to wind himself into the inmost recesses and labyrinths of the Indian detail, what part, I say, it became such a member of parliament to take, when a minister of state, in conformity to a recommendation from the throne, has brought before us a system for the better government of the territory and commerce of the East.

One phrase here is worthy of remark: 'in conformity to a recommendation from the throne'. This is, of course, a reference to the King's Speech, at the opening of the parliamentary session. Then, as now, such a speech was entirely the work of Ministers, outlining the legislative programme of the administration: in this case, the Fox-North one. George III detested the Fox-North Coalition and had seriously contemplated abdicating rather than submit to it (see Chapter III above, p. 226). In the context, to treat the Coalition's programme as responsive 'to a recommendation from the throne' is mockery in courtly guise. The mockery seems extraordinarily imprudent, in the circumstances. Burke knew, from Charles Jenkinson, that George was hostile to the East India Bill, and would use his influence against it in the Lords. Burke also knew that the king felt himself to be the Coalition's prisoner, that he longed to escape, and that the East India Bill, in the Lords, offered a promising escape route. To use the phrase 'a recommendation from the throne' here seems like rattling the bars, behind which the royal tiger was pent up. Could Burke have been deliberately taunting the king, hoping to provoke a constitutional crisis, in the expectation that the crisis would result in the desired reduction of the powers of the Crown? If so it was a grave miscalculation.

Those who opposed the East India Bill generally did not try to defend the East India Company: it was unpopular and its abuses were by now notorious (largely, but not wholly, because of the exertions of Burke and his Select Committee, from 1781 on). The strongest argument of the Bill's opponents was that a legislative encroachment on the Company's Charter implicitly undermined *all* Charters, and so all the human rights guaranteed by these. Burke comes powerfully to grips with this argument:

> As to the first of these objections; I must observe that the phrase of 'the chartered rights of men', is full of affectation; and very unusual in the discussion of privileges conferred by charters of the present description. But it is not difficult to discover what end that ambiguous mode of expression, so often reiterated, is meant to answer.
>
> The rights of men, that is to say, the natural rights of mankind, are indeed sacred things; and if any public measure is proved mischievously to affect them, the objection ought to be fatal to that measure, even if no charter at all could be set up against it. If these natural rights are further affirmed and declared by express covenants, if they are clearly defined and secured against chicane, against power, and authority, by written instruments and positive engagements, they are in a still better condition: they partake not only of the sanctity of the object so secured, but of that solemn public faith itself, which secures an object of such importance. Indeed this formal recognition, by the sovereign power, of an original right in the subject, can never be subverted, but by rooting up the holding radical principles of government, and even of society itself. The charters, which we call by distinction great, are public instruments of this nature; I mean the charters of King John and King Henry the Third. The things secured by these instruments may, without any deceitful ambiguity, be very fitly called the chartered rights of men.
>
> These charters have made the very name of a charter dear to the heart

of every Englishman – But, Sir, there may be, and there are charters, not only different in nature, but formed on principles the very reverse of those of the great charter. Of this kind is the charter of the East India Company. Magna Charta is a charter to restrain power, and to destroy monopoly. The East India charter is a charter to establish monopoly, and to create power. Political power and commercial monopoly are not the rights of men; and the rights to them derived from charters, it is fallacious and sophistical to call 'the chartered rights of men'. These chartered rights, (to speak of such charters and of their effects in terms of the greatest possible moderation) do at least suspend the natural rights of mankind at large; and in their very frame and constitution are liable to fall into a direct violation of them.

Burke then refers to the extensive powers still to be retained by the Company, even after the East India Bill becomes law.

But granting all this, they must grant to me in my turn, that all political power which is set over men, and that all privilege claimed or exercised in exclusion of them, being wholly artificial, and for so much, a derogation from the natural equality of mankind at large, ought to be some way or other exercised ultimately for their benefit.

If this is true with regard to every species of political dominion, and every description of commercial privilege, none of which can be original self-derived rights, or grants for the mere private benefit of the holders, then such rights, or privileges, or whatever else you choose to call them, are all in the strictest sense a trust; and it is of the very essence of every trust to be rendered accountable; and even totally to cease, when it substantially varies from the purposes for which alone it could have a lawful existence.

This, I conceived, Sir, to be true of trusts of power vested in the highest hands, and of such as seem to hold of no human creature. But about the application of this principle to subordinate derivative trusts, I do not see how a controversy can be maintained. To whom then would I make the East India Company accountable? Why, to Parliament to be sure; to Parliament, from whom their trust was derived; to Parliament, which alone is capable of comprehending the magnitude of its object, and its abuse; and alone capable of an effectual legislative remedy. The very charter, which is held out to exclude Parliament from correcting malversation with regard to the high trust vested in the Company, is the very thing which at once gives a title and imposes a duty on us to interfere with effect, wherever power and authority originating from ourselves are perverted from their purposes, and become instruments of wrong and violence.

Having systematically demolished the strongest argument of his opponents, Burke appears to pause for a moment in his act. He refers to the reluctance he had felt about interfering with the Company's rights:

The strong admission I have made of the Company's rights (I am conscious of it) binds me to do a great deal. I do not presume to condemn those who argue a priori, against the propriety of leaving such extensive political powers in the hands of a company of merchants. I know much is, and much more may be said against such a system. But, with my particular ideas and sentiments, I cannot go that way to work. I feel an insuperable reluctance in giving my hand to destroy any established institution of government, upon a theory, however plausible it may be.

In that last sentence, Burke states the precise principle on which, seven years later, he will denounce the destroying theorists of the French National Assembly. This is yet another example of the profound consistency of Burke's mind, in all four of our themes.

In this part of the speech, where he is referring to the reluctance with which he approached the problem, Burke adopts a calm detached tone, resembling that of a neutral. He even defends the Company, at one point, against the aristocratic criticism that merchants are not fit persons to exercise political power. 'I have known merchants with the sentiments and the abilities of great statesmen; and I have seen persons in the rank of statesmen, with the conceptions and character of pedlars' (Shelburne). But the calm of this passage is a rhetorical device. Burke's explanation of his reluctance to interfere with the Company is a prelude to a recital of the enormities which alone could have overcome the depth of his reluctance:

To justify us in taking the administration of their affairs out of the hands of the East India Company, on my principles, I must see several conditions. 1st. The object affected by the abuse should be great and important. 2d. The abuse affecting this great object ought to be a great abuse. 3d. It ought to be habitual, and not accidental. 4th. It ought to be utterly incurable in the body as it now stands constituted. All this ought to be made as visible to me as the light of the sun, before I should strike off an atom of their charter.

Burke then establishes his four conditions. For his first condition – 'the object great and important' – he describes the extent of the Company's dominions:

With very few, and those inconsiderable intervals, the British dominion, either in the Company's name, or in the names of princes absolutely dependent upon the Company, extends from the mountains that separate India from Tartary, to Cape Comorin, that is, one-and-twenty degrees of latitude!

In the northern parts it is a solid mass of land, about eight hundred miles in length, and four or five hundred broad. As you go southward, it becomes narrower for a space. It afterwards dilates; but narrower or broader, you possess the whole eastern and north-eastern coast of that vast country, quite from the borders of Pegu – Bengal, Bahar, and Orissa, with Benares (now unfortunately in our immediate possession) measure 161,978 square English miles; a territory considerably larger than the whole kingdom of France. Oude, with its dependent provinces, is 53,286 square miles, not a great deal less than England. The Carnatic, with Tanjour and the Circars, is 65,948 square miles, very considerably larger than England; and the whole of the Company's dominion comprehending Bombay and Salsette, amounts to 281,412 square miles; which forms a territory larger than any European dominion, Russia and Turkey excepted. Through all that vast extent of country there is not a man who eats a mouthful of rice but by permission of the East India Company.

Having estimated the population of British India, in 1783, at around thirty millions, he continues:

My next enquiry to that of the number, is the quality and description of the inhabitants. This multitude of men does not consist of an abject and barbarous populace; much less of gangs of savages, like the Guaranies and Chiquitos, who wander on the waste borders of the river of Amazons, or the Plate; but a people for ages civilized and cultivated; cultivated by all the arts of polished life, whilst we were yet in the woods. There, have been (and still the skeletons remain) princes once of great dignity, authority, and opulence. There, are to be found the chiefs of tribes and nations. There is to be found an antient and venerable priesthood, the depository of their laws, learning, and history, the guides of the people whilst living, and their consolation in death; a nobility of great antiquity and renown; a multitude of cities, not exceeded in population and trade by those of the first class in Europe; merchants and bankers, individual houses of whom have once vied in capital with the Bank of England; whose credit had often supported a tottering state, and preserved their governments in the midst of war and desolation; millions of ingenious manufacturers and mechanicks; millions of the most diligent, and not the least intelligent, tillers of the earth. Here are to be found almost all the religions professed by men, the Braminical, the Mussulmen, the Eastern and the Western Christians.

Burke clearly senses some resistance from his parliamentary audience, to this phase of his argument, for he adds that he has been trying 'to awaken something of sympathy for the unfortunate natives, of which I am afraid we are not perfectly susceptible, whilst we look at this very remote object through a false and cloudy medium.'

There follows the recital of abuses by the Company, which makes up the bulk of the speech. There is a magnificent passage, contrasting the effects of Company rule with those of previous Asian rulers of India:

The several irruptions of Arabs, Tartars, and Persians, into India were, for the greater part, ferocious, bloody, and wasteful in the extreme: our entrance into the dominion of that country was, as generally, with small comparative effusion of blood; being introduced by various frauds and delusions, and by taking advantage of the incurable, blind, and senseless animosity, which the several country powers bear towards each other, rather than by open force. But the difference in favour of the first conquerors is this; the Asiatic conquerors very soon abated of their ferocity, because they made the conquered country their own. They rose or fell with the rise or fall of the territory they lived in. Fathers there deposited the hopes of their posterity; and children there beheld the monuments of their fathers. Here their lot was finally cast; and it is the natural wish of all, that their lot should not be cast in a bad land. Poverty, sterility, and desolation, are not a recreating prospect to the eye of man; and there are very few who can bear to grow old among the curses of a whole people. If their passion or their avarice drove the Tartar lords to acts of rapacity or tyranny, there was time enough, even in the short life of man, to bring round the ill effects of an abuse of power upon the power itself. If hoards were made by violence and tyranny, they were still domestic hoards; and domestic profusion, or the rapine of a more powerful and prodigal hand, restored them to the people. With many disorders, and with few political checks upon power, Nature had still fair play; the sources of acquisition were not dried up; and therefore the trade, the manufactures, and the commerce of the country flourished. Even avarice and usury itself operated, both for the preservation and the employment of national wealth. The husbandman and manufacturer paid heavy interest, but then they augmented the fund from whence they were again to borrow. Their resources were dearly bought, but they were sure; and the general stock of the community grew by the general effort.

But under the English government all this order is reversed. The Tartar invasion was mischievous; but it is our protection that destroys India. It was their enmity, but it is our friendship. Our conquest there, after twenty years, is as crude as it was the first day. The natives scarcely know what it is to see the grey head of an Englishman. Young men (boys almost) govern there, without society, and without sympathy with the natives. They have no more social habits with the people, than if they still resided in England; nor indeed any species of intercourse but that which is necessary to making a sudden fortune, with a view to a remote settlement. Animated with all the avarice of age, and all the impetuosity of youth, they roll in one after another; wave after wave; and there is nothing before the eyes of the natives but an endless, hopeless prospect of new flights of birds of prey and passage, with appetites continually renewing for a food that is continually wasting. Every rupee of profit made by an Englishman is lost for ever to India. With us are no retributory superstitions, by which a foundation of charity compensates, through ages, to the poor, for the rapine and injustice of a day. With us no pride erects stately monuments which repair the mischiefs which pride had produced, and which adorn a country, out of its own spoils. England has erected no churches, no hospitals, no palaces, no schools; England has built no bridges, made no high roads, cut no navigations, dug out no reservoirs. Every other conqueror of every other description has left some monument, either of state or beneficence, behind him. Were we to be driven out of India this day, nothing would remain, to tell that it had been possessed, during the inglorious period of our dominion, by any thing better than the ouran-outang or the tiger.

There is nothing in the boys we send to India worse than the boys whom we are whipping at school, or that we see trailing a pike, or bending over a desk at home. But as English youth in India drink the intoxicating draught of authority and dominion before their heads are able to bear it, and as they are full grown in fortune long before they are ripe in principle, neither nature nor reason have any opportunity to exert themselves for remedy of the excesses of their premature power. The consequences of their conduct, which in good minds, (and many of theirs are probably such) might produce penitence or amendment, are unable to pursue the rapidity of their flight. Their prey is lodged in England; and the cries of India are given to seas and winds, to be blown about, in every breaking up of the monsoon, over a remote and unhearing ocean.

Burke is aware, however, yet again of resistance among his listeners, and he again adapts his tone, in order to bring them round. He holds himself in, and acknowledges that he is doing so. In the following passage, he is referring to his Select Committee, which had now spent three years in investigating the Company's system of extortion:

I shall certainly endeavour to modulate myself to this temper; though I am sensible that a cold style of describing actions which appear to me in a very affecting light, is equally contrary to the justice due to the people, and to all genuine human feelings about them. I ask pardon of truth and nature for this compliance. But I shall be very sparing of epithets either to persons or things. It has been said (and, with regard to one of them, with truth) that Tacitus and Machiavel, by their cold way of relating enormous crimes, have in some sort appeared not to disapprove them; that they seem a sort of professors of the art of tyranny, and that they corrupt the minds of their readers by not expressing the detestation and horror that naturally belong to horrible and detestable proceedings. But we are in general, Sir, so little acquainted with Indian details; the instruments of oppression under which the people suffer are so hard to be understood; and even the very names of the sufferers are so uncouth and strange to our ears, that it is very difficult for our sympathy to fix upon these objects. I am sure that some of us have come down stairs from the committee-room, with impressions on our minds, which to us were the inevitable results of our discoveries, yet if we should venture to express ourselves in the proper language of our sentiments, to other gentlemen not at all prepared to enter into the cause of them, nothing could appear more harsh and dissonant, more violent and unaccountable, than our language and behaviour. All these circumstances are not, I confess, very favourable to the idea of our attempting to govern India at all. But there we are; there we are placed by the Sovereign Disposer: and we must do the best we can in our situation. The situation of man is the preceptor of his duty.

That last sentence is a good example of the Burkean aphorism. Entering into particular abuses, Burke comes to the case of the Begums of Oudh, and therefore to Hastings. He does not denounce him, directly, but he quotes from him, copiously and effectively, and details a number of his extortions. The following is a lucid summary of the Company's system, under Warren Hastings:

The invariable course of the Company's policy is this: Either they set up some prince too odious to maintain himself without the necessity of their assistance; or they soon render him odious, by making him the instrument of their government. In that case troops are bountifully sent to him to maintain his authority. That he should have no want of assistance, a civil gentleman, called a Resident, is kept at his court, who, under pretence of providing duly for the pay of these troops, gets assignments on the revenue into his hands. Under his provident management, debts soon accumulate; new assignments are made for these debts; until, step by step, the whole revenue, and with it the whole power of the country, is delivered into his hands. The military do not behold without a virtuous emulation the moderate gains of the civil department. They feel that, in a country driven to habitual rebellion by the civil government, the military is necessary; and they will not permit their services to go unrewarded. Tracts of country are delivered over to their discretion. Then it is found proper to convert their commanding officers into farmers of revenue. Thus, between the well paid civil, and well rewarded military establishment, the situation of the natives may be easily conjectured. The authority of the regular and lawful government is every where and in every point extinguished. Disorders and violences arise; they are repressed by other disorders and other violences. Wherever the collectors of the revenue, and the farming colonels and majors move, ruin is about them, rebellion before and behind them. The people in crowds fly out of the country; and the frontier is guarded by lines of troops, not to exclude an enemy, but to prevent the escape of the inhabitants.

As Burke went on, the resistance of certain Members made itself audible. He was telling the story of the Begums of Oudh:

So far as to the objects of the spoil. The instrument chosen by Mr. Hastings to despoil the relict of Sujah Dowlah was her own son, the reigning Nabob of Oudh. It was the pious hand of a son that was selected to tear from his mother and grandmother the provision of their age, the maintenance of his brethren, and of all the ancient household of his father. [Here a laugh from some young members] – The laugh is seasonable, and the occasion decent and proper. ['Seasonable' is a reference to the approach of Christmas.]

At the beginning of his consideration of the Company's abuses he had set out four conditions. He goes on:

I am now come to my last condition, without which, for one, I will never readily lend my hand to the destruction of any established government; which is, That in its present state, the government of the East India Company is absolutely incorrigible.

Of this great truth I think there can be little doubt, after all that has appeared in this House. It is so very clear, that I must consider the leaving any power in their hands, and the determined resolution to continue and countenance every mode and every degree of peculation, oppression, and tyranny, to be one and the same thing. I look upon that body as incorrigible, from the fullest consideration both of their uniform conduct, and their present real and virtual constitution.

If they had not constantly been apprized of all the enormities committed in India under their authority; if this state of things had been as much a discovery to them as it was to many of us; we might flatter ourselves that the detection of the abuses would lead to their reformation. I will go further: If the Court of Directors had not uniformly condemned every act which this House or any of its Committees had condemned; if the language in which they expressed their disapprobation against enormities and their authors had not been much more vehement and indignant than any ever used in this House, I should entertain some hopes. If they had not, on the other hand, as uniformly commended all their servants who had done their duty and obeyed their orders, as they had heavily censured those who rebelled; I might say, These people have been in an error, and when they are sensible of it they will mend. But when I reflect on the uniformity of their support to the objects of their uniform censure; and the state of insignificance and disgrace to which all of those have been reduced whom they approved; and that even utter ruin and premature death have been among the fruits of their favour; [1] I must be convinced, that in this case, as in all others, hypocrisy is the only vice that never can be cured.

In contrasting the hollowness of the Court of Directors' impeccable, and ostensible, instructions to its 'servants' in India, Burke comes to the case of Nuncomar:

Hanged in the face of all his nation, by the judges you sent to protect that people; hanged for a pretended crime, upon an ex post facto British act of parliament, in the midst of his evidence against Mr. Hastings. The accuser they saw hanged. The culprit, without acquittal or enquiry, triumphs on the ground of that murder: a murder not of Nuncomar only, but of all living testimony, and even of evidence yet unborn. From that time not a complaint has been heard from the natives against their governors. All the grievances of India have found a complete remedy.

Men will not look to acts of parliament, to regulations, to declarations, to votes, and resolutions. No, they are not such fools. They will ask, what conduct ends in neglect, disgrace, poverty, exile, prison, and gibbet? These will teach them the course which they are to follow. It is your distribution of these that will give the character and tone to your government. All the rest is miserable grimace.

In concluding his main argument, when Burke says 'you' he is referring to the formal approval by the Commons of his Select Committee Reports.

The fact is, that for a long time there was a struggle, a faint one indeed, between the Company and their servants. But it is a struggle no longer. For some time the superiority has been decided. The interests abroad are

[1] A reference to the fate of Lord Pigot.

become the settled preponderating weight both in the Court of Proprietors, and the Court of Directors. Even the attempt you have made to enquire into their practices and to reform abuses, has raised and piqued them to a far more regular and steady support. The Company has made a common cause, and identified themselves, with the destroyers of India. They have taken on themselves all that mass of enormity; they are supporting what you have reprobated; those you condemn they applaud; those you order home to answer for their conduct, they request to stay, and thereby encourage to proceed to their practices. Thus the servants of the East India Company triumph, and the representatives of the people of Great Britain are defeated.

I therefore conclude, what you all conclude, that this body, being totally perverted from the purposes of its institution, is utterly incorrigible; and because they are incorrigible, both in conduct and constitution, power ought to be taken out of their hands; just on the same principles on which have been made all the just changes and revolutions of government that have taken place since the beginning of the world.

The speech really ends there, as far as its contribution to the Great Melody is concerned. It is an important contribution. This speech is qualitatively different from any of Burke's previous utterances over India. For the first time, he is speaking without constraint. He is speaking for a Bill, designed to his own political specifications, and written by himself. He has carried his party with him, and overcome their waverings. He can now speak out his own mind, because his mind now dominates his party. In the passages I have quoted from 'Fox's India Bill', Edmund Burke is speaking out of the full conviction of his heart and mind. It is under these conditions, and almost only under these, that the Great Melody is best heard. Although it can also be heard under other conditions; more faintly, and sometimes eerily.

I have yet to quote from the peroration to the speech, the eulogy of Charles James Fox, which seemed to many contemporaries its finest part. I don't agree, and I would not rate this peroration as fully part of the Great Melody, for I find it to be flawed. Yet it is worth quoting in part because, though there is falsity in it, yet it is a generous falsity, and moving in its context:

And now, having done my duty to the Bill, let me say a word to the author. I should leave him to his own noble sentiments, if the unworthy and illiberal language with which he has been treated, beyond all example of parliamentary liberty, did not make a few words necessary; not so much in justice to him, as to my own feelings. I must say then, that it will be a distinction honourable to the age, that the rescue of the greatest number of the human race that ever were so grievously oppressed, from the greatest tyranny that was ever exercised, has fallen to the lot of abilities and dispositions equal to the task; that it has fallen to one who has the enlargement to comprehend, the spirit to undertake, and the eloquence to support, so great a measure of hazardous benevolence. His spirit is not owing to his ignorance of the state of men and things; he well knows what snares are spread about his path, from personal animosity, from court intrigues, and possibly from popular delusion. [1] But he has put to hazard his ease, his security, his interest, his power, even his darling popularity, for the benefit of a people whom he has never seen. This is the road that all heroes have trod before him. He is traduced and abused for his supposed motives. He will remember, that obloquy is a necessary ingredient in the composition of all true glory: he will remember, that it was not only in the Roman customs, but it is in the nature and constitution of things, that calumny and abuse are essential parts of triumph. These thoughts will support a mind, which only exists for honour, under the burthen of temporary reproach. He is doing indeed a great good; such as rarely falls to the lot, and almost as rarely coincides with the desires, of any man. Let him use his time. Let him give the whole length of the reins to his benevolence. He is now on a great eminence, where the eyes of mankind are turned to him. He may live long, he may do much. But here is the summit. He never can exceed what he does this day.

The falsities are obvious. Fox was not 'the author' of the Bill. Burke was the author. The great task to which Fox had, somewhat reluctantly, set himself did not just 'fall to his lot,' it was imposed on him by the awe which Burke inspired in him. Fox did indeed 'well know what snares are spread about his path' and he had tried not to go any further down that path. It was Burke who, by a vigorous application of the Eleventh Report, had driven him on. These falsities of form are dictated by the parliamentary setting, in which Burke's praise must be couched in a form appropriate to Fox's position as leader, and to his own as follower. The realities were different. But under the falsities of the form there is a genuine warmth in the praise. The feelings involved are not those of a follower applauding a leader, but of a teacher applauding a pupil. Pupil-to-teacher had been the relation of Fox to Burke from the beginning, and so it remained. On

[1] The first two of the snares Burke had in mind would snap tight when the East India Bill went to the Lords ten days later. The personal animosity was that of the king towards Fox. The effects of what Burke regarded as 'popular delusion' were felt in the General Election of the following year (see below pp. 330–336).

the India business, the great teacher had been worried about his beloved, brilliant, wayward pupil. Being worried, he had been a bit stern with him. The sternness had worked, the pupil had done well, and praise is now called for. The warmth of the praise reflects affection for the pupil, admiration for his great talents, and also the depth of Edmund Burke's relief that Charles James Fox is still with him.

Perhaps, after all, the peroration really does belong in the Great Melody. But you need to listen carefully.

The vote at which Burke's speech was aimed – the vote to go into committee – passed handsomely: 217 to 103. Shortly afterwards, the Bill went to the Lords and to its fate.

On 11 December, the King sprang the trap, on the Fox-North Coalition. On that day the King gave his confidant, Lord Temple (Richard Grenville Temple, second Earl of that name), the following statement in writing: 'His Majesty allowed Earl Temple to say, that whoever voted for the India Bill was not only not his friend, but would be considered by him as an enemy; and if these words were not strong enough, Earl Temple might use whatever words he might deem stronger and more to the purpose.'[1] This was, of course, a terrifying threat to any lord: it meant being completely cut off from all State patronage, both for oneself and one's family. So it is not surprising that the East India Bill should have been decisively defeated in the Lords, as it was on 17 December 1783. Next day, the King sent the following message to North: 'Lord North Is by this required to send Me the Seals of His Department, and to acquaint Mr. Fox to send those of the Foreign Department. Mr. Frazer or Mr. Nepean will be the proper Channel of delivering them to Me this Night; I choose this method as Audiences on such occasions must be unpleasant.'[2] Burke's own dismissal, as Paymaster General, followed on 19 December. As L. G. Mitchell says in his book on Charles James Fox (p. 72): 'The royal coup had been in preparation for at least a week.' And the King had not been alone in preparing it. He was working closely with his confidential political agents, Charles Jenkinson, John Robinson, and Richard Atkinson (1735–85; the last was acting for the East India Company). And it is clear that, on this occasion at least, they were acting, not merely as the King's agents but as his advisers. We find Atkinson writing to Robinson, on 3 December, eight days before the coup: 'Everything stands prepared

---

[1] *Corr.* V, 119. Temple was Pitt's brother-in-law.
[2] *Corr. Geo. III*, Vol. VI, p. 476.

for the blow, if a certain person has courage to strike it.' Clearly, advice had been given, and the king was hesitating as to whether to take it.

All this conforms with Burke's view of the king and his political entourage. This was the 'court intrigue', which he well knew to be at work against the East India Bill, and had expressly warned against in his speech of December, sending it on its way to the Lords. This is what Burke meant by his metaphor of the Double Cabinet (see Introduction, li–liii). A set of confidential advisers – what in later days would be called 'a kitchen Cabinet' – was conspiring to get the king to use his prerogative powers to destroy his official Cabinet. This is the rankest heresy, according to Namierite doctrine. Sir Lewis Namier, with his blazing certitude that he understood the late eighteenth-century better than any person who actually lived in it, decreed that the Double Cabinet was 'a product of Burke's fertile and malignant imagination'. Burke was seeing things that simply weren't there, according to Namier. But the things were there, and they triumphed in December 1783.

Granted the discrepancy between Namierite doctrine and the reality of the December 1783 conspiracy and coup, it is impossible not to admire the delicacy and discretion with which that distinguished Namierite Lucy Sutherland, in *The East India Company in Eighteenth Century Politics*, Oxford, 1952 (p. 403) alludes to the doctrinally unmentionable presence of advisers, around the king in that crisis. She refers to 'Charles Jenkinson emerging from his silence to play on behalf of the King a discreet part as an intermediary and perhaps something more.'

'And perhaps something more' is a cryptic half-acknowledgement of something offensive to Namierite ears, and unmentionable by Namierite lips. Charles Jenkinson was something much, much more than 'an intermediary', generally an *ad hoc* role, exhausted on a single occasion. He was the king's confidential political agent, reporting to him regularly, over many years. It is true that there is no record of Jenkinson's offering the king advice, in writing: he volunteers information only. Jenkinson was not a man to offer advice to his sovereign, without being asked for it. But neither was he the man to withhold advice, if his sovereign did ask for it. Implicit in the role of confidential agent is that of confidential adviser, when the principal feels in need of advice. And the king was badly in need of advice. He didn't need advice as to 'what to do'. He knew exactly what he wanted to do: to sack Fox and North and their friends whom he hated because he felt they had betrayed him. What he wanted to know was whether he could safely sack them, while they still commanded a safe majority in the Commons. North had advised him, in March 1782, that if he rejected the advice of a large majority in the House of Commons, he ran a high risk of losing his throne. Did that still apply now, if he sacked Fox and North and had to face a hostile Commons majority?

In seeking an answer to that question, the king must certainly have consulted his confidential agents, of whom Jenkinson was the chief. Who else was there to consult? He could hardly consult his official advisers, Fox and North, about whether it would be safe to sack them. The kind of advice George needed, and Jenkinson and his coadjutors were there to provide, when asked, was the kind of advice that consisted largely of information. Jenkinson certainly did not advise the king about what he ought to do. That kind of advice was a Rockingham-Burke sort of thing, not a Jenkinson sort of thing. What the king needed was an assessment of the political situation, which would tell him the limits within which he was free to act. From Atkinson's letter of 3 December to Robinson (see above pp. 330–1), we can see that the assessment has already been furnished, that it is positive – in the sense that the King can safely sack Fox and North – and that the agents/informants/advisers are hoping that the king will have the nerve to act on it. Eight days later, he did so act.

Why was it safe for the king to defy a House of Commons majority in 1783, whereas, in the crisis of the previous year, to defy such a majority might have cost him his throne? The reason is that, in 1782, defiance meant holding on to Ministers who had become unpopular, both in the Commons and in the country. In 1783, in contrast, defying a Commons majority meant sacking unpopular Ministers over an unpopular measure. The king's ace of trumps, in the 1783 circumstances, was his power – a power then altogether unrestricted – to dissolve Parliament. In the 1782 circumstances, dissolution would have done the King no good; it would have given him a House of Commons even less to his taste than the House he actually had. But in 1783–4 a dissolution could be expected to bring in a more satisfactory House of Commons, from the king's point of view. That Jenkinson understood all that perfectly well can be seen from the fact that, just at this point, he ratted on North, whom he had supported in parliament for more than a decade. That Jenkinson advised the king that he could sack Fox and North with impunity is a completely safe assumption; even though there is no piece of paper, in Jenkinson's handwriting, extant to prove it.

In that connection, Lucy Sutherland's reference to Jenkinson's 'emerging from his silence' at this time is revealing, concerning the assumptions of her school. For there is no way of knowing whether Jenkinson (or anyone else) was silent, at any particular time. When Sutherland refers to 'silence' she means a documentary gap. But the two are not the same; not by any means. A documentary gap often reflects a period of particularly intense communication. The people concerned are not in correspondence, because they are in daily conversation. Most of the correspondence between the Rockingham leaders, for example, took place during the parliamentary recess, when the leaders were separated. When parliament was in session, they didn't need to write, because they could talk to one another. Similarly, when George had something particularly important to discuss with Jenkinson or Robinson, he didn't need to correspond with them; he could summon them to his presence. Then, as now, many of the most important things didn't get written down. What an eerie place, by contrast, is eighteenth century London, once it has undergone Namierisation! This is a world in which no one ever talks to anyone else. All communication is in writing. The spaces between the bouts of penmanship are filled by silence. Anything that doesn't get written down doesn't happen.

Let us now return to the development of the political crisis of 1783–4, which had such a powerful impact on the life of Edmund Burke. After dismissing North and Fox, the king first sent for the chosen instrument of their destruction to be chief Minister. Temple accepted, and resigned three days later (possibly fearing impeachment). The king then sent for William Pitt, then aged twenty-four. Pitt, although he knew himself to be in a minority in the Commons, continued as Chief Minister for three months, enduring repeated voting defeats, and violent Whig attacks for unconstitutional conduct. He could have advised the King to dissolve parliament, but did not do so. 'The overthrow of the coalition and the accession of Pitt were the results of a carefully prearranged plan which was exceptional in character, even at that time of irregular political methods.'[1] The planners were the King's confidential agents, Jenkinson, Robinson and Atkinson; also the former (and

[1] W. T. Laprade, 'Public Opinion and the General Election of 1784', *English Historical Review* xxxi (1916) pp. 224–237.

future) Lord Chancellor, Lord Thurlow. Pitt had had a 'secret conference' with Robinson on 15 November, three days before the royal coup, and Robinson had been able to convince Pitt that the ensuing elections could be won, provided Robinson was given the time he needed for their management.[1] Pitt then agreed to accept office in an Administration which would be in a minority.

To head an Administration without a Commons majority would later become impossible; even at that time, it was regarded by the Whigs as unconstitutional. Yet Pitt advised the king against an immediate dissolution. The royal use of the Lords to overthrow a Government with a Commons majority was deemed to have shocked a great many people, and it has been felt that Pitt needed time, to allow the shock to die down before he could safely face a general election. But Pitt, and the king, had more solid reasons for delaying dissolution. Time was needed until 'the necessary agreements could be made with borough-managers and men of influence for securing a majority in the new Parliament.'[2]

When the Commons met, on 17 December, Mr. Baker of Hertford, a personal friend of Burke, rose in his place and proposed a Resolution in the following terms: 'That it is now necessary to declare that to report any opinion or pretended opinion of His Majesty upon any Bill or other proceedings depending on either House of Parliament, with a view to influencing the votes of the Members, is a high crime and misdemeanour derogatory to the honour of the Crown, a breach of the fundamental privilege of Parliament, and subversive of the Constitution of this country.'[3] Against this Resolution, Pitt moved the Order of the Day but was defeated. The Resolution was obviously intended as a prelude to the Impeachment of Lord Temple, and this would have followed, had the Fox-North majority in the Commons remained stable, but this was not to be. Pitt held on grimly as chief Minister despite this resounding defeat in the Commons.

Fox, with a Commons majority behind him, facing Pitt's minority Administration, was elated and looked forward to an early return to power.[4] Burke does not seem to have shared this elation. Nothing

[1] C. E. Fryer, 'The General Election of 1774', *History* ix, pp. 221–3.

[2] W. T. Laprade, 'William Pitt and Westminster Elections', *American Historical Review* xviii (1912–13) pp. 253–274.

[3] Earl Stanhope *Life of the Right Honourable William Pitt* (Three vols. London, 1879) 119. By noting that Baker was a personal friend of Burke's, Stanhope appears to suggest that Burke prepared the Resolution. This was probably the case.

[4] Mitchell, *Charles James Fox*, pp. 79–80.

of the kind appears in his *Correspondence*; on the contrary. On 1 January 1784, when a dissolution was generally believed to be imminent, he wrote to his friend John Noble to ask for his support for two Whig candidates in the coming election. Burke foresees that they will be difficult: 'There is no doubt that many are ready to begin an attack under the Guidance of the secret influence [i.e. of the Crown] upon every member of Parliament who is resolved to assert the privileges and dignity of the two Houses, and particularly of the foundation of all the rights of the Subject, the House of Commons.'[1]

In the event the dissolution, which Burke and most others had believed to be imminent at the beginning of January, did not occur until 25 March. Pitt in the meantime fought a long, cool, effective rearguard action in the Commons, and the impressive Fox-North majority steadily dwindled, as a result of Northite defections. Jenkinson and Robinson had been working on the Northites – their former party colleagues – to show them that the way back into royal favour was to start voting for Pitt. About 50 of them 'succumbed to royal favours, royal threats'.[2] By late March, 1784, Fox's majority was reduced to just one vote. Pitt now felt politically strong enough to go to the country. By this time Robinson and Atkinson had completed their homework in the boroughs, using public funds, company funds, secret service funds and promises of titles. When Pitt dissolved Parliament in March 1784, therefore, the membership of the new House was no longer in doubt. Lists of the members who had been agreed upon were already being handed around in Westminster.[3] The elections of March 1784 were, accordingly, a disaster for the followers of Fox and North who lost 89 seats (mostly Northite). It is generally acknowledged that the influence of the Crown and of the East India Company played a significant part in this result, their joint efforts being co-ordinated by Robinson and Atkinson. It is held that there were also other factors: many followers of both Fox and North are said to have resented the 'unnatural' and 'unprincipled' alliance between the two leaders. 'Fox's India Bill' was unpopular in itself, because it was widely seen as being aimed, not at reform, but at getting the loot of India into the same unprincipled hands as had clutched at power through coalition. That was the picture presented by most of the London Press, in the three months between the dismissal of the Coalition and the General Election. Much of the press

[1] *Corr.* V, 121–2.
[2] Mitchell, *op. cit.*, p. 91.
[3] Laprade, 'William Pitt' etc.

campaign was fuelled and paid for by the East India Company, and by Paul Benfield in particular. In any case, John Robinson, in his calculations, took no account of public opinion, only of bribes. [1]

From Nadir to Impeachment

Burke's political situation, as the 1784 parliamentary session opened, was deeply depressing. The measure which had brought down the Fox-North Coalition was Burke's India Bill, even though it carried Fox's name. The Bill was also at the centre of Pitt's successful election campaign. On Burke's shoulders, therefore, rested most of the responsibility for the political demise of 'Fox's Martyrs', as the 89 coalition followers who lost their seats were known. One might expect, therefore, that he would have little influence over his colleagues in the new Parliament. One might expect, in particular, that any attempt by him to suggest India, as a principal focus for opposition in the new Parliament, would have been treated with derision: there was no more unpromising topic, for the opposition. It was because of India, after all, that they were in opposition. Yet, against all the odds, Burke was to carry not only his own colleagues but eventually a majority of this very parliament, with him in impeaching Warren Hastings, former Governor-General of Bengal, before the bar of the House of Lords. This was an extraordinary achievement, and it provides a measure of the persuasive powers which Burke could exert, when engaged on a matter about which he felt deeply, and had thought deeply.

A year earlier, in the previous Parliament, Burke had entered into a solemn pledge, concerning Warren Hastings: 'Burke pledged himself to God, to his country, to that House and to the unfortunate people of India, to bring to justice as far as in him lay, the greatest delinquent that India ever saw.' [2] In the new Parliament he now set out, in what seemed extremely adverse political conditions, to fulfil that pledge.

The first opportunity came on 28 July, when he rose to oppose Pitt's East India Bill. He opposed it for its inadequacies, as compared

---

[1] Laprade, *Public opinion* etc.
[2] *Parl. Hist.* xxiii, 800 (speech of 17 April 1783) quoted in *Writings and Speeches V, 194* n.

with 'Fox's East India Bill', but he did not attack it very strongly. It appeared to be a serious reform measure partly along the lines of Fox's Bill, and the principle on which it was based – 'supervision' rather than 'control' was one which Burke had long favoured, during earlier periods in opposition. Clearly his main object in this speech was to signal the renewal, in the new Parliament, of his attack on Warren Hastings. That attack took up most of his speech, and furnished its conclusion 'that he had no personal cause of dislike to Mr. Hastings; he felt no prejudice against him: on the contrary, when he first sat in the select committee, he felt a strong prepossession in his favour, that the lofty panegyrics he had heard of him; so much so, that the friends of Sir Elijah Impey had upbraided him with being greatly partial to the Governor-General. If that partiality was now no more, it was because it had been rooted out by the discoveries he had made in the Company's records, while he sat in the select committee: All he wanted was, that the House would give him an opportunity to defend the reports, and to make good all the charges they had brought against the Governor-General. Since he saw he was not likely to obtain that, he would not say any thing more against the bill, but simply to enter his protest against it in the name of the injured natives of India, whose grievances were to be inquired into and redressed by – those who had occasioned them.'

The speech on Pitt's East India Bill does not fall into the Great Melody class. But much of one delivered two days later, the 'Speech on Almas Ali Khan', does fall into this category. In an editorial note introducing the speech, P. J. Marshall writes: 'Burke's contributions to the debate on 30 July are vivid evidence that he was in a disturbed and anxious state of mind during the summer of 1784, but they are also some of the most moving expressions of his concern and compassion for India. Embittered by the defeat of the Coalition, by what he took to be criticism by his colleagues of his part in its fall, and by public ridicule of him by supporters of the new government, he was determined to justify himself and to force what he saw as an an apathetic and complacent public to accept the existence of the Indian abuses, which "had left on his mind such an impression of horror, as had frequently deprived him of sleep".' V, 460.

In the speech Burke claims that, under Hastings,

a confederacy was formed, for the sole purpose of extolling the India government as a good one, and the Governor as unimpeachable. The whole drift of this crooked policy, was to keep the poor natives wholly out of sight. We might hear enough about what great and illustrious exploits were daily performing on that conspicuous theatre by Britons: But unless some dreadful catastrophe was to take place – unless some hero or heroine was to fall – unless the tragedy was to be a very deep and bloody one; – we were never to hear of any native's being an actor! No. The field was altogether engrossed by Englishmen; and those who were chiefly interested in the matter actually excluded. . . . He now appeared in behalf of those Indians, whom our barbarous policy had ruined and made desperate. Their grievances were unparalleled in history, and seemed to increase in proportion as they became unable to bear them. The English establishment among them appeared to have no other subject, than to accumulate their oppression and distress.

Burke then comes to Warren Hastings and his dealings with Almas Ali Khan, the largest *amil*, or revenue administrator, in Oudh, a principality then subject to the absolute and arbitrary rule of Warren Hastings. Burke had come into possession of Hastings's instructions sent to John Bristow, Resident at Lucknow on 23 October 1782 as to how Almas Ali Khan is to be dealt with:

If he [Almas] has been guilty of any criminal offence to the Nabob his master, for which no immunity is provided in the engagement, or he shall break any one of the conditions of it, I do most strictly enjoin you, and it must be your special care to endeavour, either by force or surprize, to secure his person, and bring him to justice: by bringing him to justice, I mean that you urge the Nabob, on due conviction, to punish him with death, as a necessary example to deter others from the commission of the like crimes; nor must you desist till this is effected. – I cannot prescribe the means: but to guard myself against that obloquy to which I may be exposed by a forced misconstruction of this order, by those who may hereafter be employed in searching our records for cavils and informations against me, I think it proper to forbid, and protest against, the use of any fraudulent artifice or treachery to accomplish the end which I have prescribed; and as you alone are privy to the order, you will of course observe the greatest secrecy that it may not transpire: but I repeat my recommendation of it as one of the first and most essential duties of your office.

Knowing the political conditions in Oudh, and Hastings's *modus operandi*, Burke sees that the instructions are a carefully wrapped-up order to have Almas Ali Khan murdered, so that his money can be seized.

Alas! the situation and property of this man, like a great many of his countrymen, destroyed him, attracted the attention, stimulated the avarice, and brought down the vengeance of the British on his head. The crime of having money was imputed to this unfortunate prince, which, like the sin against the Holy Ghost in Christian theology, in India politics can never be forgiven. It seemed impossible, in this instance, to plunder without murder. The bloody edict is therefore issued. Mark how soon the fatal science in that country is brought to perfection! No matter what is done, provided the manner of doing it be properly managed. Yet he had heard of a letter, and of a murder, or something very like it, recited in that letter; an extract of which had come to his hand. From this extract he learned that orders had been sent to arrest Almas Ali Cawn: but this gentleman-like business must be done in the most gentleman-like manner. The Chief must be taken, and he must also be put to death; but all this must be contrived as to imply no treachery. Here was honour of a very singular and nice description – Plunder, peculation, and even assassination, without treachery! – Such was the extreme refinement which distinguished the cruelties of the East. All possible delicacy was even to be shown in the exercise of a ferocity, the foulest and the most atrocious that ever blackened the prostitution of usurped authority.

As editor of Volume V of *Writings and Speeches*, P. J. Marshall uncritically accepts Hastings's version of his reasons for giving those instructions: 'By 1782 his loyalty to the Wazir [alias Nawab] was suspect and there were rumours that he might throw off his allegiance altogether. Hastings ordered that he be brought to heel, by violence if necessary.' (*Writings and Speeches* V, 464, n. 1.) I find it depressing to read this sort of thing, from the pen of a distinguished scholar, in the late twentieth century. The authority of the Wazir/Nawab, in the 1780s was a fiction, and so was the idea of 'loyalty' to him. Rumours about rebellious plots were a regular part of the Hastings system, as a prelude to the seizure of someone's wealth. The Begums of Oudh got this treatment, and so did the Rajah of Benares, Chait Singh. The rumours were the pretext, in all cases, for drastic action, though no evidence, or confirmation of any of them, was ever produced. And Marshall's summary of Hastings's instructions is euphemistic. Hastings did not order that Almas 'be brought to heel, by violence if necessary'. He ordered that 'you urge the Nabob, on due conviction, to put him to death.' 'Urge' in the context of Hastings's Oudh, meant 'order', it meant getting some form of death-sentence ('due conviction') out of the helpless Nawab, to clear Hastings of the intended murder. But the misty, myopic late-Victorian retrospect on the India of Warren Hastings has a remarkably long half-life, into our own day.

Burke's speeches on India in 1783 and 1784, were often met with derisive laughter, but it seems that the laughter, during this particular speech, was more persistent and concerted than usual, and that the head of the new Administration, the young William Pitt, was giving a lead in this. Burke takes him up on it: 'It became the Minister of a great and generous nation, instead of laughing at the miseries, of his fellow-creatures, to regard these important calls with all his attention. Good God! he exclaimed, What must the whole world think of a young man, who could hear of oppression, peculation, rapine, and even murder, not with insensibility only, but with levity – with laughter! Whatever sport it was to the Treasury Bench, it was, he could assure them, no sport to the poor helpless men, who daily saw the effects of their industry, the means of their subsistence, extorted from them, and their families reduced to abjection and want!' There is some reason to believe that this went home. Pitt was later to acknowledge that his contemptuous treatment of Burke's case, in the early years of his Administration, was unwarranted (see below p. 358).

The religious dimension, always present, but not often explicit, in Burke's thinking about India, is more obtrusive in this speech than anywhere else. And the negative side of Burke's feelings towards England finds more open expression here than it ever did before. And it is significant that the negative feelings towards England are intertwined with the religious dimension. The following passage is coming from deep down in Burke's psyche:

He, for his own part, thought, the dreadful procedure of Providence was so strongly and obviously marked, as to have escaped no man but those who wished not to observe it – He believed from his heart, the vengeance of heaven to be raised against this country. By authorising the massacres which had been so foully perpetrated and repeated in India, Britain was now become a land of blood – Much innocent blood had been shed, and he doubted was still shedding – But an avenger would certainly appear and plead the cause of the wronged with those who had wronged them – Yes, the arm of God was abroad – His righteous visitation was already begun, and who could tell where it might end? He knew with accuracy how to discriminate the good from the bad, those who had, from those who had not, imbrued their hands in the blood of their fellow creatures. The instruments of his wrath were infinite, and would be exercised without ceasing or interval, till the redress of the wretched, and the punishment of the oppressors were completed. This great work Providence was visibly carrying on against a country, who, by its crooked policy, had ripened itself for destruction. What were the infatuation which seized us so generally, the debt which hung about our neck, with a weight which precipitated our downfall; our want of union, our want of principle, and our want of consequence, but certain indications of a malediction which the dreadful wretchedness we had entailed on a people much better than we, had brought at last on our own heads?

Burke's next speech on India, 'On Nabob of Arcot's Debts', (28 February 1785)[1] is one of his greatest, and marks a turning point in the debate over India. After this speech, the tide begins to turn, in Burke's favour. 'Almas Ali Khan' and 'Nabob of Arcot' are mostly in different keys, but part of the same Melody. 'Nabob of Arcot' is largely cooler and less emotional than 'Almas', but in its close, the same emotions appear, under rather better, but still imperfect, control. Its background is as follows: Paul Benfield and his colleagues in the Council at Madras were in the habit of lending, or purporting to lend, huge sums of money to the Nawab (or Nabob) of Arcot, who was their prisoner and puppet at Madras, just as the Nawab of Oudh was prisoner and puppet of Warren Hastings in Bengal. By autumn 1784 the Company's Court of Directors had decided that a fund from the revenues of the Carnatic – south-eastern India – would be set up for debt repayment, but the directors insisted that claims on the fund could only be accepted after some form of examination. The directors were, however, overruled by the new Board of Control set up under Pitt's India Act. The Board decided that the Nabob's debts, as stated by his creditors, were to be paid, in full, without inquiry of any kind. Burke believed that this startling decision by the Board of Control was the result of a corrupt bargain, reached between Henry Dundas (who, as well as being Navy Treasurer, handled India affairs for Pitt, and picked the Board of Control) and the Nabob's 'creditors', for their financial and other assistance to the Pitt campaign in the elections of 1784. P. J. Marshall, generally reserved about Burke's allegations, cannot find much wrong with this one:

'Burke's allegations of political corruption in Britain may again have an element of exaggeration, but there seems to be real substance to them. In its simplest form an "Arcot squad" of MPs, welded into a unit by common interest and for sale to the Government, did not exist. But individuals concerned with the debts certainly put all their weight behind Pitt and expected some reward. The terms in which the

[1] *Writings and Speeches* V, 478–617.

Board of Control altered the directors' dispatch show a remarkable similarity to the representations which such individuals pressed upon Dundas and his advisers.' That last sentence seems to represent what would, nowadays, be called 'the smoking gun'.

Burke directed his attack against Dundas and Pitt. Dundas was particularly vulnerable, because, in the previous Parliament, he had been a major ally of Burke in exposing Indian abuses. Dundas was now himself involved in the very type of transaction which he had formerly sought to expose. But Pitt was also vulnerable, though in a different way. Like his father, Chatham, the younger Pitt had a high reputation for probity, which he valued and liked to flaunt. The 'Nabob' transaction did not sit well with such a reputation. I believe that Pitt must have suffered, as he listened to Burke's speech on the Nabob of Arcot's debts, and that Pitt's suffering, on that occasion, contributed to his *volte face*, in the matter of Warren Hastings, in the following year (below pp. 354–6). Burke asked:

Whether the Chancellor of the Exchequer, and the Treasurer of the Navy, [Pitt and Dundas] acting as a Board of Control, are justified by law or policy, in suspending the legal arrangements made by the Court of Directors, in order to transfer the public revenues to the private emolument of certain servants of the East India Company, without the enquiry into the origin and justice of their claims, prescribed by an act of Parliament?

It is not contended, that the act of parliament did not expressly ordain an enquiry. It is not asserted that this enquiry was not, with equal precision of terms, specially committed under particular regulations to the Court of Directors. I conceive, therefore, the Board of Control had no right whatsoever to intermeddle in that business. There is nothing certain in the principles of jurisprudence, if this be not undeniably true, that when a special authority is given to any persons by name, to do some particular act, that no others, by virtue of general powers, can obtain a legal title to intrude themselves into that trust, and to exercise those special functions in their place. I therefore consider the intermeddling of ministers in this affair as a downright usurpation. But if the strained construction, by which they have forced themselves into a suspicious office (which every man, delicate with regard to character [i.e. reputation], would rather have sought constructions to avoid) were perfectly sound and perfectly legal, of this I am certain, that they cannot be justified in declining the enquiry which had been prescribed to the Court of Directors. If the Board of Control did lawfully possess the right of executing the special trust given to that court, they must take it as they found it, subject to the very same regulations which bound the Court of Directors. It will be allowed that the Court of Directors had no authority to dispense with either the substance, or the mode of enquiry prescribed by the act of parliament. If they had not, where, in the act, did the Board of Control acquire that capacity? Indeed, it was impossible they should acquire it. – What must we think of the fabric and texture of an act of parliament which should find it necessary to prescribe a strict inquisition; that should descend into minute regulations for the conduct of that inquisition; that should commit this trust to a particular description of men, and in the very same breath should enable another body, at their own pleasure, to supersede all the provisions the legislature had made, and to defeat the whole purpose, end, and object of the law? This cannot be supposed even of an act of parliament conceived by the Ministers themselves, and brought forth during the delirium of the last session.

Burke lays down a general principle, to which he senses resistance:

Fraud, injustice, oppression, peculation, engendered in India, are crimes of the same blood, family and cast, with those that are born and bred in England. To go no farther than the case before us; you are just as competent to judge whether the sum of four millions sterling ought, or ought not, to be passed from the public treasury into a private pocket, without any title except the claim of the parties, when the issue of fact is laid in Madras, as when it is laid in Westminster. [1]

As Burke knew, of course, if the millions in question were to come from the British taxpayer, the scandal of their transfer, in such circumstances, would have brought down Pitt's Administration. But as the money was to be paid by natives of India, parliamentary interest in the transaction was limited.

Henry Dundas, in opposing Fox's motion for papers about the Nabob of Arcot's debts, was refusing relevant information to Parliament. On this ground Burke launches a devastating attack on Dundas:

It is to perpetuate the abuses which are subverting the fabric of your empire, that the motion is opposed. It is therefore with reason (and if he has power to carry himself through, I commend his prudence) that the right honourable gentleman makes his stand at the very outset; and boldly refuses all parliamentary information. Let him admit but one step towards enquiry, and he is undone. You must be ignorant, or he cannot be safe. But before his curtain is let down, and the shades of eternal night shall veil our eastern dominions from our view, permit me, Sir, to avail

[1] *Writings and Speeches* V, 488.

myself of the means which were furnished in anxious and inquisitive times, to demonstrate out of this single act of the present Minister, what advantages you are to derive from permitting the greatest concern of this nation to be separated from the cognizance, and exempted even out of the competence, of parliament. The greatest body of your revenue, your most numerous armies, your most important commerce, the richest sources of your public credit, (contrary to every idea of the known settled policy of England) are on the point of being converted into a mystery of state. You are going to have one half of the globe hid even from the common liberal curiosity of an English gentleman ... Here a grand revolution commences. Mark the period, and mark the circumstances. In most of the capital changes that are recorded in the principles and system of any government, a public benefit of some kind or other has been pretended. The revolution commenced in something plausible; in something which carried the appearance at least of punishment of delinquency, or correction of abuse. But here, in the very moment of the conversion of a department of British government into an Indian mystery, and in the very act in which the change commences, a corrupt, private interest is set up in direct opposition to the necessities of the nation. A diversion is made of millions of the public money from the public treasury to a private purse. It is not into secret negotiations for war, peace, or alliance, that the House of Commons is forbidden to enquire. It is a matter of account; it is a pecuniary transaction; it is the demand of a suspected steward upon ruined tenants and an embarrassed master, that the Commons of Great Britain are commanded not to inspect. The whole tenor of the right honourable gentleman's argument is consonant to the nature of his policy. The system of concealment is fostered by a system of falsehood. False facts, false colours, false names of persons and things, are its whole support.

Then Burke returns to 'the young Minister', to Pitt himself, linking him personally to Benfield and his associates:

In my opinion the courage of the minister was the most wonderful part of the transaction, especially as he must have read, or rather the right honourable gentleman says, he has read for him, whole volumes upon the subject. The volumes, by the way, are not by one tenth part so numerous as the right honourable gentleman has thought proper to pretend, in order to frighten you from enquiry; but in these volumes, such as they are, the minister must have found a full authority for a suspicion (at the very least) of every thing relative to the great fortunes made at Madras. What is that authority? Why no other than the standing authority for all the claims which the Ministry had thought fit to provide for – the grand debtor – the Nabob of Arcot himself. Hear that Prince, in the letter written to the Court of Directors, at the precise period, whilst the main body of these debts were contracting. In his Letter he states himself to be, what undoubtedly he is, a most competent witness to this point. After speaking of the war with Hyder Ali in 1768 and 1769, and of other measures which he censures (whether right or wrong it signifies nothing) and into which he says he had been led by the Company's servants; he proceeds in this matter – 'If all these things were against the real interests of the Company, they are ten thousand times more against mine, and against the prosperity of my country, and the happiness of my people; for your interests and mine are the same. What were they owing to them? to the private views of a few individuals, who have enriched themselves at the expense of your influence, and of my country; for your servants HAVE NO TRADE IN THIS COUNTRY; neither do you pay them high wages, yet in a few years they return to England, with many lacks of pagodas.[1] How can you or I account for such immense fortunes, acquired in so short a time, without any visible means of getting them?'

Burke succinctly describes the working of the Nabob of Arcot's debts:

If this body of private claims of debt, real or devised, were a question, as it is falsely pretended, between the Nabob of Arcot as debtor, and Paul Benfield and his associates as creditors, I am sure I should give myself but little trouble about it. If the hoards of oppression were the fund for satisfying the claims of bribery and peculation, who would wish to interfere between such litigants? If the demands were confined to what might be drawn from the treasures which the Company's records uniformly assert that the Nabob is in possession of; or if he had mines of gold or silver, or diamonds (as we know that he has none) these gentlemen might break open his hoards, or dig in his mines, without any disturbance from me. But the gentlemen on the other side of the House know as well as I do, and they dare not contradict me, that the Nabob of Arcot and his creditors are not adversaries, but collusive parties, and that the whole transaction is under a false colour and false names. The litigation is not, nor ever has been, between their rapacity and his hoarded riches. No; it is between him and them combining and confederating on one side, and the public revenues, and the miserable inhabitants of a ruined country, on the other. These are the real plaintiffs and the real defendants in the suit. Refusing a shilling from his hoards for the satisfaction of any demand, the Nabob of Arcot is always ready, nay, he earn-

[1] 'Each pagoda being worth about eight shillings . . .' Burke's *Annual Register* 1774 p. 115; one lakh = 100,000 (rupees etc.)

estly, and with eagerness and passion, contends for delivering up to these pretended creditors his territory and his subjects. It is therefore not from treasuries and mines, but from the food of your unpaid armies, from the blood withheld from the veins, and whipt out of the backs of the most miserable of men, that we are to pamper extortion, usury, and peculation, under the false names of debtors and creditors of state.

Then Burke swoops to punish Dundas, who had rashly advanced, as an argument in favour of paying the creditors' claims in full, that payment in this way had been approved by the Presidency (or council) of the Company at Madras. Paul Benfield and his extortionist colleagues constituted a majority of the Council in question at the material time. Turning to Dundas, Burke says:

The right honourable gentleman, with an address peculiar to himself, every now and then slides in the Presidency of Madras, as synonymous to the Company. That the Presidency did approve the debt, is certain. But the right honourable gentleman, as prudent in suppressing, as skilful in bringing forward his matter, has not chosen to tell you that the Presidency were the very persons guilty of contracting this loan; creditors themselves, and agents, and trustees for all the other creditors. For this the Court of Directors accuse them of breach of trust; and for this the right honourable gentleman considers them as perfectly good authority for those claims. It is pleasant [i.e. amusing] to hear a gentleman of the law quote the approbation of creditors as an authority for their own debt.

Burke recalls how the creditors themselves, in 1781, had been willing to abate their claims by 25 per cent. Then he turns on Pitt, in his capacity as Chancellor of the Exchequer, for having met the creditors' claims in full:

But what corrupt men, in the fond imaginations of sanguine avarice, had not the confidence to propose, they have found a Chancellor of the Exchequer in England hardy enough to undertake for them. He has cheered their drooping spirits. He has thanked the peculators for not despairing of their commonwealth. He has told them they were too modest. He has replaced the twenty-five per cent. which, in order to lighten themselves, they had abandoned in their conscious terror. Instead of cutting off the interest, as they had themselves consented to do, with the fourth of the capital, he has added the whole growth of four years usury of twelve per cent. to the first over-grown principal; and has again grafted on this meliorated stock a perpetual annuity of six per cent. to take place from the year 1781. Let no man hereafter talk of the decaying energies of nature. All the acts and monuments in the records of peculation; the consolidated corruption of ages; the patterns of exemplary plunder in the heroic times of Roman iniquity, never equalled the gigantic corruption of this single act. Never did Nero, in all the insolent prodigality of despotism, deal out to his praetorian guards a donation fit to be named with the largess showered down by the bounty of our Chancellor of the Exchequer on the faithful band of his Indian Sepoys.

After much detailed and cogent argument the emotional temperature rises, and that imagery of physical corruption, which betrays the arousal of 'the Irish level' of his psyche (as in the 1780 Bristol Guildhall speech) makes its appearance.

That debt forms the foul putrid mucus, in which are engendered the whole brood of creeping ascarides, all the endless involutions, the eternal knot, added to a knot of those inexpugnable tape-worms which devour the nutriment, and eat up the bowels of India.

Then back to Paul Benfield and the 1784 election:

But it was necessary to authenticate the coalition between the men of intrigue in India and the minister of intrigue in England, by a studied display of the power of this their connecting link. Every trust, every honour, every distinction, was to be heaped upon him, Benfield. He was at once made a director of the India Company; made an alderman of London; and to be made, if ministry could prevail (and I am sorry to say how near, how very near they were prevailing) representative of the capital of this kingdom [a reference to the seat at Westminster, hotly contested and narrowly won, by Fox against Benfield, supported by Pitt and George III]. But to secure his services against all risque, he was brought in for a ministerial borough. On his part, he was not wanting in zeal for the common cause. His advertisements shew his motives, and the merits upon which he stood. For your minister, this worn-out veteran submitted to enter into the dusty field of the London contest; and you all remember, that in the same virtuous cause, he submitted to keep a sort of public office or countinghouse, where the whole business of the last general election was managed. It was openly managed by the direct agent and attorney of Benfield. It was managed upon Indian principles, and for an Indian interest. This was the golden cup of abominations; this the chalice of the fornications of rapine, usury, and oppression, which was held out by the gorgeous eastern harlot; which so many of the people, so many of the nobles of this land, had drained to the very dregs. Do you think that no reckoning was to follow this lewd debauch? that no payment was to be demanded for this riot of public drunkenness and

national prostitution? Here! you have it here before you. The principal
of the grand election manager must be indemnified; accordingly the
claims of Benfield and his crew must be put above all enquiry.

Burke realises that public opinion, in spite of what was obviously
a corrupt political deal, will tend to acquit Pitt personally, as he
will (rightly) not be suspected of having enriched himself by the
transaction. Burke is at pains to establish the exact nature of the link
between the high-minded Pitt and the low-minded Benfield. This is
a classic treatment of the relationship between avarice and ambition:

I know that the ministers will think it little less than acquittal, that they
are not charged with having taken to themselves some part of the money
of which they have made so liberal a donation to their partizans, though
the charge may be indisputably fixed upon the corruption of their politics.
For my part, I follow their crimes to that point to which legal presumptions and natural indications lead me, without considering what species
of evil motive tends most to aggravate or to extenuate the guilt of their
conduct. But if I am to speak my private sentiments, I think that in a
thousand cases for one it would be far less mischievous to the public,
and full as little dishonourable to themselves, to be polluted with direct
bribery, than thus to become a standing auxiliary to the oppression,
usury, and peculation of multitudes, in order to obtain a corrupt support
to their power. It is by bribing, not so often by being bribed, that wicked
politicians bring ruin on mankind. Avarice is a rival to the pursuits of
many. It finds a multitude of checks, and many opposers, in every walk
of life. But the objects of ambition are for the few; and every person
who aims at indirect profit, and therefore wants other protection than
innocence and law, instead of its rival, becomes its instrument. There is
a natural allegiance and fealty due to this domineering paramount evil,
from all the vassal vices, which acknowledge its superiority, and readily
militate under its banners; and it is under that discipline alone that avarice
is able to spread to any considerable extent, or to render itself a general
public mischief. It is therefore no apology for ministers, that they have
not been bought by the East India delinquents, but that they have only
formed an alliance with them for screening each other from justice,
according to the exigence of their several necessities.

As he approaches the end of his speech Burke's anger at political
corruption takes on, once more, the horrid imagery of physical corruption:

It is difficult for the most wise and upright government to correct the
abuses of remote delegated power, productive of unmeasured wealth,

and protected by the boldness and strength of the same ill-got riches. These abuses, full of their own wild native vigour, will grow and flourish under mere neglect. But where the supreme authority, not content with winking at the rapacity of its inferior instruments, is so shameless and corrupt as openly to give bounties and premiums for disobedience to its laws; when it will not trust to the activity of avarice in the pursuit of its own gains; when it secures public robbery by all the careful jealousy and attention with which it ought to protect property from such violence; the commonwealth then is become totally perverted from its purposes; neither God nor man will long endure it; not will it long endure itself. In that case, there is an unnatural infection, a pestilential taint fermenting in the constitution of society, which fever and convulsions of some kind or other must throw off; or in which the vital powers, worsted in an unequal struggle, are pushed back upon themselves, and by a reversal of their whole functions, fester to gangrene, to death; and instead of what was but just now the delight and boast of the creation, there will be cast out in the face of the sun, a bloated, putrid, noisome carcass, full of stench and poison, an offence, a horror, a lesson to the world.

Burke chooses to end on a dying fall. He acknowledges his own isolation, and the repugnance which this topic inspires even in his own friends.

I know on what ground I tread. This subject, at one time taken up with so much fervour and zeal, is no longer a favourite in this House. The House itself has undergone a great and signal revolution. To some the subject is strange and uncouth; to several harsh and distasteful; to the reliques of the last parliament it is a matter of fear and apprehension. It is natural for those who have seen their friends sink in the tornado which raged during the late shift of the monsoon, and have hardly escaped on the planks of the general wreck [the general election], it is but too natural for them, as soon as they make [mark?] the rocks and quicksands of their former disasters, to put about their new-built barks, and, as much as possible, to keep aloof from this perilous lee shore.

The tone of this passage should not be taken for one of resigned acceptance. Burke is really needling his friends, shaming them into giving him more support. Fox, in particular, should feel the weight of the implied reprimand, and respond to it, in the direction desired. And he did.

Burke closed on a note of quiet determination:

For one, the worst event of this day, though it may deject, shall not break or subdue me. The call upon us is authoritative. Let who will shrink back, I shall be found at my post. Baffled, discountenanced, subdued, discredited, as the cause of justice and humanity is, it will be only the dearer to me. Whoever therefore shall at any time bring before you any thing towards the relief of our distressed fellow-citizens in India, and towards a subversion of the present most corrupt and oppressive system for its government, in me shall find, a weak I am afraid, but a steady, earnest, and faithful assistant.

Of the scene when Burke sat down, P. J. Marshall writes, 'Nathaniel Wraxall (see Chapter III above, p. 211), an M.P. who actually was connected with the Nawab of Arcot and was not therefore an impartial witness, described the extremely hostile reception given to Burke when he finally finished speaking. Ministers chose to ignore him, and "Burke's violence recoiling on himself, a loud cry of question arose from every part of the assembly. Not a word was uttered in reply, Pitt disdaining to refute allegations which his character sufficiently repelled. The vote was taken and the papers were refused by 164 votes to 69."'[1]

Pitt was wise not to attempt a reply; no serious reply was possible. Burke was on absolutely solid ground, as both contemporaries and historians have agreed. Lord Cornwallis – Hastings's reforming successor as Governor-General – told Dundas: 'You only consented that their fraudulent and infamous claims should be put into any course of payment, because you could not help it.'[2]

N. C. Philips sums up the relation of this transaction to the 1784 General Election: 'The Board's decision on the debts was undoubtedly unjust, and the evil that it supposedly aimed at checking was actually encouraged. The evidence afforded by the Board's handling of this Arcot question supports the view that Pitt, through the

---

[1] *Writings and Speeches* V, 552 n. Marshall also quotes a felicitous contemporary tribute to the speech: 'Every thing is borne out with an energy of reasoning and a vehemence of rhetoric of which, while they both rise to the highest pitch, it is difficult to decide whether it be the one or the other that carries conviction with the most irresistible force to our hearts. *English Review* vi (1785) p. 208.

[2] Letter of 4 November 1788; quoted in N. C. Philips, *The East India Company, 1781–1834* (Manchester U.P. 1940). Charles Cornwallis (1738–1805), first marquess, was opposed to taxing American colonists but when war came scored two important victories. In 1782, thanks to the incapacity of other British generals, he was forced to surrender at Yorktown. In India, as Commander-in-Chief and Governor-General, he again distinguished himself militarily and, so says the *Chambers Biographical Dictionary*, 'by unwearying efforts to promote the welfare of the natives'. In 1798 he crushed the rebellion in Ireland and 'showed a rare union of vigour and humanity'.

agency of Dundas, Atkinson, Macpherson and Call, had received political support from the Arcot interest in the general election, and that Dundas had in return promised to procure a settlement of the creditors' claims on the Nawab without preliminary investigation.' (Philips, *op. cit.* p. 40). Some years later one of the Arcot extortionists, James Macpherson, wrote to the confidential agent John Robinson: 'There are apprehensions of Burke's being in the Board of Control. . . . If they will agree, all the fat will be in the fire.'

The best answer to Burke's speech from the point of view of a practical politician, as Pitt was, consisted not of rational argument but of shouting – from his followers – and then voting, with the majority supplied by the 1784 election. But Pitt, as well as being an excellent practical politician, was also a fastidious human being. As such he can have enjoyed, neither the speech itself, nor his own inability to answer it, nor the mindless bawling of his own troops. I think, from the sequel, that he may have begun to wonder whether it was a good idea, from the point of view of his own reputation, to go on standing between Edmund Burke and the abuses of India.

Burke, towards the end of the Speech on the Nabob of Arcot's Debts, acknowledged and emphasised his isolation. But he was already beginning to move out of isolation, through the sheer force of that speech. By the following year not merely Charles James Fox, but William Pitt as well, will be helping him towards the impeachment of Warren Hastings.

*   *   *

Only a few faint strains of the Melody are heard over the next three years, before it fully resumes, with the actual Impeachment. The intervening years were occupied with rallying his own party to the cause of impeachment, and then in presenting the case to the Commons.

In February 1785 Hastings, troubled by reports of proceedings in Parliament, sailed for home. On 20 June Burke gave notice to the Commons: 'That if no other gentleman would undertake the business, he would, on a future day, make a motion respecting the conduct of a gentleman just returned from India.' This was the first specific move in the process that would lead to the Impeachment. By the end of the year Fox is worried about where Burke is heading, and enlists the improbable aid of Philip Francis. Burke has now been working closely with Francis over Indian affairs for four years, but about this time Francis seems to have tried, or pretended to try, to help Fox bring Burke under control. Holden Furber, the Editor of Volume V of the *Correspondence*, writes (page 240, n. 2): 'Burke appears to have been in some disagreement with Francis and Fox about the Opposition's tactics on India for the new session. While Francis and Fox apparently wished to introduce resolutions which must meet the approbation of almost every body Burke wanted a comprehensive and direct attack on Hastings.'

Francis had invited Burke in November, to his house at Sheen to meet Fox. From Burke's reply it can be seen that he foresees, and resents, an impending effort to talk him round:

> I shall be with you on Saturday next, if some accident that I dont foresee should not prevent me. I have lately passed a very pleasant day with Mr. Fox here. I shall be happy in having the same satisfaction renewed, with the improvements it must receive at Sheen.
>
> I do not well see how the East can be kept out of our Conversation; but if I were to choose, it should make mere matter of conversation; and not the Subject of a Business consultation. There can be no difference between us on the general principles of Indian politicks. On the same abstract View of things the plan of Conduct you propose must meet the approbation of almost every body. Therefore any further discussion of the Subject as an affair of parliamentary management is unnecessary. When you or he [Fox] bring any India question before the House, the single Vote, to which I am reduced, will be given to Justice in the first place; in the next to you and to Mr. Fox. If I were to enter into any further detail, besides the indecorum of making a man's personal feelings a Topic in the consideration of a great publick concern, I should fall into the more disgusting impropriety of Teizing you upon points, on which I have more than once troubled you already. If a man is disabled from rendering any essential Service to his principles or his party, he ought at least to contrive to make his conversation as little disagreeable as he can to the Society which his friends may still be indulgent enough to hold with him. [1]

This letter is interesting. It runs counter to the generally accepted picture of Francis as 'egging Burke on' against Hastings. And it shows Burke as clearly determined to decide, and prosecute, Indian policy on his own, without deference to the views of his party leader. He was going to go ahead anyway, even without Francis, against Hastings; his party and his leader could follow, or not, as they chose. And it was the Party that gave in, not Burke. One can only speculate

---

[1] *Corr.* V, 240; letter of 23 November 1785.

about Francis's motives, in apparently trying to hold back Burke, from attacking Hastings. Had Francis's craving for revenge abated since the days when he imagined himself to be Nuncomar's ghost? I doubt it. I think that, after four years in close contact with Burke, Francis knew that there was now no possibility of deflecting Burke from attacking, and seeking to impeach, Hastings. So Francis could safely ingratiate himself with the party leader, by 'helping' him in an enterprise which would certainly fail, to the 'helper's' secret relief. The 'Junius' side of Francis was reconciled with the 'Nuncomar' side.

Before the new sessions began, in January 1786, Burke was able to secure a united opposition. A meeting at the Duke of Portland's house 'decided to adopt the impeachment as an opposition measure'.[1] The Arcot speech and Burke's unyielding determination had clearly made their impact, on Fox and his friends.

In February Burke first declared his intention to impeach Warren Hastings. He ruled out an alternative legal procedure:

> His invincible objection to a bill of pains and penalties would of course lead him to the proposition of another mode; and this, at once ancient and constitutional, was a bill of impeachment; yet, even in the adoption of this measure, he would not endeavour to introduce the usual practice of first moving an immediate bill of impeachment, and next constituting a committee for the purpose of discovering and arranging articles, in order that they might serve as its foundation; a recourse which, in his humble opinion, carried with it an appearance of warmth and prejudice exceedingly repugnant to the justice, dignity, and honour of the House. With their permission, he should move for papers, from the contents of which he would endeavour to collect the several articles into their necessary points of view, and when these should, in the contemplation of the House seem (as, without rancour and, in the cool spirit of impartial justice, he could venture to intimate his belief that they would seem) charges of an atrocious nature, he then designed to move for an impeachment at the bar of the House of Lords.[2]

Pitt, in reply, was cautious, but not unyielding: 'Every paper which was material to elucidate the subject ought to be produced. He was neither a determined friend nor foe to Mr. Hastings; but he was resolved to support the principles of justice and equity.' Pitt added: 'Should the right hon. gentleman bring fully home to Mr. Hastings the violent imputations of atrocious crimes, he, for his own part,

[1] Marshall, *Impeachment of Warren Hastings*, p. 38.
[2] *Parl. Hist.* xxiv, 1060–1095.

far from screening, would wish to bring down upon him the most exemplary punishment.' In the event, Burke got most, though not all, of the papers he needed for the impeachment. For the first time, in the House of Commons elected in 1784, Burke is making progress with his Indian business; more progress indeed than he had expected, for he had written to Francis, before the opening of the new Session: 'We know that we bring before a bribed tribunal a prejudged cause.'[1]

On 4 April 1786, 'Mr. Burke in his place [having] charged Warren Hastings, esq., late Governor-General of Bengal, with sundry high crimes and misdemeanours, presented to the House several Articles of charge. All the said Articles were delivered in at the table and read.'[2] The Clerk of the House, John Hatsell, was impressed, which is unusual, in any age, and therefore significant. Four days after the presentation of the first charges Hatsell wrote to a friend: 'I don't see how they will get rid of Mr. Burke.'[3]

Warren Hastings appeared before the Commons, by leave, to offer his own defence, on 1 May. It was generally admitted that the defence was a disaster. It was extremely long and boring, and abounded in prevarications, some of which had later to be withdrawn and replaced by others, to the great embarrassment of his supporters. In seeking to prove that his 'political conduct was invariably regulated by truth, justice and good faith,' he had set himself an impossible task. Had he pleaded necessity of State, and the need for rigour in the governance of India, he could probably have averted his impeachment. As it was, his Defence did his cause great harm. A number of respected independent country gentlemen now began to support the impeachment.[4] Yet the impeachment was still uphill work in the Commons. On 2 June the first Article – Hastings's Conduct of the Rohilla war – was defeated by 116 votes to 67.

After that vote 'it was widely anticipated', as P. J. Marshall says, 'that the impeachment would make no further progress.'[5] Then, on 13 June, the breakthrough came. This was in the debate over the 'Benares' article – Hastings's treatment of Rajah Chait Singh (see above p. 284). Pitt declared himself convinced by one element in this Article: 'The fine which [Hastings] determined to levy was beyond

[1] *Corr.* V, 241; letter of 10 December 1785.
[2] *Parl. Hist.* xxiv, 1394.
[3] Quoted in Marshall, *Impeachment*, p. 44.
[4] Marshall, *Impeachment*, Chapter III.
[5] *Impeachment*, p. 45.

all proportion exorbitant, unjust and tyrannical; he should therefore, certainly, on the present charge, agree to the motion that had been made, not considering himself as thereby committed to a final vote of impeachment.'[1] After that declaration, the Article was carried: Yeas 119; Noes 79. Subsequent charges were also carried, whether Pitt voted in favour of them or not. It seems that Pitt's vote was taken as a signal that the question of impeachment was no longer a party matter, but one on which Members were free to vote according to their consciences. And it soon became clear that, under those conditions, a majority of Members were by now convinced that Hastings deserved to be impeached.

Pitt's decision to vote for impeachment on the 'Benares' Article astonished Members on both sides at the time, and has been the subject of much speculation since. Marshall lists several of the 'ingenious explanations' offered, but finds that 'it seems to have been the unanimous opinion of all those who were in close contact with him that he had judged the case entirely on what he had believed to be its merits, and without any ulterior calculations.'[2]

One has to remember, however, that all of 'those who were in close contact' with Pitt were his political friends and likely to interpret his surprise decision in the most favourable way. It is not, I think, likely that 'ulterior calculations' were altogether absent from Pitt's mind. He was a skilful politician, and he would have assessed the political context, before reaching his decision. The opinion of the independent members had been moving against Hastings over the past two months, and even Hastings's followers had been dismayed by his incredible defence. It might not seem politic, to appear to be protecting Hastings. To do so might remind people of that shady transaction over the Nabob of Arcot's debts. And Pitt would want that to be forgotten, as speedily as possible. It was forgotten by his admirers – his faithful biographer, Earl Stanhope, omits all mention of the transaction. I don't doubt that such considerations did pass through Pitt's mind, as they would pass through the mind of any other competent politician, in a comparable situation. But I don't doubt, either, that he did make a serious study of the case, on the merits, and that he found, as did other Members, that there was a good case for impeachment.

I suspect indeed that Pitt's feelings, as his penetrating mind

[1] *Parl. Hist.* xxvi, 91–115.
[2] *Impeachment*, p. 47.

explored the records, may have been oddly similar to those of Burke, after he had undertaken the same exercise, in 1781. That is to say, that when Pitt realised the extent of the Indian oppressions, he too became, at least, somewhat ashamed of his own past record on India. He had more reason to be ashamed than Burke, and was in fact less ashamed, but there was a certain kinship of feeling, as he implicitly acknowledged in a later speech (see below p. 358). Burke's satisfaction at the progress during that session is apparent from a letter to a friend during the recess: 'It is since you left England that we have Closed our Campain; and we did close it as well as a defeated, rallying and defensive army could hope to do[:] that is we got off with reputation. Some of our army more to their conviction than their original good Liking have found that they have not come off the worse for Listening a little to the Counsels of an old friend. India is no longer new to the Ears or understandings of the nation, you know that one great difficulty in our way was the opinion that nothing relative to the East was to be made Intelligible or, to come nearer to the truth there was something like a resolution taken; not to know or to care any thing about it. That difficulty is in a great measure got over. Enough however in Conscience remain.'[1]

The remaining Articles were adjourned into the next Session. Burke was in no hurry, as he knew opinion, once it had turned in his favour, would be likely to be still more favourable after the recess. In February, 1787, Sheridan introduced the Article on Oudh, which was the strongest set of the charges against Hastings.[2] In introducing these charges, Sheridan began by referring to the vote by the House in favour of Impeachment of Hastings on the Benares charge. That vote, he said, had 'vindicated the character of his right hon. friend (Mr. Burke) from the slanderous tongue of ignorance and perversion. They had, by their vote on that question, declared, that the man who brought the charges was no false accuser; that he was not motivated by envy, by malice, nor by any unworthy motives to blacken a spotless name; but that he was the indefatigable, persevering, and, at length, successful champion of oppressed multitudes, against their tyrannical oppressor.' This speech marks Burke's greatly enhanced position within his party, following the progress of the impeachment in the previous year. Sheridan had not previously been

---

[1] *Corr.* V, 281; letter of 29 September 1786, to Thomas Lewis O'Beirne.
[2] The different Articles were parcelled out among different members of Fox's party, with Burke managing the general progress of the impeachment, and no doubt coaching each member on the evidence for his particular Article.

an enthusiast for the India cause; in November 1783, he had been the intermediary in the attempted deal with Hastings (see above p. 315). After the 1784 General Election Sheridan was certainly among the Members who wanted to hear no more about India. If he was now fully behind Burke in the impeachment, so was the whole of his party, for the time being. The Oudh Article carried by a vote of more than two to one: Yeas, 175; Noes, 68, much better than on Benares. The impeachment by the House of Commons was now unstoppable.

Burke now wants to keep up the momentum. On 2 April he opposed a motion for adjournment: 'He hoped that the House would not consent to further delay.' In a tactical move, for the sake of 'unanimity', Burke accepts a procedural point of Pitt in preference to one of Fox, thus symbolising that there is no longer any difference between the parties, but an effective unity, concerning the impeachment. For Burke, this is an ecstatic moment, the consummation of six years of unstinting, and often apparently hopeless, effort:

> The effects of the enquiry with a view to impeachment had been glorious both in that House and without doors. Without doors men's minds had been changed, rooted prejudice had been eradicated, conviction had followed, and all the world confessed that the House of Commons were engaged in a grave and important proceeding essential to the establishment of the national character for justice and equity. Within doors all the various modes and styles of eloquence had been called forth, to the admiration of the House, and to its infinite honour and advantage. Looking round him and seeing who were near him [Fox and Pitt?], he scarcely dared venture to speak further on a subject on which recent experience had proved, that he found many masters and younger than himself: but the topic operated as an excitement to the display of all the finer powers of the human understanding. It has gone much further, softening almost into a common bond of union the hitherto-obdurate hearts of violently contending politics; sheathing the sword of embattled party, and lowering its hostile front.

Burke's impression that public opinion was moving in his favour was correct. P. J. Marshall writes: 'By the time Hastings was impeached, nearly every section of British political opinion was prepared to accept that serious crimes had been committed in India. While Burke and Fox led the attack on Hastings, George III wrote of "shocking enormities in India that disgrace human nature".'[1]

[1] *Impeachment*, pp. xvii–xviii.

On that April day of 1787 Burke is experiencing what Pope – in a phrase dear to Burke – had called 'the sunshine of the soul'. (Burke had applied this phrase to Philip Francis, of all people!) We should not grudge him this moment of hard-earned euphoria. He had lived much with horror, most of which he kept to himself. The abiding horror of his particular Irish predicament had erupted, in a single epiphany, in the Bristol Guildhall, in 1780. In the following year, as his mind came to grips with the realities of Warren Hastings's India, his Irish horror took the accusing form of a tormented India. In April, 1787, the accuser is appeased. In bringing Warren Hastings to justice, Burke has done what was demanded of him. It is now Warren Hastings, alone, who is accused. Burke has done his duty and is free. This is what is at the core of his rejoicing. (All conjecture of course; the reader will decide to what extent it seems to fit.)

On 25 April 1787, according to the *Parliamentary History* 'Mr. Burke brought up the first seven Articles of Impeachment against Mr. Hastings which were read pro forma at the table and ordered to be printed.' On 9 May two members, from outside the new consensus of the House, protested against sending the impeachment to the Lords. Pitt sternly reprimanded these speakers. According to the *Parliamentary History*, Pitt 'felt himself totally at a loss to conceive how it could be reconciled to the honour, the conscience or the justice of that House, to stop short of sending up the Impeachment to that place, where alone it ought to undergo its ultimate discussion. He admitted that he once was of opinion, that the language of those who chiefly promoted the present proceedings, was too full of acerbity, and much too passionate and exaggerated; but when he found what the nature of the crime alleged was, and how strong was the presumption that the allegations were true, he confessed that he could not expect that gentlemen, when reciting what they thought actions of treachery, actions of violence and oppression, and demanding an investigation into those actions, should speak a language different from that which would naturally arise from the contemplation of those actions.'

Succeeding generations of critics have found Burke's language against Hastings 'too full of acerbity, and much too passionate and exaggerated'. Burke's exoneration on that charge, after reflection, by the greatest of his contemporary opponents, a notably cool and temperate politician, is therefore worthy of note.

Next day, 'After the Articles of Impeachment were all read, amended, and agreed to, Mr. Burke moved, "That the said Warren

Hastings Esq be impeached of High Crimes and Misdemeanours."'
The following motion was then carried: "That Mr. Burke go to the
Lords, and, at their bar, in the name of the House of Commons, and
of all the Commons of Great Britain, do impeach Warren Hastings,
Esquire, late Governor-General of Bengal, of High Crimes and Mis-
demeanours; and acquaint the Lords, that this House will, with all
convenient speed, exhibit Articles against him and make good the
same."' The *Parliamentary History* goes on: 'The majority of the
House immediately attended Mr. Burke to the bar of the House of
Peers, where Mr. Burke solemnly impeached Mr. Hastings in the
form above recited. . . . On the 14th [May] Mr. Burke carried the
Articles of Impeachment up to the Lords.'

On 10 December 1787 – that is, after an interval proportionate to
the dignity of their House – 'The Lords acquainted the Commons
that they had appointed the 13 February next, for the Trial of Warren
Hastings Esq. at the bar of the House of Lords'. [1]

*   *   *

Macaulay, in his essay on Warren Hastings, writes of Burke's 'vortex': 'Burke had in his vortex whirled away Windham.' There is no
more striking example of the 'vortex effect' than the decision of
the House of Commons, in December 1787, to impeach Warren
Hastings.

IMPEACHMENT BEFORE THE LORDS

Macaulay's famous description of the scene at Westminster Hall,
as the Impeachment trial of Warren Hastings opened, has to be
reproduced here, because of the high significance of that scene in the
career of Edmund Burke, in which it represented a kind of ambiguous
and precarious apotheosis.

'The place was worthy of such a trial. It was the great hall of
William Rufus; the hall which had resounded with acclamations at
the inauguration of thirty Kings; the hall which had witnessed the
just sentence of Bacon and the just absolution of Somers[2]; the hall

---

[1] *Parl. Hist.*, xxvi, 1314.
[2] William III's Lord Chancellor, whose impeachment by the Commons, in 1701,
was rejected by the Lords.

where the eloquence of Strafford had for a moment awed and melted a victorious party inflamed with just resentment; the hall where Charles had confronted the High Court of Justice with the placid courage which has half redeemed his fame. Neither military nor civil pomp was wanting. The avenues were lined with grenadiers. The streets were kept clear by cavalry. The peers, robed in gold and ermine, were marshalled by the heralds under Garter King-at-Arms. The judges, in their vestments of state, attended to give advice on points of law. Near a hundred and seventy lords, three-fourths of the Upper House, as the Upper House then was, walked in solemn order from their usual place of assembling to the tribunal. The junior baron present led the way – Lord Heathfield, recently ennobled for his memorable defence of Gibraltar against the fleets and armies of France and Spain. The long procession was closed by the Duke of Norfolk, Earl Marshal of the realm, by the great dignitaries, and by the brothers and sons of the King. Last of all came the Prince of Wales, conspicuous by his fine person and noble bearing. The grey old walls were hung with scarlet. The long galleries were crowded by such an audience as has rarely excited the fears or the emulation of an orator. There were gathered together, from all parts of a great, free, enlightened, and prosperous realm, grace and female loveliness, wit and learning, the representatives of every science and of every art. There were seated round the Queen the fair-haired young daughters of the house of Brunswick. There the Ambassadors of great Kings and Commonwealths gazed with admiration on a spectacle which no other country in the world could present. There Siddons, in the prime of her majestic beauty, looked with emotion on a scene surpassing all the imitations of the stage. There the historian of the Roman Empire thought of the days when Cicero pleaded the cause of Sicily against Verres; and when, before a senate which had still some show of freedom, Tacitus thundered against the oppressor of Africa. There were seen, side by side, the greatest painter and the greatest scholar of the age. The spectacle had allured Reynolds from that easel which has preserved to us the thoughtful foreheads of so many writers and statesmen, and the sweet smiles of so many noble matrons. It had induced Parr to suspend his labours in that dark and profound mine from which he had extracted a vast treasure of erudition – a treasure too often buried in the earth, too often paraded with injudicious and inelegant ostentation; but still precious, massive, and splendid. There appeared the voluptuous charms of her to whom the heir of the throne had in secret plighted his faith [Mrs.

Fitzherbert]. There, too, was she, the beautiful mother of a beautiful race, the Saint Cecilia, whose delicate features, lighted up by love and music, art has rescued from the common decay. There were the members of that brilliant society which quoted, criticised, and exchanged repartees, under the rich peacock-hangings of Mrs. Montague. And there the ladies whose lips, more persuasive than those of Fox himself, had carried the Westminster election against palace and treasury, shone round Georgiana Duchess of Devonshire.'

For Burke, as one of the two protagonists at the centre of that gorgeous scene; that day – 13 February, 1788 – had to be a day of pride and joy, but also of anxiety. As Manager, and opener of the case which the House of Commons was about to present to the House of Lords, Burke occupied, at that moment, a more central position, within the British political order, than he had ever before occupied, or ever would again. Burke's feelings towards that order were, as we have seen, inherently ambivalent. On that February day, the positive side of his feelings was surely predominant. But it was a precarious predominance. What if the impeachment should fail, in the House of Lords? Burke's negative feelings were in reserve for that contingency. As he approached Westminster Hall, Burke certainly knew that his chances of success in his great enterprise were, in human terms, small. In the Lords, the influence of the Crown and of the Company were stronger than in the Commons, and both were favourable to Warren Hastings. There were also the lawyers in the Lords to be considered. What was impending in the Lords was a legal proceeding: a trial. In the Commons, what had taken place had been a political debate: Burke had had to do no more than convince the Commons of the *probability* that serious crimes had been committed in India, under the Governor-Generalship of Warren Hastings. But, before the Lords, Burke would be required to do much more than this: to prove beyond reasonable doubt that Warren Hastings, personally, had committed these crimes or ordered others to commit them.

Both Burke and Hastings thought that proof was an impossibility, in the circumstances, under the ordinary rules of evidence. Burke knew that Hastings himself (oddly enough) had acknowledged the impossibility of obtaining proof of oppression: 'In the charge of oppression, although supported by the cries of the people and the most authentic representations, it is yet impossible to obtain legal proofs of it.' [1] Burke had argued in the Commons, and would now

[1] Company Minutes, 2827–9, cited by Burke in his Speech in Reply [to Hastings's Defence]; Eighth Day. Hastings was then seeking discretionary powers for himself, to deal with charges against subordinate officials.

argue in the Lords, that an Impeachment should not be held to the ordinary standards of proof and rules of evidence that applied to common crime in the ordinary courts. What should apply, he argued were 'the enlarged and solid principles of state morality'. By this he meant that a high official, under impeachment, should be found guilty, if it could be shown that the governmental system which he operated was criminally oppressive, even if it could not be shown that he, personally, had explicitly directed any specific act of criminal oppression.

This was a reasonable argument, but Burke, who was usually realistic in his assessment of probabilities, can have had little hope that his argument would prevail. Lawyers, brought up on the ordinary rules of evidence, were unlikely to be impressed by a layman – Burke had studied law but had never practised – talking about the principles of State morality. Then there was the additional handicap that the Articles of Impeachment were not lawyerlike documents. They had been drawn up, by Burke and Francis, at a time when they did not believe there was any serious prospect of carrying the impeachment through the Commons, on its way to the Lords. So the Articles were drawn up, not in the form best calculated to secure a conviction in the Lords, but in the form best calculated to make an impact on public opinion, outside Parliament. This made the Articles most unseaworthy vessels, in which to face the long and stormy legal passage of impeachment in the Lords.

But if all that were not enough, Burke knew that the Chancellor, Edward, first Baron Thurlow (1731–1806), who would preside over the impeachment, was a friend of Hastings, and hostile to the Articles. (Like Sir Elijah Impey, Thurlow had been at school with Hastings, at Westminster; Hastings was fortunate in his school-friends.) But even if he had not been a friend of Hastings, Thurlow would not have liked those Articles: few lawyers could have liked them; Thurlow dismissed them in conversation, as fiction: 'Robinson Crusoe'.

So the prospects, as Edmund Burke entered Westminster Hall for the impeachment of Warren Hastings, did not look bright. But then they had not looked bright in the Commons either, before Pitt's astonishing 'conversion' to impeachment. In the Lords, too, something surprising might happen. In any case Burke, when once he was committed to a course, did not allow himself to be daunted or deflected by the improbability of success. He had stuck to his American course for over fifteen years (1766–1782), during most of which success seemed most improbable. His India course lasted fourteen years, from 1781, when he first became fully committed to it, to 1795, when it ended with the dismissal of the charges against Warren Hastings. When Burke entered Westminster Hall, on 13 February 1788, he had still half his India course to run.

From Fanny Burney's diary for 13 February, 1788: 'I shuddered, and drew involuntarily back, when, as the doors were flung open, I saw Mr. Burke, as Head of the Committee, make his solemn entry. He held a scroll in his hand, and walked alone, his brow knit with corroding care and deep labouring thought, – a brow how different to that which had proved so alluring to my warmest admiration when first I met him! so highly as he had been my favourite, so captivating as I had found his manners and conversation in our first acquaintance, and so much as I had owed to his zeal and kindness to me and my affairs in its progress! How did I grieve to behold him now the cruel Prosecutor (such to me he appeared) of an injured and innocent man!'[1]

Fanny Burney was a lady-in-writing to the queen, who was even more partial to the side of Hastings than most of the rest of the court (though the king had his doubts). But Fanny Burney was also an acute observer, with a good eye for 'business' in the stage sense of the word. Having reported Thurlow's speech calling on Warren Hastings to be ready to answer the charges, Fanny Burney already detected what would prove to be a crucial feature of the trial: Thurlow's predilection for the prisoner: 'This speech, uttered in a calm, equal, solemn manner, and in a voice mellow and penetrating, with eyes keen and black, yet softened into some degree of tenderness while fastened full upon the prisoner.'

Burke's opening speech lasted for four days, and was generally felt, even by hostile critics, to be worthy of the occasion. Fanny Burney attended on the second day, and has left a remarkable account of the impression made by the speech on a highly intelligent witness who was strongly predisposed in favour of the accused: 'At length the Peers' procession closed, the Prisoner was brought in, and Mr. Burke began his speech. It was the second day of his harangue; the first I had not been able to attend.

'All I had heard of his eloquence, and all I had conceived of his great abilities, was more than answered by his performance. Nervous, clear, and striking was almost all that he uttered: the main business,

---

[1] *Diary and Letters of Madame d'Arblay*, 1842–1846, 7 vols; Vol. IV, p. 56.

indeed, of his coming forth was frequently neglected, and not seldom wholly lost; but his excursions were so fanciful, so entertaining, and so ingenious, that no miscellaneous hearer, like myself, could blame them. It is true he was unequal, but his inequality produced an effect which, in so long a speech, was perhaps preferable to greater consistency, since, though it lost attention in its falling off, it recovered it with additional energy by some ascent unexpected and wonderful. When he narrated, he was easy, flowing, and natural; when he declaimed, energetic, warm, and brilliant. The sentiments he interspersed were as nobly conceived as they were highly coloured; his satire had a poignancy of wit that made it as entertaining as it was penetrating, his allusions and quotations, as far as they were English and within my reach, were apt and ingenious; and the wild and sudden flights of his fancy, bursting forth from his creative imagination in language fluent, forcible, and varied, had a charm for my ear and my attention wholly new and perfectly irresistible.

'Were talents such as these exercised in the service of truth, unbiased by party and prejudice, how could we sufficiently applaud their exalted possessor? But though frequently he made me tremble by his strong and horrible representations, his own violence recovered me, by stigmatizing his assertions with personal ill-will and designing illiberality. Yet, at times I confess, with all that I felt, wished, and thought concerning Mr. Hastings, the whirlwind of his eloquence nearly drew me into its vortex.'[1]

Yet, powerful as it is, the speech opening the impeachment is not as fully and spontaneously Burkean as the speeches on Fox's East India Bill, Almas Ali Khan, or the Nabob of Arcot's debts. In those, Burke was speaking as an individual Member of Parliament, knowing that his friends were in broad agreement with him on the subject under discussion, and feeling free to speak his mind as he pleased. The situation in Westminster Hall was very different. Burke is not speaking for himself: he is pleading the case of the House of Commons at the bar of the House of Lords. He is also responsible to his Committee: his fellow-Managers of the Impeachment. As I read the speech, I felt that Burke was to some extent trying to hold himself back; as he had done, for example in the Reports of the Select Committee. Yet I have to acknowledge that that is certainly not the impression of an attentive contemporary who actually heard the

[1] Diary IV, 95–6, 16 February 1788. Macaulay may well have had the conclusion of the above passage in mind when he wrote: 'Burke had in his vortex whirled away Windham' (see above p. 359)

speech, Fanny Burney. If the 'whirlwind of his eloquence' nearly drew the queen's lady-in-waiting 'into its vortex', the impact of the speech, as delivered, clearly had elemental force.

Inevitably, in addressing the Lords, Burke had to cover much of the same ground as he had already covered in the Commons. I shall refer here only to passages which open new ground.

Near the beginning Burke leads into a theme of supreme importance to him, throughout his pursuit of Warren Hastings:

> My Lords, the business of this day is not the business of this man, it is not solely whether the prisoner at the bar be found innocent or guilty, but whether millions of mankind shall be made miserable or happy.
>
> Your Lordships will see, in the progress of this cause, that there is not only a long, connected, systematic series of misdemeanors, but an equally connected system of maxims and principles invented to justify them. Upon both of these you must judge. According to the judgment that you shall give upon the past transactions in India, inseparably connected as they are with the principles which support them, the whole character of your future government in that distant empire is to be unalterably decided. It will take its perpetual tenor, it will receive its final impression, from the stamp of this very hour.
>
> It is not only the interest of India, now the most considerable part of the British empire, which is concerned, but the credit and honor of the British nation itself will be decided by this decision. We are to decide by this judgment, whether the crimes of individuals are to be turned into public guilt and national ignominy, or whether this nation will convert the very offences which have thrown a transient shade upon its government into something that will reflect a permanent lustre upon the honor, justice, and humanity of this kingdom. [1]

Formally, Burke is speaking on behalf of the Commons of Great Britain, but it is hardly the Commons of Great Britain that put that last sentence into his mouth. Burke's own positive and negative feelings towards England can be seen here, held in a balance. In the trial of Warren Hastings, England herself is on trial, for Burke. If Warren Hastings is found guilty England is innocent; and *vice versa*. If Burke is holding himself in, generally speaking, something of what is being held in comes near to the surface there, for a moment. From this, he moves to an argument, by which his case must stand or fall: the argument that the ordinary rules of evidence should not apply to an impeachment:

[1] *Works* IX, 331.

My Lords, there is another consideration, which augments the solicitude
of the Commons, equal to those other two great interests I have stated,
those of our empire and our national character, – some thing that, if
possible, comes more home to the hearts and feelings of every Englishman: I mean, the interests of our Constitution itself, which is deeply
involved in the event of this cause. The future use and the whole effect,
if not the very existence, of the process of an impeachment of high crimes
and misdemeanors before the peers of this kingdom upon the charge of
the Commons will very much be decided by your judgment in this cause.
This tribunal will be found (I hope it will always be found) too great for
petty causes: if it should at the same time be found incompetent to one
of the greatest, – that is, if little offences, from their minuteness, escape
you, and the greatest, from their magnitude, oppress you, – it is impossible that this form of trial should not in the end vanish out of the Constitution. For we must not deceive ourselves: whatever does not stand with
credit cannot stand long. And if the Constitution should be deprived, I
do not mean in form, but virtually, of this resource, it is virtually deprived
of everything else that is valuable in it. For this process is the cement
which binds the whole together; this is the individuating principle that
makes England what England is. In this court it is that no subject, in no
part of the empire, can fail of competent and proportionable justice; here
it is that we provide for that which is the substantial excellence of our
Constitution, – I mean, the great circulation of responsibility, by which
(excepting the supreme power) no man, in no circumstance, can escape
the account which he owes to the laws of his country. It is by this process
that magistracy, which tries and controls all other things, is itself tried
and controlled. Other constitutions are satisfied with making good subjects; this is a security for good governors. It is by this tribunal that
statesmen who abuse their power are accused by statesmen and tried by
statesmen, not upon the niceties of a narrow jurisprudence, but upon the
enlarged and solid principles of state morality. It is here that those who
by the abuse of power have violated the spirit of law can never hope for
protection from any of its forms; it is here that those who have refused
to conform themselves to its perfections can never hope to escape through
any of its defects. It ought, therefore, my Lords, to become our common
care to guard this your precious deposit, rare in its use, but powerful in
its effect, with a religious vigilance, and never to suffer it to be either
discredited or antiquated. For this great end your Lordships are invested
with great and plenary powers: but you do not suspend, you do not
supersede, you do not annihilate any subordinate jurisdiction; on the
contrary, you are auxiliary and supplemental to them all. [1]

---

[1] *Works* IX, 332–3.

Burke argues that justice to the Indians requires this enlargement of judicial procedure:

> But your Lordships will maintain, what we assert and claim as the right of the subjects of Great Britain, that you are not bound by any rules of evidence, or any other rules whatever, except those of natural, immutable, and substantial justice.
>
> I have too much confidence in the learning with which you will be advised, and the liberality and nobleness of the sentiments with which you are born, to suspect that you would, by any abuse of the forms, and a technical course of proceeding, deny justice to so great a part of the world that claims it at your hands. Your Lordships always had an ample power, and almost unlimited jurisdiction; you have now a boundless object. It is not from this district or from that parish, not from this city or the other province, that relief is now applied for: exiled and undone princes, extensive tribes, suffering nations, infinite descriptions of men, different in language, in manners, and in rites, men separated by every barrier of Nature from you, by the Providence of God are blended in one common cause, and are now become suppliants at your bar. For the honor of this nation, in vindication of this mysterious Providence, let it be known that no rule formed upon municipal maxims (if any such rule exists) will prevent the course of that imperial justice which you owe to the people that call to you from all parts of a great disjointed world. For, situated as this kingdom is, an object, thank God of envy to the rest of the nations, its conduct in that high and elevated situation will undoubtedly be scrutinized with a severity as great as its power is invidious.

With great boldness, Burke now argues that the Lords may be bribed, and that the results of bribery may take the form of a decision that the ordinary rules of evidence are to apply to an impeachment.

> It is well known that enormous wealth has poured into this country from India through a thousand channels, public and concealed; and it is no particular derogation from our honor to suppose a possibility of being corrupted by that by which other empires have been corrupted, and assemblies almost as respectable and venerable as your Lordships' have been directly or indirectly vitiated. Forty millions of money, at least, have within our memory been brought from India into England. In this case the most sacred judicature ought to look to its reputation. Without offence we may venture to suggest that the best way to secure reputation is, not by a proud defiance of public opinion, but by guiding our actions in such a manner as that public opinion may in the end be securely defied, by having been previously respected and dreaded. No direct false

judgment is apprehended from the tribunals of this country; but it is feared that partiality may lurk and nestle in the abuse of our forms of proceeding. It is necessary, therefore, that nothing in that proceeding should appear to mark the slightest trace, should betray the faintest odor of chicane. God forbid, that, when you try the most serious of all causes, that, when you try the cause of Asia in the presence of Europe, there should be the least suspicion that a narrow partiality, utterly destructive of justice, should so guide us that a British subject in power should appear in substance to possess rights which are denied to the humble allies, to the attached dependants of this kingdom, who by their distance have a double demand upon your protection, and who, by an implicit (I hope not a weak and useless) trust in you, have stripped themselves of every other resource under heaven!

I do not say this from any fear, doubt, or hesitation concerning what your Lordships will finally do, – none in the world; but I cannot shut my ears to the rumors which you all know to be disseminated abroad. The abusers of power may have a chance to cover themselves by those fences and intrenchments which were made to secure the liberties of the people against men of that very description. But God forbid it should be bruited from Pekin to Paris, that the laws of England are for the rich and the powerful, but to the poor, the miserable, and defenceless they afford no resource at all! God forbid it should be said, no nation is equal to the English in substantial violence and in formal justice, – that in this kingdom we feel ourselves competent to confer the most extravagant and inordinate powers upon public ministers, but that we are deficient, poor, helpless, lame, and impotent in the means of calling them to account for their use of them! An opinion has been insidiously circulated through this kingdom, and through foreign nations too, that, in order to cover our participation in guilt, and our common interest in the plunder of the East, we have invented a set of scholastic distinctions, abhorrent to the common sense and unpropitious to the common necessities of mankind, by which we are to deny ourselves the knowledge of what the rest of the world knows, and what so great a part of the world both knows and feels. I do not deprecate any appearance which may give countenance to this aspersion from suspicion that any corrupt motive can influence this court; I deprecate it from knowing that hitherto we have moved within the narrow circle of municipal justice. I am afraid, that, from the habits acquired by moving within a circumscribed sphere, we may be induced rather to endeavor at forcing Nature into that municipal circle than to enlarge the circle of national justice to the necessities of the empire we have obtained.

This is the only thing which does create any doubt or difficulty in the minds of sober people. But there are those who will not judge so equitably. Where two motives, neither of them perfectly justifiable, may be assigned, the worst has the chance of being preferred. If, from any appearance of chicane in the court, justice should fail, all men will say, better there were no tribunals at all. In my humble opinion, it would be better a thousand times to give all complainants the short answer the Dey of Algiers gave a British ambassador, representing certain grievances suffered by the British merchants, – 'My friend,' (as the story is related by Dr. Shaw,) 'do not you know that my subjects are a band of robbers, and that I am their captain?' – better it would be a thousand times, and a thousand thousand times more manly, than an hypocritical process, which, under a pretended reverence to punctilious ceremonies and observances of law, abandons mankind without help and resource to all the desolating consequences of arbitrary power.

In that passage, which is at the core of Burke's case against Hastings, the negative side of Burke's feelings towards the English ruling class and system of Government is sufficiently in evidence. He explains that he is putting a system of iniquity upon trial in the person of its chief practitioner, Warren Hastings.

As to the criminal, we have chosen him on the same principle on which we selected the crimes. We have not chosen to bring before you a poor, puny, trembling delinquent, misled, perhaps, by those who ought to have taught him better, but who have afterwards oppressed him by their power, as they had first corrupted him by their example. Instances there have been many, wherein the punishment of minor offences, in inferior persons, has been made the means of screening crimes of an high order, and in men of high description. Our course is different. We have not brought before you an obscure offender, who, when his insignificance and weakness are weighed against the power of the prosecution, gives even to public justice something of the appearance of oppression: no, my Lords, we have brought before you the first man of India, in rank, authority, and station. We have brought before you the chief of the tribe, the head of the whole body of Eastern offenders, a captain-general of iniquity, under whom all the fraud, all the peculation, all the tyranny in India are embodied, disciplined, arrayed, and paid. This is the person, my Lords, that we bring before you. We have brought before you such a person, that, if you strike at him with the firm and decided arm of justice, you will not have need of a great many more examples. You strike at the whole corps, if you strike at the head.

Central to Hastings's defence was the contention that actions in India are not to be judged by the same moral standards as apply in Europe. Burke, towards the close of the second day of his speech, vigorously attacks this contention:

My Lords, we positively deny that principle. I am authorized and called upon to deny it. And having stated at large what he [Hastings] means by saying that the same actions have not the same qualities in Asia and in Europe, we are to let your Lordships know that these gentlemen have formed a plan of geographical morality, by which the duties of men, in public and in private situations, are not to be governed by their relation to the great Governor of the Universe, or by their relation to mankind, but by climates, degrees of longitude, parallels, not of life, but of latitudes: as if, when you have crossed the equinoctial, all the virtues die, as they say some insects die when they cross the line; as if there were a kind of baptism, like that practised by seamen, by which they unbaptize themselves of all that they learned in Europe, and after which a new order and system of things commenced.

This geographical morality we do protest against; Mr. Hastings shall not screen himself under it; and on this point I hope and trust many words will not be necessary to satisfy your Lordships. But we think it necessary, in justification of ourselves, to declare that the laws of morality are the same everywhere, and that there is no action which would pass for an act of extortion, of peculation, of bribery, and of oppression in England, that is not an act of extortion, of peculation, of bribery, and oppression in Europe, Asia, Africa, and all the world over. This I contend for not in the technical forms of it, but I contend for it in the substance.

Mr. Hastings comes before your Lordships not as a British governor answering to a British tribunal, but as a subahdar, as a bashaw of three tails. He says, 'I had an arbitrary power to exercise: I exercised it. Slaves I found the people: slaves they are, – they are so by their constitution; and if they are, I did not make it for them. I was unfortunately bound to exercise this arbitrary power, and accordingly I did exercise it. It was disagreeable to me, but I did exercise it; and no other power can be exercised in that country.' This, if it be true, is a plea in bar. But I trust and hope your Lordships will not judge by laws and institutions which you do not know, against those laws and institutions which you do know, and under whose power and authority Mr. Hastings went out to India. Can your Lordships patiently hear what *we* have heard with indignation enough, and what, if there were nothing else, would call these principles, as well as the actions which are justified on such principles, to your Lordships' bar, that it may be known whether the peers of England do not sympathize with the Commons in their detestation of such doctrine? Think of an English governor tried before you as a British subject, and yet declaring that he governed on the principles of arbitrary power! His plea is, that he did govern there on arbitrary and despotic, and, as he supposes, Oriental principles. And as this plea is boldly avowed and maintained, and as, no doubt, all his conduct was perfectly correspondent to these principles, the principles and the conduct must be tried together.

I have quoted extensively from the first two days of the opening speech, because it was in that part that Burke laid down what he called 'the general grounds' of the charges against Warren Hastings. The second two days, dealing with particulars need not detain us so long. Yet there is one case, raised by Burke on the third day, which merits attention because it has been a main focus of the adverse comment concerning his conduct of the impeachment. This is the case of Rajah Devi Singh, tax farmer of Rangpur. Burke came across this case in a late stage of the preparation of the impeachment. He first mentions the case in a letter of 3 January 1788, to Philip Francis. The editors of the relevant volume of the *Correspondence* establish the background: 'This letter introduces one of the most controversial episodes in the Impeachment: Burke's use of the reports of atrocities in the collection of revenue in Rangpur. Rangpur was a district in northern Bengal which, together with Dinajpur and Edrakpur, had been farmed in 1781 at a high assessment for which Raja Devi Singh was security. In February 1783 there were widespread disturbances in Rangpur against Devi Singh's collectors. John Paterson (d. 1809), a Servant of the East India company, was instructed by the Supreme Council to inquire into the causes of the unrest, and reported that it had been provoked by extortionate demands enforced by the use of torture, of which he provided lurid and detailed descriptions.'[1]

In a letter to Francis, Burke shows himself determined to use the Paterson report on torture, but worried about how to use it: 'However I have read most attentively the first Volume of the Rangpore memoirs, (there are three in all. I have not yet seen the two last) and have so noted it as to make an Index to it a very easy work. Oh! what an affair – I am clear that I must dilate upon that; for it has stuff in it, that will, if any thing, work upon the popular Sense. But how to do this without making a monstrous and disproportioned member; I know not.'[2]

On the third day of the impeachment Burke comes to the question of the use of torture. He has been examining the general system of extortion, the seizure of money and property: 'I come now to the last stage of their miseries. Everything visible and vendible was seized and sold. Nothing but the bodies remained.' Then Burke comes to the Paterson report:

[1] *Corr.* V, 372, tn.
[2] *Ibid.* c. 3 January 1788.

And here, my Lords, began such a scene of cruelties and tortures as I believe no history has ever presented to the indignation of the world, – such as I am sure, in the most barbarous ages, no politic tyranny, no fanatic persecution, has ever yet exceeded. Mr. Paterson, the commissioner appointed to inquire into the state of the country, makes his own apology and mine for opening this scene of horrors to you in the following words: 'That the punishments inflicted upon the ryots, both of Rungpore and Dinagepore, for non-payment, were in many instances of such a nature that I would rather wish to draw a veil over them than shock your feelings by the detail, but that, however disagreeable the task may be to myself, it is absolutely necessary, for the sake of justice, humanity, and the honor of government, that they should be exposed, to be prevented in future'.

My Lords, they began by winding cords round the fingers of the unhappy freeholders of those provinces, until they clung to and were almost incorporated with one another; and then they hammered wedges of iron between them, until, regardless of the cries of the sufferers, they had bruised to pieces and forever crippled those poor, honest, innocent, laborious hands, which had never been raised to their mouths but with a penurious and scanty proportion of the fruits of their own soil; but those fruits (denied to the wants of their own children) have for more than fifteen years past furnished the investment for our trade with China, and been sent annually out, and without recompense, to purchase for us that delicate meal with which your Lordships, and all this auditory, and all this country, have begun every day for these fifteen years at their expense. To those beneficent hands that labor for our benefit the return of the British government has been cords and hammers and wedges. But there is a place where these crippled and disabled hands will act with resistless power. What is it that they will not pull down, when they are lifted to heaven against their oppressors? Then what can withstand such hands? Can the power that crushed and destroyed them? Powerful in prayer, let us at least deprecate and thus endeavor to secure ourselves from the vengeance which these mashed and disabled hands may pull down upon us. My Lords, it is an awful consideration: let us think of it. [1]

It might have been better if Burke had ceased his recital of torture there, at the end of that moving passage, leaving one atrocity to speak for all the rest. He decided otherwise. He recited the catalogue of atrocities contained in the Paterson report, including the details of revolting cruelties perpetrated in Rangpur against women. A contemporary account describes the impact of this recital on Burke himself, and on his audience: 'Here Mr. B. leant his head upon his lap

[1] *Works* X, 84–5.

unable to proceed, so greatly was he oppressed by the horror which he felt at this relation. The effect of it was visible through the whole audience a lady, who was in the Great Chamberlain's box fainted away.'[1]

Burke has been blamed, both for sensationalism and for irrelevance in his treatment of the case of Devi Singh. In the charge of sensationalism, there is at least some force: Burke had found 'stuff in it that will, if anything, work upon the popular Sense'. But I cannot see that there is anything reprehensible in this. Burke believed in the reality of these atrocities, which he laid at Hastings's door. His best hope of getting the Lords to convict Hastings seemed to be to arouse public opinion. Why should he not use the report of the atrocities to arouse public opinion? What the effects on public opinion actually were is another matter. The eminent Shakespearian critic and editor, Edmund Malone, was present for most of the opening speech. He wrote to Lord Charlemont: 'I suppose you have heard much of Burke's astonishing performance on the business of Hastings. I had the good fortune to hear him on the first, second and fourth day; but could not get a ticket on the third, when he gave so pathetick a description of the tortures that had been practised in India. All the papers have made sad stuff of his most delicate touches, on a point of so nice a nature that nothing but the most consummate art could have guarded him against ridicule.'[2]

The charge of irrelevance is based on the fact that the Paterson Report accused Devi Singh and his agents, not Hastings. But this is a distinction without a difference. Hastings had appointed Devi Singh tax-farmer in Rangpur. Devi Singh was part of a system of extortion which was headed by Hastings. And the tortures practised by Devi Singh's agents were also part of that system. It is true that a Commission set up 'to make a fresh inquiry' into what Paterson had reported found that: 'The most Dreadful of the Cruelties stated in Mr. Paterson's letter to have been exercised to enforce the payment of Revenue . . . have no existence.'[3] But that Commission was set up by Hastings. Its report, too, was part of the system. The relation of Devi Singh's fief to Hastings's empire is well established by the following passage concerning Richard Goodlad, the Company's – that is to say Hastings's – Collector in Rangpur: 'Paterson's report

---

[1] *Trial of Warren Hastings*, p. 42. The lady was Mrs. Sheridan, Macaulay's 'St Cecilia' (above, p. 361).

[2] *Corr.* V, 379.

[3] *Corr.* V, 383, n. 1.

alleged that Devi Singh's agents had collected an extortionate revenue by the use of torture, and that Richard Goodlad, the Collector of Rangpur, had made no attempt to restrain them.' Goodlad defended himself by pleading ignorance – claiming that '. . . if this Tyranny and Extortion actually prevailed, no Complaints were ever preferred to me to induce me to suspect it', and he was acquitted by the Supreme Council. With rather more candour, he admitted to another Company Servant that, '*had he gone out of his way to hear complaints*, the collection of revenue from the district would have fallen short of the assessed total' (my italics – C.C.O'B). The Supreme Council which acquitted Goodlad was Hastings's Council, and fully under his control. Hastings's own comprehensive verdict on the Rangpur affair (21 January 1785) is characteristic:

'I entirely acquit Mr. Goodlad of all the charges: he has disproved them. It was the duty of the accuser to prove them. Whatever crimes may be established against Rajah Devi Sing, it does not follow that Mr. Goodlad was responsible for them; and *I so well know the character and abilities of Rajah Devi Sing, that I can easily conceive that it was in his power both to commit the enormities which are laid to his charge, and to conceal the grounds of them from Mr. Goodlad,* who had no authority but that of receiving the accounts and rents of the district from Rajah Devi Sing, and occasionally to be the channel of communication between him and the Committee' (my italics – C.C.O'B).

The passage was quoted by Burke on the fourth day of his speech opening the impeachment, and the parts I have italicised are highly revealing. It is to be presumed that it is because Hastings 'so well knew the character and abilities of Rajah Devi Singh' that he appointed him as tax-farmer in Rangpur. Which is to say that such 'enormities' as the character and abilities of Devi Singh could commit were intended by Hastings as the means of getting the maximum that could be extorted from the people of Rangpur. The case of Devi Singh, far from being irrelevant to the impeachment, is one of the best-documented examples of the workings of Hastings's system.

In his peroration Burke offered a highly idealised version of the Parliament of Great Britain, as it was in the 1780s:

My Lords, is it a prosecutor you want? You have before you the Commons of Great Britain as prosecutors; and I believe, my Lords, that the sun, in his beneficent progress round the world, does not behold a more glorious sight than that of men, separated from a remote people by the material bounds and barriers of Nature, united by the bond of a social and moral community, – all the Commons of England resenting, as their own, the indignities and cruelties that are offered to all the people of India.

Do we want a tribunal? My Lords, no example of antiquity, nothing in the modern world, nothing in the range of human imagination, can supply us with a tribunal like this. My Lords, here we see virtually, in the mind's eye, that sacred majesty of the crown, under whose authority you sit, and whose power you exercise. We see in that invisible authority, what we all feel in reality and life, the beneficent powers and protecting justice of his Majesty. We have here the heir-apparent to the crown, such as the fond wishes of the people of England wish an heir-apparent of the crown to be. We have here all the branches of the royal family, in a situation between majesty and subjection, between the sovereign and the subject, – offering a pledge in that situation for the support of the rights of the crown and the liberties of the people, both which extremities they touch. My Lords, we have a great hereditary peerage here, – those who have their own honor, the honor of their ancestors and of their posterity to guard, and who will justify, as they have always justified, that provision in the Constitution by which justice is made an hereditary office. My Lords, we have here a new nobility, who have risen and exalted themselves by various merits, – by great military services which have extended the fame of this country from the rising to the setting sun. We have those who, by various civil merits and various civil talents, have been exalted to a situation which they well deserve, and in which they will justify the favor of their sovereign, and the good opinion of their fellow-subjects, and make them rejoice to see those virtuous characters that were the other day upon a level with them now exalted above them in rank, but feeling with them in sympathy what they felt in common with them before. We have persons exalted from the practice of the law, from the place in which they administered high, though subordinate, justice, to a seat here, to enlighten with their knowledge and to strengthen with their votes those principles which have distinguished the courts in which they have presided.

My Lords, you have here also the lights of our religion, you have the bishops of England. My Lords, you have that true image of the primitive Church, in its ancient form, in its ancient ordinances, purified from the superstitions and the vices which a long succession of ages will bring upon the best institutions. You have the representatives of that religion which says that their God is love, that the very vital spirit of their institution is charity, – a religion which so much hates oppression, that, when the God whom we adore appeared in human form, He did not appear in a form of greatness and majesty, but in sympathy with the lowest of the people, and thereby made it a firm and ruling principle that their welfare was the object of all government, since the Person who was the Master of Nature chose to appear Himself in a subordinate situation. These are the considerations which influence them, which animate them, and will animate them, against all oppression, – knowing that He who is called first among them, and first among us all, both of the flock that is fed and of those who feed it, made Himself 'the servant of all'.

My Lords, these are the securities which we have in all the constituent parts of the body of this House. We know them, we reckon, we rest upon them, and commit safely the interests of India and of humanity into your hands. Therefore it is with confidence, that, ordered by the Commons,

I impeach Warren Hastings, Esquire, of high crimes and misdemeanors.

I impeach him in the name of the Commons of Great Britain in Parliament assembled, whose Parliamentary trust he has betrayed.

I impeach him in the name of all the Commons of Great Britain, whose national character he has dishonored.

I impeach him in the name of the people of India, whose laws, rights, and liberties he has subverted, whose properties he has destroyed, whose country he has laid waste and desolate.

I impeach him in the name and by virtue of those eternal laws of justice which he has violated.

I impeach him in the name of human nature itself, which he has cruelly outraged, injured, and oppressed, in both sexes, in every age, rank, situation, and condition of life. [1]

We are certainly not to take this presentation of King, Lords and Commons literally, as representing Edmund Burke's opinion of the King, Lords and Commons of Great Britain, as he actually knew these. He could, in another context, be cynical and acerbic about all three. About 'the lights of our religion', for example, he had written in the previous year – in an assessment of the impeachment's chances in the Lords:'I am sorry to say that the most sacred part of that house is precisely that in which we can confide the least. The humility of the Bishops will leave the honour of vindicating the Christian religion to others.' [2]

But it would be quite wrong, also, to assume that he has his tongue in his cheek; which would be an awkward posture for a peroration. Burke, as usual, is profoundly in earnest. But he is not talking about the House of Lords as it actually is. He is conjuring up, on this solemn occasion, an image of a Platonic ideal of the House of Lords, in the hope of inducing the actual House – or some of its members

[1] *Works* X, 142–145.
[2] *Corr.* V, 341; letter to Thomas Burgh (1 July 1787).

– to try to live up to that ideal. The image he is conjuring up is part of himself; the positive side of his feelings towards England. He is willing England, in the persons of the Lords, to live up to what he wishes her to be. The Lords can do that if they will cast out Warren Hastings, the living embodiment of all that Burke's hostile feelings, usually suppressed, tell him that England is. The peroration is not really a description, but a kind of prayer, that England may find Grace, and repent from evil.

The immediate answer to the prayer was not promising. The Lord Chancellor spoke immediately after Burke had finished. According to the *Parliamentary History* the 'Lord Chancellor left the woolsack and opened his speech by pronouncing a very fine eulogium on Mr. Burke, for his mode of opening his charges. . . . "After this, said his lordship, I shall hold Mr. Burke to the proof of all he has asserted." The Lord Chancellor rules "that the managers should complete the whole of their case, before Mr. Hastings said a word in his defence . . . In the present impeachment, he trusted their lordships would not depart from the known established laws of the land."' [1]

Starting off with that perfidious 'eulogium', Thurlow had dealt Burke's cause two deadly blows. By ruling out any departure from 'the known established laws of the land', he had rejected Burke's case for 'enlarged principles of State morality'; thus he had made it virtually impossible to secure a conviction of Hastings on the basis of the known iniquities of his system of government. By ruling that 'the managers should complete the whole of their case, before Mr. Hastings said a word in his defence,' Thurlow was destroying Burke's hopes of arousing public opinion against Hastings. Without the drama of charges being made, with Hastings there to answer each charge as soon as it was made, the public would lose interest in the case, long before Hastings made his general answer to the charges as a whole.

Burke had now no real hope of success, but he was determined, out of a sense of duty, to keep on with the case until the bitter end, which came more than seven years later. The path he had now to tread was an increasingly lonely one. He soon became aware that the Pitt Administration, while it had supported the principle of impeachment, would give little support to the impeachment itself: 'No member of the administration served on the committee, which meant that, for the first time since the Revolution of 1688, the crown

[1] *Parl. Hist.* xxvii, 54–56; 21 February, 1788.

law officers were not associated in the prosecution of an impeachment.'[1]

Instead of actively supporting the Impeachment, the Pitt Administration – until 1790 – actually harassed its managers (see below, pp. 379–80). As early as April 1788, Pitt's Treasury is complaining to Burke about the mounting costs of the Impeachment. Burke's reply is both dignified and well-taken: 'We conceive that Justice for the People of India is an Object which will warrant a large Expence and We know that Justice for the people of India cannot be obtained in Great Britain without incurring that Expence. When we come in our Places to a vote for making it good We entertain no Doubt that We shall find ourselves able to support to our Consciences to our constituents and to the world the Share we have had in producing that Charge. We know the attention that ought to be paid to the frugal Expenditure of the Public Treasure but we shall always Steadily avow our Opinion that some thousands of Pounds from the many Millions taken with so free and so strong an hand from the People of India are properly expended in an Attempt to obtain Justice for the Injuries they have suffered.'[2]

Pitt, with his safe majority in the Commons, could of course have called off the impeachment at any time. Instead he let it drag on until 1795. His reasons for doing so are plain. The impeachment consumed the time and talents of Opposition leaders – pre-eminently, Burke – and diverted these from the Commons to the Lords. If Pitt had nipped the impeachment in the bud, he would have had Burke back in the Commons, attacking him for shielding corruption and oppression in India. It is unlikely that Pitt had forgotten his exposure to the 'Speech on Nabob of Arcot's Debts', or that he could have any wish to provoke a renewal of that experience.

At the time of supporting the passage of the impeachment through the Commons, Pitt may, as he himself suggested, have been moved, in some degree, by compassion for Indians. But once the impeachment had actually begun, Pitt's attitude towards it was dictated solely by cold calculations of political expediency. For Burke, what was still worse than Pitt's negative attitude, was that his own political colleagues speedily tired of the impeachment, and became resentful of his own commitment to it. On 20 November 1788 Georgiana, Duchess of Devonshire, noted in her diary: 'Sheridan who is heartily

[1] Marshall, *Impeachment*, p. 69.
[2] *Corr.* V, 389; Burke to the Lords Commissioners of the Treasury, 15 April 1788.

tired of Hastings trial, and fearful of Burke's impetuosity says that he wishes Hastings would run away and Burke after him.'[1]

In May 1789, as a result of an expression used by Burke in the course of the impeachment, Pitt's hostility and the exasperation of Burke's colleagues both converged on him. In opening the Sixth Article – bribery and corruption – against Hastings[2] on 21 April, Burke alluded to the fate of Nuncomar and said that Hastings 'has murdered this man by the hands of Sir Elijah Impey'.[3] Major Scott – Hastings's agent in the Commons – immediately petitioned the House to protect Hastings from allegations which were not included in any of the Articles. The editors of the relevant volume of the *Correspondence* relate the sequel: 'After an acrimonious debate, the House agreed on 27 April to receive Hastings's petition. "Notice" was taken on 30 April "that the Name of the Right honourable Edmund Burke (a Member of this House) is mentioned in the said Petition"' (*Journals of the House of Commons*, XLIV, 312), and that the subject would be discussed on the next day. Burke chose to make his answer through Frederick Montagu – (1733–1800) – one of the Committee of Managers and a particularly respected member of the Opposition – rather than to take part in the debate himself.'[4]

Burke's letter, which Montagu read to the House, is impressive, and implacable:

The House having, upon an opinion of my diligence and fidelity (for they could have no other motive), put a great trust into my hands, ought to give me an entire credit for the veracity of every fact I affirm or deny; but if they fail with regard to me, it is at least in my power to be true to myself. I will not commit myself in an unbecoming contention with the agents of a criminal whom it is my duty to bring to justice. I am a Member of a Committee of Secrecy, and I will not violate my trust, by turning

[1] *Corr.* V, 457, n. 4.

[2] There seems little doubt that Hastings did take bribes, though not on the Benfield scale. Even the hard-to-convince P. J. Marshall comes near to conceding, in one case, that even 'if the imputation of bribery remains unproven, it is unfortunate, to say the least that he should have accepted a loan from [Maharajah] Nobkissen, which soon became a present, when appointing him to a most valuable office.' (Marshall, *Impeachment*, p. 151).

[3] 'Speech on the Sixth Article – First Day': in *Works* X, 218. This was near the beginning of another four-day speech, about as long as the 'Speech on Opening the Impeachment'. But the 'Speech on the Sixth Article' neither belongs in the Great Melody nor is particularly helpful to our understanding of that, and so need not detain us here – except for the episode of 'the hands of Sir Elijah Impey'.

[4] *Corr.* V, 466, tn.

myself into a defendant, and bringing forward, in my own exculpation, the evidence which I have prepared for his conviction. I will not let him know on what documents I rely; I will not let him know who the witnesses for the prosecution are, nor what they have to depose against him. Though I have no sort of doubt of the constancy and integrity of those witnesses; yet because they are men, and men to whom, from my own situation, I owe protection, I ought not to expose them either to temptation or to danger. I will not hold them out to be importuned or menaced, or discredited, or run down, or possibly to be ruined in their fortunes, by the power and influence of this delinquent, except where the national service supersedes all other considerations. If I must suffer, I will suffer alone! No man shall fall a sacrifice to a feeble sensibility on my part, that at this time of day might make me impatient of those libels, which by despising through so many years, I have at length obtained the honour of being joined in commission with this Committee, and becoming an humble instrument in the hands of public justice.

The only favour I have to supplicate from the House is, that their goodness would spare to the weakest of their Members any unnecessary labour; by letting me know, as speedily as possible, whether they wish to discharge me from my present office. If they do not, I solemnly promise them, that with God's assistance, I will, as a Member of their Committee, pursue their business to the end – That no momentary disfavour shall slacken my diligence in the great cause they have undertaken – That I will lay upon, with the force of irresistible proof, this dark scene of bribery, peculation, and gross pecuniary corruption which I have begun to unfold, and in the midst of which my course has been arrested.

This poor Indian stratagem, of turning the accuser into a defendant, has been too often and too uniformly practised by Devi Sing, Mr. Hastings, and Gunga Goom'd Sing, and other Banyans [agents], black and white, to have any longer the slightest effect upon me, whom long service in Indian Committees has made well acquainted with the politics of Calcutta. If the House will suffer me to go on, the moment is at hand when my defence, and included in it the defence of the House, will be made in the only way in which my trust permits me to make it, by proving juridically on this accusing criminal the facts and the guilt which we have charged upon him. As to the relevancy of the facts, the Committee of Impeachment must be the sole judge, until they are handed over to the Court competent to give a final decision on their value. In that Court the agent of Mr. Hastings will soon enough be called upon to give his own testimony with regard to the conduct of his principal. The agent shall not escape from the necessity of delivering it; nor will the principal escape from the testimony of his agent.

I hope I have in no moment of this pursuit (now by me continued, in one shape or other, for near eight years) shown the smallest symptom of collusion or prevarication. The last point in which I should wish to shew it, is in this charge concerning pecuniary corruption – a corruption so great and so spreading, that the most unspotted characters will be justified in taking measures for guarding themselves against suspicion. Neither hope, nor fear, nor anger, nor weariness, nor discouragement of any kind, shall move me from this trust – nothing but an act of the House, formally taking away my commission or totally cutting off the means of performing it. I trust we are all of us [the managers] animated by the same sentiments. [1]

The Commons, on 4 May, voted by 135 to 66 that the words complained of 'should not have been spoken', but Pitt did not respond to Burke's challenge, by calling on the parliamentary majority to discharge him from the Management of the Impeachment. Burke's party colleagues, led by Fox, had defended him quite warmly in the debate, as well as voting against the motion of censure. Fox said that Burke 'had done justice to God and man, and he deserved no censure.' However, immediately after that motion had been carried, Fox tried to have the impeachment dropped. But, as John Hatsell, the Clerk of the House of Commons had observed, three years before, Burke was 'hard to get rid of'. Burke felt that he had called Pitt's bluff. He took the censure of the Commons, unaccompanied by the challenged discharge, as a mandate to continue. He said later: 'the most brilliant day of my life, and that which I most wish to live over again, was the day I appeared at the bar of the House of Lords with the censure of the Commons in my hand.' [2]

Facing the Lords, Burke defended his use of the word 'murdered':

Your Lordships do not imagine, I hope, that I used that word in any other than a moral and popular sense, or that I used it in the legal and technical sense of the word murder. Your Lordships know that I could not bring before this bar any commoner of Great Britain on a charge for murder. I am not so ignorant of the laws and constitution of my country. I expressed an act which I conceived to be of an atrocious and evil nature, and partaking of some of the moral evil consequences of that crime. What led me into that error? Nine years' meditation upon that subject.

Burke now knew that the impeachment, whatever its ultimate outcome, could not be stopped in mid-career. He had challenged Pitt on that point, and Pitt had drawn back. Only a Commons majority

[1] *Corr.* V, 466–8. "Unspotted characters" is a warning to Pitt.
[2] *Corr.* V, 472–474.

could terminate the mandate of the Managers. Fox who desperately wanted to terminate that mandate, did not control a majority. In party-political terms, Pitt now had Fox on the hook of the impeachment, and was not going to let him off it. Burke, repenting of his former party constraints over India, was now altogether indifferent to all considerations of party – including the known wishes of his nominal leader, where India was concerned. So Burke drove on, until the Lords delivered judgement – in 1795.

Many contemporaries found Burke's persistence in this matter to be absurd and futile. So have some historians – one historian writes: 'The proceedings in Westminster Hall came more and more to resemble an elaborate folly, inhabited only by Burke.'[1] That is indeed how it looks, from the point of view of a Namierite historian of Fox's party. But if we look at the matter in a wider perspective, taking into consideration the peoples of India, Burke's constancy of purpose, under adversity and ridicule, over fourteen years, has in it something of the sublime. He set out to establish a principle which was quite new, in relation to the governance of India: that the servants of the East India Company – the representatives of British power in India – shall be held accountable, for their treatment of Indians. Until Burke interested himself in the matter, no Company servant had ever been held accountable on that score. By holding Warren Hastings pinned at the bar of the House of Lords for nearly eight years, Burke established the principle of accountability, in a way that nobody, connected with the government of India, or of the Empire generally, would ever forget. The ultimate acquittal did not erase the memory of the ordeal. As V. A. Smith, author of the *Oxford History of India*, puts it: 'Though the faults of many lesser men transcended those of Hastings as his ability exceeded theirs, it was fitting that the responsibility for misgovernment and acts of high-handedness should be fixed upon the head rather than on lesser men . . . The arraignment of Hastings and the ending of all his further prospects gave warning to the Company's servants in general that no lesser man could expect his actions to go without scrutiny or his faults without reproof.'

This view is not universal. Penderel Moon writes in his biography of Hastings: 'Did the impeachment serve any useful purpose? It is commonly thought that Burke's denunciations of Hastings, however unjust in themselves, did at least focus public attention on the abuses

---

[1] Mitchell, *Charles James Fox*, p. 115.

of the Company's rule, and that out of the impeachment a new order of things arose in India. This notion is mistaken. The iniquities of the Company's servants were not brought to public notice by the speeches at Hastings' trial – they had been notorious and the constant theme of parliamentary discussion throughout the preceding twenty years, and all the essential measures which brought about a reform were taken before and not after the impeachment.'[1] The idea of a 'mistaken notion' in that passage is achieved by a trick in presentation. The trick is to make it appear that Burke's 'denunciations of Hastings' began with the impeachment. As we have seen Burke's attacks on Hastings had been sustained for seven years before the formal impeachment opened.

Hastings's successor, Lord Cornwallis, brought an end to the system of extortion that had prevailed for a quarter of a century of British rule in India. The beginning of the clean-up did precede the actual Impeachment. But the impetus towards the clean-up had been provided almost entirely by Edmund Burke, from 1781 on, mainly through the Reports of his Select Committee, and the adoption of these by the House of Commons.

*   *   *

By the second half of 1789 the French Revolution was already beginning to replace India as Burke's principal preoccupation. There is one aspect of this which it seems appropriate to dispose of here: that Burke's quarrel with Fox, over the French Revolution, had its origins in the strained relations that already existed between the two men, over the Impeachment. If this hypothesis were just another example of the trivialising itch – a notion that Burke picked a quarrel with Fox over France, because he felt Fox had let him down, over India – we could afford to pass it over in silence. But there is some truth in this particular hypothesis. Relations certainly were strained by the end of 1789. Burke wrote to Francis on 17 December of the 'desertion and treachery of friends'.[2] Fox is certainly aimed at here.

The two men were seeing less of one another, in 1789, than formerly. This was partly due to the sheer volume of work which the management of the impeachment involved for Burke – most of it outside the House – and partly a result of the growing divergence between them over the impeachment. Burke writes to Fox on 11 May

[1] Moon, *Hastings*, pp. 323–4.
[2] *Corr.* VI, 55–8.

1789: 'It is unlucky, that things are so circumstanced, that we seldom can meet; and that, with us, an explanation cannot always follow on the heels of a misapprehension.'[1] This was a careful fence-mending letter, written just after the 'hands of Sir Elijah Impey' crisis (see above pp. 379–81). If their relations had been in their normal, pre-impeachment condition in the second half of 1789, the two men would have met and talked, privately, about the French Revolution. Had they done so, the quarrel – and the consequent split in the Whig Party – could have been avoided. If Burke had been able to communicate to Fox his own misgivings over the Revolution – at a stage when these were no more than misgivings – Fox's rising enthusiasm for it could have been significantly cooled, because of his immense respect for Burke. As it was, Fox had publicly committed himself, before he was aware how Burke was thinking, on this subject. And, if Burke had not already been angry with Fox, over India, he would have sought him out, for private remonstrance, at the first sign of Fox's enthusiasm for the French Revolution, manifested privately in November 1789, and publicly in February 1790. As it was, the old teacher publicly denounced his formerly beloved pupil, regarding him as doubly delinquent: over France, and over India (see below, Chapter V).

Each phase of the Great Melody affects all the others and sometimes, as here, with melancholy personal consequences both for Burke and his friends. But that was a price Burke was willing to pay – and willing for his friends to pay – in any cause to which he felt fully committed. He had felt committed to India since 1781. He was committed to opposing the French Revolution by January 1790. Burke then saw Fox as standing in the way of both commitments. He was impelled by the elemental forces of his nature to thrust Fox aside, in order to be able to honour his own commitments, to India and to France; and, more obscurely, to Ireland.

---

[1] *Corr.* V, 473.

V
France 1789–1791

I feel an insuperable reluctance in giving my hand to destroy any established institution of government, upon a theory, however plausible it may be.

EDMUND BURKE, 1 December 1783,
speaking on Fox's East India Bill.

'Mr Fox rose to reply: but his mind was so much agitated, and his heart so much affected by what had fallen from Mr Burke, that it was some minutes before he could proceed. Tears trickled down his cheeks, and he strove in vain to give utterance to feelings that dignified and exalted his nature. The sensibility of every member of the House appeared uncommonly excited upon the occasion.' (p. 425)

BURKE'S FIRST REACTION TO THE FRENCH REVOLUTION

The earliest known comment by Edmund Burke on the French Revolution is in a letter to Lord Charlemont of 9 August 1789:

> As to us here our thoughts of every thing at home are suspended, by our astonishment at the wonderful Spectacle which is exhibited in a Neighbouring and rival Country – what Spectators, and what actors! England gazing with astonishment at a French struggle for Liberty and not knowing whether to blame or to applaud! The thing indeed, though I thought I saw something like it in progress for several years, has still something in it paradoxical and Mysterious. The spirit it is impossible not to admire; but the old Parisian ferocity has broken out in a shocking manner. It is true, that this may be no more than a sudden explosion: If so no indication can be taken from it. But if it should be character rather than accident, then that people are not fit for Liberty, and must have a Strong hand like that of their former masters to coerce them. Men must have a certain fund of natural moderation to qualify them for Freedom, else it become noxious to themselves and a perfect Nuisance to everybody else. What will be the Event it is hard I think still to say. To form a solid constitution requires Wisdom as well as spirit, and whether the French have wise heads among them, or if they possess such whether they have authority equal to their wisdom, is to be seen; In the meantime the progress of this whole affair is one of the most curious matters of Speculation that ever was exhibited.[1]

By the end of the following month, Burke's negative view of the Revolution has hardened. His friend William Windham (1750–1810, MP for Norwich), who had visited Paris, from mid-August to

[1] *Corr.* VI, 10.

6 September, wrote to him on 15 September in an optimistic vein: 'What is said of the disorder and irregularity of the national assembly has, I think, a great deal of exaggeration: at least, if a due consideration be had of all the circumstances. My prediction was, (and accounts which I heard since my being there, have contributed to confirm it) that they would very soon become perfectly orderly.'

The attitude – 'things are settling down' – was widespread in the months immediately after the fall of the Bastille, especially among Burke's friends, the Whigs. It became even more general in 1790, a year of apparent tranquillity. Burke never shared it. In his reply to Windham, on 27 September, he civilly, but firmly, rejects this assessment:

> That they should settle their constitution, without much struggle, on paper, I can easily believe; because at present the Interests of the Crown have no party, certainly no armed party, to support them; But I have great doubts whether any form of Government which they can establish will procure obedience; especially obedience in the article of Taxations. In the destruction of the old Revenue constitution they find no difficulties – but with what to supply them is the Opus. You are undoubtedly better able to judge; but it does not appear to me, that the National assembly have one Jot more power than the King; whilst they lead or follow the popular voice, in the subversion of all orders, distinctions, priveleges impositions, Tythes, and rents, they appear omnipotent; but I very much question, whether they are in a condition to exercise any function of decided authority – or even whether they are possessed of any real deliberate capacity, or the exercise of free Judgement in any point whatsoever; as there is a Mob of their constituents ready to Hang them if They should deviate into moderation, or in the least depart from the Spirit of those they represent.[1]

Here we find, already, the essentials of the view of the Constitution-forming phase of the Revolution, which Burke was to develop, in the following year in *Reflections on the Revolution in France*.

Ten days later an event occurred which suggested that Burke, not Windham, had got it right. On 5 and 6 October a crowd of 30,000 Parisians, men and women, marched to Versailles and forced their way into the palace shouting '*A Paris! A Paris!*'. Louis XVI, prompted by Lafayette, gave way, with the words: 'My friends, I

---

[1] *Corr.* VI, 25. Windham later fully came round to Burke's view of the Revolution; see below p. 487.

shall go to Paris, with my wife and my children: it is to the love of my good and faithful subjects that I entrust my most precious possessions.' The royal family then made their way from Versailles to the Tuileries, in the midst of the crowd, which included women carrying pikes. The significance of the *journées* of 5th and 6th October is assessed by a modern French historian as follows: 'The sun had ceased to set at Versailles in the splendid isolation determined by Louis XIV. The October rain brought back the King to the Tuileries, which he was not to leave, except for prison, and then the scaffold.'[1]

The news of the fateful *journées* reached Burke on 10 October. He wrote to his son Richard:

This day I heard from Laurence who has sent me papers confirming the portentous State of France – where the Elements which compose Human Society seem all to be dissolved, and a world of Monsters to be produced in the place of it – where Mirabeau presides as the Grand Anarch; and the late Grand Monarch makes a figure as ridiculous as pitiable. I expect to hear of his dismissing the Regiment he has called to his aid, for drinking his health, and [for] their listening to a french God save the King, and that he has chosen a corps of Paris Amazons for his Body Guard.[2]

On 4 November, a young Parisian acquaintance of the Burkes, Charles-Jean-François Depont (1767–96), wrote Burke the letter to which *Reflections on the Revolution in France* were to be, in form, a reply. Depont asks for assurance 'that the French are worthy to be free, that they will know how to distinguish liberty from licence, and a legitimate government from a despotic power [and] that the Revolution which has begun will succeed.' Burke's original reply to Depont – later greatly expanded to become *Reflections* – is mild and judicious in tone, without any of the fierceness of the later version. In his letter, Depont had said he would never forget that his heart had beaten for the first time at the name of *Liberty* 'when I heard you talk about it'. Burke takes this up with gentle, stately irony:

Besides as you are pleased to think that your splendid flame of Liberty was first lighted up at My faint and glimmering taper, I thought you had

[1] *Journées Révolutionnaires*, by Denis Richet, in the *Dictionnaire Critique de la Révolution Française* (Paris, 1988) p. 116. Richet here ignores the five-day episode of the flight to Varennes in June 1791, treating it no doubt as no more than an incident within the Tuileries captivity.

[2] *Corr.* VI, 30.

a right to call upon me for my undisguised sentiments on whatever related to that Subject.

He goes on:

Permit me then to continue our conversation, and to tell You what the freedom is that I love and that to which I think all men intitled. It is not solitary, unconnected, individual, selfish Liberty. As if every Man was to regulate the whole of his Conduct by his own will. The Liberty I mean is social freedom. It is that state of things in which Liberty is secured by the equality of Restraint; A Constitution of things in which the liberty of no one Man and no body of Men and no Number of men can find Means to trespass on the liberty of any Person or any description of Persons in the Society. This kind of Liberty is indeed but another name for Justice, ascertained by wise Laws, and secured by well constructed institutions. I am sure, that Liberty, so incorporated, and in a manner, identified, with justice, must be infinitely dear to every one, who is capable of conceiving what it is. But whenever a separation is made between Liberty and Justice, neither is, in my opinion, safe . . .

   When therefore I shall learn, that in France, the Citizen, by whatever description he is qualified, is in a perfect state of legal security, with regard to his life, to his property, to the uncontrolled disposal of his Person, to the free use of his Industry and his faculties; – When I hear that he is protected in the beneficial Enjoyment of the Estates, to which, by the course of settled Law, he was born, or is provided with a fair compensation for them; – that he is maintain'd in the full fruition of the advantages belonging to the state and condition of life, in which he had lawfully engaged himself, or is supplied with a substantial, equitable Equivalent; – When I am assured, that a simple Citizen may decently express his sentiments upon Publick Affairs, without hazard to his life or safety, even tho' against a predominant and fashionable opinion; When I know all this of France, I shall be as well pleased as every one must be, who has not forgot the general communion of Mankind, nor lost his natural sympathy in local and accidental connexions.

Burke addresses his young friend about his own future, in revolutionary times:

You are now to live in a new order of things; under a plan of Government of which no Man can speak from experience. Your talents, Your publick spirit, and your fortune give you fair pretensions to a considerable share in it. Your settlement may be at hand; But that it is still at some distance is more likely. The French may be yet to go through more transmigrations. They may pass, as one of our Poets says, "thro' many varieties of untried being" before their State obtains its final form. In that progress thro' Chaos and darkness, you will find it necessary (at all times it is more or less so) to fix Rules to keep your life and Conduct in some steady course. You have theories enough concerning the Rights of Men. It may not be amiss to add a small degree of attention to their Nature and disposition. It is with Man in the concrete, it is with common human life and human Actions you are to be concerned. I have taken so many liberties with You, that I am almost got the length of venturing to suggest something which may appear in the assuming tone of advice. You will however be so good as to receive my very few hints with your usual indulgence, tho' some of them I confess are not in the taste of this enlighten'd age, and indeed are no better than the late ripe fruit of mere experience. – Never wholly seperate in your Mind the merits of any Political Question from the Men who are concerned in it. You will be told, that if a measure is good, what have you [to] do with the Character and views of those who bring it forward. But designing Men never seperate their Plans from their Interests; and if You assist them in their Schemes, You will find the pretended good in the end thrown aside or perverted, and the interested object alone compassed, and that perhaps thro' Your means. The power of bad Men is no indifferent thing.

The letter ends:

I have been led further than I intended. But every days account shews more and more, in my opinion, the ill consequence of keeping good principles and good general views within no bounds. Pardon the liberty I have taken; though it seems somewhat singular, that I, whose opinions have so little weight in my own Country, where I have some share in a Publick Trust, should write as if it were possible they should affect one Man, with regard to Affairs in which I have no concern. But for the present, my time is my own, and to tire your patience is the only injury I can do You.[1]

As the editors of the relevant volume of Burke's *Correspondence* rightly say: 'It seems clear that by the end of 1789 Burke had already made up his mind about the French Revolution.'[2]

Burke had made up his mind; and yet it has recently been argued,

[1] *Corr.* VI, 39–50.
[2] *Corr.* VI. This volume is edited, admirably, by Alfred Cobban and Robert A. Smith.

with an appearance of authority, that he had no right to make up his mind. L. G. Mitchell, in the opening paragraph of his introduction to Volume VIII, *The French Revolution, 1790–1794*, of *The Writings and Speeches of Edmund Burke* (Oxford, 1989) states: 'Edmund Burke claimed that he knew "France, by observation and enquiry, pretty tolerably for a stranger". Nothing was more disputed by his critics. In squaring up to the implications of the French Revolution, Burke was denied access to that range of information and contacts that someone like Charles James Fox could call on. His opponents made the same point in different words. According to them, Burke deliberately abstained from readily available information for fear of upsetting his prejudices. Burke was nervous of receiving Frenchmen in England because of "the very bad French which I speak." In Paris, Madame du Deffand, although finding him *"de beaucoup d'esprit"*, agreed that *"il parle notre langue avec le* [*sic.* – C.C.O'B] *plus grande difficulté"*. Not to have a mastery of French in the late eighteenth century was, in some sense, a badge of dishonour, marking a man as a provincial who could not easily move in the enlightened world of the Paris salons and the great London houses. It was a deficiency that Burke must have felt keenly.'[1]

Presumption, superficiality, naivety, snobbery and sheer obtuseness can seldom have been so confidently combined and exhibited as they are in the above passage. Consider, in the light of the Mitchellian categories of comparison, the September 1789 exchange set out above between Windham and Burke:

William Windham, like Charles James Fox, had 'access to that range of information and contacts', that was said to be 'denied' to Burke. Windham's French, we may reasonably assume, was superior to Burke's and Windham 'could easily move in the enlightened world of the Paris salons'.[2]

---

[1] *Writings and Speeches* VIII. See my Introduction for an examination of this eccentric and defective compilation (Volume VIII, not the series) p. lix above. Actually, Fox's French was probably no better than Burke's. When Fox visited Amiens, during the peace of Amiens, he had an argument with Bonaparte who recalled, '*Il me combattait avec chaleur en son mauvais français.*' See Stanley Ayling's *Life of Charles James Fox* (London, 1991) p. 213.

[2] Burke could, when he wanted to, move in those same salons with much less difficulty than Mitchell would imply. Horace Walpole wrote to a friend, Lady Ossory, on 11 March 1773: 'Mr. Burke is returned from Paris, where he was so much the mode, that happening to dispute with the philosophers, it grew the fashion to be christians: St Patrick himself did not make more converts.'

Furthermore, Windham had first-hand experience of revolutionary Paris, while Burke's only visit to France had taken place in 1773. In Mitchell's terms, Windham was much the better informed of the two men. Yet it was the 'provincial', linguistically-handicapped Burke, and not the polished and polyglot Windham – as Windham himself would later acknowledge – who had already seen the direction in which the Revolution was moving.

Mitchell makes the mechanical assumption that the wider the range of information available to a person, the better informed that person is. The mechanical assumption contains within itself an egalitarian assumption: that all persons are equally capable of evaluating the information available to them. But both these assumptions are false. A person endowed with superior powers of evaluation – as Burke clearly was – can be better informed, on the basis of fewer data, than an inferior evaluator, with access to more data. Also the phrase 'range of information and contacts' is misleading. In a scene of excitement and rapid change, 'contacts' are as likely to be a source of misinformation as of information. And this was particularly so of 'the enlightened world of the Paris salons' in 1789–91. The stars of those salons, in those days, were the Constitution-makers of the National Assembly. These were then sublimely confident that they were making over French society precisely to their own specifications. People like Charles James Fox (and, for a time, William Windham) took the Constitution-makers at their own valuation, and believed what they said. Burke, in contrast, believed that the Constitution-makers were Sorcerer's Apprentices: infatuated beings, who did not understand the disastrous consequences to which their efforts were doomed. Six years later, the best and brightest of the Constitution-makers, Abbé Sieyès, was to acknowledge, as a survivor of the Terror, that Burke's view of the matter had been correct. Most of the other Constitution-makers did not survive.

Taking that view of the Constitution-makers, Burke was naturally unimpressed, when regaled with 'inside information' which he knew derived ultimately from those sources. This is why his opponents claimed that he 'deliberately abstained from readily available information for fear of upsetting his prejudices.' For Burke, the question was not whether information was or was not 'readily available', but whether it was true or false.

The 'range of information' available to Burke was wider than Mitchell implies, and more solid than the kind of information most relied on by his opponents. In an important letter, of January 1790, to an unknown correspondent, Burke stated: 'As for me, I have read, and with some attention, the authorised, or rather the equally authentic documents on this subject, from the first instructions to the representatives of the several orders down to this time.'[1]

Burke relied on the published reports of the proceedings – *procès-verbal* – of the National Assembly. His spoken French was defective, though he could and did sustain animated conversations in that language with Mirabeau and others. But he could read the written language with ease, and depended on reading, in both French and English, for most of his information about the Revolution. He knew there was more to be learned about politics, and the real hopes, fears and ambitions of politicians, from the recorded adversarial proceedings of a political assembly, than from the kinds of information so 'readily available' in the gossip of the Paris salons.

The Decision to Fight the Revolution

By the end of 1789, Burke has made up his mind, in a decidedly negative way, about the character and probable future course of the French Revolution, 'through Chaos and darkness'. But his emotions are not yet engaged, and he has not yet decided that it is incumbent on him personally to oppose the Revolution. That engagement occurred, and that decision was taken, in January 1790. The moment of the engagement and of the decision is reflected in the closing sentences of that letter to an unknown correspondent from which I have just quoted. The letter ended: 'But so it is. I see some people here are willing that we should become their scholars too, and reform our state on the French model. They have begun; and it is high time for those who wish to preserve morem majorum [ancestral traditions], to look about them.'[2]

The decision to sound the alarm against English sympathisers with the French Revolution was reached in the third week of January 1790, when Burke read a pamphlet containing the proceedings of

[1] *Corr.* VI, 79.
[2] *Corr.* VI, 81.

the Revolution Society in the previous November. The Revolution Society was an old established body, consisting mainly of Dissenters, which existed to commemorate the English Revolution of 1688. The Society met annually on 4 November, William III's birthday. The 1789 meeting was the first since the fall of the Bastille, and the participants used the occasion to celebrate and extol the *French* Revolution. The proceedings consisted of a sermon by a well-known dissenting minister, the Rev. Richard Price; a resolution carried by the Society; a dinner in the London Tavern, and an address to the National Assembly. In *Reflections*, the part of the proceedings Burke concentrates on is the Price sermon. But it was the pamphlet as a whole that inflamed him, and set him to composing *Reflections*. The pamphlet firmly placed the British welcome for the French Revolution in a context of anti-Popery. The resolution carried by the Revolution Society at the London Tavern on the evening following Price's sermon, ran: 'This Society, sensible of the important advantages arising to this Country by its deliverance from Popery and Arbitrary Power, and conscious that, under God, we owe that signal blessing to the Revolution, which seated our Deliverer, King William the Third on the Throne; do hereby declare our firm attachment to the civil and religious principles which were recognised and established by that glorious event and which has preserved the succession in the Protestant line; and our determined resolution to maintain and, to the utmost of our power, to perpetuate, those blessings to the latest posterity.'

On the same occasion Price moved the Congratulatory Address to the National Assembly in Paris, which was duly carried, conveyed to the Assembly and warmly welcomed there. Thus, a Society set up to celebrate the English Revolution of 1688 was emphasising the anti-Catholic character of that Revolution, while welcoming the French Revolution, which had already assumed an anti-Catholic character, notably through the annexation of Church property in November 1789. It didn't help that Dr Price was a protégé of Lord Shelburne (by now, Marquess of Lansdowne) whom Burke suspected of having fomented the Gordon Riots. Burke's feelings about what he read of the excesses of the Paris revolutionary mob in 1789 blended, in his imagination, with his still vivid memories of that London Protestant mob of nine years before. In his writing and speeches on the French Revolution, Burke frequently refers to the Gordon Riots.

Nor was it entirely a matter of imagination. The London Corresponding Society, which has been described as 'the most active, the most extreme and the best organised' of the pro-Jacobin societies, was founded by a Scot named Thomas Hardy,[1] a disciple of Lord George Gordon. Lord George himself is said to have sung the French Revolutionary hymn *Ça Ira!* in Newgate Prison immediately before he died on 1 November 1793 (the third anniversary of the publication of *Reflections*). The link between Protestant zealotry and British zeal for the French Revolution was real, and understandably alarming to Edmund Burke.

The Revolution Society's proceedings had to impinge painfully on the buried 'Irish layer' of Burke's psyche. In particular, the language of the resolution carried by the Society immediately after Price's sermon reminded him of just how anti-Catholic the Glorious Revolution, which he was committed to revere, had actually been. It made his Jacobite ancestors walk, and reproach him for having betrayed his people. As over India, with similar forces in operation nine years earlier (see Chapter IV above, especially p. 328), the inner conflict released tremendous psychic energies, driving Burke on in a passionate commitment to another cause: France, as well as India, with Ireland as ultimate driving force. Burke had sound intellectual reasons for the positions he adopted over both India and France. He had set out these reasons cogently and, for the most part, calmly and he had taken up a position opposed to the French Revolution on intellectual grounds, *before* his emotions became involved, as they did in January 1790. But the element of the obsessive, discerned by contemporaries, in the passion and pertinacity of his commitment in both cases, comes from the intensity of the internal conflict, at the level of the Irish layer.

Immediately after contemplating the Revolution Society's proceedings, he set out to expand the letter to Depont into the great tract *Reflections on the Revolution in France*, which was published in the following November. In the meantime, he took the earliest opportunity to make a parliamentary statement, strongly hostile to the French Revolution. The leader of the Whigs, Charles James Fox, had been gushing with enthusiasm for the French Revolution ever since the news of the Fall of the Bastille had reached England. 'How much the greatest event it is that has ever happened in the world and how much the best!' Fox had written with sublime confidence on 30 July 1789.[2] Burke can hardly have known of that particular expression

---

[1] See H. N. Brailsford, *Shelley, Godwin and their Circle* (London and Norwich, 1914) p. 33.
[2] *Memorials and Correspondence of Charles James Fox*, Vol. II, p. 361.

of Fox's enthusiasm for the Revolution, but the enthusiasm itself was known to the whole political world. Burke now set out to fire a warning shot across the bows of his leader in the Commons.

The debate in which Burke made his first parliamentary statement on the French Revolution was on the Army Estimates, in early February 1790, a little less than seven months after the Fall of the Bastille. Burke spoke, as was usually his way, late in the debate, on Day Two (9 February) after both Fox and Pitt had spoken twice. Declaring his uncompromising and comprehensive hostility to the French Revolution, and his fears of British friendship towards it, Burke said:

> The French had shown themselves the ablest architects of ruin that had hitherto existed in the world. In that very short space of time they had completely pulled down to the ground, their monarchy, their church, their nobility, their law, their revenue, their army, their navy, their commerce, their arts and their manufactures. Our friendship and our intercourse with that nation had once been, and might again become more dangerous to us than their worst hostility.[1]

Fox had applauded the extension of Revolutionary citizenship to the soldiers of the French Army. Burke now, gently but gravely, remonstrated with him over this, and revealed that the strength of his own commitment against the Revolution was so great that it could lead to a breach between Burke and the Whigs:

> He was sorry that his right hon. friend [Mr Fox] had dropped even a word expressive of exultation on that circumstance: or that he seemed of opinion that the objection from standing armies was at all lessened by it. That it was with a pain inexpressible he was obliged to have even the shadow of a difference with his friend, whose authority would be always great with him, and with all thinking people. That the house must perceive, from his coming forward to mark an expression or two of his best friend, how anxious he was to keep the distemper of France from the least countenance in England, where he was sure some wicked persons had shown a strong disposition to recommend an imitation of the French spirit of reform. He was so strongly opposed to even the least tendency towards the means of introducing a democracy like theirs, as well as to the end itself, that much as it would affect him, if such a thing could be attempted and that any friend of his could concur in such measures (he was far, very far, from believing they could), he would part with his best friends and join with his worst enemies to oppose either the means or

[1] *Parl. Hist.* xxviii, 323–374.

the end; and to resist all violent exertions of the spirit of innovation, so distinct from all principles of true and safe reformation; a spirit well calculated to overturn states, but perfectly unfit to amend them.

Fox seems to have been altogether unprepared for this, for he rose, according to the *Parliamentary History*, 'with a concern of mind which it was almost impossible to describe'. In words that have been already quoted (see Chapter II above, pp. 160), he acknowledged his immense intellectual indebtedness to Burke. He went on: 'Never would he lend himself to support any cabal or scheme, formed in order to introduce any dangerous innovation into our excellent constitution'. Burke accepted this olive branch with a civility within which we can sense a degree of reserve: 'What he said had drawn from his right hon. friend an explanation [no less] satisfactory to his mind than he was persuaded it was to the House and to all who heard it.'

Such reconciliation as there was, was immediately marred by an intervention by Richard Brinsley Sheridan, the next in eminence at this time to Fox and Burke, in the leadership of the Whigs. Sheridan said that he felt it, 'a duty to declare that he differed decidedly from his right hon. friend in almost every word that he uttered respecting the French Revolution.' Burke curtly replied that 'henceforth his hon. friend [Sheridan] and himself were separated in politics.'

Pitt wound up the debate by declaring that 'he agreed with Mr Burke in every point he had urged relative to the late commotions in France.'[1]

Burke remained, formally, a member of the Parliamentary Opposition, and a follower of Charles James Fox, for more than a year after that parliamentary exchange. But he was no longer at home, politically or even spiritually, in the party of Fox and Sheridan. For Burke, the difference over the Revolution in France nullified the remaining areas of agreement. The enormity of the dangers stemming from that Revolution changed the priorities of British politics also. The dour struggle which Burke and his friends had waged against the influence of the Crown, from 1766 to 1789, was now over, as far as Burke was concerned. The new threat to the very existence of all monarchy made it necessary for true friends of the British Constitution to abate their criticisms of George III. Burke quietly gave notice of this shift in his priorities in an intervention on 10

[1] *Ibid.*

March 1790, a month and a day after his first challenge to Fox. Burke took an opportunity – a rather tenuous one, in terms of parliamentary procedure – to raise the matter of Dunning's Resolution, in favour of diminishing the power of the Crown: 'He was well known not only to have taken a part in laying down the principle stated in the resolution in question, but to have acted upon it in more than one instance.' Burke then added: 'That the resolution did not apply at present in any thing like the proportion it had applied at the time it was voted.' He was giving notice in that last form of words, that the French Revolution had already taken him out of the ranks of active opposition.

Inevitably, he was soon to be charged, by both Whigs and radicals, with having 'changed his principles over the French Revolution'. It is a charge that has echoed down the years, well into our own time. I believe it to be groundless, but I shall reserve full consideration to later in this chapter, in the context of his *Appeal from the New to the Old Whigs* (1791), which contains his fullest answer to it. There is a related charge, however, which is strictly relevant to the present stage of the story: the opening of the rift with Fox. This charge is that Burke's supposed 'change of principles' was motivated by pique at Fox's failure to give him adequate support over the impeachment of Warren Hastings. In that form, the charge is a travesty. Only a dull and superficial mind could impute eloquence and argument of the order of Burke's writings and speeches against the French Revolution to so petty a motive as personal pique. (Burke himself was later to make this point in *Letter to a Noble Lord* (1796). See Chapter VI below, pp. 535–541). That said, it is true that Burke did deeply resent, by late 1789, what he called 'the desertion and Treachery' of his friends, the Whig leaders.[1]

Burke's resentment against Fox, in connection with Warren Hastings, was not a causal factor in the formation of Burke's views and feelings over the Revolution in France. That formation proceeded quite independently of their relations. But the coolness between them, brought about by divergences over the Impeachment, did affect the *mode* in which the rift over the French Revolution developed. It is even possible that there would have been no personal rift, between Fox and Burke, over the French Revolution, had there not been the

---

[1] *Corr.* VI, 55–8. To Philip Francis, 17 December 1789. Fox and Sheridan are not named in this letter, but they were the principal co-managers in the Impeachment and Burke clearly had them in mind. Disraeli, in *Sybil*, ascribes Burke's hostility to the French Revolution to his supposed need to be revenged on Fox.

earlier rift over the Impeachment. I don't mean by that, that Burke could have changed the embattled position he had taken up, from January 1790 on, against the Revolution in France. That was never a possibility. But he might have talked Fox round, as he had done so often before (see above p. 249, and pp. 313–16). Had relations been as cordial as, say, at the time Burke prepared 'Fox's East India Bill' (1783–4), he would have sought Fox out, personally, at the first sign of Fox's attraction to the French Revolution. Burke would have talked with his friend, walked up and down with him, as he had done before, and gently sought to convince him of his error. He might well have succeeded, for his authority over Fox was great, as Fox himself acknowledged. Unlike some of Burke's contemporaries, and some later writers, Fox was himself sufficiently intelligent to be aware of Burke's intellectual superiority. So, had the two still been on a footing of real friendship, Burke might have at least dissuaded Fox from further public, and especially parliamentary, eulogies of the Revolution, and the unity of the Whigs might have been saved.

As it was, Burke was already angry with Fox, and Fox's enthusiasm for the French Revolution made him angrier still. So instead of talking privately with Fox, Burke challenged him publicly on the floor of the House of Commons. A rift developed which was to become an irreparable breach, by May of 1791.

THE *REFLECTIONS*

The period February 1790 to April 1791 may be seen as a period of parliamentary truce between Edmund Burke, on the one hand, and Charles James Fox and most of the rest of the Whigs, on the other. But outside parliament there occurred, during this period, a major event which greatly increased the hostility of the Whigs towards Burke. That event was the publication of Burke's *Reflections on the Revolution in France* on 1 November. For a modern reader, the *Reflections* are the most readily accessible of Burke's works, in the sense that this is the only book by Burke which is in print. I would assume that most people who are sufficiently interested in Burke to read this study will either already have read it or will do so, so I shall not devote as much space to the book as I would if the text were not readily available. Still, I shall make some general points about it and quote some key passages.[1]

The full title, as set out on the title page of its first edition, is:

REFLECTIONS
on the
REVOLUTION IN FRANCE
And On The
PROCEEDINGS IN CERTAIN SOCIETIES
IN LONDON
Relative to that event
In A
LETTER
Intended to have been sent to a Gentleman
In Paris

As recounted earlier in this chapter (p. 389) the book began as a reply to Charles-Jean-François Depont 'a very young gentleman' in Paris, who had asked for reassurance regarding the future course of the French Revolution. The original letter explains, calmly and courteously, why Burke cannot provide the desired reassurance: 'You may have subverted Monarchy, but not recovered freedom ... You are now to live in a new order of things; under a plan of Government of which no Man can speak from experience ... The French may be yet to go through more transmigrations.' Those three sentences are developed at length in the *Reflections*, which are also still, in form, a letter to the same correspondent. But the *Reflections* are in other aspects very different, in character and tone, from the original letter, thanks to Burke's having learnt of those 'proceedings of certain societies' in London, in which unrestricted admiration for the French Revolution was expressed, and a desire to emulate it in England was implied. Burke felt great alarm and anger at those proceedings, and having denounced them in the Commons, in February 1790, he set out to write a tract, to warn the British public against the dangers

---

[1] For a more extended commentary see my introduction to the Penguin Classics edition of *Reflections on the Revolution in France*.

of any such tendencies. That tract, in the form of a letter, is the *Reflections*.

His passionate indignation against the French Revolution – and above all against any attempt to imitate it in the British Isles – is evident in *Reflections*, sustains it, and is the source of a part of its power. But a part only. The text takes up nearly 300 pages. I reckon that 90 per cent of that is taken up with argument and analysis. There is an emotional undercurrent throughout, but it breaks through to the surface only rarely. When it does, the resultant rhetoric is spectacular. The most spectacular such passage – that about the Queen of France, as Burke saw her in 1773 – has been quoted far more often than anything else in the book. Repetition of this quotation has created the misleading impression that *Reflections* consists mostly of gorgeous rhetoric. There is, in reality, very little rhetoric, quantitatively speaking. Most of the book is made up of plain and cogent argument. Passion is present, but Burke keeps it well under control, except on the rare occasions when he decides not to do so.

The grand distinguishing feature of the *Reflections* is the power of Burke's insight into the character of the French Revolution, then at an early stage. This insight is so acute as to endow him with prophetic power. He sees what way the Revolution is heading. No one else seems to have done so, at the time. The spring and summer of 1790 – the period in which Burke wrote the *Reflections* – was the most tranquil stage, in appearance, in the history of the Revolution. It was a period of constitution-making, of benevolent rhetoric and of peaceful jubilation, as in the *Déclaration de Paix au Monde* (21 May 1790) or in the *Fête de la Fédération*, on 14 July 1790, celebrating the first anniversary of the Fall of the Bastille.

Contemplating that attractive scene, in the spring and summer of 1790, most people seem to have assumed that the French Revolution *had already taken place* and that all that remained was to reap its benign consequences. Burke sensed that the Revolution was only beginning. In the penultimate paragraph of the *Reflections*, Burke warned that the French 'commonwealth' could hardly remain in the form it had taken in 1790: '. . . but before its final settlement it may be obliged to pass, as one of our poets says,' 'through great varieties of untried being', and 'in all its transmigrations to be purified by fire and blood.'

Reading the *Reflections* with an undergraduate class in New York, in the 1960s, I found that my students assumed that the direst events of the Revolution – the September Massacres, the Terror, the executions of the King and Queen – had already taken place when the *Reflections* was written. In reality, those events all lay in the future, both when the *Reflections* was written, and when it was published. And yet there is a sense in which those events are already present in the *Reflections*. They are present in the sense that the ferocious dynamic which Burke ascribes to the Revolution, even in 1790, became visible to the world, through those events of 1792–4.

Burke not merely foresaw 'transmigrations, fire, and blood'. Late in his book (page 342 of the *Penguin Classics* edition) he foresaw how those transmigrations would end up, in military despotism:

It is known, that armies have hitherto yielded a very precarious and uncertain obedience to any senate, or popular authority; and they will least of all yield it to an assembly which is to have only a continuance of two years. The officers must totally lose the characteristic disposition of military men, if they see with perfect submission and due admiration, the dominion of pleaders; especially when they find, that they have a new court to pay to an endless succession of those pleaders, whose military policy, and the genius of whose command (if they should have any) must be as uncertain as their duration is transient. In the weakness of one kind of authority, and in the fluctuation of all, the officers of an army will remain for some time mutinous and full of faction, until some popular general, who understands the art of conciliating the soldiery, and who possesses the true spirit of command, shall draw the eyes of all men upon himself. Armies will obey him on his personal account. There is no other way of securing military obedience in this state of things. But the moment in which that event shall happen, the person who really commands the army is your master; the master (that is little) of your king, the master of your assembly, the master of your whole republic.

The seizure of power by Napoleon Bonaparte – the event predicted in this remarkable passage – occurred on 18 Brumaire (9 November) 1799, nine years after the publication of the *Reflections*, and more than two years after the death of the author.

Burke's astonishing capacity to see into the ways in which events were moving derived, not from any mystical intuition, but from penetrating powers of observation, judicious inference from what was observed, and thorough analysis of what was discerned by observation and inference. Burke had immense respect for *circumstances*, and observed them with proportionate attentiveness. There is a passage about circumstances, in relation to liberty, very near the beginning of the *Reflections*, which is fundamental to Burke's political thinking, not only in *Reflections* but generally. In this he is referring to the congratulations conveyed by the English Revolution Society to the French National Assembly, in November 1789, on France's achievement of liberty:

I flatter myself that I love a manly, moral, regulated liberty as well as any gentleman of [the Revolution] society; be he who he will; and perhaps I have given as good proofs of my attachment to that cause, in the whole course of my public conduct. I think I envy liberty as little as they do, to any other nation. But I cannot stand forward, and give praise or blame to any thing which relates to human actions, and human concerns, on a simple view of the object, as it stands, stripped of every relation, in all the nakedness and solitude of metaphysical abstraction. *Circumstances (which with some gentlemen pass for nothing) give in reality to every political principle its distinguishing colour, and discriminating effect. The circumstances are what render every civil and political scheme beneficial or noxious to mankind* [my italics – C.C.O'B]. Abstractedly speaking, government, as well as liberty, is good; yet could I, in common sense, ten years ago, have felicitated France on her enjoyment of a government (for she then had a government) without enquiry what the nature of that government was, or how it was administered? Can I now congratulate the same nation upon its freedom? Is it because liberty in the abstract may be classed amongst the blessings of mankind, that I am seriously to felicitate a madman, who has escaped from the protecting restraint and wholesome darkness of his cell, on his restoration to the enjoyment of light and liberty? Am I to congratulate an highwayman and murderer, who has broke prison, upon the recovery of his natural rights? This would be to act over again the scene of the criminals condemned to the gallies, and their heroic deliverer, the metaphysic Knight of the Sorrowful Countenance.

When I see the spirit of liberty in action, I see a strong principle at work; and this, for a while, is all I can possibly know of it. The wild *gas*, the fixed air is plainly broke loose: but we ought to suspend our judgement until the first effervescence is a little subsided, till the liquor is cleared, and until we see something deeper than the agitation of a troubled and frothy surface. I must be tolerably sure, before I venture publicly to congratulate men upon a blessing, that they have really received one. Flattery corrupts both the receiver and the giver; and adulation is not of more service to the people than to kings. I should therefore suspend my congratulations on the new liberty of France, until I was informed how it had been combined with government; with public force; with the discipline and obedience of armies; with the collection of an effective and well-distributed revenue; with morality and religion; with the solidity of property; with peace and order; with civil and social manners. All these (in their way) are good things too; and, without them, liberty is not a benefit whilst it lasts, and is not likely to continue long. The effect of liberty to individuals is, that they may do what they please: We ought to see what it will please them to do, before we risque congratulations, which may be soon turned into complaints. Prudence would dictate this in the case of separate insulated private men; but liberty, when men act in bodies, is *power*. Considerate people, before they declare themselves, will observe the use which is made of *power*; and particularly of so trying a thing as *new* power in *new* persons, of whose principles, tempers, and dispositions, they have little or no experience, and in situations where those who appear the most stirring in the scene may possibly not be the real movers (*Penguin* ed. pp. 89–91).

I have considered, so far, only the reasoned arguments, which take up most of the text. But the passages in which Burke tries to convey to his readers his own feelings about the Revolution, though less extensive than the rational ones, had probably greater impact. The emotional is used to reinforce the rational, for he is convinced that the Revolution in France is defective both in reason and in feeling. He writes: 'But it seems as if it were the prevalent opinion in Paris, that an unfeeling heart, and an undoubting confidence are the sole qualifications for a perfect legislator (*Penguin* ed. p. 281). This is a key-passage, for Burke's approach to all the four areas of our concern. Burke sees the over-confidence of decision-makers as necessarily cruel in its consequences. There is a word for the area where over-confidence and cruelty overlap. The word is 'arrogance'. In combating the Protestant ascendancy in Ireland, the taxers and punishers of the American colonists, the extortionist rulers of India and finally the Jacobins, Burke is fighting a long war, on changing fronts, against the arrogance of power.

By the second half of 1790, the atrocities which had accompanied the first phase of the Revolution (July–October 1789) were fading from memory. The Whigs and radicals glossed over them as essentially irrelevant; transient episodes in the early history of a Revolution whose generally benign character seemed to them well established in 1790. Burke, on the other hand, regards these atrocities as inherent in the nature of the Revolution, and indicative of its future course. So Burke recalls a day which the Whigs would prefer to forget: the *journées révolutionnaires*, 6 and 7 October 1789:

History will record that on the morning of the 6th of October 1789, the king and queen of France, after a day of confusion, alarm, dismay, and slaughter, lay down, under the pledged security of public faith, to indulge nature in a few hours of respite, and troubled melancholy repose. From this sleep the queen was first startled by the voice of the centinel at her door, who cried out to her, to save herself by flight - that this was the last proof of fidelity he could give – that they were upon him, and he was dead. Instantly he was cut down. A band of cruel ruffians and assassins, reeking with his blood, rushed into the chamber of the queen, and pierced with an hundred strokes of bayonets and poniards the bed, from whence this persecuted woman had but just time to fly almost naked, and through ways unknown to the murderers had escaped to seek refuge at the feet of a king and husband, not secure of his own life for a moment.

This king, to say no more of him, and this queen and their infant children (who once would have been the pride and hope of a great and generous people) were then forced to abandon the sanctuary of the most splendid palace in the world, which they left swimming in blood, polluted by massacre and strewed with scattered limbs and mutilated carcases. Thence they were conducted into the unprovoked, unresisted, promiscuous slaughter, which was made of the gentlemen of birth and family who composed the king's body guard. These two gentlemen, with all the parade of an execution of justice, were cruelly and publickly dragged to the block, and beheaded in the great court of the palace. Their heads were stuck upon spears and led the procession; whilst the royal captives who followed in the train were slowly moved along, amidst the horrid yells and shrilling screams, and frantic dances, and infamous contumelies and all the unutterable abominations of the furies of hell in the abused shape of the vilest of women. After they had been made to taste, drop by drop, more than the bitterness of death, in the slow torture of a journey of twelve miles, protracted to six hours, they were, under a guard composed of those very soldiers who had thus conducted them through this famous triumph, lodged in one of the old palaces of Paris now converted into a Bastile for kings (*Penguin* ed. pp. 164–5).

This narration is the prelude to the most famous passage in all of Burke's writings:

It is now sixteen or seventeen years since I saw the queen of France, then the dauphiness, at Versailles; and surely never lighted on this orb, which she hardly seemed to touch, a more delightful vision. I saw her just above the horizon, decorating and cheering the elevated sphere she just began to move in, – glittering like the morning-star, full of life, and splendour, and joy. Oh! What a revolution! and what an heart must I have, to contemplate without emotion that elevation and that fall! Little did I dream when she added titles of veneration to those of enthusiastic, distant, respectful love, that she should ever be obliged to carry the sharp antidote against disgrace concealed in that bosom; little did I dream that I should have lived to see such disasters fallen upon her in a nation of gallant men, in a nation of men of honour and of cavaliers. I thought ten thousand swords must have leaped from their scabbards to avenge even a look that threatened her with insult. – But the age of chivalry is gone. – That of sophisters, oeconomists, and calculators, has succeeded; and the glory of Europe is extinguished for ever. Never, never more, shall we behold that generous loyalty to rank and sex, that proud submission, that dignified obedience, that subordination of the heart which kept alive, even in servitude itself, the spirit of an exalted freedom. The unbought grace of life, the cheap defence of nations, the nurse of manly sentiment and heroic enterprise is gone! It is gone, that sensibility of principle, that chastity of honour, which felt a stain like a wound, which inspired courage whilst it mitigated ferocity, which ennobled whatever it touched, and under which vice itself lost half its evil, by losing all its grossness (*Penguin* ed. pp. 169–170).

This passage was written at a fairly early stage in the composition of the *Reflections*, and in the white heat of the emotions aroused in Burke by his discovery of the proceedings of the Revolution Society. The reasoned arguments which make up most of the Reflections as we now have them were probably the products of later stages of composition. In February 1790, Burke sent 'the manuscript draft and the proofs for the early part of the work' to Philip Francis.[1] From Francis's reply, dated 19 February, we know that the draft and proofs already contained the romantic passage about the queen. Burke had asked for Francis's critical comments. He got them: 'Waving all discussion concerning the Substance and general tendency of this printed Letter, I must declare my opinion that what I have seen of it, is very loosely put together. In point of writing at least the manuscript you showed me first, was much less exceptionable. Remember that this is one of the most singular, that it may be the most distinguished and ought to be one of the most deliberate acts of your life. Your writings have hitherto been the delight and instruction of your own Country. You now undertake to correct and instruct another Nation, and your appeal in effect is to all Europe. Allowing you the liberty to do so in an extreme case, you cannot deny that it ought to be done with

---

[1] For Francis, see Chapter IV, *passim*.

special deliberation in the choice of the topics, and with no less care and circumspection in the use you make of them. Have you thoroughly considered whether it be worthy of Mr Burke, of a Privy Councillor, of a man so high and considerable in the House of Commons as you are, and holding the station you have obtained in the opinion of the world to enter into a war of Pamphlets with Doctor Price? If he answers you as assuredly he will (and so will many others) can you refuse to reply to a person whom you have attacked? If you do, you are defeated in a battle of your own provoking, and driven to fly from ground of your own choosing. If you do not, where is such a contest to lead you, but into a vile and disgraceful, tho' it were ever so victorious, an altercation? *Dii Meliora* that if you will do it, away with all jest and sneer and sarcasm. Let every thing you say be grave, direct and serious. In a case so interesting as the errors of a great nation, and the calamities of great individuals, and feeling them so deeply as you profess to do, all manner of insinuation is improper, all jibe and nickname prohibited. In my opinion all that you say of the Queen is pure foppery. If she be a perfect female character you ought to take your ground upon her virtues. If she be the reverse it is ridiculous in any but a Lover, to place her personal charms in opposition to her crimes. Either way I know the argument must proceed upon a supposition; for neither have you said anything to establish her moral merits, nor have her accusers formally tried and convicted her of guilt.'[1]

Francis's brusquely negative reaction was not limited to the bit about the queen. He ended his letter by calling on Burke – in the rather painfully jocular tone which had characterised much of the correspondence between these two men – to abandon the whole enterprise which was to become the *Reflections*: 'Look back, I beseech you and deliberate a little, before you determine that this is an office that perfectly becomes you. If I stop here it is not for want of a multitude of objections. The mischief you are going to do yourself is, to my apprehension, palpable. It is visible. It will be audible. I snuff it in the wind. I taste it already. I feel it in every sense and so will you hereafter when I *vow to God* (a most elegant phrase) it will be no sort of consolation to me to reflect that I did every thing in my power to prevent it. I wish you were at the De–l for giving me all this trouble. And so farewell.'

Burke was deeply hurt by Francis's letter, which he answered on

[1] *Corr.* VI, 85–87.

the following day.[1] He was especially hurt by Francis's treatment of the passage about the queen:

> I tell you again that the recollection of the manner in which I saw the Queen of France in the year 1774 [really, 1773] and the contrast between that brilliancy, Splendour, and beauty, with the prostrate Homage of a Nation to her, compared with the abominable Scene of 1789 which I was describing did draw Tears from me and wetted my Paper. These Tears came again into my Eyes almost as often as I lookd at the description. They may again. You do not believe this fact, or that these are my real feelings, but that the whole is affected, or as you express it, "downright Foppery". My friend, I tell you it is truth – and that it is true, and will be true, when you and I are no more, and will exist as long as men – with their Natural feelings exist. I shall say no more on this Foppery of mine.

Burke, as we might expect, was altogether unshaken in his determination to persevere in his enterprise:

> But I intend no controversy with Dr Price or Lord Shelburne or any other of their set. I mean to set in a full View the danger from their wicked principles and their black hearts; I intend to state the true principles of our constitution in Church and state – upon Grounds opposite to theirs.

The letter ends:

> Believe me always sensible of your friendship; though it is impossible that a greater difference can exist on Earth between any Sentiments on those Subjects than unfortunately for me there is between yours and mine.

Francis, no doubt mindful of Richard Burke's admonition, refrained from replying. But immediately after the *Reflections* were published (which was on 1 November 1790) Francis sent Burke his comments on it (3 to 4 November). The letter is a classic of tact-

---

[1] *Corr.* VI, 88–92. This letter was enclosed in one from Edmund's son Richard, asking Francis not to draw Edmund aside from the many and great labours he has on hand by any further letters of this kind. He added: 'Are you so little conversant with my father, or so inslaved by the cant of those, who call themselves his friends only to injure *themselves* through time, as to feel no deference for his judgment, or to mistake the warmth of his manner for the heat of his mind? Do I not know my father at this time of day? I tell you, his folly is wiser than the wisdom of the common herd of able men'.

lessness. Francis assures Burke that he is prepared to defend him, in public: 'On the occasion, whether the occasion demanded and the parties deserved so much of your Notice as you have given them, you had a right to decide, as you have done, for yourself. On that point, you may be perfectly sure that I shall never say another word, unless it be to support and defend you to the utmost of my power. That is my Office now.' He goes on to recall his previous criticisms of Burke's style: 'While I thought the measure was in suspense, I had another duty to perform; and I gave you my thoughts, not prudently and cautiously as I might have done, but frankly and cordially as I ought to do. Away with all that sort of reason, which banishes the affections. You see that I have not neglected my Studies, and that I have profited by them already.'[1]

That was bad enough. But the passage that puts Francis in the ranks of the enemy – in terms of Burkean values – is the following: 'We do not pillage and massacre quite so furiously as our ancestors used to do. Why? Because those Nations are more enlightened: – because the Christian Religion is, de facto, not in force in the world. Suspect me not of meaning the Christian Religion of the Gospel. I mean that, which was enforced, rather than taught, by priests, by bishops, and by cardinals; which laid waste a province, and then founded a Monastery; which, after destroying a great portion of the human species, provided as far as it could for the utter extinction of future population by instituting numberless retreats for Celibacy; which set up an ideal being, called the Church, capable of possessing property of all sorts for the pious use of its Ministers, incapable of alienating, and whose property its usufructuaries very wisely said it should be sacrilege to invade: – that religion in short, which was practised or professed, and with great Zeal too, by tyrants and villains of every denomination.'[2] From Burke's point of view, Francis is here putting himself in line with Lord Shelburne, Dr Price and the Revolution Society.

Burke's reply (dated 19 November) is the end of a rather strained sort of friendship – within a genuine alliance – which had subsisted between them for eight years. In his first sentence, Burke briskly demolishes Francis's attempted overture: 'I am very much obliged to you for your kind resolution to defend my late Publication against your better judgment.' Burke does not accept that Francis's letter is

---

[1] *Corr.* VI, 151.
[2] *Corr.* VI, 152–5.

the letter of a friend: 'Your paper has much more the character of a piece, in an adverse controversy, carried on before the tribunal of the Nation at large, than of the animadversion of a friend on his friend's performance.' To Francis's uneasy condescension, Burke opposes assured condescension: 'All that you have said against the despotism of Monarchies, you must be sensible that I have heard a thousand times before, though certainly not so neatly and sharply expressed.'

'Neatly and sharply' – terms of thinly concealed disparagement in the context – prepare the way for the following deadly shaft, towards the end of the letter: 'I decline Controversy with you; because I feel myself overmatched in a competition with such talents as yours.' I believe Burke is here telling Francis that he knows him to be Junius, and does not hold Junius, in particularly high esteem. The single reference to Francis's anti-Catholic language is in the guarded manner habitually assumed by Burke, when this particular topic arises: 'I cannot think the religion of the Gospel, which you speak of with love and respect, or any other, can be promoted by the kind endeavours of those, who do not so much as pretend to be any other than Atheists.'[1]

While the anti-Catholic side of the Revolution was the one that made the heaviest impact on Burke, at a deep emotional level, it was not a side that he cared to show himself specifically affected by, or wished to stress in controversy. He knew, after all, only too well, that many Englishmen, like the members of the Revolution Society, were well disposed to the Revolution precisely because of its anti-Catholic side. So he stresses what he calls its Atheism. Burke knew well, of course, that almost all the revolutionary leaders regarded themselves – or at least presented themselves – as Deists, not Atheists. Burke chose not to observe this distinction. For one thing, it was a distinction without a difference, in his eyes. People who denied all revealed religion and mocked all Churches, were as bad as atheists. Also, it was controversially effective to call the revolutionaries atheists. That made them uncomfortable company for preachers like Dr Price. At the end of his letter, Burke indicates the terms on which he wishes his relations with Francis to be conducted for the future. 'These are opinions, I have not lightly formed, or that I can lightly quit. Therefore let us end here all discussion on the subject. There is another, on which I have the happiness of more agreement with you.'

[1] *Corr.* VI, 170–173.

In short, the two were to remain allies, over Warren Hastings, and no more than allies.

It is interesting, and rather surprising, that Francis swallowed the rebuff, and continued the relationship within the terms laid down by Burke. He had been put in his place, and accepted that. This seems out of character. Both as Junius and as the avenger of Nuncomar, Francis had been vindictiveness personified. His meekness, when reproved by Burke, is therefore remarkable. It is true that Francis had an interest in continuing the alliance against Hastings. But even after Burke had snubbed Francis over the *Reflections*, Francis wrote about him with a deep respect, such as he is never known to have accorded to any other human being whom he knew personally. Francis was referring to the Ninth Report of the Select Committee on India (see Chapter IV above, p. 306). He wrote: 'As to the ninth report, which is indeed a masterpiece of human wisdom, the fact is I wrote a very small part of it, and, as to the composition, corrected the whole.

'On memory only, and speaking without book, I think I can say with truth that there is not one material principle or deduction in it which may not be fairly and honestly traced back to some antecedent opinions of my own, dilated on and expanded by a superior power. In some respect I am the acorn. But, if you want to see the oak in all its beauty, dignity, and strength, read the ninth report, the sole undoubted property of the commanding mastermind of Edmund Burke.

'It is true he sucked the saccharine juices out of all vegetation, even from such a wild weed as myself, and turned it to his purpose; but he alone was the wonderful artificer who made the wax, the comb and the honey'.[1]

Not least among the remarkable achievements of Edmund Burke is the taming of Junius – Nuncomar – Francis.

Burke had expected 'the Miscreants', of the pro-Jacobin faction to 'darken the air with their arrows' when the *Reflections* appeared, and they did. Of the many pamphlets which attacked the book, by far the most successful, in popular readership and acclaim, was Tom

[1] Quoted in *Junius Revealed* by H. R. Francis (London, 1894) p. 29. The date of that reference is 'April 27th 1791'. At first I thought this must be a mistake, since the reference has a 'posthumous' feel to it. However, I now accept the date given by H. R. Francis. I do so in the light of the following sensitive interpretation by Owen Dudley Edwards: 'Could it not be a statement in the light of the popular Whig feeling that Burke was dead, as far as party allegiance was concerned, with resultant diminution or dismissal of his former achievements? This would account for the tone as though Burke was dead.' (Letter to author.)

Paine's *The Rights of Man* (March 1791). Burke, as a matter of policy, ignored Paine's book, in public. In private, he recognised its efficacy, for its own public, by comparing it to Junius. *The Rights of Man* contained two phrases about Burke, which 'made their fortune', as the French say, by being widely repeated. One accounted for Burke's supposed 'change of principles' by depicting him as 'praising the aristocratic hand that hath purloined him from himself'. This is at least an elegant formulation of that perennial hypothesis of venality. The second phrase was an even more serviceable and durable contribution to Paine's side of the controversy. This was his statement that Burke 'pities the plumage and forgets the dying bird'. This is a brilliant formula, for it succinctly dehumanises all the victims of the Revolution, by turning them into feathers. The phrase became part of the rhetorical armoury of later generations of revolutionaries, and has been used to squelch sympathy with the victims of the Russian and Chinese revolutions.[1]

Two other pamphlets against the *Reflections* merit at least passing attention. Mary Wollstonecraft, in *A Vindication of The Rights of Man* (1790) wrote: 'Reading your *Reflections* warily over, it has continually struck me, that had you been a Frenchman, you would have been, inspite of your respect for rank and antiquity, a violent revolutionist Your imagination would have taken fire.' It is true that if we can imagine Burke as having been born in, say Arras, circa 1760, he might well have been a French revolutionary. As it was, the circumstances of his actual birth, in the Dublin of 1729, were part of the preparation of the counter-revolutionary of 1790. Yet Mary Wollstonecraft's observation remains perceptive. Time would show that there were some forms of revolutionary impulses – even pro-Jacobin impulses – with which Edmund Burke could feel a twinge of sympathy (see Chapter VI below, pp. 573–5).

The other pamphlet of interest to students of Burke is James Mackintosh's *Vindiciae Gallicae* (1791). Mackintosh, at this time, thought little of Burke's arguments, but was impressed by the resourcefulness of his rhetoric: 'He can cover the most ignominious retreat by a brilliant allusion. He can parade his arguments with masterly generalship where they are strong. He can escape from an intolerable position into a splendid declamation. He can sap the most impregnable conviction by pathos and put to flight a host of syllogisms with a

---

[1] I found this Paine tag used in 1977 about Northern Ireland, in a manner which cast the Protestant working-class of Belfast in the role of 'the plumage'.

sneer. Absolved from all the laws of vulgar method, he can advance a groupe of magnificent horrors to make a breach in our hearts, through which the most undisciplined rabble of arguments may enter in triumph.' Like many another, Mackintosh had his early admiration for the French Revolution completely dispelled by the events of 1792–4. By the end of the decade, he completely reverses his 1791 judgment. He now sees the magnificence of Burke's rhetoric as concealing not the weakness but the force of his arguments. Burke, according to the Mackintosh of 1799 'is only not esteemed the most severe and sagacious of reasoners, because he was the most eloquent of men, the perpetual force and vigour of his arguments being hid from vulgar observation by the dazzling glories in which they were enshrined.'

The Quarrel with Fox
April–May 1791

Burke had decided, from the beginning, to ignore extra-parliamentary attacks on his book by radical 'miscreants'. He was much more concerned about reactions among the parliamentary Whigs, to whom he still nominally belonged. For nearly six months there were no clear reactions, in public, nor any developments, among the Whigs, that called for a reaction on Burke's part. Most Whigs disapproved of the *Reflections*, but there seems to have been a *consigne* to avoid public discussion of the book. Still, there was a question which, even if not publicly raised, would not go away. The question was: Could the author of the *Reflections* remain in a party whose leader was an enthusiast for the French Revolution, and had the support, in that, of most of his followers?

It was Fox himself who precipitated Burke's negative answer to that question, in a Commons debate on 15 April 1791: 'Now that the situation of France altered, that she had erected a government, from which neither insult nor injustice was to be dreaded by her neighbours, he was extremely indifferent concerning the balance of power. With regard to the change of system that had taken place in that country, Mr Fox said that he knew different opinions were entertained on that point by different men, and added, that he for one, admired the new constitution of France, taken together, as the most stupendous and glorious edifice of liberty, which had been erected on the foundation of human integrity in any time or country'.[1]

As it happened, the Constitution which Fox so admired was to be unceremoniously scrapped by the French Revolutionaries themselves in the following year. Fox continued to eulogise the French Revolution even after the demolition of the 'most stupendous and glorious edifice.' The *History* states: 'As soon as Mr Fox sat down, Mr Burke rose, in much visible emotion, but the cry of "Question" being general, he unwillingly gave way to the division which immediately after took place.' According to a footnote, 'Mr Fox is known to have regretted the injudicious zeal of those who would not suffer Mr Burke to answer him on the spot. The contention, he said, might have been fiercer and hotter, but the remembrance of it would not have settled so deep, nor rankled so long in the heart.'

It probably wouldn't have made any substantial difference. It is hard to believe that Fox, when he produced – on the floor of the House, in Burke's presence – that effusion of superlatives about the French Constitution, did not intend to drive Burke from the party. The intention may not have been fully conscious – and Fox's subsequent conduct suggests that it was not – but it must have been there. Fox knew how strongly Burke felt about this, and a breach had been threatened in February of the previous year (see above pp. 396–7). In the circumstances, and after the publication of the *Reflections*, Fox's extravagant praise of the French Constitution was an intolerable provocation.[2]

I believe that Fox had, for some years, resented Burke's intellectual and moral ascendancy over him – which had cost him and his party dear, over 'Fox's East India Bill' – and that he was now in revolt against that ascendancy, and probably egged on by Sheridan. Because Fox still retained much of his old affection and veneration for Burke, it was a painful revolt, but he persisted in it. In summary accounts, the breach between Burke and Fox appears as the affair of a day. In fact, there was a sustained parliamentary struggle, beginning with

[1] *Parl. Hist.* xxix, 249. Debate on the Armament against Russia.

[2] Not all historians agree. According to another view, 'Fox's studied moderation in the dispute seemed to place Burke traditionally in the wrong at least.' E. A. Smith, *Whig Principles and Party Politics, Earl Fitzwilliam and the Whig Party, 1748–1833* (Manchester U.P. 1975) p. 126. In the actual debate Burke appeared more inflexible than Fox. But it was Fox who had chosen to ignore Burke's warning of the previous year, and to breach the tacit parliamentary truce.

Fox's provocation of 15 April and continuing through three further days of parliamentary debate – 21 April, 6 May and 11 May – with repeated interventions by both parties. The drama of the occasion was enhanced by the fact that the parties were two of the three greatest debaters of the period (the third being William Pitt). And the fact that it was a great parliamentary duel between champions of debate made it even more difficult for either champion to give way.

The business before the House on 21 April was the Quebec Bill. Burke saw in this an opportunity to discuss the French Revolution, on the rather tenuous pretext that Quebec, being a French-speaking province, might conceivably be offered the new French Constitution. Fox tried, but in vain, to dissuade Burke from broaching this discussion. Perhaps Fox, at this stage, hoped to avoid the breach which he had already provoked. His conflicting feelings, over Burke, were inherently unstable. The *Parliamentary History* introduces its account of the 21 April debate with the words: 'From the moment of the debate on the 15 April on Mr Baker's Motion relative to the war with Russia, a rupture between Mr Burke and Mr Fox was distinctly foreseen. On the morning of the 21st April, the day appointed for the re-commitment of the Quebec Bill, Mr Fox, for the last time paid Mr Burke a visit, accompanied by a common friend. Mr Burke talked over with them the plan of all which he intended to say, opened the different branches of his argument, and explained the limitations which he meant to impose on himself. Mr Fox, on his part, treated him with confidence, and mentioned to him a political circumstance of some delicacy. What it precisely was, Mr Burke declined telling, even in the heat of altercation. But from the tenor of the charge, which he seems most eager to refute, and from some intimations in one of Mr Fox's answers, we may form a reasonable conjecture. The king, it seems was represented to have used some expressions favourable to Mr Fox. In order, therefore, to secure himself in his situation, the minister [Pitt] was asserted to have given out the watch-word that Mr Fox was a republican, and it was supposed that in pursuance of this plan, he instigated Mr Burke to the discussion. Mr Burke undecided his friend by relating the fact as it was [presumably] that the discussion was provoked by Mr Fox [which was the case]. Still it was requested by Mr Fox that at least the discussion might not take place on the recommitment of the Quebec Bill, but Mr Burke was unwilling to forego an opportunity which he could not hope to find again in any other business than before parliament, or likely to come before it. They walked however to Westminster together, and together entered the House.'[1]

Fox began the debate by intimating, without any new provocation, that he would not disavow the one that was already on record (that of 15 April): 'Mr Fox said than when the bill came again to be discussed, from the great respect which he entertained for some of his friends, he should be extremely sorry to differ from them, but he should never be backward in delivering his opinion, and he did not wish to recede from anything which he had formerly advanced.'

Burke's reply was measured, but unyielding. However, its conclusion was emollient, in relation to Fox, personally:

> Mr Burke said he did not wish to call forth public opinion unnecessarily, or to provoke a debate with the right hon-gentleman, because he was his friend, and so he wished to consider him, but his principles were even dearer to him than his friendship. He did not wish to meet his friend as his adversary and antagonist. If it should so happen that he must defend his principles he would do it; though it would distress his body and mind to think that he and his friend must have that difference. He thought when he rose before he had spoken guardedly. He did not know whether anything which he said had occasioned the remarks which had been made. His opinions on government he thought, were not unknown: the more he had considered the French revolution, the more sorry he was to see it. On the 12th of February [actually 9 February 1790] he had thought it necessary to speak his opinion very fully on the French Revolution but since that time he had never mentioned it [i.e. in the Commons] either directly or indirectly; no man, therefore could charge him with having provoked the conversation [sic] that had passed.

Burke seems to imply here that he believed that the discussion of 9 February 1790 had been followed by an implicit parliamentary truce between Fox and himself. Fox was free to say what he liked about the Revolution, outside Parliament, and Burke was free to write about it, in the opposite sense. But the two men could only work together, as members of the same parliamentary party, if the topic on which they both felt so strongly in opposing senses, was altogether avoided, within the walls of parliament. And there was no present difficulty about avoiding it, in parliamentary terms, for there was nothing about the French Revolution on the parliamentary agenda in 1791. France and England were still at peace. In order to

---

[1] *Parl. Hist.*, xxix, 361–2.

bring that subject up, in debate, that year, you had first to drag it in to a discussion on another topic. Fox was the first to drag it in to a debate about Russia on 15 April. Burke retaliates, by dragging it into debate on Quebec, on 21 April.

Burke was not alone in believing that there should be a parliamentary truce over the French Revolution, unless and until the business of the House should require otherwise. A member spoke in that sense at the outset of the debate of 21 April. According to the *Parliamentary History* 'Mr Powys complained that the debate had turned irregularly both in retrospect [15 April] and anticipation [21 April] and hinted that Mr Fox should have imitated the example of Mr Burke, in writing, rather than speaking there in the House of Commons of the French Revolution.'

It is clear, from the record, that it was Fox, not Burke, who had initiated the parliamentary quarrel over the French Revolution.

Burke ended his speech of 21 April on a conciliatory note with respect to Fox personally, but without any concessions of principle:

> He thought it right to say, that it was his intention to give his opinion on certain principles of government at the proper moment in the future progress of the bill. Whether they should agree or disagree, the debate on the bill, whenever it came, would show; but he believed he was most likely to coincide in sentiment with the other side of the House. Mr Burke said he did not believe his right Hon. Friend did mean the other night to allude offensively to the affairs of France, though, at the moment, he had thought it necessary to rise and make some observations which accident prevented.[1]

The exchange of 21 April was a prelude only: the substantive, and decisive, debate came on 6 May, when the House resumed the discussion of the Quebec Bill. Burke, at the onset of the discussion, used that Bill as a pretext for a frontal assault on the French Constitution, which Fox had unreservedly extolled on 15 April:

> Were we to give [the people of Quebec] the French Constitution – a constitution founded on principles dramatically opposed to ours, that could not assimilate with it on a single point: as different from it as wisdom from folly, as vice from virtue, as the most opposite extremes in nature – a constitution founded on what was called the rights of man. As soon as this system arrived among them [the French], Pandora's box, replete with every mortal

---

[1] *Parl. Hist.* xxix, 367.

evil, seemed to fly open, hell itself to yawn, and every demon of mischief to overspread the face of the earth. Blacks rose against whites [in Haiti], whites against blacks, and each against one another in murderous hostility; subordination was destroyed, the bonds of society torn asunder, and every man seemed to thirst for the blood of his neighbour

Black spirits and white
Blue spirits and grey
Mingle, mingle, mingle[1]

All was toil and trouble, discord and blood, from the moment that this doctrine was promulgated among them; and he verily believed that wherever the rights of man were preached, such ever had been and ever would be the consequences.

France, who had generously sent them the precious gift of the rights of man, did not like this image of herself reflected in her child, and sent out a body of troops, well seasoned too with the rights of man, to restore order and obedience. These troops, as soon as they arrived, instructed as they are in the principle of government, felt themselves bound to become parties in the general rebellions and, like most of their brethren at home began asserting their rights by cutting off the head of their general. Ought this example to induce us to send to our colonies a cargo of the rights of man? As soon would he send them a bale of infected cotton from Marseilles.

Burke looked on the French constitution 'not with approbation but with horror, as involving every principle to be detested, and pregnant with every consequence to be dreaded and abominated.'

Burke and Fox were now in absolute opposition to one another on a specific point: the French Constitution of 1790/91. Fox had seen that Constitution as inspired; Burke as ruinous. The clash of principles was irreparable. So far, both men had treated one another, personally, with respect. Fox now, however, in reply to Burke's fierce attack on Fox's beloved French Constitution, resorted to sarcasm, which envenomed the next phase of the debate.

'*Mr Fox* thought his right hon. friend could hardly be said to be out of order. It seemed that this was a day of privilege, when any gentleman might stand up, select his mark, and abuse any government he pleased, whether it had reference or not to the point in question. Although nobody had said a word on the subject of the French revolution, his right hon. friend had risen up and abused that

---

[1] Here Burke is anticipating (as often), the course of revolutionary events. The insurrection of slaves in Haiti did not break out until August 1791.

event. He might have treated the [Hindu] government, or that of China, or the government of Turkey, or the laws of Confucius precisely in the same manner, and with equal appositeness to the business of the House. Every gentleman had a right that day to abuse the government of every country as much as he pleased, and in as gross terms as he thought proper, or any government, either ancient or modern, with his right hon. friend.'[1]

Fox's implication that Burke was out of order was taken up by Fox's followers, who interrupted Burke's reply with calls of Order! Order! This deeply angered Burke, who saw the interruptions as a deliberate strategy, laid down by Fox. The interruptions were probably spontaneous, but responsive to a suggestion, contained in Fox's sarcastic reply. Fox does not seem to have discouraged the calls for order. The *Parliamentary History* goes on:

Mr Burke replied that he understood his right hon. friend's irony, but his conclusions were very erroneously drawn from his premises. If he was disorderly, he was sorry for it. His right hon. friend had also accused him of abusing government in very gross terms. He conceived his right hon. friend meant to abuse him in unqualified terms. He had called him to account for the decency and propriety of his expressions. Mr Burke said he had been accused of creating dissention among nations. He never thought the national assembly was imitated so well as in the debate then going on. M. Cazales [a right-wing member of the Assembly] could never utter a single sentence in that assembly without a roar.

[Two Members call Burke to order; one defends him.] *Mr Burke* said, he meant to take the sense of the committee, whether or not he was in order. He declared he had not made any reflection, nor did he mean any, on any one gentleman whatever. He was as fully convinced as he could be, that no one gentleman in that House wanted to alter the constitution of England. The reason why, in the first regular opportunity that presented itself, he had been anxious to offer his reflections on the subject, was, because it was a matter of great public concern, and occasion called for his observations. As long as they held to the constitution he should think it his duty to act with them; but he would not be the slave of any whim that might arise. On the contrary he thought it his duty not to give any countenance to certain doctrines which were supposed to exist in this country, and which were intended fundamentally to subvert the constitution. They ought to consider well what they were doing [Here there was a loud cry of Order! Order! and Go on!] Mr Burke said, there was such an enthusiasm for order that it was not easy to go on. If the French

[1] *Parl. Hist.* xxix, 369.

revolutionaires were to mind their own affairs, and had shown no inclination to go abroad and to make proselytes in other countries, Mr Burke
declared that neither he nor any other member of the House had any
right to meddle with them. If they were not as much disposed to make
proselytes as Louis 14th had been to make conquests he should have
thought it very improper and indiscreet to have touched on the subject.
He said he would quote the national assembly itself, and a correspondent
of his at Paris [Anacharsis Cloots] who had declared he appeared as the
ambassador of the whole human race. Repeated calls of order. Mr Burke
said an attempt was now being made, by one who had been formerly his
friend, to bring down upon him the censure of the House.

Under the strain of being shouted down by his own colleagues,
sitting all around him, Burke had reached breaking-point with Fox.
Always, up to this moment, Burke had referred to Fox as his friend.
Now, Fox has become 'one who was formerly his friend'. Burke went
on:

> It was unfortunate for him, he said, sometimes to be hunted by one party,
> and sometimes by another. He considered himself to be unfairly treated
> by those gentlemen with whom he had been accustomed to act, but from
> whom he now received extreme violence. He should, he said, if the tumult
> of order abated, proceed in the account he was going to give of the
> horrible consequences flowing from the French idea of the rights of man.

At this point, a Whig member, Lord Sheffield, put the charge of
disorder into the form of a motion: 'That dissertations on the French
constitution, and to read a narrative of the transactions in France,
are not regular or orderly on the question, that the clauses of the
Quebec bill be read a second time, paragraph by paragraph'.

Pitt, who must have relished the sight and sound of the Whigs
engaged in shouting down one of the most illustrious of their own
number, now intervened on Burke's side, over the question of order:
'*Mr Pitt* begged leave to observe, that the question of discretion, and
the question of order, ought to be kept perfectly separate. Whatever
he might feel for himself, he must beg leave to be understood, to do
complete justice to the motives of the right hon. gentleman (Mr
Burke) which he could trace to no other source than a pure regard
to the constitution of his country. But as to the motive in the hands
of the chairman, as to the question of order when they were considering what was to be the best constitution for Canada, or for any other
of the dependencies of Great Britain, it was strictly in order to allude
to the constitution of other countries.'

Pitt's statement ensured that the Commons, as a body, would not find Burke to be out of order, since Pitt had a large and disciplined majority. Lord Sheffield's motion could not carry (and was in fact withdrawn at the close of the debate, at Pitt's request). Fox now rose, however, to support that motion. It appears, from Fox's reaction to a later statement by Burke that he had not heard, or else not understood, Burke's reference, at this state of the debate, to 'one who was formerly his friend.' In support of the motion, Fox said: 'On the French Revolution he did, indeed, differ from his right hon. friend. Their opinions, he had no scruple to say, were wide as the poles asunder. But what had a difference of opinion on that, which to the House was only matter of theoretical contemplation, to do with the discussion of a practical point, on which no such difference existed? On the revolution, he adhered to his opinion, and never would retreat any syllable of what he had said. He repeated, that he thought it, on the whole, *one of the most glorious events in the history of mankind.* But when he had on a former occasion mentioned France, he had mentioned the revolution only, and not the constitution: the latter remained to be modified by experience, and accommodated to circumstances.'

This is curious. Fox here forgets – or retrospectively corrects – what he had actually said. The statement of 15 April that had provoked the parliamentary crisis between him and Burke was specifically in praise of the French Constitution. But perhaps word had reached Fox in the meantime that the Constitution, though still unfinished, was no longer *à la mode* among advanced revolutionaries. Robespierre had become president of the Jacobins in March. The constitution-makers were already near to being marked down for the guillotine. Fox went on: 'The arbitrary system of government was done away; the new one had the good of the people for its object, and this was the point on which he rested. If the committee should decide that his right hon. friend should pursue his argument on the French constitution he would leave the House, and if some friend would send him word, when the clauses of the Quebec bill were to be discussed he would return and debate them. And when he said this, he said it from no unwillingness to listen to his right hon. friend: he always had heard him with pleasure, but not where no practical use could result from his argument. When the proper period for discussion came, feeble as his powers were, compared with those of his right hon. friend, whom he must call his master, for he had taught him everything he knew in politics yet, he should be ready to maintain the principles he had asserted, even against his right hon. friend's superior eloquence to maintain, that the rights of man, which his right hon. friend had ridiculed as chimerical and visionary, were in fact the basis and foundation of every rational constitution, and even of the British constitution itself. Having been taught by his right hon. friend, that no revolt of a nation was caused without provocation, he could not help feeling a joy ever since the constitution of France became founded on the rights of man, on which the British constitution itself was founded. If such were principles dangerous to the Constitution they were the principles of his right hon. friend, from whom he had learned them. During the American war they had together rejoiced at the success of a Washington, and sympathised, almost in tears at the death of a Montgomery. From his right hon. friend he had learned that the revolt of a whole people could never be countenanced and encouraged, but must have been provoked.'

These last reminders incensed Burke, who felt that friendly private conversations of the past were being exploited in order to worst him in public debate. Fox ended this speech by a sentence that seemed to imply that Burke was being used as a catspaw by Pitt: 'They [ministerialists] might be sure of him and his sentiments without forcing on any thing like a difference between him and his right hon. friend.'

The *Parliamentary History* goes on:

Mr Burke commenced his reply in a grave and governed tone of voice, observing that, although he had been called to order so many times, he had sat with perfect composure, and had heard the most disorderly speech that perhaps ever was delivered in that House. His words and his conduct throughout had been misrepresented, and a personal attack had been made upon him from a quarter he never could have expected, after a friendship and intimacy of more than two-and-twenty years; and not only his public conduct, words and writings, had been alluded to in the severest terms, but confidential views and opinions had been brought forward, with a view of proving that he acted inconsistently. The practice now was, upon all occasions, to praise, in the highest strain, the French constitution, some indeed qualified their argument so far, by praising only the French revolution, but in that he could see no difference, as the French constitution, if they had any, was the consequence and effect of that revolution. So fond were gentlemen of this favourite topic, that whoever disapproved of the anarchy and confusion that had taken place in France, or could not foresee the benefits that were to arise out of it, were stigmatised as enemies to liberty, and to the British constitution – charges that were false, unfounded, and every way unfair. Doctrines of this kind, he thought, were extremely dangerous at all times and much more so if they were to be sanctioned by so great a name as that of the right hon. gentleman, who always put whatever he said in the strongest and most forcible view in which it could possibly appear. After what had been said, nobody could impute to him [Burke] interested or personal motives for his conduct. Those with whom he had been constantly in habits of friendship and agreement [attacked him] and from the other side of the House he was not likely to have much support; yet all he did was no more than his duty. It was a struggle, not to support any man, or set of men, but a struggle to support the British constitution, in doing which he had incurred the displeasure of all about him, and those opposite to him, and what was worst of all, he had induced the right hon. gentleman to rip up the whole course and tenure of his life, public and private, and that not without a considerable degree of asperity. His failings and imperfections had been keenly exposed, and, in short, without the chance of gaining one new friend, he had made enemies, it appeared malignant enemies, of his old friends: but, after all, he esteemed his duty far beyond any friendship, any fame, or any other consideration whatever. The right hon. gentleman in the speech just made, had treated him in every sentence with uncommon harshness. In the first place, after being fatigued with skirmishes of order, which were wonderfully managed by his light troops, the right hon. gentleman brought down the whole strength and heavy artillery of his own judgement, eloquence and abilities, upon him to crush him at once, by declaring a censure upon his whole life, conduct and opinions.

Notwithstanding this great and serious, though, on his part, unmerited attempt to crush him, he would not be dismayed; he was not yet afraid to state his sentiments in that House, or anywhere else, and he would tell all the world that the constitution was in danger.

At this point, Burke seems to have believed that Fox had organised a walk-out during Burke's speech. 'In carrying on the attack against him, the right hon. gentleman had been supported by a corps of well-disciplined troops, expert in their manoeuvres, and obedient to the word of their commander [Mr Grey here called Mr Burke to order, considering that it was disorderly to mention gentlemen in that way, and to ascribe improper motives to them].'

The *Parliamentary History* here has a footnote: 'It is probable that a little incident which happened in the course of Mr Burke's reply contributed to draw from him the expressions considered as disorderly by Mr Grey. In his speech Mr Fox had intimated an intention of leaving the House, if the Committee should suffer Mr Burke to proceed. While the latter gentleman was speaking, the former, being perhaps now resolved on a rejoinder, accidentally went toward the lobby for some light refreshment, with which he soon after returned to his place. But in the mean time about twenty other gentlemen, of those most personally attached to him, mistaking his departure for the execution of his declared intention, rose from their seats, and followed him out of the House.'

Burke, according to the *Parliamentary History*, next recapitulated the political questions

upon which he had differed from right hon. gentleman upon former occasions . . . but in the course of their long acquaintance, no one difference of opinion had ever before for a single moment interrupted their friendship. It certainly was indiscrete at any period, but especially at his time of life, to parade enemies, or give his friends occasion to desert him; yet if his firm and steady adherence to the British constitution placed him in such a dilemma, he would risk all; and, as public duty and public experience taught him with his last words exclaim, "Fly from the French constitution." [Mr Fox here whispered, that "there was no loss of friends"]. Mr Burke said Yes, there was a loss of friends – he knew the price of his conduct – he had done his duty at the price of his friend, their friendship was at an end.

The *History* goes on: 'Mr *Fox* rose to reply: but his mind was so much agitated, and his heart so much affected by what had fallen from Mr Burke, that it was some minutes before he could proceed. Tears trickled down his cheeks, and he strove in vain to give utterance to feelings that dignified and exalted his nature. The sensibility of every member of the House appeared uncommonly excited upon the occasion. Recovered at length from the depression under which he had risen, Mr Fox proceeded to answer the assertions which had caused it. He said that however events which have altered the mind of his right hon. friend, for so he must call him notwithstanding what had passed – because, grating as it was to any one to be unfriendly treated by those to whom they felt the greatest obligations, and whom, notwithstanding their harshness and severity, they found they must still love and esteem – he could not forget that, when a boy almost, he had been in the habit of receiving favours from his right hon. friend, but their friendship had grown with the years, and that it had continued for upwards of twenty-five years, for the last twenty of which they had acted together, and lived on terms of the most familiar intimacy. He hoped, therefore, that notwithstanding what had happened that day, his right hon. friend would think on past times, and, however any imprudent words or intemperance of his might have offended him, [he] would show that it had not been at least intentionally his fault. His right hon. friend had said, and said truly, that they had differed formerly on many subjects, and yet it did not interrupt their friendship . . . He enumerated, severally, what those differences of opinion had been, and appealed to his right hon. friend, whether their friendship had been interrupted on any one of these occasions.'

At that point there appeared a possibility that the personal friendship might be preserved, to some extent, despite the clash of principle. If Fox had stopped there, that possibility remained open. But the great debater is driven to carry on the debate, and win it. Fatally, Fox goes on: 'In particular,' he said, 'on the subject of the French revolution, the hon. gentleman well knows that his sentiment differed widely from his own; he knew also, that as soon as his book on the subject was published, he condemned that book both in public and private, and every one of the doctrines which it contained.'

That tore it. By formally and absolutely condemning Burke's book, *on the floor of the House*, Fox had made it impossible for the author of the *Reflections* to continue a member of the party led by the man who, speaking as leader of the party, and supported by it, had condemned his book. That was the political consequence of those words. In personal terms, the condemnation of the book took all the good out of the appeal to friendship with which Fox's speech had opened. In continuing, after condemning the book, Fox managed to make things even worse, in personal terms. Fox had apparently failed to notice Burke's fierce resentment, already declared, of Fox's use of recollections of past private conversations to furnish debating points against his old friend. Fox now proceeds to offer more in the same kind: 'With regard to his right hon. friend's enthusiastic attachment to our constitution, in preference to all others, did he remember when his majesty's speech was made in 1783 on the loss of America, in which his majesty lamented the loss the provinces had sustained, in being deprived of the advantages resulting from a monarchy, how he had ridiculed that speech, and compared it to a man's opening the door after he had left a room, and saying, "at our parting, pray let me recommend a monarchy to you." In that ridicule Mr Fox said, he had joined heartily at the time. . . .'

Fox's speech ends: 'The course he should pursue, he said, would be to keep out of his right hon. friend's way, 'till time and reflection had fitted his right hon. friend to think differently upon the subject; and then, if their friends did not contrive to unite them, he should think their friends did not act as they had a right to expect at their hands. If his right hon. friend wished to bring forward the question of the French revolution on a future day, in that case he would discuss it with him as temperately as he could; at present he had said all that he thought necessary, and, let his right hon. friend say what he would more on the subject, he would make him no farther reply.'

Parliamentary History:

Mr Burke again rose, He began with remarking that the tenderness which had been displayed in the beginning and conclusion of Mr Fox's speech was quite obliterated by what had occurred in the middle part. He regretted, in a tone and manner of earnestness and fervency, the proceedings of that evening, which he feared might long be remembered by their enemies to the prejudice of both. He was unfortunate enough to suffer the lash of Mr Fox, but he must encounter it. Under the mask of kindness a new attack, he said, was made upon his character and conduct in the most hostile manner, and his very jests brought up in judgment against him. He did not think the careless expressions and playful triflings of his unguarded hours would have been recorded, mustered up in the form of accusations, and not only have had a serious meaning imposed upon them, which they were never intended to bear, but one totally inconsistent with any fair and candid interpretation. Could his most inveterate enemy have acted more unkindly towards him? The event of that night in debates in which he had been interrupted without being suffered to explain, in which he had been accused without being heard in his defense, made him at a loss to understand what was either party or friendship. His arguments had been misrepresented. He had never affirmed that the English, like every other constitution, might not in some points be amended. He had never mentioned, that to praise our own constitution the best way was to abuse all others. The tendency of all that had been said, was to represent him as a wild inconsistent man, only for attaching bad epithets to a bad subject. With the view of showing his inconsistency, allusions had been made to his conduct in 1780 [and over] the American war ... If he thought, in 1780, that the influence of the Crown ought to be reduced to a limited standard, and with which Mr Fox himself, at the time, seemed to be satisfied, it did not follow that the French were right in reducing it with them to nothing. He was favourable to the Americans, because he supposed they were fighting, not to acquire absolute speculative liberty, but to keep what they had under the English constitution ... In France, it had been asserted by the right hon. gentleman that the largest religious tolerance prevailed. It would be judged of what nature that toleration was, when it was understood that there the most cruel tests were imposed . . . The treatment of the Nuns was to shocking almost to be mentioned. These wretched girls, who could only be animated by the most exalted religious enthusiasm, were engaged in the most painful office of humanity, in the most sacred duty of piety, visiting and attending the hospitals. Yet these had been dragged into the streets; these had been scourged by the sovereigns of the French nation, because the priest from whom they had received the sacrament, had not submitted to the test. And this proceeding had passed, not only unpunished, but uncensured. Yet, in the country in which said proceedings had happened, the largest religious toleration was said to prevail . . . Mr Burke said he was sorry for the occurrence of that day. "Sufficient for the day was the evil thereof." Yet if the good were to many, he would willingly title the evil to himself . . . With regards to pretences of friendship, he must own that he did not like them, where his character, as in the present instance, had been so materially attacked and injured.

Fox, as he had promised, made no reply to Burke. Pitt, speaking at the close of the debate, noted that Fox had found Burke to be disorderly, in discussing the French Revolution, but that Fox himself had made two speeches on that subject. Pitt found Burke to be still in order, but added, characteristically, 'although he could not but think, that every asperity and censure on that event had, for various reasons, better be avoided.' Yet he went on: 'He thought Mr Burke entitled to the gratitude of his country, for having that day, in so able and eloquent a manner, stated his sense of the degree of danger to the constitution that already existed.' This was neat. In the guise of a compliment to Burke, Pitt was making one of his sidelong, feline forays against the leader of the opposition in the Commons, insinuating that Fox was either unaware of, or collusive towards, the danger to the Constitution which Fox's colleague/opponent, Burke, had rightly sensed.

Pitt, unlike either Burke or Fox, had every reason to be pleased with the course and outcome of the debate of 6 May 1791. Pitt had come under the fire of Burke's oratorical big guns – especially in the *Speech on Nabob of Arcot's Debts* – and he knew their power so well that he had been happy to encourage Burke to find another target, through the impeachment of Warren Hastings. But that *Fox* should have become Burke's target was a splendid parliamentary windfall for Pitt. From then on Burke was Pitt's ally against Fox, although only implicitly so, up to April 1792. It was a reluctant alliance, reserved and suspicious on both sides, but it was to become an effective working alliance. From the beginning it significantly strengthened and, a few years later, greatly strengthened Pitt's parliamentary position. The alliance lasted, and grew, during the few remaining years of Burke's parliamentary career.

The breach between Burke and Fox had become irreparable by the close of parliamentary proceedings on 6 May. But the Commons debate between the two was to rumble on, for a further parliamentary day, like the last few peals of a dying thunderstorm. The occasion was the resumption, on 11 May 1791, of the Quebec Bill debate. It began with intimations of what would now be called attempts at 'damage limitation' on both sides. Fox began by raising a technicality. Burke discussed the technicality and then indicated that he held to his principles, but would stay within the rules of order, this time: 'Situated as he was, an isolated being, perfectly separated, banished from his party, there was a voice which cried to him, "Beware". For the short time he would remain in parliament (and it would be but a very short time), he would support those principles of government which were founded upon the wisdom of antiquity, and sanctioned by the experience of time. On the present bill, necessary as it was for him to be careful of what he should say, he would state the arguments that occurred to him, as they should arise, upon every clause.'

Fox spoke again, uncontroversially, and with a guardedly respectful reference to Burke. It seems, however, that at this stage, Burke got wind of some stories that the Whigs were putting out about him, and also of a press release, which was to be published on the following day (12 May) in the Whig paper, the *Morning Chronicle*. The press release ran: 'The great and firm body of the Whigs of England, true to their principles, have decided on the dispute between Mr Fox and Mr Burke, and the former is declared to have maintained the pure doctrines by which they are bound together, and upon which they have invariably acted.' The clear implication that Burke had failed to maintain 'the pure doctrines' by which the Whigs were bound together was calculated to infuriate Burke, and it did.

Parliamentary History:

Mr Burke rose. He began with observing that he had served the House and the country in one capacity or another, for twenty-six years, twenty-five of which had been spent within these walls. He had wasted so much of his life to a precious purpose, if that House should [not?] at least counteract a most insidious design to ruin him in reputation, and crown his age with infamy. For the best part of the time, he had been a very laborious and assiduous, though a very unimportant servant of the public. He had not, he declared, been treated with friendship; but if he was separated from his party, if sentence of banishment had been pronounced against him, he hoped to meet a fair, open hostility, to which he would oppose himself in a fair and manly way, for the very short period that he should continue a member of that House.

The 'insidious design' was the circulation of a story that Burke was engaged in a 'base premeditated design', in concert with Pitt, to ruin Fox's reputation by making him 'pass for a Republican' (see above, p. 416). This would keep Fox out of office, and Burke would be rewarded with a place in Pitt's Administration. Burke's closing words – or what he meant to be his closing words – ran:

> In saying what he had said on the subject, he was conscious that he had done his duty; and he hoped he had in some measure averted what otherwise might have effected the downfall of the British constitution. That being the case, separate and unsupported as he was, let not the party who had excommunicated him, imagine that he was deprived of consolation – although all was solitude without, there was sunshine and company enough within.

The last reference is to Alexander Pope's 'sunshine of the soul', the reward of a person who is conscious that he has done his duty. This would be a satisfactory close to the debate from Burke's point of view. But his experienced antagonist could see this, and moved to spoil Burke's effect. Fox intervened again, to make an offer to which Burke will have to reply: 'With regard to the right hon. gentleman's declaration, that he was separated from the party, if he was so separated, it must be his own choice; and if he should repent that separation, he might be assured his friends would ever be ready to receive him, to respect him, and to love him, as heretofore.' Burke's reply was cold and brief:

> He took notice of what had been said, that, if he would repent, he would be received. He stood, he said, a man publicly disgraced by his party, and therefore the right hon. gentleman ought not to receive him. He declared he had gone through his youth without encountering any party disgrace; and though he had then in his age been so unfortunate as to meet it, he did not solicit the right hon. gentleman's friendship, nor that of any man, either on one side of the House or the other.

And that was all. The *Parliamentary History*'s report of that last speech carries the footnote: 'Thus ended the friendship between Mr Burke and Mr Fox – a friendship which had lasted for more than the fourth part of a century.'[1]

COUNTER-REVOLUTIONARY WRITINGS OF 1791

After the debate of 11 May, Burke made no further parliamentary interventions on French affairs, during 1791. Outside parliament, as a writer, he was particularly active. He published two major tracts: *Letter to a Member of the National Assembly* (published in Paris on 27 April and in London on May 21) and *Appeal from the New to the Old Whigs* (London, 3 August). He also wrote, not for publication but for private circulation, two memoranda: *Hints for a Memorial to Monsieur de M.M.* (early 1791) and *Thoughts on French Affairs* (December). After that, Burke did not again write about French affairs until the following December (*Heads for Consideration on the Present State of Affairs*). But by then, the Revolution had already entered its most dramatic and violent phase, with the 'deposition' (alias 'suspension') of Louis XVI (August 1792).

The 1790–1791 writings about the French Revolution have a certain stability of theme, in that the Revolutionary leaders, throughout this period were themselves aiming at stability under new conditions. They were trying to institute a Constitutional Monarchy: a state of affairs which they hoped – by then rather wanly – they had achieved by 14 September, when Louis XVI formally accepted his role in the Constitution proposed by the National Assembly. Yet, while a certain stability of theme does exist in Burke's writings for this entire period, a distinction has to be made between those written before 20/21 June 1791 – when the royal family tried to escape from France – and those written after their recapture and return to revolutionary Paris, after which, concluded F. C. Montague, 'It was no longer possible to

---

[1] Strangely, the relevant volume (Volume VIII, *The French Revolution 1790–1794*) of *The Writings and Speeches of Edmund Burke* does not contain the texts of any of Burke's speeches for this period, and is also incomplete for the *Writings*. It omits *Appeal from the New to the Old Whigs*. We are promised speeches for a later volume.

pretend that the Revolution had been made with the free consent of the king.'[1]

Up to the June days, it had suited both Louis and the Revolutionary leaders to pretend that the king was giving his free consent to the revolutionary programme of the National Assembly. The external admirers of the Revolution – such as Fox and almost all the rest of the English Whigs – all accepted this version of revolutionary realities. Burke had scornfully rejected this version as early as 10 October 1789 when he had written about 'the late Grand Monarch' as making 'a figure as ridiculous as pitiable'. In the Reflections, and again in Letter to a Member of the National Assembly – the last of his writings to be composed before the attempted escape – Burke consistently presents Louis and Marie Antoinette as already prisoners. The events of June completely vindicated his insight.

The king's status as prisoner, after the journées of 5 and 6 October 1789 was not some kind of sentimental side-issue, as some later pro-Revolutionary commentators would suggest. It is central, because, at this stage, the royal prisoner was officially chief executive. France from then on was a country without an executive. The Paris mob, prompted by a faction, had transferred the nominal executive from Versailles to Paris. Henceforward power rested ultimately with the Paris mob, and primarily with whatever revolutionary factions could, in any particular crisis, most efficiently manipulate the mob. Burke had seen that with the utmost clarity from September–October 1789. In contrast, Fox, and with him most of the Whigs, took the superficial and wishful view that those events had been an aberration of the early turbulent phase of the Revolution; that the Constitution of 1790–91 was everything that it purported to be, and that France, under its benign sway, was about to enjoy the blessings of an unexampled peace, stability and liberty.

These illusions ought to have been punctured, when the king and queen were brought back to Paris on 25 June, under the grimly watchful eyes of huge, silent crowds of Parisians, who in the following year would hurl both the royal couple and their political captors to their doom, and the elaborate structures of the Constitution along with them. The English Whigs, however, clung to their illusions. The events of June 1791 were an aberration, they thought, just as the events of October 1789 had been. The

[1] Encyclopaedia Britannica, eleventh edition (1910–1911) under the entry 'French Revolution'.

noble edifice of the French Constitution was still intact. Nay, more! It was the autumn of 1791 – in the aftermath of the Flight to Varennes – which actually saw the Constitutional edifice brought to its final perfection.

On 3 September 1791 the National Assembly completed its Constitution-making work by voting the Constitutional Act. On 14 September, the prisoner-king swore fidelity to the Constitution, devised by the people from whom he had tried to escape. The English Whigs contemplated with complacency this macabre completion of a Constitutional process of which their leader had spoken in terms of such enthusiastic admiration. I quoted earlier the judgment that after Louis' flight and recapture that it 'was no longer possible to pretend that the Revolution had been made with the free consent of the king.' That judgment needs to be qualified. The flight and recapture had made it harder to sustain that pretence, but the attempt was actually made, both by the king of France and by those who had brought him back, the leaders of the national Assembly. The king and those leaders were by now acting in concert, over an agreed and incredible fiction. The agreed fiction was that Louis had not tried to escape at all; he had been abducted. Both the king and the Assembly leaders knew this was nonsense; when he fled he had left behind a declaration revoking his assent to all measures which had been laid before him while he was under restraint. This document is the definitive corroboration of Burke's view of the king's status as a prisoner, from October 1789 on.[1]

However, after June 1791, it suited both the king and the Assembly leaders to pretend that no such document existed. So they continued, after the flight to Varennes, as before, to act out the fiction that the King had been, and remained, a loyal partner in the revolutionary process. Parisians were not fooled, as became apparent in the following year, with the mob-led downfall of all who took part in the agreed fiction of 1791 and the killing of most of them. But the English Whigs, at a safe distance, and heavily committed by their enthusiastic leader to a rosy view of the French Revolution, could afford to be taken in, even by so implausible a spectacle as Louis XVI's oath to the new French Constitution, on 14 September 1791.

Burke's position, as against that of the Whigs, was vindicated, at a most critical point, by Varennes. But the Whigs did not acknowl-

---

[1] For Louis' declaration of 20 June 1791, solemnly protesting against all the acts issued during his captivity, see J. H. Stewart (Ed.) *A Documentary Survey of the French Revolution* (Macmillan, 1951) pp. 205–10.

edge that any such vindication had taken place. The agreed fiction was completely in line with their wishful interpretation of the French Revolution, from its very beginning, and was therefore acceptable to them as a body, despite its transparent flimsiness. Burke was still out in the cold. Undeterred, he persevered with the exertions which had taken him there.

We have already considered Burke's 1791 speeches against the French Revolution and Charles James Fox. The only one of Burke's writings of that year which was published before the pivotal events of 20–21 June was *Letter to a Member of the National Assembly* (Paris, April 27; London, May 21. Text in *Writings and Speeches* VIII, 294–335). It was written in January 1791, and so antedates not only the flight to Varennes, but also Burke's parliamentary quarrel with Fox. This *Letter* is essentially a postscript, or set of afterthoughts to the *Reflections*. The greatest of the afterthoughts is Burke's majestic onslaught on J. J. Rousseau, as the grand inspiration of the Revolutionaries. This was a topical subject when Burke was writing. On 22 December, less than a month before it was written, the National Assembly had decreed that 'there shall be erected to the author of *Emile* and *du Contrat Social* a statue hearing the inscription: *La Nation Française libre à J. J. Rousseau. . . .*' Burke writes:

The Assembly recommends to its youth a study of the bold experimenters in morality. Every body knows that there is a great dispute amongst their leaders, which of them is the best resemblance to Rousseau. In truth, they all resemble him. His blood they transfuse into their minds and into their manners. Him they study; him they meditate; him they turn over in all the time they can spare from the laborious mischief of the day, or the debauches of the night. Rousseau is their canon of holy writ; in his life he is their canon of *Polycletus*; he is their standard figure of perfection. To this man and this writer, as a pattern to authors and to Frenchmen, the foundries of Paris are now running for statues, with the kettles of their poor and the bells of their churches. If an author had written like a great genius on geometry, though his practical and speculative morals were vicious in the extreme, it might appear that in voting the statue, they honoured only the geometrician. But Rousseau is a moralist, or he is nothing. It is impossible, therefore, putting the circumstances together, to mistake their design in choosing the author, with whom they have begun to recommend a course of studies.

Their great problem is to find a substitute for all the principles which hitherto have been employed to regulate the human will and action. They find dispositions in the mind, of such force and quality, as may fit men, far better than the old morality, for the purposes of such a state as theirs; and may go much further in supporting their power, and destroying their enemies. They have therefore chosen a selfish, flattering, seductive, ostentatious vice, in the place of plain duty. True humility, the basis of the Christian system, is the low, but deep and firm foundation of all real virtue. But this, as very painful in the practice, and little imposing in the appearance, they have totally discarded. Their object is to merge all natural and all social sentiment in inordinate vanity. In a small degree, and conversant in little things, vanity is of little moment. When full grown, it is the worst of vices, and the occasional mimick of them all. It makes the whole man false. It leaves nothing sincere or trust-worthy about him. His best qualities are poisoned and perverted by it, and operate exactly as the worst. When your lords had many writers as immoral as the object of their statue (such as Voltaire and others) they chose Rousseau; because in him that peculiar vice which they wished to erect into a ruling virtue, was by far the most conspicuous.

We have had the great professor and founder of *the philosophy of vanity* in England. As I had good opportunities of knowing his proceedings almost from day to day, he left no doubt in my mind, that he entertained no principle either to influence his heart, or to guide his understanding, but *vanity*. With this vice he was possessed to a degree little short of madness. It is from the same deranged eccentric vanity, that this, the insane *Socrates* of the National Assembly, was impelled to publish a mad Confession of his mad faults, and to attempt a new sort of glory, from bringing hardily to light the obscure and vulgar vices which we know may sometimes be blended with eminent talents. He has not observed on the nature of vanity, who does not know that it is omnivorous; that it has no choice in its food; that it is fond to talk even of its own faults and vices, as what will excite surprize and draw attention, and what will pass at worst for openness and candour. It was this abuse and perversion, which vanity makes even of hypocrisy, which has driven Rousseau to record a life not so much as chequered, or spotted here and there, with virtues, or even distinguished by a single good action. It is such a life he chooses to offer to the attention of mankind. It is such a life, that with a wild defiance, he flings in the face of his Creator, whom he acknowledges only to brave. Your Assembly, knowing how much more powerful example is found than precept, has chosen this man (by his own account without a single virtue) for a model. To him they erect their first statue. From him they commence their series of honours and distinctions.

It is that new-invented virtue which your masters canonize, that led their moral hero constantly to exhaust the stores of his powerful rhetoric in the expression of universal benevolence; whilst his heart was incapable of harbouring one spark of common parental affection. Benevolence to the whole species, and want of feeling for every individual with whom the professors come in contact, form the character of the new philosophy. Setting up for an unsocial independence, this their hero of vanity refuses the just price of common labour, as well as the tribute which opulence owes to genius, and which, when paid, honours the giver and the receiver; and then he pleads his beggary as an excuse for his crimes. He melts with tenderness for those only who touch him by the remotest relation, and then, without one natural pang, casts away, as a sort of offal and excrement, the spawn of his disgustful amours, and sends his children to the hospital of foundlings. *The bear loves, licks, and forms her young; but bears are not philosophers* (my italics – C.C.O'B). Vanity, however, finds its account in reversing the train of our natural feelings. Thousands admire the sentimental writer; the affectionate father is hardly known in his parish.

Under this philosophic instructor in the *ethics of vanity*, they have attempted in France a regeneration of the moral constitution of man. Statesmen, like your present rulers, exist by every thing which is spurious, fictitious, and false; by every thing which takes the man from his house, and sets him on a stage, which makes him up an artificial creature, with painted theatric sentiments, fit to be seen by the glare of candlelight, and formed to be contemplated at a due distance. Vanity is too apt to prevail in all of us, and in all countries. To the improvement of Frenchmen it seems not absolutely necessary that it should be taught upon system. But it is plain that the present rebellion was its legitimate offspring, and it is piously fed by that rebellion, with a daily dole.

If the system of institution, recommended by the Assembly, is false and theatric, it is because their system of government is of the same character. To that, and to that alone, it is strictly conformable. To understand either, we must connect the morals with the politics of the legislators. Your practical philosophers, systematic in every thing, have wisely began at the source. As the relation between parents and children is the first among the elements of vulgar, natural morality, they erect statues to a wild, ferocious, low-minded, hard-hearted father, of fine general feelings; a lover of his kind, but a hater of his kindred. Your masters reject the duties of this vulgar relation, as contrary to liberty; as not founded in the social compact; and not binding according to the rights of men; because the relation is not, of course, the result of *free election*; never so on the side of the children, not always on the part of the parents.[1]

Definitely a part of the Great Melody.
Letter to a Member of the National Assembly contains two striking examples of Burke's powers of predictive insight. At a time of no

[1] *Writings and Speeches* VIII, 312–316.

apparent threat to the king in person, Burke predicts his execution. *Letter to a Member* is dated 19 January 1791 – before both the flight to Varennes and the Royal Oath to the Constitution. The king did not come to be guillotined until 21 January 1793. Burke writes almost exactly two years earlier:

> Nothing that I can say, or that you can say, will hasten them by a single hour, in the execution of a design which they have long since entertained. In spite of their solemn declarations, their soothing addresses, and the multiple oaths which they have taken, and forced others to take, they will assassinate the king when his name will no longer be necessary to their designs; but not a moment sooner. They will probably first assassinate the queen, whenever the renewed menace of such assassination loses its effect upon the anxious mind of an affectionate husband. At present, the advantage which they derive from the daily threats against her life, is her only security for preserving it. They keep their sovereign alive for the purpose of exhibiting him, like some wild beast at a fair; as if they had a Bajazet in a cage. They chose to make monarchy contemptible by exposing it to derision, in the person of the most benevolent of their kings.[1]

It is worth noting that – if we equate the guillotining of Louis and Marie Antoinette with assassination as Burke would – he is right about the only event which he actually predicts: the assassination of the king. He also foresees (without specifically predicting) the execution of the queen. He is wrong only about something of which he spoke in terms of probability: the order of the two assassinations. Marie Antoinette was not guillotined until 16 October 1793.

Burke's capacity to predict, years ahead of time, certain events – intensification of revolution; execution of king and queen; emergence of military despotism – came from his early and profound insight into the general character and tendencies of the Revolution. In matters of timing and tactics, long-distance prediction was impossible. Burke knew Marie Antoinette was much more unpopular than Louis, and he therefore naturally assumed that she would be killed first. What could not be foreseen in early 1791, was that the king would be singled out, in late 1792, for execution first, because he was relatively popular. Thus the threat to him would draw the *indulgents* – the relative 'soft-liners' among the revolutionaries – to try to save him, so leading to their own destruction, and to the ascent of Robespierre

[1] *Writings and Speeches* VIII, 309.

to the supreme power, by means of the compromising of his greatest rival. As Michelet was to write, 'They were aiming at Danton, through the King': '*Derrière le Roi, on visait Danton.*'

Burke could not foresee the tactics which Robespierre – little known outside France in early 1791 – would pursue in late 1792. But he did foresee, and clearly predict in *Letter to a Member*, the rise to power, within the Revolution, of people of the Robespierre type, ousting the 'moderates' who held the leadership of the Assembly in 1789–91. Burke writes, of those who called themselves the moderates:

> These, if I conceive rightly of their conduct, are a set of men who approve heartily of the whole new constitution, but wish to lay heavy on [i.e. to distance themselves from] the most atrocious of those crimes, by which this fine constitution of their's has been obtained. They are a sort of people who affect to proceed as if they thought that men may deceive without fraud, rob without injustice, and overturn every thing without violence. They are men who would usurp the government of their country with decency and moderation. In fact they are nothing more or better, than men engaged in desperate designs, with feeble minds. They are not honest; they are only ineffectual and unsystematic in their iniquity. They are persons who want not the dispositions, but the energy and vigour, that is necessary for great evil machinations. They find that in such designs they fall at best into a secondary rank, and others take the place and lead in usurpation, which they are not qualified to obtain or to hold. They envy to their companions, the natural fruit of their crimes; they join to run them down with the hue and cry of mankind, which pursues their common offences; and then hope to mount onto their places on the credit of the sobriety with which they shew themselves disposed to carry on what may seem most plausible in the mischievous projects they pursue in common. But these men naturally are despised by those who have heads to know, and hearts that are able to go through the necessary demands of bold, wicked enterprizes. They are naturally classed below the latter description, and will only be used by them as inferior instruments. They will be only the Fairfaxes of your Cromwells.[1]

Burke here predicts in January 1791, the transit of power, within the Revolution, which would come about, in the second half of 1792. And it was this transit, of course that led directly to what Burke had also foreseen; the execution/assassination of the king and queen of France.

[1] *Writings and Speeches* VIII, 333.

Of Burke's 1791 writings on the French Revolution, the *Letter to a Member of the National Assembly* is the only one to have been published before Varennes. But he did write another paper early in 1791, though it wasn't published before the bid to escape. This was *Hints for a Memorial to be delivered to Monsieur M.M. (Writings and Speeches* VIII, 336–338). L. G. Mitchell, the editor of Volume VIII, describes *Hints for a Memorial* as 'little more than a fragment'. It is in fact complete and the brevity is appropriate to its purpose. The person it was intended for was the Comte de Montmorin, at the time Foreign Minister of France. (In 1792, after the fall of the monarchy, Montmorin was among those murdered by the mob.) Burke clearly intended this document for the eyes of Lord Grenville, then Foreign Secretary in Pitt's administration, and then of Pitt himself, and of George III. It is a draft of an *aide-mémoire* to be delivered – if Pitt approved – by the British Ambassador in Paris to the French Foreign Minister, in a *démarche* which would be a preliminary to the breaking off of diplomatic relations between Britain and France. It opens: 'The King my Master, from his sincere desire of keeping up a good correspondence with his Most Christian Majesty, and the French nation, has for some time beheld with concern, the condition into which that sovereign and nation have fallen.' It ends: 'If unfortunately, a due attention should not be paid to these his Majesty's benevolent and neighbourly offers, or, if any circumstances should prevent the Most Christian King from acceding (as his Majesty has no doubt he is well disposed to do) to the healing mediation in favour of himself and all his subjects, his Majesty has commanded me to take leave of this Court, as not conceiving it to be suitable to the dignity of his Crown, and to what he owes to his faithful people, any longer to keep a public Minister at the Court of a Sovereign who is not in possession of his own liberty.'

In the *Letter to a Member of the National Assembly (Writings and Speeches* VIII, 305–8) Burke said that the progress of the French Revolution could now be arrested only by the use of outside force. *Hints for a Memorial* shows him offering to the British Government advice in conformity with that public position. Pitt was not even nearly ready to take Burke's advice. Although the recapture of the king and queen, in June, greatly reinforced Burke's case, neither this, nor the deposition of the king in August, altered Pitt's mind. Britain did not recall her Ambassador from Revolutionary France until January 1793, after Louis's execution. War, actually declared by France, followed in February.

Second in importance after *Reflections*, in the canon of Burke's writings in the controversy over the French Revolution, is *An Appeal from the New to the Old Whigs*[1]. The full title of the pamphlet is: *An Appeal from the New to the Old Whigs in consequence of some later discussions in Parliament – relative to the Reflections on the French Revolution*. It belongs incontestably in the Great Melody – its presence there has the sanction of W. B. Yeats himself, whose favourite it was out of all Burke's works.

An Appeal was written immediately after Burke's parliamentary quarrel, of April–May 1791, with Charles James Fox. Its general purpose was to defend Burke against the charges of inconsistency levelled against him by Fox and his followers. The Whigs claimed that Burke's position over the French Revolution was inconsistent, both with the Whig tradition in general, and with his own personal position, when he had worked with the Whigs, especially in relation to the American Revolution and also to the power of the Crown. In *An Appeal* Burke sets out to show his full consistency both with the Whig tradition, and with his own past words and actions. The core-passage specifically and directly defends Burke's consistency. (It was published anonymously, in August 1791, and speaks of Burke in the third person):

> I pass to the next head of charge – Mr. Burke's inconsistency. It is certainly a great aggravation of his fault in embracing false opinions, that in doing so he is not supposed to fill up a void, but that he is guilty of a dereliction of opinions that are true and laudable. This is the great gist of the charge against him. It is not so much that he is wrong in his book (that, however, is alleged also) as that he has therein belied his whole life. I believe, if he could venture to value himself upon anything, it is on the virtue of consistency that he would value himself the most. Strip him of this, and you leave him naked indeed.
>
> In the case of any man who had written something and spoken a great deal, upon very multifarious matter, during upwards of twenty-five years' public service, and in as great a variety of important events as perhaps have ever happened in the same number of years, it would appear a little

[1] Inexplicably, and without attempted explanation, *An Appeal from the New to the old Whigs* (1791) is omitted from Volume VIII *The French Revolution 1790–1794*, of *The Writings and Speeches of Edmund Burke*. One wonders in what volume it is intended to publish this work. Or is it to be left out altogether? After Volume VIII, anything could happen. Lacking a modern scholarly edition, by the delinquency of the editor of Volume VIII, I am here using the text in *Works* IV, 61–215, the Nimmo edition of 1899 (see Sources).

hard, in order to charge such a man with inconsistency, to see collected by his friend a sort of digest of his sayings, even to such as were merely sportive and jocular. This digest, however, has been made, with equal pains and partiality, and without bringing out those passages of the writings which might tend to show with what restrictions any expressions quoted from him ought to have been understood. From a great statesman he did not quite expect this mode of inquisition. If it only appeared in the works of common pamphleteers, Mr. Burke might safely trust to his reputation. When thus urged, he ought, perhaps, to do a little more. It shall be as little as possible; for I hope not much is wanting. To be totally silent on his charges would not be respectful to Mr. Fox. Accusations sometimes derive a weight from the persons who make them to which they are not entitled from their matter.

He who thinks that the British Constitution ought to consist of the three members, of three very different natures, of which it does actually consist, and thinks it his duty to preserve each of those members in its proper place and with its proper proportion of power, must (as each shall happen to be attacked) vindicate the three several parts on the several principles peculiarly belonging to them. He cannot assert the democratic part on the principles on which monarchy is supported, nor can he support monarchy on the principles of democracy, nor can he maintain aristocracy on the grounds of the one or of the other or of both. All these he must support on grounds that are totally different, though practically they may be, and happily with us they are, brought into one harmonious body. A man could not be consistent in defending such various, and, at first view, discordant, parts of a mixed Constitution, without that sort of inconsistency with which Mr. Burke stands charged.

As any one of the great members of this Constitution happens to be endangered, he that is a friend to all of them chooses and presses the topics necessary for the support of the part attacked, with all the strength, the earnestness, the vehemence, with all the power of stating, of argument, and of coloring, which he happens to possess, and which the case demands. He is not to embarrass the minds of his hearers, or to encumber or overlay his speech, by bringing into view at once (as if he were reading an academic lecture) all that may and ought, when a just occasion presents itself, to be said in favour of the other members. At that time they are out of the court; there is no question concerning them. Whilst he opposes his defence on the part where the attack is made, he presumes that for his regard to the just rights of all the rest he has credit in every candid mind. He ought not to apprehend that his raising fences about popular privileges this day will infer that he ought on the next to concur with those who would pull down the throne; because on the next he defends the throne, it ought not to be supposed that he has abandoned the rights of the people.

A man, who, among various objects of his equal regard, is secure of some, and full of anxiety for the fate of others, is apt to go to much greater lengths in his preference of the objects of his immediate solicitude than Mr. Burke has ever done. A man so circumstanced often seems to undervalue, to vilify, almost to reprobate and disown, those that are out of danger. This is the voice of Nature and truth, and not of inconsistency and false pretence. The danger of anything very dear to us removes, for the moment, every other affection from the mind. When Priam had his whole thoughts employed on the body of his Hector, he repels with indignation, and drives from him with a thousand reproaches, his surviving sons, who with an officious piety crowded about him to offer their assistance. A good critic (there is no better than Mr. Fox) would say that this is a master-stroke, and marks a deep understanding of Nature in the father of poetry. He would despise a Zoïlus who would conclude from this passage that Homer meant to represent this man of affliction as hating or being indifferent and cold in his affections to the poor relics of his house, or that he preferred a dead carcass to his living children.

Mr. Burke does not stand in need of an allowance of this kind, which, if he did, by candid critics ought to be granted to him. If the principles of a mixed Constitution be admitted, he wants no more to justify to consistency everything he has said and done during the course of a political life just touching to its close. I believe that gentleman had kept himself more clear of running into the fashion of wild, visionary theories, or of seeking popularity through every means, than any man perhaps ever did in the same situation.

He was the first who, on the hustings, at a popular election, rejected the authority of instruction from constituents, – or who, in any place, has argued so fully against it.[1] Perhaps the discredit into which that doctrine of compulsive instructions under our Constitution is since fallen may be due in a great degree to his opposing himself to it in that manner and on that occasion.

The reforms in representation, and the bills for shortening the duration of Parliaments, he uniformly and steadily opposed for many years together, in contradiction to many of his best friends. These friends, however, in his better days, when they had more to fear from his loss than now they have, never chose to find any inconsistency between his acts and expressions in favor of liberty and his votes on those questions. But there is a time for all things.

Against the opinion of many friends, even against the solicitation of some of them, he opposed those of the Church clergy who had petitioned the House of Commons to be discharged from the subscription. Although

[1] At Bristol in 1774; see Chapter I, p. 74.

he supported the Dissenters in their petition for the indulgence which he had refused to the clergy of the Established Church, in this, as he was not guilty of it, so he was not reproached with inconsistency. At the same time he promoted, and against the wish of several, the clause that gave the Dissenting teachers another subscription in the place of that which was then taken away. Neither at that time was the reproach of inconsistency brought against him. *People could then distinguish between a difference in conduct under a variation of circumstances and an inconsistency in principle* [my italics – C.C.O'B.]. It was not then thought necessary to be freed of him as of an incumbrance.

These instances, a few among many, are produced as an answer to the insinuation of his having pursued high popular courses which in his late book he has abandoned. Perhaps in his whole life he has never omitted a fair occasion, with whatever risk to him of obloquy as an individual, with whatever detriment to his interest as a member of opposition, to assert the very same doctrines which appear in that book. He told the House, upon an important occasion, and pretty early in his service, that, "being warned by the ill effect of a contrary procedure in great examples, he had taken his ideas of liberty very low in order that they should stick to him and that he might stick to them to the end of his life."

At popular elections the most rigorous casuists will remit a little of their severity. They will allow to a candidate some unqualified effusions in favor of freedom, without binding him to adhere to them in their utmost extent. But Mr. Burke put a more strict rule upon himself than most moralists would put upon others. At his first offering himself to Bristol, where he was almost sure he should not obtain, on that or any occasion, a single Tory vote, (in fact, he did obtain but one,) and rested wholly on the Whig interest, he thought himself bound to tell to the electors, both before and after his election, exactly what a representative they had to expect in him.

"The *distinguishing* part of our Constitution," he said, "is its liberty. To preserve that liberty inviolate is the *peculiar* duty and *proper* trust of a member of the House of Commons. But the liberty, the *only* liberty, I mean is a liberty connected with *order*; and that not only exists with order and virtue, but cannot exist at all *without* them. It inheres in good and steady government, as in *its substance and vital principle*."

The liberty to which Mr. Burke declared himself attached is not French liberty. That liberty is nothing but the rein given to vice and confusion. Mr. Burke was then, as he was at the writing of his Reflections, awfully impressed with the difficulties arising from the complex state of our Constitution and our empire, and that it might require in different emergencies different sorts of exertions, and the successive call upon all the various principles which uphold and justify it. This will appear from what he said at the close of the poll.

"To be a good member of Parliament is, let me tell you, no easy task, – especially at this time, when there is so strong a disposition to run into the perilous extremes of *servile* compliance or *wild popularity*. To unite circumspection with vigor is absolutely necessary, but it is extremely difficult. We are now members for a rich commercial *city*; this city, however, is but a part of a great *nation*, which however, is itself but part of a great *empire*, extended by our virtue and our fortune to the farthest limits of the East and of the West. *All* these widespread interests must be *considered*, – must be *compared*, – must be *reconciled*, if possible. We are members for a *free* country; and surely we all know that the machine of a free constitution is no *simple* thing, but as *intricate* and as *delicate* as it is valuable. We are members in a *great and ancient* MONARCHY; *and we must preserve religiously the true, legal rights of the sovereign, which form the key-stone that binds together the noble and well-constructed arch of our empire and our Constitution.* A constitution made up of *balanced powers* must ever be a critical thing. As such I mean to touch that part of it which comes within my reach." [Burke's italics throughout.]

In this manner Mr. Burke spoke to his constituents seventeen years ago. He spoke, not like a partisan of one particular member of our Constitution, but as a person strongly, and on principle, attached to them all. He thought these great and essential members ought to be preserved, and preserved each in its place, – and that the monarchy ought not only to be secured in its peculiar existence, but in its pre-eminence too, as the presiding and connecting principle of the whole. Let it be considered whether the language of his book, printed in 1790, differs from his speech at Bristol in 1774.

With equal justice his opinions on the American war are introduced, as if in his late work he had belied his conduct and opinions in the debates which arose upon that great event. On the American war he never had any opinions which he has seen occasion to retract, or which he has ever retracted. He, indeed, differs essentially from Mr. Fox as to the cause of that war. Mr. Fox has been pleased to say that the Americans rebelled "because they thought they had not enjoyed liberty enough." This cause of the war, *from him*, I have heard of for the first time, It is true that those who stimulated the nation to that measure did frequently urge this topic. They contended that the Americans had from the beginning aimed at independence, – that from the beginning they meant wholly to throw off the authority of the crown, and to break their connection with the parent country. This Mr. Burke never believed. When he moved his second conciliatory proposition, in the year 1776, he entered into the discussion of this point at very great length, and, from nine several heads of presumption, endeavored to prove that charge upon that people not to be true.

If the principles of all he has said and wrote on the occasion be viewed with common temper, the gentlemen of the party will perceive, that on a supposition that the Americans had rebelled merely in order to enlarge their liberty, Mr. Burke would have thought very differently of the American cause. What might have been in the secret thoughts of some of their leaders it is impossible to say, As far as a man so locked up as Dr. Franklin could be expected to communicate his ideas, I believe he opened them to Mr. Burke. It was, I think, the very day before he set out for America that a very long conversation passed between them, and with a greater air of openness on the Doctor's side than Mr. Burke had observed in him before, In this discourse Dr. Franklin lamented, and with apparent sincerity, the separation which he feared was inevitable between Great Britain and her colonies. He certainly spoke of it as an event which gave him the greatest concern. America, he said, would never again see such happy days as she had passed under the protection of England. He observed, that ours was the only instance of a great empire in which the most distant parts and members had been as well governed as the metropolis and its vicinage, but that the Americans were going to lose the means which secured to them this rare and precious advantage. The question with them was not, whether they were to remain as they had been before the troubles, – for better, he allowed, they could not hope to be, – but whether they were to give up so happy a situation without a struggle. Mr. Burke had several other conversations with him about that time, in none of which, soured and exasperated as his mind certainly was, did he discover any other wish in favor of America than for a security to its *ancient* condition. Mr. Burke's conversation with other Americans was large, indeed, and his inquiries extensive and diligent. Trusting to the result of all these means of information, but trusting much more in the public presumptive indications I have just referred to, and to the reiterated solemn declarations of their Assemblies, he always firmly believed that they were purely on the defensive in that rebellion. He considered the Americans as standing at that time, and in that controversy, in the same relation to England as England did to King James the Second in 1688. He believed that they had taken up arms from one motive only; that is, our attempting to tax them without their consent, – to tax them for the purposes of maintaining civil and military establishments. If this attempt of ours could have been practically established, he thought, with them, that their Assemblies would become totally useless, – that, under the system of policy which was then pursued, the Americans could have no sort of security for their laws or liberties, of for any part of them, – and that the very circumstance of *our* freedom would have augmented the weight of *their* slavery.

Considering the Americans on that defensive footing, he thought Great Britain ought instantly to have closed with them by the repeal of the taxing act. He was of opinion that our general rights over that country would have been preserved by this timely concession. When, instead of this, a Boston Port Bill, a Massachusetts Charter Bill, a Fishery Bill, and Intercourse Bill, I know not how many hostile bills, rushed out like so many tempests from all points of the compass, and were accompanied first with great fleets and armies of English, and followed afterwards with great bodies of foreign troops, he thought that their cause grew daily better, because daily more defensive, – and that ours, because daily more offensive, grew daily worse. He therefore, in two motions, in two successive years, proposed in Parliament many concessions beyond what he had reason to think in the beginning of the troubles would ever be seriously demanded.

So circumstanced, he certainly never could and never did wish the colonists to be subdued by arms. He was fully persuaded, that, if such should be the event, they must be held in that subdued state by a great body of standing forces, and perhaps of foreign forces. He was strongly of opinion that such armies, first victorious over Englishmen, in a conflict for English constitutional rights and privileges, and afterwards habituated (though in America) to keep an English people in a state of abject subjection, would prove fatal in the end to the liberties of England itself; that in the mean time this military system would lie as an oppressive burden upon the national finances; that it would constantly breed and feed new discussions, full of heat and acrimony, leading possibly to a new series of wars; and that foreign powers, whilst we continued in a state at once burdened and distracted, must at length obtain a decided superiority over us. On what part of his late publication, or on what expression that might have escaped him in that work, is any man authorized to charge Mr. Burke with a contradiction to the line of his conduct and to the current of his doctrines on the American war? The pamphlet is in the hands of his accusers: let them point out the passage, if they can.[1]

Having read everything that Burke is known to have written, and everything that he is recorded as having said, and having studied every phase of his career, I find this defence against the charge of inconsistency – over supposedly taking 'a new line' over the French Revolution – to be fully justified. There were some inconsistencies in his career; the greatest, which was noted in Chapter IV, was the fundamental incompatibility between his earliest and later speeches over India. But that Indian inconsistency – or change of mind – has no relevance to the controversy over the French Revolution. There is no inconsistency there. Nobody who had studied Burke's works carefully, before the French Revolution, should have expected him to welcome it. There

[1] *Works* IV (1899), 92–103.

is one statement of Burke's, made nearly six years before the French Revolution (not quoted in *An Appeal*), which sums up the basic principle on which Burke was to resist the French Revolution, when it came. Burke was speaking against Warren Hastings on 1 December 1783. In explaining his initial reluctance to attack the East Indian Company's Rule, Burke expressed his 'insuperable reluctance . . . to destroy any established system of government upon a theory'.[1] Burke had thus succinctly defined the intellectual basis of what became his opposition to the French Revolution, nearly six years before the Revolution took place. Never were charges of inconsistency more lightly made, or more perfunctorily sustained, than the charges of inconsistency levelled by the Whigs and radicals – and some later historians – against Edmund Burke, over the French Revolution.

The most eloquent and the most profound passage in *An Appeal* is Burke's defence of what he calls 'natural aristocracy' (a term to which he gives a wide definition) against the levelling tendencies and projects of the French Revolutionaries:

A true natural aristocracy is not a separate interest in the state, or separable from it. It is an essential integral part of any large body rightly constituted. It is formed out of a class of legitimate presumptions, which, taken as generalities, must be admitted for actual truths. To be bred in a place of estimation; to see nothing low and sordid from one's infancy; to be taught to respect one's self; to be habituated to the censorial inspection of the public eye; to look early to public opinion; to stand upon such elevated ground as to be enabled to take a large view of the widespread and infinitely diversified combinations of men and affairs in a large society; to have leisure to read, to reflect, to converse; to be enabled to draw the court and attention of the wise and learned, wherever they are to be found; to be habituated in armies to command and to obey; to be taught to despise danger in the pursuit of honor and duty; to be formed to the greatest degree of vigilance, foresight, and circumspection, in a state of things in which no fault is committed with impunity and the slightest mistakes draw on the most ruinous consequences; to be led to a guarded and regulated conduct, from a sense that you are considered as an instructor of your fellow-citizens in their highest concerns, and that you act as a reconciler between God and man; to be employed as an administrator of law and justice, and to be thereby amongst the first benefactors to mankind; to be a professor of high science, or of liberal

---

[1] *Writings and Speeches* V, 387. See epigraph above. Burke's Indian inconsistency, in his early speeches, is thus explained by a consistency in his thinking, at a deeper level.

and ingenuous art; to be amongst rich traders, who from their success are presumed to have sharp and vigorous understandings, and to possess the virtues of diligence, order, constancy, and regularity, and to have cultivated an habitual regard to commutative justice: these are the circumstances of men that form what I should call a *natural* aristocracy, without which there is no nation.

The state of civil society which necessarily generates this aristocracy is a state of Nature, – and much more truly so than a savage and incoherent mode of life. For man is by nature reasonable; and he is never perfectly in his natural state, but when he is placed where reason may be best cultivated and predominates. Art is man's nature. We are as much at least, in a state of Nature in formed manhood as in immature and helpless infancy, Men, qualified in the manner I have just described, form in Nature, as she operates in the common modification of society, the leading, guiding, and governing part. It is the soul to the body, without which the man does not exist. To give, therefore, no more importance, in the social order, to such descriptions of men than that of so many units is a horrible usurpation.[1]

'Art is man's nature.' Burke had long since rejected the eighteenth century's tendency to oppose the natural to the artificial, and to exalt the former over the latter. His first book, published in 1756, was called *A Vindication of Natural Society*. The title, like the book itself, is ironic. Burke was seeking to show that the arguments for 'natural religion' – that is to say a form of religion without revelation, church or dogma – could be turned into a case for 'natural society' – that is to say a form of society devoid of its existing institutions. In the preface to the second edition of *A Vindication*, he abandoned the ironic mode and directly explained the purpose of the book: 'The design was to show that, without the exertion of any considerable forces, the same engines which were employed for the destruction of religion, might be employed with equal success for the subversion of government.'

They might be, and they were, in France, assiduously during the thirty-three years that separated the publication of *A Vindication* from the outbreak of the French Revolution. The 'engines which were employed for the destruction of religion' by the *philosophes*, led by Voltaire, also inadvertently – as far as Voltaire was concerned – subverted the French system of government. They did so by desacralising, delegitimising and ultimately dislodging the keystone of that system, the Monarchy. Once the 'divinity doth hedge a king' was

[1] *Works* IV, 174–176.

gone – because all intervention of divinity was gone – the king of France was helplessly exposed. He had become not merely an ordinary mortal, but a peculiarly guilty mortal, for he had to be seen as the principal beneficiary in a prolonged fraud, organised by a hated church. The nobility, of whose honour the Most Christian King had been the fount, lost their honour when its fount was deligitimised, and they were exposed as secondary beneficiaries in the great ecclesiastical swindle. The guillotine awaited all the criminals.

In *A Vindication of Natural Society*, Burke had described the nature of the pre-revolutionary process, then at a very early stage. *A Vindication* is therefore an outstanding example of Burke's capacity to foresee what is about to happen, out of the depths of his insight into what is already happening. Burke understood the long-term effects of the activity of the anti-Christian *philosophes* at a time when they themselves had no idea that they were subverting the State (with which Voltaire at least had no quarrel), through their attacks on the Church.

A Vindication is also an outstanding example of Burke's *consistency*, over a third of a century. He had denounced, in its embryo, in 1756, the same phenomenon he was to fight in its mature form, from 1790 to his death in 1797: forty-one years after the publication of *A Vindication*. In the circumstances, it might seem strange that in his *Appeal from the New to the Old Whigs*, where Burke's principal object is to establish the consistency of his position over the French Revolution, with his past conduct, he should make no mention of *A Vindication of Natural Society*, that majestic illustration of the very form of Burkean personal consistency which Burke was now at pains to establish. The omission had to be deliberate. Burke might easily have forgotten a pertinent *obiter dictum* he had made in a speech (like the one about destruction 'upon a theory' – see epigraph above), but he couldn't have forgotten a whole book, and that his very first one.

That curious omission from *An Appeal* is linked, I believe, with another curious omission, in *A Vindication* itself. Burke is consistent, even in his omissions. The omission, in *A Vindication*, consists in leaving out the French intellectuals, the main carriers of what Burke was talking about. What he was attacking was the anti-Christian phase of the Enlightenment, a phase which, by the 1750s, had seen significant progress in France – under the brilliant leadership of Voltaire – and little progress anywhere else, at that time. Burke's real enemy – and an enemy worthy of his steel –

was Voltaire. Yet, in *A Vindication*, he makes no mention of Voltaire, or of any of the other French *philosophes*, whose depredations he certainly has in mind. His ostensible target is a relatively minor figure in that movement of ideas: Henry St. John, Viscount Bolingbroke (1678–1751), an English politician of the early eighteenth-century, who was, as a 'philosopher', a disciple of Voltaire, and the leading one in Britain.

Here again, Burke's position of 1756 is deeply consistent with his position of 1790. In both cases, his primary targets are British importers of French ideas which he finds both abhorrent and dangerous. The importers targeted were Bolingbroke in the 1750s, and Richard Price and his friends in 1789–90. The articles of importation, in both cases, were products of one identical manufacturing process: early products and late ones. But what may still seem odd is that in *A Vindication* – most unlike *Reflections* in this – there is no mention of the original manufacturers. *A Vindication* contains no direct allusion to Bolingbroke's mentor and hero, Voltaire. The nearest Burke comes, in that book, to referring to the French anti-Christian *philosophes*, is in the sentence in the preface, 'such are the reasonings which this noble writer and several others have been pleased to dignify with the name of philosophy.'

In studying Burke, I have often found that, whenever there is an unexpected silence, a failure to refer to something obviously relevant, or a cryptically guarded formulation, the probable explanation is usually to be found at 'the Irish level': the suspect and subterranean area of emotional access to the forbidden world of Roman Catholicism. The omissions in both *A Vindication* and *An Appeal* fall in sensitive areas for Burke, in relation to Catholicism and his links with it. In his public persona as a good Protestant Whig, he could appropriately attack Bolingbroke, for attemping to subvert the Church of England, and thus inadvertently subverting the British Constitution. But to attack Bolingbroke's mentor Voltaire would be something else. What Voltaire was best known for was attacking Roman Catholicism. To attack Voltaire, therefore, for attacking religion, would be to emerge as a defender of Roman Catholicism. Burke was prepared to run risks, and incur losses, in defence of tolerance for Roman Catholics, but he always tried to avoid giving his enemies a handle against him by saying anything that might reinforce the suspicion that he personally was a crypto-Catholic. That seems to provide an adequate explanation for that omission from *A Vindication*.

The omission from *An Appeal* of any reference to *A Vindication* is closely similar. If he had cited *A Vindication*, and brought out its close relevance to the pre-revolutionary process in France, he could have triumphantly established his own personal consistency in resisting the ideological trends that did so much to produce the French Revolution. But by introducing that argument, Burke, while vindicating his personal consistency, would be raising questions about his Whig orthodoxy. Zeal in the frustration of efforts to undermine the Roman Catholic Church was hardly a Whig tradition. It was even less characteristic of the Old Whigs, to whom Burke was appealing, than of the New Whigs, with whom Burke was breaking. Many of the Old Whigs – including Locke – were veterans of the Popish Plot. All of them had used anti-Catholicism, with enthusiasm, to drive James II from his throne. *Lilliburlero* is not an ecumenical ditty, but it was the great tune of the Old Whigs. Burke knows all this, but does not want to talk about it. Nor does he want to talk about *A Vindication*, in the context of the French Revolution: a conjuncture, which would expose his vulnerable flank: his pro-Catholic sympathies, inappropriate to a proper Whig. Burke was a sound Whig, in most ways. It was only the anti-Catholic element in Whiggery that made him uncomfortable. He had done his best in his own time, to filter that element out of Whiggery, and with considerable success, through his influence over Rockingham, Fox and others. But enough is still around, even in 1790, to make him sometimes uneasy, and on his guard.

In *An Appeal from the New to the Old Whigs*, there are, along with much solid argument and splendid eloquence, elements of both understatement and overstatement. Burke's personal consistency in the matter of the French Revolution is understated (because of the failure to mention *A Vindication*). His Whig orthodoxy is overstated, especially with regard to the Old Whigs. This great tract ends, regrettably, on a false note: 'The Whigs of this day have before them, in this Appeal, their constitutional ancestors; they have the doctors of the modern school. They will choose for themselves. The author of the *Reflections* has chosen for himself. If a new order is coming on, and all the political opinions must pass away as dreams, which our ancestors have worshipped as revelations, I say for him, that he would rather be the last (as certainly he is the least) of that race of men than the first and greatest of those who have coined to themselves Whig principles from a French die, unknown to the impress of our fathers in the Constitution.' This is exactly the same false note as had been struck in *On Conciliation with America*, seventeen years before (see Chapter III above, p. 51). Burke's real ancestors were Irish Jacobites, not English Whigs. He is speaking, in both these passages, in a persona that does not fit his inner being. His rare false notes, and his evasions and other oddities, all occur in contexts where 'the Irish level' is relevant. But the Irish level is also the source of some of his most penetrating insights. Only a mind accustomed from its earliest years to looking intently on the confines of religious and political affairs would have been likely to discern, – in the anti-Catholic writings of the mid-eighteenth-century – the germs of the coming French Revolution.

Burke's last statement in the 1789–91 series of writings and speeches on the French Revolution – and also his last statement written while France was still ostensibly a monarchy – is *Thoughts on French Affairs* (*Writings and Speeches* VIII, 338–386; December 1791).

Thoughts, like *Hints for a Memorial*, is prepared not for publication but for the eyes of Grenville, Pitt and possibly the king. Unlike *Hints*, however, *Thoughts* is not a draft, intended to take form as an official British document, but a memorandum in which Burke makes a detailed case for breaking off relations with France. Much of the memorandum is taken up by a *tour d'horizon* of the positions of the European powers, in relation to Revolutionary France, as these stood towards the end of 1791, the last full year of European peace. This appraisal is of considerable historical interest, but need not detain us here. In this context, by far the most important part of *Thoughts* is a passage, unparalleled in Burke's public writings on the subject, comparing the French Revolution to the Reformation. Having noted that England's Glorious Revolution 'did not extend beyond its territory', he goes on:

> The present Revolution in France seems to me to be quite of another character and description; and to bear little resemblance or analogy to any of those which have been brought about in Europe, upon principles merely political. *It is a Revolution of doctrine and theoretick dogma* [Burke's italics]. It has a much greater resemblance to those changes which have been made upon religious grounds, in which a spirit of proselytism makes an essential part.
>
> The last Revolution of doctrine and theory which has happened in Europe, is the Reformation. It is not for my purpose to take any notice here of the merits of that Revolution, but to state one only of it's effects.

That effect was *to introduce other interests into all countries, than those which arose from their locality and natural circumstances* [Burke's italics]. The principle of the Reformation was such, as by it's essence, could not be local or confined to the country in which it had it's origin. For instance, the doctrine of 'Justification by Faith or by the Works', which was the original basis of the Reformation, could not have one of it's alternatives true as to Germany, and false as to every other country. Neither are questions of theoretick truth and falsehood governed by circumstances any more than by places. On that occasion, therefore, the spirit of proselytism expanded itself with great elasticity upon all sides; and great divisions were everywhere the result.

These divisions however, in appearance merely dogmatick, soon became mixed with the political; and their effects were rendered much more intense from this combination. Europe was for a long time divided into two great factions, under the name of Catholick and Protestant, which not only often alienated State from State, but also divided almost every State within itself. The warm parties in each State were more affectionately attached to those of their own doctrinal interest in some other country than to their fellow citizens, or to their natural Government, when they or either of them happened to be of a different persuasion. These factions, wherever they prevailed, if they did not absolutely destroy, at least weakened and distracted the locality of patriotism. The publick affections came to have other motives and other ties.

It would be to repeat the history of the last two centuries to exemplify the effects of this Revolution.

Although the principles to which it gave rise, did not operate with a perfect regularity and constancy, they never wholly ceased to operate. Few wars were made, and few treaties were entered into in which they did not come in for some part. They gave a colour, a character, and direction to all the politicks of Europe.

These principles of internal, as well as external division and coalition, are but just now extinguished. But they who will examine into the true character and genius of some late events, must be satisfied that other sources of faction, combining parties among the inhabitants of different countries into one connexion, are opened, and that from these sources are likely to arise effects full as important as those which had formerly arisen from the jarring interests of the religious sects. The intention of the several actors in the change in France, is not a matter of doubt, It is very openly professed.

In the modern world, before this time, there has been no instance of this spirit of general political faction, separated from religion, pervading several countries, and forming a principle of union between the partizans in each. But the thing is not less in human nature.

If Burke had used that comparison in his public works, he would

have been making the largest possible present to Protestant sympathisers with the French Revolution, which is the very last thing he
wanted to do. But *Thoughts on French Affairs* is essentially a State
Paper, containing an *argumentum ad hominem* aimed at Pitt. The
message Burke sought to convey to Pitt was that the French Revolution was potentially as explosive an event, in social and political
and military terms, as the Reformation had been. That warning was
amply borne out, from early in the following year, throughout the
remainder of the century, and well into the next one (and beyond it
through 1917). But in late 1791 the Pitt Administration was not
inclined to listen to Burke. Lord Grenville, the Foreign Secretary,
returned *Thoughts on French Affairs* 'without a word of Observation'. Pitt who also had a copy, said nothing either. Burke was hurt,
and very much alone.[1]

This seems an appropriate point to try to sum up the state of
Burke's relations with Administration – that is to say with George
III and Pitt – during this early phase of the French Revolution.

Burke's relations with George III were transformed as a result of
the French Revolution. On Burke's side – once he had made up his
mind against the Revolution – his long struggle to curb the power
of 'the Court' was over. Burke made this clear in public statements
(see above pp. 427–8). There was no change of principle. It was simply
that emphasis on limiting the power of the monarch was no longer
appropriate, when the very existence of monarchy was being challenged. And in any case, for reasons which we shall be considering,
the struggle was no longer necessary. On the king's side, once he
had read *Reflections on the Revolution in France*, Burke – whose
capacities George had long appreciated – almost became the apple
of the royal eye. On 21 March 1791 Jane Burke proudly reported to
her brother-in-law a conversation between George III and Burke:
'You have been of *use to us all*, it is a general opinion, is it not so
Lord Stair? . . . It is, said Lord Stair; – Your Majesty's adopting it,
Sir, will make the opinion general, said Ned – I know it is the general
opinion, and I know that there is no Man who calls himself a Gentleman that must not think himself obliged to you, for you have supported the cause of the Gentlemen.'[2] The king also approved of
Letter to a Member of the National Assembly: 'I lose no time in
informing you that I have this morning had an opportunity of know-

---

[1] See letter of 29 February 1792 to his son Richard, *Corr.* VII, 81.
[2] *Corr.* VI, 237–9.

ing, from the best Authority, that His Majesty has perused it with much attention, and that he expressed very great satisfaction at the whole of it, particularly those parts which relate to Rousseau, Mirabeau and the new Organization of the Courts of Justice.'[1]

If the George III of 1791 had dominated his own Administration, as he had done through Lord North, from 1770–1782, Burke's advice (of 1791, in *Thoughts on French Affairs*) would have been heeded, and Burke probably called to join the Administration himself. But George III did not dominate Administration in the period of the French Revolution, as he had in the period of the American Revolution. The effective head of the Administration was now the Chief Minister. That was how Burke – and the rest of the Whigs – had always thought it ought to be. They had won their struggle, but they were the losers by it. Paradox piled on paradox. The ultimate eighteenth-century beneficiary of the long Constitutional efforts of the Whigs – William Pitt – had come to office, in 1784, through the most blatant exercise of personal initiative and authority, on the part of the monarch, that that reign had known (see Chapter IV above, pp. 328–33). Yet that very fact drained the king's authority and left Pitt the master. George could not do without Pitt, and Pitt knew this. The king had been driven to stage the coup of 1784, by his desperate anxiety to rid himself of the Whigs, who had broken his will over America (see Chapter III above, pp. 224–234). But once Pitt had replaced the Fox – North Coalition, George could not afford to offend Pitt, by refusing to take his advice, because if he did, he ran the risk of another Coalition with Whigs in it, inevitably including the hated Fox. This was the stable basis of Pitt's authority.

The king, whatever the political constraints upon him, might not have accepted Pitt's authority so meekly if his own character had remained what it was in the 1770s. But his character seems to have been changed as a result of his bout of mental illness (November 1788–February 1789). On 24 February, after his recovery, Burke observed: 'But his Mind is subdued and broken; perfectly under the command of others.' (E.B. to Thomas Burgh; *Corr V*, 449). On 4 April Burke wrote: 'The King goes thro' ordinary conversations pretty much in his ordinary manner: But otherwise he is much and materially alterd. He is in the most complete subjection to those who are called his attendants and in reality are his Keepers. With regard to others, all Jealousy with regard to his authority a distinguishing

---

[1] James Bland Burges to Edmund Burke, 5 May 1971, *Corr. VI*, 252–3.

feature of his Mind, is compleatly gone.' (E.B. to Lord Charlemont; *Corr V.* 461).

Politically, the George III–Pitt–Burke relationship, for this period, may be defined as follows: both George III and Burke were stuck with Pitt, because both of them now depended on him to keep the Whigs out. As far as Burke was concerned, Pitt was not nearly as hostile to the French Revolution as he ought to be. But Pitt was at least basically hostile to it, in his own tepid way, whereas Fox and his friends actually liked the Revolution. So Burke had no alternative but to support Pitt. And Pitt knew this, also.

From Pitt's point of view, Burke was an extremely useful ally but an ally whom he didn't have to cultivate, and whom he didn't particularly wish to cultivate. Both temperamentally and in political background, Burke and Pitt were remote from one another. Temperamentally, Burke was warm-hearted, hot-tempered, given to exaggeration in moments when his emotions were aroused. Pitt was cold and cultivated coldness. It was part of his authority. He appeared in the character of the phlegmatic Englishman, partial to understatement, impervious to enthusiasm. With Pitt as the foil, Burke's Irishness comes out especially strong. And I have the impression that Pitt deliberately exploited this in debating with Burke, especially in 1784–6. Pitt even overplays the phlegmatic Englishman to show Burke up as an overheated outsider. By 1791 the contrast was well established and Pitt does no more than remind his hearers of it gently by an aside about 'acerbities'. Burke had become an ally, but Pitt could still not resist putting him in his place.

The political background was no more conducive to friendship than was the temperamental one. Pitt's father, the Earl of Chatham, by accepting office in 1767, without the Rockinghams, broke the ranks of the Whigs, and led to fifteen years in the wilderness for Burke and his friends. Chatham's acceptance was regarded by the Rockinghams, and especially by Burke, as a betrayal. Burke, who was rarely uncharitable towards political opponents (with the exception of Shelburne), is quite startlingly vindictive towards Chatham. The savage sentence in his account of the end of the dying Chatham's famous last speech in the House of Lords, on 7 April 1778, is unique in the whole canon of Burke's writing, in its combination of bitterness and callousness: 'Lord Chatham fell upon the bosom of the Duke of Portland, in an apoplectick fit, after he had spit his last Venom.'[1]

---

[1] E.B. to Richard Champion, his Quaker friend in Bristol, *Corr. III*, 427.

That remark was in a private letter and Pitt would probably not have known of it. But he would have known, in a general way, of Burke's antagonism to his father, and the younger Pitt was not disposed to view with favour the enemies of the elder Pitt (unless they proved essential to his political advantage). Still, cool as it was, the political alliance between the two men lasted through the rest of Burke's parliamentary career, which ended in 1794.

At the close of this section, concerned as it is mainly with Burke's writing and speeches of 1790–91, I should like to make a general point about these particular utterances, as a whole. They have a marked unity. They were all written (or spoken) during a particularly quiet phase of the Revolutionary process: for Paris and the rest of France remained outwardly, though sullenly, tranquil even after the Flight to Varennes, for the rest of 1791, and well into 1792, up to the first French Revolutionary declaration of war, in April of that year. And these utterances are all distinguished by Burke's extraordinary and sustained capacity to pierce through the superficial tranquillity and look into the seething core of the Revolution in France, which had yet to burst out upon the world.

What he had to say when it did burst will be considered in its place. But the body of utterance we have just considered is complete in itself. It constitutes what I shall call the *clairvoyant* stage of Burke's statements on the French Revolution. In the final sentence of the 'Burke' entry in the great *Dictionnaire critique de la Révolution Française* (Paris 1988) Gérard Gengembre refers to '*ce regard étranger, d'une clairvoyance pénétrante. . . .*' In the English translation, unfortunately, the translator has no equivalent for *clairvoyance*. French *clairvoyant* means 'clear-sighted'; its synonym is *perspicace*; the earliest *OED* example is in that sense too. But *clairvoyance* also has an association, in parapsychology, with *perception extrasensorielle*. And this is the part of Burke's entire *oeuvre* in which his unique political genius is most astonishingly apparent.

EARL FITZWILLIAM.

'The disastrous news, my dear Sir, of Earl Fitzwilliam's recall is come;
and Ireland is now on the brink of a Civil war.' (p. 515)

VI
France, Ireland, India
1791–1797

I think I can hardly overrate the malignity of the principles of Protestant ascendancy, as they affect Ireland; or of Indianism, as they affect these countries, and as they affect Asia; or of Jacobinism as they affect all Europe, and the state of human society itself. The last is the greatest evil. But it readily combines with the others, and flows from them.

EDMUND BURKE, 26 May 1795 (*Corr.* VIII, 254).

William Pitt. 'Cold as ice themselves, they never could kindle in our breasts a spark of that zeal which is necessary to a conflict with an adverse zeal . . .' – Edmund Burke (p. 556)

After the great parliamentary quarrel-scene with Fox, in May 1791, Burke did not again speak in the Commons on French affairs, for nearly a year, until 30 April 1792. There were adequate political reasons for a spell of parliamentary silence, on this particular subject. Not one of the Whigs, in either House, had publicly taken his side against Fox. He knew, however, that several Whigs – some of the most important of them – privately agreed with him, at least to a considerable extent, over the French Revolution, and were worried about Fox's enthusiasm for it, and especially about the enthusiasm of Fox's extra-parliamentary allies. Yet they much liked Fox and, perhaps even more important, they detested Pitt, especially for what they regarded as his unconstitutional part, in collusion with George III, in the crisis of 1783 and the elections of 1784.

The leading Whigs in this category were the Duke of Portland and Earl Fitzwilliam, Whig magnates in the Rockingham tradition: high-minded, virtuous, cautious, and conservative; liberal in tendency, and a little slow. Both had great influence, when they chose to exert it, which was seldom. Portland was the nominal leader of the Party, and had presided over what was (nevertheless) generally known as the Fox-North coalition. In practice, both in Government and in opposition, he allowed Fox to take the lead, until 1794. Portland and Fitzwilliam generally worked together, on the fairly infrequent occasions on which they chose to exert themselves seriously, in political matters. Burke was much closer to Fitzwilliam than to Portland, and it was through winning over Fitzwilliam that he expected to win over Portland also.

Fitzwilliam (1748–1833) was Rockingham's heir, in material terms, and he saw himself as Rockingham's heir in moral and intellectual terms also, and sincerely strove to be worthy of that heritage. Much of the heritage in question, as we have seen, derived ultimately from Burke, through his decisive influence over Rockingham, in the later phases of that statesman's career. Fitzwilliam was hardly fully aware of that, but an unusual kind of spiritual relationship did develop between Burke and Fitzwilliam, through Rockingham. On Rockingham's death, on 1 July 1782, Burke had transferred his allegiance, almost formally, not to Portland or Fox, the heirs to the parliamentary leadership, but to Fitzwilliam: 'If you felt only common grief on the late melancholy Event I should offer you common consolation. But there is something so very right, and so perfectly honourable to you, and so very much your own, in your thoughts, and bringing before you any thing that had any kind of relation to him. You have his place to fill and his example to follow; and you are the only man in the world to whom this would not be a work of the greatest difficulty. But to you it is so natural, that it is only going on in your own Course, and inclining with the bent of your ordinary dispositions. You are Lord Rockingham in every thing, To say this is not to flatter you; and I think it impossible it should displease you. I am so much convinced of this, that I have no doubt that you will take it in good part that his old friends, who were attached to him by every tie of affection, and of principle, and among others myself, should look to you, and should not think it an act of forwardness and intrusion to offer you their Services.'[1] Fitzwilliam, for his part, knowing Rockingham's respect for Burke's judgment, always heard him attentively, was swayed by him, and even when he resisted his advice, felt uneasy about having to resist it.

There is an alternative interpretation – the usual reductionist one – which has to be considered here, if briefly. If Namier's view of Burke as a servant of 'the men whose livery he happened to be wearing' has any validity, then the livery was that of Fitzwilliam, from 1782 to 1794 (after which date Edmund's son Richard inherited the livery). This view, as often, has a certain superficial plausibility: Fitzwilliam's inheritance from Rockingham included the patronage of the borough of Malton, for which Burke sat in the Commons, from his defeat at Bristol in 1780 to his retirement in 1794. Also Fitzwilliam was Burke's patron, in a pecuniary sense: Burke accepted, on various occasions, quite large sums of money from him; as he had earlier done from Rockingham.

On Namierite assumptions – and on general worldly assumptions, prevalent also in Burke's time – this should have made him Fitzwilliam's mouthpiece. But it demonstrably didn't work out that way.

[1] *Corr.* V, 6–7.

Burke's public campaign against the French Revolution was acutely uncomfortable for Fitzwilliam, personally and politically. It was personally uncomfortable, because of Fitzwilliam's close friendship with Charles James Fox. And it was politically uncomfortable because it played into the hands of the detested Pitt. The political position common to Portland and Fitzwilliam, in relation to Burke on the French Revolution, in 1790–1792, is well defined by a historian of the Whigs, and biographer of Fitzwilliam: 'Anything which might divide the party or alienate the public was to be avoided, and Burke's insistence on what must as yet seem a hypothetical threat to the principles of the constitution was an unwelcome diversion from the real business of politics.'[1]

This being so, Burke was subjecting his relationship with his patron and benefactor to a considerable strain, by insisting on attacking the French Revolution's admirers in England, among whom the most conspicuous figure was Fitzwilliam's friend, and the leader of his party in the Commons, Charles James Fox. If the relationship between Fitzwilliam and Burke had been that imagined by Namier and others, the relation between a lord and his servant, the lord, at this point, would have sent his cheeky servant packing. Nothing of the kind happened. The tone of the correspondence between the two, at this time of their greatest political divergence, is uniformly cordial and full of mutual respect. The only thing that slightly troubled their relationship, on a personal plane, during this period, is that Fitzwilliam twice attempts to renew his financial subventions to Burke, and Burke twice refuses, giving as reason the continuing political divergence between himself and Fitzwilliam.[2] If Burke had been the kind of person he was depicted as being, by Namier and others, he would have taken Fitzwilliam's money, and shut up about the French Revolution. What he did, as in so many other instances, was the exact opposite.

Burke never desisted, from February 1790 on, from his attack on the French Revolution and its English sympathisers. But he was careful how he chose the ground of his attacks. During the second half of 1791 and the first quarter of 1792 he fought the battle through correspondence, through conversation with powerful individuals, and above all through his great series of political tracts. In the Commons he held his peace. His great object, in parliamentary politics,

[1] E. A. Smith, *Whig Principles and Party Politics: Earl Fitzwilliam and the Whig party, 1748–1833* (Manchester, 1975) pp. 120–1.
[2] *Corr.* VI, 271–6.

after his personal break with Fox, was to win over Fitzwilliam and Portland, and with them as many Whigs as possible. It would only hinder the attainment of this objective were he to keep on attacking Fox in the Commons while Fitzwilliam and Portland were still giving Fox general support in the Lords. Burke continued to work on the opinions of parliamentarians, but he was doing so through political tracts, rather than through speeches. The timing of his publications took account of the parliamentary calendar. Thus the *Reflections* were timed to appear on the eve of the opening of Parliament in the 1790 winter session.[1]

There was another consideration behind the parliamentary truce. Burke had to wait for the French Revolution to catch up, as it were, on his vision of it. To many of his British contemporaries, that vision seemed almost crazily alarmist, at the time of the break with Fox. The month of the break saw the promulgation by the National Assembly of the *Déclaration de Paix au Monde* (22 May, 1790): a document that deeply moved the poets, Wordsworth and the German Friedrich Klopstock, and many other impressionable souls. This was the high-water mark of pacific revolutionary internationalism: the happy flowering of enlightenment cosmopolitanism. So what on earth did Burke think he was talking about?

The month that followed, with the king's flight and recapture, may have sobered the admirers of revolution a little, but only a little. After that, things seemed to return to normal, with further messages of reassurance to the world. Burke knew that the appearances of stability were utterly deceptive and that the leaders of the Assembly, the framers of the Constitution of 1790–91, and of documents like the *Déclaration de Paix au Monde* had been discredited among their own followers, first by Louis' attempted flight and then by his continued acceptance as Chief Executive under the Constitution, despite his detestation of the Revolution; (known through the declaration he made when he fled to Varennes. See Chapter V above, pp. 432–34). Burke had seen from very early on that harder and fiercer revolutionaries would take the place of the Sorcerer's Apprentices of 1789–91. By late 1791, these harder men were already beginning to set the pace. But the change of pace was not yet perceptible to most outsiders. On the contrary, Louis XVI's acceptance of the Constitution in September appeared to inaugurate a new era, in which the fruits

[1] See Frank O'Gorman, *The Whig Party and the French Revolution* (London, 1967) p. 55.

of the Revolution might still be secured without undue violence.[1] Burke would not speak again in parliament on the subject until the change had become unmistakable and alarming, in April 1792.

Meanwhile he was active against the Revolution, not only in his writings, but also in international correspondence. The *Reflections* had made him famous throughout Europe, hated by the revolutionaries, and revered by their enemies. He became the intellectual focal point, in Britain, for the European counter-revolution. Louis's brothers, the Comte de Provence (later Louis XVIII) and the Comte d'Artois (later Charles X), had succeeded in escaping from France in June 1791. Burke's hopes for a restoration (with limited reforms) now centred on those exiled princes, for he had given up Louis for lost, after his accepting the Constitution of 1791, which he did in September. Burke now favoured counter-revolutionary war against the French regime of which Louis was the nominal head. 'I am afraid' Burke wrote on 16 August 1791, 'that the war in favour of Monarchy must be against the Monarch as well as against the Rebels'.[2]

Marie-Antoinette had read the famous passage about herself in the *Reflections*, and had wept as she read it. But by the force of things, she was now on the other side, as far as Burke was concerned. Both she and Louis had become compliant prisoners of the Revolution since their recapture, and the king was already preparing to swear allegiance to the Constitution. Furthermore, she hated the exiled princes and was said to fear that to become the objects of a restoration headed by them would be even worse than revolutionary captivity. Burke wrote to her in August, respectfully and compassionately, but with an underlying sternness, advocating silence, as the best recourse of imprisoned royalty:

Circumstances require that my Words should be few: My Sentiments demand that they should be faithful. They cannot be ceremonious.

Since the commencement of these troubles you had a part to act which has fixed the Eyes of the world upon you. You have sufferd much affliction; but you have obtained great glory. Your conduct at this great Crisis will determine whether affliction and shame together are to attend on your Life and your memory as long as both shall last. Your place, your dangers, your interest, your fame, the great Objects of your fears, and

[1] O'Gorman, *Whig Party etc.* p. 79.
[2] *Corr.* VI, 339–341. He was convinced as early as January 1791 that the Revolution could be overcome only by armed force: 'You have an armed tyranny to deal with, and nothing but arms can bring it down.' *Corr.* VI, 210–213.

hopes, will not suffer your conduct to be governd by little politicks.

It cannot be supposed for an instant that you can think of recommending any settlement whatsoever, which must dishonour prescribe, and banish all the Kings friends and those of the Monarchy and the Church and to place the whole power of the Kingdom in the hands of their known Enemies who have never omitted any indignity or insult to your person or your fame and have made several attempts on your Life.

For Gods sake have nothing to do with Traitors. Those men can never be seriously disposed to restore the Nation, the King, yourself or your Children, who have been the authors of your common ruin. If they had the inclination, their power has not solidity, consistency, or means of permanence, sufficient to enable them to keep any engagements they may seem to make with you. Their whole power is to hurt you; To serve you they have none.

If the King accepts their pretended constitution you are both of you undone for ever.[1]

As noted earlier, Louis did accept the Constitution in the next month.

The letter, in the form that Burke wrote it, never reached Marie Antoinette, but a summary of it was 'put into her hand'. There is no record of how she reacted, but it must have had a chilling effect, coming from the author of that gorgeous tribute to her youthful self. But both the tribute and the admonition were actions in one and the same cause, products of a heart and a mind dedicated to resisting the French Revolution. That passage in the *Reflections* came from the heart, the letter from the mind. In August also Burke sent his son, Richard Burke (1758–94), to Coblenz to meet Louis-Stanislas-Xavier, the Comte de Provence, the future Louis XVIII, at this time next in line to the throne of France after Louis XVI and the Dauphin. The Comte, who was clever and an author of pamphlets, admired the *Reflections*. He and his exiled court received Richard warmly and the Comte appointed the Chevalier de la Bintinaye to be '*Auprès de M. Burke*' in England.[2] The Comte de Provence was then at the head of the counter-revolutionary movement in Europe. He was clearly grateful for Burke's assurance of support, which was helpful to him from a propaganda point of view, since Burke's name carried great weight with counter-revolutionaries – among whom there were many tendencies, often in conflict – and he also hoped to benefit

---

[1] *Corr.* VI, 349–51. Burke sent a similar message to Louis, through Richard Burke (*Corr.* VI, 318–22).

[2] Richard Burke to Edmund Burke, 16 August, 1791, *Corr.* VI, 342–7.

from Burke's influence with the British ministers: an influence which was real, though limited.

The Burke mission to Coblenz, followed by the quasi-accreditation of a princely representative '*Auprès de M. Burke*', made up a strange episode, and one indicative of Burke's unique significance in the European politics of the 1790s. He had no office, and would never again hold any. He belonged to no party, and never again would belong to one. In the political life of Great Britain he appeared to be entirely isolated, although he was in fact on the eve of making a political breakthrough. Yet even at the apparent nadir of his political fortunes, the radiations of his mind, and the resonance of his words, penetrate the entire civilised world. Princes are thinking about him and so are revolutionaries: the King of Poland writes to him, and so does the Pope.

In Britain too, even at the deepest point of his isolation, Burke remained a force to be reckoned with. The Whigs, as a body now hated and feared him (though not as much as they were to do a few years later: see below pp. 501–3). Pitt and his ministers valued him as an ally against the Whigs, but knew him to be an uncontrollable ally, and therefore to be handled warily though with respect. One would expect Pitt, and especially his Foreign Secretary, William Windham Grenville (1759–1834), to have been infuriated by Burke's presumption in setting up, as it were, an alternative Foreign Office of his own, as exemplified by Richard's mission to Coblenz, and the 'accreditation' of La Bintinaye. If so, they gave no outward sign of resentment. I suspect, although there is no record of such a transaction, that Burke informed Grenville in advance and received at least his tacit approval. The British Government could have no dealings with what was in effect a government in exile, since Britain still recognised the revolutionary government in Paris: a government still nominally headed by Louis. But it may have suited the British to keep channels open to the Comte de Provence, through private individuals who could be disavowed officially, and dismissed as negligible. When La Bintinaye arrived in England, in September, Burke asked Henry Dundas, Pitt's closest collaborator, and Grenville to see him. Dundas refused but Grenville agreed 'to show him any little attention in my power.'[1]

[1] *Corr.* VI, 396–8.

IRELAND 1790–92:
THE BURKES AND THE CATHOLIC COMMITTEE
1790–1792

I suggested in Chapter IV that Ireland – in particular Burke's relation to the Irish Catholics – had something to do with his commitment to India. In the early 1790s Burke once more had an opportunity to be of direct service to the Irish Catholics. Serving them at any time during the eighteenth century was a hazardous affair and at this time it presented new hazards, and somewhat paradoxical ones, from Burke's point of view. On 13 August 1790 Thomas Hussey (1741–1803), later President of Maynooth College and first Catholic Bishop of Waterford, wrote to Burke transmitting a letter from the Catholic Committee to his son Richard 'as a Professional Gentleman'.[1] This first overture to Richard asked his help in drafting an Appeal to the nation. A year later came an offer of appointment as agent to the Committee. With Edmund's approval Richard accepted appointment in September. His father took a strong advisory interest in Richard's activities as agent. Yet the Burke involvement with the Catholic Committee sat rather awkwardly with Edmund's general position on the French Revolution. That position was never definitely incompatible with his position on Ireland, but there was a marked tension between the two.

The Catholic Committee had been in existence since the 1760s, but it became inactive after 1783, when the Irish Volunteers' Convention in Dublin avoided committing itself to Catholic enfranchisement. The Committee revived suddenly in 1790 under the stimulus, direct and indirect, of the French Revolution and the Declaration of the Rights of Man and of the Citizen. Directly, the Revolution and its Declaration encouraged the disfranchised Catholics by making political disfranchisement on 'religious' grounds, appear in conflict with the spirit of the age. They also helped indirectly, by the encouragement they gave to those radical Dissenters, mainly Belfast Presbyterians, who had come to favour the enfranchisement of Catholics as part of a general enlargement of the franchise, leading to a radicalisation of politics. Such people had been active in the later stages of the Irish Volunteer movement, and had received a setback with the failure of the Dublin Convention of 1783 (see Chapter III above, pp. 248–9).

[1] *Corr.* VI, 133.

Their hopes of a brighter future for Irish radicalism were rekindled by the French Revolution. Under that stimulus, and aided by the skilful and energetic radical lawyer and publicist, Theobald Wolfe Tone (1763–1798), himself a deist of Anglican background, radical dissenters founded the Society of United Irishmen in Belfast in October, 1791.[1] A Dublin Society of the same name was founded in November, also with Tone's participation. The Society of United Irishmen, as its name implied, was open to all Irishmen, irrespective of religion, and it was firmly committed to full enfranchisement of Catholics, and removal of all Catholic legal and political liabilities. On those grounds alone, the leaders of the Catholic Committee – of whom the most prominent were the wealthy merchants John Keogh and Edward Byrne – valued the United Irishmen as allies. Yet some eminent Catholics, such as the leading Catholic landowner, Lord Kenmare, broke with the Catholic Committee, in this period, partly because of its associations with the Northern radicals. Some of the senior Catholic clergy also held aloof from the Committee on the same grounds, and even those who on the whole sided with the Committee had their misgivings. Thomas Hussey, who had acted as intermediary between the Committee and the Burkes, was one of the latter. Hussey's ambivalence appears shortly after he had put Richard in touch with the Catholic Committee. He wrote to Richard: 'Should these Kingdoms be involved in a war, a further toleration to the Catholics of necessity should compel, what true Policy ought to offer voluntarily i.e. enfranchisement. Hitherto the Catholics of that Country have proceeded with proper deference, and submission to the laws, in their application for redress, notwithstanding the endeavors of *neighboring* Countries, suggesting to them to wrest by *force*, and *violence*, what, I hope, they will never mention, but with moderation, and temper. Sublimated, however, as mens minds are by the *french disease*, (as it is not improperly called) one cannot foresee, what a continuation of oppressive laws may work upon the minds of people: and those of the Irish Catholics are much altered within my own Memory; and they will not in future bear the lash of

---

[1] These remarks on Wolfe Tone are apropos Tone's reputation in 1790–1, and not his later fame as a revolutionary leader and martyr. For Tone and the United Irishmen see especially Marianne Elliott's two valuable works, *Wolfe Tone: Prophet of Irish Independence* (Yale U.P. 1989) and *Partners in Revolution: The United Irishmen and France* (Yale, 1982). There are also important essays in Hugh Gough and David Dickson (eds.) *Ireland and the French Revolution* (Irish Academic Press, Dublin, 1990).

Tirranny and oppression which I have seen inflicted upon them, without their resisting or even complaining.'[1] In September 1791, when Richard Burke agreed to serve as agent for the Catholic Committee 'the *french disease*' was even more rife: the Society of the United Irishmen at once abetted the Committee's work. Richard, with Edmund's full approval, was now in a kind of tacit alliance with the ideological enemies, in Ireland, of his father's book.

After the *Reflections* had reached Ireland, followed by Paine's *Rights of Man*, politically-minded and literate people became divided between those who agreed with Burke and those who agreed with Paine. Wolfe Tone wrote: 'In England, Burke had the triumph completely to decide the public; fascinated by the eloquent publication, which flattered so many of their prejudices, and animated by their unconquerable hatred of France, . . . the whole English nation, it may be said, retreated from their first decision in favour of the glorious and successful efforts of the French people . . . But matters were very different in Ireland, an oppressed, insulted, and plundered nation. In a little time the French Revolution became the test of every man's political creed.' Paine had won, in Ireland, Tone thought, and certainly the United Irishmen were all Paine people.[2] An Irish friend of Burke's was of a different opinion: concerning the reception in Ireland of the *Reflections*: 'It is impossible to conceive how greatly [Burke's] admirers on this occasion exceed in numbers those who are of another opinion . . . his print [of *Reflections*] and bits of his hair are sought for and produced, or worn as tokens of being of the same sentiments, and admiring the work.'[3]

It is unlikely that Richard Burke saw any tokens of that kind on people with whom he became associated in Ireland. The leaders of the Catholic Committee were discreet, but they tended to share the general outlook of their United Irish friends, who were Paine people and not Burke people; not by any means. Why then, did they employ Burke's son? It is generally agreed that they did so in order to ensure Burke's support. But his support for the enfranchisement of Catholics had been apparent for nearly thirty years, often to his detriment. It looks as if what was needed was a sign of approval specifically for the Catholic Committee, then engaged on a controversial, and not obviously Burkean, course. Richard's appointment would tend to reassure those Catholics who were worried about '*the french*

[1] *Corr.* VI, 134.
[2] *Autobiography* of Theobald Wolfe Tone (London, 1893) Vol. I, p. 38.
[3] *Corr.* VI, 193: quoting letter of 23 December 1790 from Thomas Barnard.

disease'. It seems likely indeed that it was Thomas Hussey, himself worried about '*the french disease*', who recommended Richard's appointment.

It might have been expected that Burke's influence, working through his devoted son, might tend to separate the Catholics from their United Irish allies (for those Dissenters who favoured Catholic enfranchisement were all, or almost all, by the end of 1791, at least sympathisers with the United Irishmen). Yet Burke opposed any such separation, in 1791–2, although the Pitt Administration (which Burke otherwise supported) was actively trying to bring about such an outcome, and so advising the Irish government. On 15 September 1791 Edmund wrote to Richard. 'The Ministers in Ireland are mad or think the Catholics so in proposing an open Rupture between them and the Protestant Dissenters before the State-Church thinks fit to put those people so much upon a footing as to balance each other. But for them to make an open Quarrel with a great, perhaps the greatest party in the Country for no other Reason than that they offer them the whole of what they themselves possess, whilst the others are making an hard bargain upon a most scanty and penurious distribution of what they have given without any limit or measure whatsoever to those with whom they have the folly to desire the others to quarrel. It is too much to propose to rational Creatures in their Situation. It is what they would have accepted some time ago, because they would have done any thing, with any consequences, for the slightest hope of the most triffling relaxation. But now they stand on the firm bottom of Legal protection, and of several of the modes of acquiring and keeping property, and they can negotiate for the rest upon some Terms consistent with common Sense.'[1]

At first sight, this position might seem un-Burkean. Burke had opposed any tendency to an alliance between Catholics and radical Dissenters in 1783, six years before there was any French Revolution to be considered. How, then, could he find such an alliance acceptable in 1791, when the Dissenters in question had become enthusiastic supporters of the French Revolution?

The answer lies in the different political circumstances – always a key consideration for Burke – in Ireland. In 1783 there was no major open political movement of Catholics demanding enfranchisement.

---

[1] *Corr.* VI, 462. The 'firm bottom' referred to here is that furnished by the Catholic Relief Acts (1778–82), largely shaped by Burke.

In 1791 there was. In 1783 the radical Dissenters, whose basic demand was for widening the property franchise, included Catholic enfranchisement in the package, in the hope of broadening the support for their general programme. Burke believed the Catholics should not be drawn in that direction. In general, he was suspicious of proposals for enlarging the franchise, and there were specific reasons, affecting the interests of the Catholics, for opposing such a measure in late eighteenth-century Ireland. The kind of measure the radical Dissenters had in mind in 1783 would have put political power into the hands of the Irish middle-classes, who were then overwhelmingly Protestant (with a high proportion of Dissenters who, outside Belfast, were by no means all pro-Catholic). A middle-class Protestant parliament, in the 1780's, would be likely to be even more resistant to Catholic enfranchisement than a landlord Parliament. So the offer of the radical Dissenters, in 1783, however, well-intentioned, would turn out, in practice, to be a trap, so Burke thought. In 1791, however, there was no question, at least as far as the Catholic Committee was concerned, of any political bargain. Radical Dissenters were still in favour of a wider property-franchise, but they were offering unreserved support, politically gratis, to the declared objective of the Catholic movement. Both the Pitt and the Dublin Castle Administrations were advising the Catholics to repudiate that support. But Burke knew that the people who gave that advice had no present intention of conceding full Catholic enfranchisement. The advice was given in the hope of avoiding any such outcome, by splitting the supporters of enfranchisement. Burke's long and deep commitment to Catholic enfranchisement swung him towards countering a tactic devised by its adversaries, for its frustration.

Both the Catholic commitment and the tactic were in fundamental accord, in 1791–3, though in surface tension, with Burke's commitment against the French Revolution and its influence, both in Ireland and in Britain. Burke saw the stigmatised condition of the Irish Catholics – their not being treated as full and equal citizens – as the factor that laid them most open to the seductions of Jacobin ideology. If they were fully enfranchised, Burke thought they would fall more under the influence of their natural leaders – Catholic clergy, gentry, merchants – who themselves would be more resistant to radical influences, once their own status was securely accepted. In short, Burke accepted a degree of tactical alignment with the radicals, in order to defeat them later on, at the level of political strategy. As often, though not always, an apparent inconsequence on Burke's part turns out, when carefully scrutinised, to exemplify a deep underlying coherence and consistency of thought, feeling and purpose.

Burke's hopes of what might be achieved through the tactical alignment, necessarily yielded to foreboding, after the Irish Parliament, in February 1792, contemptuously rejected the Catholic petition for enfranchisement. The concession of full enfranchisement might perhaps have turned the Catholics away from the radicals; the rejection of enfranchisement implied the sealing of a Catholic-radical alliance with potential revolutionary implications (which were to become apparent three years later). Both Burkes were deeply apprehensive. On 23 February Richard wrote to Edmund saying that the Catholics stand 'in an ugly predicament; for the northern allies are the only ones who have stood forward and to whom they in great measure owe (as I think) the Parliamentary support they have had.'

'Our petition has had a companion in its misfortune; the Belfast petition [for enfranchisement of Dissenters]. Dissenter and Catholic are turn'd a drift together – Thus hand in hand; but whether with wandering steps and *slow*, God knows. The marriage however is not yet made to couple the two parties.'[1]

As can be seen from these comments, Richard inherited, or had acquired by example, some part of his father's political insight and powers of expression. His own political efforts were, however, unfortunate. He was tactless in the extreme. He talked down to important people, including Portland and Fitzwilliam, and wrote them didactic letters of inordinate length. Even his adoring father refers sadly to his 'ample letters'. His indiscretions earned him many enemies, in Britain, in Ireland and in Europe, and many scathing accounts of him are on record, from people of widely differing political views. Probably the fairest account comes from Wolfe Tone, who succeeded Richard, in the summer of 1792, as agent to the Catholic Committee: 'Richard Burke, with a considerable portion of talents from nature and cultivated, as may be well supposed, with the utmost care by his father who idolized him, was utterly deficient in judgement, in temper and especially the art of managing. In three or four months, during which he remained in Ireland, he contrived to embroil himself, and in a certain degree, the Committee, with all parties in Parliament, the Opposition as well as the Government, and finally, desiring to drive his employers into measures, of which they disapproved . . . he

[1] *Corr.* VII, 68–74.

ended his short and troubled career by breaking with the Catholic Committee.'[1]

The evidence of intelligence, especially in Richard's many letters to his father, is hard to reconcile with the abundant evidence of his blundering in practice. But there is something feverish, both about many of his letters, and about his reported conduct. I suggest that the disease – tuberculosis – which was to destroy him in 1794, to the affliction of his father's last three years of life, was already at work in 1791. Even if Richard had been a more effective, and healthier, agent, he could not have accomplished what the Catholic Committee wanted him to do. A majority in the Irish Parliament which enjoyed 'legislative independence' since 1782, was implacably opposed in 1791–2 to Catholic enfranchisement (as distinct from forms of Catholic relief which did not admit any Catholics to any share of political power). Real, as distinct from formal, political authority still resided in the British Government. The Catholic Committee wanted Richard Burke, its agent in Britain, to persuade (no doubt with his father's assistance) Pitt's Administration to put enough pressure on the Irish Parliament to bring about Catholic enfranchisement. The Irish executive, in Dublin Castle, was controlled from London and could swing votes through the patronage at its disposal. But Pitt did not want to do this, in 1791–2. In principle, Pitt was in favour of Catholic enfranchisement. In practice, his Administration, like most other British Administrations, usually wanted Ireland to be governed with as little trouble, and as little cost, as possible. On the whole the course that seemed to promise the least trouble and the least cost was to refrain from irritating the Irish ruling class, now embattled under the new and provocative title the 'Protestant Ascendancy'. This meant leaving the Catholics disfranchised. The calculations that led Pitt to pursue this policy in 1791–2 were not likely to be changed by long letters from Richard Burke. He could report no progress and was dismissed in consequence by his impatient employers, in July 1792. Richard never accepted his dismissal, which was ambiguously worded, and as it happened by far his most effective work, towards the objectives of the Committee was performed at the end of the same year under dramatically altered circumstances (see below, pp. 496–7).

William Pitt, in conniving, for the moment, at the continuing disfranchisement of Catholics, was impenetrably armoured against criti-

---

[1] *Life of Theobald Wolfe Tone*, Vol. I, p. 51. Richard was dismissed by the Committee on 30 June 1792, but did not understand the polite letter (drafted by Wolfe Tone himself) as the dismissal which it actually was.

cism from the Opposition, including Burke. Pitt, after all, was doing no more than paying the most scrupulous respect to the 'legislative independence' of the Irish Parliament. It was the Whigs who had granted that independence, nine years before. They were hardly in a position to criticise Pitt for respecting it too much. (Such criticism would in any case have been difficult in the British Parliament under the rules of procedure, since the very notion of 'legislative independence' for 'Ireland' seemed to preclude it). And they were precluded by their fundamental principles from demanding that the Catholics should be emancipated in the only way that the Irish Parliament could ever be induced to emancipate them; that is to say by bribing the Members, through the use of Crown patronage – which is how the Irish Parliament was induced to abolish itself and its legislative independence, nine years later, three years after Burke's death. The Whigs could not possibly condone the use of Crown patronage for any kind of corruption; they had been fighting that all their political lives. And least of all could they condone Crown corruption for the purpose of undermining a legislative independence they had prided themselves on having created. Not by any means a promising ground for effective opposition.

Most Whigs probably did not care much about the difficulties of opposing Pitt's Irish policy since they cared little about the 'disabilities of the Irish Catholics'. But for Burke, who did care deeply about the disabilities, the impossibility of carrying out an effective parliamentary campaign against Pitt's Irish policy must have been intensely frustrating. Burke had got himself into one of his false positions on 'legislative independence'; this was always more likely to happen to him over Irish matters than over anything else. When legislative independence was first mooted by Henry Grattan, in 1781, he had been greatly alarmed. (See Chapter III above, pp. 243–5: 'Will no one stop this madman, Grattan?'). Real legislative independence, for an entirely Protestant Parliament, would mean perpetual disenfranchisement for the Irish Catholics. Burke had been inhibited, for reasons already considered, from conveying to his Whig colleagues the nature and strength of his opposition to legislative independence. Eventually, finding that what was proposed was something considerably less than full independence, he came round and acquiesced in the proposed version, which he subsequently hailed for its completeness (while in reality all that he felt satisfied about was its *in*completeness). He now found that the concept of 'legislative independence', even in the limited version it had assumed, could still be used for the purposes he had originally feared: the denial of the franchise to the Catholics. And Burke was estopped by his own past words and actions, from any direct attack on 'legislative independence', and by his basic Whig principles, from any public condonation of the only means by which the Irish Parliament could be induced to accept Catholic enfranchisememt; which was, by Crown bribery.

On Irish or Irish-related affairs, up to now, Edmund Burke had always preferred to work behind the scenes as much as possible: as over Catholic Relief in 1778. On America, on India and on France, he had made major speeches in Parliament, and had written major tracts for publication. But on Ireland he had spoken relatively little, often in self-defense, and often cryptically. The 'corruption' passage in the 1780 Bristol Guildhall speech remained absolutely exceptional, as a cry from the heart concerning the condition of the Irish Catholics (and of the Burkes). The *Tract Relative to the Laws against Popery*, of the early 1760s, was (see Chapter I above, p. 82) intended for circulation among influential people, not for publication, and was never published in his lifetime. His first major public statement on Ireland is the *Letter to Sir Hercules Langrishe*, of 3 January 1792[1]. In form it was a personal letter but its length, sixty printed pages, and presentation, suggest it was always intended to be published, as it was, in February. Feeling unable to give effective support to the Irish Catholics either behind the scenes or on the floor of the House, he decided to try an appeal to the Irish Parliament itself, through the person of one of its most distinguished members. Burke knew that the chances of making any impact there were quite low, but that kind of consideration seldom deterred him from trying, if only for acquittal of conscience; indeed this was frequently a strong motive with him. (A subsidiary motive was probably to help Richard, with the Catholic Committee.) He was also probably glad of an occasion – now that he was free from all party ties and all political ambitions – to speak far more freely in public about those matters on which he had exercised so much reticence for so long.

Langrishe had once been 'an eloquent advocate of Catholic relief'. In 1791, however, he was in favour of relief, short of enfranchisement. He was favourably inclined to the 'moderate' demands of those land-owning Catholics (headed by Lord Kenmare), who had resigned from the Catholic Committee in December 1791,[2] because of what

[1] *Works*. IV, 241–306.
[2] *Corr*. VII, 6, n. 1.

they saw as its extremism, and suspect connections with the radical Dissenters of Belfast who had set up the Society of United Irishmen in October of that year. Langrishe had outlined proposals embodying the aspirations of the Kenmare group in the Irish House of Commons on 25 January 1792. The proposals, later embodied in a Bill, which carried, removed Catholic disabilities in four fields – law, education, intermarriage and apprenticeships – but they did not provide for enfranchisement.

Langrishe's January proposals were the occasions for Burke's letter. Privately, he did not trust Langrishe very far.[1] But his past exertions on behalf of measures of Catholic emancipation entitled him to some respect, and Burke also shared at least a part of his reservations about those radical Dissenters and their pro-French tendencies. Burke now set out to try to convince Langrishe (and others) that further resistance to Catholic enfranchisement would drive the Catholics into the arms of the radical Dissenters and ultimately of the French.

Burke was replying to a letter written to him by Langrishe on 10 December 1791, in order to commend to him the 'Herculean' proposals for limited Catholic relief. In making this case, Langrishe offered a constitutional argument which touched Burke at the most sensitive point in his political psyche. The State had to be fully Protestant, Langrishe had argued, because 'it was declared so at the Revolution. It was so provided in the acts for settling the succession of the crown: – the king's coronation oath was enjoined in order to keep it so. The king, as first magistrate of the state, is obliged to take the oath of abjuration, and to subscribe the Declaration; and by laws subsequent, every other magistrate and member of the state, legislative and executive, are bound under the same obligation.'

Burke rebuts Langrishe effectively on the Coronation Oath:

Before we take it for granted that the king is bound by his coronation oath not to admit any of his Catholic subjects to the rights and liberties which ought to belong to them as Englishmen, (not as religionists,) or to settle the conditions or proportions of such admission by an act of Parliament, I wish you to place before your eyes that oath itself, as it is settled in the act of William and Mary:

'Will you to the utmost of your power maintain the laws of God, the

---

[1] See, for example, Burke's negative reference to 'the Herculean faction' in the Irish House of Commons. (*Corr.* VII, 204; letter of 9, 10 September 1792 to Richard Burke jr.) Richard, for his part, thought Langrishe 'a rogue'.

true profession of the Gospel, and the Protestant Reformed Religion *established by law*? And will you preserve unto the *bishops* and clergy of this realm, and to the churches committed to *their* charge, all such rights and privileges as by law do or shall appertain unto them, or any of them? – All this I promise to do' [Burke's italics].

In these coronation engagements of William III, I do not find one word to preclude him from consenting to any arrangement which Parliament may make with regard to the civil privileges of any part of his subjects.

In marking the Coronation Oath, Burke emphasises those words which show that it is an oath to support one specific Church only, and not Protestantism-in-general. From this inroad into his adversary's position, he goes on to open up a wide-ranging attack against the idea of a privileged position of Protestantism-in-general over Catholics-in-general, as being something sanctioned by the Revolution Settlement.

For reasons forcible enough at all times, but at this time particularly forcible with me, I dwell a little the longer upon this matter, and take the more pains, to put us both in mind that it was not settled at the Revolution that the state should be Protestant, in the latitude of the term, but in a defined and limited sense only, and that in that sense only the king is sworn to maintain it. To suppose that the king has sworn with his utmost power to maintain what it is wholly out of his power to discover, or which, if he could discover, he might discover to consist of things directly contradictory to each other, some of them perhaps impious, blasphemous, and seditious upon principle, would be not only a gross, but a most mischievous absurdity. If mere dissent from the Church of Rome be a merit, he that dissents the most perfectly is the most meritorious. In many points we hold strongly with that church. He that dissents throughout with that church will dissent with the Church of England, and then it will be a part of his merit that he dissents with ourselves: a whimsical species of merit for any set of men to establish. We quarrel to extremity with those who we know agree with us in many things; but we are to be so malicious even in the principle of our friendships, that we are to cherish in our bosom those who accord with us in nothing, because, whilst they despise ourselves, they abhor, even more than we do, those with whom we have some disagreement. A man is certainly the most perfect Protestant who protests against the whole Christian religion. Whether a person's having no Christian religion be a title to favor, in exclusion to the largest description of Christians, who hold all the doctrines of Christianity, though holding along with them some errors and some superfluities, is rather more than any man, who has not become recreant and apostate from his baptism, will, I believe, choose to affirm. The countenance given from a spirit of controversy to that negative religion may by degrees encourage light and unthinking people to a total indifference to everything positive in matters of doctrine, and, in the end, of practice too. If continued, it would play the game of that sort of active, proselytizing, and persecuting atheism which is the disgrace and calamity of our time, and which we see to be as capable of subverting a government as any mode can be of misguided zeal for better things.

After some skirmishing points, Burke next moves to establish a distinction never before publicly pointed out by him, although implicitly always present in his long commitment to Catholic relief. This is a distinction between the general principles of the Glorious Revolution and some of its actual practices, especially in Ireland, and in relation to Catholics:

I therefore pass by all this, which on you will make no impression, to come to what seems to be a serious consideration in your mind: I mean the dread you express of "reviewing, for the purpose of altering, the *principles of the Revolution*." This is an interesting topic, on which I will, as fully as your leisure and mine permits, lay before you the ideas I have formed.

First, I cannot possibly confound in my mind all the things, which were done at the Revolution with the *principles* of the Revolution. As in most great changes, many things were done from the necessities of the time, well or ill understood, from passion or from vengeance, which were not only not perfectly agreeable to its principles, but in the most direct contradiction to them. I shall not think that the *deprivation of some millions of people of all the rights of citizens, and all interest in the Constitution, in and to which they were born,* was a thing comfortable to the *declared principles* of the Revolution. This I am sure is true relatively to England (where the operation of these *anti-principles* comparatively were of little extent); and some of our late laws, in repealing acts made immediately after the Revolution, admit that some things then done were not done in the true spirit of the Revolution. But the Revolution operated differently in England and Ireland, in many, and these essential particulars. Supposing the principles to have been altogether the same in both kingdoms, by the application of those principles to very different objects the whole spirit of the system was changed, not to say reversed. In England it was the struggle of the *great body* of the people for the establishment of their liberties, against the efforts of a very *small faction*, who would have oppressed them. In Ireland it was the establishment of the power of the smaller number, at the expense of the civil liberties and properties of the far greater part, and at the expense of the political liberties of the whole. It was, to say the truth, not a revolution, but a conquest: which is not to say a great deal in its favor. To insist on everything done in Ireland at the Revolution would be to insist on the severe and jealous policy of a conqueror, in the crude settlement of his new acquisition, as a *permanent* rule for its future government [Burke's italics throughout].

There follows a brief description of the situation in Ireland in the aftermath of the Glorious Revolution:

The new English interest was settled with as solid a stability as anything in human affairs can look for. All the penal laws of that unparalleled code of oppression, which were made after the last event, were manifestly the effects of national hatred and scorn towards a conquered people, whom the victors delighted to trample upon and were not at all afraid to provoke. They were not the effect of their fears, but of their security. They who carried on this system looked to the irresistible force of Great Britain for their support in their acts of power. They were quite certain that no complaints of the natives would be heard on this side of the water with any other sentiments than those of contempt and indignation. Their cries served only to augment their torture. Machines which could answer their purposes so well must be of an excellent contrivance. Indeed, in England, the double name of the complainants, Irish and Papists, (it would be hard to say which singly was the most odious,) shut up the hearts of every one against them. Whilst that temper prevailed, (and it prevailed in all its force to a time within our memory,) every measure was pleasing and popular just in proportion as it tended to harass and ruin a set of people who were looked upon as enemies to God and man, and, indeed, as a race of bigoted savages who were a disgrace to human nature itself.

Next, in the same letter, comes the famous definition of the Penal System:

It was a machine of wise and elaborate contrivance, and as well fitted for the oppression, impoverishment, and degradation of a people, and the debasement, in them, of human nature itself, as ever proceeded from the perverted ingenuity of man.

These passages completely demolished (without mentioning) the idyllic picture of Ireland's share in the blessings of the British Constitution which Burke had presented to the Commons eighteen years before (see Chapter II above, pp. 151–2). They also seriously qualify the no less idyllic and much more recent general picture of the Glorious Revolution offered in the peroration of *An Appeal from the New to the Old Whigs*. The ageing Burke has dropped pretences, and emerged from concealment, in matters of great moment to him. The pretences had been only occasional, and the two examples cited are the only major ones, among his published works. But the conceal-ment had been habitual with him since his boyhood, and must have been hard to break from. He had never indeed concealed his detes-tation of the Penal Laws themselves. What he had concealed – with the exception of a single isolated outburst in the Bristol Guildhall speech of 1780 – was the extent of his emotional identification with the historical experience of the conquered people. This was a final sacrifice for him to make in the cause of the Irish Catholics, whose emancipation he hoped to help to complete before his death, by unreserved support for the efforts of the Catholic Committee.

In writing to Langrishe, Burke stresses the continuity of his own thinking on these matters: 'Though my hand but signs it, my heart goes with what I have written. Since I could think at all, those have been my thoughts.' We may be sure that these had indeed always been his thoughts. But he had kept much of them to himself, up to now. His strategy with regard to Irish affairs, especially Irish Catholic affairs, had been such, during most of his life, as to preclude Ireland's becoming a major theme of Burke's oratory, or of that part of his writing what most resembles his oratory. Ireland profoundly affects the Great Melody, but mostly indirectly, through inflections, mainly on the themes of India and France, and sometimes on America also. The *Letter to Sir Hercules Langrishe*, by itself, constitutes most of that part of the Great Melody which is directly about Ireland.

Burke acknowledges that what he has written has become, through its length, more like a dissertation than a letter. This had also been the case with that 'Letter to a gentleman in Paris', which turned into *Reflections on the Revolution in France*. But much more than the *Reflections*, the 'Letter' to Langrishe preserves the tone of a real letter. Burke is really directing his argument at Langrishe, though he hopes to reach others with it too. He never forgets the person he is writing to, as he does in long sections of the *Reflections*. And he uses the (relative) informality of the letter form to dazzling effect, in swift changes of mood and pace. The paragraph I am about to quote starts with a burst of rollicking sarcastic humour: the sort of thing the Commons liked but Johnson disapproved of as 'low'. But then Burke suddenly stops laughing. He makes the abrupt transition magnifi-cently, with one of the most profound examples of the Burkean aphorism. The rest of the paragraph is a penetrating assessment of the dangerously impalpable *modus operandi* of the prejudices referred to earlier with such hilarity.

Burke begins by assuming, not entirely without artifice, that Langrishe, being a child of the Enlightenment, is altogether superior to the vulgar prejudices Burke is about to consider:

> As little shall I detain you with matters that can as little obtain admission into a mind like yours: such as the fear, or pretence of fear, that, in spite of your own power and the trifling power of Great Britain, you may be conquered by the Pope; or that this commodious bugbear (who is of infinitely more use to those who pretend to fear than to those who love him) will absolve his Majesty's subjects from their allegiance, and send over the Cardinal of York to rule you as his viceroy; or that, by the plenitude of his power, he will take that fierce tyrant, the king of the French, out of his jail, and arm that nation (which on all occasions treats his Holiness so very politely) with his bulls and pardons, to invade poor old Ireland, to reduce you to Popery and slavery, and to force the free-born, naked feet of your people into the wooden shoes of that arbitrary monarch. I do not believe that discourses of this kind are held, or that anything like them will be held, by any who walk about without a keeper. *Yet I confess, that, on occasions of this nature, I am the most afraid of the weakest reasonings, because they discover the strongest passions* [my italics – C.C.O'B.]. These things will never be brought out in definite propositions. They would not prevent pity towards any persons; they would only cause it for those who were capable of talking in such a strain. But I know, and am sure, that such ideas as no man will distinctly produce to another, or hardly venture to bring in any plain shape to his own mind, he will utter in obscure, ill-explained doubts, jealousies, surmises, fears, and apprehensions, and that in such a fog they will appear to have a good deal of size, and will make an impression, when, if they were clearly brought forth and defined, they would meet with nothing but scorn and derision.

Burke had often encountered that particular fog, especially in his youth in Ireland, and had become accustomed to keeping his mouth shut, when it was around him. But now he could speak out. He knows that the most effective argument at his disposal, in relation to the Parliament of which Langrishe is a member, is that it is no longer safe to keep the Catholics disenfranchised. If members of the Established Church insist on that, they will push the Catholics into the arms of the radical Dissenters, the United Irishmen, and so in the direction of revolution:

You are to weigh, with the temper [coolness] which is natural to you, whether it may be for the safety of our establishment that the Catholics should be ultimately persuaded that they have no hope to enter into the Constitution but through the Dissenters. . . .[1]

Suppose the people of Ireland divided into three parts. Of these, (I speak within compass,) two are Catholic; of the remaining third, one half is composed of Dissenters. There is no natural union between those descriptions. It may be produced. If the two parts Catholic be driven into a close confederacy with half the third part of Protestants, with a view to a change in the Constitution in Church or State or both, and you rest the whole of their security on a handful of gentlemen, clergy, and their dependents, – compute the strength *you have in Ireland*, to oppose to grounded discontent, to capricious innovation, to blind popular fury, and to ambitious, turbulent intrigue.[2]

The publication of *A Letter to Sir Hercules Langrishe* was ill received in Dublin Castle. The Lord Lieutenant, Lord Westmorland, in a letter to Pitt, referred to Richard Burke as bent on 'inflammation' in Ireland and went on: 'If the Father is a Friend of Peace it was most injudicious to publish that inflammatory Letter to Sir Hercules Langrishe.'[3] Burke was certainly a sincere 'Friend of Peace', in that he believed that Catholic enfranchisement would work in that direction. Yet Westmorland had a point too. Language such as Burke was using necessarily did have an inflammatory effect, as long as enfranchisement was denied. So, against an Administration still committed to that denial, Burke's language was certainly inflammatory. But Burke, not unreasonably, put the blame for all the inflammation on the unjust and unwise denial of enfranchisement, and not on his own critique of that policy.

The *Letter to Sir Hercules Langrishe* was a public document and thus, though more candid than had been usual with Burke, on this subject, less than completely so. A passage in an unfinished letter to Richard in the following year provides a rare glimpse into Burke's uncensored feelings concerning the history of Ireland. He is discussing Protestant arguments about titles to land:

---

[1] 'Our establishment' is here that of the Church of Ireland. Langrishe may well have taken the expression, coming from Burke, with a pinch of salt.

[2] *Letter to Sir Hercules Langrishe* in *Works* IV, 245; 260; 262–4; 271–2; 274–5; 280–1; 302; 305.

[3] *Corr.* VII, 48, n.1.

They would not set men upon calling from the quiet sleep of death any Samuel, to ask him by what act of arbitrary monarchs, by what inquisitions of corrupted tribunals and tortured jurors, by what fictitious tenures invented to dispossess whole unoffending tribes and their chieftains [incomplete]. They would not conjure up the ghosts from the ruins of castles and churches, to tell for what attempt to struggle for the independence of an Irish legislature, and to raise armies of volunteers without regular commissions from the crown in support of that independence, the estates of the old Irish nobility and gentry had been confiscated. They would not wantonly call on those phantoms to tell by what English acts of Parliament, forced upon two reluctant kings, the lands of their country were put up to a mean and scandalous auction in every goldsmith's shop in London, or chopped to pieces and cut into rations, to pay the mercenary soldiery of a regicide usurper. They would not be so fond of titles under Cromwell, who, if he avenged an Irish rebellion against the sovereign authority of the Parliament of England, had himself rebelled against the very Parliament whose sovereignty he asserted, full as much as the Irish nation, which he was sent to subdue and confiscate, could rebel against that Parliament, or could rebel against the king, against whom both he and the Parliament which he served, and which he betrayed, had both of them rebelled.[1]

This passage shows how fervently Burke shared the views and feelings general among the Irish Catholic gentry concerning the history of their country.

THE REVOLUTION SPREADS FROM FRANCE
1792–1793

1792 was a breakthrough year for Burke, in the sense that this was the year that the French Revolution began unmistakably to live up to his vision of it. On 20 April, the National Assembly declared war on Austria.[2] The Declaration affirmed, in the name of the National Assembly, that it 'adopts in advance all foreigners who, abjuring the

---

[1] A Letter to Richard Burke, Esq. on Protestant Ascendancy in Ireland: *Works* VI, 408.

[2] In historical retrospect, the body which declared war (technically on the King of Hungary and Bohemia) is known as 'The Legislative Assembly', elected in October, 1791 after the 'National Constituent Assembly' had completed its Constitution. But the Declaration of War is in the name of 'The National Assembly'.

cause of its enemies, range themselves under its banners and conse-crate their efforts to the defence of its liberty. . . .'[1] Jacques Brissot, the leader of the dominant Girondin faction in the Assembly, pro-claimed the war to be 'a universal crusade for liberty'. At the popular level, the slogan was one of class-war; 'War on the castles, peace to the cabins.' French Revolutionary expansionism, both military and ideological, was now in full spate.

The theory of Fox and Sheridan that the French Revolution was no more than a French internal affair was now in ruins. The pro-French radical societies with which they had flirted ceased to look like groups of harmless enthusiasts and appeared in the sinister guise of people who might be 'ranged under the banners' (in the language of the French Declaration of War on Austria) of a foreign revolutionary assembly. In particular, the formation, by a group of younger Whig parliamentarians, of the Association of the Friends of the People, was acutely embarrassing to the Whig leadership, as it appeared to link the Whigs in Parliament to those who might be ranged under those banners. The Association had been set up on 11 April, little more than a week before the proclamation of 'the universal crusade for liberty'.[2] For the Whigs, this was an unfortunate coincidence.

The time had come for Burke to break the parliamentary silence, over these matters, which he had observed since the breach with Fox. The parliamentary occasion, on 30 April 1792, was better suited to his purposes than to those of his adversaries. This was a 'Debate on Mr Grey's Motion relative to Parliamentary Reform'. The author of the Motion, the young Charles Grey, has been described as 'a restless and disruptive force' in the Whig Party.[3] He was, at this time, more radical than Fox and Sheridan, and had helped to found the Association of Friends of the People. Burke's remaining friends among the Whigs, headed by Portland and Fitzwilliam (see above pp. 461–63) to whom he pinned his hopes, strongly disapproved of Grey and his friends. Grey's theme, Parliamentary Reform, was the main demand of the radical pro-French clubs in the 1790's. Burke had long been suspicious of schemes for Parliamentary Reform (other

---

[1] The text of the declaration (in translation) is in J. H. Stewart (ed), *A Documen-tary Survey of the French Revolution* (Toronto, 1951) pp. 286–288.

[2] E. A. Smith, *Whig Principles and Party Politics*, p. 137, calls the formation of this Association 'the decisive event in the Whig split'. In isolation, it could not have been so, but it became a crux, for conservative Whigs, in the new context created by French Revolutionary expansionism, in its April flood.

[3] O'Gorman, *The Whig Party etc.* p. 8.

than removal of religious barriers) and he was of course adamantly opposed to any reform measures that might benefit the English sympathisers with the French Revolution. So, in the propitious conditions of late April, Grey's motion gave Burke an excellent opportunity to attack the Whig radicals, in the knowledge that many Whigs would be in secret agreement with what he had to say. Burke's attack, as recorded in the *Parliamentary History* was short and sharp:

> There were in this country men who scrupled not to enter into an alliance with a set in France of the worst traitors and regicides that had ever been heard of – the club of the Jacobins. He asked if this was a time for encouraging visionary reforms in this country.[1]

The use of the words 'regicides' is remarkable. Louis XVI was still on his throne, and there were as yet no legal charges against him. But Burke had believed, from very early on, that regicide was implicit in the nature of the French Revolution. Fox's reply was vague, low-key, and cannot have been satisfactory to Grey and his friends. It seems to have encouraged Burke in the hope that Fox might distance himself from the sympathisers with the French Revolution, now that its dangerous character had become so much more obvious. He soon found an opportunity to make a public overture to Fox. On 11 May 1792, the anniversary of the last of the parliamentary debates which had constituted the public breach between them, there was a debate on Fox's 'Motion for the Repeal of Certain Statutes respecting Religious Opinions'.[2]

The overture to Fox was an awkward affair: a little stilted, a little hollow, as if he were forcing himself, in a good cause. He began by praising Fox for 'the delicacy used by the right hon. gentleman in matters of religion. Not one word had dropped from him irreligious or even indifferent.' The implication, as to the real character of Fox's ideas about religion, was plain enough, though presumably unintended in the context. Even more artificially, Burke went on to claim to have arrived, through Fox's speech, at a most satisfactory 'discovery'. Another cause of satisfaction to him was deduced from the discovery 'that the House was untainted by those false principles which had been so amply circulated without doors.' The so-called discovery was really an offer: If Fox would now repudiate 'those false principles', Burke was prepared to forget that Fox had ever been

[1] *Parl. Hist.* xxix, 1322.
[2] *Parl. Hist.* xxix, 1372–1403.

'tainted' by them. Fox's reply was uncompromisingly negative: 'His opinions of the French Revolution were precisely the same now as they had ever been. The right hon. gentleman's book was a libel on every free constitution in the world.' Whatever real, live French Revolutionaries might actually do, Charles James Fox would remain true to the idealised view of the French Revolution that he had formed at the very beginning, in July 1789 (see above p. 396). Burke, for his part, saw the news from France as irrefutable confirmation of the validity of the analysis contained in the book which Fox had once again condemned.

The chasm between them actually widened during the debate. The Pitt Administration, alarmed by the implications of the new 'universal crusade for liberty', was preparing to introduce restrictions on pro-French propaganda – the proclamation 'on seditious Writings', debated in the Commons on 28 May 1792. Those measures during the next three years would be the principal targets of Whig parliamentary rhetoric, couched in traditional Whig terms. Burke in this debate pre-emptively defends limited coercion in principle, as a means for preventing worse evils: 'A reasonable, prudent, provident and moderate coercion, may be a means of preventing acts of extreme ferocity and vigour; for by propagating excessive and extravagant doctrines, such extravagant disorders take place, as require the most perilous and fierce corrections to oppose them.'[1]

Rebuffed by Fox, Burke now concentrated on splitting the Whigs, bringing as many of them as possible to support the Ministry, in preparation for the coming war with France. His main hopes were in Earl Fitzwilliam and the Duke of Portland. Fitzwilliam at least was now thoroughly alarmed.[2] In the Commons, the able and energetic William Windham (1750–1810) set up a small Burkean 'Third Party' and became a target of bitter hostility from his former colleagues, the Whigs. Both Fitzwilliam and Portland were now slowly overcoming their objection to coalition, but their ideas of coalition were still unrealistic. Portland was thinking of a coalition not headed by Pitt, and including Fox. Pitt, well aware of the disarray of the Opposition, had no intention of agreeing to anything of the kind. Some Whigs, during this pivotal year, were torn between loyalty to Fox and growing awareness of the weight of Burke's argument over the French Revolution. One such was a contemporary of Windham and later a

[1] *Parl. Hist.* xxix, 1382.
[2] Smith, *Whig Principles*, pp. 137–140: also O'Gorman, *Whig Party*, pp. 90–100.

full disciple of Burke, Sir Gilbert Elliot (1751–1814). There is a
remarkable letter in which Elliot expressed the torment of mind he
felt, at having to resist Burke's 'authority'. Elliot, who had long been
on friendly terms with Burke, mainly over Indian affairs, had written
to Burke proposing to visit him at Beaconsfield on 7 April and had
received a reply agreeing. He sent on the reply to his wife. Noting 'a
little stiffness' in it, he went on: 'The truth is, that I have had a horror
at this meeting, and that he does not know how to feel on the subject
either. I believe his disposition towards me to be affectionate and
kind as usual, but I know his sanguine character so well that I cannot
doubt of his being at heart deeply hurt and affected at my withdrawing myself from the [Indian] proceeding of last year. My own wish,
and a very anxious one it is, is to return to the most unlimited
cordiality and affection with him in point of private and personal
friendship; but, besides that I am unable to go all lengths with him
on the subject which most engrosses his mind – *the French question*,
I have felt so sensibly the evil of admitting any sway over my mind
so powerful and sovereign as his was, and have found myself so often
led to a fluctuation of opinion on important points by yielding first
to the influence of his authority, and then having to combat the same
point with my own reason, and I think the particular subject of his
present attention is so likely to lead to questions of immense moment
on which every man should form an opinion of *his own*, and regulate
his conduct by an unbiased and *temperate* judgment, that I cannot
again surrender myself so unconditionally even to Burke; and this is
a resolution, which I *must* acquaint him with.'[1]

   This is the only first-hand account that has come down to us of
what it felt like to come within the Burkean field of force or 'vortex'
and to offer resistance to it. Elliot's experience is surely the clue
to much in the political behaviour of Rockingham, of Fox, and of
Fitzwilliam; even, though to a much lesser extent, of Pitt; and therefore also of a great part of the political pattern of the late eighteenth
century. Elliot's account establishes the folly of estimating Burke's
political influence by the magnitude of the offices he held. Elliot is
not responding to a former Paymaster of the Forces. He is struggling
to resist 'any sway over my mind so powerful and sovereign as his
was'. What we are witnessing, through Elliot's testimony, is a force
in human affairs that fascinated one of the great novelists of our own
time, François Mauriac: *la puissance des esprits sur les esprits qui*

---

[1] *Corr.* VII, 121.

leur sont inférieurs. That factor accounts for more in history than historians of the more mechanistic schools allow for.

The visit to Beaconsfield went off better than had been expected and Elliot wrote again to his wife: 'I am very much relieved in my mind by the renewal of my intercourse with Burke, as that subject has weighed pretty heavily on me ever since I left town last May. His reception of me was full of kindness, and I have reason to be satisfied that there is much less difference in his affection for me than in the case of any other of his friends, with perhaps the exception of Elliot [apparently William Elliot (d. 1818), a friend and relative of Gilbert] and the Duke of Portland. But with all this, I own I did not feel perfectly comfortable. He talked his own language about the French Revolution, and his difference with his former friends on that subject, as freely as if I had no share in their dissent from him. . . .' Later, Elliot came completely round to Burke's point of view over the French Revolution. His wife probably already knew that he would.

In July and August, the French Revolution made another surge forward, in the direction predicted by Burke. The Girondins, heirs to the Constitution-makers of 1790–1791, had opted for war, in the hope of generating patriotic enthusiasm, and uniting the nation behind them, silencing the more radical revolutionaries who accused them of betraying the Revolution, in collusion with Louis. There was no mistake about the patriotic enthusiasm – the *Marseillaise* was written in April, in the first days of the war with Austria – but the rest of the Girondin programme went badly wrong. The war itself went badly at first, and military failures were blamed on the treachery of the king and his pseudo-revolutionary allies. The blow fell on 10 August, when an insurrectionary republican Commune massacred Louis's Swiss Guard and overthrew the Monarchy. The Girondins were discredited and doomed. The Constitution of 1790–1791 had collapsed, as Burke had said it would. And as Burke had also said, a new generation of revolutionaries, harder and more purposeful – Danton, Robespierre and others – took the places of the confident Utopian innovators who had opened the way for them. The royal family were transferred to prison in the Temple. Other prisons were full of suspects arrested as counter-revolutionaries, including many clergy and religious. The Prussian Army were besieging Verdun and threatening Paris. For four days armed revolutionary mobs roamed the city, entering the prisons and massacring the prisoners. The mobs were encouraged by the Commune and unchecked by an Assembly whose members were terrified for their own lives. The royal family were protected, for the time being, by the Assembly and the Commune; presumably as hostages.

On 17 August Edmund Burke wrote to James Bland Burges (1752–1824), the Foreign Under-Secretary, who had just sent him some of the accounts received by the Government concerning the fall of the French Monarchy and the imprisonment of the Royal Family. Burke wrote: 'I am infinitely obliged to you for your constant attention to my feelings. I certainly am much interested in what happens in France, the Effects and example of which I am certain cannot be confined to that Kingdom. Even if they could there is enough to shock and afflict any person, whose heart is not wholly alienated from his Species. I looked for some such an Event for a long time. But Let these things be never so much expected they still confound one when they happen.' Burke went on to put a question intended to push Pitt in the direction of a breach with the new republic. It concerned the position of Lord Gower, then British Ambassador in Paris. Gower had, of course been accredited to Louis, now in effect deposed. The Commune had declared the king deposed; the Assembly declared him merely 'suspended'. It was a distinction without a difference: Louis never again exercised even the slightest semblance of power. He remained a prisoner in the Temple up to his execution. In his letter Burke asked: 'Will Lord Gower continue in Paris? If he should, will his old Commission and credentials serve him, or must he have a new one to the new power set up by the Jacobins? I do by no means envy his Situation; which, whatever other advantages it may have, does not shine in point of Dignity.'

On the day Burke's letter was written, a despatch was sent to Lord Gower 'instructing him to return to England, reiterating the King's neutrality on the internal affairs of France and his solicitude for the personal situation of their Most Christian Majesties and their royal family.' This was much less than what Burke wanted, which was a complete breach with Revolutionary France, followed by war. But at least the recall of the British Ambassador was a step in the right direction.

On the same day, Burke wrote to Fitzwilliam, giving him the news from France, and striking while the iron was hot. After an introductory paragraph about sheep-breeding – a hobby the two had in common – Burke got down to business:

> I stand in need of avocations of this Kind to dissipate painful feelings, and unpleasant reflexions, and still more unpleasant prognostications.

All Europe seems to me to be collecting from various causes, and on various principles some new and grievous malady, from the contagion of which I am far from thinking that this Country is likely to be exempted. The Events which have lately happend in France, though by me, and by most others I believe, perfectly foreseen in all the extent of their atrocity, are nearly as shocking and disgusting to me as if they had come upon me quite unexpectedly. I have not, I confess, the same humane Sympathy with the actors in all these Horrours, which has made many Gentlemen think that the blessings of the French System of the Rights of man had been bought at an unusually cheap purchase: But it is paid for by instalments – and the Price may to them at last appear more adequate to the real value of the Object. Their appetite is pretty sharp – But be their hunger for the destruction of every thing, to which the vulgar Idea of Dignity had hitherto been annexed, be [*sic.*] never so sharp, (and I know how sharp it is) one would think it has been nearly satiated. I know the bitter hatred which many persons in a certain party entertain against Priests, nobility, and Kings, But one would think they might relent a little at the murder of such a multitude of Clergy and the famine and dispersion of such numbers more, an hundred thousand at least of both Sexes. The expatriation, spoliation, and ruin of twenty five thousand Princes, noblemen, and Gentlemen – and truly as to Kings and Queens, it is hard to satisfye their Hunger and thirst for their persecution, if they are not now glutted. I do suppose, that such a Termination of the misery and captivity of three years, attended with humiliations and mortification of every sort, could hardly be exceeded by any Effort of imagination; and this but preparatory to the dreadful Death that awaits them.[1]

So far, Burke is on common ground; he knew Fitzwilliam's feelings about all this were the same as his own. But now Burke points the political moral, first against Fox, Fitzwilliam's friend, and then against Fitzwilliam himself:

Surely all this will be enough to satiate even Mr Fox, and Mr Sheridan, or Dr Priestley – or whoever carries these Triumphs the farthest. If this King and Queen had been guilty of all the Crimes that ever were committed by Kings and Queens from the beginning of the world they have surely expiated them all in their own persons. Yet Mr Foxes Newspaper chooses to tell the people of England and of Europe, that the Horrors of this tragic narration, many facts of which it details correctly, was owing, to the "want of *Candour*" (want of Candour truly) in the miserable Victims, and that they themselves were the authors of all the Crimes from which they suffered. Mr Foxes paper only describes the Calamities of

[1] *Corr.* VII, 169; 170–3.

these unfortunate people to aggravate the load of their affliction. This Paper professes to convey to France the Sentiments of the Independent people of England. This Paper for two years past has stimulated the French to all their excesses. It laments indeed the excesses which have been committed, but it laments them only on account of the ill consequences they may have on their blessed Scheme of Liberty. Thank God that I have been completely seperated from all the Partizans of that sort of Liberty. If I cannot, as I cannot, preserve the Freedom of others from its Tyranny, I have hitherto at least preserved my own. I am not in the way of being Witness to the insolent Triumph and savage Joy of these philosophic and patriotick fomentors of all that degrades and debases human Nature. I know, that the Faction in France which looked not a little to names in England, could not have stood their Ground without English countenance. It is most certain, though very extraordinary, that these people had their Eyes fixed on England for every thing, and that even an Alehouse Club was important to them. How much more the first and most splendid names in this Country carrying with them the weight and Sanction of great Parties.

That last startling sentence is the nub of the whole letter. Here Burke, implicitly but unmistakably, accused Fitzwilliam and Portland of a share in responsibility – through the 'countenance' they had given, and were still continuing to give, to Fox's pro-French-Revolution policy – for the bloody and destructive course of the Revolution itself. Subsequent developments were to show that Burke's words were not wasted, though they took effect more slowly than he wished.

The letter to Fitzwilliam was written two weeks before the September Massacres, the news of which could only reinforce Burke's message. As the year closed the French Revolution was intensifying and expanding. On 20 September the Duke of Brunswick's invading force was defeated at Valmy. The newly elected National Convention proclaimed the Republic, 'one and indivisible'. On 19 November the Convention, in the First Propagandist Decree, declared 'that it will grant fraternity and aid to all peoples'. In December the Austrian Netherlands was annexed, under the name of 'Belgium'. Savoy, Nice and the Rhineland were also declared to be returned to the Motherland.

Fitzwilliam and Portland hoped that the eyes of Fox and Sheridan would be opened by the course of events in Europe. On the contrary, Fox seemed to be exhilarated by the triumphs of the Revolution he had loved so steadfastly from its beginnings. By late

November Portland was beginning to suspect Fox of wanting a revolution in England. As the Duke put it, in his rather mealy-mouthed way, 'I am sorry to say that I fear I observed symptoms of no very strong indisposition to submit to the experiment of a new and possibly a republican system of government.'[1] His fears were to be confirmed in the following month. On 4 December Fox, at the Whig Club, toasted 'the friends of liberty all over the world' and professed himself 'an advocate for the rights of the people'. Fitzwilliam gloomily commented: 'When coupled with the times . . . his commenting upon them at all does not meet with my approbation.' But Fox was already reconciling himself to the probable loss of Fitzwilliam and Portland and their following: 'I grow doubtful of preserving those connexions which I love and esteem as much as ever.'[2]

The Whig Party was now moving, slowly but inexorably, towards disintegration. Burke and Fox, from their opposing sides, drove the process on. By the end of 1792 Fox seemed in more of a hurry than Burke was, for Burke was anxious not to seem too far ahead of Portland and Fitzwilliam, while Fox had apparently written them off.

On 11 December 1792, in Paris, the trial of Louis XVI for treason began. Two days later, at Westminster, the new session of Parliament opened, following scenes of turmoil – in Britain itself. In the Commons, the Address of Thanks, moved by Pitt included the words: 'That we learn with concern, that not only a spirit of tumult and disorder has shown itself in acts of insurrection, which required the interposition of a military force in support of the civil magistrate, but that the industry employed to excite discontent has appeared to proceed from a design to attempt, in concert with persons in foreign countries, the destruction of our happy constitution, and the subversion of all order of government.'[3]

Fox denied it all. Considering the recent and current transactions in France, Fox's followers were in surprisingly boisterous mood that December. When Windham rose to speak he was 'interrupted with loud cries'. Burke came to Windham's aid with a point of order and went on to speak himself: 'He, for his own part, declared himself to be, not a defender of ministry or opposition, but of the country. The French had declared war against all kings, and of consequence

[1] Letter of 24 November, 1792, quoted in Smith, *Whig principles*, p. 145.
[2] Smith, *Whig principles*, p. 150.
[3] *Parl. Hist.* xxx, 6.

against this country, if it had a king. The question now was not, whether we shall carry an address to the king, but whether we should have a king at all.' Burke did not, at this stage, attack Fox. But Fox intervened again, stating flatly: 'France had justice completely on her side,' an astonishing formula, considering the nature of the judicial proceedings unfolding in France while Fox was speaking. He thought that Britain 'ought immediately to acknowledge the government of France and to adopt all honourable means of procuring peace.' Fox urged that the British Ambassador be sent back to Paris. Burke replied, rather mildly, considering the provocation: 'And what was the peculiar time when we were desired to despatch an ambassador to them? At the very moment perhaps when the merciless savages had their hands red with the blood of a murdered king. The Koran which France held out was the declaration of the rights of man and universal fraternity; and with the sword she was determined to propagate her doctrines, and conquer those whom she could not convince.'

Fox drove on. Five days later, he introduced in the Commons a formal 'Motion for sending a Minister to Paris to Treat with the Provisional Government of France'. Burke's speech against the Motion showed, in its conclusion, that his patience was wearing thin: 'Let no ambassador go thither from Great Britain. If we condescend to acknowledge them by sending an ambassador might they not insult him by saying Who sent you? The king or the people? . . . . They talk as if England were not in Europe. I say we are now engaged in actual war . . . If there must be a war, it had arisen from the proceedings of those among themselves, who by their seditious practices, had provoked it.'[1]

As the execution of Louis drew nearer, the Whigs showed signs of awareness that they had been overreaching themselves. On 20 and 21 December the House debated 'the Situation of the Royal Family of France'. Sheridan, opening for the Whigs, appealed to the French authorities for 'justice, mercy and magnanimity'. Burke would have none of this: 'Mr Burke was not one who looked up to the leaders of the Revolution in France for justice, magnanimity or mercy – he was not willing to apply to them, in any way, for the exercise of those virtues. The truth was, the king was in the custody of assassins, who were both his accusers and his judges, and his destruction was inevitable.' During this debate, the Pitt Administration presented a

---

[1] *Parl. Hist.* xxx, 111, 20 December 1792.

copy of 'the Instructions dated 17 August sent to Earl Gower, his Majesty's ambassador to the most Christian king, signifying his Majesty's pleasure that he should quit Paris'. The instructions expressed 'solicitude for the personal situation of their Most Christian Majesties'[1] and warned 'that any acts of violence could not fail to produce one universal sentiment of indignation throughout every country in Europe.' Fox declared his 'concurrence' with these instructions, and so did Sheridan. The *Parliamentary History* records Burke as observing that these 'manly declarations' of Fox and Sheridan 'deserved the highest approbation'. I am not sure whether this observation was ironic, or intended to encourage retreat. In any case it did not presage any reconciliation, for a week later Burke again strongly attacked Fox, saying: that 'any person who had seen the French business in the bud, and who now saw it fully blown and matured, and yet still wished to maintain any connexion between France and this country, must, in every respect, meet with his entire disapprobation.'[2]

This speech of 21 December became famous as the 'dagger speech': 'He mentioned the circumstances of three thousand daggers having been bespoke at Birmingham by an Englishman, of which several had been delivered. It was not ascertained how many of these were to be exported, and how many were intended for home consumption. [Here Mr Burke drew out a dagger which he had kept concealed, and with much vehemence of action threw it to the floor]. This, said he, pointing to the dagger, is what you are to gain by an alliance with France: wherever their principles are introduced, their practice must follow.' The Foxites, naturally, ridiculed this bit of business, and it was probably a mistake on Burke's part to provide them with, as it were, a handle. In later times, the dagger was to become an heirloom and a tool for those historians who try to make Burke look ridiculous and negligible. Yet the dagger that fell flat should not mislead us. Burke at this time was at the height of his influence, in relation to the French Revolution. No sensible person, by the end of 1792, could any longer regard Burke's diagnosis, in the *Reflections*, as alarmist. Burke had indeed, at the beginning of 1790, 'seen the French business in the bud' and all could see it now 'fully blown and matured'. The Foxites might laugh at Burke, but others contemplated him with immense respect. Pitt, as we shall see, took care to consult

[1] *Parl. Hist.* xxx, 143, 21 December 1792.
[2] *Parl. Hist.* xxx, 181, 21 December 1792. Debate on the Aliens Bill.

with him, in the midst of the great European crisis of the winter of 1792–3.

Burke, ever since the fall – or completion of the fall – of the French monarchy, in August, had been urging Pitt to declare war on Revolutionary France. The case for that became stronger, with Louis' execution, on 21 January 1793. On 24 January the Foreign Secretary, Grenville, informed the French Ambassador that his functions were 'now entirely terminated by the fatal death of his late Most Christian Majesty' and that 'the king can no longer permit your residence here'. The National Assembly retaliated, on February 1, by declaring war on 'the King of England'.[1]

On the eve of war with France, Burke was in close contact with Ministers, and on 8 February 1793, when the French declaration reached England, Pitt immediately sent him a copy. Consultations between them continued after the outbreak of war, and on 13 February Burke is reported as having attended a meeting of the Cabinet.[2] On 6 March, Burke, Windham and Sir Gilbert Elliot met Pitt and Dundas. Elliot has left a valuable account of how Burke exerted his influence, on that occasion: 'Pitt was of course all civility, and desired that we would never make the smallest scruple of applying for any information we wished, or suggesting anything we thought useful, promising to attend to it with great care, and assuring us of a perfectly confidential communication of all information. He gave us a good deal of satisfaction concerning naval preparations, and on all other points gave us encouraging information. Burke gave him a little political instruction, in a very respectful and cordial way, but with the authority of an old and most informed statesman; and although nobody ever takes the whole of Burke's advice, yet he often, or rather always, furnishes very important and useful matter, *some part* of which sticks and does good. Pitt took it all very patiently and cordially.'[3]

IRELAND AT WAR

Over Irish affairs also, the conditions of late 1792 and early 1793 were conducive to the taking of 'some' of Burke's advice. This period, which included the outbreak of war between the French Republic

[1] J. H. Stewart, *Documentary Survey, etc.*, pp. 396–401.
[2] *Corr.* VII, 348.
[3] *Corr.* VII, 349, tn.

and the King of Great Britain and Ireland, was the time of Burke's greatest influence with Pitt, and he used this influence to bring about a major measure of Catholic emancipation. On 3 December the General Committee of the Roman Catholics of Ireland, a new and popularly elected body (see below p. 499), drew up a petition to the king to be given a share 'in the advantages of the Constitution'. The strategy of petitioning the king directly, thus bypassing the Irish Administration and Parliament, was one advised by Edmund and Richard Burke. The Catholic delegation, with the petition, arrived in London on 18 December. The delegates relied on Richard as their agent despite his earlier dismissal by the Catholic Committee proper, under the far less propitious circumstances of the previous July. Following a private interview between Richard and Pitt on Christmas Day 1792, the delegates were presented to George III on 2 January.[1]

A major Catholic Relief Bill followed in April in the Irish Parliament and was carried, with the decisive support of the British Administration (despite the fiction of 'legislative independence'). The Catholic Relief Act of 1793 removed almost all the remaining Catholic disabilities. By far the most important major exception was that Catholics, while admitted to the franchise, were still excluded from Parliament. The attempt – ultimately inspired by Burke – to remove that exception, more than two years later, was to end in disaster (see below pp. 511–21). But for the moment he was happy, having achieved most of what he had hoped to achieve for Ireland. Things were going well for him, both in Britain and Ireland. They were to continue to go well, for a little more than a year.

Pitt's motive in bringing about what was (despite its limitations) a major measure of Catholic Relief, was obviously to reduce the danger of insurrection, in case of a French landing. Yet the danger would not go away. Burke was acutely aware of it in the months immediately following the French declaration of war. This appears from a letter he wrote to Henry Grattan, on 8 March 1793, to congratulate him on the Catholic Relief Act. Burke refers to 'the mutinous Spirit which is in the very constitution of the lower part of our compatriots of every description, and now begins to ferment with tenfold force by the leven of republicanism, which always existed, though without much Noise in the Northern parts of the Kingdom but now becomes more evident and requires no small

---

[1] See T. H. D. Mahoney, *Edmund Burke and Ireland* (Harvard, 1960) pp. 196, 211–214.

degree both of firm and of prudent management.'[1] Burke is here referring to what we are likely to think of, in retrospect, as early rumblings preceding the great rebellion which broke out in 1798, the year after his death. The main carriers of revolutionary feelings and ideas were the United Irishmen, a movement strongest among the Dissenters of Belfast, and the Defenders, strong in Catholic Ireland. How revolutionary either of these bodies was, at the time of the outbreak of the war with France, is open to question. Ostensibly, the Society of the United Irishmen, at its inception, had purely consti-tutional objectives, centred on reform of the franchise, and no doubt many of its members aimed at no more. But there is some evidence that its founders had bolder ambitions. The relevant entries in Theo-bald Wolfe Tone's journal are decidedly conspiratorial, from the beginning: '*October 12* [1791]: Mode of doing business [of United Irishman] by a Secret Committee who are not known or suspected of co-operating, but who in fact direct the movement of Belfast'. '*17 August 1792: The King of France dethroned. Very glad of it . . .*' '*25 October 1792 This is the King's* [George III] *accession. How many more accessions shall we have?*' '*26–31 January, 1793.* The King of France was beheaded on the 21st January. *I am sorry it was neces-sary*' [Tone's italics][2].

Burke would have been horrified if he had known that these were the real sentiments of the man who had succeeded his son, Richard, as agent of the Catholic Committee. Burke was right about that 'leven of republicanism', but he did not realise how near that leven had got to the Committee whose declared objectives he and his son supported so strongly. The middle-class Catholics of the Committee had also made contact in the course of their agitation, with the other main carriers of revolutionary feelings and ideas: the Defenders. The Defenders were a complex social and political movement, among Catholics. The movement had agrarian, sectarian, millenarian and revolutionary aspects. It has been described as 'anti-Protestant, anti-English and anti-settler'.[3] In the early 1790's the anti-Protestant aspect of the Defender movement made it an awkward potential partner for the 'anti-sectarian' United Irishmen. Tone's diary (for 12 August 1792) records an approach from 'sundry Defenders' who

[1] *Corr.* VII, 361.

[2] The diary is published as part of *The Life of Theobald Wolfe Tone*, by his son, W. T. W. Tone (2 vols, Washington, 1826).

[3] Thomas Bartlett, 'Select Documents XXXVIII, Defenderism in 1795', *Irish Historical Studies* XXIV (1985), pp. 373–392.

asked him to conduct their defence at the next assizes. Tone adds: 'That may not be'. Whatever scruples the United Irishmen may have had about the Defenders at this date were, however, to disappear in the second half of the decade when the two apparently quite disparate societies became overlapping parts of one large confused revolutionary movement.

The rank-and-file Defenders were mostly poor peasants, and the wealthy merchants who led the Catholic Committee would normally have had little contact with them. But in the second half of 1792 the Catholic Committee had engaged in staging elections for a Catholic Convention (which met that December) in order to establish the breadth of the demand for Catholic enfranchisement. 'In the course of this campaign,' writes Marianne Elliott, 'the Catholic delegates naturally came into contact with the Defenders.'[1]

The Catholic Committee appears to have been the only body during this period, to have been in touch with *both* the societies – the United Irishmen and the Defenders – which were later to become revolutionary allies (1795–1798). The Catholic Committee's activities in 1792 may therefore be seen as a possible catalyst, or agent of cross-fertilisation, preparing the way for the revolutionary alliance. If the matter is looked at in that light, the involvement of Burke, the great counter-revolutionary, with the Catholic Committee, in its radical phase, from 1790 on, may appear a startling paradox. Lord Kenmare, who broke with the Catholic Committee in 1790, because he feared the revolutionary potential, seems more consistent, and indeed he was so. Kenmare was consistently conservative. Burke was conservative in the 1790s, in relation to Britain, in the sense that he was determined to defend the British Constitution against its Jacobin and pro-Jacobin enemies. But he was not conservative in relation to Ireland, where the benefits of the British Constitution were denied to the majority of the population, including his relatives. He obviously did not want Jacobinism to spread to Ireland. But he was well aware that the *fear* of the spread of Jacobinism represented the best hope of securing full Catholic enfranchisement. The Catholic Committee, in their cordial relations with the United Irishmen were exploiting that fear, and Edmund Burke was not above abetting them, within limits, in that exploitation.

Burke and Tone – who met only once – were radically opposed to

[1] Elliott, 'The Origins and Transformation of Early Irish Republicanism', *International Review of Social History* XXIII (1978); pp. 405–428.

one another, in relation to the French Revolution. But they were allies, in the early 1790s, in relation not only to Catholic enfranchisement in principle but in supporting the Catholic Committee's programme for securing it, through popular agitation, with an implicit threat behind it. They were agreed, tacitly, on an immediate objective, and on a tactic for achieving it. As regards longer-term objectives, the two remained utterly opposed. Burke hoped that the removal of all Catholic disabilities would have a tranquillising effect, diminish the attractions of Jacobinism, and strengthen the connection between Ireland and Great Britain. Tone hoped that the struggle of enfranchisement, the resistance to it, and the spread of revolutionary ideas, would destroy sectarian differences, and produce a new Ireland, emancipated both from British rule and from Catholic superstition. Neither dream was to be fulfilled. Both turned to nightmare, in 1795–8.

In the first two years of the war with France, however (1793–4), the thought of possible revolution in Ireland, though never entirely absent from Burke's mind, was not among his most pressing preoccupations. Richard Burke's connection with the Catholic Committee had come to an end in 1792, and the Committee itself went into abeyance in 1793, perhaps partly because of the Catholic Relief Act of that year, but mainly because of the great difficulty of conducting an open, popular agitation in time of war. At the same time the Society of United Irishmen, in its original form, dwindled to nearly nothing. With Britain at war with France, pro-French propaganda became almost impossible: in any case the French Revolution no longer looked attractive, to many of those who had idealised it in 1790–1. The real revolutionaries, probably a minority of the original membership, bided their time, or went underground. The idea of a rapprochement between radical Dissenters and radical Catholics, which had been real enough in 1790–1, seemed to have faded in 1793–4. Defenders were still engaged in sporadic violence in this period. But hardly anyone could imagine any kind of alliance between Defenders and United Irish Dissenters, sectarian Catholics and anti-sectarian Protestants.

BURKEANS JOIN PITT
1793–4

Concern about Ireland was permanent with Burke, and always linked with his other concerns. But his primary concern, from 1793 on, was the prosecution of the war with revolutionary France. Burke's main contribution to that was to be the consolidation of parliamentary support for the war effort by ensuring the defection of as many Whigs as possible from Fox's leadership. In February when a resolution of the Whig Club had confirmed their attachment to Fox and repudiated 'calumnies' against him, Burke and about forty others, including Windham and Elliot, resigned from the Club.

As Fitzwilliam and Portland had approved the pro-Fox resolution of the Whig Club, Burke's resignation in protest constituted an implicit rebuke to them. In September, Burke made the rebuke explicit, with *Observations on the Conduct of the Minority*, an indictment, under fifty-four heads, of Fox's misdeeds, in relation to the French Revolution.[1] In the covering letter with which he sent this formidable document to Portland, Burke pointed the moral: 'No man, who is connected with a party, which professes publickly to admire, or may be justly suspected of secretly abetting, this French revolution, who must not be drawn into its vortex, and become the instrument of its designs.'[2] As George III and Lord North had found over America, and as Hastings and Pitt had found over India, so now Portland and Fitzwilliam were finding Burke 'hard to get rid of' over France.

October 1793, brought the trial and execution of Marie Antoinette. 'Oh God!' wrote Burke, 'The Charge! and the last article particularly!' (The last article stated that Marie Antoinette 'committed indecencies with her own son, too shocking to mention'). 'All this,' Burke went on, 'is but the unfolding of the Jacobin system.' The fact that Burke had foreseen that unfolding did not lessen his horror as he contemplated both the transactions in France and their acceptance by his former friends. The advent of the Terror, towards the end of 1793, made no change in the attitude of the Foxites: 'The entire unfolding of the Jacobin system has made no change in them whatsoever.'[3]

[1] *Writings and Speeches*, VIII, 402–452.
[2] *Corr.* VII, 436–8.
[3] Letters to Windham, 24 October and 25 November, *Corr.* VII, 460–2; 489–91.

A few days later Burke wrote to Fitzwilliam declining some offer of financial assistance, because he regarded Fitzwilliam's continued support for Fox as incompatible with confidence in Burke himself:

> I send back enclosed the Papers, which you were so good to send to me, with a thousand thanks. My dear Lord, the Debt of gratitude is never to be cancelled; and whilst honour, Virtue, and benignity are entitled to the love and esteem of Mankind you ever must have an uncontrovertible Title to my cordial and respectful attachment: But when confidence and good opinion on your side no longer exist, you must be sensible, that an intercourse of this kind cannot continue. [He went on:] I am not at all surprised, that the Jacobins should represent me after *their* manner. That their representations should have so much weight with you, is not what I equally expected – But the thing is done and I say no more of it in the way of discussion, I shall only say in justice to my intentions that I am not conscious to myself of having been wanting to the demands of publick principle, or private friendship. I am however come to a time of Life, in which it is not permitted that we should trifle with our Existence. I am fallen into a State of the world, that will not suffer me to play at little Sports, or to enfeeble the part I am bound to take, by smaller collateral considerations. I cannot proceed, as if things went on in the beaten circle of Events, such as I have known them for towards half a Century. The moral State of Mankind fills me with dismay and horrour. The Abyss of Hell itself seems to yawn before me. I must act, think, and feel according to the exigencies of this tremendous season.[1]

Both Fitzwilliam and Portland now capitulated and broke with Fox. On Christmas Day Portland told Fitzwilliam of his intention to notify Fox of his determination 'to support the war with all the effect and energy in my power' and to end connexion with the Friends of the People. Although Fox led the Whigs in the Commons, Portland ranked as leader of the party as a whole. In that capacity – and treating Burke as still a Whig in the sense that he himself was – Portland invited him to the Whigs' eve-of-session meeting on 20 January 1794, at Burlington House. It must have been a most uncomfortable meeting. Portland 'made a strong and decisive speech declaring his support for the Ministry'[2] – and urging the same course on his followers. Henceforward, in both Houses, 'the Portland Whigs' were a separate party, speaking and voting against the Foxites, in favour of the war and of measures of repression against Jacobin

[1] *Corr.* VII, 494–7.
[2] E. A. Smith, *Whig Principles*, p. 163.

propaganda. The 'Portland Whigs' rather like 'Fox's East India Bill' were both essentially Burkean creations.

Fitzwilliam went with Portland. In February in the Lords, Burke's old bugbear, the former Earl of Shelburne, now Marquess of Lansdowne, proposed a motion for peace with France. Fitzwilliam opposed him, on thoroughly Burkean lines: 'With regard to peace with France, we could have no hopes of it under the present system, unless we were prepared to sacrifice everything that was dear to us. . . . His Lordship contended that the safety of the country, the preservation of the constitution, of everything dear to Englishmen and to their posterity depended upon the preventing the introduction of French principles, and the new-fangled doctrine of the rights of man; and that this could only be effected by the establishment of some regular form of government in that country upon which some reliance might be placed.'[1]

The creation of the 'Portland Whigs', with the accretion of support which that brought to the war against the French Revolution, was a major political victory for Burke. He now worked to consolidate that victory through the creation of a Coalition Government.

INDIA: CLOSING THE IMPEACHMENT
1794

In mid-1794 Burke was finally to acquit himself of the impeachment of Warren Hastings. The monumental task of managing the impeachment during the more than six years between the opening speech (February 1788) and the Speech in Reply (28 May–6 June 1794) cannot be adequately considered here; the sheer tedium of the thing would be too daunting. Yet the reader wishing to understand the life and character of Edmund Burke should at least be aware of that self-imposed, totally unrewarded labour in the service of the peoples of India. Burke's eloquence in the greatest of his Indian speeches is not the airy kind, off the top of a brilliant head. It is earned; it is something spun out of his very entrails.

The Speech in Reply was, and it was intended to be, his last major speech, and his longest. As a whole it is not among his great speeches, although it has its great moments, and it contains the final strain

[1] Smith, *Whig principles*, p. 164.

of the Indian part of the Great Melody. Its mood is one of grim
determination in the discharge of duty to the end: an end which
Burke knew was likely to be bitter, as he made clear near the beginning: 'The wreck and fragments of our cause (which has been dashed
to pieces upon rules by which your Lordships have thought fit to
regulate its progress) await your final determination.'[1] The rules
which hemmed Burke in were those which required the Managers to
show that Warren Hastings personally had committed crimes, or
directly and explicitly ordered their commission. It was not enough
to show that Hastings had been at the head of a system of criminal
extortion; any crimes committed must be brought home to him personally and individually. The fact that he was Governor-General,
head of a system, was treated as irrelevant. Against such rules, the
impeachment could not succeed.

In opening the impeachment, Burke had hoped to arouse public
opinion sufficiently to make the Lords fear the consequences of
acquitting Warren Hastings and, out of that fear, relax their
interpretation of the rules. Burke had therefore, as in the case of Devi
Singh, worked on the emotions of his audience: emotions which he
shared. This might have worked, if the hearings had been completed
in 1788–9, when there was still intense public interest in the case.
But the Lord Chancellor and others interested in acquitting Hastings
had spun the proceedings out, to Burke's frustration. By 1794 public
opinion had absolutely lost interest in the impeachment. Next door,
in France, that summer, the Terror was raging. The impeachment
was yesterday's news.

In his Opening Speech, before a fashionable throng in Westminster
Hall, Burke had stressed the cruelty of Hastings's system. In the
Speech in Reply, with nobody listening to him except a few unimpres-
sionable peers, Burke stressed the system's fraudulent nature. Perhaps
he hoped that some peers who would not be likely to be moved by
the thought of suffering Indians might resent frauds, invented for the
deception of people like themselves. One such was the fiction that
Hastings was the servant of the Company's Court of Directors, while
in reality it was the other way round; another the fiction that the
Nawab of Oudh was an independent prince, whereas he was in
reality the slave of Warren Hastings. There were many others. Burke
here comes forward in the role of one who is giving the Lords a
conducted tour behind the scenes of the Hastings India. This was, in

[1] *Works* XI, 157.

particular, the theme of the Fourth Day of the Speech in Reply:

> I only think it necessary that your Lordships should truly know the actual state of that country, and the ground upon which Mr Hastings stood. Your Lordships will find it a fairy land, in which there is a perpetual masquerade, where no one thing appears as it really is, – where the person who seems to have the authority is a slave, while the person who seems to be the slave has the authority. In that ambiguous government everything favors fraud, everything favors peculation, everything favors violence, everything favors concealment.[1]

And then, after the production of a number of telling exhibits:

> Now, my Lords, was there ever such a discovery made of the arcana of any public theatre? You see here, behind the ostensible scenery, all the crooked working of the machinery developed and laid open to the world. You now see by what secret movement the master of the mechanism has conducted the great Indian opera, – an opera of fraud, deceptions, and harlequin tricks. You have it all laid open before you. The ostensible scene is drawn aside; it has vanished from your sight. All the strutting signors, and all the soft signoras are gone; and instead of a brilliant spectacle of descending chariots, gods, goddesses, sun, moon, and stars, you have nothing to gaze on but sticks, wire, ropes, and machinery. You find the appearance all false and fraudulent; and you see the whole trick at once.[2]

A few such touches apart, the Speech in Reply is mostly a piece of dogged, conscientious, sustained exposition. But there is just one long passage, from the First Day's Speech, which is clearly part of the Great Melody. Indeed it is part of the genesis of Yeats's lines, providing them with their concluding 'it'. The passage is the extra-ordinary panegyric on 'sympathetic revenge', which concludes with a contingent curse on the House of Lords if they dare to acquit Hastings. I have italicised the 'it' phrase:

> If it should still be asked why we show sufficient acrimony to exact a suspicion of being in any manner influenced by malice or a desire of revenge, to this, my Lords, I answer, Because we would be thought to know our duty, and to have all the world know how resolutely we are resolved to perform it. The Commons of Great Britain are not disposed

[1] *Works* XI, 381.
[2] *Works* XI, 413.

to quarrel with the Divine Wisdom and Goodness, which has moulded up revenge into the frame and constitution of man. He that has made us what we are has made us at once resentful and reasonable. Instinct tells a man that he ought to revenge an injury; reason tells him that he ought not to be a judge in his own cause. From that moment revenge passes from the private to the public hand; but in being transferred it is far from being extinguished. My Lords, it is transferred as a sacred trust to be exercised for the injured, in measure and proportion, by persons, who feeling as he feels, are in a temper to reason better than he can reason. Revenge is taken out of the hands of the original injured proprietor, lest it should be carried beyond the bounds of moderation and justice. But, my Lords, it is in its transfer exposed to a danger of an opposite description. The delegate of vengeance may not feel the wrong sufficiently: he may be cold and languid in the performance of his sacred duty. It is for these reasons that good men are taught to tremble even at the first emotions of anger and resentment for their own particular wrongs; but they are likewise taught, if they are well taught, to give the loosest possible rein to their resentment and indignation, whenever their parents, their friends, their country, or their brethren of the common family of mankind are injured. Those who have not such feelings, under such circumstances, are base and degenerate. These, my Lords, are the sentiments of the Commons of Great Britain.

Lord Bacon has very well said, that "revenge is a kind of wild justice." It is so, and without this wild austere stock there would be no justice in the world. But when, by the skilful hand of morality and wise jurisprudence, a foreign scion, but of the very same species, is grafted upon it, its harsh quality becomes changed, it submits to culture, and, laying aside its savage nature, it bears fruits and flowers, sweet to the world, and not ungrateful even to heaven itself, to which it elevates its exalted head. The fruit of this wild stock is revenge regulated, but not extinguished, – revenge transferred from the suffering party to the communion and sympathy of mankind. This is the revenge by which we are actuated, and which we should be sorry, if the false, idle, girlish, novel-like morality of the world should extinguish in the breast of us who have a great public duty to perform.

This sympathetic revenge, which is condemned by clamorous imbecility, is so far from being a vice, that it is the greatest of all possible virtues, – a virtue which the uncorrupted judgment of mankind has in all ages exalted to the rank of heroism. To give up all the repose and pleasures of life, to pass sleepless nights and laborious days, and, what is ten times more irksome to an ingenuous mind, to offer oneself to calumny and all its herd of hissing tongues and poisoned fangs, in order to free the world from fraudulent prevaricators, from cruel oppressors, from robbers and tyrants, has, I say, the test of heroic virtue, and well deserves such a distinction. The Commons, despairing to attain the heights of this virtue, never lose sight of it for a moment. For seventeen years they have, almost without intermission, pursued, by every sort of inquiry, by legislative and by judicial remedy, the cure of this Indian malady, worse ten thousand times than the leprosy which our forefathers brought from the East. Could they have done this, if they had not been actuated by some strong, some vehement, some perennial passion, which, burning like the Vestal fire, chaste and eternal, never suffers generous sympathy to grow cold in maintaining the rights of the injured or in denouncing the crimes of the oppressor?

My Lords, the Managers for the Commons have been actuated by this passion; my Lords, they feel its influence at this moment; and so far from softening either their measures of their tone, they do here, in the presence of their Creator, of this House, and of the world, make this solemn declaration, and nuncupate this deliberate vow. *that they will ever flow with the most determined and unextinguishable animosity against tyranny, oppression, and peculation in all, but more particularly as practised by this man in India; that they never will relent, but will pursue and prosecute him,* **and** *it, till they see corrupt pride prostrate under the feet of justice.* We call upon your Lordships to join us; and we have no doubt that you will feel the same sympathy that we feel, or (what I cannot persuade my soul to think or my mouth to utter) you will be identified with the criminal whose crimes you excuse, and rolled with him in all the pollution of Indian guilt, from generation to generation. Let those who feel with me upon this occasion join with me in this vow: if they will not, I have it all to myself.[1]

'Pursue and prosecute him and *it . . .*' This is Yeats's 'it'.

The 'perennial passion' which Burke ascribes to the Commons, in whose name he is conducting the impeachment, is very much his own. The words 'whenever their parents, their friends, their country and the common family of mankind are injured' are significant. In Burke's psyche, other voices, as well as those of Indians, are calling for revenge. Like Hamlet, Burke is listening to his father's ghost.

Burke had now completed his work, not only in the impeachment, but in parliament. Although the Lords did not hand down their verdict until the following year, Burke's own work on the case ended on 16 June 1794, with the conclusion of his Speech in Reply. Without delay he accepted the Chiltern Hundreds, and retirement. On 20 June 1794, his last day in the House of Commons, Pitt proposed a vote of thanks to the Managers of the Impeachment: 'It was a task

[1] *Works* XI, 178–81.

of great length, labour and difficulty, and had been performed by the hon. managers with indefatigable industry, unparalleled assiduity, and laudable obedience to the desires of that House. He was confident that the example of Mr Hastings would deter other governors from a repetition of the practices which marked his administration'.

Pitt added a word of warning to Hastings's friends in the House: 'And he asked those who had shown themselves hostile for the impeachment to reflect seriously before they gave a negative to the motion; for he doubted much whether an unanimous vote of that House (honourable though it was) would be so honourable to the managers as a vote of thanks marked with the discriminating negative of those who felt themselves irritated and stung by the faithful and admirable discharge of the task imposed on them by their country.'

Hastings's friends concentrated their attack on Burke. As the first of their speakers, one Sumner, said, he would not object to thanking the Managers, 'provided [thanks] could be given without their bestowing their thanks at the same time on the leading manager [Burke] who had by his conduct disgraced and degraded the House of Commons. . . .' Windham and Francis opposed any such proviso. So did Fox — generously, in view of all that had passed. He said that he 'disclaimed all separation between the rest of the managers and the right hon. member so eminently qualified, not only by nature but by his particular study and attention, to be, as he was termed, their leader in this business, and with whom it was their boast and glory to be identified.'

The vote of thanks to the Managers, including Burke, was carried by 50 votes to 21. The Speaker then conveyed the thanks of the House: 'The subject, to which your attention has been directed, was intricate and extensive beyond example: you have proved, that it was well suited to your industry and eloquence, the exertions of which have conferred honour, not on yourselves only, but on this House, whose credit is intimately connected with your own. A forcible admonition has been given, on this occasion, to all persons in situations of national trust, that they can neither be removed by distance, nor sheltered by power, from the vigilance and authority of this House . . .'

Burke then replied on behalf of the Managers:

Mr Burke said, that by the orders of the House when the thanks were given, he and his brother managers were tongue-tied, and had no means whereby to express their gratitude but by their submission to those orders. But he thought he would be wanting in gratitude if he did not, the moment the penalty of silence was removed, seize the first opportunity to express his own satisfaction, and that of his fellow managers, on the occasion. They had laboured to discharge their duty, they had completed the task, and they were paid by the thanks of that House, the first reward men could receive.

TRAGEDY
AUGUST 1794

So ended a Parliamentary career of nearly thirty years. Earl Fitzwilliam had agreed that Richard Burke would succeed to the seat at Malton, for which his father had sat since his defeat for Bristol in 1780. Edmund and Richard travelled to Malton together, and Richard was elected for the borough on 18 July, 1794. Ten days later tragedy struck. On 28 July, Richard went down with an acute and unmistakable attack of tuberculosis of the trachea. On 2 August he died, in the presence of his father and mother. As he lay dying, he asked if it was raining. His father told him that the noise was the wind rustling through the trees. Richard then spoke his last words: three lines from Adam's morning hymn in Book V of *Paradise Lost*, a favourite passage of his father's:

> His praise ye winds, that from four Quarters blow,
> Breathe soft or loud; and wave your tops, ye Pines,
> With every Plant, in sign of Worship wave.

Burke's devoted young friend and volunteer assistant, French Laurence, has left an account of Edmund and Jane on the day of Richard's death: 'The behaviour of our two poor remaining friends is such as might be expected from them by those who rightly knew both their sensibility and their strength of reason: though perhaps for the exertion of the latter under so severe a dispensation, we hardly gave them sufficient credit. During the first day the father was at times, as I have heard, truly terrible in his grief. He occasionally worked him[self] up to an agony of affliction, and then bursting away from all controul, would rush to the room where his son lay, and throw himself headlong, as it happened, on the body, the bed, or the floor. Yet at intervals he attended and gave directions relative to every little arrangement, which their situation rendered necessary, pleasing himself most with thinking what would be most consonant to the living wishes and affections of his lost Son: at intervals too he would argue against the ineffectual sorrows of his wife. She on the other hand sometimes broke into fits of violent weeping, sometimes shewed a more quiet but more determined grief, and at other times again a more serene composure than her husband. Instead of dashing herself down, like him, she only lamented, that when on Thursday by an accidental fall she sprained her wrist, "it had not been her neck": but when her husband attempted to persuade her, that she had no business still to remain in the House, she answered steadily, "*No Edmund*: while he remains here, I will not go". – I am happy however to inform you, that on Saturday evening she took and gave a promise, that neither of them would ever enter more the chamber, where their Son lay. They have repented, but have fulfilled their mutual promises, and she has consented, notwithstanding her resolution above mentioned, to leave the House this day.'[1]

It seems that Burke, after his son's death, refused a peerage that Pitt had offered him. Pitt's biographer writes: 'It was now desired I cannot say with truth to honour Mr Burke, but rather to honour the peerage by his accession to its ranks. There was also, so I have heard, the design, as in other cases of rare merit, to annex by an Act of Parliament a yearly income to the title during two or three lives. Already was the title chosen as Lord Beaconsfield. Already was the patent preparing. Just then it pleased Almighty God to strike the old man to the very earth by the untimely death of his beloved son, his only child. Richard Burke expired on the 2nd. of August, 1794. There ended Burke's whole share of earthly happiness. There ended all his dreams of earthly grandeur. Thenceforth a Coronet was to him a worthless bauble which he must decline to wear.'[2]

Edmund Burke had now a little less than three years to live. In personal terms the years after the death of his son, with the blighting of all his fond and ardent hopes for him, were a period of utter desolation, as his own letters and those of his friends, attest. But his public activity was undiminished (except for the very last months): its quality even in some ways enhanced. R. B. McDowell, the most perceptive of living Burke scholars, has written in his Introduction to Volume VIII of the *Correspondence*: 'On 2 August Richard Burke, the only son on whom his father's affections and ambitions centred,

---

[1] French Laurence to Mrs W. Haviland (Burke's niece, née Mary French) 4 August 1794, *Corr*. VII, 563–6.
[2] Earl Stanhope, *Life of the Rt. Hon. William Pitt*, Vol. 2, p. 244.

died. Burke was profoundly and grievously shaken. What is remarkable is, not that he was deeply afflicted, but how successfully he rallied and with what intellectual and emotional power he expressed himself during the following three years. It might almost be said that the blow of his son's death acted on him as a stimulus, bringing home to him the immediacy of catastrophe in the political sphere. If his happiness was shattered, Europe's future was imperilled, and Burke, like Job to whom he compared himself, drew general lessons from his afflictions.'

From the frequent references to Richard, in the correspondence of those years, it is clear that Burke drew consolation from the causes he had shared with his son, in their common passionate commitments, concerning France and Ireland. There is a sense of posthumous collaboration, and also one of atonement, for Burke accused himself of having kept his son too much to himself, and perhaps asked too much of him. Yet these funereal or morbid preoccupations are evident only in asides. In intellectual combat, they became transmuted into exaltation. The last of his published political writings – *Letter to a Noble Lord* (1796) and *Letters on a Regicide Peace* (1796–7) – are distinguished from his earlier writings and speeches, not at all by any melancholy undertones, but on the contrary, by their exceptional élan, coruscating wit and reckless high spirits. They are marked by that quality which Yeats most admired in Nietzsche: 'a curious, astringent joy'.

IRELAND
1794–5
BURKE'S VICEROY

It was the opportunity of playing a part in shaping the Irish policy of the new government which seems to have rekindled Burke's interest in politics after Richard's death
R. B. McDOWELL, Burke's *Correspondence*,
Volume VIII, Introduction.

In July 1794, the month between Edmund's retirement and Richard's death, a new Government had been formed in London. Pitt's Administration, then under stress from French Revolutionary victories in Holland and in Italy, had been strengthened by the accession to it of the 'Portland' (or Burkean) Whigs. Four of these joined the Administration, which benefited from the support of their following in both Houses of Parliament. This was the outcome for which Burke had been working since 1791. Three of the new Ministers – Portland, Fitzwilliam and William Windham – were his friends. Fitzwilliam was about to be Viceroy of Ireland, and he, on Irish affairs, was entirely Burke's disciple. Like Burke, he believed in the complete removal of all Catholic disabilities, and specifically in completing enfranchisement, by giving Catholics the right to sit in Parliament. Fitzwilliam also followed Burke in believing that nothing would go right in the administration of Ireland without the removal of what Burke called the 'Junto', a tightly knit group of officials, well-endowed with sinecures, and resistant to Catholic claims. These officials, of whom the most conspicuous were the Beresford family, were removable at the pleasure of the viceroy, at least in theory.

E. A. Smith, in his political biography of Fitzwilliam,[1] refers to his 'Burkean principles', and to his 'passionate conviction' that the Burkean measures must be applied in Ireland. On Burke's side, the appointment of Fitzwilliam as viceroy had been among his objectives from the beginning of his efforts to effect a juncture between Pitt and those Whigs over whom he had influence. As early as September, 1792, nearly two years before the formation of the coalition, Richard Burke had suggested to Fitzwilliam the possibility of the viceroyalty, and had found that the Earl 'seem'd to interest himself strongly in the business'.[2]

The allocation of Ireland to Fitzwilliam, in the Administration of 1794, is indicative of the strong influence of Edmund Burke over the formation of the coalition. Subsequent events were to demonstrate, painfully, the limitations of that influence over the coalition's actual conduct, where Ireland was concerned. It came near to breaking up in October, over Ireland and Fitzwilliam. There was a delay in the appointment of the Viceroy – Pitt is said to have 'become alarmed at the way his new allies seemed to assume they could treat Ireland as their own administrative preserve'.[3] Windham wrote to Burke: 'One cannot but suspect, that it is at the bottom a determination to maintain in Ireland, what he [Pitt] has brought himself to consider as *his* power in opposition to the D. of P. [Duke of Portland].'[4]

'The D. of P.' was a manner of speaking. Portland was a timid,

[1] *Whig Principles and Party Politics*, p. 175.
[2] R.B. to E.B. *Corr.* VII, 185.
[3] *Corr.* VIII, Introduction, xiv.
[4] *Corr.* VIII, 60.

irresolute figure, as his long tolerance of Fox's philo-Jacobinism demonstrated. Pitt could not possibly have thought of Portland as some
kind of 'power' in opposition to his own. The opposing power, in
relation to Ireland, was outside the Cabinet. Fitzwilliam in Ireland,
would seek to execute policies laid down for him by Burke. Pitt knew
this, and found it unacceptable. While the so-called 'Portland Whigs'
were still followers of Fox, Pitt had needed Burke, in order to prise
them loose. By agreeing to make Fitzwilliam Viceroy in Ireland, Pitt
was making a major concession to Burke. But once the Coalition was
formed, Burke's political work was done, as far as Pitt was concerned. Pitt no longer needed him, and Fitzwilliam, the colleague
over whom Burke had most influence, was becoming a nuisance.

Burke's main and over-riding concern was to avert a collapse of
the coalition which would benefit the Jacobins and their English and
Irish sympathisers. With deep reluctance, he quitted his bereaved
retirement at Beaconsfield and went to London, to try to save the
coalition and Fitzwilliam's viceroyalty. 'Nothing', he wrote to
Loughborough, the coalition's Lord Chancellor, 'can be in itself so
disagreeable to me as to go to London to show to the world the face
of a man marked by the hand of God.'[1]

But he went, and with some help from him and Henry Grattan,
the immediate crisis was resolved. On 15 November the 'Portland
Whig' leaders met with Pitt and Grenville, in Downing Street, and
agreed, or believed they had agreed, on terms on which Fitzwilliam
could proceed to Ireland as Viceroy.

Burke's journey to London in November appears as a tragic mis-
take. His arrival on the scene could only serve to remind Pitt that
Fitzwilliam would be Burke's viceroy and not his own. From the
sequel, it is clear that Pitt's 'agreement' at the meeting was feigned.
He never had any intention of allowing Fitzwilliam any scope in
Ireland, to walk his Burkean way. For Pitt, the advantage of allowing
Fitzwilliam to proceed to Ireland was that that journey separated
Fitzwilliam from Portland, physically. Portland, with Fitzwilliam at
his side, and stiffened by Fitzwilliam's Burkean sense of purpose,
could be difficult, as he had shown in the Coalition negotiations. But
Portland on his own would be easy.[2] William Pitt was an excellent
judge of men, and a ruthless operator.

---

[1] *Corr.* VIII, 70.
[2] 'Portland was one of the most easily influenced men who ever rose to the high
offices he held. He was usually influenced by the last person who had his ear. In this
instance Fitzwilliam was away, and Pitt confronted him with arguments which His
Grace weakly accepted'. Mahoney, *Edmund Burke and Ireland*, p. 270.

So Fitzwilliam went to Ireland and his political doom. He arrived in Ireland, amid popular rejoicing, on 4 January 1795. He immediately took on the Junto, the network of senior officials who had dominated the tenure of his predecessor, Lord Westmorland. By mid-January, Fitzwilliam had removed from office five of these officials, headed by the First Commissioner of the Revenue, John Beresford, and the Attorney-General, Arthur Wolfe. Fitzwilliam was here complying with Burke's specific instructions: 'You must therefore directly criminate the Irish Jobbery, or you are defeated; and defeated, I cannot well say, with how much disgrace.'[1]

In removing the officials, Fitzwilliam was not in breach of the Downing Street agreement, which had stipulated only that the Irish Chancellor, John Fitzgibbon, be left in place, which he was. Pitt grumbled about the dismissals, but did not press that particular matter. The issue that precipitated Fitzwilliam's fall was not the dismissals, which Burke had urged on him, but the issue of Catholic enfranchisement, which Burke was not urging. In a long letter of the previous September – the tenor of which may have surprised Fitzwilliam – Burke had played down the intrinsic importance of the matter of 'the eligibility of Catholics to Parliament', since so few Catholics would be in a position to benefit from it: 'The second point – the eligibility of the Catholicks to Parliament – Its collateral effects may or may not be important, as they may tend more or less to satisfye the desires of one description of the people, or to raise Jealousy and alarm in the other. This is a matter of great uncertainty, as every thing not dependent on reason, but on the occasional feelings of the people must ever be. It cannot be well judged of but at the moment of Execution: but as an independent measure standing upon its intrinsick merits only, I think it a matter of (very) little importance indeed.'[2]

Clearly, Burke saw the new Viceroy's most important task as cleaning-up the Administration, through breaking up the power of the anti-Catholic and jobbing Junto. He hoped to avoid an early confrontation (over enfranchisement) which might wreck the Viceroy and restore the Junto. It was Henry Grattan, not Burke, who now brought that confrontation on.[3] Under the Downing Street agreement, the Viceroy was not to take an initiative in bringing on

[1] *Corr.* VIII, 53–7.
[2] *Corr.* VIII, 21.
[3] James Cunniff's 'Edmund Burke's Reflections on the Coming Revolution in Ireland' (*Journal of the History of Ideas*, xlviii, Jan.–Mar. 1986) is in general a

the question of enfranchisement, and he did not do so. What he should do if someone else did so, was not determined.

On 12 February 1795 Grattan, after discussion with Fitzwilliam, formally asked leave to introduce his Catholic Relief Bill. Fitzwilliam strongly recommended acceptance, and was widely known to desire it. When Pitt showed the Viceroy's despatches to the king, he thundered against 'letters from the Lord Lieutenant of Ireland, which to my greatest astonishment propose the total change of the principles of government which have been followed by every administration in the kingdom since the abdication of King James II . . . venturing to condemn the labour of ages and wanting an adoption of ideas which every man of property in Ireland and every friend to the Protestant religion must feel diametrically contrary to those he has imbibed in his youth.'[2] Considering that George had already signed a number of Catholic Relief Acts, from 1778 to 1793, the reaction to this one may seem surprisingly violent. But it was hardly unprompted. Pitt would have made known to the king his sense that Fitzwilliam was going too far. And the king would have known that Fitzwilliam could be repudiated without the risk of losing Pitt, and of getting something with Fox in it.

Fitzwilliam was now doomed, as a viceroy repudiated by the king, and not defended by his colleagues. It was Portland, on 21 February, who broke the news to Fitzwilliam 'that he no longer had the confidence of his colleagues'.[3] Two days later came Fitzwilliam's official recall. Lord Camden, a faithful follower of Pitt, was nominated in his place. Fitzwilliam departed from a mourning Dublin on 25 March. Thomas Hussey had not been alarmist but accurate, when he wrote to Burke: 'The disastrous news, my dear Sir, of Earl Fitzwilliam's recall, is come; and Ireland is now on the brink of a civil war.'[4]

We cannot know whether a Viceroyalty on Burkean lines would really, if sustained, have had all the benign effects that both Burke and Fitzwilliam hoped of it. We do know that Fitzwilliam's recall,

useful contribution, but gets this one wrong. It is not true to say, as Cunniff does, that Burke 'encouraged Fitzwilliam to attempt so much in so short a time'. The record (above p. 514) shows Burke as trying to hold Fitzwilliam back in the critical matter of rushing to complete Catholic Emancipation, which is what precipitated his fall.

[2] *English Historical Documents, 1783–1832* (ed. A. Aspinall and E. A. Smith, 1969) p. 158.

[3] *Corr.* VIII, 156, tn.

[4] *Corr.* VIII, 162–3; 27 February 1795.

after the high hopes kindled by his appointment and by his known intentions, set in motion the cycle of agitation, conspiracy and repression that were to result, after Burke's death, in the Great Rebellion of 1798. The concession of Catholic representation in Parliament, if made in 1795, would probably have given little joy to Catholics. As Burke said, it affected very few people. But the dismissal of a viceroy, for having been prepared to accept this measure of Catholic enfranchisement, outraged Catholics generally, and gave great encouragement to the revolutionaries among them.

To Burke, Fitzwilliam's recall was of course nothing less than the reversal of almost all Burke's hopes for Ireland (with one exception, the founding of Maynooth College – see below). In these trying circumstances what is remarkable is how cool a head he kept; how steady in his priorities, refusing to be carried away against Pitt, yet keeping intact his friendship with Fitzwilliam, without breaking off his relations with Portland, and also without any element of double-dealing. E. A. Smith, writing about the onset of the Coalition's Irish crisis, refers to Burke's 'perplexity and anxiety, his mind almost unhinged by the recent tragedy of the death of his son, Richard.'[1] That may seem a plausible hypothesis, and it fits well into the historiographical tradition whereby, if Burke's conduct cannot be accounted for on some sordid assumption, then the man must have been off his head at the time. Not that Smith personally is hostile to Burke, but this sort of thing was still in the air, in 1975. (Nor is it quite yet gone.) In reality, Burke's conduct in this great crisis, for him and his friends, is one of the most remarkable examples in history of a great capacity for reason, managing to keep a torrent of emotions under control. Burke fiercely resented what Pitt had done. But he still saw Pitt as the indispensable leader in the anti-Jacobin cause. Everything else had to be subordinated to that, since the Jacobins threatened everything: England, Ireland, all Europe.

On 13 March 1795, when Fitzwilliam's recall was known, Burke wrote a long, tenderly supportive letter to him. The key passage runs:

> Before I could abandon you I must first abandon all my opinions, all my feelings, all my principles. Before I could abandon you, I must forget, that I have a King, that I have a Country, that I have a friend: I must forget that once I had a son – who at a very early period of his Life

[1] E. A. Smith, *Whig Principles*, p. 183.

risqued it in the field rather than suffer the slightest glance upon your fame.[1] Had it pleased God to keep him here to this more trying hour, he would have fought this other kind of battle, under your auspices with a resolution worthy of you, and of himself, and of the Cause. Whatever an enfeebled mind in an old and shattered carcass could do, I have done for this fortnight past. I thought, and do still think, Mr Pitts power necessary to the Existence of the antient order in Europe. But that which nothing else could destroy he may destroy himself. I am in Truth overwhelmed with Grief, shame, and anguish. But my reason, such as it is, remains.[2]

The crucial words here are 'and do still think'. Burke is not about to break publicly with Pitt, or advise others to do so, even over Fitzwilliam's recall. Fitzwilliam, very naturally, was inflamed against Pitt and Portland, and Burke must have wondered how his friend would receive his indication of continuing support for the coalition around these two leaders. Fitzwilliam's reply brought reassurance: 'The letter I have received from you this morning has been a cordial to my soul.'[3] Fitzwilliam would no longer serve in the Pitt-Portland Administration, but he would continue to support it in the Lords over the war with France. Much later, he would make his peace with Fox, but not in Burke's lifetime. The coalition, with Burke's help, survived the strain of the Viceroy's dismissal.

Fitzwilliam left Ireland on 25 March, 'his carriage attended by silent crowds and passing through Dublin streets draped with mourning.'[4] The arrival of his successor, Lord Camden, precipitated a riot in Dublin. Fitzwilliam's recall set a vicious spiral in motion, which would culminate in the Great Rebellion, three years later.

Burke was distressed, but not deflected from his course, by the dismissal. His general view of the condition of British politics became more pessimistic, and this tendency was reinforced by developments in the Hastings case. By 20 March, four days before Fitzwilliam's departure from Ireland, the Committee of the House of Lords, which was considering its verdict on Hastings, had rejected the first two Charges to come before it. Acquittal followed a month later. Burke

[1] This refers to a duel fought by young Richard on 12 March 1784 with someone who, in his presence, had used the word 'blackguard' about Fitzwilliam. (*Corr.* V, 130–3.)
[2] *Corr.* VIII, 188–96.
[3] *Corr.* VIII, 211.
[4] E. A. Smith, *Whig Principles*, p. 207.

wrote to Grattan: 'We have had an Eastern, and a Western Chief Governour before the Publick. Mr Hastings is acquitted by the House of Lords. Lord Fitzwilliam is condemned by the Cabinet. All this, however strange, is not contradictory.'[1]

The deep ambivalence of Burke's feelings, towards England and the heritage of the Glorious Revolution, produced angel figures and devil figures. For many years, Rockingham had been the angel, and Shelburne the devil. After Shelburne had been forced out of office, and out of active politics, with Burke's help, it was Warren Hastings who succeeded him, in the devil role. After Rockingham's death, Fitzwilliam was the successor angel: 'You are Lord Rockingham in everything'.[2] So the comment about 'an Eastern and a Western Chief Governor' means that a devil has been acquitted and an angel condemned. The negative side of Burke's feelings towards England and the heritage of the Glorious Revolution, has gained an edge over the positive side. The idealised view of the British Constitution, apparent in *On Conciliation with America* (1774), in the peroration of the speech opening the impeachment of Hastings (1788), in the *Reflections* (1790) and in the conclusion of *An Appeal for the New to the Old Whigs* (1791), never again makes an appearance, after this traumatic March of 1795. The cloud-capped towers, the gorgeous palaces, which Burke had liked to evoke on appropriate occasions, are now dismantled, like Warren Hastings' 'Indian opera' (see above, p. 505). From now on Burke's references to the actual working of British politics are bleak, and sometimes savagely sardonic.

There is a shift, that March, but its extent should not be overestimated. The devil–angel trauma of March, 1795, was mild in comparison with that of July 1782, when Shelburne had succeeded Rockingham. Hastings had been acquitted, but at least he had not become head of the Administration, as Shelburne had done. Its head now was Pitt, who was neither an angel-figure nor a devil-figure in Burke's eyes. He still saw Pitt as indispensable to the struggle against Revolutionary France and he still saw both Britain and Ireland, with all the faults of their rulers, as eminently worth defending against the dark forces which were threatening to take them over.

Burke was at first puzzled about Pitt's reasons for treating Fitzwilliam as he did. It didn't seem in character. As he wonders about

[1] *Corr.* VIII, 206.
[2] *Corr.* V, 6.

it, the depth of Burke's respect for Pitt, even at this most trying moment, becomes apparent:

It appears to me like some strange, hideous and illsorted dream. If it had been for a Wench, the madness had been more excuseable, for being with authentick Precedent; and it would have had something of a wild Generosity in it: But the whole of this, has, I know not what air of Chicanery and pettifogging in it; I do not know how to spell and put it together, with the name of the most eloquent tongue, the clearest head, and the most powerful mind for official Business of the time we live in.[1]

That was written before Fitzwilliam's actual dismissal was known. After that, Burke can no longer account for these transactions as 'chicanery and pettifogging'. He now discerns a deeper motive. In his key letter to Henry Grattan, on 20 March (the one in which he refers to the two Chief Governors) he says, 'It is possible they look to a Sansculotick peace.'

In the same letter, Burke shows himself aware of Pitt's hostility to himself, and makes a veiled reference to its relevance to Fitzwilliam's dismissal:

God knows how earnestly I wished Mr. Pitts stability and greatness. I wish it still. I am afraid, I am not equally regarded by him. Indeed it is natural, that he and the rest, from the summit of human glory and prosperity, should not discern me in the mud of my obscurity and wretchedness. I have done all I could to bring them together, to keep them together, and, after a breach, to reconcile them. I agree with you, that this Quarrel cannot be on its ostensible Grounds. I have perhaps more reason than you have to think so. If it stood on those Grounds I am quite sure, that nothing on earth could more easily have been compromised. But, to the last hour, no sort of compromise or Treaty was listened to. There must be some sort of original Sin. For something or other, Lord Fitzwilliam, in a signal and unexampled punishment, is to be made, at every hazard, a striking example.[2]

This passage requires a little exegesis. The first two sentences, registering Burke's awareness of Pitt's negative feelings towards him, are straightforward enough. The third sentence with the reference to the 'mud of my obscurity' rings false; it is one of Burke's not infrequent, and never quite successful displays of humility. Burke had

[1] *Corr.* VIII, 157.
[2] *Corr.* VIII, 207.

long known – at least since Pitt's abandonment of Warren Hastings – that Pitt's negative feelings towards him did not include contempt. In the rest of the paragraph, the key words are: 'For something or other . . .' Burke is here referring to Pitt's resentment of Burke's influence over certain members of his coalition administration.

In the following month, which brought peace between France and Prussia, Burke felt sure that Pitt was contemplating a British peace, and that that had been behind the treatment of his viceroy. Burke wrote to Fitzwilliam: 'Indeed the moment I found them determined finally to break with your Lordship, I had no kind of Doubt that they thought they had peace in prospect. Otherwise, the part they acted would be beyond the ordinary insanity of the violent passions.'[1]

Superficially, this looks like one of Burke's wilder notions. That an Irish Viceroy should be removed, in the circumstances which have been described, because Pitt was aiming at peace with Revolutionary France, seems quite implausible. Yet it can be seen to fit. Pitt did make peace overtures to France before the end of 1795, and it is probable that he had had such an overture in mind from about the time the coalition was formed. In that month, July 1794, Robespierre fell. The Thermidorians, who succeeded him, were not proselytising ideologists but pragmatists, after their fashion. Pitt, also above all a pragmatist, after his own fashion, thought it possible to do business with them, and was to make the attempt in 1795–6. And it was apparent, from the very moment of the Coalition's formation that Fitzwilliam would be a most inconvenient member of an Administration whose leader was looking for peace with Revolutionary France. According to E. A. Smith, 'it was Fitzwilliam above all who had urged upon a seemingly reluctant Cabinet in June 1794 Burke's policy of total war against the revolution.'[2] That stand marked Fitzwilliam out, in Pitt's eyes, as the most potentially refractory member of his new Coalition. In the event of a serious attempt at peace with Revolutionary France, Fitzwilliam would be the main source of trouble within the Cabinet, because he was the most attached to Burke's ideas. Pitt found Burke's support, from outside the Cabinet, useful, but the last thing he wanted, inside the Cabinet, was a convinced Burkean, liable to resign at the wrong moment, over the wrong issue, at the Master's call. Against that background, Pitt's

[1] *Corr.* VIII, 231; letter of 14 April 1795.
[2] *Whig Principles*, p. 194.

treatment of Fitzwilliam becomes more intelligible. To get rid of Fitzwilliam over Irish affairs, about which few in Britain cared very much, was preferable to waiting for him to jump, in the midst of a major political crisis, over a central issue: peace with France. Burke, for his part, understood what Pitt was up to, and was waiting for him. As long as Pitt continued to wage war, Burke would support him, but at the first serious attempt at peace with Revolutionary France, Burke would attack: not Pitt personally, but his attempt at 'a Sansculotick Peace'. Or, as he would later put it, 'a Regicide Peace.'[1] Contemplating the relations between Burke and Pitt, as these stood, under the bruised Coalition, in the Spring of 1795, I am reminded of a phrase of Maxim Gorki's about Tolstoy and God: 'With God he maintains very suspicious relations. They are like two bears in one den.'

IRELAND: MAYNOOTH COLLEGE
1795

As far as Ireland was concerned – specifically, Catholic Ireland – Burke concentrated, after Fitzwilliam's recall, on what could be saved, out of the wreck of almost all his Irish hopes. What could be saved consisted essentially of the national Catholic seminary, what became the Royal College, Maynooth. 'We shall take over this Irish College. As to the Rest, everything is gone beyond my reach. I have only to lament,' Burke wrote to Thomas Hussey (in September 1795). He had been involved with the project for the creation of a Catholic seminary since the end of 1793, as a result of an appeal he had received from the Roman Catholic Bishop of Cork, Francis Moylan. Burke declined direct association with the project, but he advised putting it into the hands of two nominees of his, and his advice was accepted. The two nominees were his son Richard and Hussey, the latter being his closest associate over Catholic affairs. This was clearly intended to ensure that the new seminary should be established according to Burkean prescriptions.

Before the French Revolution, Irish Catholic priests had received their education mostly in French-speaking seminaries in North-

---

[1] Below, pp. 542–69. With 'Regicide Peace', Burke aimed at getting George III's attention, and turning his influence against the peace moves.

Western Europe. The Revolution made this system impossible. France had broken with the Papacy in July 1790, by passing the Civil Constitution of the Clergy, which was formally condemned by the Pope in the following April. Henceforward, wherever the Revolutionary writ ran, the only priests tolerated were the 'Constitutional priests', excommunicated by Rome. The Irish Catholic hierarchy, firmly attached to the Papacy, and therefore rejecting any priests (or 'priests') who might be trained under Revolutionary auspices, urgently needed a seminary, or seminaries, of their own. Pitt's Administration, at war with France, was favourable to the endowment of such an institution. The Irish Administration – before Fitzwilliam's appointment – was prepared to accept that, but would have liked to use endowment as an instrument by which it could exercise control over the Catholic hierarchy. Burke was fiercely opposed to this. He advised Hussey to accept the Government's money, and to account for it annually to the House of Commons. For the rest, he went on, 'All other interference whatsoever, if I were in the place of these Reverend persons, I would resist; and would much rather, trust to Gods good Providence, and the contributions of your own people, for the Education of your Clergy than to put into the hands of your known, avowed, and implacable Enemies, – into the hands of those, who make it their merit and their boast, that they are your Enemies, [and to] the very foundations of your morals and your religion.'[1]

Fitzwilliam, as usual, fell in with Burke's Irish advice, and the foundation of a Catholic National Seminary, responsible to the Hierarchy, and not to the Irish Administration, was acceptable. But after Fitzwilliam's recall it seemed that the Administration would have its way with the new college. The [British] Act for the Better Education of Persons Professing the Popish or Roman Catholic Religion (35 Geo. III, c. 21), which received the Royal Assent on 5 June, 1795, appointed trustees for Maynooth. They included the Irish Chancellor, John Fitzgibbon, Earl of Clare. Fitzgibbon (1749–1802) was the most inveterate and effective enemy of the Irish Catholics, and had played a significant part in the shipwreck of Fitzwilliam's Viceroyalty.[2]

Burke, when he heard the Trustees' names, was outraged. He wrote to Hussey:

[1] E.B. to Thomas Hussey, 17 March 1795; *Corr.* VIII, 199–205.
[2] Fitzgibbon had advised the king that he could not approve the proposed measure of Catholic enfranchisement 'without a direct breach of his Coronation Oath'. (*Corr.* VIII, 192, n.3). See above, pp. 511–21.

I hear, and am extremely alarmed at hearing, that the Chancellor, and the chiefs of the Benches are amongst your Trustees. If this be the Case, so as to give them the power of intermeddling, I must fairly say, that I consider, not only all the Benefits of the institution to be wholly lost – but that a more mischievous project never was set on foot. I should much sooner make your College, according to the first act of Parliament; a subordinate department of our Protestant university – absurd as I always thought that plan to be, than make you the instrument, of the Instruments, of the Jobbing System. I am sure that the constant meddling of the Bishops and the Clergy with the Castle, and of the Castle with them, will infallibly set them ill with their own body. All the weight, which hitherto the Clergy have had in keeping the people quiet will be wholly lost, if once this should happen. At best you will soon have a marked Schism; and more than one kind: and I am very greatly mistaken – if this very thing is not intended, and diligently and systematically pursued. I am steadily of my old opinion, that this affair had better be wholly dropped; and the Government boon, with civility and acknowledgement, declined, than to subject yourselves and your religion to your known and avowed Enemies – who connect their very Interest with your humiliation, and found their own Reputation on the destruction of yours.[1]

In the end Maynooth turned out to be what Burke had intended: an essentially autonomous Roman Catholic institution, controlled by the Irish Catholic Hierarchy and by them alone, through the Catholic Trustees. It appears from the attendance at the first two meetings of the Trustees, shortly after Burke's letter to Hussey, that there was an informal understanding to that effect from the beginning. The first meeting, on 25 June 1795, in the Lord Chancellor's Chamber in the House of Lords, was attended by all the Trustees, with the Lord Chancellor in the Chair. This was clearly a *pro forma* meeting. The first business meeting occurred next day, in John's Lane Chapel. The official centenary history of the college states: 'None of the Protestant ex-officio Trustees was present at this, or most of the subsequent meetings.'[2] Such self-effacement was far from characteristic of Fitz-

---

[1] *Corr.* VIII, 263.

[2] Most Rev. John Healy, *Maynooth College: Its Centenary History, 1795–1895* (Dublin, 1895) p. 110. T. H. D. Mahoney sees Burke as defeated in this matter: 'Burke was strongly opposed to the inclusion of the Chancellor and the judges among the trustees, but necessity forced the Catholics to accept this arrangement despite the wishes of their good friend' (*Edmund Burke and Ireland*, p. 275). This is a misreading. The arrangement in question was nominally accepted, but substantively nullified. In this, as well as in some other matters, Mahoney shows himself rather too literally-minded to be an altogether reliable guide to the often camouflaged realities of life in eighteenth-century Ireland.

gibbon and his legal colleagues. It is clear that there must have been a prior arrangement with Pitt's Administration – meaning, in a matter of such importance, with Pitt himself – that the ex-officio Trustees should not attempt to interfere with the running of Maynooth. So its constitution turned out to be in practice what Burke intended it to be, despite superficial appearances to the contrary.

To endow a Catholic educational foundation, and then concede to it *de facto* autonomy, was a major break both with the theory and practice of the past in Ireland. Socially, culturally, and even politically, this was a more important concession to the Catholics, than even the completion of Catholic enfranchisement would have been. (Although neither this nor any other concession could undo the disastrous effect of the sudden *refusal* of Catholic enfranchisement, once that appeared to have been promised.) One can only speculate why Pitt, after having had Fitzwilliam recalled, then conceded so much. No doubt there was an element of compensation to the Catholics. But I suspect that he was also thinking of Burke, and of the dangers of driving him too far. Pitt's Machiavellian ruthlessness was always accompanied by a judicious sense of limits. The combination was what made him so great a statesman.

What was rescued from the wreckage of Fitzwilliam's viceroyalty, mainly by Burke, was something large and solid. Maynooth College celebrates its bicentenary in 1995. It was the first national institution, under Irish Catholic control, to come into being since the total defeat of the Catholic cause, more than a hundred years before. Directly and indirectly, it has shaped generation after generation of Irish Catholics. It has been much criticised, both by Irish liberals and by a more influential group: Irish republicans, self-proclaimed heirs of the United Irishmen of the period of Maynooth's foundation. Without Burke, it might never have come into being, and might never have preserved its autonomy as a Catholic institution.

Maynooth was from the beginning thoroughly conservative, but also subversive, and both qualities were in tune with Burke's ideas and feelings. Its conservatism, like Burke's, rested on the correct perception that Jacobinism was fundamentally hostile to Catholicism (as later avatars of Jacobinism also were). Its subversiveness rested in being directed against the social order, the Protestant ascendancy – which had just reasserted itself. Burke was on Maynooth's side in that also. Finally, the Maynooth spirit, also from the beginning, was one of benign paternalism. Its authorities gave devoted service to the needs of the Irish people, as they perceived those needs. It was for

Maynooth to teach, and for the people to obey, and learn. Of that, too, Burke approved, in the circumstances of the time. He never idealised the Irish masses of his day. He thought they were in a dreadful condition, and needed to be taken in hand by their own natural leaders, and protected against themselves. That was high among the reasons for the foundation of Maynooth. It runs counter to most of our modern ideas, but in the conditions of Catholic Ireland at the end of the eighteenth century, it made sense.

Burke's share in the foundation of Maynooth was the last in the series of his contributions to the rehabilitation of the Irish Catholics, which had begun more than thirty years before, with the *Tracts on the Penal Laws*. He had hoped to see Catholic Emancipation completed, but that was to be deferred to the generation of Daniel O'Connell. But the main series of emancipation measures – beginning with the Catholic Relief Act of 1778 and ending with that of 1793 – had been carried, under Burke's influence well before O'Connell's day. This is not to depreciate O'Connell's role. The last stage of Catholic Emancipation, which was O'Connell's, was won by a colossal popular agitation. The first stage, that of 1778 was won by discreet lobbying, led by Burke, behind the scenes. The second stage, that of 1793, was won by the royal reception of a petition, the way for which was prepared by Burke and his son, also behind the scenes. Naturally, the last stage, O'Connell's, had far greater emotional impact and therefore historical resonance, than the first two.

IRELAND AFTER FITZWILLIAM'S RECALL
1795–1796

Maynooth apart, Burke was a helpless spectator, as far as Ireland was concerned, from the recall of Fitzwilliam until his own death, a little more than two years later. The Irish Administration was now firmly back in the hands from which Burke had tried to wrench it, and those in power were bent on a policy of pre-emptive repression of an incipient Catholic rebellion. Pitt's Administration, through the recall of Fitzwilliam, had taken the decision to give the Junto its head. Pitt knew that repression might lead to disaster – perhaps indeed conciliation and repression were only alternative roads to disaster, in the 1790s. But if the Junto's policies – the practical embodiment of 'legislative independence' – should fail, then Pitt had a remedy in reserve – the Union of Great Britain and Ireland.

Burke could not hope to turn Pitt from an Irish policy for which he had come near to sacrificing the Coalition. The Coalition had held, with some help from Burke, and he was still committed to supporting it as long as the alternative was Fox and a pro-Jacobin policy. The French Revolution, in Burke's mind, took precedence over everything else, including Ireland. But emotionally, that precedence was painful. His correspondence for this period reflects a high degree of ambivalence. He wrote to a friend in March 1795: 'Well! they all amaze me, – Princes, Dukes, Marquisses, Chancellors of the Exchequer, Secretaries of State! – My heart is sick; my stomach turns; my head grows dizzy; The world seems to me to reel and stagger. The Crimes of Democracy, and the madness and folly of Aristocracy alike frighten and confound me. The only refuge is in God who sees thro' all these mazes.'

Burke was, of course, opposed to all Jacobins, Irish as well as English, and of course French. But his feelings towards the Irish Jacobins were significantly different from his feelings towards the English ones. All his many comments on the latter, from the moment he first realised their existence, in November 1789, are implacably hostile, and usually contemptuous. He does not often refer to the Irish Jacobins, but when he does, his tone is more respectful. The most conspicuous of them in 1795 was Arthur O'Connor (1763–1852), the only member of the Irish Parliament to make a speech there along 'United Irish' lines. (O'Connor later escaped arrest by going to France, became a general in the French Army, and married a daughter of Condorcet.) In his most famous speech, delivered on 4 May 1795 after Fitzwilliam's recall, O'Connor attacked the political and administrative abuses of the time and hinted that if they were not speedily redressed, the Irish people might look for foreign aid. Burke wrote to Fitzwilliam:

It should seem as if young o'Connor gave himself his full swing. I am sorry for it: He has good parts; and on his Uncle Longfields Death he will have a large fortune. I saw him at Bath about three years ago. He was then an enthusiast; an admirer of Rousseau, and the French writers, – but, as I thought, very tractable; and had taken, on the whole, a very proper direction. What became of him after that time I never knew: I saw he had a mind of great energy, and was capable of much good or of much Evil. I am very sorry to say, that the Course they are pursuing in

Ireland will Jacobinize all the Energies and all the active Talents of that Country. These are very considerable; and the popular mind is more susceptible of any emotion there than it is here. Jacobinism is the Vice of men of Parts; and, in this age, it is the Channel in which all discontents will run.

Clearly O'Connor's speech made a strong impression on Burke, for he refers to it again a few days later, in a letter to Thomas Hussey:

In Parliament the Language of your friends (one only excepted) was what it ought to be. But that one Speech, though full of fire and animation, was not warmed with the fire of heaven. I am sorry for it. I have seen that Gentleman but once. He is certainly a man of parts; but one who has dealt too much in the Philosophy of France. Justice, Prudence, Tenderness, moderation, and Christian Charity, ought to become the measures of tolerance, and not a cold apathy, or indeed rather a savage hatred, to all Religion, and an avowd contempt of all those points on which we [Christians] differ, and on those about which we agree.[1]

There is a suggestion here of Milton contemplating Satan. O'Connor is on the wrong side, but there is something splendid about him all the same. Burke never wrote in that vein about any of the English Jacobins. Of course the circumstances – always a prime Burkean concern – were greatly different. The Irish revolutionaries had something to be revolutionary about; the English ones did not, in Burke's view.

Burke saw that many Catholics were becoming Jacobinised, but he did not cease to sympathise with them on that account. He put the blame for the rapid spread of Jacobinism, after Fitzwilliam's recall, squarely onto the shoulders of the Protestant Ascendancy (a term popularised in the 1790s by members of the Ascendancy itself, and replacing the older and less offensive term 'Protestant interest').[2]

Together with 'Indianism' and 'Jacobinism', 'Protestant Ascendancy' now formed a malign triad in Burke's mind. On 26 May 1795, Burke again wrote to Hercules Langrishe, an Ascendancy member but a moderate one:

[1] *Corr.* VIII, pp. 215–6; 242–3; 245–6.
[2] See W. J. McCormack, 'Ascendancy and Tradition' in *Anglo-Irish Literary History from 1789 to 1939* (Oxford, 1985); also James Kelly, 'The Genesis of Protestant Ascendancy: the Rightboy Disturbances of the 1780's and their Impact upon Protestant opinion' in Gerard O'Brien (ed.), *Parliament, Politics and People: Essays in Eighteenth Century Irish History* (Dublin, 1989) pp. 93–124.

In the Catholic Question I considered only one point. Was it [full enfran-
chisement] at the time, and in the circumstances, a measure which tended
to promote the concord of the citizens? I have no difficulty in saying it
was; and as little in saying that the present concord of the citizens was
worth buying, at a critical season, by granting a few *capacities*, which
probably no one man now living is likely to be served or hurt by. When
any man tells *you* and *me* that, if these places were left in the discretion
of a Protestant Crown, and these memberships in the discretion of Protestant electors, or patrons, we should have a Popish official system, and
a Popish representation, capable of overturning the establishment, he
only insults our understandings. When any man tells this to *Catholics*,
he insults their understandings and he galls their feelings. It is not the
question of the places and seats; it is the real hostile disposition, and the
pretended fears, that leave stings in the minds of the people. I really
thought that in the total of the late circumstances, with regard to persons,
to things, to principles, and to measures, was to be found a conjunction
favourable to the introduction, and to the perpetuation, of a general
harmony, producing a general strength which to that hour Ireland was
never so happy as to enjoy. My sanguine hopes are blasted, and I must
consign my feelings on that terrible disappointment to the same patience
in which I have been obliged to bury the vexation I suffered on the defeat
of the other great, just, and honourable causes in which I have had some
share; and which have given more of dignity than of peace and advantage
to a long, laborious life. Though, perhaps, a want of success might be
urged as a reason for making me doubt of the justice of the part I have
taken, yet, until I have other lights than one side of the debate has
furnished me, I must see things, and feel them too, as I see and feel them.
*I think I can hardly overrate the malignity of the principles of Protestant
ascendency, as they affect Ireland; or of Indianism, as they affect these
countries, and as they affect Asia; or of Jacobinism as they affect all
Europe, and the state of human society itself. The last is the greatest evil.
But it readily combines with the others, and flows from them* [my italics
– C.C.O'B.]. Whatever breeds discontent at this time will produce that
great master-mischief most infallibly. Whatever tends to persuade the
people that the *few*, called by whatever name you please, religious or
political, are of opinion that their interest is not compatible with that of
the *many*, is a great point gained to Jacobinism. Whatever tends to irritate
the talents of a country, which have at all times, and at these particularly,
a mighty influence on the public mind, is of infinite service to that formidable cause. Unless where Heaven has mingled uncommon ingredients, of
virtue in the composition – *quos meliore luto finit proecordia Titan* –
talents naturally gravitate to Jacobinism. Whatever ill humours are afloat
in the state, they will be sure to discharge themselves in a mingled torrent
in the *Cloacâ Maximâ* of Jacobinism. Therefore people ought well to

look about them. First, the physicians are to take care that they do nothing to irritate this epidemical distemper. It is a foolish thing to have the better of the patient in a dispute. The complaint, or its cause, ought to be removed, and wise and lenient arts ought to precede the measures of vigour. They ought to be the *ultima*, not the *prima*, not the *tota* ratio of a wise government. God forbid, that on a worthy occasion authority should want the means of force, or the disposition to use it. But where a prudent and enlarged policy does not precede it, and attend it too, where the hearts of the better sort of people do not go with the hands of the soldiery, you may call your constitution what you will, in effect it will consist of three parts, (orders, if you please,) – cavalry, infantry, and artillery, – and of nothing else or better.[1]

By the autumn of 1795, the cycle of seditious conspiracy and governmental repression was far advanced in Ireland, and already taking the form of incipient political–sectarian civil war. Its epicentre, at this time, was in Co. Armagh, where the (Protestant) Peep O'Day Boys were fighting the (Catholic) Defenders and where the Orange Order was founded, in September 1795. Its members immediately set about the mass expulsion of thousands of Catholics from those rural areas – in Tyrone, Down and Fermanagh, besides Armagh – where Protestants were sufficiently numerous to be able to undertake such an enterprise. These disturbances were known as 'the Armagh outrages'. As Thomas Bartlett writes: 'It was on the anvil of these expulsions that the alliance between Defenders and United Irishmen was forged sometime early in 1796.'[2]

The Catholic Archbishop of Dublin, Dr Troy, issued a pastoral letter in August denouncing the Defenders and shortly afterwards parties of Defenders surrendered their arms. Burke disapproved of these developments, since he thought the Catholic clergy too inclined to advise their flocks to submission, under repression and provocation. In February, he had written to Fitzwilliam:

All the Miseries of Ireland have originated, in what has produced all the

---

[1] *Corr.* VIII, 253–255. This letter is included in *Works* as 'Second Letter to Sir Hercules Langrishe', for the first, see above, pp. 476–83. The emphasis of this letter differs from the advice offered by Burke to Fitzwilliam at the time of his appointment as Viceroy. In the advice Burke was preoccupied with tactics and, above all, timing. Writing to Langrishe, after the disaster, Burke returns to basic principles.

[2] Select Documents XXXVIII: 'Defenders and Defenderism in 1795' in *Irish Historical Studies* XXIV (1985) p. 375.

miseries of India, a servile patience under oppression, by the greatest of all misnomers called prudence.[1]

Pursuing the same line of thought, Burke now opposed the disarming of the Defenders. He wrote to Thomas Hussey:

> We are not in a pleasant way any where. In Ireland I fear as ill almost as can be. In truth all these distempers pass my Skill. The Catholicks have foolishly, in all senses disarmed themselves. If the disarmament had been common to all descriptions of disorderly persons the Measure would have been excellent. But when one description of armed Rioters consent to become peaceful Subjects, to keep up another set of armed Rioters, and those too the original Rioters who first provoked the Rest is a policy belonging to our unhappy time and Country.[2]

By the end of the year Burke's position over Ireland was so complex and involved as to be almost untenable. His heart and head were at variance. He had first become emotionally committed to the anti-Jacobin cause in November 1789, on discovering that Protestant bigots in England were welcoming the French Revolution, because of its anti-Catholic character. But in Ireland, by 1795, Protestant bigots were anti-Jacobin, or at least were making use of anti-Jacobinism for anti-Catholic purposes. Burke's Catholic sympathies – and specifically his sympathies with those Catholics who were disposed to resist repression and provocation – drew him toward the side of the Irish Catholic pro-Jacobins, a category which included the Defenders.

In 1795–6, the Defender refugees from the Ulster fringes were spreading throughout Ireland. According to Marianne Elliott: 'The Catholic refugees from Ulster were more effective agents of revolution than the intellectual United Irish leaders could ever have been.'[3] Yet the Defenders and the United Irish leaders soon formed an alliance, which was to be at the root of the Great Rebellion of 1798. On 22 January 1796 Camden, who had succeeded Fitzwilliam as viceroy, wrote to Portland that the Defenders swore, not only to be true to one another, 'but to be united and correspond with the society of United Irishmen'.[4]

---

[1] *Corr.* VIII, 144–8.
[2] *Corr.* VIII, 351–2.
[3] Elliott: 'The Origins and Transformations of Irish Republicanism', *International Review of Social History*, xxiii (1978), pp. 405–428.
[4] Cited in Bartlett, 'Defenders', p. 375.

Burke, at the time when he wrote against the disarming of Defenders, probably did not know about their emerging alliance with the United Irishmen. It could hardly have surprised him, however, since he was acutely aware that conditions in Ireland after Fitzwilliam's recall were highly propitious to the spread of Jacobinism. Still, in the context of 'the Armagh outrages', it would have been natural for Burke to think of Defenders as primarily innocent Catholics, trying to hold on to their homes against assaults from Protestant bigots. Archbishop Troy, in denouncing the Defenders, showed himself more aware of their revolutionary potential. The Defenders have been described as 'anti-Protestant, anti-English and anti-settler'.[1] They were in fact no less sectarian than their Orange adversaries, and the apparent paradox of their alliance with the 'anti-sectarian' United Irishmen has been noted. There was a related paradox in the admiration of this violently Catholic body for anti-Catholic Revolutionary France, and their expectations from that quarter. But Defender documents reveal a real confusion of Catholic millenarian hopes with Jacobin jargon. There are references to 'the present United States of France and Ireland' and to 'the Tree of Liberty', and there is a Defender catechism of 1795 which runs: 'Are you concerned? I am. To what? To the National Convention. What do you design by that cause? To quell all nations, dethrone all kings and to plant the true religion that was lost at the Reformation. Who sent you? Simon Peter, the head of the Church. Signed by order of the Chief Consul.'[2]

Not only did the Defenders propagate millenarian ideas – so did some of the putatively enlightened United Irishmen. In 1795–6 millenarian prophecies associated with Colmcille were dispensed by Catholic United Irishmen to Catholics in Co. Derry, while Protestant United Irishmen dispensed the same prophecies – no doubt with somewhat different glosses – to Protestants in Co. Antrim.[3]

The late rays of the Enlightenment as they penetrated the mists of

[1] Bartlett, 'Defenders', p. 376.
[2] Bartlett, 'Defenders', pp. 378–9.
[3] See James S. Donnelly, 'Propagating the Cause of the United Irishmen', *Studies* LXIX, Spring 1980, pp. 5–23. Sometimes the millenarian preaching crossed community lines, with unfortunate results, in at least one case. Donnelly tells of an absent-minded preacher of the Millennium, the Reformed Presbyterian, William Gibson, of Co. Antrim: 'Forgetting the United Irish ideal of Presbyterian Catholic unity, Gibson was said at times to relapse into identification of the pope with the scarlet whore of Babylon, only to make amends to offended Catholic listeners by pointing out the immediate destruction of the British monarchy.'

rural Ireland, in the middle of the last decade of the eighteenth century, produced some strange and ominous rainbows. Altogether the situation was so confusing that it is not surprising that Burke's relation to it was also somewhat confused. Politically, this mattered little: Burke's influence over Irish affairs, so significant over three decades, had collapsed. The last, ripe fruit of that influence was the foundation of Maynooth College. 'As to the Rest', as he had written to Thomas Hussey in September 1795, 'everything has gone beyond my reach. I have only to lament.'

It is tempting to think of Burke as a Greek chorus, commenting on the unfolding of a tragedy whose outcome he is powerless to deflect. But the analogy is not close. Unlike the chorus, Burke had played a significant part at a decisive moment in the tragedy.[1] He had done more than anyone to prepare the way for Fitzwilliam's viceroyalty. He had laboured long to make possible the Coalition which appointed Fitzwilliam ·as Viceroy. It was Burke who had instilled in Fitzwilliam the principles over Irish affairs on which he acted during the Viceroyalty. Fitzwilliam's arrival as Viceroy, imbued with Burkean principles, appeared to represent the triumph of everything Burke had been working for, where Ireland was concerned, throughout his political career.

To say that the apparent triumph then turned to disaster would be inadequate. The apparent triumph – the euphoria that welcomed Fitzwilliam – was an integral part of the total disaster. Historians agree that it was the high hopes aroused by Fitzwilliam's arrival, combined with the rage excited by the circumstances of his recall, which precipitated an upsurge of revolutionary feelings among many Catholics. Obviously, the panic which Fitzwilliam's arrival excited among the Protestant Ascendancy, combined with the vindictive triumphalism aroused by the circumstances of his recall, accounted for the ferocity of the subsequent anti-Catholic repression. All in all, it was the tragic course of Fitzwilliam's viceroyalty, more than any other set of events, which prepared the way the for Great Rebellion, three years later. It would have been better for the Irish – all varieties of them – if his benevolent viceroyalty had never been. In this case, more than in most, the road to Hell was indeed paved with good intentions. And the best of those intentions were those of Edmund Burke.

---

[1] Owen Dudley Edwards reminds me that the chorus in the *Eumenides* of Aeschylus did play a significant part in the tragedy.

There is only one letter in which he acknowledged his own share in the responsibility for the disaster, and the deep distress occasioned to him by that knowledge. This is the crucial letter of 13 March 1795, to Fitzwilliam; the first written in the knowledge that his recall has now been decided:

My lord you say, that you hope I too will not abandon you. I abandon my friend! How could such a thought come into your head? I abandon you, who am responsible to you for the advice I gave you to coalite with this Ministry, and to accept your Late Office of chief Governour of Ireland! I abandon you, who, (if I could suppose myself in your place) would do the very same things, and more of the same kind! – I abandon you who would have pulled down much more of that crazy and infected Structure that loads my native Country, than you have done; and who have advised the permitting any part of it to stand, only on the pressure of the most rigid and odious Necessity. [He added:] I am in Truth over-whelmed with grief, shame and anguish.[1]

There are no further references of that kind. In his other letters written while the consequences of Fitzwilliam's recall were unfolding, Burke, quite legitimately, puts the full blame on those who were responsible for the recall, and does not allude to any share, in the responsibility for the dire trend of events, which may have been incurred by those who had raised the high hopes, and deep resentments, which had accompanied the original appointment of the hapless viceroy. But I don't doubt that the feelings of personal responsibility, and associated 'grief, shame and anguish', of which we get a glimpse in that letter to Fitzwilliam, lingered and tormented Burke throughout the ever-darkening sequel to the Fitzwilliam Viceroyalty, which had been his beloved brain-child.

[1] *Corr.* VIII, 188–96.

BURKE AND PITT

Burke had no cause to reproach himself. Not only had his intentions been in the highest degree benevolent and personally disinterested, but his plans had been most carefully laid, and based on a lifetime of thought and inquiry, concerning Ireland and its relation to Britain. The only error he made – but that a fatal one – was to misread the meaning of Pitt's acquiescence in Fitzwilliam's appointment as Viceroy. It was not that Burke underestimated Pitt – he never did that – but that he had underestimated himself in relation to Pitt. He had failed to allow for Pitt's resentment at the tendency towards the formation of a distinct Burkean section within William Pitt's new Administration. Pitt was determined to nip that in the bud. The unfortunate Fitzwilliam was the bud.

Pitt, being essentially a power-politician, as distinct from a cause-politician (that much rarer breed), had considered Burke with the lucid attentiveness with which such a politician considers a force which may enlarge, or advance, or encroach upon, his own power, depending on the circumstances. Burke had been seen as a threat over Pitt's dubious Indian involvement, in the mid-1780s. Later, from the beginning of the 1790s, with the breach with Fox, Burke offered the prospect of an accretion to Pitt's power-base, and was courted accordingly, although always with some reserve. Then when the hoped for accretion materialised, in the form of the coalition, it emerged that some of the members seemed to think of themselves, not as Pitt's supporters, but as his conditional allies, more under Burke's influence than Pitt's. That was what had to be stopped. Pitt reckoned that Burke would swallow the bitter pill of the recall. He knew the depth of Burke's commitment to the struggle against Revolutionary France, and he also knew of his conviction that Pitt was the essential leader in that struggle. Those factors ensured Burke's continued support for the Coalition, after Fitzwilliam's recall. It was the rational subordination of the lesser to the greater, within a strong emotional field of force. Those words 'Grief, shame and anguish', in the March letter to Fitzwilliam, are followed by, 'But my reason, such as it is, remains.'

'Rational subordination of the lesser' – the lesser being the Irish Catholics, abandoned by Pitt to their fate – had to feel like a betrayal, at a certain level of the Burkean psyche. That feeling, and an inner revulsion from Pitt and 'the greater' may partly account for the otherwise surprising tenderness, in certain references, towards the potential allies, in Ireland, of Burke's greatest enemies in the world at large: the Jacobins. 'Rational subordination' still held, but the emotional price was high.

DETRACTORS COUNTER-ATTACKED

Towards the end of 1795, the centre of Burke's attention was deflected from the doom-laden scene in Ireland by developments at Westminster which were to provide the genesis for his last published writings: *Letter to a Noble Lord* and *Letters on a Regicide Peace* (24 February and 20 October 1796). The occasion for the composition of *Letter to a Noble Lord* was an attack by two Whig peers, the Duke of Bedford and the Earl of Lauderdale, in the Lords on 13 November 1795 on the pension which had been granted to Burke in the previous year, on his retirement from Parliament. The pension was of £1,200 a year, and a peerage had also been proposed. Pitt's biographer, Earl Stanhope, believed that Burke refused the peerage, after his son's death.[1] However that may be, the pension was accepted. It enabled Edmund to pay his debts and to be assured, during his last illness, that his widow would not have to face a life of poverty. (Jane died in 1812, fifteen years after Edmund.)

Inevitably, Burke's many enemies, among the Whigs and radicals, triumphed. The secret of Burke's 'Apostasy' – Lauderdale's word – was now out. He had written the *Reflections*, in 1790, because he was in quest of the pension he managed to get four years later. That accounted for everything. It was the thirty pieces of silver. As Carl B. Cone wrote: 'His representation as a Judas Iscariot and a sycophant was cruel and maddening as well as untrue.'[2] But Burke had received an enormous amount of abuse and innuendo – more than any other politician – in his long political career. In *Letter to a Noble Lord* he called it 'the hunt of obloquy, which ever has pursued me with a full cry through life.' Most of these attacks came from anonymous writers in the corrupt press of the time, faceless and un-

---

[1] *Life of Pitt* II, p. 244. Later writers believe that the peerage was given up before Richard's death: Cone, *Burke and the Nature of Politics; the Age of the French Revolution*, p. 447, n.129. The pension was the work of Burke's friends in the Coalition Administration of 1794, with Pitt's consent.

[2] Cone, *op. cit.*, p. 449.

accountable tormentors. Burke did not answer those ever. The Duke of Bedford, on the other hand was a marvellous target. He was a member of the Whig leadership: 'one of the main pillars of the party,'[1] Charles James Fox had called him.

He was also vulnerable. The Bedford family, since the days of Henry VIII, had been beneficiaries of Crown patronage on a colossal scale. Thus, by attacking Burke's modest pension, the Duke had unwittingly laid himself open to the most devastating *argumentum ad hominem* in the history of English controversy. But *Letter to a Noble Lord* is more than that; it is also the nearest that Burke comes to an *apologia pro vita sua*. It contains, with much else, Burke's grave and succinct rebuttal to the charge of venality that dogged him throughout his life, and has clung to his reputation ever since:

> His Grace thinks I have obtained too much. I answer, that my exertions, whatever they have been, were such as no hopes of pecuniary reward could possibly excite; and no pecuniary compensation can possibly reward them. Between money and such services, there is no common principle of comparison: they are quantities incommensurable.[2]

I referred to this passage as 'a rebuttal' and in itself it is no more than that. But when we take into consideration also the totality of Burke's writing and speeches, as these have come down to us, the rebuttal becomes a refutation. Those writings and speeches are indeed 'such as no hopes of pecuniary reward could possibly excite.'

Burke goes on to distinguish between his own efforts as a reformer and the revolutionary innovations which the Duke defends. Burke here gives full vent to the horror and hatred which the French Revolution inspires in him. The imagery of corruption, which I believe to be associated with the disturbance of the Irish level in Burke's psyche,

---

[1] *Corr.* VIII, 395, n.3.

[2] *Works* V, p. 179. I have also before me as I write a copy of the first edition of this work. The full title is *A Letter from the Right Honourable Edmund Burke to a Noble Lord on the attacks made upon him and his pension, in the House of Lords by the Duke of Bedford and the Earl of Lauderdale in the present sessions of Parliament*. It is a pamphlet of 80 pages. This first edition, with 'from the Author' in manuscript on the half-title page, was sent to me from New York, by Deirdre Levinson Bergson, and is my most treasured possession. It arrived just as I was finishing Chapter IV. When I read the inscription, 'my hair sat up'. As Kipling puts it in 'My Own True Ghost Story' (1888). 'It is a mistake to say that hair stands up. The skin of the head tightens, and you can feel a faint bristling all over the scalp. That is the hair sitting up.' The *Letter to a Noble Lord* with the inscription 'from the Author' forms the Message from the Master referred to in the Dedication.

is strongly present in the conclusion of the following passage:

> It cannot at this time be too often repeated, line upon line, precept upon precept, until it comes into the currency of a proverb, – *To innovate is not to reform*. The French revolutionists complained of everything; they refused to reform anything; and they left nothing, no, nothing at all, *unchanged*. The consequences are *before* us, – not in remote history, not in future prognostication: they are about us; they are upon us. They shake the public security; they menace private enjoyment. They dwarf the growth of the young; they stop our way. They infest us in town; they pursue us to the country. Our business is interrupted, our repose is troubled, our pleasures are saddened, our very studies are poisoned and perverted, and knowledge is rendered worse than ignorance, by the enormous evils of this dreadful innovation. The Revolution harpies of France, sprung from Night and Hell, or from that chaotic Anarchy which generates equivocally "all monstrous, all prodigious things", cuckoo-like, adulterously lay their eggs, and brood over, and hatch them in the nest of every neighboring state. These obscene harpies, who deck themselves in I know not what divine attributes, but who in reality are foul and ravenous birds of prey, (both mothers and daughters,) flutter over our heads, and souse down upon our tables, and leave nothing unrent, unrifled, unravaged, or unpolluted with the slime of their filthy offal.[1]

Burke compares his own arduous public career with Bedford's situation:

> I was not, like his Grace of Bedford, swaddled and rocked and dandled into a legislator: "*Nitor in adversum*" [I advance against adversity] is the motto for a man like me. I possessed not one of the qualities nor cultivated one of the arts that recommend men to the favor and protection of the great. I was not made for a minion or a tool. As little did I follow the trade of winning the hearts by imposing on the understandings of the people. At every step of my progress in life, (for in every step was I traversed and opposed,) and at every turnpike I met, I was obliged to show my passport, and again and again to prove my sole title to the honour of being useful to my country, by a proof that I was not wholly unacquainted with its laws and the whole system of its interests both abroad and at home. Otherwise, no rank, no toleration even, for me. I had no arts but manly arts. On them I have stood, and, please God, in

---

[1] *Works* V, 187. I take the disturbance of the 'Irish level' here to be due in part to the dire situation in Ireland and Burke's painfully conflicting feelings about it, and in part to his horror at the approaching conjuncture between Catholic rebellion in Ireland and Jacobin France.

spite of the Duke of Bedford and the Earl of Lauderdale, to the last gasp will I stand.

'I was not made for a minion or a tool'. Here again Burke's self-assessment is borne out by his life and work.

The first part of the tract is mainly defensive; towards the middle, Burke goes suddenly on the attack:

His Grace may think as meanly as he will of my deserts in the far greater part of my conduct in life. It is free for him to do so. There will always be some difference of opinion on the value of political services. But there is one merit of mine which he, of all men living, ought to be the last to call in question. I have supported with very great zeal, and I am told with some degree of success, those opinions, or, if his Grace likes another expression better, those old prejudices, which buoy up the ponderous mass of his nobility, wealth, and titles. I have omitted no exertion to prevent him and them from sinking to that level to which the meretricious French faction his Grace at least coquets with omit no exertion to reduce both. I have done all I could to discountenance their inquiries into the fortunes of those who hold large portions of wealth without any apparent merit of their own. I have strained every nerve to keep the Duke of Bedford in that situation which alone makes him my superior.[1]

Burke develops his attack:

The Duke of Bedford conceives that he is obliged to call the attention of the House of Peers to his Majesty's grant to me, which he considers as excessive and out of all bounds. I know not how it has happened, but it really seems, that, whilst his Grace was meditating his well-considered censure upon me, he fell into a sort of sleep. Homer nods, and the Duke of Bedford may dream; and as dreams (even his golden dreams) are apt to be ill-pieced and incongruously put together, his Grace preserved his idea of reproach to *me*, but took the subject-matter from the crown grants *to his own family*. This is "the stuff of which his dreams are made." In that way of putting things together his Grace is perfectly in the right. The grants to the House of Russell were so enormous as not only to outrage economy, but even to stagger credibility. The Duke of Bedford is the leviathan among all the creatures of the crown. He tumbles about his unwieldy bulk, he plays and frolics in the ocean of the royal bounty. Huge as he is, and whilst "he lies floating many a rood," he is still a creature. His ribs, his fins, his whalebone, his blubber, the very spiracles through which he spouts a torrent of brine against his origin, and covers me all over with the spray, everything of him and about

[1] *Works* V, 196–7.

him is from the throne. Is it for *him* to question the dispensation of the royal favor?

I really am at a loss to draw any sort of parallel between the public merits of his Grace, by which he justifies the grants he holds, and these services of mine, on the favorable construction of which I have obtained what his Grace so much disapproves. In private life I have not at all the honor of acquaintance with the noble Duke; but I ought to presume, and it costs me nothing to do so, that he abundantly deserves the esteem and love of all who live with him. But as to public service, why, truly, it would not be more ridiculous for me to compare myself, in rank, in fortune, in splendid descent, in youth, strength, or figure, with the Duke of Bedford, than to make a parallel between his services and my attempts to be useful to my country. It would not be gross adulation, but uncivil irony, to say that he has any public merit of his own to keep alive the idea of the services by which his vast landed pensions were obtained. My merits, whatever they are, are original and personal; his are derivative. It is his ancestor, the original pensioner, that has laid up this inexhaustible fund of merit which makes his Grace so very delicate and exceptious about the merit of all other grantees of the crown. Had he permitted me to remain in quiet, I should have said, "'Tis his estate: that's enough. It is his by law: what have I to do with it or its history?" He would naturally have said, on his side, "'Tis this man's fortune. He is as good now as my ancestor was two hundred and fifty years ago. I am a young man with very old pensions; he is an old man with very young pensions: that's all."[1]

Burke reviews the career of the founder of the Bedford family fortunes, a courtier of Henry VIII. And he warns the inheritor of these fortunes against his incongruous and unnatural allies, the Jacobins:

They are the Duke of Bedford's natural hunters; and he is their natural game. Because he is not very profoundly reflecting, he sleeps in profound security: they, on the contrary, are always vigilant, active, enterprising, and, though far removed from any knowledge which makes men estimable or useful, in all the instruments and resources of evil their leaders are not meanly instructed or insufficiently furnished. In the French Revolution everything is new, and, from want of preparation to meet so unlooked-for an evil, everything is dangerous. Never before this time was a set of literary men converted into a gang of robbers and assassins; never before did a den of bravoes and banditti assume the garb and tone of an academy of philosophers.

Let me tell his Grace, that an union of such characters, monstrous as

[1] *Works* V, 198–200.

it seems, is not made for producing despicable enemies. But if they are formidable as foes, as friends they are dreadful indeed. . . .[1]

Whatever his Grace may think of himself, they look upon him, and everything that belongs to him, with no more regard than they do upon the whiskers of that little long-tailed animal that has been long the game of the grave, demure, insidious, spring-nailed, velvet-pawed, green-eyed philosophers, whether going upon two legs or upon four.[2]

From a whale and a mouse, Burke turns the hapless Duke into an ox, for the slaughter:

It is not a singular phenomenon, that, whilst the sans-culotte carcass-butchers and the philosophers of the shambles are pricking their dotted lines upon his hide, and, like the print of the poor ox that we see in the shop-windows at Charing Cross, alive as he is, and thinking no harm in the world, he is divided into rumps, and sirloins, and briskets, and into all sorts of pieces for roasting, boiling, and stewing, that, all the while they are measuring him, his Grace is measuring me, – is invidiously comparing the bounty of the crown with the deserts of the defender of his order, and in the same moment fawning on those who have the knife half out of the sheath? Poor innocent!
Pleased to the last, he crops the flowery food,
And licks the hand just raised to shed his blood.

In his conclusion, Burke invokes the memory of Bedford's uncle, the Whig naval hero, Admiral Keppel. Keppel was of Dutch descent, and Holland – rebaptised the 'Batavian Republic' – was then in the power of Revolutionary France. Bedford had said that he could not 'conceive what claims a man could have upon the country who by his writings could involve it in all the horrors of war'. Burke tells Bedford that Keppel would agree with Burke on the necessity of war with the revolutionary and expansionist French Republic. The peroration of *Letter to a Noble Lord* is also the prelude to *Letters on a Regicide Peace*. Burke here tells Bedford that Keppel could never have accepted the transformation of Holland by the Jacobins:

He was no great clerk, but he was perfectly well versed in the interests of Europe, and he could not have heard with patience that the country of Grotius, the cradle of the law of nations, and one of the richest repositories of all law, should be taught a new code by the ignorant flippancy

[1] *Works* V, 213.
[2] *Works* V, 217.

of Thomas Paine, the presumptuous foppery of La Fayette, with his stolen rights of man in his hand, the wild, profligate intrigue and turbulency of Marat, and the impious sophistry of Condorcet, in his insolent addresses to the Batavian Republic.

Could Keppel, who idolized the House of Nassau, who was himself given to England along with the blessings of the British and Dutch Revolutions which consolidated and married the liberties and the interests of the two nations forever, – could he see the fountain of British liberty itself in servitude to France? Could he see with patience a Prince of Orange expelled, as a sort of diminutive despot, with every kind of contumely, from the country which that family of deliverers had so often rescued from slavery, and obliged to live in exile in another country, which owes its liberty to his house?

Would Keppel have heard with patience that the conduct to be held on such occasions was to become short by the knees to the faction of the homicides, to entreat them quietly to retire? or, if the fortune of war should drive them from their first wicked and unprovoked invasion, that no security should be taken, no arrangement made, no barrier formed, no alliance entered into for the security of that which under a foreign name is the most precious part of England? What would he have said if it was even proposed that the Austrian Netherlands [Belgium] (which ought to be a barrier to Holland, and the tie of an alliance to protect her against any species of rule that might be erected or even be restored in France) should be formed into a republic under her influence and dependent upon her power?

But above all, what would he have said, if he had heard it made a matter of accusation against me, by his nephew, the Duke of Bedford, that I was the author of the war? Had I a mind to keep that high distinction to myself, (as from pride I might, but from justice I dare not,) he would have snatched his share of it from my hand, and held it with the grasp of a dying convulsion to his end.

It would be a most arrogant presumption in me to assume to myself the glory of what belongs to his Majesty, and to his ministers, and to his Parliament, and to the far greater majority of his faithful people: but had I stood alone to counsel, and that all were determined to be guided by my advice, and to follow it implicitly, then I should have been the sole author of a war. But it should have been a war on my ideas and my principles. However, let his Grace think as he may of my demerits with regard to the war with Regicide, he will find my guilt confined to that alone. He never shall, with the smallest color of reason, accuse me of being the author of a peace with Regicide. – But that is high matter, and ought not to be mixed with anything of so little moment as what may belong to me, or even to the Duke of Bedford.

I have the honor to be, &c.
Edmund Burke.[1]

[1] *Works* V, 196–229.

Peace with France? Burke against Pitt

The four *Letters on a Regicide Peace* are the last in the series of Burke's great polemics against the French Revolution. As early as March 1795, Burke had foreseen that Pitt would make a move in the direction of peace with France. The move was actually made that autumn, following the adoption in August by the Directory – which had come to power after the fall of Robespierre – of the 'Constitution of the Year III'. Article I of the new constitution proclaimed 'The rights of man in society are liberty, equality, security, and property.'[1] Fraternity had vanished, and in its place had come 'security and property', Pitt interpreted the new constitution as meaning that the French Revolution was now at last 'settling down.' Burke for his part, liked the new constitution no better than he had liked its predecessor, and he foresaw, correctly that the new one would be no more effective than the old one had been. Actually, the most significant political document of 1795–6 was not the 'Constitution of the Year III', but General Bonaparte's Proclamation to the Army of Italy on 27 March: 'Soldiers, you are naked, ill fed! The Government owes you much; it can give you nothing. Your patience, the courage you display in the midst of these rocks, are admirable; but they procure you no glory, no fame is reflected upon you. I seek to lead you into the most fertile plains in the world. Rich provinces, great cities will be in your power. There you will find honour, glory, and riches. Soldiers of Italy, would you be lacking in courage or constancy?'[2]

Liberty, Equality and Fraternity are here seen as yielding place to 'honour, glory and riches' as motivating forces for the French revolutionary armies. The property rights guaranteed by the 'Constitution of the Year III' were the rights of those *French* people who owned property in 1796. The property of France's neighbours, however, was still an object of annexation by their French Liberators. In that sense, France was still a revolutionary nation. The fact that loot, not liberty, was now the motivating force did not make France any less dangerous a neighbour. France might be 'settling down' in the sense that the slogans of 1789–1794 had lost much of their charm, but France was not about to settle down

[1] J. H. Stewart, *A Documentary Survey of the French Revolution*, p. 572.
[2] *Documentary Survey*, p. 672.

within its old frontiers. Post-Robespierre France was decidedly more expansionist than Robespierre's France had been. General Bonaparte, the 'popular general' whose rise to supreme power had been predicted by Burke in 1790 in *Reflections* (see above p. 403), was already beginning his ascent in 1796. Pitt's peace initiative of 1795–6, was therefore a misguided enterprise. Burke saw this, and prepared his attack.

The first definite intimation that peace with France was in the wind came to Burke with a letter from William Eden (first Baron Auckland, 1744–1814), enclosing a pamphlet of his own composition entitled *Some Remarks on the Apparent Circumstances of the War in the Fourth Week of October 1795*. The pamphlet argued that the time had come for considering a peace with France. Auckland was a friend and ally of Pitt's, and his nearest neighbour at Holwell. Auckland's pamphlet was probably written at Pitt's request and it was probably also at Pitt's suggestion that the author sent a copy of the pamphlet to Burke, in order to draw a reaction. This was rather imprudent on Auckland's part, for his political record was not such as to attract Burke's approbation. Auckland had deserted the Whig opposition in 1785, in order to become Pitt's special envoy to France. Before that, in 1780, he had been Chief Secretary to Lord Carlisle in Ireland and had become a friend and ally of the Irish Chancellor, John Fitzgibbon, who was hostile to everything Burke stood for and had done more than anyone else except Pitt to destroy Fitzwilliam's viceroyalty (see above pp. 511–21).[1]

Burke's reply to Auckland was implacably negative: 'If the plan of politics there recommended (pray excuse my freedom) should be adopted by the King's councils, and by the good people of this kingdom (as, so recommended, undoubtedly it will), nothing can be the consequence but utter and irretrievable ruin to the Ministry, to the Crown, to the Succession, to the importance, to the very existence of this country.' Auckland sent Burke's letter to Pitt, who replied: 'I return Burke's letter, which is like other rhapsodies from the same pen, in which there is much to admire, and nothing to agree with.'[2]

Pitt was a little premature there. The real 'rhapsody' was only then in the process of composition. Burke had already begun work on the

---

[1] In 1798, after Burke's death, Fitzgibbon, clearly with a view to damaging his posthumous reputation in England, sent Auckland 'two popish letters' of Burke's, apparently acquired by Dublin Castle.

[2] *Corr.* VIII, 335.

Letters on a Regicide Peace. These *Letters* are written with a single purpose in mind: to force Pitt to continue the war with revolutionary France, until the restoration of the Monarchy. The *Letters* have neither the scope nor the profundity of insight of *Reflections*, and the proportion of rhetoric and invective to analysis is much higher. Yet the *Letters* are an astonishing production. They are the work of a dying man, yet they contain the fieriest, the most animated, of Burke's writings. Burke, in his letter to Auckland, had spoken of himself as 'a dejected old man, buried in the anticipated grave of a feeble old age, forgetting and forgotten in an obscure and melancholy retreat.' Yet this late work of that dejected old man is distinguished above all by its sheer exuberance and knockabout high spirits. The enjoyment which Burke felt in the writing of it communicates itself to the reader on almost every page. Clearly he enjoyed the combined operation of ridiculing Auckland while thereby conveying an implicit warning to Pitt.

Something like this had happened three times before. In all four cases a period of constraint had been followed by a tremendous release of energy. The first was the silence over American affairs generally observed by the Rockinghams from 1768 to 1774 (see Chapter II above). That constraint ended when the Rockinghams decided to protest against the Penal Acts. The results of the consequent release of energy included two of Burke's greatest speeches 'On American Taxation' (1774) and 'On Conciliation with America' (1775). The second case occurred over India. That period of constraint extended from Burke's discovery, in 1773, that his heart was at variance with his party over India, until the time, ten years later, when he was able to bring his party round to his point of view (see Chapter IV above, p. 328). The release of energy this time produced the great speeches which began with 'On Fox's East India Bill', and included 'On Nabob of Arcot's Debts'. The period which preceded the writing of *Reflections* (1788–9) was also one of constraint through strained relations with his Whig colleagues. Fox's enthusiasm for the French Revolution liberated Burke from that constraint, and so released a new outburst of energy.

The period of constraint before the composition of *Letters on a Regicide Peace* was much shorter, but probably more distressing than the three others. It stretched from March 1795, with the news of Fitzwilliam's recall, to October of that year, when Burke learns of Pitt's intention to try to conclude a peace with France. Burke had continued to support Pitt, after Fitzwilliam's recall, only because he considered Pitt to be indispensable for the conduct of the indispensable war, against revolutionary France. From Burke's point of view, Pitt was now attempting to desert his post, and it became a congenial duty to drive him back to it. Burke's thralldom to Pitt, as long as Pitt was faithful to the war, had been profoundly uncongenial, because of Burke's feelings at how Pitt had treated his friend Fitzwilliam, and along with him, Burke's own people, the Catholics of Ireland. The exuberance in the *Letters on a Regicide Peace* reflects his joy in being released from that self-imposed thralldom, and released from it by the very same sense of duty that had imposed it in the first place.

Burke nowhere in the *Letters* attacks Pitt personally, because he felt that Pitt was still needed, provided he could be kept at his post. He alludes to Pitt only on one occasion, and then with restraint. It is with Pitt's minions that Burke clashes, addressing Pitt through them, implicitly.

Of the four *Letters on a Regicide Peace*, two were published on 26 October 1796, during Burke's lifetime; the other two were published posthumously. The first letter to be written was the one that figures as 'Fourth Letter' in Volume VI (pp. 9–112) of the published *Works*. The target of this letter is Auckland's pamphlet seen as Pitt's *ballon d'essai*. Burke's own letter is addressed, significantly, to Earl Fitzwilliam:

> A piece has been sent to me, called "Some remarks on the Apparent Circumstances of the War in the Fourth Week of October, 1795," with a French motto: *Que faire encore une fois dans une telle nuit? Attendre le jour.* The very title seemed to me striking and peculiar, and to announce something uncommon. In the time I have lived to, I always seem to walk on enchanted ground. Everything is new, and, according to the fashionable phrase, revolutionary. In former days authors valued themselves upon the maturity and fulness of their deliberations. Accordingly, they predicted (perhaps with more arrogance than reason) an eternal duration to their works. The quite contrary is our present fashion. Writers value themselves now on the instability of their opinions and the transitory life of their productions. On this kind of credit the modern institutors open their schools.

Burke makes game of Auckland's affected precision in chronology, mocking the author with the wetness of his chosen date.

> In comes a gentleman at the fag-end of October, dripping with the fog of that uncertain season. . . .

The ruling Directory, in Paris at that time, were no longer talking about the country as 'the Republic, one and Indivisible', but were referring simply to 'France'. Similarly, the peace which Auckland proposes is 'peace with France'. Burke will not let him get away with that:

> That hostile power, to the period of the fourth week in that month, has been ever called and considered as an usurpation. In that week, for the first time, it changed its name of usurped power, and took the simple name of *France*. The word France is slipped in just as if the government stood exactly as before that Revolution which has astonished, terrified, and almost overpowered Europe. "France," says the author, "will do this," – "it is the interest of France," – "the returning honor and generosity of France," &c., &c., – always merely France: just as if we were in a common political war with an old recognized member of the commonwealth of Christian Europe, – and as if our dispute had turned upon a mere matter of territorial or commercial controversy, which a peace might settle by the imposition or the taking off a duty, with the gain or the loss of a remote island or a frontier town or two, on the one side or the other. This shifting of persons could not be done without the hocuspocus of *abstraction*. We have been in a grievous error: we thought that we had been at war with *rebels* against the lawful government, but that we were friends and allies of what is properly France, friends and allies to the legal body politic of France. But by sleight of hand the Jacobins are clean vanished, and it is France we have got under our cup.

'The power of bad men is no indifferent thing,' Burke had written at an earlier date, with Shelburne in mind. The former terrorists, now Thermidorians, were still in power in Paris, and Burke will not allow his adversary to 'slip them out of view' for the purpose of peace-making.

Burke next attacks are on Auckland's central argument which is that the extent of the conquests of the French revolutionaries should not excite alarm:

> But if there are yet existing any people, like me, old-fashioned enough to consider that we have an important part of our very existence beyond our limits, and who therefore stretch their thoughts beyond the *pomoerium* [bounds] of England, for them, too, he has a comfort which will remove all their jealousies and alarms about the extent of the empire of Regicide. *"These conquests eventually will be the cause of her destruction."* So that they who hate the cause of usurpation, and dread the power of France under any form, are to wish her to be a conqueror, in order to accelerate

her ruin, A little more conquest would be still better. Will he tell us what dose of dominion is to be the *quantum sufficit* for her destruction? – for she seems very voracious of the food of her distemper. To be sure, she is ready to perish with repletion; she has a *boulimia*, and hardly has bolted down one state than she calls for two or three more. There is a good deal of wit in all this; but it seems to me (with all respect to the author) to be carrying the joke a great deal too far. I cannot yet think that the armies of the Allies were of this way of thinking, and that when they evacuated all these countries, it was a strategy of war to decoy France into ruin, – or that, if in a treaty we should surrender them forever into the hands of the usurpation, (the lease the author supposes,) it is a master-stroke of policy to effect the destruction of a formidable rival, and to render her no longer an object of jealousy and alarm. This, I assure the author, will infinitely facilitate the treaty. The usurpers will catch at this bait, without minding the hook which this crafty angler for the Jacobin gudgeons of the new Directory has so dexterously placed under it.

Every symptom of the exacerbation of the public malady is, with him, (as with the Doctor in Moliere,) a happy prognostic of recovery. – Flanders gone. *Tant mieux.* – Holland subdued. Charming! – Spain beaten, and all the hither Germany conquered. Bravo! Better and better still! – But they will retain all their conquests on a treaty. Best of all! – What a delightful thing it is to have a gay physician, who sees all things, as the French express it, *couleur de rose!* What an escape we have had, that we and our allies were not the conquerors!

Then Burke ridicules the most important of Auckland's arguments: that the revolutionaries have changed their character:

Are they not the very same ruffians, thieves, assassins, and regicides that they were from the beginning? Have they diversified the scene by the least variety, or produced the face of a single new villany? Oh! but I shall be answered, "It is now quite another thing; – they are all changed. You have not seen them in their state dresses; – this make an amazing difference, The new habit of the Directory is so charmingly fancied, that it is impossible not to fall in love with so well-dressed a Constitution; – the costume of the *sans-culotte* Constitution of 1793 was absolutely insufferable. The Committee for Foreign Affairs were such slovens, and stunk so abominably, that no *muscadin* ambassador of the smallest decree of delicacy of nerves could come within ten yards of them; but now they are so powdered, and perfumed, and ribanded, and sashed, and plumed, that, though they are grown infinitely more insolent than they were in their rags, (and that was enough,) as they now appear, there is something in it more grand and noble, something more suitable to an awful Roman Senate receiving the homage of dependent tetrarchs. Like that Senate, (their perpetual model for conduct toward other nations,) they permit their vassals (during their good pleasure) to assume the name of kings, in order to bestow more dignity on the suite and retinue of the sovereign Republic by the nominal rank of their slaves." All this is very fine, undoubtedly; and ambassadors whose hands are almost out for want of employment may long to have their part in this august ceremony of the Republic one and indivisible, But, with great deference to the new diplomatic taste, we old people must retain some square-toed predilection for the fashions of our youth.

I am afraid you will find me, my Lord, again falling into my usual vanity, in valuing myself on the eminent men whose society I once enjoyed. I remember, in a conversation I once had with my ever dear friend Garrick, who was the first of actors, because he was the most acute observer of Nature I ever knew, I asked him how it happened, that, whenever a senate appeared on the stage, the audience seemed always disposed to laughter. He said, the reason was plain: the audience was well acquainted with the faces of most of the senators. They knew that they were no other than candle-snuffers, revolutionary scene-shifters, second and third mob, prompter, clerks, executioners, who stand with their axe on their shoulders by the wheel, grinners in the pantomime, murderers in tragedies, who make ugly faces under black wigs, – in short, the very scum and refuse of the theatre; and it was of course that the contrast of the vileness of the actors with the pomp of their habits naturally excited ideas of contempt and ridicule.

So it was at Paris on the inaugural day of the Constitution for the present year. The foreign ministers were ordered to attend at this investiture of the Directory; – for so they call the managers of their burlesque government. The diplomacy, who were a sort of strangers, were quite awe-struck with the "pride, pomp, and circumstance" of this majestic senate; whilst the *sans-culotte* gallery instantly recognized their own insurrectionary acquaintance, burst out into a horse-laugh at their absurd finery, and held them in infinitely greater contempt than whilst they prowled about the streets in the pantaloon of the last year's Constitution, when their legislators appeared honestly, with their daggers in their belts, and their pistols peeping out of their side-pocket-holes, like a bold, brave banditti, as they are.

Auckland gives the Directory credit for the fall of Robespierre. Burke comments:

I hear another inducement to fraternity with the present rulers. They have murdered one Robespierre. This Robespierre, they tell us, was a cruel tyrant, and now that he is put out of the way, all will go well in France. Astraea will again return to that earth from which she has been an emigrant, and all nations will resort to her golden scales. It is very extraordinary, that, the very instant the mode of Paris is known here, it becomes all the fashion in London. This is their jargon. It is the old *bon-ton* of robbers, who cast their common crimes on the wickedness of their departed associates. I care little about the memory of this same Robespierre. I am sure he was an execrable villain. I rejoiced at his punishment neither more nor less than I should at the execution of the present Directory, or any of its members. But who gave Robespierre the power of being a tyrant? The present virtuous constitution-mongers. He was a tyrant; they were his satellites and his hangmen, Their sole merit is in the murder of their colleague, They had expiated their other murderers by a new murder. It has always been the case among the banditti. They have always had the knife at each other's throats, after they had almost blunted it at the throats of every honest man. These people thought, that, in the commerce of murder, he was like to have the better of the bargain, if any time was lost; they therefore took one of their short revolutionary methods, and massacred him in a manner so perfidious and cruel as would shock all humanity, if the stroke was not struck by the present rulers on one of their own associates. But this last act of infidelity and murder is to expiate all the rest, and to quality them for the amity of an humane and virtuous sovereign and civilized people. I have heard that a Tartar believes, when he has killed a man, that all his estimable qualities pass with his clothes and arms to the murderer; but I have never heard that it was the opinion of any savage Scythian, that, if he kills a brother villain, he is, *ipso facto*, absolved of all his own offences. The Tartarian doctrine is the most tenable opinion. The murderers of Robespierre, besides what they are entitled to by being engaged in the same tontine of infamy, are his representatives, have inherited all his murderous qualities, in addition to their own private stock. But it seems we are always to be of a party with the last and victorious assassins. I confess I am of a different mind, and am rather inclined, of the two, to think and speak less hardly of a dead ruffian than to associate with the living. I could better bear the stench of the gibbeted murderer than the society of the bloody felons who yet annoy the world. Whilst they wait the recompense due to their ancient crimes, they merit new punishment by the new offences they commit. There is a period to the offences of Robespierre. They survive in his assassins. "Better a living dog," says the old proverb, "than a dead lion." Not so here. Murderers and hogs never look well till they are hanged, From villany no good can arise, but in the example of its fate. So I leave them their dead Robespierre, either to gibbet his memory, or to deify him in their Pantheon with their Marat and their Mirabeau.

Then Burke comes to the terms, as summarised by Auckland, on which the Directory might agree to peace.

But hear still further and in the same good strain the great patron and advocate of amity with this accommodating, mild, and unassuming power, when he reports to you the law they give, and its immediate effects: – "They amount," says he, "to the sacrifice of powers that have been the most nearly connected with us, – the direct or indirect annexation to France of all the ports of the Continent from Dunkirk to Hamburg, – an immense accession of territory, – and, in one word, *The Abandonment of the Independence of Europe!*" This is the *Law* (the author and I use no different terms) which this new government, almost as soon as it could cry in the cradle, and as one of the very first acts by which it auspicated its entrance into function, the pledge it gives of the firmness of its policy, – such is the law that this proud power prescribes to abject nations. What is the comment upon this law by the great jurist who recommends us to the tribunal which issued the decree? "An obedience to it would be" (says he) "dishonorable to us, and exhibit us to the present age and to posterity as submitting to the law prescribed to us by our enemy."

Here I recognize the voice of a British plenipotentiary: I begin to feel proud of my country. But, alas! the short date of human elevation! The accents of dignity died upon his tongue. This author will not assure us of his sentiments for the whole of a pamphlet; but, in the sole energetic part of it, he does not continue the same through an whole sentence, if it happens to be of any sweep or compass. In the very womb of this last sentence, pregnant, as it should seem, with a Hercules, there is formed a little bantling of the mortal race, a degenerate, puny parenthesis, that totally frustrates our most sanguine views and expectations, and disgraces the whole gestation. Here is this destructive parenthesis: "Unless some adequate compensation be secured *to us.*" *To us!* The Christian world may shift for itself, Europe may groan in slavery, we may be dishonored by receiving law from an enemy, – but all is well, provided the compensation *to us* be adequate. To what are we reserved? An *adequate* compensation "for the sacrifice of powers the most nearly connected with us"; – an *adequate* compensation "for the direct or indirect annexation to France of all the ports of the Continent from Dunkirk to Hamburg"; – an *adequate* compensation "for the abandonment of the independence of Europe"! Would that, when all our manly sentiments are thus changed, our manly language were changed along with them, and that the English tongue were not employed to utter what our ancestors never dreamed could enter into an English heart!

On the repudiation by the Directory of the principle of Equality:

The Regicides, they say, have renounced the creed of the Rights of Man, and declared equality a chimera. This is still more strange than all the rest, They have apostatized from their apostasy. They are renegadoes from that impious faith for which they subverted the ancient government, murdered their king, and imprisoned, butchered, confiscated, and banished their fellow-subjects, and to which they forced every man to swear at the peril of his life. And now, to reconcile themselves to the world, they declare this creed, bought by so much blood, to be an imposture and a chimera. I have no doubt that they always thought it to be so, when they were destroying everything at home and abroad for its establishment. It is no strange thing, to those who look into the nature of corrupted man, to find a violent persecutor a perfect unbeliever of his own creed. But this is the very first time that any man or set of men were hardy enough to attempt to lay the ground of confidence in them by an acknowledgment of their own falsehood, fraud, hypocrisy, treachery, heterodox doctrine, persecution, and cruelty. Everything we hear from them is new, and, to use a phrase of their own, *revolutionary*; everything supposes a total revolution in all the principles of reason, prudence, and moral feeling. If possible, this their recantation of the chief parts in the canon of the Rights of Man is more infamous and causes greater horror than their originally promulgating and forcing down the throats of mankind that symbol of all evil. It is raking too much into the dirt and ordure of human nature to say more of it.

Burke rejects a call for good feeling towards the France of the Directory, expresses his own hatred towards it, and qualifies that hatred:

But, after all, for what purpose are we told of this reformation in their principles, and what is the policy of all this softening in ours, which is to be produced by their example? It is not to soften us to suffering innocence and virtue, but to mollify us to the crimes and to the society of robbers and ruffians. But I trust that our countrymen will not be softened to that kind of crimes and criminals; for if we should, our hearts will be hardened to everything which has a claim on our benevolence. A kind Providence has placed in our breasts a hatred of the unjust and cruel, in order that we may preserve ourselves from cruelty and injustice. They who bear cruelty are accomplices in it. The pretended gentleness which excludes that charitable rancor produces an indifference which is half an approbation. They never will love where they ought to love, who do not hate where they ought to hate.[1]

Then Burke turns to the English Jacobins, and how greatly a peace

---

[1] Compare the passage on 'sympathetic revenge' in Burke's concluding *Speech in the Impeachment of Warren Hastings*, above, p. 506.

with the Directory would magnify their influence in England. This part of the argument is closely aimed at Pitt, who had headed, with Burke's approval, the repression of Jacobin propaganda in Britain:

> Gentlemen who not long since thought with us, but who now recommend a Jacobin peace, were at the time sufficiently aware of the existence of a dangerous Jacobin faction within this kingdom. A while ago they seemed to be tremblingly alive to the number of those who composed it, to their dark subtlety, to their fierce audacity, to their admiration of everything that passes in France, to their eager desire of a close communication with the mother faction there. At this moment, when the question is upon the opening of the communication, not a word of our English Jacobins. That faction is put out of sight and out of thought. "It vanished at the crowing of the cock." Scarcely had the Gallic harbinger of peace and light begun to utter his lively notes, than all the cackling of us poor Tory geese to alarm the garrison of the Capitol was forgot.[1] There was enough of indemnity before. Now a complete act of oblivion is passed about the Jacobins of England, though one would naturally imagine it would make a principal object in all fair deliberation upon the merits of a project of amity with the Jacobins of France. But however others may choose to forget the faction, the faction does not choose to forget itself, nor, however gentlemen may choose to flatter themselves, it does not forget them.

After a Regicide Peace, the French Embassy in London will be the centre of Jacobin intrigue: 'A French Ambassador at the head of a French party, is an evil which we have never experienced.' Burke foresees the possibility of civil war in Britain, following on a peace with revolutionary France:

> There never was a political contest, upon better or worse ground, that by the heat of party-spirit may not ripen into civil confusion. If ever a party adverse to the crown should be in a condition here publicly to declare itself, and to divide, however unequally, the natural force of the kingdom, they are sure of an aid of fifty thousand men, at ten days' warning, from the opposite coast of France.

The second of the *Letters on a Regicide Peace* (which appears in Volume V of *Works* as the first *Letter*, pp. 233–341) leaves Auckland's pamphlet behind. This Letter, headed 'On the Overtures of Peace,' opens on a philosophical key. Burke meditates on the course of human history:

---

[1] This is the only reference by Burke to himself as a Tory, but it is facetious. He no more thought of himself as a Tory than as a goose.

It is often impossible, in these political inquiries, to find any proportion between the apparent force of any moral causes we may assign and their known operation. We are therefore obliged to deliver up that operation to mere chance, or, more piously, (perhaps more rationally,) to the occasional interposition and irresistible hand of the Great Disposer. We have seen states of considerable duration, which for ages have remained nearly as they have begun, and could hardly be said at ebb or flow. Some appear to have spent their vigor at their commencement. Some have blazed out in their glory a little before their extinction. The Meridian of some has been the most splendid. Others, and they the greatest number, have fluctuated, and experienced at different periods of their existence a great variety of fortune. At the very moment when some of them seemed plunged in unfathomable abysses of disgrace and disaster, they have suddenly emerged. They have begun a new course and opened a new reckoning, and even in the depths of their calamity and on the very ruins of their country have laid the foundations of a towering and durable greatness. All this has happened without any apparent previous change in the general circumstances which had brought on their distress, The death of a man at a critical juncture, his disgust, his retreat, his disgrace, have brought innumerable calamities on a whole nation. A common soldier, a child, a girl at the door of an inn, have changed the face of fortune, and almost of nature.[1]

From that, Burke turns to the recent course of the history of France:

Deprived of the old government, deprived in a manner of all government, France, fallen as a monarchy, to common speculators might have appeared more likely to be an object of pity or insult, according to the disposition of the circumjacent powers, than to be the scourge and terror of them all: but out of the tomb of the murdered monarchy in France has arisen a vast, tremendous, unformed spectre, in a far more terrific guise than any which ever yet have overpowered the imagination and subdued the fortitude of man. Going straight forward to its end, unappalled by peril, unchecked by remorse, despising all common maxims and all common means, that hideous phantom overpowered those who could not believe it was possible she could at all exist, except on the principles which habit rather than Nature had persuaded them were necessary to their own particular welfare and to their own ordinary modes of action. But the constitution of any political being, as well as

[1] 'This sentence,' writes Owen Dudley Edwards, 'seems to allude to the common soldier who slew Archimedes, and then to Jesus and Mary. The previous sentence seems to allude to Pericles, Themistocles and Alcibiades' (letter to author).

that of any physical being, ought to be known, before one can venture to say what is fit for its conservation, or what is the proper means of its power. The poison of other states is the food of the new Republic. That bankruptcy, the very apprehension of which is one of the causes assigned for the fall of the monarch, was the capital on which she opened her traffic with the world.

The Republic of Regicide, with an annihilated revenue, with defaced manufactures, with a ruined commerce, with an uncultivated and half-depopulated country, with a discontented, distressed, enslaved, and famished people, passing, with a rapid, eccentric, incalculable course, from the wildest anarchy to the sternest despotism, has actually conquered the finest parts of Europe, has distressed, disunited, deranged, and broke to pieces all the rest, and so subdued the minds of the rulers in every nation, that hardly any resource presents itself to them, except that of entitling themselves to a contemptuous mercy by a display of their imbecility and meanness. Even in their greatest military efforts, and the greatest display of their fortitude, they seem not to hope, they do not even appear to wish, the extinction of what subsists to their certain ruin. Their ambition is only to be admitted to a more favored class in the order of servitude under that domineering power.

Burke correctly predicts a long war, and then stresses its unique character:

There is much to be done, undoubtedly, and much to be retrieved. We must walk in new ways, or we can never encounter our enemy in his devious march. We are not at an end of our struggle, nor near it. Let us not deceive ourselves: we are at the beginning of great troubles. . . .

We are in a war of a *peculiar* nature, It is not with an ordinary community, which is hostile or friendly as passion or as interest may veer about – not with a state which makes war through wantonness, and abandons it through lassitude. We are at war with a system which by its essence is inimical to all other governments, and which makes peace or war as peace and war may best contribute to their subversion. It is with an *armed doctrine* that we are at war, It has, by its essence, a faction of opinion and of interest and of enthusiasm in every country. To us it is a Colossus which bestrides our Channel. It has one foot on a foreign shore, the other upon the British soil. Thus advantaged, if it can at all exist, it must finally prevail. Nothing can so completely ruin any of the old governments, our's in particular, as the acknowledgment, directly or by implication, of any kind of superiority in this new power. This acknowledgement we make, if, in a bad or doubtful situation of our affairs, we solicit peace, or if we yield to the modes of new humiliation in which alone she is content to give us an hearing. By that means the terms cannot be of our choosing, – no, not in any part.

Burke's thesis of 'an armed doctrine' is open to serious question, in the post-Thermidorian period about which he was writing. As Burke himself had noted, in the first of his *Letters on a Regicide Peace*, the Thermidorians had apostasised from most of the doctrines which had earlier been sacred to the revolutionaries. Insofar as there was any 'doctrine' guiding the destinies of post-Thermidorian France, it was the doctrine proclaimed by Bonaparte to his troops in Italy: the doctrine of 'honour, glory and riches'. If that could be classified as a 'doctrine', it was certainly an armed one, and of terrifying efficiency.

Whatever about the nature of the 'armed doctrine', Burke was right to see that post-Thermidorian France was a manically expansionist power, with which peace could not be concluded, without total submission. Pitt's assumption that the Directory was a normal power, with which business could be done, was unfounded, as Pitt was now beginning to find out for himself. As Burke writes:

In one point we are lucky. The Regicide has received our advances with scorn. We have an enemy to whose virtues we can owe nothing, but on this occasion we are infinitely obliged to one of his vices. We owe more to his insolence than to our own precaution. The haughtiness by which the proud repel us has this of good in it, – that, in making us keep our distance they must keep their distance too. In the present case, the pride of the Regicide may be our safety. He has given time for our reason to operate, and for British dignity to recover from its surprise. From first to last he has rejected all our advances. Far as we have gone, he has still left a way open to our retreat.

Burke goes on to argue that the Regicides cannot even discuss peace without sowing 'the seeds of tumult and sedition':

For they never have abandoned, and never will they abandon, in peace, in war, in treaty, in any situation, or for one instant, their old, steady maxim of separating the people from their government.

Then Burke gives us one of his last great set-pieces: the picture of the royal ambassadors at the regicide levée:

To those who do not love to contemplate the fall of human greatness, I do not know a more mortifying spectacle than to see the assembled majesty of the crowned heads of Europe waiting as patient suitors in the antechamber of Regicide. They wait, it seems, until the sanguinary tyrant Carnot shall have snorted away the fumes of the undigested blood of his sovereign. Then, when, sunk on the down of usurped pomp, he shall have sufficiently indulged his meditations with what monarch he shall next glut his ravening maw, he may condescend to signify that it is his pleasure to be awake, and that he is at leisure to receive the proposals of his high and mighty clients for the terms on which he may respite the execution of the sentence he has passed upon them. At the opening of those doors, what a sight it must be to behold the plenipotentiaries of royal impotence, in the precedency which they will intrigue to obtain, and which will be granted to them according to the seniority of their degradation, sneaking into the Regicide presence, and, with the relics of the smile which they had dressed up for the levee of their masters still flickering on their curled lips, presenting the faded remains of their courtly graces, to meet the scornful, ferocious, sardonic grin of a bloody ruffian, who, whilst he is receiving their homage, is measuring them with his eye, and fitting to their size the slider of his guillotine.

Burke returns to the subject of the long war, and touches, through generalisations, on the reasons for Pitt's inadequacy as a war-time leader:

They never entered into the peculiar and distinctive character of the war. They spoke neither to the understanding nor to the heart. Cold as ice themselves, they never could kindle in our breasts a spark of that zeal which is necessary to a conflict with an adverse zeal; much less were they made to infuse into our minds that stubborn, persevering spirit which alone is capable of bearing up against those vicissitudes of fortune which will probably occur, and those burdens which must be inevitably borne, in a long war. I speak it emphatically, and with a desire that it should be marked, – in a *long* war; because, without such a war, no experience has yet told us that a dangerous power has ever been reduced to measure or to reason.

Burke reflects on the French Revolutionary achievement in the sphere of manners:

Manners are of more importance than laws. Upon them, in a great measure, the laws depend, The law touches us but here and there, and now and then. Manners are what vex or soothe, corrupt or purify, exalt or debase, barbarise or refine us, by a constant, steady, uniform, insensible operation, like that of the air we breathe in. They give their whole form and color to our lives. According to their quality, they aid morals, they supply them, or they totally destroy them. Of this the new French legislators were aware; therefore, with the same method, and under the same authority, they settled a system of manners, the most licentious, prostitute, and abandoned that ever has been known, and at the same time the most coarse, rude, savage, and ferocious. Nothing in the Revolution, no, not to a phrase or a gesture, not to the fashion of a hat or a shoe, was left to accident. All has been the result of design; all has been matter of institution. No mechanical means could be devised in favor of this incredible system of wickedness and vice, that has not been employed. The noblest passions, the love of glory, the love of country, have been debauched into means of its preservation and its propagation. All sorts of shows and exhibitions, calculated to inflame and vitiate the imagination and pervert the moral sense, have been contrived. They have sometimes brought forth five or six hundred drunken women calling at the bar of the Assembly for the blood of their own children, as being Royalists or Constitutionalists. Sometimes they have got a body of wretches, calling themselves fathers, to demand the murder of their sons, boasting that Rome had but one Brutus, but that they could show five hundred. There were instances in which they inverted and retaliated the impiety, and produced sons who called for the execution of their parents. The foundation of their republic is laid in moral paradoxes. Their patriotism is always prodigy. All those instances to be found in history, whether real or fabulous, of a doubtful public spirit, at which morality is perplexed, reason is staggered, and from which affrighted Nature recoils, are their chosen and almost sole examples for the instruction of their youth.

Burke summarises his objection to Jacobin morality in one sentence: 'They think everything unworthy of the name of public virtue, unless it indicates violence on the private.'

Some of those who had floated the 'Regicide Peace' idea had argued, by way of precedent, that European powers had not hesitated to conclude agreements with Algiers, a polity of pirates. Burke plays happily with this notion:

I never shall so far injure the Janizarian Republic [Algiers] as to put it in comparison, for every sort of crime, turpitude, and oppression, with the Jacobin Republic of Paris. There is no question with me to which of the two I should choose to be a neighbor or a subject. But, situated as I am, I am in no danger of becoming to Algiers either the one or the other. It is not so in my relation to the atheistical fanatics of France. I *am* their neighbor; I *may* become their subject. Have the gentlemen who borrowed this happy parallel no idea of the different conduct to be held with regard to the very same evil at an immense distance and when it is at your door? when its power is enormous, as when it is comparatively as feeble as its distance is remote? when there is a barrier of language and usages, which prevents corruption through certain old correspondences and habitudes, from the contagion of the horrible novelties that are introduced into everything else? I can contemplate without dread a royal or a national tiger on the borders of Pegu. I can look at him with an easy curiosity, as prisoner within bars in the menagerie of the Tower, But if, by *Habeas Corpus*, or otherwise, he was to come into the lobby of the House of Commons whilst your door was open, any of you would be more stout than wise who would not gladly make your escape out of the back windows. I certainly should dread more from a wild-cat in my bedchamber than from all the lions that roar in the deserts behind Algiers. But in this parallel it is the cat that is at a distance, and the lions and tigers that are in our antechambers and our lobbies. Algiers is not near; Algiers is not powerful; Algiers is not our neighbor; Algiers is not infectious. Algiers, whatever it may be, is an old creation; and we have good data to calculate all the mischief to be apprehended from it. When I find Algiers transferred to Calais, I will tell you what I think of that point.

Burke now, for the first time, refers explicitly to Pitt, the implicit target of the whole polemic. The passage is a ceremonious and solemn warning and it contains an allusion to the recall of Fitzwilliam:

In wishing this nominal peace not to be precipitated, I am sure no man living is less disposed to blame the present ministry than I am. Some of my oldest friends (and I wish I could say it of more of them) make a part in that ministry. There are some, indeed, "whom my dim eyes in vain explore." In my mind, a greater calamity could not have fallen on the public than the exclusion of one of them. But I drive away that, with other melancholy thoughts. A great deal ought to be said upon that subject, or nothing. As to the distinguished persons to whom my friends who remain are joined, if benefits nobly and generously conferred ought to procure good wishes, they are entitled to my best vows; and they have them all. They have administered to me the only consolation I am capable of receiving, which is, to know that no individual will suffer by my thirty years' service to the public. If things should give us the comparative happiness of a struggle, I shall be found, I was going to say fighting (that would be foolish) but dying, by the side of Mr. Pitt. I must, add, that, if anything defensive in our domestic system can possibly save us from the disasters of a Regicide peace, he is the man to save us. If the finances in such a case can be repaired, he is the man to repair them. If I should lament any of his acts, it is only when they appear to me to have no resemblance to acts of his. But let him not have a confidence in himself which no human abilities can warrant. His abilities are fully equal (and that is to say much for any man) to those which are opposed to him. But if we look to him as our security against the consequences of a Regicide peace, let us be assured that a Regicide peace and a constitutional ministry are terms that will not agree. With a Regicide peace the king cannot long have a minister to serve him, nor the minister a king to serve. If the Great Disposer, in reward of the royal and the private virtues of our sovereign, should call him from the calamitous spectacles which will attend a state of amity with Regicide, his successor will surely see them, unless the same Providence greatly anticipates the course of Nature. Thinking thus, (and not, as I conceive, on light grounds,) I dare not flatter the reigning sovereign, nor any minister he has or can have, nor his successor apparent, nor any of those who may be called to serve him, with what appears to me a false state of their situation.

In the peroration to this, the second of these *Letters*, Burke acknowledges the character of the *Letters on a Regicide Peace* as a whole as 'testamentary'. At the time of the publication of the third (and the first posthumuous)he had less than a year to live. The testamentary passage runs:

In this crisis I must hold my tongue or I must speak with freedom. Falsehood and delusion are allowed in no case whatever: but, as in the exercise of all the virtues, there is an economy of truth. It is a sort of temperance, by which a man speaks truth with measure, that he may speak it the longer. But as the same rules do not hold in all cases, what would be right for you, who may presume on a series of years before you would have no sense for me, who cannot, without absurdity, calculate on six months of life. What I say I *must* say at once. Whatever I write is in its nature testamentary, It may have the weakness, but it has the sincerity, of a dying declaration.

The third *Letter* (second in Volume V of *Works*, pp. 342–383) is headed 'On the Genius and Character of the French Revolution as it regards other Nations'. It begins by acknowledging the redoubtable character of his adversaries:

It is a dreadful truth, but it is a truth that cannot be concealed: in ability, in dexterity, in the distinctness of their views, the Jacobins are our superiors. They saw the thing right from the very beginning. Whatever were the first motives to the war among politicians, they saw that in its spirit, and for its object, it was a *civil war*; and as such they pursued it. It is a war between the partisans of the ancient civil, moral, and political order of Europe against a sect of fanatical and ambitious atheists which means to change them all. It is not France extending a foreign empire over other nations: it is a sect aiming at universal empire, and beginning with the conquest of France. The leaders of that sect secured *the centre of Europe*; and that secured, they knew, that, whatever might be the event of battles and sieges, their *cause* was victorious. Whether its territory had a little more or a little less peeled from its surface, or whether an island or two was detached from its commerce, to them was of little moment. The conquest of France was a glorious acquisition. That once well laid as a basis of empire, opportunities never could be wanting to regain or to replace what had been lost, and dreadfully to avenge themselves on the faction of their adversaries.

As against that picture, Burke evokes the memory of the common run of British politicians, the kind of people who had laughed at his speeches:

In truth, the tribe of vulgar politicians are the lowest of our species. There is no trade so vile and mechanical as government in their hands. Virtue is not their habit. They are out of themselves in any course of conduct recommended only by conscience and glory. A large, liberal, and prospective view of the interests of states passes with them for romance, and the principles that recommend it for the wanderings of a disordered imagination. The calculators compute them out of their senses. The jesters and buffoons shame them out of everything grand and elevated, Littleness in object and in means to them appears soundness and sobriety, They think there is nothing worth pursuit, but that which they can handle, which they can measure with a two-foot rule, which they can tell upon ten fingers.

Continuing his analysis of the energies released by the French Revolution, Burke considers the roles of philosophers and politicians:

In the Revolution of France, two sorts of men were principally concerned in giving a character and determination to its pursuits: the philosophers and the politicians. They took different ways, but they met in the same end. The philosophers had one predominant object, which they pursued with a fanatical fury, – that is, the utter extirpation of religion. To that every question of empire was subordinate. They had rather domineer in a parish of atheists than rule over a Christian world. Their temporal ambition was wholly subservient to their proselytizing spirit, in which they were not exceeded by Mahomet himself. They who have made but superficial studies in the natural history of the human mind have been taught to look on religious opinions as the only cause of enthusiastic zeal and sectarian propagation. But there is no doctrine whatever on which men can warm, that is not capable of the very same effect. The social nature of man impels him to propagate his principles, as much as physical impulses urge him to propagate his kind. The passions give zeal and vehemence. The understanding bestows design and system. The whole man moves under the discipline of his opinions. Religion is among the most powerful causes of enthusiasm. When anything concerning it becomes an object of much meditation, it cannot be indifferent to the mind. They who do not love religion hate it, The rebels to God perfectly abhor the Author of their being. They hate Him 'with all their strength.' He never presents Himself to their thoughts, but to menace and alarm them. They cannot strike the sun out of heaven, but they are able to raise a smouldering smoke that obscures him from their own eyes. Not being able to revenge themselves on God, they have a delight in vicariously defacing, degrading, torturing, and tearing in pieces His image in man. Let no one judge of them by what he has conceived of them, when they were not incorporated, and had no head. They were then only passengers in a common vehicle. They were then carried along with the general motion of religion in the community, and, without being aware of it, partook of its influence. In that situation, at worst, their nature was left free to counterwork their principles. They despaired of giving any very general currency to their opinions; they considered them as a reserved privilege for the chosen few. But when the possibility of dominion, lead, and propagation presented themselves, and that the ambition which before had so often made them hypocrites might rather gain than lose by a daring avowal of their sentiments, then the nature of this infernal spirit, which has "evil for its good," appeared in its full perfection. Nothing, indeed but the possession of some power can with any certainty discover what at the bottom is the true character of any man. Without reading the speeches of Vergniaud, Français of Nantes, Isnard, and some others of that sort, it would not be easy to conceive the passion, rancor, and malice of their tongues and hearts. They worked themselves up to a perfect frenzy against religion and all its professors. They tore the reputation of the clergy to pieces by their infuriated declamations and invectives, before they lacerated their bodies by their massacres. This fanatical atheism left out, we omit the principal feature in the French Revolution, and a principal consideration with regard to the effects to be expected from a peace with it.

The other sort of men were the politicians. To them, who had little or not at all reflected on the subject, religion was itself no object of love or hatred. They disbelieved it, and that was all. Neutral with regard to that object, they took the side which in the present state of things might best answer their purposes. They soon found that they could not do without the philosophers; and the philosophers soon made them sensible that the destruction of religion was to supply them with means of conquest, first at home, and then abroad. The philosophers were the active internal agitators, and supplied the spirit and principles: the second gave the practical direction. Sometimes the one predominated in the composition, sometimes the other. The only difference between them was in the necessity of concealing the general design for a time, and in their dealing with foreign nations: the fanatics going straight forward and openly, the politicians by the surer mode of zigzag. In the course of events this, among the causes, produced fierce and bloody contentions between them; but at the bottom they thoroughly agreed in all the objects of ambition and irreligion, and substantially in all the means of promoting these ends.

Without question, to bring about the unexampled event of the French Revolution, the concurrence of a very great number of views and passions was necessary. In that stupendous work no one principle by which the human mind may have its faculties at once invigorated and depraved was left unemployed; but I can speak it to a certainty, and support it by undoubted proofs, that the ruling principle of those who acted in the Revolution *as statesmen* had the exterior aggrandizement of France as their ultimate end in the most minute part of the internal changes that were made.[1]

That final point about aggrandisement is of course crucial to the debate of 1796. If the French were as bent on aggrandisement as Burke believed them to be, then there was no hope of a tolerable peace, either with the Directory on any of its successors until expansionist France could be defeated in war:

From all this what is my inference? It is, that this new system of robbery in France cannot be rendered safe by any art; that it must be destroyed, or that it will destroy all Europe; that to destroy that enemy, by some means or other, the force opposed to it should be made to bear some analogy and resemblance to the force and spirit which that system exerts; that war ought to be made against it in its vulnerable parts. These are my inferences. In one word, with this republic nothing independent can coexist.[2]

The fourth and last of the *Letters on a Regicide Peace* (Letter III in *Works* V, 384–508) is a kind of postscript, for by this time the attempt at a peace had ended in humiliating failure. Lord Malmesbury, Pitt's envoy to the Directory had been contemptuously expelled from France (19 December 1796). This final Letter is entitled: 'On the rupture of the negotiation; the terms of peace proposed; and the

[1] *Works* V, 361–4.
[2] *Works* V, 377–8.

resources of the country for the continuance of the war.' It begins:

The Declaration which brings up the rear of the papers laid before Parliament contains a review and a reasoned summary of all our attempts and all our failures, – a concise, but correct narrative of the painful steps taken to bring on the essay of a treaty at Paris, – a clear exposure of all the rebuffs we received in the progress of that experiment, – an honest confession of our departure from all the rules and all the principles of political negotiation, and of common prudence in the conduct of it, – and to crown the whole, a fair account of the atrocious manner in which the Regicide enemies had broken up what had been so inauspiciously begun and so feebly carried on, by finally, and with all scorn, driving our suppliant ambassador out of the limits of their usurpation.

Even after all that I have lately seen, I was a little surprised at this exposure. A minute display of hopes formed without foundation and of labors pursued without fruit is a thing not very flattering to self-estimation. But truth has its rights, and it will assert them. The Declaration, after doing all this with a mortifying candor, concludes the whole recapitulation with an engagement still more extraordinary than all the unusual matter it contains. It says that "His Majesty, who had entered into the negotiation with *good faith*, who had suffered *no* impediment to prevent his prosecuting it with *earnestness and sincerity*, has now *only to lament* its abrupt termination, and to renew *in the face of all Europe the solemn declaration*, that, whenever his enemies shall be *disposed* to enter on the work of general pacification in a spirit of conciliation and equity, nothing shall be wanting on his part to contribute to the accomplishment of that great object."

If the disgusting detail of the accumulated insults we have received, in what we have very properly called our 'solicitation' to a gang of felons and murderers, had been produced as a proof of the utter inefficacy of that mode of proceeding with that description of persons, I should have nothing at all to object to it. It might furnish matter conclusive in argument and instructive in policy; but, with all due submission to high authority, and with all decent deference to superior lights, it does not seem quite clear to a discernment no better than mine that the premises in that piece conduct irresistibly to the conclusion. A labored display of the ill consequences which have attended an uniform course of submission to every mode of contumelious insult, with which the despotism of a proud, capricious, insulting, and implacable foe has chosen to buffet our patience, does not appear to my poor thoughts to be properly brought forth as a preliminary to justify a resolution of persevering in the very same kind of conduct, towards the very same sort of person, and on the very same principles. We state our experience, and then we come to the manly resolution of acting in contradiction to it. As it is not only confessed by us, but made a matter of charge on the enemy, that he had given us no encouragement to believe there was a change in his disposition or in his policy at any time subsequent to the period of his rejecting our first overtures, there seems to have been no assignable motive for sending Lord Malmesbury to Paris, except to expose his humbled country to the worst indignities, and the first of the kind, as the Declaration very truly observes, that have been known in the world of negotiation.[1]

Burke then reviews the debate on the Declaration. It revealed, in his view, the degradation of both the great parties:

That day was, I fear, the fatal term of *local* patriotism. On that day, I fear, there was an end of that narrow scheme of relations called our country, with all its pride, its prejudices, and its partial affections. All the little quiet rivulets, that watered an humble, a contracted, but not an unfruitful field, are to be lost in the waste expanse, and boundless, barren ocean of the homicide philanthropy of France. It is no longer an object of terror, the aggrandizement of a new power which teaches as a professor that philanthropy in the chair, whilst it propagates by arms and establishes by conquest the comprehensive system of universal fraternity. In what light is all this viewed in a great assembly? The party [Pitt's] which takes the lead there has no longer any apprehensions, except those that arise from not being admitted to the closest and most confidential connections with the metropolis of that fraternity. That reigning party no longer touches on its favorite subject, the display of those horrors that must attend the existence of a power with such dispositions and principles, seated in the heart of Europe. It is satisfied to find some loose, ambiguous expressions in its former declarations, which may set it free from its professions and engagements. It always speaks of peace with the Regicides as a great and an undoubted blessing, and such a blessing as, if obtained, promises, as much as any human disposition of things can promise, security and permanence. It holds out nothing at all definite towards this security. It only seeks, by a restoration to some of their former owners of some fragments of the general wreck of Europe, to find a plausible plea for a present retreat from an embarrassing position. As to the future, that party is content to leave it covered in a night of the most palpable obscurity. It never once has entered into a particle of detail of what our own situation, or that of other powers, must be, under the blessings of the peace we seek. This defect, to my power, I mean to supply, – that, if any persons should still continue to think an attempt at foresight is any part of the duty of a statesman, I may contribute my trifle to the materials of his speculation.

[1] *Works* V, 385–387.

As to the other party [Fox's Whigs], the minority of to-day, possibly the majority of to-morrow, small in number, but full of talents and every species of energy, which, upon the avowed ground of being more acceptable to France, is a candidate for the helm of this kingdom, it has never changed from the beginning. It has preserved a perennial consistency. This would be a never failing source of true glory, if springing from just and right; but it is truly dreadful, if it be an arm of Styx which springs out of the profoundest depths of a poisoned soil. The French maxims were by these gentlemen at no time condemned. I speak of their language in the most moderate terms. There are many who think that they have gone much further. – that they have always magnified and extolled the French maxims, – that, not in the least disgusted or discouraged by the monstrous evils which have attended these maxims from the moment of their adoption both at home and abroad, they still continue to predict that in due time they must produce the greatest good to the poor human race. They obstinately persist in stating those evils as matter of accident, as things wholly collateral to the system.

It is observed, that this party has never spoken of an ally of Great Britain with the smallest degree of respect or regard: on the contrary, it has generally mentioned them under opprobrious appellations, and in such terms of contempt or execration as never had been heard before. – because no such would have formerly been permitted in our public assemblies. The moment, however, that any of those allies quitted this obnoxious connection, the party has instantly passed an act of indemnity and oblivion in their favor. After this, no sort of censure on their conduct, no imputation on their character. From that moment their pardon was sealed in a reverential and mysterious silence. With the gentlemen of this minority, there is no ally, from one end of Europe to the other, with whom we ought not to be ashamed to act. The whole college of the states of Europe is no better than a gang of tyrants. With them all our connections were broken off at once. We ought to have cultivated France, and France alone, from the moment of her Revolution. On that happy change, all our dread of that nation as a power was to cease. She became in an instant dear to our affections and one with our interests. All other nations we ought to have commanded not to trouble her sacred throes, whilst in labor to bring into an happy birth her abundant litter of constitutions. We ought to have acted under her auspices, in extending her salutary influence upon every side. From that moment England and France were become natural allies, and all the other states natural enemies. The whole face of the world was changed. What was it to us, if she acquired Holland and the Austrian Netherlands? By her conquests she only enlarged the sphere of her beneficence, she only extended the blessings of liberty to so many more foolishly reluctant nations. What was it to England, if, by adding these, among the richest and most peopled countries of the world, to her territories, she thereby left no possible link of communication between us and any other power with whom we could act against her? On this new system of optimism, it is so much the better: so much the further are we removed from the contact with infectious despotism. No longer a thought of a barrier in the Netherlands to Holland against France. All that is obsolete policy. It is fit that France should have both Holland and the Austrian Netherlands too, as a barrier to her against the attacks of despotism. She cannot multiply her securities too much; and as to our security, it is to be found in hers. Had we cherished her from the beginning, and felt for her when attacked, she, poor, good soul, should never have invaded any foreign nation, never murdered her sovereign and his family, never proscribed, never exiled, never imprisoned, never been guilty of extrajudicial massacre or of legal murder. All would have been a golden age, full of peace, order, and liberty, – and philosophy, raying out from Europe, would have warmed and enlightened the universe; but, unluckily, irritable philosophy, the most irritable of all things, was put into a passion, and provoked into ambition abroad and tyranny at home. They find all this very natural and very justifiable.[1]

Burke points out that on the day of the Declaration – 27 December 1796 – a great French fleet with a great army aboard was just leaving Bantry Bay. This was the expedition headed by Hoche. Theobald Wolfe Tone had successfully solicited its creation by the Directory and was himself aboard. The expedition failed because bad weather made it impossible to land the troops, and the fleet itself was then dispersed by storms. But the knowledge that the French were serious about sending forces to Ireland gave hope and encouragement to those planning the rebellion that was to break out in 1798. The Declaration, issued just as the French were leaving Bantry Bay, committed Britain to engage in negotiations again, should the Directory be willing. Burke comments:

It was on the very day of the date of the wonderful pledge, in which we assumed the Directorial government as lawful, and in which we engaged ourselves to treat with them whenever they pleased, – it was on that very day the Regicide fleet was weighing anchor from one of your harbors, where it had remained four days in perfect quiet. These harbors of the British dominions are the ports of France. They are of no use but to protect an enemy from your best allies, the storms of heaven and his own rashness. Had the West of Ireland been an unportuous coast, the French

---

[1] *Works* V, 393–397.

naval power would have been undone. The enemy uses the moment for hostility, without the least regard to your future dispositions of equity and conciliation. They go out of what were once your harbors, and they return to them at their pleasure. Eleven days they had the full use of Bantry Bay, and at length their fleet returns from their harbor of Bantry to their harbor of Brest. Whilst you are invoking the propitious spirit of Regicide equity and conciliation, they answer you with an attack. They turn out the pacific bearer of your "how do you dos," Lord Malmesbury; and they return your visit, and their "thanks for your obliging inquiries," by their old practised assassin, Hoche. They come to attack – what? A town, a fort, a naval station? They come to attack your king, your Constitution, and the very being of that parliament which was holding out to them these pledges, together with the entireness of the empire, the laws, liberties, and properties of all the people. We know that they meditated the very same invasion, and for the very same purposes, upon this kingdom, and, had the coast been as opportune, would have effected it.[1]

In the conclusion of this final letter Burke comes near to threatening Pitt with impeachment should he renew his effort to negotiate a peace with revolutionary France:

As to the great majority of the nation, they have done whatever, in their several ranks and conditions and descriptions, was required of them by their relative situations in society: and from those the great mass of mankind cannot depart, without the subversion of all public order. They look up to that government which they obey that they may be protected. They ask to be led and directed by those rulers whom Providence and the laws of their country have set over them, and under their guidance to walk in the ways of safety and honor. They have again delegated the greatest trust which they have to bestow to those faithful representatives who made their true voice heard against the disturbers and destroyers of Europe. They suffered, with unapproving acquiescence, solicitations, which they had in no shape desired, to an unjust and usurping power, whom they had never provoked, and whose hostile menaces they did not dread. When the exigencies of the public service could only be met by their voluntary zeal, they started forth with an ardor which outstripped the wishes of those who had injured them by doubting whether it might not be necessary to have recourse to compulsion. They have in all things

[1] *Works* V, 411–2. Burke here refrains from mentioning that if the strong French army on the ships in Bantry Bay had been able to land there, they could have occupied all Ireland with ease. But this particular situation was fraught with problems for him. See below pp. 569–79.

reposed an enduring, but not an unreflecting confidence. That confidence demands a full return, and fixes a responsibility on the ministers entire and undivided. The people stands acquitted, if the war is not carried on in a manner suited to its objects. If the public honor is tarnished, if the public safety suffers any detriment, the ministers, not the people, are to answer it, and they alone. Its armies, its navies, are given to them without stint or restriction. Its treasures are poured out at their feet. Its constancy is ready to second all their efforts. They are not to fear a responsibility for acts of manly adventure. The responsibility which they are to dread is lest they should show themselves unequal to the expectation of a brave people. The more doubtful may be the constitutional and economical questions upon which they have received so marked a support, the more loudly they are called upon to support this great war, for the success of which their country is willing to supersede considerations of no slight importance. Where I speak of responsibility, I do not mean to exclude that species of it which the legal powers of the country have a right finally to exact from those who abuse a public trust: but high as this is, there is a responsibility which attaches on them from which the whole legitimate power of the kingdom cannot absolve them; there is a responsibility to conscience and to glory, a responsibility to the existing world, and to that posterity which men of their eminence cannot avoid for glory or for shame, – a responsibility to a tribunal at which not only ministers, bit kings and parliaments, but even nations themselves, must one day answer.[1]

Those of the *Letters on a Regicide Peace* which were published on Burke's lifetime had success with the public: 'Unpleasant as was the prospect of a long war,' Carl B. Cone writes, 'people seemed to appreciate Burke's defiant and frank acknowledgement of it. They read his pamphlets eagerly and approvingly, Thirteen editions were issued.'[2] And Burke's acute sense of timing had not deserted him. The publication of those two *Letters* (20 October 1796) came just two days before Lord Malmesbury arrived in Paris on his ill-fated Embassy to the Directory.[3] One thinks of the timing of the Eleventh Report of the Select Committee, set at the right moment to shatter Fox's attempts to make peace with Hastings (see Chapter IV above, p. 315).

In the long battle of wills and minds between Burke and Pitt, Pitt had beaten Burke, and hurt him deeply in the process, over

---

[1] *Works* V, 507–8.
[2] *Burke and the Nature of Politics, The Age of the French Revolution*, p. 499.
[3] *Corr.* IX, Introduction, xxiii.

Fitzwilliam's viceroyalty. But in the battle over peace with the Direc- tory, it was Burke who prevailed, because of his superior understand- ing of the French Revolution, and the military expansionism emerging out of it. Pitt, despite his strong personal inclination to peace, would be still at war with France, when he died in 1806, nine years after Burke's death. And when peace eventually came, nine years after Pitt's death, it was the kind of peace which Burke, not Pitt, had always insisted it must be: peace with a restored monarchy. Pitt himself, at the time when Burke was developing the 'Regicide Peace' thesis, showed in the very manner of rejecting that thesis, his sense of the authority behind it: 'The unguarded and warm expressions' of 'that great man, Mr Burke should not,' he said, 'be regarded as an expression of Government policy.'[1]

Burke, from 1795 on, had little regard either for Pitt or Fox person- ally, but he remained obliged to support Pitt, because the alternative was Fox: 'I have no partiality at all to him [Pitt] or to his measures against which latter nothing but the accelerated motion of my illness could have hindered me from publishing my Opinion before this time, but between my disapprobation of Mr Pitts measure [measures?] and my horrour of those, of Mr Fox, there is some difference.'[2] Some three months before his death he refers grimly to 'the very ministers whom I *must by the necessities of the case support* [Burke's italics].'[3]

IRELAND
1796–1797

The 'necessities' imposed by the nature of the Pitt–Fox alternative, in the context of the war with France, weighed particularly heavily on Burke in relation to Ireland, the chief topic of most of his last letters. Once Pitt's attempt at peace-making had failed, Burke is com- pelled to renew support to him; this is painful where Ireland is con- cerned. The exuberance of *Letter to a Noble Lord* and of parts of *Letters on a Regicide Peace* – in the brief period of the revolutionary crisis when Burke was free to attack Pitt – never appears again. Much in these last letters is expressive of deep inner conflict.

[1] *Parl. Hist.* xxxii, 1132: quoted in *Corr.* IX, Introduction, xxii.
[2] *Corr.* IX, 264.
[3] *Corr.* IX, 315; letter of 26 April 1797.

In November 1796 John Keogh – Richard Burke's old chief in the Catholic Committee – wrote to Edmund offering to keep him 'truly informed' about the Irish situation, and to carry any message he might choose to send (to the Catholics, that is). Burke's reply is cold and guarded. By this time, he did not trust Keogh, regarding him as far gone in Jacobinism. Burke draws attention to his own declining health, and to his total lack of influence 'for a good while' over Irish affairs. Then he takes up, with marked ambivalence, a phrase of Keogh, who had said, 'I know you are so uncourtly as to be a true Irishman.' Burke wants Keogh to know that he is both a true Irishman and a true Englishman, but he has unusual difficulty in formulating this particular thought:

> You do me Justice in saying in your Letter of July, that I am a "true Irishman". Considering as I do England as my Country, of long habit, of long obligation and of establishment, and that my primary duties are here, I cannot conceive how a Man can be a genuine Englishman without being at the same time a true Irishman, tho' fortune should have made his birth on this side the Water. I think the same Sentiments ought to be reciprocal on the part of Ireland, and if possible with much stronger reason.

He goes on to attack all ideas of separating Ireland from England, and implicitly warns Keogh against his Protestant friends in the United Irishmen:

> I conceive, that the last disturbances, and those the most important, and which have the deepest root, do not originate, nor have they their greatest strength amongst the Catholicks; but there is, and ever has been, a strong Republican, Protestant Faction in Ireland, which has persecuted the Catholicks as long as persecution would answer their purpose; and now the same faction would dupe them to become accomplices in effectuating the same purposes; and thus either by Tyranny or seduction would accomplish their ruin.

Burke then alludes specifically to the founder of the United Irishmen, Wolfe Tone, and to his connections with the Catholic Committee. (Tone had left Ireland for America in June 1795, after it was discovered that he had been in contact with a captured French agent, the Rev. William Jackson. By November 1796 Tone was in France, on the staff of General Hoche, awaiting orders to sail to Ireland, with the expedition that miscarried at Bantry Bay in December). Burke tells Keogh:

It was with grief I saw last year with the Catholic Delegates a Gentleman who was not of their Religion or united to them in any avowable Bond of a public Interest, – acting as their Secretary, in their most confidential concerns. I afterwards found that this Gentlemans Name was implicated in a Correspondence with certain Protestant Conspirators and Traitors, who were acting in direct connexion with the Enemies of all Government and all Religion. – He might be innocent and I am very sure, that those who employed and trusted him [Keogh and the Catholic Committee], were perfectly ignorant of his treasonable correspondences and designs if such He had in dangerous connexion – But as he has thought proper to quit the Kings Dominions about the time of the investigation of that Conspiracy, unpleasant inferences may have been drawn from it.

I never saw him but once, which was in your Company, and at that time knew nothing of his Connexions character, or dispositions.[1]

In a letter to French Laurence, Burke described Keogh as 'a man that on the whole I think ought not to be slighted, tho' he is but too much disposed to Jacobin principles and connexions in his own nature and is a Catholic only in Name – Not but that whole Body contrary to its Nature has been driven by Art and Policy into Jacobinism, in order to form a pretext to multiply the Jobs and to increase the power of that foolish and profligate Junto to which Ireland is delivered over as a Farm.'[2]

In that last sentence was the nub, for it was Pitt who had driven the Irish Catholics into Jacobinism, by delivering Ireland over to the Castle Junto 'as a Farm'. And Burke was stuck with Pitt, because the alternative was Fox, and the English Jacobins. 'Jacobinism' in England was seen as fuelling both sides in the incipient civil war in Ireland. Burke wrote again to French Laurence on 23 November 1796: 'The Jacobin Opposition take this up to promote sedition in Ireland; and the Jacobin Ministry will make use of it to countenance Tyranny in the same Place.' In the meantime he wrote also to Fitz-

---

[1] *Corr.* IX, 112; 113; 113 n.2; 114–6. Tone later discussed Burke with Tom Paine in Paris. Tone mentioned that he had 'known Burke in England, and spoke of the shattered state of his mind, in consequence of the death of his only son, Richard. Paine immediately said that it was the Rights of Man which had broken his heart, and that the death of his son gave him occasion to develop the chagrin which had preyed upon him ever since the appearance of that work. I am sure the Rights of Man have tormented Burke exceedingly, but I have seen myself the workings of a father's grief upon his spirit, and I could not be deceived. Paine has no children!' W. T. Wolfe Tone, *Life of Theobald Wolfe Tone* (Washington, 1826) II, 348.

[2] *Corr.* IX, 120: letter of 18 November 1796. Writing to Fitzwilliam, Burke described Keogh as 'a franc Jacobin' and in league with Fox (*Corr.* IX, 120–6). However, he later agreed that his letter to Keogh had been 'too repulsive' (*Corr.* IX, 139).

william: 'We are in a perpetual dilemma between Tyranny and Jacobinism; the Jacobinism too tasting of Tyranny, and the Tyranny rankly savouring of Jacobinism.'

From Maynooth, Thomas Hussey, the President of the new college, informed Burke of the rapid spread, and revolutionary programme, of the United Irishmen: 'They are urging these cursed Sentiments thro'out the Country; and under the name of United Irishmen, this evil is extending beyond imagination. Many thousands, I am assured, are weekly sworn, thro' the Country in such a secret manner, and form, as to evade all the law in those cases.' He added: 'I am terrified at what I foresee regarding my own unfortunate native Country. To *pass by Parliament*, and *break the connexion with Great Britain*, is, I am informed, the plan of the United Irishmen.'

Hussey was right about the new United Irish programme. The original programme of the Society of United Irishmen had been of 'Whig' type aiming at reform of the Irish Parliament. (Some of its members, including Tone, probably had more far-reaching designs even then.) But in May 1795, after Fitzwilliam's recall, a new oath-bound United Irish Society was formed, with a separatist, and there-fore revolutionary, programme. Many of the thousands who were now sworn as United Irishmen were probably also Defenders. Pro-gress towards full-scale rebellion was now accelerating and irre-versible.

Burke's reply to Hussey's letter is the most important and compre-hensive of his late writings on Ireland. The circumstances of its com-position, indeed, are such as to justify our taking it as Burke's political testament with regard to Ireland. The letter, dated by the editor as 'post 9 December 1796', opens:

> This morning I received your Letter of the 30th November from May-nooth. I dictate my answer from my Couch, on which I am obliged to lie for a good part of the Day. I cannot conceal from you, much less can I conceal from myself, that, in all probability I am not long for this world. Indeed things are in such a Situation independently of the Domestic wound [Richard's death] that I never could have less reason for regret in quitting the world than at this moment; and my End will be, by several, as little regretted.[1]

The gist of this long letter is contained in two remarkable para-graphs. In the first, Burke establishes a critical distinction between

[1] *Corr.* IX, 161–172.

Jacobinism in general and, in particular, the type of Jacobinism to which Irish Catholics are being driven by official policy towards them in the second half of the 1790s:

> You state, what has long been but too obvious, that it seems the unfortunate policy of the Hour, to put to the far largest portion of the Kings Subjects in Ireland, the desperate alternative, between a thankless acquiescence under grievous Oppression, or a refuge in Jacobinism with all its horrors and all its crimes. You prefer the former dismal part of the choice. There is no doubt but that you would have reasons if the election of one of these Evils was at all a security against the other. But they are things very alliable and as closely connected as cause and effect. That Jacobinism, which is Speculative in its Origin, and which arises from Wantonness and fullness of bread, may possibly be kept under by firmness and prudence. The very levity of character which produces it may extinguish it; but the Jacobinism which arises from Penury and irritation, from scorned loyalty, and rejected Allegiance, has much deeper roots. They take their nourishment from the bottom of human Nature and the unalterable constitution of things, and not from humour and caprice or the opinions of the Day about privileges and Liberties. These roots will be shot into the Depths of Hell, and will at last raise up their proud Tops to Heaven itself. This radical evil may baffle the attempts of Heads much wiser than those are, who in the petulance and riot of their drunken power are neither ashamed nor afraid to insult and provoke those whom it is their duty and ought to be their glory to cherish and protect.

In the second paragraph, Burke cautions Hussey against justifying the practices of the Irish Administration, even with the objective of averting rebellion:

> I have told you, at a great length for a Letter, very shortly for the Subject and for my feelings on it, my sentiments of the scene in which you have been called to act, – on being consulted you advized Sufferers to quiet and submission; and giving Government full credit for an attention to its duties you held out, as an inducement to that submission, some sort of hope of redress. You tryed what your reasons and your credit could do to effect it. In consequence of this piece of Service to Government you have been excluded from all communication with the Castle; and perhaps you may think yourself [lucky] that you are not in Newgate. You have done a little more than in your circumstances I should have done. You are indeed very excusable from your motive; but it is very dangerous to hold out to an irritated people Any hopes that we are not pretty sure of being able to realize. The Doctrine of Passive obedience, as a Doctrine, it is unquestionably right to teach; to go beyond that, is a sort of deceit;

and the people who are provoked by their Oppressors do not readily forgive their friends, if whilst the first persecutes, [and] the others appear to deceive them. These friends lose all power of being serviceable to that Government in whose favor they have taken an illconsidered Step. Therefore my Opinion is, that untill the Castle shall shew a greater disposition to listen to its true friends than hitherto it has done, it would not be right in you any further to obtrude your services. In the mean time upon any new Application from the Catholics you ought to let them know simply and candidly how you stand.

Hussey's position was not as passive as Burke might have seemed to imply. As Catholic Bishop of Waterford, Hussey publicly called, during this period, for the repeal of the remaining Penal Laws: not as a favour but as a moral right. This caused the Protestant oligarchy to regard him as a dangerous agitator. The vigilant Sir Richard Musgrave (see Chapter I, pp. 37–8 and pp. 59–60) described him in October 1797 as 'an infamous incendiary . . . now living in the greatest intimacy with Messrs Fox, Grey and Sheridan.' Actually, Hussey was far closer to Burke than to Fox and his friends. In 1798 Hussey joined the other Catholic Bishops in enjoining 'peaceable and loyal submission'. I am indebted for these references to a valuable paper on Hussey by Daire Keogh.[1]

It would not be unfair to summarise these two paragraphs as meaning:

1. That resort to rebellion, by people oppressed as are the Irish Catholics in the 1790s, is justifiable, and

2. That a minister of religion should therefore refrain from actively exerting himself to avert such a rebellion.

This is a perfectly understandable position for a sympathiser with the Catholics to take up, in 1796, and it is also in accordance with the previously established pattern of Burke's views in Ireland. The reference to 'scorned loyalty, and rejected Allegiance', for example, recalls Burke's letter to his son Richard of four years earlier (see above, pp. 483–4). But the tension between this specific position, on Ireland, and Burke's general position, of fierce anti-Jacobinism, must have been almost intolerable. This letter was written in December 1796, the month when a French fleet anchored in Bantry Bay. What would Burke's position have been, had the French Army, carried by

[1] D. Keogh, 'Thomas Hussey' in *Waterford History and Society*, ed. T. Power (Dublin, 1992).

that fleet, been able to land in Ireland (as a much smaller French force was able to do in 1798, after Burke's death)? He was fully committed – most recently by *Letters on a Regicide Peace* – to fierce resistance against any such attempt. Yet the success of such a resistance would necessarily entail the bloody repression of rebels with whom Burke at heart sympathised. No wonder Burke told Hussey that he felt 'little reason for regret in quitting the world' at the end of 1796. He knew that the longer he lived, the greater the risk that he might witness, in the land where he was born, a war in which his head would be on one side, and his heart on the other. Had he lived just a year longer, into the summer of 1798, he would have witnessed just such a war. He would have followed his head, and the general anti-Jacobin cause, but at the cost of terrible emotional torments.[1]

I believe he was already experiencing, in imagination, a foretaste of those torments. The idea of 'heart and head at variance' is a simplification, although a suggestive one. In the more complex reality, there were rational as well as emotional components, in Burke's attitude towards policy in Ireland, in the late 1790s, and in his attitude towards the general Jacobin threat, in the same period.

There were rational grounds for deep dissatisfaction with the Pitt Administration's policy pursued in Ireland after Fitzwilliam's fall. Henry Grattan, who had no such links as Burke had with the Catholic people, shared his disapproval. And Pitt himself, into whose political decisions emotion did not enter, implicitly recognised, after the 1798 disaster, failure of the policy he had condoned. The solution he then attempted – Union of Great Britain and Ireland, combined with Catholic Emancipation – was as essentially Burkean in conception, in the circumstances of 1800, as Fitzwilliam's viceroyalty had been, in the circumstances of 1795. There is a peculiar irony here. Pitt's policy in 1800, on Catholic emancipation, foundered on the rock of George III's conviction that the completion of emancipation would be a breach of his Coronation Oath. But that rock appears to have been put there by Pitt himself (together with Fitzgibbon) in 1795, in order to crush the Burkean tendency within his Coalition. That was why

---

[1] That he would indeed have favoured repression of such a rebellion is clear, for example, from the following passage in a letter to Fitzwilliam on 20 December 1796 (*Corr.* IX, 189): 'The other party [Catholics] can do nothing at all but aggravate the Tyranny by provoking it, unless by the aid of a foreign Jacobin force and in that Case their Victory would be the utter subversion of human Society itself, of all religion, all Law, all order, all humanity, as well as of all property.'

he was unable to bring the king round, in 1800, in the way he could usually do.

Similarly, Burke's general anti-Jacobinism had, as we have seen, its emotional as well as its rational aspects. Those Catholic associations which caused Burke to sympathise, up to a point, with Irish pro-Jacobinism in the late 1790s, were the same as had aroused him to combat Jacobinism, and English pro-Jacobinism, in November 1790. It is difficult to imagine a more painfully complex dilemma both of head and heart, than Burke found himself in, while he helplessly contemplated the unfolding of the Irish tragedy, in the last months of his life.

Early in January, 1797, Burke learned the news of the arrival of the French fleet – with Hoche's army of 14,000 men aboard – in Bantry Bay, and of its subsequent dispersal by storm. He wrote to William Windham, now his only confidant in Pitt's Administration, to congratulate him on an escape which, as Burke implies, the Administration had done nothing to deserve:

> But the fate of that expedition is, I trust, now decided by an Arm stronger than ours, and by a Wisdom capable of counteracting our Folly. – Yes, My Dear Friend, I do tremble, lest the boldness of these Men in risquing every thing, and our negligence or Misfortune in not providing for any thing, may not always find the Heavens so propitious. I confess I tremble at the danger whilst I am rejoicing in the escape. However I sincerely congratulate you upon it. I consider you so much as a Friend to whom I am used to disburthen myself, that I forget I am writing to a Minister with whom I ought to have managements when I discuss anything relative to the Conduct of his Colleagues. The want of a Steady intelligence both from Paris, and from Brest, is a thing I cannot comprehend; because I am sure it might have been obtained. God bless you I am very faint, and perhaps peevish, but ever most truly Yours.' Windham replied: 'I perfectly agree with you on every sentiment respecting the danger, to which Ireland has been exposed, and the total want of judgement and foresight in providing anything like a proper defence.[1]

Meanwhile, the English Jacobins had also been busy. Burke had founded a school at Penn, near Beaconsfield, for the sons of Royalist refugees from France. He gave much of his time to this project, in his last years, and enjoyed the company of the boys. In January the school was attacked by a stone-throwing mob. The news was kept

[1] *Corr.* IX, 223–5.

from Burke. A friend wrote that Jane Burke would tell her husband about it 'when she shall think his spirits equal to such a precarious state, and of course his Friends are very anxious to keep every thing from him which may create *new Griefs*, and these poor Boys have been almost his only comfort since he lost his own Son.'[1]

In the nineteenth-century edition of Burke's *Works* (Vol. VI, pp. 415–29), there appears a letter entitled, *Letter on the Affairs of Ireland, 1797*. This is the same letter as appears in the modern edition of the *Correspondence* (Vol. IX, pp. 253–63) under the heading 'To Unknown', February 1797.

From its place in the canon of Burke's writings, this letter might appear to be his 'political testament' on Ireland, as I described his letter of December 1796 (see above, pp. 572–5) to Thomas Hussey. However, the Hussey letter remains the testament: the last vigorous effort of Burke's mind at grips with its most difficult dilemma. In it, Burke, with powers then only beginning to decline, is addressing someone he knows well and trusts completely, about the inward nature of problems with whose general outlines both men were only too familiar. 'To Unknown', by contrast, might be marked 'for beginners'. Burke's unknown correspondent is much younger, a contemporary of Richard, and it appears from the letter that the 'Unknown' did not know that Burke had done his best to avert Fitzwilliam's recall. He writes:

> Your mistake with regard to me lies in supposing that I did not, when his removal was in agitation, strongly and personally represent to several of his Majesty's Ministers, to whom I could have the most ready access, the true state of Ireland and the mischiefs which sooner or later must arise from subjecting the Mass of the people to the capricious and interested domination of an exceeding small faction and its dependencies.[2]

In this letter, gently instructing his young friend about the rudiments, Burke sketches the outlines of the problems whose depths he had grimly contemplated, in the letter to Hussey. For anyone who had followed Burke's copious commentary on Irish affairs, especially since the recall of Earl Fitzwilliam, there is nothing new in the political analysis contained in the *Letter to Unknown*. Indeed, Burke's shorter remaining letters referring to Ireland are of interest to us today mainly as showing how closely he continued to follow the

[1] *Corr.* IX, 226, n.2; letter from Mrs Crewe to Caroline Fox.
[2] *Corr.* IX, 254.

news from Ireland almost to the day of his death. (See *Corr.* IX, 333–371, covering the period 12 May to 3 July 1797.)

The important aspect of *Letter to Unknown* is the glimpse it affords into Burke's personal situation in the February before his death:

> In the state of my mind, so discordant with the tone of ministers, and still more discordant with the tone of Opposition, you may judge what degree of weight I am likely to have with either of the parties who divide this Kingdom; even tho' I were endowed with strength of body, or were possessed of any active situation in the Government which might give success to my endeavours. But the fact is, since the day of my unspeakable calamity, except in the attentions of a very few old and compassionate friends, I am totally out of all social intercourse. My health has gone down very rapidly; and I have been brought hither with very faint hopes of Life, and enfeebled to such a degree, as those, who had known me some time ago, could scarcely think credible. Since I came hither my Sufferings have been greatly aggravated, and my little strength still further reduced; so, that though I am told the Symptoms of my disorder begin to carry a more favourable aspect, I pass the far larger part of the twenty four hours, indeed almost the whole, either in my Bed, or lying upon the Couch, from which I dictate this. Had you been apprized of this circumstance you could not have expected any thing, as you seem to do, from my active exertions.

A month later, he offers his friend and confidant French Laurence death-bed reflections on his own career, and in particular on Ireland:

> What I say may have no weight; but it is possible that it may ténd to put other men of more ability, and who are in a situation where their abilities may be more useful, into a train of thinking. What I dictate may not be pleasing either to the great or to the multitude; but looking back on my past public life, though not without many faults and errors, I have never made many sacrifices to the favour of the great, or to the humour of the people. I never remember more than two instances in which I have given way to popularity; and those two are the things of which, in the whole course of my life, now at the end of it, I have the most reason to repent. Such has been the habit of my public life, even when individual favour and popular countenance might be plausibly presented to me as the means of doing my duty the more effectually. But now, alas! of what value to me are all those helps or all those impediments. When the damp chill sweat of death already begins to glaze our visage, of what moment is it to us whether the vain breath of man blows hot or cold upon it? But our duties to men are not extinguished with our regard to their opinions.

A country, which has been dear to us from our birth, ought to be dear to us, as from our entrance, so to our final exit from the stage upon which we have been appointed to act; and in the career of the duties which must in part be enjoyments of our new existence, how can we better start, and from what more proper post, than the performance of those duties which have made occupations of the first part of the course allotted to us?[1]

India = Ireland?
1796–1797

The Indian preoccupation in Burke's last years is reflected in the *Correspondence* much less extensively, but appears as even more intense. I believe this is a significant contrast, and I shall consider the nature of its significance a little later. The acquittal of Warren Hastings in 1795 was of course for Burke a bitter blow, but not an unexpected one. But what was exquisitely distressing was the decision by the Board of Control of the East India Company – responsible ultimately to Pitt's Administration – to grant an annuity of £4,000 to Warren Hastings. What distressed Burke most was a perceived symmetry between Hastings's annuity and Burke's own pension. The symmetry lay in the fact of the grants to the two men, not in the amounts. Hastings's annuity was worth more than three times the amount of Burke's pension.

Furiously, Burke wrote on 6 March 1796 to Henry Dundas, who was responsible for Indian affairs:

It is with pain inexpressible, I am driven to the Step I *must* take. Costs and damages, to an immense amount are given by you, on the publick Estate administered by the East India company, to Mr Hastings, against the House of Commons. That House has charged him with robbing that fund; and the people from whose labours the fund arises; and we reward that Robbery, by a new Robbery. I cordially wished well to your India administration; and, except in one Instance in the beginning, I never, even whilst I was otherwise in warm opposition, opposed it; hoping, that redress would be given to India; and that this Gang of Thieves called the

---

[1] *Corr.* IX, 274–5. On the reference to 'popularity', R. B. McDowell, the editor of *Corr.* IX, comments: 'Burke may be referring to his support of John Wilkes during the Middlesex election dispute (see vol. II) and to his support of the petitioning movement in 1780 (see vol. IV, 199—200).' See Chapter II, above.

Court of Directors and proprietors would be kept in some order. But there am I, acting under your own *individual* Authority, as well as *publick* authority attempted to be disgraced with the present age, and with all Posterity. But it shall never be said, either by the present Age or by Posterity, that the blood of India has been compromised by a Pension to the accuser and another to the party accused. I shall therefore, I hope, before the End of next week present a Petition to the House of Commons; and know whether they will confess themselves false accusers – whether they will deliberately betray those whom they have employd in their accusation, and whether the only satisfaction, they will give to undone nations as the result of their twenty four years Enquiry into their Grievances, is an enormous sum of Money, from their Substance, to reward the person they have charged as the authour of their Grievances.[1]

Burke wrote in a similar vein to Fitzwilliam, to Portland, to Windham, to Speaker Addington and to Chancellor Loughborough. In the letter to Loughborough he returns to the blood-guilt theme:

Oh no! It shall never be said, never, never, that the cause of the people of India, taken up for twenty years in Parliament, has been compromised by pensions to the accused and the accuser. The blood of that people shall not be on my head.[2]

The idea of a Petition to the Commons, in the circumstances, was hopelessly impracticable, and a product of emotional shock. Fitzwilliam, as a good friend should in such circumstances, gently talked Burke out of this project. Having pointed out the odds against success, he concludes: '– No, my dear Burke, you cannot stir – You must rest the character of your cause, upon the judgement of the last House of Commons, when all parties, contending about every thing else, agree'd alone on this – This, back'd by the indelible notoriety of the crimes you labour'd with such meritorious toil and efforts to bring to condign punishment and thereby to vindicate the character of the country at large, from any disgraceful concurrence with the crimes of an Individual, must bear out your cause and character, before that tribunal which will do it justice, an impartial Posterity.'[3] Burke acquiesced, with deep reluctance, and an increment of guilt. He writes to French Laurence: 'But what a dreadful example it is to

---

[1] *Corr.* VIII, 401–2.
[2] *Corr.* VIII, 401–2; 406–7.
[3] *Corr.* VIII, 410–411. Posterity has not proved altogether worthy of Fitzwilliam's confidence in its impartiality: see Introduction.

add myself to the number of those who have successively betrayed the poor people of India.'[1]

Burke's strongest emotional preoccupation, in his dying months was over India, at least overtly. It is on this issue – and apparently on this alone – that he craves vindication, through the preparation and publication of a history of the impeachment of Warren Hastings. Burke, on his retirement from Parliament in 1794 had entrusted this task to his friend French Laurence, who was co-adviser to Jane Burke as executrix of his will. In an impassioned passage in a letter written a little less than a year before his death, Burke reminds his friend of the charge laid upon him:

As it is possible that my stay on this side of the Grave, may be yet shorter, than I compute it, let me now beg to call to your Recollection, the solemn charge and trust I gave you on my Departure from the publick Stage. I fancy I must make you the sole operator, in a work, in which, even if I were enabled to undertake it you must have been ever the assistance on which alone I could rely. Let not this cruel, daring, unexampled act of publick corruption, guilt, and meanness go down – to a posterity, perhaps as careless as the present race, without its due animadversion, which will be best found in its own acts and monuments. Let my endeavours to save the nation from that Shame and guilt, be my monument; The only one I ever will have. Let every thing I have done, said, or written be forgotten but this. I have struggled with my active Life; and I wish after death, to have my Defiance of the Judgments of those, who consider the dominion of the glorious empire given by an incomprehensible dispensation of the Divine providence into our hands as nothing more than an opportunity of gratifying for the lowest of their purposes, the lowest of their passions – and that for such poor rewards, and for the most part, indirect and silly Bribes, as indicate even more the folly than the corruption of these infamous and contemptible wretches. I blame myself exceedingly for not having employd the last year in this work and beg forgiveness of God for such a Neglect. I had strength enough for it, if I had not wasted some of it in compromising Grief with drowsiness and forgetfulness; and employing some of the moments in which I have been rouzed to mental exertion, in feeble endeavours to rescue this dull and thoughtless people from the punishments which their neglect and stupidity will bring upon them for their Systematick iniquity and oppression: But you are made to continue all that is good of me; and to augment it with the various resources of a mind fertile in Virtues, and cultivated with every sort of Talent, and of knowledge. Above all make out the cruelty of this pre-

[1] *Corr.* VIII, 419.

tended acquittal, but in reality this barbarous and inhuman condemnation of whole Tribes and nations, and of all the abuses they contain. If ever Europe recovers its civilization that work will be useful. Remember! Remember! Remember![1]

Burke wrote that letter from Bath, where his doctors had ordered him to take the waters. He also recorded his physical condition:

But my flesh is wasted in a manner which in so short a time no one could imagine. My limbs look about to find the Rags that cover them. My strength is declined in the full proportion; and at my time of life new flesh is never supplied; and lost strength is never recoverd. If God has any thing to do for me here [on earth] – here he will keep me. If not, I am tolerably resigned to his Divine pleasure.

In the following February, less than six months before his death, Burke again reminds his friend of that injunction over India:

But you remember, likewise, that when I came hither at the beginning of last summer, I repeated to you that dying request which I now reiterate, That if at any time, without the danger of ruin to yourself, or over-distracting you from your professional and parliamentary duties, you can place in a short point of view, and support by the documents in print and writing which exist with me, or with Mr Troward, or yourself, the general merits of this transaction, you will erect a cenotaph most grateful to my shade, and will clear my memory from that load, which the East India Company, King, Lords, and Commons, and in a manner the whole British Nation, (God forgive them) have been pleased to lay as a monument upon my ashes. I am as conscious as any person can be of the little value of the good or evil opinion of mankind to the part of me that shall remain, but I believe it is of some moment not to leave the fame of an evil example, of the expenditure of fourteen years labour, and of not less (taking the expense of the suit, and the costs paid to Mr Hastings, and the parliamentary charges) than near £.300,000. This is a terrible example, and it is not acquittance at all to a publick man, who, with all the means of undeceiving himself if he was wrong, has thus with such incredible pains both of himself and others, persevered in the persecution of innocence and merit. It is, I say, no excuse at all to urge in his apology, that he has had enthusiastic good intentions. In reality,

[1] Letter of 28 July 1796; *Corr.* IX, 62–3. The injunction was obeyed, by the inclusion of all the major India speeches in *Works*.

you know that I am no enthusiast, but [according] to the powers that God has given me, a sober and reflecting man. I have not even the other very bad excuse, of acting from personal resentment, or from the sense of private injury – never having received any; nor can I plead ignorance, no man ever having taken more pains to be informed. Therefore *I* say, *Remember*.[1]

At the time of that last *Remember*, Burke was still in Bath. The disease which was destroying him (believed to have been tuberculous enteritis) had hitherto been confined to his stomach. By February, it was beginning to affect his head. As he wrote in the same letter: 'They have taken the town and are now attacking the citadel.' As the phrase itself reveals, the citadel was still defended. It may seem strange that the last letters should show him much more affected, in a personal way, by the affairs of India, than by those of Ireland. Certainly there is nothing, among the copious references to Ireland in his surviving letters of 1796–7, that corresponds to the throb of guilt and thirst for vindication that appear, with urgent and insistent repetition, in his last references to India. Yet, if we consider only the context, he had much less to worry about, in those last years, over the affairs of India, than over those of Ireland. Over India, he had fought – for fourteen years, 1781 to 1795 – against a system, and against the man who had presided over that system and symbolised it for Burke. As against the man, the struggle was a stalemate, and Hastings's annuity a deep symbolic affront and injury. But in relation to the system – which was what affected the people of India – Burke had won. The systematic practice of maximal extortion, conducted by the servants of the Company, which had flourished under Hastings, had been suppressed by his successors, in large part because of the reports of the Select Committee and the adoption of these by the House of Commons: all of which was almost entirely due to the personal exertions of Edmund Burke. The people of India by the end of his life were uncontestably better off by reason of his exertions on their behalf.

It was otherwise with the people of Ireland, and notably with the Irish Catholics: Burke's people whom he had sought to serve; not just for fourteen years, as with India, but throughout his life. That people were now headed towards a disaster which was visibly looming up while he lay dying. And the chain of events leading immediately towards that disaster had been started by the recall

---

[1] *Corr.* IX, 237–8; letter dated 10, 12 February 1797.

of Fitzwilliam: that is to say by the explosive failure of Burke's long-prepared Grand Experiment designed to save the Catholics of Ireland. And once that experiment had failed, Burke was constrained by his wider commitment, against the French Revolution, not merely to leave that people to their fate, but actively to side with Pitt, who was ultimately responsible for the continuation and exasperation of their oppression, through the consequences of Fitzwilliam's recall. Burke acknowledged that that people had just cause for rebellion. Yet, whenever the justifiable rebellion should come, he would be obliged, by his wider commitment, to support its repression.

There is material enough, there, surely for a store of guilt feelings concerning Ireland, and it is not possible, given the pattern of his life, and the nature of the political situation, in the late 1790s, that the dying Burke was not afflicted by such feelings. Yet they found no direct expression, regarding Ireland, in his last letters. It is over India that he accuses himself, and craves vindication. On an almost absurdly inadequate ground – that of failing to present a petition to the Commons against Hastings's annuity – he speaks of adding himself 'to the number of those who have successively betrayed the poor people of India'. I believe that this is the psychological equivalent of a physiological 'referred pain'. I have suggested earlier that guilt-feelings about India were related, in his psyche, to guilt-feelings about Ireland. All his life, he had been accustomed to bottling up a large part of his feelings about Ireland. By 1796–7 the old reasons for bottling up had gone, but a new and imperative one had come. Guilt-feelings about Ireland, in the ghastly circumstances of his dying years, were simply too much for his conscious mind to bear. The feelings that were repressed over Ireland came out over India, where they were bearable, because largely imaginary. The urgent need to forget certain things, over Ireland, lent the urgency to his repeated cry over India: *Remember*!

In suggesting that Burke must have experienced, subconsciously, strong feelings of guilt over Ireland, as he lay dying, I am not saying that he deserved to experience such feelings. He did not. Intellectually and morally, his overall position, including his position over Ireland, was entirely tenable and entirely honourable. He fervently believed that the victory of Jacobinism would be bad, not merely for England and Europe, but also specifically for Ireland. And the people in Ireland with whom he was in most communication at this time, and whose influence he had done much to strengthen – the Catholic clergy – not merely agreed with him on that but went further along that line than Burke judged it appropriate to do.[1]

There is a popular impression that, while 'the Bishops' felt like that, the clergy as a whole did not. This view is based mainly on the knowledge that some priests took a prominent part in the 1798 Rebellion, in Co. Wexford. Recent research has shown, however, that those priests were few, and odd. In the valuable essay 'The Role of the Catholic Priest in the 1798 Rebellion in Wexford' by Kevin Whelan (in *Wexford History and Society*, edited by Kevin Whelan and William Nolan, Dublin, 1987), Dr Whelan shows that out of 85 priests in Co. Wexford 'a maximum total of eleven' can be regarded as 'having been actively involved in rebellion.' Of the eleven, one was crazy, while 'at least seven' had a noticeable drink problem. Several Wexford priests preached against the United Irishmen. One of them, Father Michael Lacy, published an advertisement condemning the United Irishmen's principles as 'tending to sow the seeds of dissent between Protestant and Catholic and to revive old prejudices against each other'. Considering the declared objectives of the United Irishmen at their foundation, this was a highly paradoxical diagnosis, but it proved to be true, in the sectarian massacres of the 'United Irish' rebellion of 1798. Most of the clergy knew much more about the French Revolution than their flocks did, and were against it. They did not share, for example, the illusion, strong among the Defenders, that the French Revolutionaries were Catholics. The Catholic clergy in Ireland, at the close of the eighteenth century, were close to their people and devoted to their interests. The clergy certainly did not see Burke's anti-Jacobinism, which they shared, as any kind of betrayal of their people. Hussey may well have felt him, indeed, to be insufficiently zealous in the anti-Jacobin cause, through his reluctance to support the clergy's efforts to avert a rebellion, which they knew would be ruinous.

Burke all his life, as he often said (for example to John Keogh, see above pp. 570–1) had felt loyalty both to England and Ireland: inherently an uneasy combination. He had sought, with considerable success, to resolve the contradictions, by promoting reconciliation

---

[1] His advice to Thomas Hussey (see above pp. 572–4), not to exert himself in trying to avert rebellion, was essentially irrational, since he would have had to support the repression of the rebellion which he wanted Hussey not to try to avert. This rare piece of irrationality confirms, to my mind, the existence of strong guilt-feelings on Burke's part in this area at this time.

between England and Ireland. But in his last phase, from Fitz-william's recall to his own death in July, 1797, he had no hope of any further progress along those lines. Relations between England and Ireland were getting much worse and fast, and by decision of an English Prime Minister. Yet Burke never wavered, even in the worst of that crisis, in his support for Pitt, provided only that Pitt himself did not waver in his support for the war against revolutionary France.

Whatever tumults of inner feelings there may have been, Burke always put that struggle above everything else, where practical decisions had to be made. In it he attained a great inner harmony, a union of mind and heart. He had been against the French Revolution on intellectual grounds – because of his awareness of the dangers of radical innovation 'upon a theory' – before he became emotionally committed to the struggle against it. It was in the specific area of Ireland, that that union of heart and mind was vexed to distraction. Yet there was a sense in which that union did extend to Ireland also, though with greater difficulty than to anything else. If, as I believe, there was an inner voice, whispering to Burke that he might be betraying the Irish Catholics, there was another, inner voice that had a solid answer to that. This was that the French Revolutionaries, the enemies of all religion, were especially virulent enemies of Cath-olicism – as they had just shown in La Vendée – and that the Irish Catholics were therefore high on the list of those who needed to be defended against them. The pastors of that community thoroughly agreed with that view, and adhered to it even more consistently than Burke himself did. Yet he knew that many young Irish Catholics did not see it that way, and in his heart he had some sympathy with them.

Religion was always important to Burke, so naturally it was especi-ally important during these last years and months. As he wrote to French Laurence in July 1796, 'If God has anything to do for me here [on earth] – here he will keep me. If not, I am tolerably resigned to the Divine pleasure.' 'Tolerably'. A touch there again of what Maxim Gorky, called the Tolstoyan relation to God, 'two bears in one den'. Certainly, Burke, as he lay dying in Bath, appeared to his intimates as a religious figure, as William Wilberforce, who visited him very near the end, tells us: 'Burke was lying on a sofa much emaciated; and Windham, Laurence, and some other friends, were round him. The attention shown to Burke by all that party was just like the treatment of Ahithophel of old. "It was as if one went to inquire of the oracle of the Lord".'[1]

Wilberforce brought Burke the news of the mutiny of Spithead: 'And it was with Burke's emphatic demand for strong measures [against the mutineers] ringing in his ears that Windham left to attend a Cabinet meeting in London.'[2]

The Spithead and Nore mutinies – the most dangerous period for England in the whole war with France – darkened Burke's last months. He wrote to French Laurence on 12 May 1797: 'I should not be surprized at seeing a French army convoyed by a British Navy to an attack upon this Kingdom.' It is against that background that we have to understand Burke's otherwise startling last instructions – given orally to his kinsman Edward Hoyle, three days before his death – concerning his own burial: he wanted to be buried: 'unknown, the spot unmarked and separate from his son, wife and Brother on *account of the French Revolutionists* [Burke's emphasis].[3]

Cone rightly remarks: 'This was no evidence of a wandering mind.' That the French Revolutionaries might conquer England was a reasonable contingency to provide for, in the summer of 1797; they never looked nearer to attaining that great objective than at that moment. Nor was it unreasonable to consider that some of the victorious French Revolutionaries (or of their English allies) might desecrate Burke's grave. It is true that Jacobinism, by this late date, was no longer the dominant force in Paris that Burke sometimes seemed to suggest it was. The dominant force was now no longer ideological egalitarian conviction, but militant French nationalism, fuelled by a devouring appetite for loot and glory. But the militant French nationalists hated Burke quite as much as the original Jacobins had done, and possibly more. The High Priest of French revolutionary nationalism, Jules Michelet, was born in the year Burke died, but his hatred of Burke, as the arch-enemy of *La Grande Nation*, was

---

[1] R. I. Wilberforce, *Life of Wilberforce* (London, 1838) Vol. II, p. 211: quoted in *Corr.* IX, Introduction, xxiv. The principal bond between William Wilberforce (1759–1833) and Burke was that Burke had been in the distinguished minority, along with Pitt and Fox, which had voted in favour of Wilberforce's proposals for the abolition of the slave trade, in April, 1791. This was the last great cause in which Burke and Fox acted together; the final breach between them came in May. Wilberforce was an intimate of Pitt, which would account for the slightly sardonic tone in this last portrait of Burke among his disciples.

[2] *Corr.* IX, Introduction, xxiv.

[3] *Corr.* IX, 332–40 and Cone *op. cit.* p. 507.

obsessive and vindictive. If Burke could arouse such hatred among such people, long after his death, what would it have been like in the 1790s had the Revolution in France moved to England? It is not fantastic, but probable that zealots in the French cause would have dug up Burke's bones and dumped them on some kind of dung-heap. It was only sensible to make it a bit harder for them to act in this way.

At some time close to Burke's death Fox made an attempt 'to arrange a last reconciliatory meeting with him'. Jane Burke wrote back, on Edmund's behalf: 'Mrs Burke presents her compliments to Mr Fox, and thanks him for his obliging inquiries. Mrs Burke communicated his letter to Mr Burke, and, by his desire, has to inform Mr Fox that it has cost Mr Burke the most heart-felt pain to obey the stern voice of his duty in rending asunder a long friendship, but that he deemed this sacrifice necessary; that his principles remain the same; and that in whatever of life yet remained to him, he conceives that he must live for others and not for himself. Mr Burke is convinced that the principles which he has endeavoured to maintain are necessary to the welfare and dignity of his country, and that these principles can be enforced only by the general persuasion of his sincerity. For herself, Mrs Burke has again to express her gratitude to Mr Fox for his inquiries.'[1]

There seems at first sight a contradiction between this cold rebuff and the last words of Burke's Will and Testament, written nearly three years before. In the will, Burke had written: 'If the intimacy which I have had with others has been broken off by a political difference on great Questions concerning the state of things existing and impending, I hope they will forgive whatever of general Human infirmity or my own particular infirmity, has entered into that contention. I heartily entreat their forgiveness. I have nothing more to say.'[2]

One might ask why, if Burke is prepared (implicitly) to 'entreat' Fox to forgive him, he is not prepared to forgive Fox? The question seems to the point, but it blurs a distinction which was clear to Burke: between forgiveness and the kind of reconciliation that Fox was looking for. Forgiveness was a personal matter and Burke as a devout Christian, no doubt forgave all his enemies, as individuals, while he prepared for death. But the 'last reconciliatory meeting' which Fox proposed would have had political implications, which

---

[1] *Corr.* IX, 373. Jane Burke's reply is dated by the editor 'ante 9 July 1797'.
[2] *Corr.* IX, Appendix, 375–8.

Burke refused. The meeting would have signified that the differences of principle, to which he had attached such importance in his lifetime, were not of such great importance after all, in the final perspective. But Burke wants the political world to know that these principles are of transcendent importance to him, and that Fox is still outside the pale, in terms of those principles. That is what Burke means by the final phrase of the rejection: 'these principles can be enforced only by the general persuasion of his sincerity.'

If Burke and Fox had both lived until after Waterloo – when Burke would have been eighty-seven – there could have been no difficulty, on Burke's side, about receiving Fox. But to receive the great French apologist in the shadow of French triumphs, in the summer of 1797, would have been striking the flag of resistance in the face of the advancing enemy. There is a contemporary drawing, published that summer, entitled 'French Telegraph making Signals in the Dark'. The drawing shows Fox signalling with a dark lantern to a fleet which is advancing from a coast marked '*République*'. There is no defending fleet in sight. The picture depicts the scene which was Burke's last nightmare: a mutinous English fleet carrying a French army towards British ports. Burke did indeed see Fox as sending welcoming signals in that direction (see for example *Observations on the Conduct of the Minority*; above p. 501). So one can understand why Charles James Fox was not admitted to the deathbed of Edmund Burke.

Burke died shortly after midnight on 9 July. Jane was with him, and French Laurence, who reported Burke's 'dying advice and request' to Fitzwilliam 'steadily to pursue that course in which he now is. He can take no other that will not be unworthy of him'[1]. Burke feared that Fitzwilliam might be about to rejoin the Foxites. One of Burke's last letters – that of 12 May 1797 to French Laurence[2] – has been interpreted as meaning that Burke actually favoured the replacement of Pitt's Government 'by a coalition headed by Fox and Sheridan' (Mahoney, *Edmund Burke and Ireland*, p. 305.) This is a wild misreading. There is a passage which, taken in isolation, might be understood in that sense. The context, however, refutes it. The letter was intended to be shown to Fitzwilliam, and the whole passage is a tactfully worded warning that, if he were to agree to take part in a Foxite Administration, he would be falling into a trap. Mahoney calls the letter 'a pretty muddled performance'.

[1] *Corr.* IX, 373–4.
[2] *Corr.* IX, 332–40.

It is, in fact remarkably lucid and well calculated as a quiet death-bed warning.

Laurence goes on: 'Mrs Burke, of whom you and Lady Fitzwilliam will I am sure be most anxious to hear, shews a fortitude truly worthy of the character which we have ever known her to possess. She feels that she has duties to discharge, for the sake of which she thinks herself bound to take every care of life, though in itself it has no longer any pleasure for her. Her behaviour is most unaffectedly heroic.' The letter ends: 'Oh! my dear Lord, what an incalculable loss have his family, his friends, and his countrymen suffered in that wonderful man, pre-eminent no less in virtues than in genius and in Learning! So kind to all connected with him, so partial to those whom he esteemed, ever preferring them in all things to himself; yet so zealous and resolute a champion in the cause of Justice, social order, morals and Religion. The private vanishes before the public calamity. When he fell, these kingdoms, Europe, the whole civilized world, lost the principal prop that remained, and were shaken to their very centers.'[1]

That was the view of an intimate friend. But there were many who felt that way, if less keenly. George Canning wrote: 'There is but one event, but it is an event for the world. Burke is dead.'

There is a tradition, with some weight behind it, that Burke, just before he died, received the last rites of the Roman Catholic Church. According to the Centenary History of Maynooth, 'It is said that he died a Catholic, and that his friend, Dr Hussey, the first President of Maynooth, received him into the Church'.[2] That formula is probably simplistic. It is not likely, from all we know of Burke, that he saw himself as leaving one Church to be 'received into' another. He believed in those large parts of Christianity that were common to Anglicanism and Roman Catholicism, and did not concern himself with those doctrinal parts which divided them. It was in that spirit, I feel sure, that he sent for Dr Hussey. I don't doubt that he did send for him, if only because to do so would be a consolation for Jane Burke, which would have been a great concern for him. There is a discreet sentence in that last letter of French Laurence's which seems to refer to that transaction: 'From some confidential directions which he gave me I know that he considered his dissolution as fast approaching, but not so instant as it proved to be.'

On this point I consulted the distinguished historian Monsignor

[1] *Corr.* IX, 373–4.
[2] Most Rev. John Healy; *Maynooth College, Its Centenary History* (Dublin, 1895) p. 100, n.2.

Patrick J. Corish, who is now at work on a new history of Maynooth. He replied: 'Burke died in 1797, Hussey in 1803. In February 1808 a letter appeared in the *Irish Magazine* stated to be from "one of the Maynooth Professors" claiming that Hussey "attended Burke spiritually in his last illness." There is a touch of *Private Eye* about the *Irish Magazine*, but *Private Eye* has been known to get things right! W. J. Fitzpatrick's *Secret Service under Pitt*, p. 386, says the same thing. This book was published in 1892. Fitzpatrick never gives his sources, but his overall accuracy is remarkable. He would not say a thing without having good reason to believe it true. So Hussey may have reconciled Burke: if Burke sent for any friend it would have been Hussey. Once again, however, extreme care would have been taken to guard the secret.'

I am most grateful for this communication, which tends to confirm my own opinion that Burke did send for Hussey, but too late.

The funeral service at Beaconsfield, on 15 July 1797, according to the Anglican rite, had the character of a solemn tribute to a pillar of the State. The pall-bearers were: William Windham (Secretary of State for War); Murrough O'Brien, Earl of Inchiquin; Earl Fitzwilliam; the Duke of Devonshire; Sir Gilbert Elliot; Henry Addington, Speaker of the House of Commons; the Duke of Portland, and Lord Loughborough (Lord Chancellor). The combined presence of Fitzwilliam and Portland is worthy of note. The two men, formerly close friends and colleagues, had not met since one had dismissed the other, in harrowing circumstances, more than two years before. French Laurence, inviting Fitzwilliam to be pall-bearer wrote: 'Will you my dear Lord, allow me to name your Lordship for one of the Pall-bearers, to shew the last respect to the memory of a man, who while living ever loved you most affectionately and ardently? It may however be right to advertize your Lordship that from some late most kind messages, and from his having borne the pall over poor young Richard, it will be impossible to pass over the Duke of Portland on this melancholy occasion.' No force less than that of their common reverence for Edmund Burke could have induced those two men to take part together in any public event.

The pall-bearers were the leaders of the Portland (or Burkean), Whigs. Politically, the chief bond between them was their common hostility to the French Revolution. Burke's other three great causes are less clearly represented. Ireland indeed was worthily represented by Fitzwilliam, who had paid dearly for his commitment to Burkean principles, in the crash of his viceroyalty. Sir Gilbert Elliot had worked closely with Burke over India, in the management of the impeachment of Warren Hastings. America, the earliest of Burke's public causes, was not represented. Of Burke's closest collaborators in that cause three were dead: Rockingham, Dowdeswell, and Lord John Cavendish. The fourth, Charles James Fox, knew that he would not be welcome.

Few Foxites would have wished to be present at Beaconsfield on that July day, especially after Burke's death-bed rebuff to their leader. Yet there was one Foxite member of Parliament there; not among the pall-bearers, but in the crowd of mourners. This was Philip Francis. He had been despatched into outer darkness by Burke, seven years before, because of his scoffing reaction to *Reflections*; and Francis agreed with Fox, not Burke, over the French Revolution. Yet he came down to Beaconsfield, to an uncongenial social–political gathering, and what must have been a chilly reception. He is a lonely figure in that crowd, and a moving one. He was a proud and selfish man, yet he deliberately went down to face what he knew would be an uncomfortable experience, and a somewhat humiliating one. And he did so, only in order to show respect to a man who had snubbed him. Francis had changed indeed! The dark bond of India had held under the rending strain of France. It was a complex and ambiguous bond, and it was a haunted one. Burke's 'India' contained a brooding presence of Ireland, and Philip Francis, in that cortège, is attended as always by the shade of Nuncomar.

Remember!

EPILOGUE:
'Wickedness is a Little More Inventive'

On three of our four main themes, Burke's stand has ceased, or almost ceased, to be controversial, for our own times. Hardly anyone would now defend the system of negative political discrimination based on religious affiliation, which Burke had to fight in Ireland. Hardly anyone would defend the policy of introducing new taxes for the American colonists, or the Penal Acts passed in consequence of the resistance to those taxes, or the war that was levied to enforce those Penal Acts. Few would defend the system of extortion in India, which is acknowledged to have been practised under the Governor-Generalship of Warren Hastings; although Hastings, personally, still has some defenders (principally his biographers).

The stand against the Revolution in France, in contrast, is still seriously challenged. Several modern writers still cling to the position popularised in the 1790s by the Painite radicals and the Foxite Whigs: that Burke's hostility to the French Revolution made him an apostate from his previous liberal position. Burke's own cogent arguments to the contrary seem to have fallen on deaf ears. Even a writer normally so scrupulous in the observance of fine distinctions as is Sir Isaiah Berlin once felt able to include Burke in a list of 'reactionary thinkers.'[1] Yet if Burke had died in 1789, at the age of sixty, instead of in 1797, at the age of sixty-eight, nobody could conceivably have labelled him as a reactionary thinker. He was well-

[1] See the essay 'Alleged Relativism in Eighteenth Century European Thought' in Berlin's The Crooked Timber of Humanity: Chapters in the History of Ideas (London, 1990). The full reference (on page 78) is: 'There is so far as I can see, no relativism in the best-known attacks on the Enlightenment by reactionary thinkers – Hamann, Justus Möser, Burke, Maistre'. But Burke nowhere attacks the Enlightenment as a whole. He was himself, intellectually, a child of the early Enlightenment, that of Locke and Montesquieu. He was hostile to the anti-Christian character of the later Enlightenment under Voltaire's influence and he was also hostile to the ambiguous and emotion-led neo-religiosity of Rousseau. But see my appendix, 'An Exchange with Sir Isaiah Berlin', in which Sir Isaiah has the last word.

established, by the earlier date, as a liberal thinker, a sound Whig. It has not been demonstrated, to say the least of it, that his response to the entirely new phenomenon of the French Revolution was such as to invalidate, retrospectively, the whole tenor of his political thought, and consign it *en bloc* to the reactionary category. Fox, Paine and many others, saw the French Revolution as continuous with the English and American ones. Burke's far more powerful mind registered both the immensity and the terrible originality of the French Revolution.

His own contention concerning the integrity and consistency of his political thought, from the American Revolution to the Revolution in France, has never been refuted, nor do I believe it to be susceptible of refutation. Yet it can be neglected, or ignored, and I found it significant that one of the finest political thinkers of our time should once have fallen into that trap.[1]

The best succinct definition of Burke's position on the French Revolution is that of Philippe Raynaud: 'A la fois libérale et contre-révolutionnaire. . . .'[2] To many English-speaking readers the juncture of the terms 'liberal' and 'counter revolutionary' would have something shocking about it. It seems to be widely assumed, in most circles to the left of the centre, that a true liberal must be sympathetic, if not necessarily to all revolutions, at least to the French one, whose intellectual origins were in the later Enlightenment and whose most memorable rhetoric is resolutely liberal. Yet surely there is validity, from a liberal point of view, in the Burkean distinction between limited revolutions – like England's Glorious Revolution and the American Revolution – and limitless revolutions, totally innovative ones like the revolution in France, which claim to extend the boundaries of liberty, but in fact result in successive mutations of despotism.

From today's perspective, we can best see Burke's writings against the French Revolution as the first great act of intellectual resistance to the first great experiment in totalitarian innovation. That first experiment failed, and turned into military despotism, as Burke had predicted it would. Yet it left behind a memory of spectacular events,

[1] Elsewhere in the same volume in the essay 'Joseph de Maistre and the Origins of Fascism'. Sir Isaiah writes very well about the differences between Burke and Maistre, who was indeed a genuinely reactionary thinker (pp. 128–133). But arranging thinkers in lists is always a dangerous business. And again, see the appendix.
[2] Preface to the modern French edition of *Réflexions sur la Révolution de France* (Hachette, 1989) p. lvi.

of drama, of rhetoric, of glory, of a sublime vision of what society might be, once the rule of *les purs* had been substituted for that of *les corrompus* (Robespierre's terms). There was matter there for emulation, and the emulators have not been lacking.

The first and most durable emulators have been the Marxists. Marx and Engels, and later Lenin, Trotsky and Stalin, had all the qualities that Burke abominated in the French Revolutionaries: radical repudiation of all existing institutions and arrangements; absolute confidence in their own competence to build a new and far better society; willingness to kill their contemporaries in great numbers, for the supposed benefit of posterity; contemptuous hostility to all religion, and a programme for its enforced elimination from the world.

The continuity of Marxism with the French Revolutionary tradition is generally no more than implicit. Marx was concerned with asserting his own originality, and not with acknowledging indebtedness to predecessors. Yet the continuity is there, and nowhere more apparent than in Marx's venomous hostility to Edmund Burke. In a footnote to *Capital* Marx enthusiastically adopted the venality theory, so dear to Burke's hostile contemporaries, the English pro-Jacobins, and to some later historians: 'The sycophant – who in the pay of the English oligarchy played the romantic *laudator temporis acti* against the French Revolution just as, in the pay of the North American colonies at the beginning of the American troubles, he had played the liberal against the English oligarchy – was an out-and-out vulgar bourgeois.'[1]

In the main body of Marxist writing, the continuity with the French Revolution is implied by a claim to *surpass* that Revolution. Marx had already, in his own opinion and in that of his followers, surpassed the French Revolution by laying, in *Capital*, the scientific basis which the earlier revolutionaries had lacked. Also, the Marxist Revolution, when it came, would be inherently superior to the French one, since it would, according to Marx, be a proletarian revolution, whereas the French had been a bourgeois one.[2] So much for the theory of the thing. In reality the resemblance between the Marxists and their French predecessors was very close indeed and where they

---

[1] *Capital* I (Moscow, 1959) p. 760, n. 2.

[2] If the French Revolution was bourgeois, it is not immediately apparent why Burke, as 'an out-and-out bourgeois', according to Marx, should have been so hostile to it. But Marxism could account for all such 'contradictions' without difficulty, on the verbal plane.

differed most obviously – which was in point of originality – the French had the advantage. The French were the first to have the audacity to attempt to reconstruct an entire system of government 'upon a theory'. The French were therefore the grand pioneers in the domain of universal innovation; the Marxists were the second wave, with precedents to work on, and to analyse, criticise and 'surpass'.

And the Marxists did indeed surpass the Jacobins in that they went further down the road of radical innovation than their predecessors had done. With two major exceptions, the French Revolutionaries had respected private property. (The two exceptions were the nationalisation of Church property in October 1789, and the systematic looting of 'liberated' foreign territories, after the outbreak of the European War, in April 1792.) The Marxists, in contrast, decreed the systematic abolition of private property. This enormous innovation heralded a correspondingly great extension of the powers wielded by the revolutionary leaders over their subjects-to-be. From a Burkean point of view, this meant that the heirs of the Jacobins represented a more virulent strain than that which Burke, in his lifetime, had had to combat. Different strains, but the same disease.

The Marxist intellectuals of the nineteenth and twentieth centuries talked in terms of different concepts to those used by the French Revolutionaries, but in their character and style, the new Jacobins were clones of the old ones. The Marxists talked a lot about the Proletariat, and assigned a high value, in theory, to its historic role. In practice, the Proletariat was to supply the troops which would put the Marxists into possession of absolute power. And the Marxists were not themselves members of the Proletariat, but exceptionally aggressive and arrogant intellectuals; in those qualities, exactly like the people who led the French Revolution, in all its phases.

The role of the Proletariat, within the Marxist system, corresponds closely to the role of Rousseau's General Will within the French Revolution. For the French Revolutionaries, of all tendencies, Rousseau's *Du Contrat Social* was authoritative, and the General Will, the key concept of that work, became a kind of tutelary deity of that Revolution.[1] Like other deities, the General Will is an elusive and inscrutable Supreme Authority. As Rousseau says: 'The General Will is always right (*droite*) but the judgment which guides it is not always

[1] Not only did Robespierre exalt the General Will, but the Thermidorians, who murdered Robespierre, sought to surpass him in the lavishness of their homage to the teachings of Jean-Jacques. See my essay 'Virtue and Terror: Rousseau and Robespierre', in *Passion and Cunning* (1986).

enlightened.' So Rousseau, in Chapters VI and VII of *Du Contrat Social*, appoints to the service of the General Will a personage variously described as a 'guide' or 'legislator'. It is the guide's job, in Rousseau's words, to show the General Will how 'to see objects as they are, sometimes as they ought to appear to it'. Robespierre was precisely such a guide.

Rousseau's General Will was the supreme authority, but liable to error, and requiring the services of a guide-interpreter (alias legislator) to make its purposes clear to itself, as well as to others. Marx's Proletariat possesses precisely the same combination of characteristics. This combination is without parallel, except in contexts which are avowedly supernatural. The combination is no accident, but a measure of Marx's indebtedness to the Jacobin tradition and to its moral and intellectual Master. That continuity is evident, not only in concepts, but also in style. Rousseau had shown the world the power of confident and peremptory affirmation, untrammelled by any care for evidence. Marx in his most popular and influential writings – notably the *Communist Manifesto* – followed the same pitch. He later, in *Capital*, assembled a vast body of 'evidence' around a predetermined conclusion. But the 'evidence' was accepted only by those who had already yielded to the peremptory affirmations.[1]

The continuity between French Revolutionary practice and Marxist practice became apparent after the Bolsheviks had seized power in the Russian Empire. The Bolsheviks, from the beginning of their enterprise, had placed it in the tradition of the French Revolution, and of the Paris Commune of 1871, itself an episode within the same tradition. It is reported that when Lenin and his group of returning revolutionary exiles were aboard their train on the way to the Finland Station in 1917, they burst into song when the train crossed the Russian frontier. The song they sang was the Marseillaise.

The Russian Communists surpassed their French predecessors in the extent and duration of the Terror they practised. Although Terror, as Burke saw, underlay the whole of the French Revolution, what historians call the Terror – that is the Terror associated with the name of Robespierre – lasted less than two years, from the summer of 1792 to the summer of 1794. Leaving aside the period of both Red and White Terror, in the Russian Civil Wars, Stalin's Terror, in

[1] Rousseau's influence over Marx has been inadequately appreciated. Marx himself dissimulated it, in order to enhance his own originality. Freud did the same thing with Nietzsche.

varying forms, lasted from 1934 to 1941 and was renewed for a further eight years from the end of the war in Europe to Stalin's death, in 1953. The number of the victims also expanded hugely. The victims of Robespierre and his associates were numbered in tens of thousands, but Stalin's victims were numbered in millions, as also were the victims of the Chinese Communists, together with those of Pol Pot in Cambodia.

The scale of the Terror appears proportionate to the scale of the innovation attempted. The French Revolution, inside France, practised only limited incursions on property, mainly church property and that of emigrés. Twentieth-century Communist Revolutions were not confined to politics and religion, but were also revolutions in property relations, and so encountered far wider and deeper resistance, necessitating far greater Terror. Stalin's Terror began with the enforcement of rural collectivism. It greatly exceeded the French Terror in scope, but it had a close precedent, of which Stalin was certainly aware, within the French Revolution. The Jacobins, in 1793–4, sent portable guillotines into the villages, to terrorise the villagers into parting with their grain, in exchange for almost worthless *assignats*. Stalin's 1936 Constitution was completely in the French Revolutionary tradition, both in its copious use of benevolent and liberal formulae and in the total irrelevance of these formulae to actual revolutionary practice.

In style also, and in moral exigence, the Russian and Chinese Revolutions took after the French one. Show trials were part of the machinery of government, and so were other rituals designed to show the supremacy of State morality. Burke had been particularly disgusted by the Jacobins' staging of public performances, in which children denounced their parents, or parents their children, as traitors to the Revolution. Such performances and multiple variations on them, became routine under the Russian and Chinese revolutions.

Under the Communists, as under the Jacobins, professions of 'public virtue' were used to suppress the practice of all the 'private virtues' hitherto honoured by ordinary human beings. The point here is that it was the French Revolution which set the precedent for the later, and even more terrible efforts at changing whole societies 'upon a theory'. In resisting that effort in his own time, Burke was also warning future generations against similar efforts.

The Communists were the direct heirs of the Jacobins. The debt of the other great Revolution of the twentieth century, the National Socialist one, is far from being so obvious, yet it exists. In principle,

Hitler rejected the French Revolution, partly because it was French, and partly because its rhetoric – though not its practice – reflected those Enlightenment values which Hitler rejected *in toto*. And Hitler rose to power as a result of his street-wise effectiveness as a populist anti-Communist. Nonetheless, there were two aspects of the French and Russian Revolutions which could not fail to attract Hitler's attention and arouse his emulation. The first was the audacity of innovations on the scale attempted by those two revolutions. The second was the ferocity with which the two sets of revolutionaries repressed all efforts at resistance to their innovations.

National Socialism descended from, and went further than, the *völkisch* tradition of nineteenth-century Germany. The *völkisch* ideal, known as *Volkstum* was nationalist, anti-semite, racist and militarist. It was also revolutionary. Following the first German attempt at revolution, in 1848, Richard Wagner wrote: 'The Revolution, redeemer and creator of a new world blessing . . . I, the Revolution, am the ever-rejuvenating, ever-fashioning Life. . . . For I am Revolution, I am the ever-fashioning Life, I am the only God. . . . The incarnated Revolution, the God become Man,. . . . proclaiming to all the world the new Gospel of Happiness.'[1]

Wagner was *völkisch* to the core and his apocalyptic revolution would have been militantly anti-semitic and racist, as is clear from his racially anti-semitic *Das Judentum in der Musik*, published in 1850. The German revolutionaries of 1848 had their heads full of an intoxicating mixture of French Revolutionary mystique and *völkisch* ideas. The abortive 1848 Revolution thus represents a stage in the transition and mutation of revolutionary ideas between France and Germany. The National Socialist Revolution of 1933–45 was the culmination of that process. As Heine had written, already before 1848: 'A drama will be enacted in Germany in comparison with which the French Revolution will appear a harmless idyll.'[2]

The Third Reich was the most far-reaching effort ever made in reconstructing human society 'upon a theory'. The theory was that of 'racial hygiene', and the Holocaust was an application of that

[1] Wagner, *The Revolution* (1849) PW 8:234, 238, quoted in Paul Lawrence Rose, *Revolutionary Anti-Semitism in Germany from Kant to Wagner* (Princeton, 1990). Rose's book is a pioneering one, which demolishes the notion that German nationalism, racism and anti-semitism were a monopoly of the Right. See also the same author's *Wagner, Revolution and Rage* (London 1992).

[2] *Almansor* (1820); quoted in Rose, *op. cit.* p. 164. As Rose says later in the same study (p. 261), 'It is dangerous to apply to German revolutionism the simple Left and Right labels of Western liberal politics.'

theory. The Holocaust would have been replicated on a world-wide scale, had the outcome of World War Two permitted continued and expanded application of the theory. The particular theory adopted by the National Socialists owes nothing to the French Revolution. What the French Revolution, and its legitimate descendant the Russian Revolution, provided for Hitler was not theory but example: the greatest examples in all history, before Hitler, of the recasting of societies 'upon a theory'. Hitler despised their particular theories, but he followed their examples – and hugely surpassed them – in the audacity and ferocity with which he applied his own particular 'theoretick dogma'.

The course and consequences of the three great revolutions of the twentieth century constitute confirmation, on an awesome scale, of Burke's warnings against attempts to reconstruct whole societies 'upon a theory'.

Yet I should not like to end this Epilogue with an exclusive concentration on the Burke of the last period (1790–1797). We read 'Burke on the French Revolution' badly, if we fail to keep in mind that this is the same Burke as 'Burke on the American Revolution', 'Burke on India', and 'Burke on Ireland'. The same Burke, but confronting different *circumstances*, and assigning different priorities in the light of the circumstances. From January 1790 until his death nearly eight years later, Burke gave the highest priority to the struggle against the French Revolutionaries and their English admirers. He saw the Grand Design of the Revolutionaries as constituting, in that period, the greatest threat to ordered liberty and human happiness. But he never attributed to the Revolutionaries a monopoly of evil, nor did he ever suggest that everything that went wrong in human society was attributable to ambitious projects based 'upon a theory'. The forms of misgovernment against which he struggled over America, India and Ireland were only marginally affected by theories and had their origin mainly in ordinary human vices and defects such as arrogance, greed, stupidity and wishful thinking. Burke's writings on the Revolution in France have a special relevance to the early and middle parts of the twentieth century: a period in which grandiose revolutionary projects, whether based on 'theories' of Right or Left, had high prestige and glamour, and short interludes of apparently dazzling success. But the late twentieth century has seen the spectacular failure of Revolution-based-upon-theory, and a comprehensive and heart-felt rejection of the theory by the great majority of the many and varied peoples who had been forced to live under it, and often to pay lip-service to it.

In the changed circumstances, it would be unBurkean to place quite as much emphasis as would have been appropriate formerly, on Revolutionary Grand Designs. The climate of the last decade of the twentieth century does not appear propitious to the formation of such projects. The dangers of the times are likely to be mostly non-theoretical and to result from visceral responses to conflicting economic, national, ethnic, and even religious stimuli. And these responses are being shaped to a great extent by those same age-old human vices and defects against which Burke had struggled over America, India and Ireland, as well as over France.

For my last quotation from Burke, I have chosen a passage from *Reflections on the Revolution in France* which is peculiarly relevant to the period of bewilderingly rapid and improvised transitions in the domains and former domains of the failed Revolutions-upon-theory in the last decade of the Twentieth Century. In it Burke detaches himself from the immediacies of the struggle against the Revolution, in order to reflect on the moral lessons of history, and the question of the Versatility of Evil. The passage was provoked by the Revolutionaries' enacting of a play before the National Assembly – in order to incite persecution of Catholics – in which the Cardinal of Lorraine is shown as plotting what Burke describes as 'the infamous massacre of St Bartholomew', in 1572. (A sad, ironic detail is that the play was by Marie-Joseph de Chénier, younger brother of the greater poet André Marie de Chénier, a former revolutionary who, disgusted by the excesses of his former colleagues, became a moderate, and was guillotined in 1794.) Burke writes:

We do not draw the moral lessons we might from history. On the contrary, without care it may be used to vitiate our minds and to destroy our happiness. In history a great volume is unrolled for our instruction, drawing the materials of future wisdom from the past errors and infirmities of mankind. It may, in the perversion, serve for a magazine, furnishing offensive and defensive weapons for parties in church and state, and supplying the means of keeping alive, or reviving dissensions and animosities, and adding fuel to civil fury. History consists, for the greater part, of the miseries brought upon the world by pride, ambition, avarice, revenge, lust, sedition, hypocrisy, ungoverned zeal, and all the train of disorderly appetites, which strike the public with the same

troublous storms that toss
The private state, and render life unsweet.

These vices are the *causes* of those storms. Religion, morals, laws, prerogatives, privileges liberties, rights of men, are the *pretexts*. The pretexts
are always found in some specious appearance of a real good. You would
not secure men from tyranny and sedition, by rooting out of the mind
the principles to which these fraudulent pretexts apply? If you did, you
would root out every thing that is valuable in the human breast. As these
are the pretexts, so the ordinary actors and instruments in great public
evils are kings, priests, magistrates, senates, parliaments, national
assemblies, judges, and captains. You would not cure the evil by resolving, that there should be no more monarchs, nor ministers of state, nor
of the gospel; no interpreters of law; no general officers; no public councils. You might change the names. The things in some shape must remain.
A certain *quantum* of power must always exist in the community, in
some hands, and under some appellation. Wise men will apply their
remedies to vices, not to names; to the causes of evil which are permanent,
not to the occasional organs by which they act, and the transitory modes
in which they appear. Otherwise you will be wise historically, a fool in
practice. Seldom have two ages the same fashion in their pretexts and
the same modes of mischief. Wickedness is a little more inventive. Whilst
you are discussing fashion, the fashion is gone by. The very same vice
assumes a new body. The spirit transmigrates; and, far from losing its
principle of life by the change of its appearance, it is renovated in its new
organs with the fresh vigour of a juvenile activity. It walks abroad; it
continues its ravages; whilst you are gibbeting the carcass, or demolishing
the tomb. You are terrifying yourself with ghosts and apparitions, whilst
your house is the haunt of robbers. It is thus with all those, who attending
only to the shell and husk of history, think they are waging war with
intolerance, pride, and cruelty, whilst, under colour of abhorring the ill
principles of antiquated parties, they are authorizing and feeding the
same odious vices in different factions, and perhaps in worse.[1]

Those last four words should be borne in mind as we contemplate
some of the patterns emerging in the disintegrating empire of ruined
Communism, in the aftermath of the longest-lasting and most formidable innovative effort in human history.

[1] *Reflections*, Penguin Classics ed. pp. 247–9.

Appendix: An Exchange with Sir Isaiah Berlin

Extract from my review in the *New York Review of Books*, April 1991, of Isaiah Berlin's *The Crooked Timber of Humanity: Chapters in the History of Ideas*. The book covers many subjects and writers, and ranges over several centuries. My article has been edited and the letters between us that follow it slightly edited, in order to keep the appendix mainly on Burke.

. . . I agree fully with Isaiah Berlin's anti-Utopian position: that is, with his contention that the belief that a Utopia can be constructed on earth, combined with the urge to bring about its construction, has resulted in practice in a colossal multiplication of human misery. But I should like to pursue this argument into a domain that Berlin does not explore in this collection of essays. That domain is the French Revolution, considered as the first major effort to construct a secular Utopia, and the model for all subsequent efforts of this kind.

All revolutions in Europe, before the French one, were either not secular or not Utopian. Early Utopias were theocratic in concept like John of Leiden's regime in Munster in the early sixteenth century. The first English revolution, that of the mid-seventeenth century, was also theocratic, in its Utopian aspects: the Rule of the Saints. The second English revolution, of 1688, known to its heirs as the Glorious Revolution, was not Utopian at all, but deliberately limited, pragmatic, and pluralist. The double objective was to end the arbitrary and Romanist rule of James II, *without* reviving the theocratic Utopia of the Rule of the Saints.

The American Revolution began out of quite limited grievances and objectives, and certainly without any Utopian agenda. As soon as definite revolutionary purpose emerged, the model was England's Glorious Revolution, with George III cast in the role of James II. It is true that the American Revolution, unlike the Glorious one, had millenarian overtones. The words *Incipit Novus Ordo Seclorum* on the Great Seal, as adopted by the Continental Congress, might be taken as indicating some form of Utopian design, but this would be misleading. The choice by the Founding Fathers of these words from Virgil's Fourth Eclogue – which European Christendom had held to be sacred prophecy – was essentially a claim to divine approval; a new chapter was opening in God's dispensation for the world. The idea that human hands should radically transform the structure of American society, as that structure stood in 1782, was entirely absent.

The Glorious Revolution was essentially a dynastic and sectarian adjustment. The American Revolution was essentially the secession of colonists from an empire. The first real full-blooded secular revolution, the first large and determined attempt to construct a secular Utopia, after a wholesale destruction of existing arrangements – together with those *people* who were seen to represent and defend these arrangements, was the French Revolution.

Throughout the nineteenth century, and up to the Russian Revolution, the French Revolution was seen, by revolutionaries, everywhere, not exactly as a model, but as a measure of what had to be surpassed or – as far as the French were concerned – completed. The French Revolution had been betrayed: by the Thermidorians, by Bonaparte, or – as Michelet believed – by priests and women. Next time, there must be no betrayal. In the meantime, the French Revolution remained as the great demonstration that it was indeed possible for people with ideas to seize power and put their ideas into practice. It was thus the license, the model, and the comfort of Utopians of every description.

By the middle of the nineteenth century, the Marxists were the most obvious heirs of the French Revolution, in the sense that their proletarian revolution was destined to surpass that bourgeois one. Bourgeois though it was, the Marxists loved it, especially in its bloodiest phase. It is said that Lenin and his followers, returning from exile in 1917, sang the Marseillaise as they crossed the frontier into Russia. In France itself, the Communist party long held the allegiance of the working class, through its claim to be the party which was the true heir to the French Revolution, and destined to complete and perfect its work.

That the Left and the Marxists in particular were heirs to the French Revolution, in the sense described above, is generally accepted. What is not so obvious is that *right-wing* revolutionaries were also its heirs. Whatever your radical program might be, and however widely it might be at variance with the programs of any of the French revolutionaries, the French Revolution still demonstrated that it was possible to seize power and put ideas into effect. The exact nature of the ideas was less important than the demonstration of the possibility.

Isaiah Berlin points out – in the last essay in the book – that nationalism was not a monopoly of the Right in Germany. Nor was the heritage of the French Revolution a monopoly of the Left. The revolutionary proceedings in Germany in 1848 were profoundly ambiguous. The desire to make a German revolution that would be bigger than the French one was patently there, and also the desire to achieve a united Germany. But what would this revolutionary united Germany be like? We can find some clue to that in the contemporary writing of Richard Wagner. Wagner's revolutionary enthusiasm, in the relevant period is beyond all doubt. In *The Revolution* (1849) Wagner wrote:

> The Revolution, redeemer and creator of a new world blessing . . . I, the Revolution, am the ever-rejuvenating, every-fashioning Life. . . . For I am Revolution, I am the ever-fashioning Life, I am the only God. . . . The incarnated Revolution, the God become Man . . . proclaiming to all the world the new Gospel of Happiness.

At the time when Wagner wrote that, the only Revolution *actually achieved* that could possibly arouse feelings of that order was the French one. So it seems clear that he, like the 1848 revolutionaries in general, desired a German revolution that would be as spectacular as the French one, but would transcend it. The passage quoted contains, of course, no clue at all to the actual content of the redeeming revolution. But one clue is contained in another work of Wagner's of the same year: *Das Judentum in der Musik* (1849). This is the first major anti-Semitic tract of a secular and racist type. Nor was Wagner unusual, among German revolutionaries of the time (often misleadingly designated as 'liberal'). Paul Lawrence Rose has amply demonstrated the anti-Semitic and racist character of the German revolutionary tradition in the nineteenth century in his recent pioneering study, *Revolutionary Anti-Semitism in Germany from Kant to Wagner*.[1] The German revolution was already marked out to be *völkisch*: that is, both nationalist and racist. The Nazi revolution – for it was one – had its roots in the *völkisch* tradition. As Heinrich Heine had written in 1820 'A drama will be enacted in Germany in comparison with which the French Revolution will appear a harmless idyll.'

For the German revolutionary tradition in the nineteenth century, the Enlightenment component in the rhetoric of the French Revolution remained largely alien. The relevance of the Revolution consisted in that spectacular demonstration of possibility. After 1917, that demonstration was no longer directly relevant. The Russian Revolution offered a far more exciting demonstration that revolution was possible *in the twentieth century*. But the second demonstration owed quite a lot to the first.

My contention that the *völkisch* revolutionary tradition was encouraged by the recollection of the French Revolution is open to argument. The place of the French Revolution in the Marxist tradition is not.

What I find surprising in *The Crooked Timber* is that the idea of the French Revolution *as Utopia* does not get explored. For surely the French Revolution deserves consideration as the first major realisation of a Utopian project: the construction of a perfect society, owing nothing to the past. Isaiah Berlin rightly identifies the destructive potential of Utopia, but he seems to confine it to Marxism and to twentieth-century revolutions.

[1] (Princeton University Press, 1990).

I can only guess at the reasons for so large an omission. I have three guesses. The first concerns the nature of the 'history of ideas' tradition. The historian of ideas generally scrutinises the writings of important thinkers. He often scrutinises them with major historical events in mind, and the possible bearing on those events of the ideas he is scrutinising. But he does not scrutinise the events themselves, though he makes occasional reference to them. In this sense, the history of ideas is rather like classical tragedy; the rough stuff goes on off stage.

Still, I don't think this hypothesis altogether explains the omission, from a discussion of Utopia, of the first example of realised Utopia. My second guess is that Isaiah Berlin may find the theme of the French Revolution intrinsically uncongenial. The French Revolution looks after all like a case of Enlightenment culminating in Terror. Isaiah Berlin, as a true child of the Enlightenment, might well find that a painful paradox. Yet the victims of the Terror – and the far more numerous victims of the wars of French territorial expansion, beginning with the Revolution – were victims, not of Enlightenment but of one of its enemies: nationalism.

What the Enlightenment did was to create an emotional vacuum, which was filled by nationalism. The French nation took the place of God. The king's head was cut off to cries of *Vive la Nation!* The insistence of *La Grand Nation* on dominating all other European nations plunged Europe into war for almost a quarter of a century. For all that, the Enlightenment had only an indirect responsibility. Yet the responsibility, though indirect, was real through the creation of that cosmic emotional vacuum. That painful paradox recedes, but will not altogether go away.

My third guess is probably the nearest to the mark. This is that Isaiah Berlin thinks the French Revolution was in some basic sense a liberating event, and so not to be placed in the category of destructive Utopias, along with the Communist revolutions of the twentieth century. This view of the matter is indicated by Berlin's inclusion of Edmund Burke in a list of 'reactionary' thinkers, along with Hamann, Möser, and Maistre: a galley on which Burke would never have voluntarily embarked. And the only reason why Burke could possibly be classified as 'reactionary' is his strong and consistent opposition to the French Revolution.

In reality, Burke was no more a reactionary than Isaiah Berlin. He was a liberal and pluralist opponent of the French Revolution. Philippe Raynaud in his excellent preface to the most recent French translation of *Reflections on the Revolution in France*[1] precisely defines Burke's position when he describes him as 'liberal and counter-revolutionary.' The French Revolution was abundantly productive of liberal documents and liberal speeches, but its transactions were not in accord with those documents and speeches. The *Déclaration des Droits de l'Homme et du Citoyen* is no better a guide to the realities of the French Revolution than Stalin's Constitution of 1936 was a guide to the realities of life in the Soviet Union. Similarly Burke, in

[1] (Hachette, Paris, 1989).

attacking the French Revolution and its would-be imitators in Britain, was no more reactionary than was George Orwell when he attacked the Russian Revolution and *its* would-be imitators in Britain. And Orwell, too, was classified as a reactionary by the friends of the revolution which he attacked.

Burke perceived and attacked what a later age would call the totalitarian tendencies in the French Revolution, and he discerned these tendencies from very early on, years before the Terror. He is a pluralist, a defender of diversity against the claims of revolutionary absolutism, as appears from the following sentence in the third of the *Letters on a Regicide Peace*:

All the little quiet rivulets, that watered an humble, a contracted, but not an unfruitful field, are to be lost in the waste expanse and boundless, barren ocean of the homicide philanthropy of France.

Nor did Burke, as Berlin suggests in the same passage, deliver any 'attacks on the Enlightenment' as a whole. Burke was himself a child of the Enlightenment, in its earlier phases and forms: the Enlightenment of Locke and Montesquieu. He did attack that branch of the Enlightenment – the Enlightenment of Voltaire and the Encyclopaedists – that was hostile to Christianity and to the whole Judeo-Christian tradition. Burke's Enlightenment was ecumenical.

I am sorry that Isaiah Berlin should have included Burke in that list of reactionaries, for Burke and Berlin are in reality kindred spirits. Berlin, indeed, seems to realise this when, in his essay on Maistre, he develops a perceptive contrast between Burke and the *real* reactionary that Maistre was. I think, on consideration, Berlin might be prepared to take Burke out of that list.

My observations above on the French Revolution have the limited purpose of showing that that revolution belongs in the category of attempted Utopias culminating in Terror. The French Revolution was much more shortlived, in terms of the durability of the regime which it established, than the Russian and Chinese Revolutions have been. In the French case the attempt at Utopia ended, with the end of the Terror in which it had culminated, in July 1794, with the fall of Robespierre's 'Republic of Virtue' just five years after the fall of the Bastille. In the year after the fall of Robespierre, the Thermidorian' Constitution of the Year III' signalled the abandonment of Utopia by substituting for 'Liberty, Equality, Fraternity' the words "liberty, equality, security and property." And in the year after that General Bonaparte introduced a new and more dynamic formula when he promised the hungry soldiers of his army of Italy 'honour, glory and riches'. Napoleon's Empire was to continue the military expansionism of its revolutionary predecessors, and also their practice of systematically looting the countries they claimed to be liberating.

Undoubtedly the Revolution brought considerable benefits to large groups of French people; the most conspicuous winners, and the most faithful defenders of the revolutionary gains, being those who acquired *les biens nationaux*: the lands and other property confiscated from the Catholic Church. The fall of the same Church was accompanied by citizenship for Protestants and Jews. The bourgeoisie benefited, principally by an enhancement of its status, through the fall of the nobility. Many peasants gained, but some were amongst the greatest losers of all. The war waged by the Convention against the refractory peasantry of La Vendée was ferocious to the verge of genocide. Finally, among the benefits conferred by the French Revolution, we must include much of the legislation passed by the Convention, and embodied by the Emperor Napoleon in the Code Civil.

Many people, in retrospect, think of the benefits of the French Revolution as outweighing their 'cost,' often counted as comprising only the decapitation of a couple of thousand persons in Paris. If we add those more informally despatched *en masse* in the provinces, including La Vendee, the death toll rises far higher although the exact numbers will never be known. If we add in the deaths which were a result of French military aggrandizement – which began under the Revolution and continued under Napoleon the cost was enormous in human terms.

That people think of the French Revolution more sympathetically than they do of the Russian one is largely due to the fact that the French attempt to achieve Utopia was of far shorter duration than the Russian one. Suppose, on the one hand, that the Russian revolution had found its Thermidor in 1922. We would be likely today to be talking about the benefits that revolution brought to the peasantry. Suppose, on the other hand, that, in July of 1794, it was the Thermidorians who lost, and Robespierre and his friends who won. That might easily have happened. It may be that the determining factor was an accident: the wound to Robespierre's jaw that silenced the voice that had held all political France in mortal fear since the death of the king in January 1793. If the Thermidorians had lost, the Republic of Virtue would have continued in being, with institutionalised Terror as its standing resource.

My point is that it is wrong, in terms of Isaiah Berlin's own anti-Utopian value scheme to treat an opponent of the first attempt to realise Utopia – the French one – as being *ipso facto* a reactionary.

I have been exploring an omission, and the omission is sufficiently capacious to invite such an exploration. But in concluding, I wish to stress the riches actually contained in the essays that make up *The Crooked Timber*. Though I have quoted abundantly, the quotations, being selected to illustrate a theme, don't fully bring out the flavour of the text as a whole. One of the delights of reading Isaiah Berlin is furnished by the asides; the little nuggets which his sense of humour leads him to pick up, for our delectation, out of the field of his voluminous and varied reading. I shall conclude with two of these nuggets. The first is from Metternich, the master of the unenthusiastic: 'If I had a brother, I would call him cousin.' The second is from Faguet, parodying Rousseau's 'Man is born free, but everywhere is found enslaved and in chains.' Faguet offers a parallel observation about sheep:

Dire: les moutons sont nés carnivores, et partout ils mangent de l'herbe, serait aussi juste.

(It would be equally correct to say that sheep are born carnivorous and everywhere eat grass.)

As a confirmed Rousseau-basher myself, I have to acknowledge that this remark of Faguet's is the neatest deflation of Rousseau ever achieved. I am grateful to Isaiah Berlin for that discovery, as for much else.

All Souls College
Oxford
10 April 1991

Dear Conor,

Your piece in the *NYRB* about my book of essays. I must offer you my
gratitude for the very handsome and generous way in which you have
treated them. All my life I have regarded myself as being systematically
over-estimated – this is a sincere view – I think by everybody except the
slightly loony Left and slightly loony Right, from which I have received a
good many knocks in my day. This estimate is something I have never been
against – long may it continue – until my dying day; after that, I don't mind
what happens. So, let me say again that I am deeply in your debt, both
about our agreements and our disagreements. I understand that you would
like me to reply to you in the *Review*, so that we could have an exchange.
But I would rather send you my views personally and privately; and if you
then want to react to them in some fashion, whether privately or publicly,
that would be your choice. . . .

I really should not argue with you about Burke. I know virtually nothing
about him except what most people know – the image handed down in
history books, and conversation, which is plainly not good enough. Of
course you are right – he should not have come into my list of
reactionaries. . . . Burke was only too justified in seeing through the fallacy
and danger of utopian universalism: all honour to him. The parallel with
Orwell is brilliant – some of Orwell's interpreters, as you know, say that it
was not really the Soviet Union at which his satires were directed. That is
rubbish, as we both know. But when you say that Burke was a liberal
pluralist, I am not sure. Yes, of course, in a way; he does derive from Locke
and Montesquieu and perhaps earlier Christian sources e.g. Hooker too.
Even more from Hume's Tory stress on custom – his defence of Indians and
Americans is a defence of traditional values. . . . What drew Maistre to
Burke, it seems to me, is not only the attack on natural man, but his
opposition to liberal individualism, and still more to democracy. Also his
doctrine of freedom, like Montesquieu's, tells us that man is only free to
do what is right – there is no freedom of choice to act according to
one's, perhaps deeply mistaken, convictions. If these beliefs are perceived as

anti-social or disgusting in some other way, then they infringe freedom. But liberty is surely what we normally mean by the word: freedom to be wrong as well as right, wicked as well as virtuous except that in the case of too much wrong or wickedness it is right to restrain such conduct. But restraint is not freedom; Locke and Montesquieu and Burke, it seems to me, in a curious way identical. Do you disagree?

Now back to natural man. It may well be a dangerous fiction; but do we not think that there are such things as human rights, as opposed to British, Indian, American and Iraqi rights, all of which are founded on different traditions? Would Burke accept that? As a Christian no doubt he should, but does he? Why does he hate Priestley and Price, as disturbers of the deep peace of the peacefully grazing British kine? Is this not in some way a genuine defence of some kind of *ancien régime*, though not perhaps to the degree to which my maverick colleague in All Souls, Jonathan Clark, tries to make out. After all, what drew Maistre to him was something deeply illiberal: respect for hierarchy; and for rule by a gentlemanly elite (whether hereditary or created by moderately recent wealth). Should one describe a man with such views as a liberal pluralist? Still, you are fundamentally right, ànd I withdraw his name from the proscribed list of reactionaries, and am willing to consider that the claims by T. S. Eliot and Oakeshott to regard him as a direct ancestor, and the fact that Gentz translated the *Reflections* for the benefit of Metternich and his lot, should not be held too sternly against him. In short, I think you are more right about this than I, and withdraw in mild disorder. . . .

Why do I not mention the French Revolution, except in a very passing way? This is because I do not believe that the French Revolution – even as a feeling, and not simply as a movement founded on doctrines – departs in any significant way from the eighteenth-century Encyclopaedists, who seem to me to be the originators of universalist infallible utopianism. I don't think that the French Revolution was nationalistic, although perhaps it became so in the last years of the eighteenth century, and certainly under the Napoleonic conquest. When people called somebody *un bon patriote*, they didn't mean, it seems to me, a good Frenchman, a good son of his country, but a member of the splendid new society, dedicated to liberty, equality, fraternity etc. When the Revolutionaries attacked Germany, it was to spread the ideas of the Revolution against horrible dynastic despotisms, and not to establish the rule of France as a nation; as the home of the truth, of liberty, of the new life, yes, but not because it was France as such that was entitled to all those conquests. . . . But of course, you are right, the French Revolution is the great original utopian experiment – the other universalist levellers are inspired by it, not so much in 1848 but certainly in 1870, 1917, Munich and Hungary in 1919, etc., etc. They might have thought about that Jesuit republic in – where was it? Peru? Paraguay? – but they didn't.

Now we come to the three causes that you put forward as having led me not to condemn the French Revolution as much as I might have done, given that I agree with Burke's warnings and analysis of what the doctrines are and what they would lead to. At this point I am obliged to begin a not too powerful self-examination, which issues in the following:

(a) You say the study of ideas leads to avoidance of the rough stuff. There is much truth in this. The French Revolution did not contain ideas not to be found in the eighteenth century thinkers whom I dealt with with some severity in a series of lectures at Bryn Mawr in 1952, repeated over the BBC, called 'Freedom and Its Betrayal' about the consequences of Helvétius, Rousseau, etc., and of all kinds of high-minded and rational doctrines in the early nineteenth century too, like Fourier and Saint-Simon; and so to the antidote in Machiavelli, Vico and Herder. The FR ideologically is pure, classical republicanism, but what is important is that what it led to – the violence of the mobs, the Terror, the dark forces – not at all what Condorcet wanted. It was the upheaval of social forces not examined, probably not dreamt of much, in the writings of the 18th-century *Philosophes* – that did put ideas into the heads of demagogues, nationalists, neo-Jacobins, old Uncle Ilyich and all. 1848 is still Girondist, non-utopian; but Marxism, of course, did look to 1793–4.

(b) You wonder whether I could quite face the idea that the Enlightenment could possibly have led to horrors. No – I did realise that the ideas of the perfect life, enforced by violence if need be, must be incompatible with any beliefs or practice that can be called liberal and humane. My thesis, after all, is that these noble-seeming ideas do lead to blood. But again, you are right. Perhaps I did not make enough of Talmon's Totalitarian Democracy; but it is not Nation which was their cry, much more *au nom du peuple!* Maistre's enemy was *le peuple*, not *la nation*. No, it is not the Enlightenment that gave birth to monsters, but the combination of that with fanaticism, nationalism, and the upheaving of elements below the surface, which the Enlightenment on the whole had no idea of, and which the breaking of the relatively civilised, if often oppressive, crust of the French 18th century allowed to emerge and spill over and wreak havoc.

(c) I cannot help but feel sympathy for the French Revolution, and to that extent some antipathy to the admirable Burke. Destructive as the consequences of the Revolution were – the line that leads to Lenin, Stalin, Pol Pot, and Mao is still not finished (China today, and some attractive regimes in the Balkans and the Far East etc.) – yet apart from emancipating atheists, radicals, Jews, etc., who had had a poor time before, it did create the tradition of the intelligentsia: of the aristocracy, of royal authority. Napoleon to some degree carried this on: liberty and equality did become widely pursued ideals, even if not very common forms of social life. Kings and churches became less sacred, and so on. Dreyfus, Vichy, were islands, dark stains, on an otherwise corrupt but democratic France. Don't you think Burke might have been somewhat Petainiste? I mean, if *mutatis mutandis*, he had been a Frenchman at the relevant time? I don't feel sure – should I? Of course, if the Thermidoreans had lost, sheer brutality, terror, etc. would have gone on. The Thermidoreans did lose in October 1917. . . . Yet the new liberal tradition. That is my defence of my *faible* for the French Revolution; I can't deny it. You are right about that, though I may not be all that difficult to penetrate. I am not, I think, one of nature's more mysterious or complicated or unfathomable creatures, and don't terribly want to be – but neither, I am happy to say, are you.

Yours ever,

Isaiah

PS. There is something I ought to have added – do you not think that perhaps it was Benjamin Constant who showed the sharpest penetration into the French Revolution and its aftermath? That cold, perceptive independent, civilised Swiss wrote better about the destruction of individual liberty and the horrors of both the Terror and, to some degree, of Bonapartist rule, than anybody. I cannot deny that his famous essay on the difference between the conceptions of liberty in the ancient and modern worlds did have a pretty strong influence on me. (Do you know his writings? In some ways more interesting than even Burke's.)

PPS. I keep thinking of things to say, but I really ought to restrain myself: only one addition: you are perfectly right when you think that my anti-utopianism has something to do with political and moral experience during the first half of the century. There is no doubt that my memories of Petrograd in 1918–20, and the political spectrum of Europe in the 1930s – wherever one looked what did one see? Stalin, Hitler, Mussolini, Franco, Salazar, dictators in the Balkans for the most part, certainly in Rumania and Hungary – I vaguely remember the names of Antonescu and Jombos de Nagibanya – I don't think anyone else remembers that Hungarian despot's name – even poor little Latvia acquired a dictator in the 30s. And against them, what? The impotent Scandinavia and Holland and Belgium; Daladier in France, Baldwin and Chamberlain in England – certainly the darkest years that I remember in peacetime. Hence my undying admiration for FDR and the New Deal. There is no doubt that that had an indelible effect on me, as you so rightly guessed.

PPPS. I agree that Faguet's gibe is marvellous; but it was made in an essay on Maistre (not, as one might think, on Rousseau) and I was saved from this misattribution by the infallible Hardy; so all is in order.

Whitewater
Howth Summit
Dublin
16 June 1991

Dear Isaiah,

I was absolutely delighted to know that you liked what I had written. As a matter of fact I was away in Japan when it arrived, and when my wife met me at the airport the first news she gave me was of the arrival of 'a marvellous letter from Isaiah Berlin'. There were joy bells that day in the O'Brien house. . . .

Your Burke passage of course, makes me particularly happy. Would I have your permission to quote your words 'he should not have come into my list of reactionaries' in my Burke book? I would also – and this may be even more important—like to quote your reservations about the idea that Burke was a liberal pluralist. I appreciate the weight of these reservations and would like the reader of the book to be able to take them on board. And I would like to quote those passages that run counter to my own view of the French Revolution.

I am glad but not at all surprised to know that we are in agreement over Rousseau. I believe that minds which are in agreement over Rousseau – one way or another – are likely also to find themselves in agreement over a wide range of historical intellectual and moral matters. If I find that a person is pro-Rousseau I class that person as basically an enemy, however agreeable they may appear in other respects. A friend of mine has just sent me a quote from Oscar Wilde's *Decay of Lying* in which Oscar says that Robespierre steps out of the pages of Rousseau.

Your P.S.: I don't know Constant as well as I might and shall now make that good.

Your PPS: Glad to have confirmation together with additional light on the roots of your anti-utopianism.

PPPS: Thanks for your clarification on the context of Faguet's gibe.

Yours ever,

Conor

All Souls College
24 June 1991

Dear Conor,

Of course you may quote anything you like from my letter. The only item which makes me, if not hesitate, at any rate wonder, is, of course, Burke. I am perfectly willing to liberate him from the ranks of the reactionaries, but I feel that my views would only be conveyed correctly if you put in all those qualifications of mine in that long letter – about his love of hierarchy, his excessive traditionalism, his belief in the rights of Englishmen, Americans, Indians, but not, it seems, human rights, which, after all, does mean something, indeed, a great deal – as I said in that letter, I don't know what his Christianity may have led him to, but even on my superficial reading I find that the emphasis is on local, regional, national, etc. rights and not on even a minimum of rights which all men may justly claim for themselves, no matter where or when they were born or live. So individualist, but a traditionalist conservative with a deep reluctance about reform, at any rate in his own times – then by all means quote anything you like, I cannot ask for a better fate than to appear in your book.

Yours ever,

Isaiah

PS. One more word about the French Revolution and my feelings – that is all they are – about it. My views, I think, such as they are, are shaped equally by tentative British empiricism (for which I was duly attacked by left-wing American sociologists, etc.) and the traditions of the Russian intelligentsia. Now the latter really were deeply influenced by, if not the events, then by the slogans and the ideas disseminated by the French revolutionaries. It does seem to me that it inspired people to attack prejudice, superstition, obscurantism, cruelty, oppression, hatred of democracy, and to struggle for various liberties – of speech, of belief, the celebrated 'inviolability of the person', which is one of the five principles enunciated by Russian liberals and contemptuously thrown aside by the Bolsheviks – and that kind of thing: the anti-Dreyfusard tradition, in short, which does go back to the French Revolution. In France the ideological divisions were, as you know, largely pro- and anti- the French Revolution; and the antis were genuine reactionaries – Barrès, Drumont, Déroulède, and of course Maurras and his disciples, Pound, Eliot, etc. Hence, if I have to line up, I line up with the Revolution – despite all the fallacies and the horrors, which are certainly there – and against the *Infame*. I am sure you detect that.

I can't deny that when my great friend Gaetano Salvemini, the authentic Italian anti-fascist, 'of the first hour', told me that his book on the French Revolution stopped in 1793, or maybe even '92, because revolution is a battle for liberty – but after a certain date it all became a tyranny and ceased to be a revolution in his sense, my heart warmed to what he said. He was a fierce old Mazzinian, and I could not help being pleased with his outburst.

> Ever yours,
>
> Isaiah

PS. Could you insert this, with any amendment you care to make, in your Appendix? I am most grateful.

T. S. Eliot, in some lecture or other, and I daresay elsewhere, repeated the usual view that Burke was the father of the central modern Conservative tradition; (his heir was Disraeli!). While this is obviously a plausible view, the truth is more complex.

General Index

fault with Hastings's ethics, 288;
on execution of Nuncomar (q.v.),
293; on North and Hastings,
298–9
*God Land: Reflections on Religion and
Nationalism* (Harvard
University Press, 1988): by
C.C.O'B., 93 n.1
Goldsmith, Oliver (1728–74):
member of Dr Johnson's
'Club', 101 n.1; couplet on EB
and Tommy Townshend,
130 n.2
Goodlad, Richard: Collector of
Rangpur under Hastings, 373; his
responsibility for torture, 373–4;
acquitted by Hastings, 374
Goodson, A.C.: 'Burke's Orphics and
Coleridge's Contrary
Understanding', lxix–lxx
Gordon, Lord George (1751–93): and
the Protestant Association, 77, 81;
and 'Gordon Riots' (1780), 77–
86, 213, 219, 395–6; the
'Gordon' vote, 218–19; and
Shelburne, 236; sings *Ça ira* in
prison, 396; *see also* Thematic
Index under 'anti-Catholicism'
Gorki, Maxim: on Tolstoy, 521, 586
Gough, Hugh: co-ed. *Ireland and the
French Revolution* (Dublin, 1990),
469 n.
Gower, George Granville Leveson
Gower, Lord (1758–1833):
British Ambassador in Paris
(1792), 490, 494, 495
Grattan, Henry (1746–1820): 'people
of Burke and of' (Yeats), 12;
Irish agitation led by (1778 ff),
192; and French Revolution, 192;
and Rousseau, *ibid*; and Irish
Volunteers, 192, 243 ff: 'masters
of Irish scene', 192; and role of an
MP, 192–3; and Free Trade, *ibid*;
resolution on legislative
independence for Ireland
defeated (1780), 197 ff; and

American war, 198–9; and
'concessions from England', 198;
and first Irish Mutiny Bill (1780),
199 ff; 'Will no one stop this
madman, Grattan?' (EB, 1780),
243, 244; and Dungannon
Resolutions, 243 ff; and
legislative independence (1780–
82), 243: cannot understand EB's
resistance to, *ibid*, glittering
language on, 245; rivalry with
Flood (1782), 245–6; 'Grattan's
Parliament', 246–7: idealised in
retrospect, 251, exclusively
Protestant composition of, *ibid*;
and Lord Northington, 246; prop
and stay of Fox-North Coalition
(1783), *ibid*; and Dublin
Convention of Irish Volunteers
(1783), 249–50; and legislative
independence (1781), 475: *see
also* Thematic Index; EB
congratulates on Catholic Relief
Act (1793), 497; helps EB avert
collapse of coalition (1794), 513;
brings on confrontation over
Catholic enfranchisement (1795),
514 ff; and Catholic Relief Bill
(1795), 515; and Fitzwilliam, 515–
9; EB writes to, on Fitzwilliam
and Warren Hastings, 518
Henry Grattan, jr: *Memoirs of the Life
and Times of the Rt Hon. Henry
Grattan* (London, 1839–46),
197, 244
Grafton, Augustus Henry Fitzroy, 3rd
Duke of (1725–1811): and control
of Parliament, 62; and
Declaratory Act indispensable to
passage of Stamp Act, 112 n.2;
Administration (1767 ff), 127 ff;
and North's offer of Coalition to
Rockingham (1780), 216; and
Gordon riots, 236; blackmailed
by *Junius* (q.v.), 279
Great Britain: *see* Britain
Great Melody: *see* Thematic Index

Thematic Index

1791), 400–10; some responses to, 412–13; *Letter to a Member of the National Assembly* (April-May 1791, Paris and London), 434–8; *An Appeal from the New to the Old Whigs* (August 1791), 440–52; *Thoughts on French Affairs* (December 1791), 452–4; *Letter to Earl Fitzwilliam* (17 August 1792) after the deposition of Louis XVI (10 August 1792), 490–2; *Letters on a Regicide Peace* (1796), 542–569.

Speeches on the French Revolution: Burke made several of these, but I do not include them in the Great Melody: none (as recorded) is of the weight, either of his American speeches, or of his Indian speeches (from 1783 on) or of his writings on the French Revolution. His speeches on the French Revolution are clearly supplementary to his writings on it. Some readers, however, may feel that the pathos and drama of his parliamentary breach with Fox (414–31) are such as to bring Burke's contributions to it into the Great Melody. I partly share this feeling, and leave the matter open.

Speeches and writings on Ireland: Both sets of these are fewer and more guarded than those on America, India and the French Revolution (above). Of the speeches there is only one passage in one speech which clearly comes from the heart and is part of the Great Melody. This is the haunted and trance-like passage beginning 'In this situation men not only shrink from the frowns of a stern magistrate; but they are obliged to fly from their very species', 82 (*Speech at Bristol*, in the Guildhall, previous to the Election, September, 1780).

Of the writings, the *Letter to Sir Hercules Langrishe* (January 1792), 476–83, belongs in the Great Melody; as do also the following, all late, and unpublished during Burke's lifetime: the passage beginning 'They would not set men calling from the quiet sleep of death any Samuel . . . (*Letter to Richard Burke* (Jr), February 1792), 484; *Letter to Earl Fitzwilliam on the news of his recall as Viceroy* (March 1795), 516–17; *Second Letter to Sir Hercules Langrishe* (May 1795), 527–9; *Letter to Thomas Hussey* (December 1796), 572–4. For the reasons why Burke's direct utterances about Ireland are so meagre and generally so guarded, see the following entries in this Thematic Index, and the passages to which they refer in the text: 'Abuse of Power', 'Ambivalences' (2 entries), 'Ancestors' (2 entries), 'Anti-Catholicism', 'Catholic Church', 'Conversions', 'Converts', 'Dissimulation, occasional, Burkean', 'Falsities, occasional, Burkean', 'Economy of truth', 'Feverishness', 'Fog', 'Glorious Revolution', 'Guilt and remorse', 'Imagery of corruption', 'Insecurity', 'Insights', 'Ireland', 'Irish level', (alias 'Catholic layer'), 'Irish Volunteers', 'Jacobites', 'Jewish converts', 'Legislative independence', 'Obloquy', 'Penal Laws', 'Philoctetes', 'Protestant Ascendancy', 'Protestantism', 'Reticence', 'Schism', 'Secretiveness', 'Self-punishment', 'Silences, Burkean', 'Whiteboys', 'Whiggery'.

George III: See General Index.

Guilt and remorse: over Ireland, 82–6; over India, 270–2; a bond between Burke and Philip Francis, 303–4: over Ireland, transferred to India, 579–85; 'accuser appeased' by Impeachment of Warren Hastings, 358; rational subordination of the lesser (Ireland) to the greater cause of anti-Jacobinism (1790's) 'had to feel like a betrayal at a certain level of the Burkean psyche', 534–5; see also entries cross-listed at end of Great Melody entry.

History: moral lessons to be drawn from, 603; 'may be used to vitiate our minds and to destroy our happiness', *ibid*.